D1328724

FIELDING'S
WALT DISNEY WORLD®
AND ORLANDO AREA
THEME PARKS

Fielding Titles

Fielding's Alaska Cruises and the Inside Passage
Fielding's Asia's Top Dive Sites
Fielding's Amazon
Fielding's Australia
Fielding's Bahamas
Fielding's Baja
Fielding's Bermuda
Fielding's Borneo
Fielding's Budget Europe
Fielding's Caribbean
Fielding's Caribbean Cruises
Fielding's Disney World and Orlando
Fielding's Diving Indonesia
Fielding's Eastern Caribbean
Fielding's England
Fielding's Europe
Fielding's European Cruises
Fielding's Far East
Fielding's France
Fielding's Freewheelin' USA
Fielding's Kenya
Fielding's Hawaii
Fielding's Italy
Fielding's Las Vegas Agenda
Fielding's London Agenda
Fielding's Los Angeles
Fielding's Malaysia and Singapore
Fielding's Mexico
Fielding's New Orleans Agenda
Fielding's New York Agenda
Fielding's New Zealand
Fielding's Paradors, Pousadas and Charming Villages of Spain and Portugal
Fielding's Paris Agenda
Fielding's Portugal
Fielding's Rome Agenda
Fielding's San Diego Agenda
Fielding's Southeast Asia
Fielding's Southern Vietnam on Two Wheels
Fielding's Spain
Fielding's Surfing Indonesia
Fielding's Sydney Agenda
Fielding's Thailand, Cambodia, Laos & Myanmar
Fielding's Vacation Places Rated
Fielding's Vietnam
Fielding's Western Caribbean
Fielding's The World's Most Dangerous Places
Fielding's Worldwide Cruises

FIELDING'S
WALT DISNEY WORLD®
AND ORLANDO AREA
THEME PARKS

By

David Swanson

Fielding Worldwide, Inc.

308 South Catalina Avenue

Redondo Beach, California 90277 U.S.A.

Fielding's Walt Disney World and Orlando Area Theme Parks

Published by Fielding Worldwide, Inc.

Text Copyright ©1997 FWI

Icons & Illustrations Copyright ©1997 FWI

Photo Copyrights ©1997 to Individual Photographers

Some maps ©MAGELLAN Geographix, Santa Barbara, California, Telephone (800) 929-4MAP, www.magellangeo.com

FIELDING WORLDWIDE INC.

PUBLISHER AND CEO	**Robert Young Pelton**
GENERAL MANAGER	**John Guillebeaux**
MARKETING DIRECTOR	**Paul T. Snapp**
OPERATIONS DIRECTOR	**George Posanke**
ELECTRONIC PUBLISHING DIRECTOR	**Larry E. Hart**
PUBLIC RELATIONS DIRECTOR	**Beverly Riess**
ACCOUNT SERVICES MANAGER	**Christy Harp**
PROJECT MANAGER	**Chris Snyder**

EDITORS

Kathy Knoles	**Linda Charlton**
Reed Parsell	**Catherine Bruhn**

PRODUCTION

Martin Mancha	**Alfredo Mercado**
Ramses Reynoso	**Craig South**

COVER DESIGNED BY	**Digital Artists, Inc.**
COVER PHOTOGRAPHERS—Front	**Orlando/Orange County Convention Bureau**
Back	**Orlando/Orange County Convention Bureau**
INSIDE PHOTOS	**Busch Entertainment Group, Orlando/Orange County Convention & Visitors Bureau, Robert Young Pelton, Sea World, Universal Studios**
3-D MAPS	**Paul Carbo**

Inquiries should be addressed to: Fielding Worldwide, Inc., 308 South Catalina Ave., Redondo Beach, California 90277 U.S.A., ☎ *(310) 372-4474*, Facsimile *(310) 376-8064*, 8:30 a.m.–5:30 p.m. Pacific Standard Time.
Website: http://www.fieldingtravel.com
e-mail: fielding@fieldingtravel.com

ISBN 1-56952-110-7

Printed in the United States of America

Letter from the Publisher

In 1946, Temple Fielding began the first of what would be a remarkable new series of well-written, highly personalized guidebooks for independent travelers. Temple's opinionated, witty and oft-imitated books have now guided travelers for almost a half-century. More important to some was Fielding's humorous and direct method of steering travelers away from the dull and the insipid. Today, Fielding's travel guides are still written by experienced travelers for experienced travelers. Our authors carry on Fielding's reputation for delivering travel experiences with a sense of discovery and style.

Designed to save travelers time and money, *Fielding's Walt Disney World and Orlando Area Theme Parks* cuts to the chase, telling readers all they need to know about the myriad attractions in the Orlando area. Whether you have a day or a week in Orlando, author David Swanson shares hundreds of insider tips.

Today, the concept of independent travel has never been bigger. Our policy of *brutal honesty* and a highly personal point of view has never changed; it just seems the travel world has caught up with us.

RYP

Robert Young Pelton
Publisher and CEO
Fielding Worldwide, Inc.

DEDICATION

To Hayley and Kyle Swanson, my niece and nephew—the most delightful research assistants a writer could ask for.

ACKNOWLEDGMENTS

Creating a thorough guidebook from the ground up around the world's largest hotel market is a monumental task. There were many who contributed their insight, opinions and support.

At the Walt Disney Company, Pam Brandon got me started on my merry road, Craig Dezern helped locate many details I might have otherwise missed, while Karen Haynes and Neil McCord helped to make sure the restaurant and resort data were up-to-date. Anne Craig and Joel Staley each spent hours with me during the painstaking fact-checking process. Thanks also to the many Disney cast members who rose above and beyond the call of duty, crowing shamelessly about their place of employment, usually without knowing they were speaking to a guidebook writer.

Tom Schroder helped uncover the expansion and energy erupting at Universal Studios, and Glenn Haddad kept me from sinking at Sea World. Danielle Saba Courtenay of the Orlando Convention and Visitor's Bureau was a tremendous aid in helping me sort through the mass of hotels, restaurants and attractions that needed to be evaluated. Thanks also to the individuals—too many to name—who helped me track down niggling details, from the exact location of a spanking new bike path, to the most recent head count of Florida's alligator population.

A number of other individuals made contributions that added greatly to the value and flavor of this guide: Betty Berzon, Bill Buyok, Brian Edmundson, Perry Glorioso, Christy Greer, Mark Podlaseck, Denise Swanson, Ed Weil and others too numerous to mention. In particular, thanks to Peter and Anthony Swanson, and Stan and Cina Podlaseck for their detailed review of the text. Thanks also to the staff at Fielding, especially John Guillebeaux for his patience and trust.

And last but certainly not least, Chris Principio, for having abundant faith in me on this grand venture.

ABOUT THE AUTHOR

David Swanson

Although David Swanson's first travels were in the back of a Volkswagen bus through the American Southwest, the Rockies and western Canada as part of annual summer trips with his family, he has been enthusiastically hoofing the globe on a regular basis since his first trip to Europe in 1982. The journals from that trip also represented his first forays into travel writing, a career that blossomed into a full-time profession after abandoning his nine-to-five in 1993. Since then, his writing has appeared in the *Los Angeles Times*, *San Francisco Examiner*, *Chicago Sun-Times*, *Dallas Morning News*, *Cleveland Plain Dealer*, *Denver Post*, *Caribbean Travel and Life*, *American Way*, *Latitudes* and a number of other newspapers and publications. Swanson is also co-author of *Fielding's Caribbean*, a region he travels to and covers regularly.

A Southern California native, he currently lives in Boston with his partner, and has gained a whole new appreciation for winter trips to sunnier climes since his move away from the West Coast. When Swanson isn't writing, he's bicycling, hiking and enjoying obscure movies, and occasionally he ponders his former career in film marketing and publicity.

WHAT'S IN THE STARS

Fielding's Five-Star Rating System for Walt Disney World and Orlando

★★★★★	**Exceptional hotels, resorts, restaurants and attractions; the best in the area**
★★★★	**Excellent in most respects**
★★★	**Average or better**
★★	**Meritorious or worth considering**
★	**Below average**

The price of an average dinner, including an appetizer or dessert, excluding alcohol, tax and tip:

$$$$	**Very expensive, $32 and up, per person**
$$$	**Expensive, $24–32**
$$	**Moderate, $16–24**
$	**Inexpensive, under $16**

Also note the Fielding's Rating Icons for additional guidance in your selections.

A NOTE TO OUR READERS

If you've had an extraordinary, mediocre or horrific experience visiting Walt Disney World and Orlando, we want to hear about it. A survey form at the end of this book will help us guide future readers. If something has changed since we've gone to press, please let us know. Those business owners who flood us with shameless self-promotion under the guise of readers' letters will be noted and reviewed more rigorously next time. If you wish to make comments beyond what the survey allows for next year's edition, send it to:

Fielding's Walt Disney World and Orlando

308 South Catalina Avenue
Redondo Beach, CA 90277
FAX (310) 376-8064
email: fielding@fieldingtravel.com

Some of the attractions, products and locations in this book are registered trademarks of The Walt Disney Company, Busch Gardens, Sea World, Universal Studios Florida and other trademark owners. The use in this guide of trademarked names including those listed below is for editorial purposes and no commercial claim to their use or suggestion of sponsorship or endorsement is made by the publisher. New trademarks are applied for almost continuously. These will be recognized and acknowledged in all subsequent editions.

Adventureland	Mickey Mouse
Audio-Animatronics	Mickey's Toontown Fair
Blizzard Beach	Pleasure Island
Bok Tower Gardens	Ripley's Believe It Or Not
Busch Gardens	River Country
Captain EO	Sea World of Florida
Church Street Station	Space Mountain
Circle Vision 360	Spaceport USA
Cypress Gardens	Splendid China
Discovery Island	Terror On Church Street
Disneyland	Tomorrowland
Disney-MGM Studios	Typhoon Lagoon
Epcot Center	Universal Studios Florida
Fantasyland	Walt Disney
Frontierland	Walt Disney World
Gatorland	Walt Disney World Resorts
Nickelodeon Studios	Water Mania
IllumiNations	Weeki Wachee Spring
Magic Kingdom	Wet'n'Wild
Medieval Times	

Fielding Rating Icons

The Fielding Rating Icons are highly personal and awarded to help the besieged traveler choose from among the dizzying array of activities, attractions, hotels, restaurants and sights. The awarding of an icon denotes unusual or exceptional qualities in the relevant category.

RATINGS
Fielding Award · Author Selection · Money Saver · Expensive · Quality · Warning · Danger · Inexpensive · Spacious · Cramped · Mild Disapproval · Crowded · Time Saving Tip

CULTURAL
Museum/Art · Interesting Architecture · History · Book Reference · Artistically Important · Musically Interesting · Cultural Archeology · Crafts · Theater · Festivals

SIGHTS
Picturesque · Great Scenery · Market · Beaches/Resorts · Cultural · Fortress · Castles · Church

WHERE TO STAY
Simple · Luxurious · Cottage · Bed & Breakfast · Scenic · Business · Honeymoon · Chateau

TRAVEL TIPS
Arrival/Departure · By Air · By Water · By Train · By Car · Bus/Local Transit · Barge · Riverboat · Calendar · Itinerary · Compass · Kids · Off the Beaten Track

ACTIVITIES

Downhill Skiing	X-country Skiing	Watersports	Sailing	Scuba Diving	Snorkeling/ Diving	Deep-sea Fishing	Freshwater Fishing
Swimming	Hiking	Walking	Relaxing	Golf	Tennis	Horseback Riding	General Sports
Cycling	Workout						

SPECIAL INTEREST

Nightlife	Singles	Romantic	Nude Beaches	Lecture	Spectacular Cuisine	Wine Tasting	Shopping
Cafe Stops	Gardening	Pro Sports	Mystery	E-Ticket Ride	Monorail	Wildlife	

Legend

Essentials

- ⛫ Hotel
- ⛺ Youth Hostel
- ✕ Restaurant
- $ Bank
- ☎ Telephone
- ℹ Tourist Info.
- ✚ Hospital
- ☕ Pub/Bar
- ✉ Post Office
- 🅿 Parking
- 🚖 Taxi
- Ⓢ Subway
- Ⓜ Metro
- Market
- Shopping
- Cinema
- Theatre
- ✈ Int'l Airport
- ✚ Regional Airport
- ★ Police Station
- ⚖ Courthouse
- 🏛 Gov't. Building

(Attractions)

- ■ Attraction
- ✈ Military Airbase
- Army Base
- Naval base
- Fort
- University
- School

Historical

- ∴ Archeological Site
- Battleground
- Castle
- Monument
- Museum
- Ruin
- Shipwreck

Religious

- Church
- Buddhist Temple
- Hindu Temple
- Mosque
- Pagoda
- Synagogue

Activities

- 🏖 Beach
- ⛰ Campground
- ⛱ Picnic Area
- ⛳ Golf Course
- Boat Launch
- Diving
- Fishing
- Water Skiing
- Snow Skiing
- Bird Sanctuary
- Wildlife Sanctuary
- Park
- Park Headquarters
- Mine
- Lighthouse
- Windmill
- Cruise Port
- View
- Stadium
- Building
- Zoo
- Garden

Physical

— — — · International Boundary	🚶🚶 Hiking Trail
- — - — - County/Regional Boundary	▬▬▬▬ Dirt Road
PARIS ⊙ National Capital	+++++++++ Railroad
Montego Bay • State/Parish Capital	**RR** Railroad Station
Los Angeles ● Major City	— — ⛴ — Ferry Route
Quy Nhon ○ Town/Village	▲ Mountain Peak
— — ⑤ — — Motorway/Freeway	Lake
⋯⋯ ⑯ ⋯⋯ Highway	River
═══════ Primary Road	Cave
═══════ Secondary Road	Coral Reef
▬ ▬ ▬ ▬ Subway	Waterfall
— — 🚲 — — Biking Routed	Hot Spring

©FWI 1995

TABLE OF CONTENTS

LIST OF MAPS

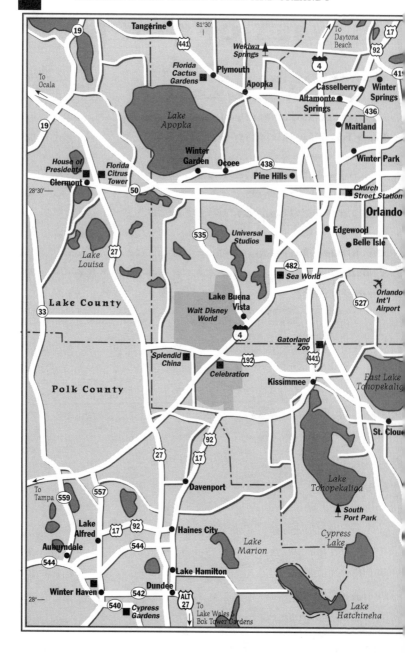

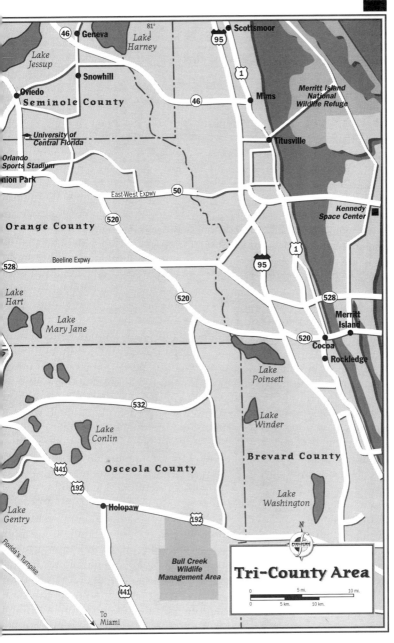

Tri-County Area

INTRODUCTION AND OVERVIEW

Orlando's daytime skyline is ever-changing.

Why Orlando?

"Orlando's destiny was sealed on Disney Day, October 1, 1971, when Disney World opened wide its gates. Since then, the swamp, once called Mosquito County, has become the top commercial tourist destination in the world. As a shrine, it is surpassed only by Kyoto, Mecca and the Vatican."

—**Priscilla Painton,** *Time Magazine*

The Walt Disney Company never ceases to amaze me in the new concepts it is willing to develop for its ever-growing legion of fans. A few years ago, the company announced plans for the **Disney Institute**, a facility that would integrate learning into a more traditional resort experience. This new venture would be located just a couple miles from the entrances to the theme parks that have made Walt Disney World famous.

When I first visited, the Disney Institute was only a few weeks away from its February 1996 opening and construction crews were operating at a feverish pitch to put the finishing touches on the buildings. Dan Higgans, a publicist for the Disney Company, was giving me a hard-hat tour of the property's educational facilities. We sauntered through one of the Institute's two kitchens, but my nose told me what was going on was anything but institutional.

Culinary arts teacher Frank Brough was leading a group of Disney employees in a test course, titled "From Field to Plate." Brough explained that the course began at Epcot's Land Pavilion, where his would-be students learned about the facility's hydroponic growing techniques. Students harvested some of the Land's vegetables and then returned to the Disney Institute's kitchen to prepare lunch. When we arrived, the best part of the two-day, six-hour course was well under way: the students were happily feasting on their vegetarian kitchen creativity. A bottle in each hand, sommelier Reid Rapport cheerfully kept the Chardonnay flowing.

Dan and I continued our tour, stopping by the Disney Institute's animation studios, where a row of computers offered students the chance to animate their imagination. Nearby, a television soundstage was a classroom for video production, and a radio station promised time on the local Disney airwaves. An 1100-seat outdoor amphitheater provided a stage for visiting musicians and others. Courses weren't limited to the arts. Sports and fitness programs (including a 25-foot rock climbing wall nestled among trees) were scheduled, as well as lifestyle and self-discovery classes and special courses for teens.

An increasingly obvious motif at Disney is the diversification of its product. The company is no longer content to be seen as strictly an amusement-park builder, and has legitimately added the word "resort" to its Walt Disney World title. Disney is successfully (and rapidly) creating a multiformity of entertainments that extend far beyond The Magic Kingdom, the original theme park that opened in 1971. By developing offerings for an increasingly divergent audience, the company hopes to corner all segments of the travel market—to become an all-purpose vacation destination for all tastes.

As I toured the Disney Institute's extensive facility, one of the themes I pessimistically returned to with Dan was the Disney Company's notorious reputation for control. True education, I argued, thrives in an environment where it is unfettered by commercial interests and business politics. How would the company keep all of these courses and teachers, brought in from a variety of professions and backgrounds, in line—on a track, as it were? What if a student of the animation program made a short subject of a Minnie Mouse striptease? What if a guest teacher led a course that swerved substantially from the company's mindset?

It was a curious dilemma, but I admired the Disney Company for the risk. And it was hardly the vacation experience I had expected at Walt Disney World.

A few days later, I visited **Katie's Wekiva River Landing**, 22 miles north of downtown Orlando. Compared to the Disney machine, this was a tiny operation: it covered only a couple acres with some campsites, four log cabins and a stack of canoes and kayaks for rent.

Our put-in point was a quiet cove set in a forest of live oak and cypress. Great blue herons sometimes visit, but more common were the coots trolling through a bank of cattails on the opposite side of the river. Katie Moncrief, my guide for an afternoon trip on the spring-fed Wekiva River, was 70 years old, but the way she deftly hoisted a kayak belied her age; in the blink of an eye, she was positioned in her watercraft and, with a single push, she floated smoothly out onto the river.

It had been years since I last used a kayak, and I was all arms. I gamely juggled a bottle of water, my paddle and notepad as I entered my boat, which was light enough to writhe nervously back and forth under my weight. My awkward push-off took an embarrassing couple of minutes, but Katie pretended not to notice as she talked to me over her shoulder and floated on downstream. Eventually, I was waterborne, though the clumsy rocking of my kayak advertised my poor balance.

Katie knows the crystal-clear Wekiva River like the back of her hand, and as I struggled to find a graceful forward momentum, she paddled effortlessly ahead, telling me about the ancient, Spanish moss-draped oaks that arch over the river, and the charming, red-bellied turtles that sprawled in the sunlight. Just as I finally gained my ability to navigate a kayak and began to keep up with her, she mentioned something about possibly seeing a gator or two.

Alligator, I asked? She nonchalantly explained that there were roughly 400 in the area and they typically sit by the edge of the river sunning themselves at mid-day. *Now* she tells me, I thought. "Keep your eye out," she added, with a smile.

It was mid-day now, and any comfort level I had previously attained in the kayak was fading away. I noticed my heart beating faster, but I wasn't sure whether it was nerves or Katie's brisk pace as she continued to extol the virtues of the river she's lived on for 22 years. Abruptly, she stopped talking and gingerly veered to the left. As I followed her, she whispered, bluntly, "Gator... big one, just over there."

Sure enough, artfully mimicking a fallen log, a nine- or 10-foot-long American alligator lurked in the water about 20 feet away. It sat motionless, although Katie warned that if we scared it, the gator would dive under the water's surface. I didn't want that. I wanted the gator right where I could see it, and it seemed to feel the same way, subtly focusing a glassy eyeball in our direction.

After a few moments watching the creature, we paddled off again downstream. My nerves settled down as Katie told me about the friendly manatees that hang out a few miles away. She described how a lone photographer in a kayak was tailed by manatees all the way up the river; the manatees even turned over the photographer's boat in a playful attempt at contact with her.

We were floating in a wilderness I didn't expect, just five miles from a major interstate and twenty minutes north of Orlando. I was ready to retire here with Katie.

Walt Disney World and Orlando are awash in misconceptions. True, what Disney and its host city proclaim to offer—exciting rides, a verdant setting, bountiful warmth, a year-round vacation playground—is there. But so often, the best memories one returns home with, such as the Disney Institute and Katie's Wekiva River Landing, are not the expected ones.

Why Fielding's?

Orlando boasts more hotel rooms and theme park attractions than any other destination in the world. Its efficient international airport is connected to departure points throughout the United States and around the globe, and a dazzling array of vacation packages is available. Orlando is a family-friendly destination, but the city and its environs are accessible to all kinds of other travelers, including those on a budget. If ever there were a "do-it-yourself" vacation, Orlando is it. Right? Dream on.

You've already entered Fantasyland

The first-time visitor will find Orlando a confounding thicket of options. Walt Disney World is a dynamic playground for all ages, but beyond Mickey and Minnie, what theme parks are worth seeing, and which are merely another run-down tourist trap? Like a scene in a snow globe, discount coupons swirl furiously around shaken guests, promising entertainment and food that is bigger, better, wilder. As for attractions, don't forget Jungleland. Gatorland. Adventureland. Adventure Island. Pleasure Island. Islands of Adventure.

Are we having fun yet? I assure you, we just sped past some winners and losers.

The truth is, many first-time visitors return home with a list of frustrations longer than the good times they hoped to remember. And, beyond Disney, most of these poor souls leave unsure of whether they saw all the best Orlando has to offer.

But *practical* information is frequently in short supply. The region's visitors are a diverse lot, so word-of-mouth about the entertainment virtue of any number of secondary attractions is slow to materialize. To test that theory, find someone who's visited Orlando for the first time and ask what they remember beyond Walt Disney World, Universal Studios and maybe Sea World. You'll probably draw a blank stare. And possibly a tacit admission that they spent a lot of money, but they don't know where it all went.

Needless to say, the lesser attractions benefit when the line is blurred on issues of quality and value-for-dollar. Therefore, this guidebook has three overriding goals:

1. To help you navigate **Walt Disney World** by providing a thorough overview of all its attractions, resorts and restaurants, with an eye toward getting you the most for your vacation investment.

2. To provide an assessment of **Universal Studios**, **Sea World** and the region's other attractions, steering you to the hits and away from the flops.

3. To hone a list of the region's best non-Disney-operated hotels and restaurants in all price categories.

In sum, we've looked to create an objective, unbiased guide to the region's many attractions. This book is not authorized or edited in any way by the Walt Disney Company or by any other Orlando organization. For the purpose of narrowing our list, during the course of two months' on-site research, 110 hotel rooms were toured, usually anonymously, along with more than 60 restaurants.

This guidebook assumes you have already been sold on the Disney vacation and have decided to travel to Walt Disney World. Although many of Disney's best customers find the company and its product unassailable, *Fielding's Walt Disney World and Orlando* makes the assumption that the World is not a perfect place and that a little well-researched assistance goes a long ways. Although a Disney vacation is not cheap, it doesn't need to be expensive. Though lines are in place for most of the day at the best Walt Disney

World attractions, there are ways to minimize your waits. And while many of Disney's restaurants are overpriced, there are values to be had.

You can select from numerous Orlando guidebooks. But unlike some of the others, neither this author nor the Fielding company has any interest in creating yet another tome that fawns and gushes over everything and everyone who can assemble a breathless press release. Since this is an unauthorized guide and Disney only supplies photos to its "authorized" publication, you will find no photos of Walt Disney World theme parks in our guide. (Fortunately the other parks were happy to supply photos.) Unless you are graced with an endless supply of time and money, you can't afford to see Walt Disney World and Orlando without *Fielding's Walt Disney World and Orlando.*

How to Use this Guidebook

Fielding's Walt Disney World and Orlando is organized in the order we think it should be used: from beginning to end. This introductory chapter will give you an overview of how Orlando became a vacation destination, including a bird's-eye view of the region, some history and a unique perspective on the Disney agenda. Also included is information about future plans for the region, some of which may be well under way or built by the time you visit.

The second chapter should be read before you go. It tells how to select a hotel and gives pointers on package tours. There are suggestions on when and how long to visit, background on airline tickets and car rentals, and valuable information on how to navigate Walt Disney World, whether using your own set of wheels or the extensive transportation system provided by Disney. This chapter also features tips for special travelers—families with small children, seniors, visitors with disabilities, gay and lesbian, and foreign visitors.

The third chapter details some of the many accommodations offered in the Orlando area, including all of the properties operated by the Disney company, and the best of the rest. The fourth chapter similarly outlines your sit-down dining options and information about the popular character meals. Fast-food and buffet eateries within the theme parks are discussed in the chapters on the various attractions that follow.

The fifth chapter explains the particulars about how Disney's paid-admission theme parks work, including important information about the confusing variety of ticket options that Disney offers and how to select the ticket package that works best for your budget and itinerary. This chapter also includes helpful tips so you can avoid the crowds, how to find the characters, information on Disney's little-known behind-the-scenes tours, and details about Walt Disney World's 25th Anniversary which will be celebrated throughout 1997. Be sure to read this chapter before you go.

Chapters six, seven and eight cover Disney's three main parks and include carefully-developed itineraries for The Magic Kingdom, Epcot and the Disney-MGM Studios that will help you visit these theme parks in an efficient manner. Chapter nine is devoted to the secondary Disney attractions—the three water parks, the zoological park Discovery Island, and the nighttime entertainment center, Pleasure Island.

The tenth and eleventh chapters of this book address the many other entertainment options available to you in and near Orlando: theme parks and attractions outside Walt Disney World, dinner theaters and activities (such as golfing, sporting events, etc.) throughout the area. Leaf through this section before you go; it will help you prioritize the long list of non-Disney attractions and activities.

In sum, as one local tourism insider told me: "First-time Orlando visitors who carefully plan their vacation before they arrive seem to have a much better time than those that don't."

Bird's-Eye View

Florida can be roughly divided into three geographical areas. Anchored by Miami and the endangered Everglades, the south is home to the state's original tourism industry, and also its growing and vibrant Hispanic culture. Northern Florida, by contrast, is part of the nation's "deep south," and includes the panhandle bordering Alabama and Georgia, and Tallahassee, the state capital. Obscurely defined central Florida is home to **Orlando** and **Walt Disney World**, but also the aerospace industry and **Kennedy Space Center**, most of the state's citrus industry, and a pair of silky white strands of sand running along the peninsula's coast.

From the air, Florida is nothing if not pancake flat—only one state, Delaware, is more plane. The highest elevation in peninsular Florida—298 feet above sea level—lies about 45 miles south of downtown Orlando. From a distance this hill at **Bok Tower Gardens** is little more than a vague rise on the horizon. A series of low ridges form a backbone down the peninsula, but the region immediately surrounding Orlando is particularly level, allowing for the area's many lakes and ponds.

AUTHOR'S OBSERVATION

Like the Bahamas off its southeastern coast, central Florida's geological structure is coralline, creating a limestone foundation. In addition to siring freshwater springs, the underground erosion of the limestone causes many sinkholes. The region's biggest collapsed sinkhole—some 300 feet across—occurred in 1981 in Winter Park (just north of Orlando). At its epicenter, the earth sank 100 feet and devoured a house, six cars, a swimming pool and part of two streets. A less-heralded, but more prominent sinkhole is the one that creates the World Showcase Lagoon at Epcot.

Indeed, the interior of the state is dotted by thousands of lakes—4511 square miles of inland water territory in all, many of these pockets created by collapses in the region's bed of limestone. Rainwater erosion causes cracks and cavities in the limestone that also produces the largest artesian spring formations in the world. Hundreds of freshwater springs bubble up throughout the area; the headwaters of the **Silver River** pour forth an average of 880 million crystal clear gallons *per day*. For a glimpse of what central Florida looked like before the turn of the century, head east from Orlando on the **Beeline**; the undeveloped flats of swamp and forest on either side of the expressway is what greeted the region's first settlers in the early and mid-18th century.

The state's ecology is strikingly diverse, but in recent years more than a few species have become endangered. The most famous *cause célèbre* has been the **West Indian manatee**. The curious mammals, sometimes called sea cows, weigh up to a ton, live in both fresh and sea water, and dine on underwater vegetation. Manatees may have once been mistaken for mermaids as they lolled near the surface of coastal waters, but today their numbers have dwindled because they are frequently injured by crab traps, pollution and ever-present speed boats. Only 2400 are thought to remain in Florida waters today, and despite extensive education efforts during the past two decades, these large marine creatures have yet to establish a recovery.

Even more endangered, the **Florida panther** was chosen by schoolchildren in 1982 to become the state animal; fewer than 50 are estimated to be alive today. As the state's population has grown, the **black bear**, **wildcat**, **gray fox** and the now-endangered **white-tailed deer** and **Key deer** have also started to drop out of sight. Although there are dim hopes for a surviving pair, the last known member of the **dusky seaside sparrow** species died at Walt Disney World's **Discovery Island** in 1987. Today, the **American crocodile** is found only in the Everglades (at last count, about 500 remain in the region). However, the **American alligator** has staged a successful comeback and is now abundant throughout the state. Currently, about 1.5 million gators live in the wild. The state is also home to the second largest population of **American bald eagles** in the country (Alaska contains the largest). Many eagles nest in the remaining wilderness in and surrounding Walt Disney World.

Florida's year-round growing cycle has made the state the nation's number one citrus grower—predominantly oranges, grapefruits and tangerines in central Florida. The region's mild winters make Florida the number two producer of vegetables and melons after California. Dairy production and beef cattle provide another significant source of income for central Florida.

AUTHOR'S OBSERVATION

In spring 1996, an alarming and unexpected series of manatee deaths rocked Florida's environmental community. One hundred fifty-eight manatees died during March and April along a 70-mile-long section of the southwestern Florida coastline around Fort Myers. Scientists were initially baffled by the die-off, but after nonstop research were finally able to announce on July 2, 1996, that the likely cause was red tide—a natural phenomenon that occurred at unusually high levels in early 1996. Coupled with the fact that many manatees had migrated farther south than usual due to an uncommonly cold winter, the creatures were exposed to the toxic organisms in large quantities. Prior to the die-off, Florida's manatee population was estimated at 2600, but with more than 300 deaths (including those from natural or other causes unrelated to the red tide) during the first six months of 1996 alone, the year had already entered the record books as the worst for manatee mortalities in Florida.

The geographical layout of Orlando and Walt Disney World is a little different from what many visitors might expect. As with many regions, the city has steadily grown during the latter half of the 20th century. Orlando has merged with surrounding towns and cities, forming an amorphous whole. "Metro" Orlando now includes tony **Winter Park**, **Maitland** and **Altamonte Springs** to the north, **Belle Isle** and **Tangelo Park** on the south. In recent years, primarily due to Disney's development, **Kissimmee** and **St. Cloud**, 15-20 miles south of Orlando, have become part of the larger community. Two primary arteries, the Florida Turnpike and I-4, form an "X" through the middle of the state, their paths crossing near **Universal Studios**, just southwest of downtown Orlando.

Thirteen miles southwest of downtown Orlando, the Walt Disney World tract has grown to encompass 30,500 acres. The Disney property extends another 11 miles south, averaging 3-7 miles in width. The southern third of the World, sliced by U.S. 192 and I-4, is largely undeveloped. Three primary Disney parks, **The Magic Kingdom**, **Epcot** and the **Disney-MGM Studios**, are set in the northern and middle portion of the World. Several smaller attractions, including **Blizzard Beach** and **Typhoon Lagoon**, as well as 15 resorts providing more than 16,000 rooms, are also nestled within this area. Finally, a chunk of property juts eastward toward a non-Disney shopping center, Crossroads Mall. This parcel is the most intensely developed portion of the World, with the **Disney Village Marketplace**, **Pleasure Island** and the **"Official Resorts of Walt Disney World"** clustered around tiny, spring-fed **Lake Buena Vista**.

History

Not a Creature was Stirring...

Although Florida had been inhabited for many years by the Apalachee, Calusa and Timucua Indians, history books tell us that Spaniards, led by Juan Ponce de Leon, who was searching for the elusive Fountain of Youth, discovered the peninsula in 1513. Thinking he had found a huge island, he named it after *La Pascua Florida*—the Feast of Flowers (or Easter). Over the next three centuries, control of the peninsula, like many Caribbean islands to the south, continually traded hands among the Spanish, French, British and, eventually, Americans.

AUTHOR'S OBSERVATION

The legend of Pocahontas and John Smith, basis for the popular 1995 animated release from the Walt Disney Company, may have its roots closer to The Magic Kingdom than Disney management might have realized. The Timucuan Indians, who inhabited much of central and northern Florida when Spaniards first arrived, were about to roast a captured soldier, Juan Ortiz, when the chief's daughter, Ulele, pleaded for his life. Ortiz went on to join a rival tribe, where he lived for 12 years until De Sota's arrival in 1539.

In 1819, after years of struggle for domination, Spain finally ceded nominal control of Florida to the United States. However, the region's new settlers had to deal with the presence of Seminole Indians (an assimilation of the earlier tribes), who had been largely left alone during Spanish rule. General Andrew Jackson castigated the Indians in 1817, leading to the First Seminole War. As president, Jackson eventually coerced the tribes into a treaty whereby they would give up Florida in exchange for territories in the West.

The Second Seminole War erupted in 1835 when a young warrior, Osceola, defiantly stabbed the papers with his knife and refused to sign the treaty. Many of the ensuing battles took place in or near what is Orlando today. The war lasted seven years, becoming possibly the most costly and bloodiest struggle in American Indian history. About 150 Seminoles escaped south to the Everglades, but the remaining survivors were resettled in Oklahoma. Orlando was founded during this period, first as Fort Gatlin, which offered protection from the wars to both the soldiers and initial settlers. As the community grew, it was named Jernigan, but the name was later changed to Orlando, possibly as a tribute to Orlando Reeves, a messenger who warned of a pending Indian attack and lost his life.

In 1845, with about 66,000 residents (at least half of them slaves), Florida was finally admitted to the Union, becoming the 27th state. Central Florida began to prosper both as cattle country and as a fertile land for cotton plantations. By 1861, however, the nation had plunged into the Civil War and Florida became the third state to secede from the Union to join the Confederacy. In 1866, at the end of the war, the state's cotton industry was in shambles, so central Florida's settlers focused their attention on cattle ranching, and eventually orange groves. The state was readmitted to the Union in 1868 after affirming the abolition of slavery.

AUTHOR'S OBSERVATION

"Cracker" is a local word used to refer to Florida's cowboys. How the term originated is a subject of some debate. Some think it refers to the crack of the bullwhip used when herding cattle (lariats and ropes weren't practical in the heavy brush of Florida's cattle ranges). Another possibility is that the term was inspired by those who ate cracked corn. Traditionally, the term was applied disparagingly to poor Southern whites, particularly the early cowboy residents of Florida.

By the end of the 19th century, Orlando had become a sort of unofficial hub of Central Florida. Schools and roads lured new settlers to the region and the two-square-mile city was incorporated by the state—by a vote of 22 men out of 85 residents—in 1875. The event was augmented by the birth of a newspaper, the *Orange County Reporter*. It was still a rough locale—an isolated frontier loaded with saloons and rowdy brawls among the cowpokes, locally known as "crackers." Alligator wrestling was popular entertainment. In 1894, Orlando suffered calamity as temperatures dropped to 24 degrees and the region's orange blossoms froze, destroying the citrus crop. The following winter, more freezing temperatures wiped out tens of thousands of trees. Conglomerates moved in, buying up the smaller grove owners who were desperate for cash. Eventually, the industry rebounded when the new trees began to bear fruit.

AUTHOR'S OBSERVATION

The groves of citrus trees that surround much of Orlando today are not native–in fact, citrus probably didn't exist in the Americas at all until Spanish explorers brought oranges over on their first voyages to the new world during the 16th century.

At the close of the century, Florida was being promoted for both its tourism and agricultural potential. By 1910, a speculative land market emerged, fueled further by the industrial demands of World War I. Orlando was among the Florida cities experiencing the fastest growth, but it all came to a crashing halt in 1929 as Wall Street went bust. Many of the region's developers became penniless overnight.

Central Florida did not emerge from the Great Depression until the late 1930s, as the nation plunged into World War II. Orlando was an important base for the Army and Air Force, bringing thousands of servicemen to the region, many of whom would later return to the city to settle. After the war, the region continued to grow, but the next big boost came when Cape Canaveral, 40 miles east of Orlando, was selected to become an Air Force base for the country's manned space program. Although the site had been in use as a missile test center since 1949, the manned flights planned during the 1950s would bring thousands of new jobs to the area, led by Martin Marietta, which acquired a 10-square-mile parcel for missile development in Orlando. In 1958, the first American satellite was deployed and, by 1961, Cape Canaveral was the launch pad for the nation's first manned space flight.

The region was pegged for continuing growth, but few proponents realized the dramatic turn of events in store that would take Orlando to new heights.

...and then Came a Mouse

The story of Walt Disney's takeover of central Florida is the stuff of legend.

In the early 1960s, buoyed by the success and acclaim that greeted Disneyland after its 1955 opening, Walt Disney began scouring the country for a location to build an East Coast counterpart. Although most of the potential consumers for such a venture were concentrated in the northeast part of the country, Disney reckoned the region's weather wouldn't be cooperative enough for a successful year-round operation. Disney set his sights on the southeast, eventually choosing Florida, which already had a tourism infrastructure in place. After touring the region by private plane, Disney settled on the Orlando area, basing his choice on existing highway access, anticipated growth, the quantity of undeveloped land available, and the fact that he didn't want to be too close to the coasts, where beaches would provide natural competition for his theme park.

Central Florida also offered Disney a way to avoid the problem of blight. In the years following the opening of the 180-acre Disneyland park in California, dozens of cheap motels had sprung up around the property. Not only were these motels an eyesore as guests approached his amusement park, but Disney wasn't getting a cut of their profits. Consequently, he planned to buy a vast chunk of territory, big enough to keep the riffraff far out of his way, and large enough to mold into a vision that went well beyond a single theme park. The only problem was that once landowners discovered what Disney's plans were, prices would skyrocket as everyone tried to get into the action. So in 1964, when the company began to buy—orange groves, pinewoods, cattle country and inaccessible swampland just southwest of Orlando—the purchaser was kept secret. Most transactions were handled in cash, correspondence was conducted through a Kansas City post office box, and speculation was successfully kept to a minimum for more than a year. The parcels purchased were of varying sizes and value, a few acres here, a few thousand there, with some land acquired for as little as $107 an acre.

The *Orlando Sentinel Star*, the city's daily newspaper, conspired to keep the stealth operation under wraps. Its publisher had discovered the identity of the mystery buyer, but recognized the enormous potential for the region, if it was allowed to succeed. It wasn't until Nov. 15, 1965, when the Disney Company was ready, that the paper finally announced the project with a gush of enthusiasm. Walt Disney had bought 27,400 acres—twice the size of Manhattan Island—for an average of $180 per acre, and Orlando would soon become "the greatest tourist city in the world." Land values beyond the Disney tract soared overnight, purportedly reaching $80,000 an acre in a matter of days.

Disney's negotiating savvy in the market had only just begun. After the official announcement, and well before making known the exact plans for development, the company launched an intense lobbying campaign among state and local elected officials. The goal: to provide the company with unprecedented free reign to dictate how the property would be developed. Disney wanted to establish an independent governing district that would have authority over issues concerning use of local tax money, building and zoning codes, and the creation and control of all-important water and drainage canals (50 miles in all). In theory, Disney's aim was to reduce red tape once the construction process began.

Well aware of the tremendous growth that Disney would bring to the region, the developer-friendly Florida State Legislature granted the authority, in effect a special taxing region, naming it the Reedy Creek Improvement

District. Whether by deliberate design or pixie-dusted serendipity, what the Disney Company obtained was virtual carte blanche autonomy to develop its property with minimal governmental input and maximum internal control. Disney was now responsible for its own building and zoning codes, utility and sewage systems, fire and police protection, transportation, roads and bridges, and more. What few realized then was just how big a tail would be wagging the state for decades to come.

AUTHOR'S OBSERVATION

In January 1996, vacant land just outside Walt Disney World near the Orlando Convention Center sold for $1 million an acre. The 17-acre parcel is scheduled to be developed as a entertainment and retail complex and will include the upscale toy store, FAO Schwarz. The price paid for the land is the highest ever in the area (outside downtown Orlando), spurred in part because the last remaining parcels in the I-Drive tourist corridor are going fast.

After a brief illness, Walt Disney died of lung cancer on Dec. 15, 1966. Although speculation was rampant as to how the company would deal with the loss of its visionary leader, less than two months after his death, Walt's brother Roy formally established the company's goals with the Florida project, now anointed **Walt Disney World**. The proposal included an amusement park mirroring Disneyland, as well as plans for hotels and recreational activities. But the focus of the February 1967 press conference was something called the Experimental Prototype Community of Tomorrow, "a living blueprint of the future," as Walt himself called it in a 25-minute announcement he had filmed before his death. Disney would create a great, glass-domed community from scratch, free from the ills of established cities, a showcase and testing ground for new products and systems.

But the first priority was building **The Magic Kingdom**. As a replication of the profitable California amusement park, this would provide the economic catalyst for all other Walt Disney World development. In 1967, the first construction phase began as hundreds of acres of swampland were diverted into efficient drainage canals. Two years later, the company announced that Walt Disney World would open in 1971. By now, with more than 9000 workers and priced at $400 million, the operation was billed as the world's largest private-construction project. Work was well under way on The Magic Kingdom and the first two Disney resorts, the **Contemporary** and **Polynesian**. Disney's California craftsmen were hard at work supporting the Florida crews with design work, architectural blueprints and scale models. The trains that were to circle the amusement park were imported from the Yucatan and completely rebuilt, a merry-go-round from New Jersey was appropriated to serve as Cinderella's Golden Carrousel, and thousands of trees and plants were sown.

The Magic Kingdom opened its doors on Oct. 1, 1971. On that first day, fewer than 10,000 admissions were recorded and, for the first few weeks attendance was low, which actually turned out to be lucky—a number of attractions were not complete. Tomorrowland, in particular, lived up to its name all too literally. But by Christmas, the park had become a prime destination for the state's residents and by the end of the first full year of operation, 10.7 million admissions had been recorded.

Meanwhile, just outside Walt Disney World's boundaries, land prices continued to rise. The Magic Kingdom-initiated construction boom was replaced by the huge growth of tourism facilities off the Disney property: hotels and motels, shopping centers and other amusements seemed to spring up wherever land could be obtained. By 1973, Orlando was called the fastest-growing metropolitan region of the country, and the problems associated with loosely regulated growth—crime, economic instability and burdensome taxes—began to take root. When the oil embargo went into effect in late 1974, the region was forced to scale back. With gas prices soaring, tourist arrivals fell off dramatically and polished new hotel rooms went empty for months at a time. Even the Disney Company was not immune to the impact and more than 600 employees were laid off.

Although the region's growth was forestalled further due to the recession of 1974–1975, tourists eventually began to return. The January 1975 opening of **Space Mountain** renewed visitor interest and, by that summer, the Disney Company seemed ready to formally cash in on Walt's dream of the city of tomorrow. Or were they? Walt Disney had been consumed by plans for a real Tomorrowland in the year leading up to his death. The Magic Kingdom and its lodging facilities were considered a means to an end; the Experimental Prototype Community of Tomorrow was Walt's vision behind it all.

Epcot was still the name for this ambitious project, but something had become lost in the translation. "What would Walt think?" had been the cautious refrain among many Disney staffers for years after his death, but the revised Epcot plans became the first clear break with Walt Disney's prime directives. This was the beginning of the Disney Company's new era, and the Epcot project was now announced as a paid-admission theme park and international shopping mall, not a community with participants living under a glass dome. Epcot would have two separate "lands," one devoted to the future and technology, the other a sort of permanent world's fair surrounding a lake. Rides and attractions would be included, though with a more educational bent than what was found at The Magic Kingdom. Unlike the earlier creation, alcohol would be served—how could you have a German pavilion without beer, or a French "land" without wine?

AUTHOR'S OBSERVATION

One of the wackiest Disney myths pertains to the remains of Walt's body. In the months leading up to his death, he became interested in cryogenics—the process of freezing a corpse immediately after death to preserve it for future resurrection. The rumor took on a life of its own over the years, fueled by a genuine (if Disney-manufactured), mystery as to where his remains really are buried; a favorite is that the stiff lies in Cinderella Castle. Although Walt's devotion to scientific advances may have been a driving factor of his inquiries into immortality, a bigger concern may have been making sure that the Disney organization followed through on his plans and dreams, particularly those involving Epcot. Hence, the commonly uttered phrase "what would Walt think" may have been less a tribute to a former leader, than a subtle threat uttered by the company's small faction who wished to carry out the man's true Epcot vision. Ironically, the phrase has taken on a whole new life of its own in recent years, murmured by a number of locals theoretically left in the cold—everyone from the Christian right, who are shocked by the Disney Company's "new morals," to competing hotel operators pinched by the company's increasing domination of the local accommodations market.

Built at an estimated cost of $900 million that severely strained the company's resources, Epcot was a risky venture during the early 1980s, but the eventual payoff has presumably been enormous. Still, the project was not without its critics: Epcot was designed to generate much of its revenue in a glaring fashion that put some visitors off. Virtually every Future World attraction was "sponsored" by a major corporation—AT&T, Exxon, General Motors, etc. Like sponsors of the Olympics, each company paid a generous sum to link its name to the gold-plated Disney image. In theory, at least, the alliance would go some distance to keep the public's mind off less-palatable corporate subjects, such as oil spills and major layoffs.

AUTHOR'S OBSERVATION

"DisneySpeak" takes two different forms. The most interesting follows Walt's personal habit of coining new words—frequently copyrighting them—to address themes or issues and making them the company's own. For instance, the company's environmental awareness program is called Environmentality, while the creative folks responsible for designing attractions are referred to as Imagineers. More coy forms of DisneySpeak are the terms Disney employees—I mean cast members—are expected to use when dealing with the public. You aren't a customer in Walt Disney World, you're a guest; employees don't wear uniforms at work, they fill costumes and play their parts on stage. Plus, when you visit, you'll partake in adventures, not rides, and so on. Stay alert, and you'll learn other words.

Epcot's World Showcase was not immune to this exchange. All the featured countries (except, curiously, Canada) paid a hefty, undisclosed sum to build their pavilions, and an annual fee to keep them open, which explains why the Third World is so glaringly under represented; it's not profitable to the Disney operation. In effect, the pavilions operate as giant kiosks to promote tourism and trade for a select 11 nations.

But the park's 1982 opening was nonetheless a solid success and the park helped Orlando secure an increasingly international tourism base. With the additional draw of another major Disney park, Orlando, its hotel facilities, tourism infrastructure and other theme parks made another leap forward.

During the early 1980s, however, beyond the fiscal boundaries of Walt Disney World and Disneyland, the Disney Company was having a tough time. In Hollywood, the G-rated Disney label had become anathema to the teenagers and baby boomers filling theaters; *The Black Hole* and *Tron* were among a number of costly misfires that sapped the company's revenue. During the spring and summer of 1984, an eventually unsuccessful takeover attempt for control of the Disney Company occurred. What was to be the future of the company that Walt built?

During 1983–1984, the company had two important movie successes, *Never Cry Wolf* and *Splash*, both rated PG, and both representing a controversial, if subtle shift away from the sterile family entertainment the company had been pegged for during the 1970s. Michael Eisner was hired as the company's new CEO following the aborted takeover, and with Eisner at the helm, the studio aggressively pursued the new film policy with increasing success, creating adult-oriented hits such as *Down and Out in Beverly Hills* and *Good Morning, Vietnam.*

Meanwhile, back in Orlando, in 1981, **Universal Studios** announced its plans to develop a major parcel of land between downtown Orlando and Walt Disney World. Universal planned to create a movie studio theme park similar to the one pioneered at its studio in Hollywood. Apparently the Disney Company was no longer content to share its turf with any other attractions that might require a day-long agenda—in 1985 the Disney Company announced that it, too, had been planning to build a movie studio theme park, the $500 million **Disney-MGM Studios**. The Disney project in concept, at least, would allow access to the vaults and rights of not one studio, but two.

Universal executives were stunned. The company's president, Sid Sheinberg, referred to Mickey Mouse as "a ravenous rat." Adding to Universal's misery, the existing Walt Disney World design and construction infrastructure allowed Disney to hustle its studio-themed attraction into place in shorter time, beating Universal's 1990 opening by a year. Universal was further embarrassed when its Florida studios opened, press corps in tow, to a series of ride malfunctions and other problems.

Disney's targets weren't limited to Universal. The company was now emboldened to fully maximize the potential of its huge property, and began pouring its now-ample financial resources into other new attractions. Orlando's popular water parks were delivered a blow when Disney opened **Typhoon Lagoon**, a water park that took an existing concept, gave it a spectacular creative overhaul, and produced a complete original. And, rather than encourage Disney customers to slip away one night and take in **Church Street Station**, a popular nighttime entertainment complex in downtown Orlando, Disney performed another one-upping by opening **Pleasure Island**, again creatively tweaking an existing concept to the gills. The year 1989 saw the opening of the **Caribbean Beach Resort**, Disney's first attempt at moderately priced lodgings. Although room rates were priced higher than the norm just off Walt Disney World property, the 2100-room Caribbean Beach sent a signal that the company wanted to dominate the local hotel market—a goal that has since largely been achieved. The *Orlando Sentinel* reported that, in 1990, the turnstiles for Disney's three main parks recorded a total of 33.7 million admissions, a figure that has since been eclipsed (actual park ticket sales are highly guarded numbers, but the 1990 figure is thought to be relatively accurate, and Disney has announced "record attendance" several times since then).

How do locals feel about the Disney Company? Cynics group them into two packs: those who work for Disney, and those who resent its all-encompassing influence. Those in the know might separate them another way: central Florida residents who remember quieter times before Disney's arrival, and those who have migrated to the city during the past decade for jobs, but have to contend with more Disney—tourists, congestion, clutter—than they bargained for. In both instances, many locals cannot afford the vacation Disney proffers at every turn.

The resentment is probably best exemplified in the August 1995 issue of *Orlando Magazine* covering the "Best of Orlando," as rated by its staff and readers. Despite dozens of categories where the company's entities were eligible, including food, activities, entertainment and more, Disney scored in only one: "Best Place to Take the Kids." In truth, much of the attitude stems from the controls Disney solicited from the state and local authorities back during the 1960s. The company has recently begun to acknowledge this strictly local public relations problem and is making a more obvious attempt to integrate itself into the community with free events targeting Orlandoans, and other offers.

Of course, deep down, Orlando residents know that if Walt Disney World packed up its show tomorrow and moved to another locale, an admittedly unlikely prospect, the city would tumble into economic crisis. Florida, which has no personal income tax, earns 21 percent of its general sales tax revenue from tourism. Disney employs a huge, continually expanding workforce—38,600 jobs, as estimated by the *Orlando Business Journal*—and the collateral tourism employment from neighboring hotels, airlines and restaurants create the city's core industry, employing at least 150,000 residents. Perhaps what Orlandoans are really responding to when they "dis" the mouse is that they feel captive to the Disney empire—good, bad, or indifferent. But how does this affect you?

INSIDER'S TIP

In March 1996, a groundbreaking alliance was established among Universal Studios, Sea World and Wet 'n' Wild. The three parks now sell a five-day Value Pass for $95.35 for adults, or $77.33 for children ages 3-9. This five-day adult pass is about $11 less than the combined admission price to each of the three parks. For Disney's rivals, the joint program is the first step in providing a competitive alternative to the multitude of incentives that discourage guests from leaving Walt Disney World.

AUTHOR'S OBSERVATION

When the Walt Disney Company bought the ABC Network in 1995, the much-anticipated and well-oiled synergy soon began to flow thick and fast. Roseanne's television family took a vacation to the World (could they really have afforded it?), with "Step by Step" and "Boy Meets World" following suit soon thereafter, while "Good Morning America" drooled extensively over the Disney Institute's opening. Said TV Guide: "Jeers to ABC for clinging a little too tightly to its corporate parent."

The Disney Agenda and You

During the late 1980s, Disney's game strategy shifted. The company's preemptive curveball thrown at Universal upped the ante for all local attractions. Now Disney not only wanted to be the leading tourism pull for central Florida, it wanted to be its exclusive draw. Moving to capture the younger, drink-and-dance crowd, Disney lobbed a bombshell at Orlando's nighttime entertainment hub, **Church Street Station**, and built **Pleasure Island**. Disney opened **Typhoon Lagoon**, only to supplement it in 1995 by an even more spectacular water park, **Blizzard Beach**; this eliminated the need for Disney's guests to take in **Wet 'n Wild** or **Water Mania**. Want to go shopping? Disney offers the **Village Marketplace**, with shops that even sell a few items without Mickey Mouse emblazoned across them. Getting married? Now Disney rents a **Wedding Pavilion**, performing up to three ceremonies daily against a backdrop of **Cinderella Castle**. Want a learning vacation? In 1996, the **Disney Institute** appropriated New York's **Chautauqua Institution** theme to capture yet another travel segment it might have missed out on before. Scheduling a convention? Walt Disney World now offers the largest convention facilities in the southeast. And in 1996, the plethora of miniature golf courses off World property got their due; Disney built **Fantasia Gardens**, a delightful pair of miniature golf courses themed from the 1940 animated classic.

AUTHOR'S OBSERVATION

Possibly the Disney Company's most audacious announcement of all came in 1994 with the plans to develop a community, named "Celebration," on the Walt Disney World property. Perhaps the closest link to Walt's original dream to build an "experimental prototype community of tomorrow," Celebration is planned as an "education-minded and health-conscious community... (with) access to a telecommunications network allowing electronic communication with both neighbors and the world." To avoid traditional housing-tract blight, the Disney Company consulted renowned architects and community developers, utilizing the lessons of contemporary tract societies in creating their plan. The first group of pre-1940s southeastern-style homes were completed for summer 1996 occupancy, and a long list of applicants await future development. Celebration is located on the south side of U.S. 192, immediately east of I-4.

With each diversifying move, Disney has built something bigger, flashier and, usually, better. With each "check" on the Orlando tourism chessboard, Disney has forced its competition to be on the defensive. The Disney Company would like you to spend every hour of your vacation, be it a day or a week, on Disney property (begging the question: can a Walt Disney World Airport be far in the future? A Disney Airline?). If there was ever an unstated mission, it would be to make Disney your one-stop shopping vacation. Today, you can book your entire trip, airfare and car included, through the **Walt Disney Travel Company**, and when you get off the plane in Orlando, just head straight for the World. Do not pass Go.

On the surface, there's nothing wrong with this. Disney creates a superlative entertainment and vacation product. The theme parks are clean and, as a group, are more imaginative than any others on the planet. The company's hotel facilities, though somewhat high-priced, are uniformly well-run and maintained, and a pleasure to stay at. In the past couple of years, Disney has begun overhauling its full-service restaurants with promising results. If you are visiting Orlando, particularly on a tight schedule (such as an extended weekend) I would not steer anyone away from signing up for the full-court Disney treatment.

However, Disney's enormous marketing mechanism is quite seductive and, accordingly, too many visitors fail to imagine the universe beyond Walt Disney World. Let's call it the captive audience theory. Those who arrive in central Florida and head straight for Walt Disney World, where they spend their entire vacation before returning home, have willingly become part of that audience. Instead, I recommend a few forays outside Fantasyland. Orlando is more than Disney. **Universal Studios Florida** delivers a different kind of entertainment from the Disney-MGM package, and the studio has eventually emerged as every bit Disney's equal. **Sea World** is an excellent marine park with, in my opinion, a better mix of education and entertainment than Epcot. **Church Street Station** may be a little rough at the edges, but as a music and club theme park, it feels a little more like the real world than what Disney offers at Pleasure Island. Just outside downtown Orlando lies **Lake Eola**, the city's inviting urban park that provides swan-shaped paddle boats, an outdoor amphitheater for Shakespeare, and a bicycle and skating path. Just north of downtown, the **Winter Park Scenic Boat Tour** visits homes of the rich and semi-famous that line several gorgeous lakes, and the people occupying the residences are hardly Disney's Audio-Animatronic creations.

INSIDER'S TIP

Books examining Walt Disney, his company and its agenda are in no short supply. Probably the definitive, most objective biography of the man is The Disney Version, *by Richard Schickel (1985, Simon and Schuster). The company's preferred take is* Walt Disney: An American Original, *by Bob Thomas (1976, Simon and Schuster). The other side of Disney is glimpsed in the controversial* Walt Disney: Hollywood's Dark Prince *by Marc Eliot (1993, Carol Publishing), which details Walt's 25-year role as an informant for J. Edgar Hoover's FBI and other peccadilloes. Disney's film animation history is splendidly told in* Of Mice and Magic, *by Leonard Maltin (1987, NAL Dutton). One of the most fascinating academic discussions of Walt Disney World and its societal role is* Vinyl Leaves, *by Stephen M. Fjellman (1992, Westview Press). John Taylor's* Storming the Magic Kingdom: Wall Street, the Raiders, and the Battle for Disney *(1988, Ballantine Books) documents the dramatic, behind-the-scenes activities during the 1984 takeover attempt and the changes in the company it produced. Finally, Joe Flower's* Prince of the Magic Kingdom: Michael Eisner and the Remaking of Disney *(1991, John Wiley and Sons), is an excellent assessment of the current Disney CEO and the challenges ahead for the company.*

Farther afield, **Busch Gardens** is a strange mix of theme park and zoo, but there are several noteworthy animal enclosures and, with the 1996 opening of **Montu**, easily the best collection of roller coasters in the state. **Kennedy Space Center**, though burdened with an inferior (compared to Disney) tourism facility, is the real thing; little can match the awe of standing within a mile of the actual Space Shuttle, let alone seeing it lift off. And Florida's beaches, the attraction Disney himself knew he couldn't compete against, are a dream.

In sum, you can join Disney's captive audience, and you'll probably have a good, perhaps great, cookie-cut Florida vacation. Or you can traipse a few miles away from the Disney thrills and experience some of what the region offers off the-beaten track. With Fielding's in hand, we'll guide you to the best of what central Florida offers, as well as through the maze of Disney attractions.

Comparisons and Expectations

A common question for West Coast residents familiar with **Disneyland** is whether a trip to Orlando is worthwhile... or even necessary. Many who have visited the Disneyland assume that Walt Disney World is simply a bigger version. Disneyland is indeed a very special amusement park, but in recent years Walt Disney World has justifiably added the word "Resort" to its title. One is an ambitious day trip, the other would be difficult to fully appreciate in a week.

But, before I go further, cards on the table. I grew up in Southern California during the 1960s, and lived for the annual family trip to Disneyland. I have a certain nostalgia that makes comparisons between Disneyland and **The Magic Kingdom** *within* Walt Disney World somewhat biased. But at the risk of offending those whose upbringing was in Florida, I'll post a few observations.

In concept, theme and layout, The Magic Kingdom is essentially a copy of Disneyland. Whether in California or Florida, you'll enter the park through Main Street and encounter the same hub-and-spoke system of themed lands leading away from a castle (Sleeping Beauty's in California, Cinderella's in Florida). Almost every ride found in the Magic Kingdom is present at Disneyland, and the differences between common attractions are usually subtle. However, the overall effect is far from a mirror image and no guest who has visited both parks can avoid comparing the two. Even the 9- and 10-year-old California relatives who joined me to sample Orlando attractions made repeated note of the differences.

Disneyland, being a little older, feels more lived in. Because it's landlocked, the park has not been able to grow outward, and so additions have been piled artfully into every conceivable nook and cranny. Disneyland is a dense and spectacular, cluttered and breathtaking vision; new attractions add to the increasingly dizzy fantasy. By contrast, The Magic Kingdom was created using the "lessons" gleaned from Disneyland's success, and therefore, pedestrian walkways are wider, crowd control is more efficient and there are fewer distracting details. On a busy day, Disneyland can feel utterly claustrophobic, whereas the Kingdom somehow manages to keep the traffic moving, and the lines seem to recess into the background.

There are several rides at Disneyland that have been replicated nowhere else: the **Matterhorn Bobsleds**, **Indiana Jones** and **Alice in Wonderland**, to name a few. Similarly, The Magic Kingdom has produced a few treats that are not yet available on the left coast: **The Hall of Presidents**, **Timekeeper** and the **ExtraTERRORestrial Alien Encounter**. And rather than quaint **New Orleans Square** plopped down next to the Rivers of America as you find in Disneyland, you have a patriotic **Liberty Square** in the Magic Kingdom.

At the risk of heresy, I'll state that the main reason to visit Orlando, for West Coasters familiar with Disneyland, is not The Magic Kingdom. Disneyland offers a special vision, and the gesture of replicating or improving on it feels hollow. Instead, Orlando's advantage is that instead of a single, 98-acre park, you have much of the 30,500-acre Walt Disney World at your disposal and you won't feel hemmed in or limited to a single, one-day Disney experience. If the crowds get you down at The Magic Kingdom, you can easily escape to an imaginative, themed resort. Three eccentric water parks dot the World. Diverse recreation opportunities are available nearby, including golf, tennis, swimming and more.

Best of all, **Epcot** and the **Disney-MGM Studios** are each an ingenious spin-off from the grand amusement park that Walt originally envisioned. Both Epcot and the Studios share one key ride with Disneyland (**Star Tours** at the studios and **Honey I Shrunk the Audience** at Epcot), but otherwise deliver a completely new experience for those familiar with the original park. Like The Magic Kingdom, both of these sizable entertainments require at least one full day to experience them.

No coastal comparison would be complete without mentioning **Sea World** and **Universal Studios**, both of which are also spin-offs from California-based inspirations. Sea World of Florida has a slightly different atmosphere from Sea World in San Diego because it is landlocked and surrounded by jungle, hardly the expected setting for an ocean-themed environment, whereas San Diego's Sea World is situated on a man-made bay and its lushest greenery is imported. A number of attractions are similar, but one key exhibit, the **Manatee habitat** in Florida, will probably never make its way to San Diego and is almost worth the price of admission alone.

Universal in Florida lacks the authentic link to film industry history that makes its Hollywood counterpart special. The backlot tram tour at Universal in California visits genuine sets from Hollywood's golden era, while the tram tour at Florida's Universal is of little interest. However, the Florida park, since it was designed first and foremost as a tourist attraction, is better laid out for visitors, and an increasing number of television shows and movies are shooting on the backlots (the television show "Seaquest" was the biggest local talent employer for several years until its 1995 cancellation). Several attractions in California—**Jaws** and **Earthquake** in particular—are greatly expanded and improved on in Florida, while a number of others—such as **Back to the Future** and **E.T. Adventure**—are virtually identical. Each park has several attractions that are not, at this time, replicated at the other. All things considered, for those who have toured Universal Hollywood in the last few years, given a choice between Universal and the Disney-MGM Studios during your Orlando visit, the latter is a better bet since visitors will find much less overlap of attractions.

But finally, comparing California and Florida is a little silly because, frankly, beyond the theme parks, they are vastly different regions. People lump the two states together because they share sunshine, beaches and oranges, yet little else can be found in common. Not only are there several unique and historic attractions in and near Orlando that are not to be found anywhere else—**Kennedy Space Center**, **Gatorland** and **Cypress Gardens**, to name some— but Orlando's culture is dramatically different.

Southern hospitality really does exist in central Florida, visible in the Cypress Gardens sight of young women in antebellum dresses posing on sprawling lawns where the whiff of a mint julep wafts faintly nearby.

The Price of Entertainment in Orlando

The theme parks (particularly the image-conscious Disney Company) rarely release the price tag of their attractions. The *Orlando Sentinel* once compiled a list of the development and construction costs for some of the region's major attractions (a few of the following figures are from other sources).

Splendid China	*$100 million*
Disney-MGM Studios's Tower of Terror	*$95 million*
Typhoon Lagoon	*$92 million*
The Magic Kingdom's Splash Mountain	*$91 million*
Epcot's Wonders of Life pavilion and Body Wars	*$90 million combined*

The Price of Entertainment in Orlando

The Magic Kingdom's new Tomorrowland and ExtraTERRORestrial	*$80 million combined*
Epcot's Test Track	*$73 million*
Blizzard Beach	*$65 million*
Universal Studios' Terminator 2 3-D	*$60 million*
Universal Studios' Jaws	*$50 million*
Universal Studios' Back to the Future	*$40 million*
Epcot's Innoventions	*$38 million*
Fantasy of Flight	*$30 million*
Epcot's Honey, I Shrunk the Audience	*$18 million*
Daytona USA	*$18 million*
Sea World's Shamu Stadium	*$14 million*

Aerial shot of downtown Orlando includes a view of Lake Eola.

TomorrOrlando

Twenty-five years ago, when The Magic Kingdom opened its doors, no one, perhaps even Walt Disney included, could have imagined the impact his vision would have on central Florida. Sure, everyone knew it would bring more tourists to the region, but did anyone then really dream that Orlando would become the single biggest hotel market in the world, with an anticipated block of 100,000 rooms built by the year 2000?

Within the World, *imagineers* are busily expanding on Walt's original vision with the recent announcement that they will build their fourth and largest Orlando theme park yet: **Disney's Animal Kingdom**. The park's centerpiece will be a giant Tree of Life—14 stories high and 50 feet wide at its base—hand-carved into a swirling tapestry of life forms. Budgeted at $766 million, Disney's Animal Kingdom will have three primary "lands" branching off from the tree, one of which will offer a safari ride through a live-animal environment. The other lands will feature creatures of the audio-animatronic kind: one will focus on the primeval world, featuring a thrill ride through the end of the dinosaur era; another will focus on mythical worlds, with unicorns, dragons and other creatures coming to life. Disney's Animal Kingdom will occupy a 500-acre parcel of land (almost five times the size of The Magic Kingdom) west of Blizzard Beach and is scheduled to open in the spring of 1998.

Disney's biggest ride set to debut in 1997 is the **Test Track** at Epcot, replacing the old **It's Fun to be Free** ride at the **World of Motion** pavilion. Advance word is that the new adventure—in essence the first thrill ride at Epcot—will represent the fastest attraction and use the longest track of any ride previously built by Disney. During the ride, say those in the know, participants become veritable crash-test dummies. Look for the Test Track to open in the spring of 1997. Disney is said to be planning another "E-Ticket" ride for Epcot's World Showcase, but a Mount Fuji attraction near the Japan pavilion (and featuring Matterhorn-style bobsleds) may be little more than a hopeful rumor.

Also set for 1997–1998 is an expansion of the Disney Village Marketplace, tentatively to be called **Downtown Disney**. The first development, scheduled to coincide with 25th anniversary festivities, was **The World of Disney**, a 50,000-square-foot superstore, the largest Disney character merchandise shop in the world. Other projects under construction as we went to press: **House of Blues**, a 1500-person capacity restaurant and music venue; **Wolfgang Puck's Cafe**, a casual setting for California cuisine and designer pizzas; and **Bongos Cuban Cafe**, a Miami Beach-themed restaurant and nightclub created by Gloria and Emilio Estefan. All three of the restaurants are scheduled to open by summer 1997. Also to open in the summer is a 14-screen addition to the **AMC Pleasure Island Theater** that will make it the largest movie complex in the state. Fall 1997 is to see the completion of a 40,000-square-foot **Virgin Megastore** for music, videos and more, and summer 1998 will mark the opening of a 1650-seat theater set to house **Cirque du Soleil**, the Montreal-based troupe of performance artists and acrobats.

Disney hotel development continues at a rapid pace. The 1921-room **Coronado Springs Resort**, to be located near the All-Stars and Disney's Animal Kingdom, will have a Southwestern flavor and includes a 95,000-square-foot convention center. Featuring hacienda-style buildings accented with terracotta tiles, the resort will be priced in the moderate range and is set to open its doors in late summer of 1997. Another All-Star Resort, possibly themed to Broadway, is rumored to be in the works, and a Mediterranean-accented resort may eventually occupy a chunk of land along the Monorail line rimming the Seven Seas Lagoon between the Contemporary Resort and the Ticket and Transportation Center.

Perhaps even bigger plans are afoot at Universal Studios, where two major additions will open in coming years as part of a $2.6 billion expansion project. The first, slated for January 1998, is the **E-Zone**, an entertainment complex mirroring the successful CityWalk complex that adjoins Universal's Hollywood studios. The 12-acre facility will feature elaborately themed restaurants, nightclubs, shops and a 16-screen movie theater. Among the creative partners involved in E-Zone are Emeril Lagasse (of New Orleans' Emeril's Restaurant fame), Shaquille O'Neal and B.B. King, who will recreate his popular Memphis club.

Immediately next door to E-Zone will be **Islands of Adventure**, a new theme park with a group of bridge-linked "is-lands" hosting a variety of attractions. Among the themed islands are: Suess Landing, based on the characters and motifs from Dr. Suess' beloved books; Isla Nublar, which houses a ride based on the hit *Jurassic Park;* and Sweethaven, a port for Popeye and his cohorts. The park, accompanied by at least two major Universal-owned hotels, is set to open in 1999; the company will, soon, like its mouse-eared neighbor to the south, add the word "resort" to its title.

AUTHOR'S OBSERVATION

Almost as entertaining as pondering today's plans for tomorrow's Orlando are the wild non-Disney concepts that never materialized. Among my favorite abandonments is **Perestroyka Palace**, *an $18 million center styled after St. Basil's Cathedral in Moscow's Red Square that was to contain a disco and facilities for diplomacy and deal-making; the project was to include a symbolic bridge over a faux Bering Strait to an Alaskan mining and trading post. Then there was* **Vedaland**, *a high-tech joint venture between the Maharishi Mahesh Yogi and magician Doug Henning to create a theme park around meditation and higher consciousness (perhaps positioning this attraction on U.S. 192 near the Medieval Times dinner theater may have been a deal breaker?).*

But these are activities for your *next* trip. Let's get to work and plan your Orlando trip for this year, today!

SEVEN BREATHTAKING CENTRAL FLORIDA VIEWS

Bok Tower Gardens
Summit Plummet at Blizzard Beach

SEVEN BREATHTAKING CENTRAL FLORIDA VIEWS

The 27th-floor dining room of Arthur's 27

The oceanside bluff next to the Kennedy Space Center shuttle liftoff pad

The California Grill and 15th floor of Contemporary Resort

The top of the incline on Kumba at Busch Gardens

Island in the Sky at Cypress Gardens

HOW THE BIG ATTRACTIONS COMPARE (BUDGETING YOUR TIME)

Attraction name	Rating	Adult Admission*	Touring Time
U.S. Astronaut Hall of Fame	★★	$10.55	1–2 hours
Blizzard Beach	★★★★	$25.39	4–6 hours
Busch Gardens	★★★	$36.15	7–10 hours
Church Street Station	★★★	$17.97	3–4 hours
Cypress Gardens	★★	$29.63	3–4 hours
Discovery Island	★★	$11.61	1–2 hours
Disney-MGM Studios	★★★★	$40.81	8–10 hours
Epcot	★★★★★	$40.81	12–16 hours
Gatorland	★★	$12.67	2–3 hours
Green Meadows Petting Farm	★★	$13	2 hours
Harry P. Leu Gardens	★★★	$3	1–2 hours
JungleLand	★	$10.65	1 hour
Kennedy Space Center	★★★	$11**	4–6 hours
The Magic Kingdom	★★★★★	$40.81	12–14 hours
Mystery Fun House	★	$8.43	30 minutes
Pleasure Island	★★★	$17.97	3–5 hours
Ripley's Believe it or Not	★★	$10.55	1 hour
River Country	★★★	$15.64	3–4 hours
Winter Park Scenic Boat Tour	★★★	$6	1 hour
Sea World	★★★★	$39.95	6–8 hours
Silver Springs	★★★	$29.63	3–4 hours
Splendid China	★★	$23.55	3–5 hours
Terror on Church Street	★★	$12.72	30 minutes
Typhoon Lagoon	★★★★	$25.39	4–6 hours
Universal Studios	★★★★	$40.81	9–12 hours
Water Mania	★★	$25.63	3–5 hours
Wet 'n Wild	★★★	$25.39	4–6 hours

*All prices include tax

**Kennedy Space Center price includes one bus tour and one IMAX film

PLANNING YOUR TRIP

Orlando International Airport handles 24 million visitors annually.

It's a safe bet you won't suffer for lack of diversions once you arrive in Orlando. There is, truly, something to please everyone. The problem is prioritizing all the activities and parks. Unless you're planning a multiweek visit, you can't cover in a single sojourn all the bases Disney and Orlando have generously laid out for you. This chapter is devoted to setting up your trip and will provide you access to all the resources that will create a memorable vacation. Before you begin locking down your plans, take a moment to procure some of the free, supplemental brochures and discount offers listed below. Although some of this material will be available after you arrive, get them before you go, and you'll be better able to plan your trip. Allow at least a month for delivery.

1. The Walt Disney Travel Company Brochure

A Disney package trip is not the only way to visit Orlando, but this 64-page pamphlet is stocked with photos and is a good resource for prices and information on the Disney Resorts. (Before you commit to a package trip, be sure to read "By Package Tour" in this chapter.) Recently, the Disney Company has also begun producing 25-minute videos that can be mailed out free of charge to prospective visitors; the videos serve as shameless infomercials for the company, but they are a decent visual aid in providing you an overview of Disney's resorts and parks. ☎ *(800) 327-2996.* Mornings, particularly Saturdays, are when this line—one of the few toll-free Disney numbers available—is least busy. If you have little patience for busy signals, call ☎ *(407) 828-3232,* or write: *The Walt Disney Travel Company Inc., P.O. Box 22094, Lake Buena Vista, Florida 32830.*

2. Universal City Travel Company

Not to be left in Disney's dust, in 1996 Universal introduced its package vacation plan, linked to Sea World, Wet 'n Wild and Busch Gardens, as well as a number of hotels primarily along the I-Drive passage (and a few in the Tampa Bay area). Some of the hotel packages are very competitive and are priced well below Disney's, though the quality of the hotels featured varies greatly. As Universal's other parks come on line toward the end of the century, the head-to-head battle between the two companies could prove very interesting. The free brochure is sure to grow in time from its current 28-page length. ☎ *(800) 224-3838.*

3. The Orlando MagiCard

This card provides reduced admissions at the major, non-Disney attractions, as well as discounts for area restaurants, hotels and car rentals. You'll receive some promotional brochures and a pamphlet called the *Official Visitor's Guide* that contains more discount offers. ☎ *(800) 255-5786.* If you have specific needs or requests, call the Orlando Convention and Visitor's Bureau directly at ☎ *(407) 363-5872* and speak to a real person.

4. Kissimmee-St. Cloud Vacation Guide

If you are considering staying at one of the many less expensive accommodations along U.S. 192, the Kissimmee-St. Cloud Visitor's Bureau also provides a brochure with discounts on local hotels and coupons for most of the major non-Disney attractions in central Florida. However, when I called and requested this material, I received nothing for weeks. Then a postcard arrived in the mail that said: "Congratulations! Due to your recent inquiry to the Kissimmee-St. Cloud Visitor's Bureau, you were selected to receive a seven day and six night vacation offer." Since the too-good-to-be-true offer expired the day after the card was postmarked, one can only assume this was a come-on; the visitor's bureau claimed to have no control over the release of its mailing list to outsiders (the Vacation Guide did eventually arrive, 11 weeks after my original request). ☎ *(800) 327-9159.*

If you have more individual needs (for instance, information for seniors, guests with disabilities, etc.), turn to "Special Travelers" in this chapter. Other important phone numbers are listed at the end of this chapter.

The Magic Kingdom Club

Also worth looking into is The Magic Kingdom Club, a Disney-created discount program. Typically, membership cards are issued free-of-charge by employers, credit unions and other organizations; check to see if you are eligible. The cards earn an approximately 5 percent discount on Disney theme park tickets, 10 percent off selected World restaurants, 10 percent off Disney Store purchases (except some collector's items) and 10 to 30 percent off rooms at Disney Resorts.

The nontransferable membership also may be purchased by the general public for $65 for two years, or $50 for seniors ages 55 and up. But, before purchasing the card, check with your employer, credit union and even with Disney (at the number below) to make sure you don't qualify for a free card (Disney maintains a list of all companies and organizations that issue the memberships).

If you will definitely be staying at a Disney Resort *and* can plan your trip several months in advance, you will probably come out ahead after springing the $65 sign-up fee, particularly if your party totals three or more. However, note that discounted room availability within the Disney Resorts is tightly controlled and must be booked months in advance, and the All-Stars Resorts are excluded from the discount program.

The Magic Kingdom Club: ☎ *(714) 781-1550.*

INSIDER'S TIP

A labyrinthine maze of ticket options—particularly for Walt Disney World—exists in Orlando, and is detailed in the "Walt Disney World Theme Parks" chapters. You'll want to read this section before you go—purchasing tickets before you leave can prove to be a real time-saver. Additionally, with Disney admission prices rising at least once a year, there's a decent chance you'll get a price break as well.

When to Go

Because the region's many attractions operate year-round and the weather is usually mild, there is no wrong time to visit Orlando. But there are periods of the year—when crowds are down, when the weather is sublime—that make for better touring than other months.

In my book, the single most important timing consideration for the Orlando region is knowing the number of strangers I'll be sharing my vacation with. Although the local tourism industry has done a number of things to spread out the crunch of visitors, the difference between a slow and a busy day at the Magic Kingdom can easily mean the difference between a 10-minute wait versus a two-hour line for Space Mountain.

The most obvious solution is to avoid the region entirely during the peak seasons when attendance at the theme parks is highest. During the Christmas vacation period and the Fourth of July weekend(s), not only are choice Disney accommodations booked to capacity months in advance, but you'll find most of the rooms between Universal and Kissimmee are solidly occupied. During these two time frames, accommodations are also priced at their highest. These aren't the only busy periods for central Florida, but if you visit during this time, you are virtually guaranteed to remember your vacation as a succession of lines and traffic.

Weather

Walt Disney World Weather provides 24-hour recorded weather information including a four-day forecast: (407) 827-4545.

Month	Average High (°F)	Average Low (°F)	Precipitation (inches)
January	67	49	2.3
February	72	51	2.9
March	75	55	3.5
April	82	61	2.7
May	86	64	2.9
June	89	71	7.1
July	89	72	8.3

Weather			
August	90	74	6.7
September	92	75	7.2
October	82	66	4.1
November	80	60	1.6
December	72	52	1.9

The second level of business, when the parks operate close to capacity, is reached during the other major holiday periods: Presidents Day weekend, the spring break period leading up to and including Easter, and the summer months in general. During these times, most or all of the Disney rooms will be filled, lines will be long at the major attractions and finding quiet and solitude will be difficult. The availability of budget accommodations outside Walt Disney World will be limited, although there will be a quantity of rooms available on short notice. If school-age visitors are traveling with you and you must visit during the summer, try mid-to-late August, when regional tourism dips slightly.

The remaining periods—roughly seven months a year—are when the parks are more manageable. Visiting during the mid-September through late-January time frame (other than the aforementioned holidays) maximizes your touring time by lessening the number and length of lines you dawdle in. Weather is generally perfect: rainfall is minimal, the days are sunny without being stifling, and rarely is anything more than a sweater required during the evenings. The December-January period can yield chilly days at the water parks, but if the sun is out and the wind is not brisk, even Blizzard Beach is enjoyable.

AUTHOR'S OBSERVATION

Though they can tear up nearby coastal areas, hurricanes usually pose little threat in landlocked central Florida. However, 1992's Andrew shut down most Orlando attractions and resulted in buckets of rain.

Finally, whenever you visit, it's important to have a plan to sidestep the crowds. You'll find tips sprinkled throughout *Fielding's Walt Disney World and Orlando* that help you understand the traffic patterns that lead to long lines, and touring plans we've developed to help you avoid them.

How Long to Go

Before setting your travel dates in stone, consider the amount of time you want to allow for your visit. The average length of stay is five nights, but shorter and longer vacations can easily be accommodated. Again, it's important to acknowledge the time period you'll be visiting. During the slower seasons, it's possible to see one big park in a day, while during the summer and holiday periods, longer operating hours only go so far to reducing the length of lines at the major attractions.

The three primary Disney parks alone require a minimum of three days total, preferably four, to enjoy them. Allow an extra day to take in a water park and/or Pleasure Island. Universal Studios also requires one long touring day. On a tight schedule, Sea World can usually be combined into the same day as another activity, such as a water park or a game of golf. A visit to either coast for Busch Gardens, Kennedy Space Center or the region's beaches will require most or all of a day, after accounting for travel time. As you can see, if you're planning even a five-day trip, particularly if it's your first to the area, you'll need to make some hard choices.

If your trip is limited to four or five days, Universal Studios and the Disney-MGM Studios share a common theme, and a little overlap. While I enthusiastically recommend visiting both attractions for guests who have the time, if you're forced to eliminate a major park from your touring schedule, high-pitched Universal appeals to teens and young adults, while the "safer" Disney-MGM park finds more fans among the pre-teen and senior set. If a water park is your cup of tea, schedule it for the morning, well before crowds arrive and force you to make it an all-day affair. If you love animals, you can fit a late-afternoon/evening visit to Sea World into a fast-paced schedule.

If your trip will allow for six or more days, I also recommend spending at least a day away from the Orlando area. The east and west coasts (Kennedy Space Center, Busch Gardens and the beaches) are the best options for families, while the gardens north and south (Silver Springs and Cypress Gardens) appeal most to an older crowd.

As you look through our description of the various attractions, you'll find some hints as to which days are the best for touring the individual parks, but that discussion can wait until after you've settled on when and how long to visit. See "Suggested Theme Park Itineraries" in "Obstacles and Opportunities" for additional touring suggestions.

Special Events

January

The **Walt Disney World Marathon** draws upwards of 10,000 entrants for a 26.2-mile race through the three major parks; ☎ *(407) 939-7810*. Disney also sponsors the **LPGA Tournament** at Lake Buena Vista Golf Course; ☎ *(407) 939-7810*. In 1996, Disney opened its racetrack at the edge of the Ticket and Transportation Center; the **Indy 200** is now an annual late-January event; ☎ *(407) 939-4639*.

February

Mardi Gras is celebrated at Pleasure Island with Zydeco and Dixieland bands, parades, Cajun and creole food, and souvenir beads and doubloons; ☎ *(407) 934-6374*. The one-week **International Carillon Festival** is held at Bok Tower Gardens and allows visitors hands-on experience at the tower's practice keyboards; ☎ *(941) 676-1408*. The **Silver Spurs Rodeo**, the largest competition in the eastern United States, draws 50,000 spectators to the three-day event, featuring champion bull riders and cowboys (a similar event takes place in July); ☎ *(407) 847-4052*. The **Houston Astros' Spring Training** continues through March at Osceola Stadium in Kissimmee; ☎ *(407) 933-5500*.

March

St. Patrick's Day brings an incursion of Leprechauns, four-leaf clovers and Irish music at Pleasure Island; ☎ *(407) 934-6374*. Disney's **Easter Parade** takes place the weekend prior to and over Easter Sunday weekend at the Magic Kingdom; ☎ *(407) 824-4321*. Cypress Gardens' annual **Spring Flower Festival** begins in March and features oversize topiaries and floral bed annuals; ☎ *(941) 324-2111*. The **Kissimmee Bluegrass Festival** is held at the Silver Spurs Rodeo grounds, drawing performers and fans for a diverse range of music including bluegrass, creole and Texas swing; ☎ *(800) 473-7773*. The **Central Florida Fair** is a 10-day event hosting rides, animals and competitions; ☎ *(407) 295-3247*. The **International Orchid Fair** takes place at World of Orchids, drawing growers from around the world (a similar event takes place in June); ☎ *(407) 396-1887*.

April

For a six-week period beginning mid-April, Epcot's popular **International Flower and Garden Festival** yields more than 3 million blooms, floral displays, topiary exhibits, demonstrations and workshops; ☎ *(407) 824-4321*. The Disney Village Marketplace celebrates **Earth Day** with exhibits, an elementary school art contest and animal presentations; ☎ *(407) 828-3800*. **Grad Nights** at the Magic Kingdom take place over two weekends, with gates opening at 11 p.m. and live music events scattered throughout the park until the wee hours; ☎ *(407) 824-4321*. The **Orlando-UCF Shakespeare Festival** takes place at Lake Eola's amphitheater, with two works performed throughout the month by noted actors; ☎ *(407) 423-6905*. The Central Florida Zoological Park's annual **Easter Egg Hunt** is scheduled on Easter morning, with more than 6000 colored eggs hidden for children ages 10 and under; ☎ *(407) 323-4450*. April is also the time for the **International Fringe Festival**, a 10-day extravaganza (downtown Orlando's biggest annual event) involving hundreds of actors, musicians, jugglers and other entertainers; they produce more than 500 performances for all ages, encompassing drama, comedy, cabaret, musicals, stories, children's theater, political satire, dance, visual arts and performance art; ☎ *(407) 648-0077.*

May

Cinco de Mayo, Mexican Independence Day, is celebrated May 5 at Epcot with special festivities; ☎ *(407) 824-4321.* The **Zellwood Sweet Corn Festival** takes place Memorial Day weekend, and provides more than 200,000 ears of corn to be consumed by attendees who also partake in carnival rides, contests and country music events; ☎ *(407) 886-0014.*

June

The **Florida Film Festival** takes place at the Enzian Theater and hosts more than 100 films from around the world and features tributes, seminars and premieres; ☎ *(407) 629-1088.*

July

The very busy **Fourth of July** period invites larger-than-usual fireworks displays at the Magic Kingdom. The **World Cooks Tour for Hunger**, a culinary competition raising funds to fight world hunger, takes place throughout Walt Disney World; ☎ *(407) 824-4321.* A **Picnic in the Park** is held on the Fourth of July at Lake Eola with games, activities and fireworks; ☎ *(407) 246-2827.*

September

Latin Rhythm Nights, featuring live Latin, jazz and salsa music, take place at Pleasure Island during the first weekend in September; ☎ *(407) 934-6374.* The annual **Disneyana** event, for devotees of Disney merchandise and collectibles, switches coasts each year, with the event scheduled for Walt Disney World in 1996, then Disneyland in 1997; ☎ *(407) 560-7232.* **Night of Joy**, a contemporary Christian music celebration requiring special tickets, occurs at The Magic Kingdom over two weekends; ☎ *(407) 824-4321.*

October

Oct. 1 is **Walt Disney World's Birthday**—see "The 25th Anniversary" in "Obstacles and Opportunities" for a list of some of the special activities planned; ☎ *(407) 824-4321.* Epcot's **Food and Wine Festival** offers a month-long series of themed dinner experiences, wine tastings, demonstrations and more, including representation by countries not depicted at World Showcase, including Spain, Greece and India; ☎ *(407) 824-4321.* The first weekend in October brings the **Central Florida Marine Trade Association Boat Show**, hosted at the Disney Village Marketplace; ☎ *(407) 828-3800.* The second weekend in October is highlighted by **Jazz Fest**, an annual event featuring name talent in the clubs and streets of Pleasure Island; ☎ *(407) 934-6374.* The **Walt Dis-**

ney World/Oldsmobile Golf Classic, an annual PGA event, takes place the third weekend in October; ☎ *(407) 939-7810.* Pleasure Island celebrates **Halloween** in a big way with a costume contest, fortune tellers and prizes; ☎ *(407) 934-6374.* **Universal Studios** is transformed into the region's biggest Halloween playground for the weekends leading up to Oct. 31; ☎ *(407) 363-8000.* Walt Disney World, Sea World, Silver Springs and Church Street Station schedule other noteworthy Halloween events.

November

The second weekend in November is highlighted by the annual **Festival of the Masters**, a juried art show covering 11 visual arts categories and taking place at the Disney Village Marketplace; ☎ *(407) 828-3800.* Beginning Thanksgiving weekend and continuing through December, the Disney parks break out in a rash of **Christmas** decorations, parades and special events; ☎ *(407) 824-4321.* The annual **Chrysanthemum Festival**, the largest display of its kind in the United States, takes place at Cypress Gardens and features more than 2.5 million blooms; the park's annual **Poinsettia Festival and Garden of Lights** begins Thanksgiving weekend; ☎ *(941) 324-2111.*

December

Mickey's Very Merry Christmas Party is a special-ticket event, usually a sellout, held several nights at the Magic Kingdom; ☎ *(407) 824-4321.* **IllumiNations** is altered for the season with a special **Holidays Around the World** show beginning Thanksgiving weekend and featuring candlelight processionals and local choir concerts. Beginning in 1995, the Disney-MGM Studios became an annual home to the **Osborne Family Christmas Decorations**, an eye-popping collection of 3 million Christmas lights; ☎ *(407) 824-4321.* Universal Studios decorates the New York Street set with a blanket of snow and also lights Hollywood Boulevard with vintage **Christmas Scenes**; ☎ *(407) 363-8000.* Sea World lights its "Christmas tree" (the 400-foot Sky Tower) and stages **Christmas in Hawaii**, with Polynesian dancers performing seasonal tunes; ☎ *(407) 363-2200.* Winter Park's Central Park is lighted by turn-of-the-century **Tiffany Windows** from the Morse Museum collection; ☎ *(407) 645-5311.* **New Year's Eve** is celebrated nightly year-round at Pleasure Island, but the real calendar date brings name talent on four stages, buffets and a fireworks show at midnight; ☎ *(407) 934-6374.* The other Disney parks also have bigger-than-usual fireworks displays for the night. Church Street Station rings in the new year with festivities and a midnight champagne toast; ☎ *(407) 422-2434.*

Some Low-Season Disclaimers

Walt Disney World, Universal and Sea World all operate their parks based on demand. During the summer months, hours are extended to spread out the crowds, and additional performances of parades and fireworks are scheduled. By contrast, a recent early November schedule found the Magic Kingdom and Disney-MGM Studios closing most nights at 7 p.m., Epcot at 9 p.m. Universal and Sea World also locked up at 7 p.m. There were no fireworks scheduled at the Magic Kingdom, and Sorcery in the Sky was performed on Saturday nights only at the Disney-MGM Studios (**IllumiNations** at Epcot seems permanently scheduled for 9 p.m. nightly year-round). The amount of live music and number of special events were greatly reduced.

Still, for touring Walt Disney World and the other parks, I'll take a 10-to-12 hour touring window during the slow, winter season *any day* over a 15-hour period in the summer when the venues have been slammed by guests. With few exceptions, you will be able to see more, enjoy more rides, and experience it all with far less congestion on the shorter, slower days than you will on the longer, busier ones. And, unless seeing several different sets of fireworks is your particular fancy, one show per trip is sufficient for most visitors.

An additional consideration is that Disney and Universal schedule annual ride maintenance for the slower months, usually a period of a couple weeks for each ride. This schedule is actually set many months in advance; call the parks when booking your trip to verify that any important attractions you want to see will be open at the time of your visit. Disney avoids scheduling closures of their major rides at the same time (for instance, **Big Thunder Mountain** and **Splash Mountain** won't be shut down simultaneously). During the winter season, Disney closes **Blizzard Beach** and **Typhoon Lagoon** in their entirety for annual refurbishing; the two facilities are each padlocked almost two months apiece. Although they avoid overlapping the closure dates of their two big water parks, and most visitors in the cooler winter season are satiated with just one water park, call in advance if you want to make sure one or both are available during your visit. Phone: ☎ *(407) 824-4321.*

Getting There

By Air

Apparently aware that first impressions count, the sleek, attractive Orlando International Airport represents the city's first contact with most of its out-of-state guests. From a sleepy runway catering to just a few hundred people daily when Walt Disney World first opened, to its current incarnation as the world's 26th largest air facility with annual arrivals exceeding 20 million, Orlando International Airport is an efficient introduction to the region's kid gloves approach to tourism. Still, most of us are primarily concerned with one thing: netting the best airfare.

In general, purchasing your tickets well in advance will land the best price. However, last-minute deals frequently pop up in a highly competitive market such as Orlando. Low-end round-trip airfare from major markets to Orlando averages about $200 from the northeast, $300 from the Midwest and $400 from the West Coast, but better deals pop onto the scene with reasonable frequency, particularly when new carriers—such as Southwest in 1995—inaugurate new or increased service to the region. Your newspaper's Sunday travel section should carry a listing of the lowest available fares. To obtain the best price, a 14- or 21-day advance purchase is usually required, with the ticket paid for within 24 hours of your reservation. Some other rules for obtaining the lowest fares include:

1. Use a travel agent.

Airline reservation attendants typically will ask for your preferred date and time of travel, and then tell you what the "best" fare is. Fair? Not if lower-priced seats are available by shifting your departure a few hours or to a different day of the week. Travel agents have access to all the airfares available. Let them know you are flexible about your exact dates and times of travel, and ask them to tell you what the requirements are for obtaining the lowest fare in the market. Some of the fare rules (such as "must depart between 11:30 a.m. and 11:59 a.m.") are highly specific and available only to those who ask. If you can bend your dates and times to when the best fares are available, frequently you'll save money.

2. Change planes.

Nonstops are available from most major markets into Orlando, but fares on itineraries requiring a change-of-plane frequently yield a lower price. After you have received a quote for the lowest nonstop fare into Orlando, ask your travel agent (or the airline, if calling direct) to check for lower fares flying via other routes. Sometimes this will require "breaking" the fare, whereby you purchase two round-trip tickets, one to the connecting city and another from that city to Orlando, but if you have the time, the slight inconvenience can sometimes save a lot of money.

3. Frequent flyer miles should not be a determining factor.

I hate to burst anyone's bubble, but the miles you earn in airline frequent flyer programs are each worth about one-and-a-half cents toward a future ticket (unless you have graduated to a program's elite level, a 1000-mile flight equals about $15 in free-ticket value). Limiting your flight options to one or two carriers whose programs you have joined is unwise if it adds substantially to your airfare. Frequent flyer miles are valuable, providing you take wing frequently enough to make them worthwhile (most airlines have now imposed expiration dates for the miles you earn), but they may not be worth the price when compared to a lower-cost ticket.

4. Consider a consolidator.

Purchasing groups of seats in blocks, consolidators sell airline tickets at 10 to 30 percent below those obtained from airlines directly. The restrictions on the tickets will not necessarily match those of the airline, and sometimes you won't even know the carrier being used until you board the aircraft—the carrier may even be a charter company. Although more common for those flying to international destinations, consolidators are increasingly becoming a part of the domestic airfare landscape and can provide excellent savings for families. The best way to shop for a consolidator is to pick up your Sunday travel section; consolidators tend to buy small ads filled with even smaller type, and herald unbelievable bargains (many of which turn out to be come-ons). Though there are a few disreputable players in this business, the real concern is that consolidators go out of business with great regularity. However, if you pay by credit card, your purchase is protected should the consolidator go under before you have a ticket in hand. It's also possible to purchase a consolidator's seats by asking your travel agency to obtain the ticket for you at the advertised fare. One last caveat: when an airline fare war is in progress, consolidators will offer little savings off the least expensive fare bought through traditional methods and will likely prove more hassle than they're worth.

5. Be on the lookout for special family deals.

Sometimes these take the shape of two-for-one offers, but these reduced airfares can appear in many forms and are prevalent in the Orlando market.

Major Domestic Carriers Flying Into Orlando International Airport	
AirTran Airways	☎ *(800) 247-8726*
American	☎ *(800) 433-7300*
American Trans Air	☎ *(800) 225-2995*
America West	☎ *(800) 235-9292*
Continental	☎ *(800) 525-0280*

Major Domestic Carriers Flying Into Orlando International Airport

Delta	☎ *(800) 221-1212*
Kiwi	☎ *(800) 538-5494*
Midway	☎ *(800) 446-4392*
Northwest	☎ *(800) 225-2525*
Southwest	☎ *(800) 435-9792*
TWA	☎ *(800) 221-2000*
United	☎ *(800) 241-6522*
USAir	☎ *(800) 428-4322*
ValuJet	☎ *(800) 825-8538*

PLANNING YOUR TRIP

The international carriers providing service to Orlando International Airport include: Air Jamaica, Bahamasair, British Airways, Canadian, Icelandair, Lacsa, Martinair, Saudi Arabian, Trans Brasil and Virgin Atlantic. A number of other foreign airlines provide service to Miami, 236 road-miles to the south (see "Foreign Visitors" in the "Special Travelers" part of this chapter).

Once you've arrived, there are airport gift shops for Disney, Universal and Sea World. If you do not have your theme park tickets, it's possible to purchase them here while you wait for your luggage to arrive (see "Tickets" in "Walt Disney World Theme Parks"). Keep these shops in mind for any last-minute gifts on the way out of Orlando.

Confirm in advance whether your hotel provides complementary transfers from the airport to your accommodations. If not, **Mears Transportation Group** ☎ *(407) 423-5566*, provides service to and from area hotels: Rates run $14 to the properties within Walt Disney World or on U.S. 192 ($25 round-trip, if purchased on the first leg of your trip); International Drive locations are $12, and $21 round-trip.

By Road

Ah, the lure of a road trip. Almost half of Orlando's out-of-state visitors arrive by car. I won't expound here on the advantages and drawbacks of driving to Florida. If you are not already a member, I recommend the invaluable services of the **American Automobile Association** (or another auto club), which can provide you with maps, discounts on theme park tickets, advise you on the best routes and more.

A few reminders for those embarking on a cross-state adventure: be sure to carry proof of auto insurance with you, as well as your current vehicle registration and a duplicate set of car keys. Before heading out, a tune-up may be in order; check your car's brakes, lights, battery, oil and air filters. Don't overextend the number of miles you assault each day, only to arrive in Orlando exhausted and anticipating the return trip through clenched teeth. Familiarize yourself with the major arteries and take the scenic route when you plan to, rather than by mistake.

The major route through Orlando is **Interstate 4**, which connects Daytona Beach on the east coast with Tampa on the west. But if you are driving in from out of state, you'll enter Florida either via I-95 (the east-coast route through Jacksonville), I-75 (from Atlanta) or I-10 (the southern route through Tallahassee). I-4 passes within three or four miles of almost every hotel listed in this book.

Approximate driving mileage between Orlando and some of the major cities in the east are: Atlanta, 447 miles; Boston, 1448 miles; Charlotte, 574 miles; Chicago, 1176 miles; Dallas, 1071 miles; Miami, 236 miles; New Orleans, 653 miles; New York, 1115 miles; St. Louis, 1011 miles; Toronto, 1374 miles; Washington D.C., 877 miles.

By Rail

Everyone gets a crack at the Disney Railroad while visiting the Magic Kingdom, but traveling to Florida by train is a time-honored method of jumpstarting a vacation. Although rail service is not substantially less expensive for adults than travel by plane, children under 16 travel at half-fare with up to two children per full-fare adult, making the train economical for families. Discounts are available for seniors, military, students and others. Amtrak offers different rail services into central Florida. The **Auto Train**, nonstop service from Washington, D.C. to Orlando, gets high marks from regulars for service and efficiency, while the **Sunset Limited** that travels through the American Southwest provides one of the country's most beautiful passages. However, the vast bulk of Florida's visitors by rail depart from the northeast and use the **Silver Meteor** or **Silver Star**.

Amtrak's Auto Train begins its daily, nonstop trek at 4:30 p.m. in Lorton, Virginia, 15 miles south of Washington, D.C., and arrives in Sanford, Florida, 24 miles northeast of Orlando, at 9 a.m. the next day. The return trip along the 861-mile route leaves Sanford at 4:30 p.m. and arrives back in Lorton the following day at 9 a.m. Round-trip, coach tickets start at $121 and cars are ferried for $341, round-trip (sleeper seats are higher). The Auto Train is a popular method of travel for many snowbirds; reservations are essential for southbound travel in the fall and northbound in the spring.

The Silver Star and Silver Meteor leave from New York daily at 10:10 a.m. and 4:05 p.m., respectively. Both trains travel the same 1129-mile passage to Orlando in a little under 24 hours with stops en route in Philadelphia, Baltimore, Washington, D.C., and a number of smaller cities. The morning Star departure tends to be a little less crowded than the afternoon Meteor, but the Meteor shaves a few hours off the trip in both directions. Northbound trips on the Meteor and Star leave Orlando daily at 12:42 p.m. and 6:25 p.m., respectively. Round-trip adult tickets on either train start at $146 out of New York or Washington, D.C.

Those traveling from the west or the south will board the Sunset Limited, which departs Los Angeles on Sundays, Tuesdays and Fridays at 10:30 p.m., and arrives in Orlando 67 hours later at 5:35 p.m. Major stops along the route include Phoenix, Houston and New Orleans. From Orlando, the westbound Sunset also leaves on Sundays, Tuesdays and Fridays, at 4:38 p.m. Round-trip adult fares start at $266 from Los Angeles.

Although the Auto Train finishes its route in Sanford, all three other trains continue south and make stops at Winter Park *(150 West Morse Boulevard)*, Orlando *(1400 Sligh Boulevard)* and Kissimmee *(111 Dakin Street, at Main)*, and continue on to Miami. However, only the downtown Orlando station has bus connections into Walt Disney World, 23 miles from the Orlando Station. For bus service via Lynx take route #34 to their downtown terminal, transfer to route #50 to Disney's Ticket and Transportation Center. Also see "Other Public Transportation" in this chapter. Car rental is available at the Orlando station through Air Rail Americar (affiliated with Payless). ☎ *(800) 228-8024.*

All above rates are subject to change. Amtrak reservations and information: ☎ *(800) 872-7245.*

By Package Tour

I'll admit up front, when it comes to describing how to buy a package tour—I cringe. We're not talking about guided tours (where you are locked into a pre-set, escorted itinerary), but referring to prepackaged vacations that allow you to shape the trip you want, delegating the booking responsibilities to a third party. In theory, by purchasing blocks of hotel rooms and airline seats, package-tour operators are able to obtain a better rate on these commodities and pass some of the savings off to you. In theory, there are two more good reasons to use a packager—they can save you time making reservations, and they offer a level of planning security prior to and during your vacation. In theory, a package tour *should* be the way to go. Unfortunately, all too often, it isn't.

The reality is that many people select package tours by determining what they can afford, and then try to fit a package into that amount. While there's nothing wrong with setting a budget, by not researching their options, many of these travelers unknowingly pay more for their vacation than necessary. And, as for the added benefits—cutting down your reservation legwork, and helping to protect you if your trip is disrupted—well, a good travel agent will provide most or all of that. But the most frustrating thing is that too frequently, the core reason to buy a package—to save money—isn't even served.

For example, I called **United Vacations** to book a proposed four-night trip in March. The first hotel the tour operator recommended was the Walt Disney World Swan, not coincidentally, the most expensive accommodations that United Vacations sells. The four-night price quoted was $2134 for two people, including round-trip airfare from Boston on United Airlines, Avis car rental, a pair of four-day Park Hopper Passes for Walt Disney World, and admission to Pleasure Island. To evaluate this package, I called United Airlines directly and obtained a quote of $168 for each airline ticket during the period I wanted to travel; I called Avis and obtained a four-day rental rate for the same car of $67; I factored in the $162 gate-price for the Disney tickets, and used the Swan's *rack* rate for a standard room—$280 per night—and came up with a price of $1847, a savings of almost $300 off the package rate. This exercise took barely 15 minutes, and if I had spent a little more time I probably could have negotiated a lower rate for the hotel room (assuming they were not heavily booked). I would also save a few dollars if I purchased my Disney tickets through The Magic Kingdom Club or AAA.

Conversely, offered an opportunity to sell me a package that worked to my advantage, the embarrassed United Vacations showed me a two-person, four-night stay at the Omni Rosen Hotel, including round-trip air from Denver, an Alamo rental car and the Disney tickets for $1587. When I made my comparisons on this package, the same features procured individually would have run $2105, more than $400 above the package price. What's more, when I called, the Omni Rosen didn't have any rooms available, at any rate, for the fourth night of my proposed visit.

As the above examples show, comparing the packages can take time. If you're hoping to save money by purchasing a package, you'll need to do a little work. On the other hand, if money is not an object and your goal is simply to streamline the procedure for obtaining your air, hotel and car arrangements, just sign on the dotted line and don't wince when the bill comes. Here are some suggestions for the rest of us:

1. Use a travel agent, on your terms.

Most travel advisers prefer to steer vacationers into a package. Because your travel agent acts as a kind of middleman between you and the package operator, selling you a package trip reduces the amount of legwork the agent is required to perform for his or her commission. However, good agents will go a step further. They will take the time to find out exactly what kind of trip you are looking for, compare packages in the price range you desire, and then evaluate how the package price compares with purchasing the various pieces—airfare, hotel, car rental, etc.—individually. No, you probably shouldn't expect them to know exactly how much tickets for a secondary attraction like **Wild Bill's Wild West Dinner Extravaganza** costs, but your agent should know that discount coupons for most non-Disney attractions are abundant in Orlando. And, he or she shouldn't consider tickets to Wild Bill's a "value added attraction," unless it's high on your list of things to do.

2. Stay focused on your objective.

As any travel agent will tell you, evaluating package trips can be time-consuming. The package companies probably don't mind. They'd prefer you focus on the pretty pictures in their brochure and overload you with details on all the amenities their package offers. Don't lose sight of your primary goal: to obtain the best rates on your airfare, hotel, transportation and tickets. By knowing the approximate cost of individual items—most of which are listed in *Fielding's Walt Disney World and Orlando*—you can better determine what savings individual packagers offer. The prices we've listed in our book are those available to the general public. If you're an AAA member, hold a Magic Kingdom Club Card, qualify for senior discounts, carry a wallet stuffed with discount coupons, or can access any of the many other deals available, factor these into your evaluation of a travel package.

3. Buy what you know you need

Standard procedure within the package tour industry is to sell clients more than they can use, thereby running up the tab. How? A typical package to Orlando will include airfare, hotel and car rental. Three cheers for the tour operators who stop there, give you a break on the price, and call it a day. But most package trips will include more, such as admission tickets, transportation, recreation and any number of items that may or may not be on your agenda. Or, worse, they may sell you things you'd *like* to see or do, but you don't realize until your trip is almost over that all the extras you've paid for (even if at a reduced rate), won't possibly fit into your vacation. Even Disney Vacation routinely incorporates admissions to Discovery Island into their packages, yet the zoological park isn't high on most visitors' agendas and relatively few of these admissions are ever even used. In short, make sure the packager isn't piling on a plethora of extras you won't use. Be particularly wary of two-for-one admissions promoted in a package you are considering. These discounts are usually provided by secondary attractions to the tour operator at little or no price and, accordingly, should have little or no bearing on the overall value of the package.

4. Compare apples to apples.

Make certain you (or your travel agent) are using valid comparisons. For instance, does the package you're evaluating deliver you to Orlando on an airline that provides convenient nonstop service while another uses a carrier that requires an out-of-the-way connection at an awkward time? Are taxes and tips covered, or are there hidden surcharges you will be expected to pick up? Brownie points to the one who gets you there more efficiently, raspberries to the one who loads you with hidden fees, and so on.

5. Deal with reputable packagers.

The industry has a wide assortment of companies providing similar-sounding offers, but the quality of service they provide before and during your trip can vary. If your flight is canceled the day of your departure, will the company assist you in making alternate arrangements, or are you on your own? If you booked a nonsmoking room but the hotel only has smoking accommodations available, is the packager there for you? Make sure the tour operator will provide unstinting local support from the moment your trip begins; your travel agent should also stand behind the package you're purchasing. Ask all the hard questions up front and you'll reduce the probability of rude surprises later.

6. Timing is everything.

Although package rates drop during the off-season, the Orlando hotel market has become so competitive that packages can't begin to match some of the deals offered when rooms go begging. Similarly, if an airfare war is in progress, it's likely the packager's negotiated airfare to Orlando won't compare with the lowest available. In either instance, ask the packager if it can match the price (they frequently will). Conversely, because it has pre-bought the space, a packager may be able to sell rooms at Disney Resorts or other properties that are officially sold out.

American Airlines Fly AAway Vacations	☎ *(800) 321-2121*
America West Vacations	☎ *(800) 356-6611*
Continental Airlines' Grand Destinations	☎ *(800) 634-5555*
Delta Dream Vacations	☎ *(800) 872-7786*
Funjet Vacations	☎ *(800) 558-3050*
Globetrotters	☎ *(800) 999-9696*
Kingdom Tours	☎ *(800) 872-8857*
United Vacations	☎ *(800) 328-6877*
Universal City Travel	☎ *(800) 224-3838*

PLANNING YOUR TRIP

USAir Vacations   ☎ *(800) 455-0123*

Walt Disney World Travel Company   ☎ *(407) 828-3232*

What to Bring

Keep it simple. Walt Disney World and Orlando pride themselves on being casual destinations and comfortable attire will serve you best, particularly during the sweltering summer months. The weather should be your chief packing concern: shorts can be worn virtually year-round, but become a near-necessity during humid July and August, when daytime highs average a sticky 90 degrees. A fanny pack is a helpful touring substitute for a purse or handbag. A wide-brimmed hat or baseball cap can provide a measure of comfort in direct sun, as will a pair of sunglasses. The summer months also bring frequent afternoon showers, so light rain gear and even an umbrella can come in handy. Every hotel listed in this book (except for a few in the "Other" section) offers pool facilities, some of them exceptional. You'll be despondent if you don't bring swimming attire. If you wear contacts, a pair of goggles can help you prevent lost lenses at the splashy water parks (they did for me).

From early November through early March, central Florida's weather is ideal for daytime touring—rain is rare and skies are sunny. However, most evenings and even a few afternoons each winter can be quite chilly; long pants and a warm jacket after dark are advised. Actually, a light sweater is a good idea year-round as long exposure to resort air conditioning can cut to the bone.

INSIDER'S TIP

Purchase and pack sundries before you go. Simple purchases at Walt Disney World, such as suntan lotion, aspirin and film, are priced 20-50 percent above what you pay at home. If you're bringing kids of any age, pack a selection of favorite snacks for them to munch on while touring the parks. Adopting this strategy can create savings to purchase souvenirs your children will remember long after a soft drink.

Jackets are required for men at **Victoria and Albert's**, otherwise, you'll stand out if you're dressed in fancy duds at most Walt Disney World restaurants.

Even at Epcot's most expensive eateries, it's not uncommon to see guests wearing shorts for a fancy dinner. In Orlando proper, a few of the restaurants we've listed cater to the city's business community, but otherwise casual dress is fine at most dining facilities.

Finally, two essentials to pack for any season: a pair of sneakers you'll feel comfortable walking in for miles (be sure to break them in prior to your trip to avoid blisters), and sunblock, preferably SPF 15 or stronger.

Transportation—Via Car

Before there was Disney, one main artery cut through Orlando, the I-4, which at one time was ample enough to serve the modest population of central Florida. In the ensuing quarter-century since Walt Disney World was launched, things have changed dramatically. The population of Orlando has skyrocketed and the hotel industry feeding it is now the largest in the country.

AUTHOR'S OBSERVATION

When driving in rainy conditions, Florida law requires the use of headlights.

Rental Car

Perhaps no other method of touring offers as much flexibility as a rental car. Although Walt Disney World transportation is free, by having a car at your disposal, you can visit the other nearby sights with ease, slip away to Crossroads Mall for a less-expensive meal than Scrooge McDuck allows, or take a day-trip to see one of Orlando's neighboring attractions such as Kennedy Space Center or Busch Gardens.

In booking your rental, carefully select your car-rental location. Generally, the lowest rates are available if you pick up your car at the airport, starting at roughly $100–135 per week for an economy model. Rates for auxiliary locations (at the resorts neighboring Walt Disney World and elsewhere) are typically 20 to 60 percent higher. However, some rental firms will waive their drop-off charge, allowing you to pick up at the airport (at the lower rate) and return the car at a pre-arranged, nearby resort. This allows visitors to use a rental car for the first portion of their trip, while relying on a shuttle or taxi for the trip back to the airport. Keep in mind that off-airport rental agencies maintain more selective hours and may not be open when your rental period concludes (or when you'd like it to begin). Most rental firms require drivers to be at least 25 years of age, but some waive the rule with an added surcharge. Florida's rental-car prices are among the most reasonable in the nation, but a few other tricks help to secure the best rates:

1. Use supply and demand to your advantage.

Although all of the major car agencies are competitive, if you call the ten major outlets and ask for a price on the exact same car model and dates, you will probably get ten different prices. This is because the agencies continually fine-tune their rates for each market based on the demand they foresee during a given time frame. Therefore, not only will the different agencies post different rates when you call on one day, but they will adjust their rates, up or down, as the weeks go by, based on the number of cars they expect to have sitting in their lots. Agencies with a surplus of cars for a given date will continue to drop their prices in an effort to entice fickle customers, while the car companies anticipating near-empty lots can afford to nudge prices up and take advantage of those who arrive at the airport without a reservation. You can make supply and demand work for you by shopping around and booking your car as soon as you have firmed your travel plans. As your travel date approaches, call the firms again and compare rates. If a lower rate is available, grab it, and then cancel your previous booking. A few days before your departure, it doesn't hurt to repeat this process again.

2. Watch where you rent.

When obtaining a car, you won't get around Florida's six percent state tax, nor its $2.05 per day road tax, but you can avoid a *third* hit—an 8.64 percent surcharge—if you avoid renting at the airport from the firms whose lots are based *off* the airport property. Only four companies (Avis, Budget, Dollar and National) are situated on the actual airport property. All other car-rental firms are required to tax their customers to shuttle them from the terminal to their lots. Check around, however, since the off-site companies frequently better the prices of the on-site firms.

3. Be flexible about your needs.

The rigid parameters a rental car agency uses to subtly separate business and leisure customers may lock you out of a good deal. For instance, as with airlines, the rates provided by most firms drop if a Saturday night stay is included. But, the lower weekend rates usually do not come into effect until noon on Thursday, and remain so only if the car is returned by noon on Monday. Weekly rates usually require you have the car in your possession at least five days and nights. Therefore, if you think you may not need a rental car for your entire vacation, flexibility usually provides several less-expensive options.

4. Understand your insurance options before you arrive.

One of the great cash cows of the industry is the notorious "collision damage waiver." Running as high as $16 per day, the sale of these policies has even been banned in some states following consumer complaints. In remaining locales, including Florida, uninformed customers are a prime target, and the use of scare tactics is not beyond the pale for some agencies. You should know two things before you arrive at the rental counter. First, does your personal auto insurance policy cover you in the event of an accident or theft of a rental car? If you have auto insurance, chances are you're already covered to some degree in a rental car—the coverage rental agencies sell is duplicated by approximately 70 percent of personal car policies. Second, you need to understand how your credit card's cardholder agreement will cover you in a rental. In essence, the free coverage—provided to Gold Master-Card or Visa Gold cardholders—is designed to supplement the insurance policy you already carry. Note: the free coverage provided by these and other charge cards is activated *only* if you decline the optional policies offered by the rental agencies.

5. Sharing the driving may be expensive.

The policies vary, but some rental agencies impose an additional driver charge of up to $5 per day if someone shares the wheel with you. Notable exceptions include Auto Club (AAA) members at some car companies, and married couples at others (although Avis also waives the charge for unmarried domestic partners).

6. Using a travel agent, or not.

A travel agency offers one-stop shopping for your airline ticket, hotel and car reservations, and should be able to compare rates and provide you the best deal. What works well in theory doesn't always function well in the real world. Calling a rental agency's toll-free number yourself will usually provide a better deal than the best delivered by a travel agent. Also, discounts provided to Sam's Club, AAA members, those holding special coupons, or for members of frequent-flier programs are not usually loaded into the reservation system that agents must use. Additionally, because a travel agent may not be attentive to lower rates as they become available, the "supply and demand" theory won't be applied after the booking is made.

AUTHOR'S OBSERVATION

In the fall of 1995, Hertz opened a new, state-of-the-art car rental facility just outside the Orlando airport. It is currently the largest Hertz rental office in the world, with 64 positions at its 320-foot service counter. The 30-acre Orlando facility is also one of the sites where Hertz now provides a computerized on-board navigation system, mounted in the front seat between driver and passenger.

You can rent a car from sites in or near Disney Village, International Drive, and along U.S. 192. National has the exclusive contract to supply cars to Walt Disney World Resort guests; National's base is the **Car Care Center**, located just north of the toll plaza for the Ticket and Transportation Center. The major car rental companies in the region and their principle locations are:

Alamo

☎ *(800) 327-9633.*

Orlando International Airport (8.64 percent off-site surcharge), Buena Vista Palace, Howard Johnson Universal, Omni Rosen, Clarion Plaza, Ho Jo Inn.

Avis

☎ *(800) 331-1212.*
Orlando International Airport, Hilton Lake Buena Vista.

Budget

☎ *(800) 527-0700.*
Orlando International Airport, Doubletree Guest Suites, Holiday Inn Maingate East, Peabody Orlando, Ramada Hotel Resort, Stouffer Renaissance.

Dollar

☎ *(800) 421-6868.*
Orlando International Airport, Courtyard by Marriott, U.S. 192 in Kissimmee.

Enterprise

☎ *(800) 325-8007.*
Orlando International Airport (8.64 percent off-site surcharge), Floridian Hotel, Hyatt Regency Grand Cypress.

Hertz

☎ *(800) 654-3131.*
Orlando International Airport (8.64 percent off-site surcharge), Marriott World Center, U.S. 192 in Kissimmee.

National

☎ *(800) 227-7368.*
Orlando International Airport, Walt Disney World Car Care Center.

Payless

☎ *(800) 541-1566.*
Orlando International Airport (8.64 percent off-site surcharge).

Thrifty

☎ *(800) 367-2277.*
Orlando International Airport (8.64 percent off-site surcharge), Grosvenor Resort, Radisson Twin Towers, Ramada Plaza Resort.

Value

☎ *(800) 327-2501.*
Orlando International Airport (8.64 percent off-site surcharge), Summerfield Suites, Econo Lodge Maingate Hawaiian.

INSIDER'S TIP

After you've signed your car rental contract, take a moment to obtain exact directions out of the airport and to your first destination. Statistics provided by rental firms show that the greatest percentage of accidents occur just as renters are leaving the airport facility after obtaining their car. Why? Travelers are anxious to begin their vacation, driving a car they are probably unfamiliar with and, in the rush to escape the airport, they make sudden or wrong turns before they've gained their bearings.

Navigating Central Florida and Orlando

Driving to your hotel after picking up a rental car at the airport is a relatively easy affair. As you leave Orlando International Airport, aim for **Route 528 West**, commonly referred to as the **Beeline Expressway**, then follow these directions:

*1. If you are headed for any of the **Disney-owned** resorts, or the **Swan** or **Dolphin**, take I-4 west six miles and exit at Epcot Center Drive (Route 536 west) and follow the signs to your hotel.*

*2. If you are bound for any of the hotels at **Disney Village**, take I-4 west four miles to Exit 27 at Crossroads Mall (Route 535 north, aka the Apopka Vineland Road); the Disney Village hotels are immediately next to I-4, and are accessed via Hotel Plaza Boulevard.*

3. If you are staying at a property listed in the "Crossroads Area and Adjacent" chapter, you'll also take I-4 west to Exit 27, then follow the directions listed for your hotel in Fielding's Walt Disney World and Orlando Area Theme Parks.

*4. If you are staying in an **International Drive** property, exit the Beeline at International Drive (also known as I-Drive); most of these hotels are north of the Beeline, but a few are south.*

*5. If you are staying at a facility located on **U.S. 192** (aka the Irlo Bronson Highway), exit the westbound I-4 at the intersection with 192 and proceed, east or west, to your hotel. However, if you are overnighting at accommodations closer to **Kissimmee** than the Maingate area, you'll want to exit the Beeline at the Florida Turnpike and proceed south on Route 441 into Kissimmee.*

One confusing issue that confronts most drivers at some point during their Orlando visit is that I-4, the region's major artery, is considered a route between the east and west coasts of peninsular Florida. In Orlando, however, the interstate runs geographically more on a north and south axis. The easiest way to keep the diagonal straight is to remember north *with* east, south *with* west.

Gas in Florida is inexpensive, but you'll pay the difference for it on Orlando's toll roads. The region has relied on toll booths to resolve some of the traffic problems created by Walt Disney World. Most of these fees are under a dollar, but they add up. When refueling your car, the last place you want to fill up is at the high-priced stations within the Disney property. Prices are lower in the nearby Crossroads Mall area, on International Drive and on

U.S. 192, where the pumps are downright cheap as you head east toward St. Cloud.

INSIDER'S TIP

If you're driving into the state for your Orlando vacation, you may be able to take advantage of the Disney-AAA Travel Center in Ocala, 83 miles northwest of Orlando. Designed for visitors who are looking for rock-bottom accommodations and who have not yet booked a hotel, the center sells rooms at the Disney Resorts, frequently at a substantial reduction over the rack rate. The hitch is they will not provide information by phone, either on room availability or the type of discounts in effect–they are strictly a walk-in service. Your best bet is mid-week and during non-holiday periods. The center is located just off I-75 in Ocala and is open daily 9 a.m. to 6 p.m. ☎ (904) 854-0770.

PLANNING YOUR TRIP

Driving Within Walt Disney World

City-dwellers are used to buildings and other landmarks to navigate our way through life on asphalt. After several weeks of driving in and around Walt Disney World, I was amazed at how often I would still miss a turn or instinctively head a direction incorrectly (based on a compass-point assumption) and have to make a multi-mile circuit out of my way to get back on track to my planned destination. Unfortunately, as often as I hoped otherwise, my mistakes weren't for lack of adequate road signage and I'd end up cursing myself for not paying attention.

Placing a high priority on a smooth flow of traffic, Disney has developed its own system of road signage that works pretty well. But the swooping, disorienting curves that provide access to Walt Disney World are somewhat indirect, designed ultimately for heightening suspense as you approach Walt's park. Although there were a few times I wished for a straight shot from the airport to my hotel, the fanciful road layout devised by Disney imagineers creatively mingles efficient traffic flow with an artful wander through the forest. My suggestions include:

1. Carry a good road map in the car at all times.

Few visitors (other than Florida residents) anticipate the difficulty of piloting through swampy, pancake-flat territory lined with trees that block any views of notable landmarks. If you are driving your own car, obtain a reliable map before you leave that identifies all the major and minor roads through Walt Disney World. If you are using a rental car, keep in mind that most of the maps provided by rental agencies insufficiently detail the World's road system. The road map on the back of the individual Disney resort maps provided at check-in is a middling substitute. Refer to your map before you fire up the engine and keep it handy.

2. Sometimes the long way is the right way.

With the opening of Pleasure Island, the Village Marketplace and other facilities, the Lake Buena Vista area has become a bog of traffic. If you're traveling from this or the Crossroads area to any of the Disney parks *other than* Typhoon Lagoon, Pleasure Island and the Village Marketplace, it is almost always faster to head for I-4 west, exiting on Epcot Center Drive West (Exit 26B). The routing appears indirect on a map, but maps don't account for traffic and stoplights.

3. Your car isn't always the fastest way.

In a number of cases where there is a single, direct public transportation line between a Disney Resort and its parks, driving your car will devour more time if you consider the chore of parking. This is particularly true when visiting The Magic Kingdom, where the parking lot is a couple of miles from the park entrance. Before heading to a destination, check at your resort's Guest Services desk to verify that you are making the right choice.

4. Avoid the jams when you can.

The worst congestion usually occurs when one of the three big parks shuts down for the night and a flood of traffic fills the roads leading away from it, impacting not only the departing park guests, but innocent visitors caught up in it. For instance, dinner at one of the Grand Floridian's restaurants will conclude on a sour note if you leave just as The Magic Kingdom closes; the resort and the park share the same road system. Familiarize yourself with what time the parks shut down and any special events likely to clog the arteries. Fortunately, these traffic jams are usually brief in nature, dissipating in relatively short order.

Public Transportation

The Walt Disney World Transportation System

Disney has set up an extensive internal transit system for its guests and, depending on who you talk to, using the Walt Disney World Transportation System is either the most frustrating part of a trip, or it's a blessing. My own view straddles these extremes, and I'll add one point that most visitors overlook: Disney has an enormous job moving thousands of guests through and around the World each day—up to a quarter-million guest trips per day during peak season. That the system works as well as it does is little short of miraculous; that it doesn't always bend to your exact needs should be forgiven.

Designed primarily to transport guests from their Disney Resort to each of the various parks, Disney's transportation system is an impressive conglomerate of vehicles, employing a huge workforce. A fleet of 12 monorails, several hundred boats (in all shapes and sizes) and 188 buses work from early in the morning till late at night to whisk you between the resorts and attractions. As a rule, if you're staying at a Disney property, there will be a single, direct line to the Disney park of your choice. The transportation to each park starts a half-hour to an hour prior to the scheduled opening time (including Surprise Mornings), and operates one-to-two hours after closing.

For most guests, the sleek **Monorail** is the preferred mode of transit. This "highway in the sky" offers two different routings: one between Epcot and the Ticket and Transportation Center, and a pair of tracks operating in opposite directions around the Seven Seas Lagoon (on this latter route, one direction, counterclockwise, is an express route between the Ticket and Transportation Center and The Magic Kingdom; the clockwise direction makes those two stops plus three at the resorts rimming the lake).

Disney's naval fleet of **watercrafts** is a colorful and diverse lot. On one end, there are the huge and efficient 600-passenger ferries that traverse the Seven Seas Lagoon between the Ticket and Transportation Center and The Magic Kingdom. Motor launches serve the Magic Kingdom, Discovery Island, Grand Floridian, Polynesian, Contemporary, Wilderness Lodge and Fort Wilderness. Slower "FriendShips" ply the water link between Epcot and The Disney-MGM Studios, stopping en route at the Swan, Dolphin, BoardWalk, Yacht and Beach Club Resorts. Lastly there's a largely unheralded, relaxing cruise down the Sassagoula River connecting the Port Orleans and Dixie Landings resorts with the Village Marketplace and Pleasure Island.

Where the system falls down is transferring you from one park to another, or from one resort to another—there is simply a limit to how many different routes are available. While this is not always a big problem, it can be if you plan to visit two parks—one of the big three and one of the smaller parks—in the same day. For example, going from Epcot to nearby Pleasure Island requires a side trip, several miles out of the way via monorail, to the Ticket and Transportation Center, where you switch to a bus and, annoyingly, pass Epcot again on your way to Pleasure Island. Worse, trying to visit another resort's dining facilities can be a exercise requiring more time than the meal itself. For instance, if you are staying at the Wilderness Lodge and want to travel to the Yacht Club Resort for lunch, you will need to take a bus to the Ticket and Transportation Center, transfer to a bus bound for the Village Marketplace, and then transfer to yet another bus bound for the Yacht Club. Or you can take one of several other, equally indirect routes. Ugh!

INSIDER'S TIP

Some of the Disney Resorts are better situated to utilize the Disney Transportation System than others. The Grand Floridian, Contemporary and Polynesian offer easy monorail service to The Magic Kingdom, Epcot and the variety of dining facilities situated around the Seven Seas Lagoon. The Epcot Resorts (Swan, Dolphin, BoardWalk, Yacht and Beach Club) also offer easy access to a number of restaurants, and are within 10 to 15 minute walking or boating distance of the entrances to Epcot and the Disney-MGM Studios. The transportation system for the Wilderness Lodge and Fort Wilderness Campground is uniformly frustrating, while the remoteness of the All-Star Resorts can contribute to slightly longer commutes.

Still, over time many visitors manage to figure out how to get around, minimize the zigzag routes, and usually find their experiences a nice relief from driving and parking hassles. And there are a number of trips that easily shorten the route as compared to driving to the same point by car. For instance, the All-Star Resorts are positioned at the opposite end of the World from The Magic Kingdom. On a non-peak admission day, driving to the park from your room will require about 10 minutes to the Ticket and Transportation Center, another five to 15 minutes to get from your car to the monorail servicing the park, and another 10 to 20 minutes on the monorail or ferry to the park entrance; a minimum of 25 minutes, and 45 minutes or more on a busy day. The same route by bus takes no more than 15 minutes to the park entrance (sidestepping the Ticket and Transportation Center), even on a relatively busy day. Now, the bus probably won't be waiting for you when you arrive at the All-Star bus stop, but even figuring the maximum anticipated wait (20 minutes between buses), there's a good chance you'll be arriving at the park entrance before the resort guests who left at the same time and drove their own cars.

The most common complaint heard from fellow visitors is that, try as they might, by the time they finally figured out exactly how the system works, their vacation was over. During my research, I spent many hours using the Disney Transportation System. I was able to uncover a few tips that will give you a running start. Keep in mind that the system isn't perfect and never will be, and if you're on a tight touring schedule you may want to rent a car to minimize time spent getting to and from destinations that require many connections.

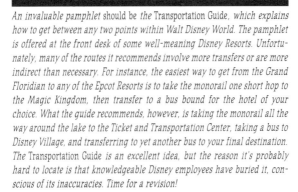

AUTHOR'S OBSERVATION

An invaluable pamphlet should be the Transportation Guide, which explains how to get between any two points within Walt Disney World. The pamphlet is offered at the front desk of some well-meaning Disney Resorts. Unfortunately, many of the routes it recommends involve more transfers or are more indirect than necessary. For instance, the easiest way to get from the Grand Floridian to any of the Epcot Resorts is to take the monorail one short hop to the Magic Kingdom, then transfer to a bus bound for the hotel of your choice. What the guide recommends, however, is taking the monorail all the way around the lake to the Ticket and Transportation Center, taking a bus to Disney Village, and transferring to yet another bus to your final destination. The Transportation Guide is an excellent idea, but the reason it's probably hard to locate is that knowledgeable Disney employees have buried it, conscious of its inaccuracies. Time for a revision!

1. Plan your trips in advance.

If you're headed to a theme park early in the morning, ask at your resort's Guest Services desk *the night before* how to get to the park, how much time to allow, and what time the service begins. If you're headed someplace other than the theme parks at any time of day, particularly one involving a connection, double-check your routing information when you board the monorail, bus or watercraft. If you will not be making a return trip directly back to your resort (via the same route in reverse), ask the driver or attendant what the best route to your next destination will be. When in doubt, call Disney's Ticket and Transportation Center office: ☎ *(407) 824-4457.*

2. Allow ample transit time.

If your routing involves just one line, your wait time should be minimal. If your trip uses two or three lines to get from point A to point B, allow at least an hour to land at your final destination. Buses are on a schedule approximately 20 minutes apart (except at peak hours, when they run somewhat more frequently), monorails run every five to 10 minutes, and boats depart every five to 15 minutes, depending on the route. If you want to take advantage of The Magic Kingdom touring plan (see: "Walt Disney World Theme Parks"), find out what time the first bus (or monorail) departs for the park entrance from your resort and position yourself at the stop a few minutes prior.

3. Always carry a detailed road map.

Walt Disney World is inventively laid out with a series of loopy, winding roads that seem deliberately designed to disorient visitors; the only (vaguely) straight line is the one from Maingate to the Ticket and Transportation Center. After a few of the twists and turns on a typical bus route, the points of a compass start to resemble something out of Alice's Wonderland. If you have a visual aid in front of you as someone is providing directions, you will become familiar with the routes. Pull out the map as you pass new destinations along your trip and the layout and proximity of the parks from one another will become more obvious, earlier in your trip.

4. Avoid peak travel periods when possible.

The various conveyances operate close to capacity in the mornings as the theme parks are opening, but the load is lighter throughout the rest of the day. The system is pushed to the limit as the parks shut down for the night, particularly if there's a closing fireworks show. If you're staying for IllumiNations or another culminating event, instead of rushing to join thousands of others exiting Epcot following its conclusion, stay seated for a few minutes after the show, or amble casually to the monorail, boat or bus depot. If you don't particularly care to watch the big finish, keep in mind there will always be a crush at the official closing time of all parks, fireworks or not. Leaving a half-hour before that point will minimize your wait for transportation.

AUTHOR'S OBSERVATION

A curious annoyance in central Florida and Walt Disney World is the lack of pedestrian access between points (except within the theme parks, of course). For instance, it's little more than a quarter-mile from the Wilderness Lodge to the Ticket and Transportation Center, but there is no path available for what would be a 10-minute walk, yet using official Disney transportation to get to the same point can take up to a half-hour. While we understand the possibility of safety issues caused by guests roaming off the track, the unwritten policy feels like an excessive gesture to protect Disney from litigation. With the exception of the walkways between the Disney-MGM Studios and Epcot (passing the Epcot Resorts), you are roundly discouraged from walking in the World.

Other Public Transportation

If you are staying in a non-Disney lodging facility, you will be much more dependent on a set of wheels you can call your own. This doesn't mean it's impossible to see Walt Disney World, Universal and Sea World using private transport systems, but there are some stumbling blocks. Predictably, the obstacles become increasingly difficult the less expensive your room and/or the farther your accommodations are situated from the World.

The easiest group of properties from which to visit the Disney parks is the "Official Resorts of Walt Disney World" located in Disney Village. Although the Westin Swan and Sheraton Dolphin are still part of the Disney Transportation System, in 1995 the other, "official" on-site properties chose to develop their own independent systems, rather than continue their (presumably more-expensive) transit contract with Disney. The Disney Village hotels use purple buses, with the Disney name scrawled in big red letters. Rather than providing service at set intervals throughout the day, "Official Resort" buses have set departure times for each hotel, generally every half-hour, with schedules concentrated in the morning and evening. You are not technically allowed to use the Disney Transportation System without purchasing a $2.50 ticket for the day (however, during research conducted over a two-month period, no one ever asked me for a resort pass identifying me as a Disney guest). All of the Disney Village properties are within an easy quarter- to half-mile walk from the Disney Marketplace and Pleasure Island, although the few footpaths are mysteriously obscure.

Beyond the Disney Village accommodations, most nearby hotels offer somewhat more limited service to the three big Disney parks. Most of these are concentrated in the Crossroads area or are the hotels closest to Maingate on U.S. 192, but there's no established rule as to who provides what. One Kissimmee property may provide three buses every morning to the main Disney parks, Sea World and Universal, while the budget facility next door may offer guests little more than a phone number to arrange their own. Keep in mind that if your hotel offers only morning and evening transit service, once you land at The Magic Kingdom, you have no route (other than via taxi) back to your hotel until the bus service resumes. If you wish to rely on hotel transportation to see the main parks, call your hotel directly and ask about the service it provides and any charges for it.

Finally, two public bus systems are available. **Lynx** is an increasingly comprehensive bus service with more than 50 routes in the Orlando Metro area. The Lynx system offers sporadic service to the Ticket and Transportation Center within Walt Disney World. Several routes also connect the U.S. 192/Kissimmee area with International Drive and downtown Orlando. A ride is 75 cents, plus 10 cents for a transfer slip. For a pamphlet, call ☎ *(407) 841-8240.*

I-Ride is a single bus line along International Drive, from Sea World north to Kirkman Road, just past Wet 'n Wild. The service runs every 10 minutes from 7 a.m. to midnight, and stops are provided every two blocks; the bus is 75 cents, plus 10 cents for a transfer slip valid on Lynx. While I-Ride is minimally valuable when staying in another area, if your hotel is positioned on International Drive, it can be a convenient service to use when touring the busy corridor's sights.

Money

How to Carry It

In the 1990s, easily the most convenient method of payment for a vacation is a credit card. American Express, Visa and MasterCard are accepted throughout Orlando's attractions, restaurants, hotels and gift shops. Discover and Diners Club can be used at most facilities catering to tourists but are not accepted at the Disney hotels or restaurants. Traveler's checks, in U.S. dollars, also remain a popular method of payment, particularly for those visiting from a foreign country. They are an excellent substitute for cash if you don't wish to carry a credit card.

Room charges are something that take on a particular significance when staying at the Disney Resorts. On check-in each member of your family (unless you designate otherwise) will receive a credit card-type room key. This plastic key-card is valid not only for charges within your resort, but also at the Disney theme parks, restaurants and gift shops. Additionally, Disney is moving toward a ticket system that will use these same cards for theme-park admission. Within Walt Disney World's borders, virtually anything beyond the ice cream and turkey-leg carts can be charged back to your Disney Resort room. If you're not someone who handles surprises well, you'll want to consider exactly who in your party actually *needs* a room charge card before divvying them out. You may also want to keep track of your room charges separately by accumulating the receipts together. Somehow, I am always astonished when I look over the final, bigger-than-expected tab at the end of my stay.

Tipping

I confess, it wasn't until I started writing about travel that I finally became acquainted with what are considered the standard tip amounts for service in the vacation industry. While ignorance is bliss (and, in this instance, cheaper to boot), here are the conventional gratuities expected for service in hotels, restaurants and the like.

Maid service: $2 per night

Bellhop or redcap (airport and train) service: 50 cents–$1 per bag

Restaurant service: 15%–20% of the bill

Bartenders: 10%–15% of the tab

Taxi or limo drivers: 15% of the fare

Valet parking attendants: $1

Phones

Following public outcry and a series of toothy articles in *Condé Nast Traveler* and elsewhere, the phone surcharge industry perpetrated by hotels—a rude shock routinely leveled on unsuspecting guests at checkout—seems to have settled back a bit. In truth, "bit" is the operative word, here. With the vast assortment of hotels available in and around Orlando, there is no general rule, but the best piece of advice I can provide is to make sure you understand exactly when and how much you will be charged when you dial out of your room, before you start calling.

For local calls, the area's budget properties usually have the best rates, charging as little as 40 cents per connection. By contrast, the Hilton at Walt Disney World Village saddles guests with a whopping $1 per local call, plus tax, presumably because a majority of its guests are convention attendees with expense accounts. Most hotels seem to hover around 75 cents per local call, though the Disney-owned properties do not charge for calls made within Walt Disney World.

Long-distance calls are a different matter. Each hotel will levy a surcharge of up to 50 percent over the regular, undiscounted rate. Hotels don't usually charge for 800 numbers, so if you expect to spend more than a few minutes on a room phone with someone outside the area, obtain a calling card from your long distance or local phone company that uses a toll-free access number. Failing that, call your party and ask them to call you back at the hotel. Double ditto for overseas calls.

Banking Services

If you run out of cash or have unexpected banking needs within Walt Disney World, your best bet is the **SunTrust Bank** on Buena Vista Drive across from the Disney Village Marketplace ☎ *(407) 828-6106*. SunTrust will provide cash advances on Visa or MasterCard credit cards, cash personal checks up to $1000 for American Express cardholders, replace lost American Express traveler's checks and even cash personal checks up to $25 on presentation of your driver's license and major credit card. In addition to the branch on Buena Vista Drive, a SunTrust Bank is located on Main Street in The Magic Kingdom.

ATMs are located at the SunTrust Bank, along International Drive, and throughout the Orlando area. You may call the two major ATM providers and obtain the closest machine to you by entering the area code and first three digits of the number you are calling from:

Cirrus: ☎ *(800) 424-7787*

Plus: ☎ *(800) 843-7587*

Special Travelers

Families with Small Children

According to the Disney Company's ongoing advertising campaign, no one will have a better time visiting The Magic Kingdom and other theme parks than children, all of whom are pictured happily embracing Mickey Mouse, riding the Jungle Cruise, etc. The reality is a little more complicated. Disney's theme parks are a dazzling conglomeration of complex imagery. And sometimes the issues parents must deal with when introducing children to the Disney machine are more gritty.

My earliest memory of going to the movies was to see *Snow White and the Seven Dwarfs*. The film had been reissued when I was four or five years old and my family went to the drive-in to see the animated masterpiece. Unfortunately, I didn't make it through the second encounter with the evil queen. Tears flying, I insisted on leaving, and was provided an ice cream cone for cold comfort. I learned then that no one does a better job of scaring the bejeesus out of small folks than Walt Disney. And today, the ride **Snow White's Adventures** at The Magic Kingdom continues to do a decent job of terrorizing new generations (it doesn't help that the witch makes more appearances in the attraction than Snow White herself).

Even Disney's solidly hyped **Character Breakfasts** can be a tragedy, or a scene from a horror movie, depending on your perspective. On both of the two occasions I sat in on a Character Breakfast, I saw pre-teens who were overjoyed at their interaction with Pluto and Goofy. However, each time there were also several preschoolers on hand traumatized by the sight of cartoon characters they loved on television but who now loomed so much larger than life (see "Character Breakfasts" in "Restaurants").

Disney's advertising campaigns frequently showcase children barely old enough to walk, but the entertainment package the company produces can be too intense for preschoolers. Yes, there are joyous experiences in spades, but the quantity and conditions in which children are required to assimilate them create a major overload. Imagine if **Dumbo the Flying Elephant**—probably Disney's most popular ride for preschoolers—landed in the parking lot of your local supermarket; your child would look forward to shopping and riding Dumbo every week. No problem, right? Now, imagine the same ride, and dozens of other luscious attractions, surrounding and competing for your child's attention, during one very long day. The youngster is tantalized at every direction, yet the length of lines mean nothing. The child's sensory preceptors go into overdrive and any ability to reason with the tyke is lost. And this is *before* factoring in something truly daunting, such as the effects of Florida's stifling summer weather conditions.

Florida's sweltering summers are probably the biggest cause of travel burn-out, particularly for young children. If you can swing it, visit during the off season, even if it means pulling the kids out of school. I'm no child development expert, but I reckon an information-packed safari to Walt Disney World has almost as much education potential as a week in school (if in doubt, ask your child's teacher, and develop a strategy for covering missed classroom time with a special report on the trip). If you *must* visit during summer, schedule a daily afternoon break (see below), carry a water bottle to minimize reliance on drinking fountains and expensive soft drinks, and provide sunglasses and hats for everyone in your party; then, double the importance of all the following suggestions.

In summation, Walt Disney World and Orlando offer a complete entertainment package, suitable for all ages. However, keep in mind that the vacation you have in mind is not necessarily the one your children are eyeing.

1. Plan flexibility.

Yes, chart a strategy for your trip, but flexibility is the key to successful theme-park touring with children. You may know they'll love Splash Mountain and that the lines are shortest in the early morning, but if the kids are standing wide-eyed in front of Dumbo at 9:01 a.m., you'll have little choice but to succumb. If you're visiting Orlando "for the kids," you'll need to sign on for their agenda to a large degree, so involve them in developing a touring plan, including the rides you'll hit first, where you plan to eat lunch, and an approximate time for an afternoon break. Beyond this, when your children have their first encounter with Dumbo (or whatever), throw caution to the wind and allow them their momentary lapse of reason.

2. Strollers.

A stroller is perhaps the best solution to avoiding burnout for younger guests. Your child may be long past the toddler stage, but by keeping youngsters off their feet for most of the day, you'll find they are more receptive to you and less frustrated by the overall experience. In the event you rent a stroller at the front gate, be sure to mark it with a business card, or something that identifies it as yours for the day. Park-provided strollers disappear by accident often enough to cause inconvenience. Hold on to your receipt in case you have to get a replacement.

3. Plan an afternoon break.

The early and mid-afternoon periods are when the theme parks reach their peak attendance for the day. Lines are longest, paths are clogged by parade-viewers, and summer heat is at its most oppressive. At this point, all but the most energetic visitors can benefit from a break in touring. Each day, before you begin your theme park assault, schedule a mini-vacation from the parks with your kids. Whether it's a long lunch away from the crowds, a nap, or a swim at the hotel pool, the time away from the hustle will be rejuvenating for everyone. Don't forget to have your hands stamped on exit so that you may return later on.

4. Switching off.

Several of Disney's most popular rides have 40- or 44-inch minimum height requirements for boarding. If you are visiting the theme parks with a child too young to partake in some attractions, you'll want to employ a "switch off" to minimize your wait in lines and maximize the number of rides you take in. It works like this: children accompany both adults in your group in the line to the ride's loading area. At that point, you'll need to inform the ride attendant that one adult will wait with the child while the other adult rides; when the first rider has finished, the child swaps sitters at the loading dock and the second adult boards the attraction. Obviously this works only when there are two adults in the party, and while riding alone isn't quite as much fun, it's better than missing some rides or, worse, waiting in line twice.

INSIDER'S TIP

Head off disappointment later by measuring your children's heights before they arrive at the parks. Some of the rides have a 40- or 44-inch height requirement that will ace out younger guests intent on riding Splash Mountain and other favorites. The minimum heights are listed in Fielding's with the description of the various rides, allowing you a chance to prepare your children in advance... or buy them heel lifts!

---

5. Set a meeting place.

The opportunities for parents and children to become separated are more numerous than the number of Disney souvenir stands. Be particularly cautious of the possibility of losing a child following parades or fireworks display, when exiting attractions with large seating capacities, and around character meetings where large groups of children congregate. Establish a meeting place where your group can relocate if someone becomes separated. The large and ill-defined Cinderella Castle area of The Magic Kingdom is *not* recommended; the base of the steps leading up to the Main Street Train Station is better. Failing reconnection, the locations of lost-children facilities at each park are listed in the "Attractions" chapters.

6. Don't forget to schedule time at the pool.

When I toured Walt Disney World with my nephew and niece, I was taken aback by their devoted fixation to the pool facilities at each hotel we visited. It wasn't until they'd been with me a couple days that I realized we needed to set aside at least an hour every day to make sure they received their dose of chlorinated fun. Months after their trip, two things they were still talking about were their visit to Blizzard Beach and the pool at the Yacht and Beach Club resorts.

7. The breakfast factor.

Hotels that offer a continental breakfast as part of their room rate are especially appealing to families. Sure, visitors like the money they're saving, but the real value lies in the fact that one can eat and run, rather than dragging the meal out and slicing valuable time off your touring schedule. Better yet, because kids see the food options laid in front of them, they're likely to get exactly what they want, and you'll keep their squirming to a minimum by not having them wait for a server or for the meal to be prepared.

INSIDER'S TIP

If traveling with children, provide each one with a disposable camera with preloaded film to use during your vacation. Better yet, buy a disposable underwater camera, which can be used at the water parks and in pools. Purchase this before you leave since any camera or film products bought in Walt Disney World will cost more.

While we've created a list of "Terror Factors," for the rides that are the most unsettling for young kids, no two children are alike. One child may be bothered by the audio-animatronic animals of the **Jungle Cruise**, while another laughs it off; put the same two children on the atmospheric **Pirates of the** **Caribbean** and their responses might be reversed. However, no one knows your child better than you. Take time to explain what the child should expect, and work up to the more dismaying attractions slowly. Kids who are forearmed about the contents of the individual attractions will be better able to experience them in the right spirit. While there's little one can do to psychologically prepare a just-tall-enough-to-ride moppet for **Space Mountain**, comparatively tame attractions such as **Snow White's Adventures** and the **Haunted Mansion** are less frightening if the child can understand it's not real (then again, that witch is awfully insistent!). When in doubt, one parent can test a ride's terror potential while the other accompanies the child on another attraction.

Terror Factor for Children*	
Ride name	Terror factor: (scale of 1 to 3)
Magic Kingdom	
Jungle Cruise	✓

Terror Factor for Children*

Pirates of the Caribbean	✓
Big Thunder Mountain Railroad	✓✓
Splash Mountain	✓✓
Tom Sawyer Island	✓ (the caves)
Haunted Mansion	✓
Snow White's Adventures	✓✓
Mr. Toad's Wild Ride	✓
ExtraTERRORestrial	✓✓✓
Space Mountain	✓✓✓
Astro Orbiter	✓✓

Epcot

Universe of Energy	✓
Body Wars	✓✓
Honey, I Shrunk the Audience	✓
Maelstrom	✓

Disney-MGM Studios

Great Movie Ride	✓✓
Star Tours	✓✓
Backstage Studio Tour	✓ (Catastrophe Canyon)
Twilight Zone Tower of Terror	✓✓✓

Universal Studios

Hitchcock: Art of Making Movies	✓
Funtastic World of Hanna-Barbera	✓
Kongfrontation	✓✓
Earthquake	✓✓
Jaws	✓✓
Back to the Future	✓✓
E.T. Adventure	✓
Horror Makeup Show	✓
Terminator 2 3-D	✓✓✓

Sea World

Wild Arctic	✓

*Based on children who meet the minimum height requirement for each ride.

Five of the Disney-owned resorts offer child care services during the evening for potty-trained kids, ages 4–12. The most popular is the **Neverland Club** at the Polynesian Resort, which provides a buffet dinner, live birds from Discovery Island, arcade and video games, a movie and an appearance by Goofy. The club charges $8 per hour (with a three-hour minimum) and is open from 5 p.m. to midnight nightly; kids reportedly love it. At $6 per hour, the **Cub's Den** at the Wilderness Lodge is a scaled-back version of the Neverland, but still provides a meal, and requires only a one-hour minimum stay. Reservations for these two facilities can be made through ☎ *(407) WDW-DINE.* The **Sandcastle Club** at the Beach Club Resort, the **Mouseketeer Club** at the Grand Floridian Resort and the **Mouseketeer Clubhouse** at the Contemporary Resort each provide more basic services for $4 an hour each evening; call the hotels directly for more information.

Disney offers several other popular programs for kids ages 6 to 15; see: "Tours for Kids" in "Obstacles and Opportunities" for more information. A number of other hotels in the area also provide child care services; check the listings under "Accommodations." For those who want to tap into baby-sitting services, there are two good options:

Fairy Godmothers. Gertrude and her staff of retired, nonsmoking Disney cast-members provide tours of the Disney parks, as well as 24-hour sitting services at any of the area hotels. ☎ *(407) 277-3724.*

KinderCare. Disney-authorized, in-room sitting service handles children of all ages. Rates start at $9 per hour for one child, with a four-hour minimum. 24-hour notice required: ☎ *(407) 827-5444.*

INSIDER'S TIP

Children of the video age greatly identify with the characters and situations they've been exposed to on television at home. Although some of the films that inspired Walt Disney World attractions such as The Lion King *and* Honey, I Shrunk the Kids, *are well-known, a number of the Disney classics that breathed life into current rides languish on video shelves in favor of flashier, newer entertainment. By viewing a few of the films at home before the trip, you can provide children a tantalizing insight into some of the park's attractions they might otherwise not fully understand. Try Disney's 1960* Swiss Family Robinson, Song of the South *(on laserdisc only) and* The Adventures of Ichabod and Mr. Toad *(released as one laserdisc or two separate featurettes on video). Older children may enjoy reading some of the classic literature that inspired some of the rides as well.*

Seniors

As with most of Florida, retirees make up a sizable portion of Orlando's guests. The city is senior-friendly and many of its attractions have particular appeal to older visitors. Traipse through **Cypress Gardens** on a weekday and anyone who appears under 50 is more likely to have recently encountered Ponce de Leon's fountain. While many seniors are either snowbirds roosting in central Florida for the winter, or those visiting from within the state, there are quite a few who make a regular pilgrimage to the region, sometimes with grandchildren and other young relatives in tow.

A number of discounts are available to seniors from hotels, car rental companies and other services. In some cases, your photo identification with birthdate will earn the discount, in others, being a member of the **American Association of Retired Persons** (AARP) is required. Some establishments have no set policy, but will provide a discount if you ask. Unfortunately, the theme parks tend to be stingy in giving seniors a break, although you should always inquire.

Some of the issues older guests face when visiting Orlando and its parks sound mundane, but they warrant acknowledgment. One of the key lessons that I've heard from seniors visiting the area is to pace yourself. Tackling the huge Disney parks requires a lot of energy and fortitude, but trying to conquer every square inch of Walt Disney World is a sure license for frustration. Don't try to do it all. Not because you can't—though no one really can on a single trip—but because you'll have a better time if you focus on savoring the experience. Bring a thick book to relax with, or spend some time people-watching (there's no place better to do this than the World). The parks are simply too extensive and detailed to fully appreciate in one trip, so don't fret it and save a little for your next visit.

If you're staying at a Disney Resort (or nearby), take a daily break from the parks. Every day around lunch-time, the Disney parks reach their maximum attendance. Until late in the afternoon, lines at attractions will be at their peak, and navigating the walkways becomes an obstacle course made up of strollers, balloons and darting children. Instead, I recommend slyly exiting the front gate (be sure to have your hand stamped for return) and heading back to your hotel for a break. Whether it's a stroll through the lobby areas, a nap, a swim in the pool or lunch, this sojourn acts as a pick-me-up for visitors of any age, and provides you a fighting chance at seeing more rides, hour-for-hour, than the people who slogged it out at the parks during the afternoon.

Having discouraged you from packing too much into your day, take particular heed of the "When to Go" section of this chapter. If you want to see as much of the parks as possible, take advantage of the months when most kids are in school and time your visit for the off-season. Not only will lines be substantially shorter, but the pace will be less hectic, the temperatures less sizzling, and prices reduced.

But the real issue most older folks are curious about is whether they'll survive the rides. Before addressing the subject directly, I'll offer an anecdote.

As a pre-teen during the mid-1960s, the Matterhorn loomed ominously over my first several trips to Disneyland. The most popular thrill ride at the park, the **Matterhorn Bobsleds** was a chorus of screams and shouts whirling furiously around the glaciated peak. By the time I was eight or nine, I had finally worked up the courage to ride the Matterhorn. Only one obstacle stood between me and the adventure this time: my grandparents who had brought me to Disneyland.

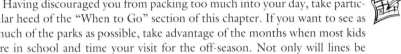

Ride name	Rattle rating (scale of 1 to 3)
Magic Kingdom	
Space Mountain	✓✓✓
Big Thunder Mountain	✓✓✓
Splash Mountain	✓✓
Astro Orbiter	✓✓
ExtraTERRORestrial	✓
Mad Tea Party	✓ (unless accompanied by teens)
Epcot	
Body Wars	✓✓✓
Disney-MGM Studios	
Star Tours	✓✓
Twilight Zone Tower of Terror	✓✓
Universal	
Funtastic World of Hanna-Barbera	✓✓
Kongfrontation	✓
Back to the Future	✓✓✓

Rattle Ratings for Seniors and Other Sensitive Guests	
Earthquake	✓✓
Jaws	✓
Terminator 2 3-D	✓
Sea World	
Wild Arctic	✓✓

Because they felt responsible for my younger brother and I, they never let us out of their sight. And as I nervously approached the mountain, I pleaded, cajoled and eventually coerced my grandmother into riding the bobsleds with me. To me, the ride was exhilarating and I had a blast. By contrast, my grandmother was whipped around more than she expected and limped out of the bobsled vowing that it would be her last roller-coaster ride.

The moral of the story is that when older visitors are accompanied by much younger ones at theme parks, a combustible mix can result. If you're traveling with teens or younger, admit that they've got more energy, and also the uncanny ability to siphon energy away from you. Make sure your agenda is met, too, and unless a hectic pace is your usual style, don't try to match younger ones ride for ride. Further, we all have different tastes, and on some rides, one member may not enjoy them as much as another. The Disney folks seem to acknowledge both extremes better than any other amusement park I've visited and there are few attractions that skew exclusively to one segment of the audience. Still, there are a number of rides in the Orlando area that will give many seniors pause.

Before warning you away from some of Walt Disney World's best adventures, however, know that many of the thrill rides are more hype and build-up than death-defying scares. One example is the **Twilight Zone Tower of Terror**, where guests are plunged into a creepy atmosphere with eye-popping effects that lead up to an abrupt, but cushioned, drop. Mentally, your mind is prepared for the worst, but except for a quick rush, few riders experience any lasting trauma. Another example of the psychological impact felt at some attractions is the contrast between **Star Tours** (at the Disney-MGM Studios) and **Body Wars** (at Epcot). Both feature an identical setup involving a flight simulator and a movie screen that displays the visual each ride is affecting. The kinds of physical tilts and dips one experiences on the two attractions are virtually identical (albeit in a different sequence), but the scenery is vastly different. Star Tours uses outtakes from the *Star Wars* trilogy to convey its "story," while Body Wars uses newly created special effects footage of a miniaturized, break-neck excursion through the human body. Curiously, most visitors have little problem with Star Tours, but Body Wars inspires vastly different reactions among some shaken guests, up to and including nausea. One can only assume it's the psychological impact of the outer space derring-do we're already familiar with compared to the visceral jolt of swooshing through a human heart via blood veins.

Still, for those guests traumatized each time they arrive at an attraction with a warning posted at its entrance, we've compiled a list of Rattle Ratings for Seniors and other Sensitive Guests, a ranking of Orlando's more thrilling rides. Note that these ratings are not the same as the Terror Factor chart for children (youngsters are usually more concerned with being spooked by Snow White's evil queen than they mind being physically shaken up). And, when a ride such as **Back to the Future** posts a "DYNAMICALLY AGGRESSIVE" sign at the front door, heed the warning. On the other hand, if you work up to some of the more modest thrills, you may soon find yourself having the time of your life on **Splash Mountain**, possibly the best all-around Disney adventure yet.

Other services provided for the region's older guests include the following:

American Association of Retired Persons (AARP)

601 East Street Northwest, Washington D.C. 20049. ☎ (202) 434-2277.
The nation's largest senior-citizen's group; carrying its card, available to those 50 and up, yields many discounts, including some unavailable to non-senior AARP members. Annual membership, $8 per person or couple.

Elderhostel

☎ (617) 426-7788.
Somewhat of a role model for the much pricier Disney Institute, Elderhostel provides study programs covering a wide variety of topics. There are several locations in and near Orlando, and courses can easily be combined with a trip to the region's attractions. Prices include simple accommodations and meals, and run $300–$350 for the six-day courses. Free catalog available.

The Mature Traveler

P.O. Box 50400, Reno, Nevada 89513. ☎ (702) 786-7419.
A popular monthly newsletter serving the senior community featuring an ample supply of tidbits about the Florida travel market, including news of special deals. Annual subscription, $29.95; sample copy, $2.

Fairy Godmothers

☎ (407) 277-3724
Gertrude and her staff of retired Disney cast members provide tours of the Disney parks, as well as 24-hour sitting services at any of the area hotels.

Holiday Assistants

7798 Indian Ridge Trail North, Kissimmee, Florida 34747. ☎ (800) 945-2045 or (407) 397-4845.
A start-up crew of current and former Disney cast members that provides unofficial tours of Disney's theme parks and other neighboring attractions. Rates start at $18 per hour with package (multi-day) rates available.

Visitors with Disabilities

For a collection of theme parks, Walt Disney World is relatively advanced in its handicapped accessibility. A number of the rides are not available to guests in wheelchairs, but most attractions will accommodate disabled visitors with relative ease. In most instances, guests in wheelchairs will be able to board rides without waiting in line. Many of these attractions require guests in wheelchairs to transfer themselves onto the ride system; Disney's employees (and those of most other parks) are not permitted to physically transfer guests, therefore an able-bodied assistant is required for these attractions.

If you are visiting the parks with a wheelchair, build a little extra touring time into your agenda than what we normally recommend, particularly at Epcot, which is spread over a very large area. Wheelchairs and "electric convenience vehicles" may be rented at the entrance to the three main parks, as well as at the Ticket and Transportation Center. Within Walt Disney World, with few exceptions, all eating facilities, restrooms and performance-oriented attractions are wheelchair-accessible. The Monorail (except the Contemporary Resort stop), ferry service between the Ticket and Transportation Center and The Magic Kingdom, and buses (every other one) are all wheelchair-accessible. The FriendShips plying the water between Epcot and the Disney-MGM Studios are *not* wheelchair-accessible at the Yacht and Beach Club dock.

All of Walt Disney World's hotel facilities feature some quantity of rooms with features for disabled guests. Handicapped room amenities vary greatly. The more expensive properties—the Grand Floridian Beach, Polynesian, BoardWalk, Yacht and Beach Club—have the best options due to larger quarters and a selection of rooms with two double beds (rather than one king, as is predominant in the handicap-accessible rooms of less-expensive properties). If you want to rely on the Walt Disney World Transportation System to see the parks, you'll want to give additional consideration to the Grand Floridian or Polynesian because of the ease of using the monorail service. Note: the monorail stop at the Contemporary is accessed by escalator only. The Epcot Resorts would make a good second choice based on transportation needs, with transit to Epcot or the Disney-MGM Studios via the footpath connecting the two parks.

Hearing-impaired guests will find listening devices at the Guest Relations desks, just inside each of the three main Disney parks. Guided tours of each of the parks are available, and sign-language interpreters can be obtained for no additional charge for these tours with two days' prior notice. Scripts and descriptions of attractions are also available from Guest Relations. Also for the hearing-impaired, TDD kits are stocked at each of the Disney hotels and televisions are close-captioned. **Sight-impaired** guests will find audio cassettes and portable tape players at the Guest Relations desk in each of the three main parks; Braille guidebooks are also available. Cast members can direct you to park relief maps with a Braille directory. Guide dogs for blind visitors are allowed access throughout most of Walt Disney World.

Disney may set the example, but **Universal Studios** stays lock-step in place behind them. Universal provides a Guide for Guests With Disabilities, available through Universal Guest Relations. ☎ *(407) 363-8000.* Visually impaired guests can obtain a portable cassette player with information about the rides at Guest Services, and hearing-impaired guests are provided tour-information scripts with descriptions of the attractions. Universal also offers a TDD line: ☎ *(407) 363-8265.* At **Sea World**, guests in wheelchairs receive a 50 percent discount off admission, and all attractions are accessible, according to a Sea World spokesperson (but no pamphlet for disabled guests is available at this time). A sign-language interpreter can be made available on two days' prior notice for guided tours. For more information, contact Sea World Guest Relations: ☎ *(407) 363-2414.* Disabled guests at **Busch Gardens** receive a similar, 50 percent break on admission, and the park also provides a brochure detailing handicap touring accessibility. Visitors with wheelchairs can visit most attractions, although guests have to transfer out of the wheelchairs to partake in most of the park's thrill rides. Busch Gardens Guest Relations can be reached at ☎ *(813) 987-5212.* For information about other area attractions and their accessibility, call directly.

For a more detailed look at planning a trip for disabled visitors, I highly recommend *Handicapped in Walt Disney World* (1993, SouthPark Publishing Group), an upbeat, informative 300-page guidebook by Peter Smith, a paraplegic who roams the world in a wheelchair. Although the book focuses on physically disabled travel, it also addresses sensory and mental disabilities. If you have difficulty locating it, you can call SouthPark and order a copy directly. ☎ *(214) 296-5657.*

Other resources include:

Walt Disney World Special Request Reservations
☎ *(407) 354-1853.*
Handles hotel reservations and vacation coordination for guests with disabilities; conducts a detailed interview to identify the special needs of each prospective guest.

Guidebook for Guests with Disabilities
☎ *(407) 824-4321.*

A free brochure published by the Walt Disney Company that provides a ride-by-ride breakdown of which attractions are accessible at the three main parks.

Holiday Assistants

7798 Indian Ridge Trail North, Kissimmee, Florida 34747. ☎ *(800) 945-2045 or (407) 397-4845.*

A start-up crew of current and former Disney cast members provide unofficial tours of the Disney's theme parks and other attractions. Rates start at $18 per hour, with package (multi-day) rates available.

Care Medical Equipment

☎ *(800) 741-2282 or (407) 856-2273.*

Provides wheelchairs, oxygen and other equipment specifically for disabled travelers, delivering directly to area hotels.

Physically Challenged Guide to Florida

The Florida Department of Commerce–Division of Tourism, 126 Van Buren Street, Tallahassee, Florida 32399. ☎ *(904) 487-1462.*

The state produces a free booklet for handicapped visitors.

Lesbian and Gay

Maybe it's the city's location at the edge of the Bible Belt, or perhaps it's the straight-laced image the mouse demands, but Orlando's vast lesbian and gay community is ill-defined and somewhat sequestered. But it's there.

A drive through the elegant residential districts of **Eola Heights** and **Lake Davis** (affectionately known locally as Lake *Bette* Davis) will visit some of the homes that have been painstakingly restored by members of Orlando's gay community. **Antique Row**, on North Orange Avenue (where it borders Lake Ivanhoe), is a frequent haunt of many gay antique collectors and their partners. The **Winter Park Shopping District** (along Park Avenue) is a popular alternative for many gays wishing to avoid the sterile trauma of a mall for window shopping. And, as in many American cities, local support for arts and culture has not been possible without the backing and involvement of the gay community.

But it's the gay and lesbian community's relationship with the Disney Company that generates the most-knowing winks. "How many straight Disney employees does it take to screw in a lightbulb on Main Street?" goes the inside joke. The answer: both of them. It's no secret within the organization, but for years Disney has been among the world's largest employers of gay men and women. In return, the community commemorates its unofficial patron saint at one of Orlando's most popular gay hangouts: a cabaret and piano bar named **Uncle Walt's**, an honor the man himself would probably have a tough time swallowing.

Walt's staunchly conservative personal outlook aside, the Disney Company has been good to its gay employees, most recently in 1995 by making health coverage available to domestic partners. This has not come without a price: many of central Florida's religious organizations—most of which seem to feel the company should celebrate only a narrow definition of family—have done their best to mount a feeble boycott of all things Disney. However, with corporate America, and Hollywood-based studios in particular, increasingly supportive of health care for domestic partners, realistically, Disney has had little choice but to quietly recognize its troops of gay employees.

The most obvious connection Walt Disney World makes with the gay community is the annual—though unofficial—**gay day** at the Magic Kingdom, typically held the first Saturday in June. Call Orlando's Gay and Lesbian Community Center for more specific information. Additionally, Disney employees are admitted to **Pleasure Island** for free on Thursday nights. It doesn't take a rocket scientist to figure out that Walt's employees put their gayest foot forward on that evening and, indeed, you'll see it yourself at the high-energy disco, **Mannequins Dance Palace**. Other, more officially gay-friendly establishments and services in the area:

Gay and Lesbian Community Center
714 East Colonial Drive, Orlando. ☎ *(407) 425-4527.*
The center provides a monthly activity calendar with a listing of gay-oriented events within central Florida, and acts as a resource for gay visitors.

Out and About Books and Gifts
930 North Mills Avenue, Orlando. ☎ *(407) 896-0204.*
Central Florida's gay and lesbian bookstore. Monday-Saturday 10 a.m.–8 p.m.; Sundays noon–6 p.m.

Uncle Walt's
I-Drive Center, 5454 International Drive, Orlando. ☎ *(407) 351-4866*
Cabaret bar Thursday–Saturday, piano bar Tuesday and Wednesday evenings, pool nightly. Open daily 4 p.m.–2 a.m.

Foreign Visitors

Wowed by the beaches and thrilled by the theme parks, foreign travelers add much of the international feel to Florida. Between Orlando and Miami's bustling airports, a growing number of foreign carriers serve Florida, delivering several million visitors annually into the central Florida region. Visitors from the United Kingdom account for almost a third of this total, followed by Brazilians, Germans and Argentinians. Among international guests, Orlando ranks as the fifth most-visited U.S. city—about one in every eight foreign visitors now makes Orlando a part of his or her U.S. vacation.

AUTHOR'S OBSERVATION

The Orlando International Airport is the second-largest airport property in the United States and serves the majority of travelers to the Orlando area— now about 23 million annually, more than double the number that flew into town yearly only a decade earlier. The number of foreign travelers using the facility has also increased dramatically, to around 3 million annually, and Orlando now represents the sixth-largest port of entry for international visitors in the United States.

What does all this mean? It exemplifies the enthusiasm that international visitors shell out to support Orlando's tourism infrastructure. Further, it means that for many foreign visitors, Orlando *is* America.

During the early 1990s, Florida developed a questionable reputation—following several robbery-motivated assaults—as being less-than-hospitable to foreigners. However, Orlando is a city vitally dependent on tourism income, and the reality is that serious crime against visitors is a rarity. When planning a trip to the United States, you'll want to consider the following areas:

1. Travel to and through central Florida

More than a dozen foreign carriers serve Orlando International Airport directly; several dozen more fly into Miami, 236 miles south of Orlando. A few also serve Tampa, 84 miles to the west. These three cities make an ideal place to begin your journey, whether you plan to cover Florida only, or several states. APEX airfares are your usually your best rate, when available, but the bucket shops in London and other cities frequently offer good deals to Florida.

Rail service in the United States is not as efficient nor as well-connected as train service in Europe, however, the eastern states are traversed by a number of lines. Three primary routes end in Florida (see: "By Rail" in this chapter), but if you're considering extensive train travel, you'll want to consider purchasing a USA Railpass, covering unlimited trips within a set time frame. Better yet, similar ticket arrangements are available for air travel, but only to foreign visitors who purchase the tickets at home. These are especially valuable if you want to see a large area of our country— remember, the United States covers a vast chunk of territory considerably larger than Europe. These touring options are best arranged for by your travel agent at home. Still, most foreign visitors see the United States the way most Americans do—by car. Aside from the peculiarities of your particular nation's driving style, pay close heed to the safety tips outlined below (also see the "Rental Car" section of this chapter). Note that some auto rental companies will contractually limit your driving to within the state of Florida.

2. Paperwork

Only Canadian citizens are exempt from carrying a passport when entering the United States (although they do need proof of residence). If you hold a round-trip ticket and sufficient funds for your visit, citizens of most western European countries, as well as Japan and New Zealand, are not required to obtain a visa to enter the United States. Visitors from other countries are usually required to apply for and obtain a tourist visa for their visit; contact the U.S. embassy closest to your home for an application and any information on special restrictions. Within the United States, all foreign embassies are located in Washington, D.C., although a number of consular offices can be found in major cities, including some in Miami. Carry a photocopy of your passport with you at all times, but separate from the actual document. In the event your passport is lost or stolen, the copy will help you procure a replacement faster.

3. Currency and Exchange Rates

Americans get by on dollars and cents, conveniently segmented into paper and coin, and written as "$" and "¢." Unfortunately, you'll rarely hear the latter referred to since most purchases involve the larger denomination. There are 100 cents for every dollar; the amount $1.50 as written equals one-and-a-half dollars, or, one dollar and 50 cents. Dollar bills come in several common amounts: $1, $5, $10, $20, $50 and $100 (the largest bill is used only for major transactions and is rarely found in cash registers).

Having provided this brief insight into the U.S. monetary system, we, as have most developed countries, are gradually becoming a "cashless society." Largely for security reasons, personal checks are becoming an increasingly uncommon form of payment, although traveler's checks in U.S. dollars are still widely accepted at businesses catering to tourists. Credit cards are becoming our preferred method of payment, and you'll find the major cards accepted widely throughout central Florida. Foreign currency is generally not accepted in Florida other than at banks (and then only at a premium), however currency may be exchanged at the Guest Relations desks of Disney's three major parks, and at the SunTrust Bank across from the Disney Village Marketplace. For hints on tipping, see "Money" in this chapter.

4. Language

Larger resorts will have some bilingual staff available; it may help, when making a booking, to identify your preferred language so that they are aware of your specific needs at check-in time. The Walt Disney Company has a foreign-exchange program in effect for its employees. As you'd expect, Epcot has large number of bilingual employees. The other language prominent in Florida is Spanish, but primarily only around Miami.

5. Safety

Despite its prevalence within American society, foreign visitors should not be overly concerned about crime and violence in the Orlando area. If you are sticking to Walt Disney World for your entire trip, you can rest assured that the area is well-patrolled; incidents involving foreign visitors are very rare. The areas along International Drive, between Universal Studios and Sea World, and along U.S. 192 are also relatively free from any serious crime. Beyond these three heavily traveled areas, a little more caution is advised, particularly where driving is concerned.

Following several episodes of violence directed at tourists driving rental cars in southern Florida (and putting a dent into the entire state's international arrivals), rental agencies have stepped up efforts to protect foreign customers. When you pick up your car, ask for explicit directions to your destination and make sure you have a good road map for the journey, no matter how brief it may be. Ask your rental agency if it has a list of the safety tips. In the event of an accident or engine problems in an area you feel uncertain of, turn your emergency blinkers on, lock the car doors, and wait in the car for police to arrive. Finally, be aware that if your driving habits make you look like a tourist, particularly if you are lost and are obviously studying a road map at the side of the road, you might become a more attractive target for what crime does exist within the region.

Photography

Surely, millions of photos are taken each year inside Walt Disney World. The imagination and talent that went into the design of the various parks makes a colorful setting for lively photos. If your camera is new or you are unfamiliar with its operation, shoot and develop a couple rolls of film prior to your trip. This will help ensure that the camera is in good working order and give you an opportunity to become comfortable with its operation. Purchase your film and an extra set of batteries before you leave (supplies are expensive in Walt Disney World); pack your film in a cool, dry place. Flash photography is not permitted inside most Disney attractions, though a high-speed film (400 ASA or higher) and a steady hand may be sufficient in some instances.

If you have camera problems while visiting, there are camera shops inside each of the three main Disney parks. Video camera rentals also are available at these locations, and two-hour film processing is offered throughout the main parks, at the Disney Village Marketplace and at many of the resorts.

HOTELS AND ACCOMMODATIONS

The Hyatt Regency Grand Cypress Resort's pool is one of the world's largest. The tri-level, half-acre pool features waterfalls, a waterslide and grotto bar.

No single decision regarding your Orlando vacation will have more impact than the one you make concerning your accommodations.

The location of your hotel will determine the amount of time you spend commuting to the attractions. Hotel amenities (or lack thereof) will either chain you to the parks for entertainment, or provide a welcome respite after long hours of touring. And the price of your accommodations can be either a secondary expense to tickets and food, or an extravagance you'll be paying off for months to come.

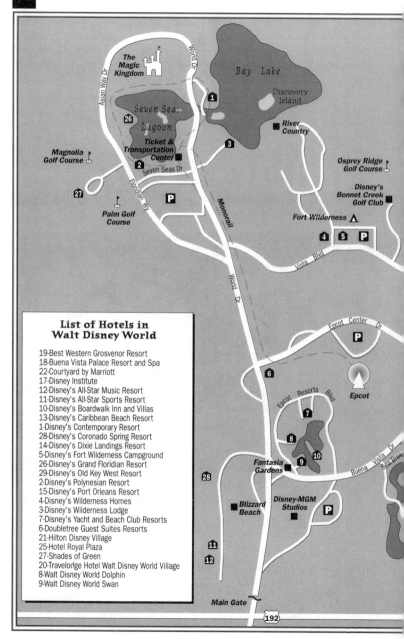

List of Hotels in Walt Disney World

19-Best Western Grosvenor Resort
18-Buena Vista Palace Resort and Spa
22-Courtyard by Marriott
17-Disney Institute
12-Disney's All-Star Music Resort
11-Disney's All-Star Sports Resort
10-Disney's Boardwalk Inn and Villas
13-Disney's Caribbean Beach Resort
1-Disney's Contemporary Resort
28-Disney's Coronado Spring Resort
14-Disney's Dixie Landings Resort
5-Disney's Fort Wilderness Campground
26-Disney's Grand Floridian Resort
29-Disney's Old Key West Resort
2-Disney's Polynesian Resort
15-Disney's Port Orleans Resort
4-Disney's Wilderness Homes
3-Disney's Wilderness Lodge
7-Disney's Yacht and Beach Club Resorts
6-Doubletree Guest Suites Resorts
21-Hilton Disney Village
25-Hotel Royal Plaza
27-Shades of Green
20-Travelodge Hotel Walt Disney World Village
8-Walt Disney World Dolphin
9-Walt Disney World Swan

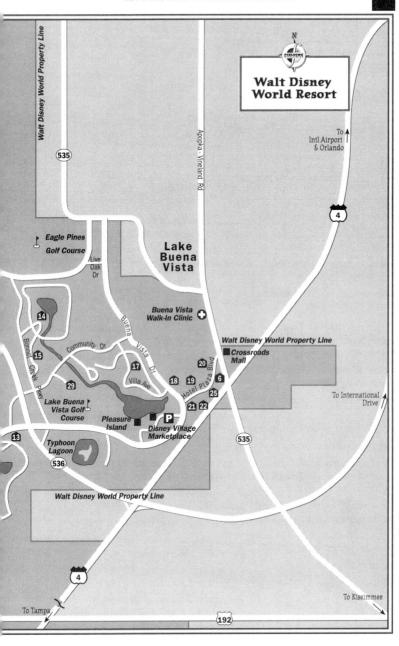

Most visitors choose a compromise between these extremes, but anyone overnighting in Orlando for the first time can be excused for being overwhelmed by the range and number of choices. More than 85,000 hotel rooms are offered in the Orlando metro area. The Walt Disney Company alone is now opening major resorts at a rate of one or more per year, with a total of 16,000 rooms available now that the BoardWalk Inn is open.

What's In A Rating?

The process of visiting, touring and evaluating hotels is not an easy one to define. Obviously, during our research period, I did not stay at all of the burrows described in this chapter. However, each hotel was thoroughly investigated, usually anonymously, to determine if it met the criteria we felt that our readers expect. For the purpose of accurate comparison, at every property I visited, I always looked at a standard room, equating apples to apples when ranking choices.

So what makes a good hotel? If you're spending $29 a night on a cut-rate roost, your expectations probably don't extend far beyond a comfortable bed in clean surroundings. However, given the surprising number of options available even at this price level, Fielding's expects a little more: a location convenient to the attractions, a selection of nearby good restaurants (preferably within walking distance), a decent pool area, a quiet night-time environment and friendly, courteous management and staff. Last, but not least, the hotel should be safe and secure, preferably using card-keys for locks.

If the price of your lodgings is a secondary consideration and you expect more than the basics from your hotel, look beyond the one- and two-star listings. For a property to attain a higher ranking, I considered the following attributes in awarding three stars or more: the size and layout of the room, furnishings, natural and other lighting sources, temperature and ventilation (any notable odor in a nonsmoking room is unacceptable), bathroom facilities, the freshness of decor and general upkeep of the room (nothing annoys my eye more than peeling wallpaper or faded bedspreads long past their prime).

I also account for the "extras" included in a room, such as a phone with voice-mail service, extra-thick towels and a bathrobe, and a coffeemaker. Even the mint on a pillow or the complimentary selection of soap and shampoo is worth considering. I weigh the facilities outside the room, including the lobby and pool area, the greenery as well as the restaurants and bars. In reality, we may spend little actual time in the hotel, but the facilities contribute greatly to our impression and memories of where we have stayed. Finally, I factor in the overall atmosphere and aura of the property. What kind of guests does the hotel cater to? Are there children running amok or rowdy conventioneers, or is the facility quiet and relaxing?

The hotel ratings we have included are designed to help you compare only the hotels featured within this book. For instance, a one-star rating for a facility does not mean it is the worst available. The rating simply reflects the minimum acceptable by Fielding's standards. Such a hotel is comparable to the other one-star properties, slightly less appealing than a two-star domicile, but better than a number of properties we chose not to include. Similarly, a five-star ranking should be used to compare a hotel against the other Orlando accommodations outlined in these pages.

Because of their unique location and reputation, I have chosen to list *all* of the hotels positioned on the Walt Disney World property, Disney-owned or not. In each case, if I did not personally stay in the facility, I made multiple visits to solidify my impressions, viewed more than one room, and then spent additional time soaking up the atmosphere, quietly gauging the hotel's strengths and weaknesses. These resorts are all judged with a tighter eye. For instance, although I didn't pop for the nightly $265 (and up) for a room at Disney's Grand Floridian, I expended innumerable hours exploring the facility over nine visits, talking with guests and employees, dining at its restaurants, drinking in the *mise-en-scène* to see if it was worth the acclaim showered on it by its regulars (it was).

AUTHOR'S OBSERVATION

Although there are excellent (and pricey) hostelries scattered throughout the area, note that none currently measures up to the industry bellwethers, the American Automobile Association Five-Diamond Award and Mobil Travel Guide's Five-Star Rating.

Off-property, with more than 200 lodging possibilities to choose from, I cast an equally discriminating eye. Dozens of hotels visited were *not* included, either due to their location or atmosphere, or because the overall facility did not measure up. When it came to evaluating the many possibilities available for under $100 a night, the key factor was value for dollar.

AUTHOR'S OBSERVATION

*Loaded with hotel and other discounts, the **Orlando MagiCard** is available free of charge from the Orlando/Orange County Convention and Visitor's Bureau. The **Kissimmee-St. Cloud Visitor's Guide** provides similar offers. If you're headed for a Disney property, obtain a **Magic Kingdom Club Card**. Similarly, be familiar with the discounts provided by membership in organizations such as an auto club or the American Association of Retired People. See "Planning Your Trip" for information about all of these, and other special deals.*

The hotel listings are broken down into five, primarily location-based groups. General directions for each of these areas are listed in the "Navigating Central Florida" section of the "Planning Your Trip" chapter. More specific directions are provided for individual hotels in their listings.

The Disney Resorts

All of these are located within Walt Disney World, and are owned and operated by the Walt Disney Company.

Disney Village

Non-Disney-owned lodgings located on the Walt Disney World property, including the nearby Swan and Dolphin.

Crossroads Area and Adjacent

The ill-defined area surrounding Crossroads Mall, near the intersection of I-4 and 535, just east of Walt Disney World.

International Drive

Hotels located on or near International Drive, between Sea World and Universal Studios.

U.S. 192 and Kissimmee

Hotels located on or near 192, south and southeast of Walt Disney World.

Other Possibilities

A few special properties situated away from the heavily touristed areas.

For most of the year, the sheer quantity of hotel rooms available in the Orlando area provides a buyer's market. Whether you are using a travel agent or negotiating for a room on your own, don't shy away from pitting one property against another. One hotel may be 90 percent occupied the week you want to visit, while another is struggling just to get half its rooms booked during the same period. Both hotels may have identical rate cards, and their age, location and amenities might be similar, but management at the second property will go further out of their way to get your business. For information on package vacations, another method of saving money, see "By Package Tour" in "Planning Your Trip."

INSIDER'S TIPS

If you are driving to Orlando from out-of-state and have not booked your accommodations in advance, stop by the Disney-AAA Travel Center in Ocala. Disney uses this facility to tempt uncommitted travelers to book rooms at a Disney Resort. Depending on what's available, rooms can be substantially discounted off the rack rate, particularly mid-week and during non-holiday travel times. Officially, the center will not quote room availability by phone, or the level of discount offered. The center is open daily from 9 a.m. to 6 p.m. and is located just off I-75 in Ocala, Florida, 86 miles northwest of Orlando. Also note that, unlike most other AAA facilities, this one sells tickets only for the Disney theme parks. ☎ (904) 854-0770.

The overall concept at Walt Disney World's Swan Hotel is to bring the outdoors inside. ©Walt Disney World Swan Hotel

The Disney Resorts

For many visitors, nothing less than staying in Walt Disney World, at a Disney Resort, will do. I can hardly blame them.

The Disney properties are uniformly well-maintained, spotlessly clean and are generally situated close or next to the Disney attractions. The hotel staffs, from entry level positions on up, are empowered to take care of their guests—most employees strive to do whatever is necessary to keep guests happy. In judging the 15 Disney Resorts for this book, it was amazing how often I would visit a property in order to see a room, only to learn that literally every chamber was occupied. Yes, the Disney properties are that popular and planning ahead, particularly during holidays, is essential if you have your heart set on a particular hotel.

Within the Disney organization, the hotels compete against each other for posting the top occupancy rates, as well as the highest repeat rates for returning guests. As a group, the Disney Resorts register at the top end when comparing occupancy rates for all hotels in the Orlando area. These hotels offer special amenities not available at the non-Disney properties, including free (and extensive) transportation within the World, and Surprise Mornings (see: "Obstacles and Opportunities"). Disney Resort guests have first choice of tee-off times at the Disney golf courses. The ability to charge to your room all of your Disney purchases—restaurants, gift shops, tickets and more—for one final transaction, is a nice (if fate-tempting) feature. And a new service allows you to have items purchased at the theme parks delivered to your room, relieving you from lugging around cumbersome purchases for the day.

But perhaps the biggest single draw for these properties, one that can't be measured in dollars, is the appeal of staying in the land of Mickey. The lure is obvious for kids. Unexpected guest appearances by the Disney characters are one little perk. The Disney Resort swimming pools are uniformly above average. While parents are checking in, Disney videos play in the lobby of every hotel, and the sleek monorail whizzes by the entrances of three of the resorts. But even adults (this writer included) are easily seduced by the Disney treatment. Who can explain why a mature grown-up is thrilled to discover Mickey Mouse soap and shampoo in his bathroom? Or why people clamor to the railing overlooking "Old Faithful," the faux geyser at the Wilderness Lodge that erupts and sprays guests every hour on the hour? It can best be summed up as the Disney mystique running at full throttle.

There is also a subtle psychological attraction to staying in Walt Disney World: if you are in Florida to *do* Disney, you will feel like a *part* of the experience by staying at a Disney property. At the hotels outside Walt Disney World, many of which are excellent in their own right, you may feel a little like a transgressor, an interloper perhaps, as you commute to and from the parks each day.

Therein lies the rub. Although there are a few exceptions, it costs a pretty penny for the privilege of staying under the Disney banner. Dollar-for-dollar, you will generally get more for your money by staying "off property." Additionally, Orlando's non-Disney attractions are decidedly easier to visit if you don't have to fight the masses flowing in and through the perimeter of Walt Disney World at most hours of the day. However, for the first-time visitor with a ready wallet, a visitor who wants to concentrate most activities within Walt Disney World, the Disney Resorts can't be beat.

INSIDER'S TIPS

The Disney Resorts have three rate structures: holiday prices (the most expensive) are in effect during Christmas vacation; regular season encompasses the summer months and the two-month period before, during and after Easter Vacation; and value season is in place for the balance of the year. The All-Star Resorts, for now, have a set price year-round; expect these rooms to fill up well in advance during busy periods.

Recommending among the different bunks is a little tricky. Walt's army of *imagineers* has done a typically inspired job of giving each resort its own singular personality. More importantly, with the 1994 opening of the All-Star Resorts, Disney can now offer rooms at a larger range of price-points, with more levels of services and amenities. But despite the wide variety of flavors (or, perhaps, because of them), Walt Disney World's millions of annual repeat customers are creatures of habit. Many of them return to the same resort year after year without trying any of the others (I'm told of one gentleman who rents the same block of rooms for his extended family at the Caribbean Beach for several weeks annually). This phenomenon is most pervasive at the Contemporary and Polynesian Resorts, the World's original properties, both of which vaunt high occupancy and return rates, yet seem particularly overpriced when comparing the different Disney facilities.

On a few fronts, I can make some general recommendations. If you're visiting without a car, it helps to be positioned on the monorail line circling the Seven Seas Lagoon (the Polynesian, Contemporary or Grand Floridian), or at one of the Epcot Resorts served by both boat and bus (the BoardWalk, Yacht and Beach Club, as well as the Swan and Dolphin discussed in the next section). Families with children will probably most appreciate the Polynesian and Beach Club for location, with the somewhat lower-priced Wilderness Lodge and Caribbean Beach representing equally appealing choices (all four of these boast excellent pool facilities, an essential for kids). Seniors or couples looking for a relaxed environment will prefer the Grand Floridian or Yacht Club, while a few rungs down the pricing ladder the Wilderness Lodge and Port Orleans provide quiet lodging. And, of course, for seeing Walt Disney World on a budget, the garish All-Star Resorts are the most reasonably priced quarters Disney offers, although some of the off-season discounts linked to the Port Orleans, Dixie Landings and Caribbean Beach can be temperate alternatives (the All-Stars are "never" discounted, according to a Disney spokesperson, at least in regard to season). For information on how to get around the World, see the "Driving Within Walt Disney World" and "Walt Disney World Transportation" sections of the "Planning Your Trip" chapter.

AUTHOR'S OBSERVATION

The Disney Resort room prices cover two adults and their children. Each additional adult in a room (beyond two) is $15. Most Disney Resorts offer rooms that accommodate four guests in two beds, while some feature a day bed or trundle bed for a fifth person. Only the Dixie Landings has a choice of rooms in either configuration, all priced equally. The Wilderness Homes, at Fort Wilderness, sleep up to six.

The Walt Disney Company does not offer a toll-free number for reservations. One central number, ☎ *(407) WDISNEY, or (407) 943-7639*, handles all inquiries and bookings for the Disney Resorts. Expect to spend some time on hold listening to the latest Disney soundtrack (the lines are least busy on Saturday mornings). Special Request Reservations handles rooms for visitors with disabilities: ☎ *(407) 354-1853*.

Finally, some of the Disney Resort perks are available at two expensive, non-Disney properties listed in the Disney Village section below. The Swan and Dolphin hotels have different lease arrangements with the Walt Disney Company than the hotels surrounding Lake Buena Vista. Guests at these two properties may partake in the daily Surprise Mornings and are welcome to use the Disney transportation system to navigate the World.

The Disney Institute

"Most of us know we really can't draw, but it's nice to be in a place where people act otherwise."

—**Jerry Adler**, Newsweek

In its never-ending quest to diversify and expand its customer base, in March 1995, Michael Eisner formally announced the long-simmering plan to develop Disney Institute, adding to and overhauling the existing facilities at Disney's Village Resort, just across the lake from Pleasure Island.

The notion had its genesis a decade ago when Eisner's wife brought him on a trip to the Chautauqua Institution, a century-old, nonprofit organization founded in upstate New York that combined a vacation with edification—brainy lectures amid the forest. After a serious examination of public affairs, classes studying the arts, and performances by distinguished artists, guests returned home exalted and ready for more. Eisner was so inspired by Chautauqua that he dreamed up a plan to duplicate its concept in Orlando as a way of seducing upscale, well-educated visitors to Walt Disney World who weren't interested in a theme park vacation.

The company spent three years developing an educational program, and the Disney Institute opened in February 1996. Despite oodles of publicity, initial reaction to the program from potential customers was lukewarm. Lower-than-anticipated bookings meant the 90-acre "campus" was never quite buzzing—though the theme parks nearby were having their best spring ever—and Disney padded classes with locals who were provided special introductory rates (without accommodations), and filled empty seats at lectures with employees. A surfeit of special offers notwithstanding, the most common observation is that the Institute is simply too expensive for middle America. Including the courses, the least expensive room currently costs more than the least expensive accommodations at the region's most expensive hotel, the Grand Floridian (though it should be noted that institute prices include the courses and other special amenities). The upmarket, goatee-and-cappuccino niche Eisner would like to lure to Orlando simply isn't buying into the concept, at least as defined by Disney.

But, as with all things Mickey, the company claims to be in this for the long haul, and will spend the time and money necessary to refine the Disney Institute until it finally hits the occupancy figures that justify the added overhead of the classes. The company never expected it to be an overnight success, and is depending heavily on word-of-mouth to be its chief sales tool in the future. Most guests that have partaken in the program are enjoying themselves and, per a Disney spokesperson, are planning return visits and recommending the institute to their friends.

Just how much education is delivered at the Disney Institute? Most of the 60-plus courses offered last two or three hours and are geared for students ages 10 and up, which means a class in cooking is limited to very basic concepts that can be appreciated by a wide audience (it's worth noting that relatively few parents are coughing up the dough to put their teens through courses in Culinary Technique, though there is a food class titled Starving Student). But, as much as the institute dabbles superficially, the Disney minds have narrowed the field to some fairly esoteric offerings that would be difficult for many visitors to accomplish at home. Hence, you can undertake a beginner's class in rock-climbing in the morning, follow it with clay animation in the afternoon and top it off that night with a lecture by a visiting luminary (recent guests have included actor Andy Garcia, late composer

Morton Gould, poet Nikki Giovanni, film-maker Jim Abrahams, and scholar Henry Louis Gates Jr., but otherwise pending guests are a closely guarded secret). Other courses take in topiary creation, Disney architecture, dance and the art of maintaining a personal journal.

What the Disney Institute excels at is providing brief excursions off the beaten track, but with a well-studied road map in hand. Surefire ingredients—such as lavishly-equipped workstations for the cooking classes, and a well-honed program for each course instructor to follow—help make sure that each class is a success, within the narrow confines of the course outline.

If Disney doesn't exactly meet your criteria for a producer of a learning vacation, Evelyn Kaye has authored *Travel and Learn: Where to Go for Everything You'd Love to Know* (1995, Blue Penguin), which tells who will take you rock climbing in the Rocky Mountains, or where to find an in-depth course in Italian cooking.

INSIDER'S TIPS

Perhaps the best introduction to the Institute is to spend a day at the facility before you decide to commit an entire vacation to the concept. The day guest program to sample Disney Institute is currently available for $49.90. This allows you to take up to three courses within one day if you are not over-nighting at the Institute (though when its success is better established, this offer may be pulled). Course reservations for day guests can be made up to 14 days in advance: ☎ (407) 827-4800.

Disney Institute, The   **$271–$389**   ★★★★

1960 North Magnolia Way, Lake Buena Vista, 32830, just off Buena Vista Drive, next to Disney Village Marketplace, ☎ *(800) 282-9282, (407) 827-1100, FAX (407) 827-4100. Rated restaurant: Seasons*
Double: $271–$389.

Situated on a lagoon facing Pleasure Island, the Disney Institute creates an alternative to the usual theme-park vacation, mingling daytime classes and evening performances into a resort setting. The courses cover eight areas of interest: entertainment arts, culinary arts, performing arts, design arts, story arts, lifestyles, gardening and the great outdoors, and sports and fitness. For now, a three-night minimum stay is required. Visitors not staying at the Institute may partake in the courses for $49 per day. Prices do not include spa services, greens fees or private golf and tennis lessons; room rates are based on double-occupancy, with additional person rates $55 to $62 per day. Accommodations are in two-story townhouses (one or two bedroom) and

bungalows, positioned among beautifully landscaped grounds and next to the Lake Buena Vista Golf Course. Townhouses have one or two king beds and a sleeper sofa, while bungalow units have two queen beds. The townhouses feature a full kitchen; bungalows have a smaller kitchenette and wet bar. The Sports and Fitness Center features a full-service spa (using Phytomer and Sothys products), and a professional basketball court, six swimming pools, four clay tennis courts, and more help round out the extensive facilities. Meal plan available for dining at Seasons. Disney Village Marketplace is a five-minute walk. Note that some of the accommodations are within late-night earshot of Pleasure Island. Amenities: tennis, health club, exercise room, Jacuzzi, sauna, balcony or patio. 457 rooms. Credit cards: A, MC, V.

AUTHOR'S OBSERVATION

Golf instruction is the most popular set of courses offered at the Disney Institute, and uses the adjacent 18-hole championship course. The golf program was developed by Gary Player, one of only four golfers to win all four of golf's "majors," while the Institute's head professional is Player's son, Wayne.

Resorts

Disney's All-Star Music Resort $69–$79 ★ ★ ★

1801 W. Buena Vista Drive, Lake Buena Vista, 32830, At south end of Buena Vista Drive, one mile south of Blizzard Beach, ☎ (407) 939-6000, FAX (407) 939-7222. Double: $69–$79.

Disney's stab at true budget accommodations yields pretty good value for dollar, particularly during high season (room rates don't fluctuate, they just become harder to come by) though the architectural and room design—a motif of oversize musical instruments and bright colors set against a neon tapestry of pop styles—is loud enough to keep you awake at night. The 10, 192-room buildings are basically identical, but are themed to jazz, calypso, rock, country and Broadway (classical didn't make the cut); rooms are best described as Disney basic, but with the company's typically high degree of maintenance and security. All rooms features two double beds and a desk; the uncontrollable air conditioning is a little annoying. There are two pools: the piano-shaped one is a tad quieter than the guitar-shaped pool offering a spurting, Three Caballeros centerpiece. Recreation and evening entertainment are to be found at the other Disney Resorts. A food court sells reasonably priced pizza, pasta and barbecue, and a bakery opens at 6 a.m. for early birds. 1920 rooms. Credit cards: A, MC, V.

Disney's All-Star Sports Resort $69–$79 ★ ★ ★

1701 West Buena Vista Drive, Lake Buena Vista, 32830, at south end of Buena Vista Drive, one-half mile south of Blizzard Beach, ☎ (407) 939-5000, FAX (407) 939-7333. Double: $69–$79.

Identical in size and layout to the All-Star Music Resort, the interchangeable Sports version continues the Paul Bunyan-size icon concept next door, with the three-story buildings adorned by baseball, football, basketball, tennis and surfing (!) themes. The main courtyard is a brash football field, with a pair of helmets big enough for a garish dwelling glaring at 40-foot-high Coca Cola cups (one of the largest pieces of product placement that this author can recall). One wag described it as "Motel 6 on acid," but a bargain in Walt Disney World is not to be taken for granted. All units have two double beds, and room layouts are cozy, but effectively utilized. Two pools provide ample cool-off time: one is shaped like a baseball diamond, the other vaults a surfing theme. A distinct advantage is the proximity of Blizzard Beach, which is almost across the street from the All-Stars. On-site food court. 1920 rooms. Credit cards: A, MC, V.

Disney's Beach Club Resort $225–$420   ★★★★

1800 Epcot Resorts Boulevard, Lake Buena Vista, 32830, one mile north of Buena Vista Drive, a half-mile west of Epcot, ☎ *(407) 934-8000, FAX (407) 934-3850. Rated restaurants: Ariel's, Cape May Cafe*
Double: $225–$420.

The Cape Cod-themed Yacht and Beach Club Resorts share a fabulous pool and the same piece of centrally located property (next to Epcot), but otherwise work hard to create their own identity and niche. The five-story, blue-and-white Beach Club creates a Disneyfied fantasy of turn-of-the-century East Coast resorts, complete with cabanas and antiquated seaside attire. The hotel draws a slightly larger contingent of families (the Yacht Club seduces a more sedate clientele). The bustling Stormalong Bay swimming lagoon is supplemented by a quiet pool at the end of the Beach Club rooms, but the network of channels, whirlpools and waterfalls at the sand-bottomed Stormalong is enchanting. A pair of tennis courts is free to guests and located just past the valet parking area (rackets and balls are obtained at the health club). A sand-floored volleyball court is available for play, while croquet and bocci ball courts are also nearby. Most rooms have two doubles and a daybed, but a few with a king/daybed combination can be requested. All rooms have balconies, though some are too small for sitting; ask for a "full" balcony at the time of reservation. Rooms on the fifth floor offer the most privacy. Striped curtains and nautical headboards further define the Nantucket-worthy decor. The two resorts share a number of restaurants and imbibing locations, including a wine bar and a '20s-style soda shop. Child care is available at the resort's Sandcastle Club (see: "Families With Small Children" in "Planning Your Trip"). Epcot is a five- to 10-minute walk, and the Disney-MGM Studios are a short boatride away. The Yacht/Beach complex is also close to the Swan, Dolphin and BoardWalk Resorts, providing many dining choices within walking distance. Amenities: tennis, health club, exercise room, Jacuzzi, sauna, balcony or patio, business services. 583 rooms. Credit cards: A, MC, V.

AUTHOR'S OBSERVATION

The five hotels immediately southwest of Epcot are sometimes referred to as the "Epcot Resorts." They include the Yacht and Beach Club, the BoardWalk, the Swan and the Dolphin. Similarly, the three hotels rimming the Seven Seas Lagoon, the Contemporary, the Polynesian and the Grand Floridian Beach, are called the "Monorail Resorts."

Disney's BoardWalk Inn and Villas $210–$495   ★★★★

2101 North Epcot Resorts Boulevard, Lake Buena Vista, 32830, half-mile north of Buena Vista Drive, opposite the Disney-MGM Studios parking lot, ☎ *(407) 939-5100. Rated restaurant: Spoodles.*
Double: $210–$495.

Disney's newest lodging facility continues the East Coast seaboard theme initiated at the Yacht and Beach Club across the water. But renowned architect Robert Stern, who also concocted the Yatch and Beach, embraces an Atlantic City flavor here, complete with a pool wrapped by a Coney Island-style roller-coaster water slide called Luna Park. The pool area at this hotel (BoardWalk) is called Luna Park. The water slide is named Keister Coaster. The 378-room BoardWalk Inn is more intimate than other Disney properties, with delightful nuances one might expect in a seaside bed-and-breakfast—within Walt Disney World, these accents are inspired. The lounge soundtrack is that of "Burns and Allen" and other 1930s radio programming, and a restored, intricately detailed miniature carousel provides a glittering centerpiece to the lobby, roofed by a barrel-vaulted ceiling. The vintage room furnishings are eclectic—like something out of your grandmother's house—and surround private courtyards and gardens. A special feature includes the 14 two-story garden suites with private entrances. The 532 vacation homes compose the adjacent BoardWalk Villas, anticipated to soon become part of the Disney Vacation Club, a time-share project where a private lounge yields unique rooftop views of IllumiNations at Epcot. An old-style dance hall, Atlantic Dance, a dueling piano bar and a sports entertainment club provide evening lures. An activity club for children, Little Toot's, and a health club, Muscles and Bustles, help round out the amenities, which also include tennis, croquet and an arcade. Walkways and boats connect the BoardWalk to Disney-MGM Studios and Epcot, and to the plethora of restaurants available in the four hotels on the other side of the water. Amenities: tennis, exercise room, Jacuzzi, business services. 910 rooms. Credit cards: A, MC, V.

Disney's Caribbean Beach Resort   **$95–$134**   ★★★

Buena Vista Drive, Lake Buena Vista, 32830, half-mile west of Epcot Center Drive (S.R. 536), just southeast of Epcot, ☎ (407) 934-3400, FAX (407) 934-3288. Rated restaurant: Captain's Tavern.
Double: $95–$134.

Reputed to be the fifth-largest resort on the planet, the Caribbean Beach was Disney's first foray into moderately priced accommodations, a sprawling conglomerate of two-story, West Indies-themed buildings ringing a tranquil lagoon behind Epcot. That the resort maintains a modicum of Robinson Crusoe escapism is a tribute to the well-conceived layout, which divides the accommodations into five "villages" named after Caribbean destinations. Each island group has different attributes: Trinidad (South) has the best bus access and is quietest, Jamaica is the most central, Martinique the most festive, etc. All villages are denoted by different pastel color schemes. The resort is centrally located, but isolated from all other activity areas within Walt Disney World; you'll want a car or will be completely dependent on the (frequent) bus service to go anywhere off the Caribbean property. A 1.4-mile promenade circles the 45-acre Barefoot Bay, ideal for walking and jogging. An island, Parrot Cay, is filled with dozens of colorful birds. Note that a number of the rooms are a fair distance from the resort's signature castle-themed pool (although small pools are nestled in each village). Corner rooms in each building are slightly larger; all units feature coffeemakers, a minibar and safe. Two doubles are standard, but about a fifth of the rooms possess a king. The resort was coming to the completion of a two-year rehab in 1996. Old Port Royale is the fluttering hub of the resort, and features a good food court offering pizza, pasta, burgers, a deli, a broiler and a bakery that opens at 6 a.m. Amenities: Jacuzzi. 2112 rooms. Credit cards: A, MC, V.

Disney's Contemporary Resort $195–$300   ★ ★ ★ ★

4600 North World Drive, Lake Buena Vista, 32830, at north end of World Dr., next to The Magic Kingdom, ☎ (407) 824-1000, FAX (407) 824-3539. Rated restaurants: California Grill, Chef Mickey's, Concourse Steakhouse.
Double: $195–$300.

Walt Disney World's first resort was this striking, 15-story concrete berm poised between Bay Lake and the Seven Seas Lagoon, on the edge of The Magic Kingdom. As the only Disney Resort within walking distance to the Kingdom, its location and its access to the monorail that buzzes right through its lobby every few minutes are still the Contemporary's biggest attributes. Although a recent makeover has added a modern color scheme (teal, cream and deep purple) for the first time since it opened, the monolithic structure is still a product of the '60s, when the resort was first conceived. The best post-renovation perk is that the top-floor dining area is now home to the fine California Grill. Guests pay a premium to stay in the A-shaped tower itself, while the least-expensive accommodations are found in the nondescript three-story condo-style wings closer to the lake. The north wing has more privacy and seclusion. Rooms in the tower are spacious by Disney standards, though note that the 6th and 7th floors on the west side vibrate slightly from the passing of the monorail, rooms on the west side also face The Magic Kingdom and its nightly fireworks display. The Contemporary is home to Disney's most extensive tennis facilities, and an abundance of watersports including parasailing is available from the marina on Bay Lake. The pool area was completely redesigned and much improved in late 1995. The Contemporary also boasts the Olympiad Health Club, a racket club and a child-care facility, the Mouseketeer Clubhouse (see: "Families with Small Children" in "Planning Your Trip"). In sum, an impressive and popular resort, but probably the most overpriced of all Disney facilities. Amenities: tennis, health club, sauna, business services. 1041 rooms. Credit cards: A, MC, V.

Disney's Dixie Landings Resort $95–$135   ★ ★ ★

1251 Dixie Drive, Lake Buena Vista, 32830, just off Bonnet Creek Parkway, one mile northeast of Epcot, ☎ (407) 934-6000, FAX (407) 934-5777. Rated restaurant: Boatwright's.
Double: $95–$135.

Positioned at the "headwaters" of the Sassagoula River, Dixie Landings is an evocative trip back to the Mississippi plantation era. Two groups of accommodations are offered—Magnolia Bend is made up of four, three-story buildings embracing the look of 1850s plantation homes, while Alligator Bayou encompasses Cajun-spiced, two-story, tin-roofed buildings, with pines gracing the grounds. Room interiors on either side of the river are nearly identical—two double beds and wood armoires accented by pastels—but Bayou rooms are slightly more rustic. Kings are available in a few dozen of the 2048 rooms, or you can add a trundle bed to the doubles to sleep a fifth person for $12 per night; corner rooms are a hair larger. In addition to tasty Boatwright's Dining Hall, a food court accented by a cotton-mill design is available for low-pressure dining throughout the day (pizza, pasta, fried chicken,

Tex Mex and more). The bakery opens a 6 a.m. daily. Six pools in all, including a theme pool on Ol' Man Island that overlooks the resort's fishin' hole. Dixie guests may also use the nearby colorful Port Orleans pool. Boat and bicycle rentals are available at Dixie Levee, while a small fleet of southern-themed boats ply the Sassagoula, connecting Dixie with the Port Orleans, Pleasure Island and the Disney Village Marketplace. Amenities: Jacuzzi. 2048 rooms. Credit cards: A, MC, V.

Disney's Grand Floridian Beach Resort $265–$505   ★ ★ ★ ★ ★

4401 Grand Floridian Way, Lake Buena Vista, 32830, on the Seven Seas Lagoon, one mile southwest of The Magic Kingdom, ☎ *(407) 824-3000, FAX (407) 824-3186. Rated restaurants: Victoria and Albert's, Flagler's, Narcoosee's, Grand Floridian Cafe. Double: $265–$505.*

Disney's most elegant property is this lavish Victorian tribute to the grand, red-shingled beachfront hotels popular at the turn of the century along the Florida coastline. A *Condé Naste Traveler* readers' survey named this the all-around best hotel in the Orlando area. Topped with opaque-and-pastel stained-glass domes, and embraced by verandas fringed with gleaming gingerbread, the resort is luxurious and immensely popular with Floridians who book weekend escapes months in advance. The main building features suites and delightful turret rooms that feel like a cozy attic. The impressive Presidential Suite was inspired by Teddy Roosevelt and his passion for adventure and sportsmanship. A group of concierge rooms adds a higher level of service and amenities. Although room furnishings vary greatly by size, price and location, most provide generous marble sinks, wood and wicker furniture and fresh spring pastels that accent the wallpaper and bedding. The hotel features five restaurants in all, plus the charming Garden View Lounge, which serves a classic high tea daily from 3 to 6 p.m. The tea room is quite busy on rainy afternoons. The vast, 8000-square-foot swimming pool is undynamic by Disney standards, but less utilized as well, which makes it ideal for relaxing—the shore of the Seven Seas Lagoon is lined with velvety white sand. A bevy of watersports is available at the resort's marina, and tennis, volleyball, croquet, an exercise room and spanking new spa are also on the property; child care is provided by the Mouseketeer Club (see: "Families with Small Children" in "Planning Your Trip"). The Palm, Magnolia and nine-hole Oak Trail golf courses are across the street. The Grand Floridian is popular with honeymooners (the Disney wedding facility is less than a half-mile away), but note that the hotel crawls with kids at all but the latest hour. The Magic Kingdom entrance is a five-minute monorail or boat hop away. Amenities: tennis, health club, exercise room, Jacuzzi, sauna, balcony or patio, club floor, business services. 901 rooms. Credit cards: A, MC, V.

Disney's Old Key West Resort $195–$225   ★ ★ ★ ★

1510 North Cove Road, Lake Buena Vista, 32830, just off Community Drive, one mile east of Epcot, ☎ *(407) 827-7700, FAX (407) 827-7710. Rated restaurant: Olivia's Cafe. Double: $195–$225.*

Mickey's time-share facilities are available to all at this expansive series of condo-style accommodations offering a Key West theme. The units are about two miles west of Disney Village, in the heart of Walt Disney World, but imagineers have successfully created an isolated village atmosphere that provides an added level of both retreat and community. Some rooms are Deluxe Studios, which are similar to a standard hotel room and sleep four, as well as offering a small kitchenette (microwave, wet bar and small fridge, but no stove or dishwasher). One-, two- and three-bedroom villas are also available, which sleep up to four, eight or 12, respectively, and feature a full kitchen and a VCR; some units contain a whirlpool tub. The resort is located in and around the Lake Buena Vista Golf Course, and its hub features a grocery store, exercise facilities and a pleasant restaurant, Olivia's Cafe. Though not cheap, these vacation homes can work out to be a good deal for families prepared to stock and use the kitchen facilities. Amenities: tennis, exercise room, Jacuzzi, sauna, balcony or patio. 704 rooms. Credit cards: A, MC, V.

Disney's Polynesian Resort $200–$395   ★★★★

1600 Seven Seas Drive, Lake Buena Vista, 32830, At the north end of World Drive, just past the Ticket and Transportation Ce, ☎ (407) 824-2000, FAX (407) 824-3174. Rated restaurant: 'Ohana.
Double: $200–$395.

A dreamy and expansive vision of the South Seas, the Polynesian opened immediately following the Contemporary in 1971, and both resorts have benefited from a quantity of repeat guests who stayed at one of the two properties on their initial visit, and aim to duplicate that first vacation in subsequent trips. The verdant lobby area was the subject of debate in early 1996 as Disney planners considered removing the lush jungle display to improve traffic flow; a decision had not been made at press time. The landscaping beyond the lobby will undoubtedly remain extensive and beautifully tended. Named after South Pacific islands, the rooms in the three-story buildings are spacious, but dated in decor; most have two queens and a daybed, though kings are found in some suites—a tapa print canopy looms for a couple feet over the bed and a ceiling fan can supplant the air conditioning for that true South Seas ambience. One building provides concierge service and added amenities; half the Moorea and Tonga rooms face the Seven Seas Lagoon and The Magic Kingdom (perfect for nighttime fireworks). The tropical pool area is surrounded by black volcanic rock and palms, and a slide keeps the kids giggling. Boat rental and watersports are available at the resort's dock, while the Palm, Magnolia and Oak Trail golf courses are across the street. The Polynesian is home to the Neverland Club, the World's most-elaborate evening child-care facility (see: "Families With Small Children" in "Planning Your Trip"). The Magic Kingdom is a five- to 10-minute monorail or boat ride away; the Ticket and Transportation Center and Epcot monorail is a five-minute walk to the east. Amenities: Jacuzzi, balcony or patio, club floor. 853 rooms. Credit cards: A, MC, V.

Disney's Port Orleans Resort $95–$134   ★★★

2201 Orleans Drive, Lake Buena Vista, 32830, just off Bonnet Creek Parkway, one mile east of Epcot, ☎ (407) 934-5000, FAX (407) 934-5353. Rated restaurant: Bonfamille's.
Double: $95–$134.

While Dixie Landings portrays 19th-century southern country living, Port Orleans embraces the Crescent City's French Quarter—wrought-iron balconies, gas-lit street lamps, cobblestone streets and flower-ringed squares. The quaint city-style atmosphere encompasses the three-story guest buildings ringed by magnolias and willows. The rooms are fronted by French doors and feature ceiling fans and two doubles, as a rule (a few contain kings; all hold a maximum of four guests). The resort's pool, Doubloon Lagoon, is a vibrant creation, guarded by a spectacular, blue, green and purple sea-serpent/water slide named Scales. Bonfamille's is supplemented by the Sassagoula Floatworks and Food Factory, a food court loaded with wonderfully garish Mardi Gras props (food service includes a cajun broiler, jambalaya, beignets, pizza and hamburgers). Note that only one bus stop services this 1008-room resort; request a room in Building 4 if transportation proximity is important (Buildings 2 and 5 are closest to the pool area and are more expensive). A boat chugs along the Sassagoula River, taking guests to Pleasure Island, the Disney Village Marketplace or upriver to Dixie Landings (Orleans guests may use the Dixie pool and fishing facilities). Despite its size, this festively decorated resort is one of the most peaceful and romantic of all Disney lodging facilities. Amenities: Jacuzzi. 1008 rooms. Credit cards: A, MC, V.

Disney's Wilderness Lodge   **$159–$300**   ★ ★ ★

901 West Timberline Drive, Lake Buena Vista, 32830, just off World Drive, one mile northeast of Ticket and Transportation Cente, ☎ *(407) 824-3200, FAX (407) 824-3232. Rated restaurants: Artist Point, Whispering Canyon Cafe.*

Double: $159–$300.

Immensely successful since its 1994 debut, Disney's enthusiastic homage to the rustic, early 20th-century lodges of America's national parks brags of the highest occupancy rate for any Disney property (96.4 percent for fiscal 1995, I'm told), and it's not hard to see why. The main building contains a cavernous, eight-story lobby with an 82-foot chimney serving as centerpiece—it colorfully mimics the geologic layers of the Grand Canyon. Beyond the soaring lobby, the resort layout is cozy, rather than sprawling, unlike most other Disney properties, and some guests may find the rooms a little tight in terms of square-footage. Units feature either two queens or the popular combo of a queen and a twin bunk (book these early); a few dozen others have a solitary king bed. Winter evenings beside the lobby fireplace are romantic, and the resort's Territory Lounge is one of the most inviting of all Disney bars. The building boasts so many Hidden Mickeys there's even a clue sheet available at the front desk (it's surprisingly hard to locate all of them, and will keep the most eagle-eyed sleuths busy for hours). The pool area is spectacular: a rock-embroidered pond with a roaring waterfall plunging nearby. Facing Bay Lake, just beyond the pool is the Fire Rock Geyser, which erupts joyously every hour on the hour; a boardwalk and trail parallels the cypress-lined shore of the lake from here. Bike and boat rental are available at the boat dock; horseback riding is a mile away at the campground. Child care is offered at the Cub's Den (see: "Families with Small Children" in "Planning Your Trip"). One notable caveat: the bus and boat connections for the Wilderness Lodge to the theme parks and other activities are the most tedious within Walt Disney World. You're better off with your own car, or else allow plenty of patience and time for commuting, particularly to other resorts for dining. Otherwise, the Wilderness Lodge is a brilliantly conceived escape. Amenities: horseback riding, Jacuzzi, balcony or patio. 728 rooms. Credit cards: A, MC, V.

Disney's Yacht Club Resort $225–$420   ★★★★

1700 Epcot Resorts Boulevard, Lake Buena Vista, 32830, One mile north of Buena Vista Drive, a half-mile west of Epcot, ☎ (407) 934-7000, FAX (407) 934-3450. Rated restaurants: Yachtman's Steakhouse, Yacht Club Galley.
Double: $225–$420.

Fronted by a lone lighthouse, and anchored by a lobby sheltered in dark brown wood, the Yacht Club has a more "masculine" design concept than its connected-at-the-hip twin, the Beach Club. The Beach Club offers family atmosphere, while the Yacht draws a larger business/convention clientele, as well as seniors—there's not even a television in the lobby to endlessly spew out Disney classics for the moppets! Which is not to say that its visitors aren't drawn to the splendid Stormalong Bay swimming area, easily the best resort swimming facility within Walt Disney World's borders. In addition, a "quiet pool" is tucked behind the building on the end facing the Dolphin and a sweep of sand fronts both hotels. A gazebo hosts up to four weddings a day during summer months, further establishing the Yacht's credentials as a more couples-oriented facility. In addition to the seaside exteriors designed by Robert Stern, the nautical embellishments extend to the rooms, where bathroom mirrors are framed in brass portholes and the headboard is shaped like a miniature ship's wheel. Most rooms have two queens and a daybed, but a few are equipped with a king and daybed. The Yacht also features a concierge floor for extra attention, and the resort's Ship Shape Health Club is second only to the Disney Institute's in quantity and variety of equipment. Croquet, volleyball and tennis are located on the beach side. A children's activity center, the Sandcastle Club, is available for baby-sitting (see: "Families With Small Children" in "Planning Your Trip"). Epcot is a 10-minute walk or boatride; Disney-MGM Studios entrance is just a little farther. The Yacht/Beach complex is also walking distance to the Swan, Dolphin and BoardWalk, offering guests a number of solid dining options. Amenities: tennis, health club, Jacuzzi, sauna, balcony or patio, club floor, business services. 630 rooms. Credit cards: A, MC, V.

Campgrounds

Disney's Fort Wilderness Campground $35–$59   ★★

Bay Lake, Lake Buena Vista, 32830, enter via Vista Boulevard, two miles east of Ticket and Transportation Center, ☎ (407) 824-2900, FAX (407) 824-3508.
Double: $35–$59.

Yes, you can camp within the forests of Walt Disney World, and there's even a front desk to receive phone messages for you. This polished, 740-acre facility extends for a mile inland from the shore of Bay Lake, just east of the Wilderness Lodge. Only two of the 20 campground loops are devoted to actual tent sites (you may rent a tent for $15 a night extra), the rest are set up for RV camping. The RV sites have electrical and water hookups, or you may book a higher-priced, deluxe site (those closest to the lake) that has sewage and cable TV hookups. Four of the loops (1600-1900) allow pets, and the grounds have two pools, free unmanned tennis courts, bike and canoe rentals, horseback riding and fishing (creeks run through the property). The Eagle Pines and Osprey Ridge golf courses are immediately east of the campground. An internal bus route connects the main entrance with the various campsites, but note that bus connections elsewhere within Walt Disney World can be somewhat problematic and a car is helpful. The Hoop Dee Doo Revue is performed nightly at Pioneer Hall next to the lake, and the same area also contains a low-key restaurant, a trading post for basic cooking and other supplies, pony rides and a petting farm. River Country is adjacent. Note that the campground's only dining spot, Crockett's Tavern, closed in summer 1996. Also see Disney's Wilderness Homes for another backwoods alternative. Amenities: tennis, horseback riding. 784 sites. Credit cards: A, MC, V.

Disney's Wilderness Homes   **$185–$220**   ★ ★ ★

Bay Lake, Lake Buena Vista, 32830, just off World Drive, one mile northeast of Ticket and Transportation Center, ☎ *(407) 824-2900, FAX (407) 824-3508.*
Double: $185–$220.

Eight of the 28 loops in Fort Wilderness Campground are devoted to 363 permanent Fleetwood trailer homes set amid cypress and pines. Most homes sleep six comfortably (a few sleep four) and feature a separate bedroom and bunk beds, making them ideal for families. The kitchen offers a microwave, electric stove, and dishwasher; a phone and TV are also provided. The Meadows Trading Post offers limited food selection as well as a laundry facility. Recreation includes tennis, fishing, biking, canoeing, horseback riding; Eagle Pines and Osprey Ridge golf courses are a mile away. The location of the homes near the entrance to Fort Wilderness (away from the lake) means you will be less-reliant on the internal campground transportation service; a car is handy, but not absolutely necessary. Also see Fort Wilderness Campground for other options in the forest. Amenities: tennis, horseback riding. 363 sites. Credit cards: A, MC, V.

Disney Village

In the mid-1970s, as plans for Epcot began to solidify following the successful opening of The Magic Kingdom, the Disney Company found itself short on two valuable commodities: guest rooms and the cash to build more. It decided to lease the land surrounding picayune Lake Buena Vista to a group of hotel conglomerates under the condition that Disney would be able to have some control over the maintenance and staff of these hotels. Hilton, Doubletree and Marriott are among the big names involved in these large facilities, termed "Official Hotels of Walt Disney World," and also referred to as the properties in Disney Village. These hotels are required to commit a part of their budget to upkeep and renovations each year and, on hiring, their employees (who work for the hotel firms, not Disney) attend a portion of the Disney training program and abide by Walt's rigid grooming standards, which include no facial hair for men, etc.

In general, these properties are well-run. All but the Swan and Dolphin are located near Lake Buena Vista and are within walking distance of Pleasure Island and the Disney Village Marketplace complex (although walkways are indirect and insufficiently marked). With the exception of the Swan and Dolphin, none of these hotels has the special atmosphere or *theming* typical of the best Disney properties. Once you're inside, you could be anywhere, which is acceptable with some guests, particularly those who attend the conventions that typically fill these hostelries (and whose attendees are not necessarily visiting for the Disney rides). In general, at the Disney Village hotels, the convention-to-vacation guest ratio varies seasonally, but averages 50/50 year-round.

Aerial view of Buena Vista Palace with Pleasure Island in the background

The two standouts are the playfully inspired Walt Disney World Swan and Dolphin, run by Westin and Sheraton, respectively. Both are located immediately southwest of Epcot and are conveniently linked to the Disney transportation network (boat to Epcot and the Disney-MGM Studios, bus to the Magic Kingdom and elsewhere). The Swan and Dolphin are included in the Surprise Morning admission policy that Disney's guests enjoy, while the other, "Official Hotels," are not. And, by virtue of their proximity to the Yacht and Beach Club and BoardWalk Resorts, the Swan and Dolphin also benefit by offering the largest selection of restaurants within a 10-minute walk. Like the other Disney Village resorts, the huge Swan and Dolphin complex frequently hosts large conventions.

Visitors looking to shave a few dollars from their Orlando vacation by staying at a non-Disney hotel will need to look beyond the facilities listed in this section. The "Official Hotels" pay a good-size chunk of revenue to lease Disney property. That cost, of course, is passed on to you. Comparable rooms located in the Crossroads Mall area (less than a mile from the Disney Village hotels) are 20 to 30 percent less than their "official" counterparts.

One facility, **Shades of Green** (formerly The Disney Inn) is not listed below. This peaceful, 288-room lodge situated between Disney's Polynesian and Grand Floridian is open only to active and retired military personnel and currently employed Department of Defense civilians. Room rates are determined by military grade and start at a bargain rate of $55 per night. An excellent choice, if you can secure it. ☎ *(407) 824-3600.*

All-Suite

Doubletree Guest Suites Resort
Walt Disney World Village $169–$375 ★ ★ ★

2305 Hotel Plaza Boulevard, Lake Buena Vista, 32830, just off I-4, at Exit 27, inside Walt Disney World, ☎ *(800) 222-8733, (407) 934-1000, FAX (407) 934-1011.*

Suite rate per day: $169–$375.

The only all-suite hotel within Walt Disney World, the Doubletree is a good choice for families who want extra room to spread out, but don't want a stiff tag for the privilege. Spacious living rooms feature a desk, sofa/bed, dining table, wet bar, refrigerator and microwave. Bedrooms have a king or two doubles, a dressing area with hair dryer, and a perfunctory, tight bathroom (with a third TV!); rooms can conceivably sleep six. The pyramidal, seven-story facility is attractive and a good value. The only drawback is that the current decor is starting to show wear and the pool area is noisy due to the hum of the nearby I-4. Affiliated car rental: Budget. Amenities: tennis, exercise room. 229 rooms. Credit cards: A, DC, D, MC, V.

AUTHOR'S OBSERVATION

We have listed the "rack rate" for each property in Fielding's strictly for comparison purposes. In theory, the rack rate for a room is the maximum price a hotel will charge during a given season; in reality, the rate is as realistic a price as a "full fare" economy airline ticket. Savvy travelers rarely pay this amount. If you are quoted the rack rate, pull out all your ammo—ask for the corporate rate, the Auto Club rate, the senior rate, even just the lower rate— and gauge the booking agent's response before trying another, equivalent property for comparison. The only time you are likely to be shut out of a lower rate is during intense demand (primarily the Christmas and Fourth of July periods), otherwise do not hesitate to ask for specials and don't be shy about pitting one hotel's prices against another's.

Hotels

Courtyard by Marriott at
Walt Disney World Village   **$159–$189**   ★ ★ ★

1805 Hotel Plaza Boulevard, Lake Buena Vista, 32830, just off I-4, at Exit 27, inside Walt Disney World, ☎ *(800) 223-9930, (407) 828-8888, FAX (407) 827-4623. Double: $159–$189.*

Beyond its trademark, 14-story atrium, this hotel is nondescript but functional, with a few amenities (room service, a poolside bar) not typically available at Marriott's Courtyard properties. Most rooms feature two doubles, but two queens may be requested and a smattering of rooms with a king can be found. All rooms have balconies and in-room Nintendo; two suites are also available. The units surround the atrium and its ground-floor cafe, surveyed by glass elevators. Two moderate-size pools plus a kiddie pool and whirlpool spa; a small exercise room features Nautilus equipment. Affiliated car rental: Dollar. Amenities: exercise room, Jacuzzi, balcony or patio. 323 rooms. Credit cards: A, DC, D, MC, V.

Hotel Royal Plaza   **$142–$252**   ★ ★ ★

1905 Hotel Plaza Boulevard, Lake Buena Vista, 32830, just off I-4, at Exit 27, inside Walt Disney World, ☎ *(800) 248-7890, (407) 828-2828, FAX (407) 827-6338. Double: $142–$252.*

This somewhat unattractive high-rise underwent a much-needed room renovation in 1995-1996. All rooms are still oversized—the largest standard units on Walt Disney World property. Some rooms have Jacuzzis and a wet bar; all have a private balcony and safe. Private patios were added to the first-floor rooms in the Lanai Section, a two-story garden wing closer to the pool and parking, but these rooms have smaller bathrooms than those in the main building. The uppermost of the 16 stories offer prime views of fireworks at Pleasure Island. A pair of top-floor celebrity suites are available—one named after Burt Reynolds, the other is Barbara Mandrell's—and a concierge level is in the works. An arcade and a manned, daytime activity area are set up for children, otherwise this hotel caters largely to the convention trade (check for hefty discounts on rack rates). Affiliated car rental: Dollar. Amenities: tennis, Jacuzzi, sauna, balcony or patio, club floor, business services. 397 rooms. Credit cards: A, DC, D, MC, V.

Travelodge Hotel Walt Disney World Village   **$139–$169**   ★ ★ ★

2000 Hotel Plaza Boulevard, Lake Buena Vista, 32830, just off I-4, at Exit 27, inside Walt Disney World, ☎ *(800) 348-3765, (407) 828-2424, FAX (407) 828-8933. Double: $139–$169.*

A better bet for families than some of the other, more convention-oriented facilities around Disney Village, this Travelodge is distinguished by its three-sided tower that climbs to an 18th-floor summit, where Toppers Nite Club booms away. The lobby area supports a winding staircase surrounded by greenery and wicker; dioramas from Disney animated classics enthrall children. The simple but generously proportioned rooms provide two queens or a king, along with a coffeemaker, hair dryer and safe. All units have private balconies with spectacular views from the upper floors; one side faces Pleasure Island, another overlooks Epcot, both the site of nightly fireworks. Four, three-room luxury suites with a glass-enclosed terrace are available on the top floor. Amenities: balcony or patio. 325 rooms. Credit cards: A, DC, D, MC, V.

Resorts

Best Western Grosvenor Resort $160–$200 ★★★

1850 Hotel Plaza Boulevard, Lake Buena Vista, 32830, just off I-4, at Exit 27, inside Walt Disney World, ☎ *(800) 624-4109, (407) 828-4444, FAX (407) 828-8120. Double: $160–$200.*

With 17,000 square feet of meeting space, the Grosvenor is geared more to conventioneers than resort guests, but it has a pleasant pool area in back, a Sherlock Holmes museum and pub, and a Disney character breakfast and dinner (see: "Character Dining" in "Restaurants"). Tennis, volleyball and a children's playground are also available. On Saturday evenings, Baskerville's hosts a Murder Watch Mystery Theater over prime rib and starring Holmes. All rooms have a small refrigerator, VCR and coffeemaker. Odd-numbered rooms face Epcot and Pleasure Island, where nightly fireworks grace the sky. Affiliated car rental: Thrifty. Amenities: tennis, exercise room, business services. 626 rooms. Credit cards: A, CB, DC, D, MC, V.

Buena Vista Palace Resort and Spa $145–$250 ★★★★

1900 Buena Vista Drive, Lake Buena Vista, 32830, just off I-4, at Exit 27, inside Walt Disney World, ☎ *(800) 327-2990, (407) 827-2727, FAX (407) 827-6034. Rated restaurants: Arthur's 27, Outback Double: $145–$250.*

This towering 27-story, 27-acre luxury property across the street from the Disney Village Marketplace received a room overhaul in 1996 and added a luxurious European Spa for guests and day visitors. The Palace offers accommodations in the main tower, which seems to rise straight up out of tiny Lake Buena Vista, as well as rooms in an adjoining, six-story suites complex; all rooms feature a king or two queens, a minibar, and private balcony or patio. Twenty rooms are eco-friendly and use EPA-recommended technology and non-allergenic pillows and blankets. Microwave ovens and refrigerators are available in the suites at an additional charge, and one floor in the tower provides concierge service. The facility boasts a 90,000-square-foot meeting and convention area, and an extensive roster of business services. Three pools are available, including one for children, a whirlpool/sauna, as well as three lighted tennis courts, volleyball courts, and a marina with bike and boat rentals. The Watercress Cafe is home to a character brunch on Sundays (see: "Character Dining" in "Restaurants"). Five-minute walk to Disney Village Marketplace. Affiliated car rental: Alamo. Amenities: tennis, health club, exercise room, Jacuzzi, sauna, balcony or patio, club floor, business services. 1014 rooms. Credit cards: A, DC, D, MC, V.

Hilton Disney Village $150–$255 ★★★★

1751 Hotel Plaza Boulevard, Lake Buena Vista, 32830, just off I-4, at Exit 27, inside Walt Disney World, ☎ *(800) 782-4414, (407) 827-4000, FAX (407) 827-3890. Double: $150–$255.*

The exterior of this sleek, 10-story, peach-and-turquoise, winged structure belies the hubbub inside one of the area's busiest properties. The long lobby is accented by pink marble and tanks of tropical fish line the walls behind the check-in desk. Rooms feature a king or two doubles with nicely appointed bathrooms and a minibar, while a concierge level on the 10th floor adds bathrobes, a continental breakfast, and other treats. Most rooms have decent views, but those overlooking Pleasure Island and its nightly fireworks display are special. The two outdoor pools are unspectacular but pleasant, and a gazebo is available for weddings and other functions. Child care is provided at the Vacation Station, and a Disney character brunch is hosted Sundays at the County Fair Restaurant (see: "Character Dining" in "Restaurants"). Extensive on-site convention and meeting facilities. The Hilton is a five-minute walk from Pleasure Island and the Disney Village Marketplace. Affiliated car rental: Avis. Amenities: health club, exercise room, Jacuzzi, sauna, club floor, business services. 814 rooms. Credit cards: A, CB, DC, D, MC, V.

AUTHOR'S OBSERVATION

The combined Swan and Dolphin facilities provide the Southeast's largest convention/resort complex: 52,000 square feet of meeting space at the Dolphin accommodating up to 2000 guests, plus a 23,000-square-foot ballroom on the Swan side. The entire resort was built at a cost of $375 million.

Walt Disney World Dolphin　　　　$245–$365　　　★★★★

1500 Epcot Resorts Boulevard, Lake Buena Vista, 32830, just off Buena Vista Drive, next to Epcot and the Disney-MGM Studios, ☎ (800) 227-1500, (407) 934-4000, FAX (407) 934-4710. Rated restaurants: Sum Chows, Juan and Only's
Double: $245–$365.

Easily central Florida's most over-the-top, eccentric hotel design is showcased at the Swan and Dolphin hotels, two postmodern resorts created by Michael Graves, who was provided a long leash by Disney officials who wanted a pair of convention-size facilities that celebrated both fantasy and architecture. The Dolphin is the home of Michael Jackson when he visits Walt Disney World (is that a selling point?). The apex of the Sheraton-managed Dolphin is a 27-story pyramid, the highest point in Walt Disney World, while two, 56-foot-tall mythical dolphins are propped on their chins at each end of the main structure. Guests enter through a giant rotunda, the main lobby, from which extend a network of corridors leading to shops, rooms and convention facilities; most of the resort's restaurants are two stories down via escalator. Hallways feature a carpet of beach towels and sand toys, and wallpaper furthering the motif with playful cabanas and clouds. Standard rooms are pretty cozy for the price, but king rooms come with a pull-out sofa sleeper. Convention business keeps the Dolphin (and Swan) hopping year-round, but a healthy block of rooms go to vacationers seduced by the excellent location at the center of Walt Disney World activities. A car is unnecessary here (and it can be quite a walk from most rooms to the non-valet area). In addition to a palm-lined walkway, the two resorts are linked by a lush pool area with grottos, slides, waterfalls, two lap pools, a kiddie pool and alcoves sheltering jacuzzis; a sand beach lines a placid cove. The resorts also share an exercise room and health club (Body by Jake), volleyball and four lighted tennis courts. Guests receive preferential tee times at the Disney golf courses. Camp Dolphin offers evening child-care services; a character brunch is held Sundays at Harry's Safari Bar and Grill (see: "Character Dining" in "Restaurants").

Dolphin guests may take advantage of not only the restaurants at the Swan, but those of the BoardWalk, Yacht and Beach Club, all of which are within a 10-minute walk. Epcot and the Disney-MGM Studios are a 10-minute boatride; The Magic Kingdom is a 15-minute bus ride. Affiliated car rental: National. Amenities: tennis, health club, exercise room, Jacuzzi, sauna, club floor, business services. 1509 rooms. Credit cards: A, DC, D, MC, V.

Walt Disney World Swan   **$250–$370**   ★★★★

1200 Epcot Resorts Boulevard, Lake Buena Vista, 32830, just off Buena Vista Drive, next to Epcot and the Disney-MGM Studios, ☎ *(800) 248-7926, (407) 934-3000, FAX (407) 934-4499. Rated restaurant: Palio.*
Double: $250–$370.

Like its sister property, the Walt Disney World Dolphin, the 12-story, arching Swan strikes some observers as a glitsy Las Vegas-meets-Florida mishap, though most (including this writer), find the resort an envelope-pushing delight—either way, it leaves a certifiable impression. The overall concept at both resorts was to bring the outdoors inside, which leads to papyrus reed columns topped by palm fronds, monkey lamps, and a carpet styled after quarry tiles and lily ponds. The entertaining Michael Graves design also includes a pair of 47-foot-high swans and two clamshell fountains perched high on the rooftops. A graceful series of stylized waves wrap around the building's exterior, while custom murals line the interior; reproductions of Picasso, Matisse and Hockney adorn corridors. By virtue of size, the Swan tends to be a little less overwhelming than the huge Dolphin, but for these rates, standard room layouts are still snug. In addition to the three-acre pool area and sandy cove, the Swan and Dolphin share a health club and exercise room, volleyball and tennis courts; guests receive the same preferential tee times enjoyed by Disney Resort guests at the Disney links. The Disney transportation network is at your disposal. Having a car here means traipsing over acres of asphalt between your room and the non-valet parking lots. Camp Swan offers evening child-care services; a character breakfast is held Saturdays at the Garden Grove Cafe (see: "Character Dining" in "Restaurants"). Swan guests may take advantage of not only the restaurants at the Dolphin, but also those at the BoardWalk, Yacht and Beach Club, all of which are within a 10-minute walk. Epcot and the Disney-MGM Studios are a 10-minute boat ride away; The Magic Kingdom is a 15-minute bus ride. Affiliated car rental: National. Amenities: tennis, health club, exercise room, Jacuzzi, sauna, balcony or patio, club floor, business services. 758 rooms. Credit cards: A, DC, D, MC, V.

Crossroads Area and Adjacent

Crossroads Mall lies at the intersection of I-4 and State Route 535, two major arteries that access Walt Disney World. Over the past two decades, many hotels have sprouted here, making the zone a prime locality for moderately priced accommodations that are convenient to the Disney attractions. Another advantage is the availability of several good, reasonably priced restaurants in the Crossroads Mall complex.

Tuck-in time at the Holiday Inn SunSpree Resort.

Due to their location, you're better off renting a car for your stay at any of these hostelries. Although most of these hotels offer bus transportation into Walt Disney World, bus service is infrequent and will rob valuable time from your touring schedule. For most of these addresses, expect about 15 to 20 minutes' drive in average traffic driving to the parking entrances of Epcot or the Disney-MGM Studios, and about 20 to 25 minutes to the Ticket and Transportation Center parking lot near the Magic Kingdom. For most of these hotels, the fastest route to the parks will be via I-4 west to Epcot Center Drive rather than taking the more direct route on oft-congested Hotel Plaza Boulevard. The exception is if you are traveling to Typhoon Lagoon, Pleasure Island or the Disney Village Marketplace, whereby you have no choice but to enter the fray of Hotel Plaza Boulevard. Sea World is about 15 to 20 minutes away and Universal is about 20 to 25 minutes east on the I-4.

INSIDER'S TIPS

Using a hotel chain's national 800 number won't always get you the best rate. Because operators manning these lines have little more than a computer terminal to access information about potentially hundreds of properties the chain oversees, unique rates frequently don't pop into view; the attendant is also probably not at liberty to cut a special deal when occupancy levels are particularly low. Additionally, they are not likely to have seen the hotel in question, and will not be able to provide detailed information about which rooms offer a view, or what special facilities the resort offers. Some of the 800 numbers listed in Fielding's connect directly to the hotel, while others connect to the central reservation office. Always ask to determine where you have reached.

All-Suite Properties

Best Western Buena Vista Suites   **$119–$179**

14450 International Drive, Lake Buena Vista, 32830, Two miles southeast of I-4 at International Drive and Route 536, ☎ (800) 537-7737, (407) 239-8588, FAX (407) 239-1401.
Suite rate per day: $119–$179.

The surrounding area, with views of power lines and a construction site, isn't much to look at, but this all-suite property flashes some of the best room deals in the area. The attractive rooms are adorned with Disney art, and offer one king or two queens, plus a sleeper sofa in the living room. A nice plus is that the two-door bathroom can be entered directly from the living room or bedroom, allowing greater privacy. Jazzy purple bedspreads and deep-hued carpets keep rooms dark, but not dingy. The kitchenette facilities include a coffeemaker, wet bar, microwave and small refrigerator; rooms also have a VCR, safe and a second TV and phone. King rooms have a whirlpool tub. The isolated (for now) location is compounded by the near-absence of eating facilities within walking distance; you'll need a car, though limited free bus transportation to the Disney parks is provided. Breakfast buffet is included in the room rate. Amenities: Jacuzzi. 280 rooms. Credit cards: A, MC, V.

Caribe Royale Resort Suites   **$159–$275**

14300 International Drive, Lake Buena Vista, 32830, two miles southeast of I-4 at International Drive and Route 536, ☎ (800) 823-8300, (407) 238-8000, FAX (407) 238-8400.
Suite rate per day: $159–$275.

This all-new, Caribbean-themed suite property was set to open November 1996 and should be a solid success. Spread over 30 acres and housing 1200 rooms, it's the largest all-suite resort in the world, and a five-minute drive into Walt Disney

World. Although the lushly landscaped, upscale resort plans to attract a mix of business/convention, group and family travelers, part of the concept is to segment these markets into different portions of the property: three separate, eight-story towers enclose a tropical pool area with waterfalls and a 75-foot water slide. Standard suites contain a pair of queen beds or a king, with a queen-size pullout in the living room; a kitchenette with microwave, fridge and wet bar is featured. Roomy, 1120-square-foot two-bedroom suites with twin-bay living rooms are also available; an executive level is offered. Free breakfast included in the rates, as is a complimentary shuttle to the World. Amenities: tennis, exercise room, Jacuzzi, balcony or patio, business services. 1218 rooms. Credit cards: A, MC, V.

Summerfield Suites Lake Buena Vista $169–$219   ★ ★ ★

8751 Suiteside Drive, Orlando, 32836, just off I-4 at Exit 27, via the Apopka Vineland Road, ☎ (800) 833-4353, (407) 238-0777, FAX (407) 238-2640.
Suite rate per day: $169–$219.
One of two Summerfield all-suite properties near Walt Disney World, this three-story complex greets visitors with a palm-lined driveway and tasteful lobby area. The one-bedroom units easily accommodate four, and are generously furnished with couches, tables, VCR and a fully equipped kitchen. Sleeping up to eight, the spacious two-bedroom units are an excellent option for larger families. A deli is on the premises; a buffet breakfast is included in the price. The patio and pool area is a pleasant respite from theme park touring. The Disney Village entrance Walt Disney World is less than a mile away. Affiliated car rental: Thrifty. Amenities: exercise room, Jacuzzi. 146 rooms. Credit cards: A, DC, D, MC, V.

Hotels

Days Inn Lake Buena Vista Resort and Suites $79–$129   ★ ★

12205 Apopka Vineland Road, Orlando, 32836, just off I-4 at Exit 27, outside Disney Village, ☎ (800) 423-3297, (407) 239-0444, FAX (407) 239-1778.
Single: $79–$129. Double: $79–$129.
One of three Days Inn properties within a block of the Disney Village entrance to Walt Disney World, this six-story complex is the biggest and offers the best value. Maroon floral hallways lead to the simply furnished rooms; two doubles or one queen are found in all units, though suites have two doubles and a pullout sofa. A small drawback—the bathrooms are poorly laid out. The 96 one-bedroom suites sleep up to six and have small kitchens, but a limited selection of dishes. Pool area is large, nondescript. Best feature is the position across the street from Crossroads Mall, where a number of fast-food joints and good, less expensive eateries lure savvy visitors. Free transport into Walt Disney World. Amenities: balcony or patio. 490 rooms. Credit cards: A, DC, D, MC, V.

Holiday Inn SunSpree Resort Lake Buena Vista$89–$122   ★ ★ ★

13351 State Route 535, Lake Buena Vista, 32830, one mile southeast of I-4 at Exit 27, ☎ (800) 366-6299, (407) 239-4500, FAX (407) 239-7713. Double: $89–$122.
One of the better-conceived area properties, this six-floor SunSpree resort is fervently dedicated to keeping kids happy despite being off Walt Disney World property (the hotel is a short mile from the Disney Village entrance). This means kids have a separate check-in desk, a hotel mascot to embrace—Max, a cuddly, six-foot

raccoon who can also tuck kids in at bedtime—and a private restaurant, The Kid's Kottage. But the best concept is "Kidsuites," a trendsetting family-friendly room that creates a private, themed environment for children to sleep in, allowing parents a little privacy. The children's room features a single and bunk bed and play area—themes include a western jail cell, a space capsule, and an igloo sponsored by Coca-Cola's polar bears; the resort planned to have 90 of these open by fall 1996. Watch for this concept to be copied soon in other area hotels and at Holiday Inns around the country. The gated pool area is attractive, though somewhat cramped, and crawling with moppets; a pair of Jacuzzis are tucked away in opposite corners. Children 12 and under eat free when accompanied by a parent—snack bar, deli and restaurant are on the premises, otherwise you'll need a car for excursions. Extensive, 2200-square-foot child care facility operates from 8 a.m. to midnight daily; $1 per hour per child. Free shuttle to the Disney parks, plus a bus to Universal and Sea World for a charge. Special discount rates for single parents. Amenities: exercise room, Jacuzzi. 507 rooms. Credit cards: A, D, MC, V.

Radisson Inn Lake Buena Vista   **$89–$129**   ★ ★ ★

8686 Palm Parkway, Orlando, 32836, just off I-4 at Exit 27, via State Route 535, ☎ (800) 333-3333, (407) 239-8400, FAX (407) 239-8025. Double: $89–$129.

Standard Radisson furnishings and decor—deep green carpets, lavender-and-pink bedspreads and celery washed walls—appoint rooms in this seven story property immediately next to Crossroads Mall. Rooms also feature a balcony and minibar, but the location, just beyond the fray of Disney Village, helps keep prices down. A small but pleasant pool area with a whirlpool and waterfall (and a slide that runs through it) will keep kids entertained for hours, as will a sand play area. A coffee shop is open for breakfast only; lunch and dinner snacks are served in the hotel's bar. Amenities: Jacuzzi, balcony or patio. 200 rooms. Credit cards: A, CB, DC, MC, V.

Wyndham Garden Hotel at Lake Buena Vista $66–$105   ★ ★ ★

8688 Palm Parkway, Lake Buena Vista, 32830, next to Crossroads Mall, off I-4 at Exit 27, ☎ (800) 996-3426, (407) 239-8500, FAX (407) 239-8591. Double: $66–$105.

Comparable to most other undynamic Wyndham properties, this six-story building lies conveniently next to the Crossroads Mall shopping center, tucked out of the way just enough that prices stay reasonable. Most rooms offer two doubles, but 35 feature a queen and pullout sofa; all utilize an attractive floral design in the fabrics. An ample bathroom provides a hair dryer and ironing board; coffeemakers and Nintendo are found in all units. Three suites are also available. A small pool area with Jacuzzi and a limited exercise room are the major activities on-site, although a pleasant lounge area next to the lobby is inviting. Amenities: Jacuzzi. 167 rooms. Credit cards: A, CB, DC, D, MC, V.

Resorts

Hyatt Regency Grand Cypress   **$185–$370**   ★ ★ ★ ★ ★

1 Grand Cypress Boulevard, Orlando, 32836, just off State Route 535 from I-4 at Exit 27, ☎ (800) 233-1234, (407) 239-1234, FAX (407) 239-3800. Rated restaurant: Hemingways.

Double: $185–$370.

A $7.5 million renovation was completed in December 1995 and provided new lustre to the rooms of this already esteemed luxury complex. The magnificent, 18-story lobby atrium soars heavenward, but is rooted in an indoor garden of immaculately groomed philodendrons, orchids and palms, fussing parrots, streams writhing with goldfish, and pieces of stately Asian art. Rooms are not large, but nicely appointed with newly installed armoires, tables, nightstands, wicker chairs, greenery and a bright tropical color scheme. A concierge level, Regency Club on the 11th floor, averages $100 more per night, and provides upgraded bathroom amenities, a private lounge for breakfast, hors d'oeuvres and cordials, and added attention. An adjoining facility next door, the Villas at Grand Cypress, features luxury condos housing up to four bedrooms with cathedral ceilings and views to the neighboring ponds and golf course greens. The 45 holes of Jack Nicklaus-designed championship golf make Grand Cypress the region's best golf resort, and central Florida's best equestrian facility is also located on the 1500-acre property. Other activities include canoeing, tennis, trails and the resort's spectacular free-form swimming pool: an evocative, jumbled mass of rock and lush vegetation that includes 12 waterfalls, grottos, whirlpools, a 45-foot slide and a suspended wooden bridge. A strip of sand fronts a 21-acre lagoon (not for swimming) and the verdant gardens and waterways continue generously around the huge property. In addition to a staffed children's activity center, Camp Hyatt *(open 7 a.m. to 11 p.m. daily)*, the Grand Cypress features a teen program, Rock Hyatt, which mingles kids ages 12 to 17 with their peers for activities both on and off the premises. The resort is frequently home to large conventions (which can change the otherwise intimate atmosphere overnight to a party scene) but few hostelries anywhere integrate business, group and leisure travelers as well as the Grand Cypress. Affiliated car rental: Enterprise. Amenities: tennis, horseback riding, health club, Jacuzzi, balcony or patio, club floor, business services. 750 rooms. Credit cards: A, DC, D, MC, V.

Marriott's Orlando World Center $154–$209   ★★★★

8701 World Center Drive, Orlando, 32821, one mile east of I-4 at Exit 26A, via State Route 536 East, ☎ (800) 621-0638, (407) 239-4200, FAX (407) 238-8777. Rated restaurant: Palm's.

Double: $154–$209.

An immense resort complex surrounded by palm-studded golf greens, the 28-story Marriott Orlando was designed with conventioneers in mind, but adds a wealth of activities and features for its guests. The 12-story, tropical atrium brims with Sabal palms, banana trees and jade plants, while 16th-century Chinese artifacts and commissioned artworks embodying Florida themes fill the corridors. Rooms are not a key sales factor: standard units feature two doubles with shopworn rose and deep green colors (avoid the fourth-floor views). Most rooms have balconies, though some face into the busy atrium lobby. The antiseptic main pool is massive— 550,000 gallons worth, the largest in central Florida—with bougainvillea-laced waterfalls, a grotto area and water slide; an indoor pool and Jacuzzi are ideal for stormy summer days. A decent Joe Lee-designed 18-hole golf course wraps around the tower, and a tough miniature golf course keeps younger duffers happy; tennis (eight lighted, Har-Tru courts), basketball, volleyball and a 24-hour health club are also available. A children's day-care area, the Lollipop Lounge, is provided. The Marriott Orlando is one of the largest convention resorts in the country, with one hall alone encompassing 50,000 square feet of space. In all, a spectacular meeting destination—and a decent resort if you don't mind the hubbub. Sizable discounts are offered for buying your room at least 14 days in advance (based on availability). Affiliated car rental: Hertz. Amenities: tennis, health club, Jacuzzi, balcony or patio, business services. 1588 rooms. Credit cards: A, DC, D, MC, V.

Marriott's World Center is a huge resort complex surrounded by palm-studded golf greens. The pool is the largest in central Florida.

INSIDER'S TIPS

Because so many of Orlando's larger hotels are geared to handle huge conventions, their rooms go wanting during periods of reduced convention activity. Over long holiday weekends and even during the summer, the published rate card goes out the window and prices can fall dramatically. For instance, in 1995 the plush new Omni Rosen dropped room rates to $39 a night to keep its hotel busy during the slow Thanksgiving period.

International Drive

A teeming artery of flashing neon, dazed visitors and crawling traffic, the heart of International Drive is where Orlando most resembles that *other* tourism conglomerate, Las Vegas. Suffice to say, it's not for all tastes, but many visitors swear by their "International" vacation.

At the southern end of International's cluster of hotels, north of the entrance to Sea World, the pace is quieter (except for the buzz of the nearby Beeline Expressway). Just north of the Beeline, several tony hotels cluster around the new Orange County Convention and Civic Center. When a big convention is on (usually during the week), this area vibrates with activity, but otherwise, these hotels maintain a more staid atmosphere. Continuing farther north the congestion enters overdrive, particularly along the stretch between Sand Lake Road and Wet 'n Wild, where a dizzying platoon of hotels, eateries, miniature golf, and more—oh, so much more—competes for your attention.

Lodgings in all styles, sizes and price range are to be found here. From the charmingly outdated Motel 6 that lies just across the freeway from Universal Studios to the dedicated opulence of the Peabody Orlando, there is something to fit any visitor's taste. The only question is one of location, and it's something to give the designated hotel booker pause.

If you are planning your first visit to Orlando and wish to concentrate your touring around Walt Disney World with just one or two days devoted to Universal and/or Sea World, you may want to stay closer to Disney than the northern International Drive accommodations will position you. If you're on a tight budget as well, continue on to the next section of this chapter and consider a room along the U.S. 192 corridor. However, if you are scheduling a repeat visit to Orlando, or if you know in advance that you'll want Disney to occupy no more than half of your vacation, then an International Drive hostelry will land you close to or right in the heart of the tourism frenzy.

HOTELS AND ACCOMMODATIONS

INSIDER'S TIPS

Don't forget that selected hotel amenities may create savings in other areas. Some properties offer a complimentary breakfast buffet (usually juice, coffee and muffins), that will save you both time and money. A room with a simple kitchen may cost a little extra, but for a stay of a week or more, a family can save a bundle on breakfast and snacks. Keep in mind that most in-room kitchen supplies are limited; if you want to plan on preparing lobster thermador, check with the hotel directly to verify what equipment and utensils are provided.

All-suite

Enclave Suites   **$79–$109**   ★ ★ ★

6165 Carrier Drive, Orlando, 32819, Exit 29 off I-4, or International Drive exit from the Beeline, ☎ *(800) 457-0077, (407) 351-1155, FAX (407) 351-2001.*
Suite rate per day: $79–$109.
Composed of three 10-story, terraced buildings pleasantly situated on the lake opposite Wet 'n Wild, the Enclave is a well-established, condo-style property suc-

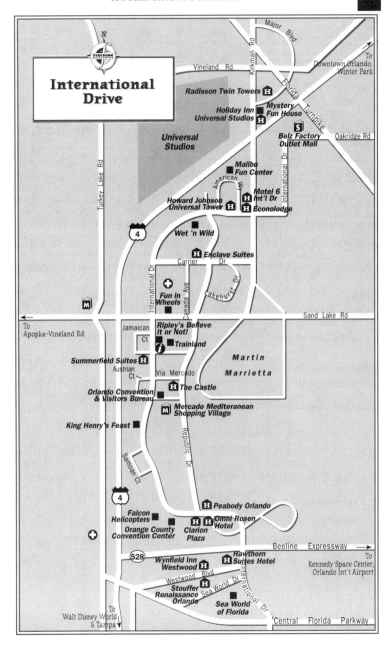

N

International Drive

Major Blvd

To Downtown Orlando, Winter Park

Kirkman Rd

Vineland Rd

Florida Turnpike

Radisson Twin Towers

Mystery Fun House

Holiday Inn Universal Studios

Belz Factory Outlet Mall

Oakridge Rd

Universal Studios

Malibu Fun Center

Motel 6 Int'l Dr

American Wy

Howard Johnson Universal Tower

Econolodge

International Dr

US 4

Wet 'n Wild

Enclave Suites

Carrier Dr

Lakehurst Dr

Fun in Wheels

Canada Ave

International Dr

Sand Lake Rd

To Apopka-Vineland Rd

Jamaican Ct

Ripley's Believe It or Not!

Trainland

Martin Marrietta

Summerfield Suites

Austrian Ct

Via Mercado

The Castle

Orlando Convention & Visitors Bureau

Mercado Mediteranean Shopping Village

King Henry's Feast

Republic Dr

Samoan Ct

US 4

Peabody Orlando

Falcon Helicopters

Omni Rosen Hotel

Orange County Convention Center

Clarion Plaza

Beeline Expressway

528

Wynfield Inn Westwood

Hawthorn Suites Hotel

To Kennedy Space Center, Orlando Int'l Airport

Westwood Blvd

Stouffer Renaissance Orlando

Sea World Dr

International Dr

Sea World of Florida

To Walt Disney World & Tampa

Central Florida Parkway

HOTELS AND ACCOMMODATIONS

cessfully catering to both business travelers and families. What you lose in service and attention is made up for in space and room amenities. Two room styles are available—the tile-floored studios feature a full kitchen, a queen-size, pull-down Murphy bed and a sleeper sofa to accommodate four. The two-bedroom suites are also a good value and sleep a total of six: the master bedroom has a queen, another has two twins, and a queensize pullout sofa resides in the living room; two bathrooms. Terrace units add only $10 to the regular price, a worthy investment. Rate includes complimentary breakfast. Ideal for longer visits, and just out of earshot of I-Drive, but still close to the action. Amenities: tennis, exercise room, Jacuzzi, balcony or patio. 321 rooms. Credit cards: A, D, MC, V.

Hawthorn Suites Hotel $109–$189   ★★★

6435 Westwood Boulevard, Orlando, 32821, just off International Drive, south of the Beeline (near Sea World), ☎ *(800) 527-1133, (407) 351-6600, FAX (407) 351-1977. Suite rate per day: $109–$189.*

Just off I-4, and one of the best of Orlando's all-suite properties, this five-story complex surrounds a laudable pool area. Units are a tad dark, but nicely furnished with mauve carpets and forest-green bedspreads. One-bedroom units provide a choice of two doubles or a king, with a double sleeper sofa to accommodate four. The two-bedroom suites can sleep up to eight using a king, two doubles and a double pullout sofa. All rooms have full kitchens (on arrival, make sure it's stocked with all the cookware you need), coffeemaker, stereo system with cassette player, a VCR and Nintendo. A healthful breakfast buffet is included in the price; 24-hour on-site convenience store in the lobby. Less than one mile from Sea World; 15 minutes to Walt Disney World. Amenities: exercise room, Jacuzzi. 150 rooms. Credit cards: A, CB, DC, D, MC, V.

Summerfield Suites International Drive $159–$239   ★★★

8480 International Drive, Orlando, 32819, Exit 29 off I-4, or International Drive exit from the Beeline, ☎ *(800) 833-4353, (407) 352-2400, FAX (407) 352-4631. Suite rate per day: $159–$239.*

Simple but tasteful design is a Summerfield specialty, and this I-Drive location works well for extended families, who can sleep up to eight in the commodious two-bedroom suites. These and the one-bedroom units include a fully equipped kitchen, desk, ironing board, computer hookup, VCR—a nice collection of amenities that works for families and business travelers alike. Smallish pool area with snack bar. Breakfast buffet included in the price, and the Mercado shopping center is across the street. Affiliated car rental: Thrifty. Amenities: exercise room, Jacuzzi, balcony or patio. 146 rooms. Credit cards: A, DC, D, MC, V.

Wynfield Inn Westwood $52–$92   ★★

6263 Westwood Boulevard, Orlando, 32821, just off International Drive, south of the Beeline (near Sea World), ☎ *(800) 346-1551, (407) 345-8000, FAX (407) 345-1508. Suite rate per day: $52–$92.*

A well-managed budget hostelry a half-mile from Sea World, the Wynfield is made up of a cluster of three-story buildings; each contains identical room layouts, with two double beds in all units. An overhaul in late 1995 helped to lighten room interiors with a tropical aura. The nearby Beeline buzzes morning, noon and night, otherwise this location is centrally located to both Disney and the I-Drive action, without being caught up in the accompanying traffic. Free scheduled transportation to Walt Disney World. 299 rooms. Credit cards: A, DC, D, MC, V.

Hotels

Castle, The   **$129–$159**   ★ ★ ★ ★

8629 International Drive, Orlando, 32819, Exit 29 off I-4, or International Drive Exit from the Beeline, ☎ *(800) 952-2785, (407) 345-1511, FAX (407) 248-8181.*

Double: $129–$159.

A loopy, dunce-capped surprise near the southern end of the I-Drive frenzy, The Castle is a newfangled Holiday Inn masquerading as a dark-edged fairy-tale palace. The nine-story structure stands out from a distance, but once inside, another world—reminiscent of "The Dark Crystal"—emerges. A "Castle Critter" looming at the front gate makes for an imposing hotel mascot, while the royal purple- and gold-embellished lobby area is accented by squawking parrots. Guest rooms (one king or two queens) feature throne chairs, ruffled gold bedposts and in-room music systems with a separate channel for more evocative sound effects, such as crashing waves. A small refrigerator, coffeemaker, ironing board and three telephones fill out the practical amenities. Two floors are devoted to the Royal Club, an executive level with embellished service. Two gardens are found on the roof, while a small courtyard contains a greenery-accented pool and jacuzzi. Textured by marble, grape velvet and gold lame, The Castle is one of Orlando's most unique hotels—not for all tastes, but a winner for those who appreciate their Grimm Fairy Tales literate, rather than Disneyfied. One drawback: service has been spotty at this relatively new (1995) property; let's hope they iron out the kinks so that the entire experience lives up to the lavish surroundings. Conveniently located behind Cafe Tu Tu Tango and Austins Steak House, with a plethora of other I-Drive restaurants within walking distance. Amenities: exercise room, Jacuzzi, club floor. 216 rooms. Credit cards: A, DC, D, MC, V.

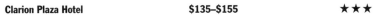

Clarion Plaza Hotel   **$135–$155**   ★ ★ ★

9700 International Drive, Orlando, 32819, Exit 29 off I-4, or International Drive exit from the Beeline, ☎ *(800) 627-8258, (407) 352-9700, FAX (407) 351-9111.*

Double: $135–$155.

A cream-colored, 14-story complex designed to be Orlando's best convention value, the Clarion is next door to the voluminous Orlando/Orange County Convention Center, and greets guests with a six-story porte cochere and marble lobby. Almost all rooms feature two doubles, but a few dozen contain a king, and there are 32 suites of varying sizes, including two Presidential units. Fifty rooms have computer-modem capability, otherwise furnishings are standard, but a good value when a convention or meeting isn't tying up rooms, and rates drop. A large swimming area offers a jacuzzi surrounded by natural rock and a cascading waterfall. Sister property: the Omni Rosen, next door. Affiliated car rental: Alamo. Amenities: Jacuzzi, business services. 810 rooms. Credit cards: A, DC, D, MC, V.

Holiday Inn Universal Studios   **$118–$159**   ★ ★ ★

5905 South Kirkman Road, Orlando, 32819, Exit 30B off I-4, across street from Universal Studios, ☎ *(800) 327-1364, (407) 351-3333, FAX (407) 351-3577.*
Double: $118–$159.

Simple but economical, this 10-story Holiday Inn property can boast of being literally across the street from Universal's entrance (although construction of Universal's new parking facilities will be a minor annoyance for the immediate future). Still, of several I-Drive-adjacent Holiday Inns, this is the best value. Rooms are basic and in decent shape, with doubles and a small balcony in all upstairs units. Safes, microwaves and small refrigerators available for a fee. Adequate pool area and a coffee shop on the premises; complimentary admission to Balley's Health Club 1.5 miles away. Amenities: balcony or patio. 257 rooms. Credit cards: A, DC, D, MC, V.

Howard Johnson Universal Tower   **$45–$79**   ★

5905 International Drive, Orlando, 32819, Exit 30A off I-4, close to Wet 'n Wild, ☎ *(800) 327-1366, (407) 351-2100, FAX (407) 352-2991.*
Double: $45–$79.

This unmistakable, 21-story cylindrical tower lodged between I-4 and International Drive is crested by a sombrero, but that's as classy as this well-trammeled property aims. A $2 million renovation in late 1996 should smooth over some of the superficial blemishes (stained and torn carpets, peeling wallpaper, etc.), but regard this solely as a budget option whose prime asset is its I-Drive location. All standard rooms contain two doubles; top-floor suites have balconies. One mile to Universal; a five-minute walk to Wet 'n Wild. 302 rooms. Credit cards: A, DC, D, MC, V.

Omni Rosen Hotel   **$180**   ★ ★ ★ ★

9840 International Drive, Orlando, 32819, Exit 29 off I-4, or International Drive exit from the Beeline, ☎ *(800) 800-9840, (407) 354-9840, FAX (407) 351-2659.*
Double: $180.

A late 1995 addition to the I-Drive scene, the Omni Rosen is a sparkling, 24-story luxury property next to the Orlando/Orange County Convention Center. Its target audience is convention and business travelers, but the freshly minted hotel has enough features to lure more than a few vacationing guests. The striking lobby vaults '50s deco themes amid smooth planes of terra cotta illuminated by natural light. Modern furnishings grace the rooms, most of which feature a pair of doubles. A small number of king rooms are available. Dusty-rose headboards and cream-colored walls make the rooms light and airy—a breath of fresh air compared to many other "contemporary" resorts. The hotel's 80 suites include three Presidential units. The stately pool includes a wading pool for children and two whirlpools; an on-site health club offers professional massage and flotation therapy. Extensive convention and meeting facilities, and an elaborately conceived signature restaurant, Everglades. Affiliated car rental: Alamo. Amenities: tennis, exercise room, Jacuzzi, club floor, business services. 1334 rooms. Credit cards: A, DC, D, MC, V.

Peabody Orlando, The   **$165–$290**   ★ ★ ★ ★ ★

9801 International Drive, Orlando, 32819, Exit 29 off I-4, or International Drive exit from the Beeline, ☎ *(800) 732-2639, (407) 352-4000, FAX (407) 351-0073. Rated restaurant: Dux.*

Double: $165–$290.

Perhaps Orlando's classiest hotel, this sister property to the famed Memphis original
retains most of its predecessor's unabashed elegance and courtly service for the Florida market. The Peabody Orlando celebrated its 10-year anniversary in fall 1996. The boxy exterior of the 27-story hotel is more imposing than grand, but the skylit lobby area sets the proper mood with acres of marble—perfect for high tea *(Monday through Friday, 3 to 4:30 p.m.).* Rooms are well-appointed and swathed in soft hues of cream, celery and beige, with views extending into Walt Disney World five miles away. Three private-access Peabody Club floors are available for a premium, offering a full-time concierge who plys guests with continental breakfast in the morning, and cookies and cocktails in the afternoon. The renowned Duck March— a red-carpet procession of five mallards from their opulent palace accommodations every morning at 11 to a private elevator, and on to a fountain in the lobby atrium— continues daily to camera-flashing acclaim; the five ducks may have foul tempers, but they have emerged as the hotel's trademark icons. On-site activities include four lighted tennis courts, a Nautilus equipped training facility, massage therapy and a sprawling Olympic-size pool ideal for lap swimming. 24-hour room service and round-the-clock eatery, the B-Line Diner. Extensive meeting and convention facilities; across the street from the Orlando/Orange County Convention Center and one mile from Sea World. Ask about hefty senior (50 and up) discount. Affiliated car rental: Budget. Affiliated airline desk: Delta. Amenities: tennis, health club, exercise room, Jacuzzi, sauna, club floor, business services. 891 rooms. Credit cards: A, DC, D, MC, V.

Radisson Twin Towers   **$119–$155**   ★ ★ ★

5780 Major Boulevard, Orlando, 32819, just off I-4 at Exit 30B, via Kirkman Road, across from Universal Studios, ☎ *(800) 333-3333, (407) 351-1000, FAX (407) 363-0106. Rated restaurant: Palm Court*
Double: $119–$155.

A night, this pair of green neon-rimmed, 18-story towers look like a vision of the Emerald City, but by day, they're just another convention hostelry trying to seduce vacationers to sample their plain, if extensive, wares. Rooms are basic, offering a choice of one king or two queens with wicker furnishings. Nice pool area out back, and a full-service restaurant providing 24-hour room service. The property preceded Universal's opening (across the street) by more than a decade, waiving extensive meeting facilities to keep the turnstile spinning with business customers, but the towers are now actively courting the leisure market with mixed success. Time will tell if the property can withstand the onslaught of Universal's ambitious hotel developments opening near the end of the century. Affiliated car rental: Thrifty. Amenities: exercise room, Jacuzzi, sauna, business services. 742 rooms. Credit cards: A, CB, DC, D, MC, V.

Motels

EconoLodge   **$29–$78**   ★

5859 American Way, Orlando, 32819, Exit 30A from I-4, just off International Drive, ☎ *(800) 327-0750, (407) 345-8880, FAX (407) 363-9366.*
Double: $29–$78.

A solid budget choice, the EconoLodge complex contains two 4-story buildings overlooking a small, bustling pool area. The well-kept rooms hold two doubles with wicker headboards (a few have a king) and standard motel amenities. Only drawback is the rush of I-4, just a stone's throw away. Universal less than a mile away; Wet 'n Wild is two blocks. Formerly known as the International Gateway Inn. 193 rooms. Credit cards: A, DC, D, MC, V.

Motel 6 International Drive   **$26–$36**   ★

5909 American Way, Orlando, 32819, Exit 30A off I-4, just off International Drive, ☎ *(800) 466-8356, (407) 351-6500, FAX (407) 352-5481.*
Double: $26–$36.

Traditional Motel 6 accommodations in three one-story rows fronting the din of I-4. Most rooms have two doubles, 10 have a single queen. Rooms are basic, but clean and have a fresh, peacock-blue carpet and white walls. Small pool area. Good location tucked just off I-Drive: one mile to Universal and a half-mile to Wet 'n Wild or Belz Factory Outlet. 112 rooms. Credit cards: A, DC, D, MC, V.

Resorts

Stouffer Renaissance Orlando Resort   **$199–$289**   ★★★★

6677 Sea Harbor Drive, Orlando, 32821, Exit 27A off I-4, or International Drive exit from the Beeline, near Sea World, ☎ *(800) 468-3571, (407) 351-5555, FAX (407) 351-9991.*
Single: $199–$279. Double: $209–$289.

Located just around the corner from Sea World, the world's largest resort atrium climbs 10 stories above the massive, airy lobby of this luxury property. Palms and flowers spring from the floor of the lobby, with waterfalls and a stream filled with Japanese carp—the centerpiece is a gilded Venetian birdcage alive with tropical birds. The big plus is the expansive guest rooms, most offering balconies that overlook either the indoor atrium or the Orlando skyline. All units feature marble bathrooms with twin sink-vanities; other amenities include in-room coffeemakers, minibars and daily newspaper delivery. Expanded service and perks are available on the 10th, executive floor, the Renaissance Club. Recreation includes an Olympic-size pool with a Mediterranean setting, tennis, volleyball and a health club providing a steam room, sauna and massage therapy; the International Golf Course is next door. A children's activity center, Shamu's Playhouse, is available for child care. Meeting facilities are extensive, and include a $12 million convention center and a vast ballroom. Affiliated car rental: Budget. Amenities: tennis, health club, Jacuzzi, sauna, balcony or patio, club floor, business services. 780 rooms. Credit cards: A, DC, D, MC, V.

U.S. 192 and Kissimmee

Up until The Magic Kingdom's 1971 opening, the town of Kissimmee was little more than a hub in the middle of dusty cattle country. Back then, the scenery included the orange groves of Osceola County rolling in the background. All that changed when Walt Disney came to Florida. That's when

Kissimmee began its dramatic transformation into a sprawling strip of moderate and inexpensive hotels. The plethora of inns dotting the U.S. 192 corridor (named Vine Street in downtown Kissimmee, and the Irlo Bronson Memorial Highway elsewhere) stretches from west of Walt Disney World to the outskirts of St. Cloud—some 15 miles in all—with nary a luxury hotel in sight. This is middle America's land of the budget vacation, and for those with the will and fortitude to make it work to their advantage, it can be an ideal position from which to conquer Walt Disney World.

Citrus groves are scattered throughout Central Florida.

However, nowhere does central Florida's astonishing quantity of accommodations become a glut more than along 192. Many properties were built more than two decades ago, and some have had difficulty weathering the fierce onslaught of competition, from their neighbors, and now from Disney with the opening of the All-Star Resorts. As such, there are losers here, most of them mom-and-pop motels long past their prime. Peeling wallpaper and outdated decor are found even in rooms overseen by national chains. The rivalry between properties has made everyone cut corners, and upkeep is one of the first "amenities" to go. However, their loss is your gain. This is where you'll rarely (if ever) hear "there's no room at the inn," and many of those rooms will frequently be priced at $30 or less in all but the busiest seasons. Sorting through the tangle of contenders was a daunting task, but we unearthed a few solid recommendations.

First, although Kissimmee's name originates from the Calusa Indian term meaning "heaven's place," I offer a few specific caveats. U.S. 192 is, literally, a corridor. The highway crawls past a seemingly endless stream of T-shirt shops, outlet stores, fast-food chains and, of course, mile after mile of accommodations; as such, it is not an aesthetically pleasing base. If you stay here, a car is an essential. Although most of these properties advertise free or reasonably priced shuttles into Walt Disney World, with few exceptions, they're inconvenient and occasionally unreliable. Lastly, although you will have an abundance of choices along the strip, the quality of food is mostly unexceptional; you'll either need to settle for less in the vicinity of your accommodations, or dine elsewhere (an option best contemplated well before the dinner hour). But, if a reasonably priced vacation is your goal, and the atmosphere of your overnighting facilities is not too important, U.S. 192 and Kissimmee are almost certain to offer a property that will fit the bill.

Finally, a clarification. The area unofficially defined as "Maingate" is the intersection of 192 and World Drive, and represents the southern entrance to Walt Disney World. Quite a few properties have woven this term into their own, along with "Eastgate" and "Westgate," the terms used by some to define on which side of the entrance they are located.

HOTELS AND ACCOMMODATIONS

AUTHOR'S OBSERVATION

A double room traditionally accommodates two people, but the specifics vary greatly from one hotel to another. A double at one property may mean a king-size bed, or a solitary queen. It could mean two queens in a room, or two double beds. A rollaway may be available, or a cot (at a charge) might be required for an extra guest. Lastly, verify that the price you are quoted is for the size of party you are bringing; some hotels limit budget rates strictly to two bodies, charging extra for each additional guest, while others will allow up to four or five in a room for the same price.

All-suite

Doubletree Guest Suites Resort
Orlando Maingate   **$149–$219**   ★★★

4787 West Irlo Bronson Highway (U.S. 192), Kissimmee, 34746, one block east of 535, six miles from Maingate entrance, ☎ *(800) 222-8733, (407) 397-0555, FAX (407) 397-0553.*
Rack rate per day: $149–$219.
Formerly the Sol Orlando Resort (and, briefly, the Melia Orlando Suites), this attractive, condominium-style property is enveloped by a Mediterranean atmosphere that creates a pleasant retreat from theme park pressures. European clientele made up the bulk of guests last year, but the change of management will likely introduce savvy Americans to the canal-laced village setting. One-, two- and three-bedroom suites sleep four, six and eight respectively, in two-story, tile-roofed villas complete with full kitchen and a garden patio overlooking the resort's duck ponds and landscaped grounds (the three-bedroom units encompass 1200 square feet of living area). On-site activities include lighted tennis, volleyball, basketball and air-conditioned racketball and squash courts; a small pool area features a jacuzzi.

Amenities: tennis, exercise room, Jacuzzi, balcony or patio. 150 rooms. Credit cards: A, DC, D, MC, V.

Homewood Suites Maingate   **$79–$189**   ★★★

3100 Parkway Boulevard, Kissimmee, 34746, half-mile north of U.S. 192, next to I-4, ☎ *(800) 255-4543, (407) 396-2229, FAX (407) 396-4833.*
Rack rate per day: $79–$189.

This two-story, condo-style hotel tucked away from the U.S. 192 traffic is advantageous for families who desire proximity to the Disney attractions and the flexibility of a suite. Most rooms feature two doubles in the bedroom, with a pullout double in the living area. All units have solid kitchens featuring full-size refrigerators with ice-makers, stove, dishwasher, microwave and coffeemakers, and a few rooms even feature wood-burning fireplaces. Smallish pool area will drive kids to the water parks, though a complimentary social hour (*evenings 5 to 7 p.m.*) keeps parents on the property. Continental breakfast included in the reasonable room rates; a shared cabana provides a gas grill for cooking. The Homewood boasts an excellent location a half-mile off 192 (1.5 miles east of Maingate), although the constant drone of nearby I-4 is a slight annoyance. Amenities: Jacuzzi. 156 rooms. Credit cards: A, DC, D, MC, V.

Residence Inn by Marriott Lake Cecile   **$119–$189**   ★★★

4786 West Irlo Bronson Highway (U.S. 192), Kissimmee, 34746, Two blocks east of 535 on U.S. 192, ☎ *(800) 468-3027, (407) 396-2056, FAX (407) 396-2909.*
Rack rate per day: $119–$189.

Though its rooms aren't the plushest of the all-suite offerings, this property claims a lovely location on the shore of Lake Cecile, and has the watersports facility on-site to prove it. Standard units are studios that sleep four in a queen/sofa bed combo and feature a working fireplace and fully equipped kitchen. Double studios have two double beds and a sleeper sofa to accommodate five; the Penthouse units sleep six in a king upstairs with its own bathroom, a queen-size Murphy bed and a sofa bed. Lakeview suites are limited and by request only; all units have a private entrance and continental breakfast is included in the rate. A small beach provides picnic tables and charcoal grills. Water activities include canoeing, sailing, paddle boats and jet skiing. Swimming is recommended in the hotel's small pool due to the motorized lake traffic. Five miles to Maingate. Amenities: tennis, Jacuzzi. 159 rooms. Credit cards: A, DC, D, MC, V.

Hostels

Hostelling International Orlando/Kissimmee Resort $23–$47   ★

4840 West Irlo Bronson Highway (U.S. 192), Kissimmee, 34746, four miles east of I-4 on U.S. 192, near intersection with Route 535, ☎ *(800) 444-6111, (407) 396-8282, FAX (407) 396-9311.*
Double: $23–$47.

Kissimmee may not be Paris, but American Youth Hostels are a good value almost anywhere, and the U.S. 192 location is no exception. Sometimes less-expensive lodgings are located nearby, but the camaraderie of backpackers and other budget travelers from around the world is hard to find elsewhere in the area. The project was initiated in late 1995 when Hostelling International took over a budget motel and began a $150,000 remodeling job. Dorm rooms feature six bunk beds and are priced $16 per night ($13 for HI members). Private rooms have one or two queen beds, and a kitchenette is featured in a few units; reservations highly recommended, particularly during summer or holiday periods. A small pool and landscaped yard lies behind the motel, and walkways lead to Lake Cecile's shoreline where guests can use free paddle boats. Needless to say, the intimate hostel environment isn't for all tastes, but it's a good bet for independent, and particularly solo, travelers. Five miles east of Maingate. Another hostel is located in downtown Orlando, but is inconvenient to most area attractions. 20 rooms. Credit cards: MC, V.

Hotels

Holiday Inn Hotel and Suites $85–$125   ★ ★ ★

5678 West Irlo Bronson Highway (U.S. 192), Kissimmee, 34746, two miles east of I-4 via Exit 25A, ☎ (800) 366-5437, (407) 396-4488, FAX (407) 396-8915. Double: $85–$125.

Located along the western edge of the Walt Disney World border, this bustling, two-story Holiday Inn pays particular attention to families, providing free sleeping bags, a game-lending library and a private kids dining area. Employees are even required to attend clown college for certification. Most rooms are standard Holiday Inn issue (two doubles or a king/sofa bed combo) with kitchenette, but the "Kidsuites" program initiated at this hotel's sister property, the SunSpree Lake Buena Vista, is being integrated into the room mix here. One- and two-bedroom suites also available. Inexpensive, licensed daycare from 2 to 10 p.m., Camp Holiday, and extensive daily activity program for children. The family-friendly atmosphere extends to pets, who are provided a dog or cat bed to sleep in the room, receive a welcome bag of treats, and may use a fenced, grassy area complete with brightly colored fire hydrants. Rates drop precipitously during the off-season. Free, scheduled transportation to the Disney theme parks. One mile west of Maingate; 10 minutes to the Disney-MGM Studios, 15 to 20 minutes to Epcot and The Magic Kingdom. Amenities: tennis, Jacuzzi. 614 rooms. Credit cards: A, CB, DC, D, MC, V.

Motels

Broadway Inn $29–$49   ★

201 Simpson Road, Kissimmee, 34744, one block north of U.S. 192, near Exit 244 off Turnpike, ☎ (800) 816-1530, (407) 846-1530, FAX (407) 846-2162. Double: $29–$49.

This simple, four-story motel facility is a good option when the other Maingate properties have filled during holiday weekends. All rooms feature two doubles, are kept clean, and rates include a continental breakfast. A Karaoke bar provides giggles nightly for the largely British clientele; a small pool area is suitable for quick cooloffs. The Broadway Inn is just off 192 between Kissimmee proper and St. Cloud, 13 miles east of Maingate and 11 miles south of the Orlando airport. 200 rooms. Credit cards: A, DC, D, MC, V.

Ho Jo Inn Maingate $60–$95   ★ ★

6051 West Irlo Bronson Highway (U.S. 192), Kissimmee, 34747, one mile east of I-4, next door to Water Mania, ☎ (800) 288-4678, (407) 396-1748, FAX (407) 649-8642.

Double: $60–$95.

A straightforward, attractive Howard Johnson motel, this cluster of white stucco buildings is easily one of the best deals in the Maingate area: clean, bright rooms in a series of three-story rows. Some rooms feature a tiny kitchenette for streamlined food preparation; a few others are "family suites," cozy efforts that segment parents and children. One drawback: the pool is too small for the number of guests, but then Water Mania lies immediately next door for serious H2O amusement. Two miles east of Maingate; 10 minutes to the Disney-MGM Studios and 15 miles to Epcot or the Ticket and Transportation Center. Amenities: Jacuzzi. 367 rooms. Credit cards: A, DC, D, MC, V.

Knights Inn Maingate East $33–$52 ★

2880 Poinciana Boulevard, Kissimmee, 34746, just off U.S. 192 behind Perkins Restaurant, three miles east of I-4, ☎ *(800) 396-8893, (407) 396-8186, FAX (407) 396-8569. Double: $33–$52.*

Spare but economical choice when the Maingate properties are full or too expensive. The one-story motel buildings are themed to Olde England and most rooms feature two doubles and simple furnishings. A few kitchenette rooms are available, along with a "Royal" room, which offers a sofa in place of one bed. $7 fee for scheduled transport to Walt Disney World attractions. Four miles to Maingate. 101 rooms. Credit cards: A, DC, D, MC, V.

Ramada Inn Westgate $43–$75 ★★

9200 West U.S. 192, Clermont, 34711, Six miles west of I-4 at Exit 25B, one mile east of U.S. 27, ☎ *(800) 365-6935, (941) 424-2621, FAX (941) 424-4630. Double: $43–$75.*

A pleasant, if predictable motel property, the Ramada Inn Westgate lies close to U.S. 27 (perfect for avoiding Orlando if you're coming in from I-75). Rooms are fresh, with a indigo-blue carpet, white and floral bedspreads, and tan wallpaper. The property is quite isolated and a car is a must, but it's suitable if you're only doing the Disney attractions—the motel is five miles west of Maingate and traffic here is less than on the Kissimmee side of the Disney entrance. Note, the motel is not in Clermont—this mailing address is 15 miles to the north of 192. 198 rooms. Credit cards: A, CB, DC, D, MC, V.

Red Carpet Inn Kissimmee East $24–$44 ★

4700 West Irlo Bronson Highway (U.S. 192), Kissimmee, 34746, five miles east of I-4, ☎ *(800) 462-6063, (407) 396-1133, FAX (407) 396-0224. Double: $24–$44.*

Basic budget accommodations are featured at this low-key motel near Jungleland. All rooms have a microwave and refrigerator, and a McDonald's is next door for fast eats. A small pool is behind the two-story structure. Simple, but clean. Six miles to Maingate. 48 rooms. Credit cards: A, DC, D, MC, V.

¢

Resorts

Inn at Maingate, The $59–$95 ★★★

3011 Maingate Lane, Kissimmee, 34747, two miles west of I-4 at Exit 25B, just off U.S. 192, ☎ *(800) 222-8733, (407) 396-1400, FAX (407) 396-0660. Double: $59–$95.*

Formerly the Radisson Inn Maingate, this large hotel was scheduled to become part of the Doubletree family in late 1996 and continues to serve a mix of business and leisure guests on the edge of Walt Disney World. The seven-story buildings house a wealth of cookie-cutter units, most of which have two doubles (some contain a king, and a few one-bedroom suites are also available). Tennis, basketball and volleyball courts, a small exercise room and undersize pool area with a Jacuzzi round out the activities. There's a full-service restaurant, plus a deli and lounge. One mile west of Maingate, just off 192. Amenities: tennis, exercise room, Jacuzzi, business services. 580 rooms. Credit cards: A, DC, D, MC, V.

Ramada Plaza Resort–Maingate at the Parkway $67–$145   ★ ★ ★

2900 Parkway Boulevard, Kissimmee, 34747, just off 192, next to I-4, ☎ *(800) 634-4774, (407) 396-7000, FAX (407) 396-6792.*

Double: $67–$145.

One of the only Kissimmee lodgings to deserve to be called a resort, and selected as "Hotel of the Year" by Ramada's franchise partners, this eight-story Ramada is located at the "intersection" of I-4 and U.S. 192. It provides excellent access to Disney's Maingate, with Sea World and Universal an unfettered 15- to 20-minute hop away. Most rooms feature two doubles, but 98 are kings, and 20 suites are available; interiors are standard mass-market domiciles. The hotel's verdant grounds are the big attraction. The largest of the two free-form pools is extensive (the best along 192) and features a waterfall and slide surrounded by lush tropical foliage. Rooms in the 1000 building are closest to the water. Tennis, volleyball and a small exercise room are available. One-and-a-half miles east of Maingate; half-mile to Water Mania. Up to five buses daily travel to the Disney attractions; free Sea World and Universal bus also provided once a day. Disney's Celebration community is across the street. Affiliated car rental: Thrifty. Amenities: tennis, exercise room, Jacuzzi, sauna. 718 rooms. Credit cards: A, CB, DC, D, MC, V.

MOST ROMANTIC CENTRAL FLORIDA RESORTS, HOTELS AND INNS

Hyatt Regency Grand Cypress

Disney's Grand Floridian Beach Resort

Peabody Orlando

Disney's Wilderness Lodge

Disney's Yacht Club Resort

Disney's Polynesian Resort

Disney's Port Orleans Resort

Park Plaza Hotel

The Castle

Chalet Suzanne

HOTELS AND ACCOMMODATIONS

Other Possibilities

If you really want to avoid the energetic spectacle of hotels positioned in or close to Walt Disney World, there are a few interesting alternatives in or near Orlando. Bedecked in ornate furnishings or antiques, none are designed for families (although all will accept them). And with the exception of Perri House (a stone's throw from the Disney property line), each of these suggestions is a hike to most of the theme parks. However, therein lies the off-the-beaten-track appeal of these quirky hostelries.

Before plunking down your deposit, request a brochure, and speak to the owner or managers about how their property works for guests. If you are comfortable with the overnighting arrangements, you may find these simpler, yet charming, facilities the highlight of your trip.

Lake Buena Vista

Bed & Breakfasts

Perri House   **$85–$90**   ★★

10417 Centurion Court (State Route 535), Lake Buena Vista, 32830, from I-4, take Exit 27 to Route 535 north; go three miles to Centurion Court, ☎ *(800) 780-4830, (407) 876-4830, FAX (407) 876-0241.*
Double: $85–$90.
Nick and Angi Perretti have turned their ranch-style abode on the edge of the Disney property line into a dedicated bird-friendly environment. The four-acre country estate is a haven for bird lovers, and identification books, bird feeders and binoculars are provided to assist in spotting the avians who frequent this area. The six guest rooms feature either a king or queen bed, private bath, and surround a swimming pool and garden all barely three miles from The Magic Kingdom, as the crow flies. Rates include a continental breakfast. Five minutes to the Disney Village entrance to Walt Disney World. Amenities: Jacuzzi. 6 rooms. Credit cards: A, D, MC, V.

Lake Wales

Inns

Chalet Suzanne Country Inn   **$135–$195**   ★★★

3800 Chalet Suzanne Drive, Lake Wales, 33853, from I-4, take U.S. 27 south 23 miles; left on Masterpiece Gardens Road, ☎ *(800) 433-6011, (941) 676-6011, FAX (941) 676-1814.*
Double: $135–$195.
Long before Walt built his Fantasyland, Chalet Suzanne spun its quirky charm for anyone who accidentally (or deliberately) stumbled into its crooked nook, just outside the small town of Lake Wales—the home of serious water-skiing fanatics. The country inn began in the 1930s, when a widow named Bertha Hinshaw built the guest rooms one at a time, eventually filling them with her spoils from 18 round-the-world expeditions. Today, there are tiles from Persia, rugs from the Orient, and ornate Norwegian ashtrays serving as soup bowls—somehow it adds up to a delight-

ful, unique experience, well away from the polished environment that the Disney company has worked to perfect. The jumble of disjointed rooms total 30, each with its own name, and its own eccentric personality. A few have whirlpool tubs, some have kitchenettes, all possess a wealth of antiques, trinkets and hand woven rugs—a choice unit is the Courtyard room with green tiled-floor and a daybed, but guests will have their own favorites. Note that a few rooms have ceilings so low as to be claustrophobic for anyone over six feet tall (advise the staff at the time of your booking). Room rate includes full breakfast. The oft-referred-to soup plant is not a vegetable, but a functioning, on-site production area for the lodge's famed canned soup developed by Bertha's son Carl; the romaine soup went to the moon with the crew of Apollo 15, and an informal tour of the factory is available. The inn's lavish restaurant is acclaimed by some, but leaves many others swooning in the wake of sky-high prices (one trick is to book the dinner/room combo in the May-November low season, which shaves at least a few dollars off the meal). Otherwise, in this land of cookie cutter accommodations, Chalet Suzanne stands out as a loopy, welcome, one-of-a-kind. Allow 45 minutes to the Disney parks; Bok Tower is a few minutes away, as is Cypress Gardens. 30 rooms. Credit cards: A, CB, DC, D, MC, V.

Orlando

Bed & Breakfasts

Courtyard at Lake Lucerne $69–$130   ★ ★ ★

211 North Lucerne Circle, East, Other, 32801, use Exit 41 from I-4, go east on Anderson, right on Delaney, right on Lucerne Circle, ☎ (800) 444-5289, (407) 648-5188, FAX (407) 246-1368.

Double: $69–$130.

Looking for an authentic slice of pre-Disney Orlando? The Courtyard at Lake Lucerne is a group of three historic homes assimilated into one elaborate bed-and-breakfast accommodation just outside downtown Orlando. The gingerbread-tinged Norment-Parry is Orlando's oldest house, built in 1883 and elegantly restored to its original Victorian splendor with American and English antiques; each of the six guest rooms was decorated by a different local designer. The sexy curves of art deco define the brash Wellborn, a 12-room apartment-style domicile complete with zebra-striped couches and cocktail shakers along with other glam details; all rooms have kitchenettes with a coffeemaker. The premiere facility is the I.W. Phillips House, an antebellum manor with French doors, ceiling fans, Tiffany stained-glass windows and antiques. Prices vary by building and amenities (Honeymoon Suites in the Norment-Parry and I.W. Phillips are the top end). Rates include a continental breakfast, and all rooms have private bath. Church Street Station and Lake Eola are a few minutes away—the surrounding neighborhood invites casual strolls. Allow 15 minutes to Universal, 20 to Sea World and a half-hour to drive to the Disney parks. Families with small children are accommodated in the Wellborn only for an additional $15 per child, per night. 23 rooms. Credit cards: A, MC, V.

Sanford

Higgans House, The   **$70–$115**   ★ ★

420 South Oak Avenue, Sanford, 32771, I-4 to Exit 51; go four miles east to Sanford, right on South Oak three blocks, ☎ *(800) 584-0014, (407) 324-9238.*
Single: $70–$115. Double: $85–$115.

An 1894 family home built by a railroad superintendent, the Higgans House is a Victorian-style bed-and-breakfast in the heart of downtown Sanford, a charming community, population, 24,000 on the shores of Lake Monroe, 25 miles north of downtown Orlando. The house was purchased in 1990 by Walter and Roberta Padgett, who have painstakingly restored it room by room. Three antique-spiced rooms are featured in the main house, each with the original heart-pine floors and cedar ceilings. An adjoining cottage has two bedrooms, two baths, a living/dining area and full kitchen and a porch. An outdoor hot tub is surrounded by a flower, vegetable and herb garden. Be sure to sample Walter's home-brewed draft and famed bread pudding with whiskey sauce. Rates include a continental breakfast of fruit and home baked muffins. Nearby is Big Tree Park, featuring "The Senator," a 3000-year-old cypress; Sanford is alive with antique and other shopping pleasures on weekends. No children under 12 allowed in the main house; no smoking inside. Allow 45 minutes to Walt Disney World theme parks. 4 rooms. Credit cards: A, D, MC, V.

Winter Park

Hotels

Park Plaza Hotel   **$80–$135**   ★ ★ ★

307 Park Avenue South, Winter Park, 32789, from I-4, use Exit 45 east; go two miles into Winter Park, left on Park Ave., ☎ *(800) 228-7220, (407) 647-1072, FAX (407) 647-4081. Rated restaurant: Park Plaza Gardens*
Single: $80–$125. Double: $90–$135.

This restored, 1922-era hostelry welcomes guests through a mahogany-finished lobby, but the real treat lies upstairs. Elegant rooms feature brass beds, Persian rugs, wicker and antique furniture, wooden ceiling fans and ferns, and open onto French Quarter-style wrought-iron balconies sporting colorful impatiens and draped by bougainvillea; breakfast is served here or in your room. Children under 5 not permitted; a concierge desk will assist with Winter Park sightseeing and shopping goals; the hotel is otherwise free of sports or other activities. The signature restaurant is distinguished and popular—the site of elegant Sunday brunches for many years. Walt Disney World theme parks are a 35- to 40-minute drive. Amenities: balcony or patio. 27 rooms. Credit cards: A, D, MC, V.

12 BEST HOTEL SWIMMING FACILITIES

Some of the resort swimming facilities in Orlando are spectacular, and a delight for all ages. Overall, Disney takes the cake, with superlative pools at all of their properties, but saddled with the task of prioritizing the best, I can't help but make a few additional notes. The extensive and dazzling series of pools and channels that fronts the Yacht and Beach Club is the best choice for families, but Stormalong Bay can be quite crowded at almost any hour of the day. The Grand Cypress provides the most relaxed pool environment with its half-acre lagoon fringed by 12 waterfalls, a grotto bar and usually surprisingly few guests. The Contemporary received a major overhaul in late 1995 and was substantially improved, while the smallish pool at the Polynesian was scheduled to go down for rehab in late 1996 for similar amendments.

   #1 Disney's Yacht and Beach Club Resorts (shared facility)

   #2 Hyatt Regency Grand Cypress

   #3 Walt Disney World Dolphin and Swan (shared facility)

   #4 Disney's Wilderness Lodge

   #5 Marriott World Center

   #6 Disney's Boardwalk Resort

   #7 Disney's Port Orleans Resort

   #8 Disney's Caribbean Beach Resort

   #9 Disney's Dixie Landings Resort

  #10 Disney's Contemporary Resort

  #11 Ramada Resort - Maingate at the Parkway

  #12 Disney's Polynesian Resort

RESTAURANTS

Planet Hollywood features film and television industry memorabilia.

Until relatively recently, dining in Orlando was an uninspiring experience. Because the city lacked any distinguishable cuisine, the better restaurants trotted out the old southern standbys (heavy on the fried fish), while the many secondary locations were content to serve mediocre food, knowing it would be a long time before their diners would come calling again. Even at Epcot, which purported to showcase international cuisine, the struggle to serve tens of thousands of meals daily inevitably dashed all higher aspirations.

However, as the number of travelers to the region has increased, diversified and become more demanding of dinner fare, local restaurants have picked up the slack and made great strides forward. Nudged on by the Mouse, dining in Metro Orlando has entered the '90s as more cosmopolitan, more ethnic and with a grander scale than ever before.

Although every franchise restaurant known to the United States is seemingly represented here, even they are spurred on to bigger things: the **McDonald's** on International Drive is the nation's largest, and other chain eateries such as **Planet Hollywood** and the **Hard Rock Cafe** give their garish formulas an extra tweak. The good news is that, outside Walt Disney World, the restaurant scene is intensely competitive—discount coupons abound in the throwaway magazines and fliers that adorn many hotel lobbies. And in a few instances, the food laid out by some of the chains is tasty *and* inexpensive.

AUTHOR'S OBSERVATION

Although southern cooking sneaks onto menus here and there, local specialties in central Florida are few and far between. Other than fresh grouper, (usually tasty however it's cooked), there's no defining dish for the region. Seafood is dependable in better restaurants and, as long as it's pale yellow and not vivid green in color, Key Lime pie is a regular favorite. Although smoked and/or fried gator tale is found on some local menus, virtually no locals eat it – it's exotic game carved mostly for tourists.

One of the biggest proponents of forward momentum on the dining front has been the ever-reflective Disney Company. In recent years, in both the theme parks and its resorts, Disney received withering customer feedback. Lately, the company has acknowledged that its eating facilities left something to be desired, and were overpriced to boot. The recent promotion of Dieter Hannig to vice president of Walt Disney World Food and Beverage is a signal of better things to come.

In charge of "everything" from the turkey-leg carts on up at both the parks and the Disney resorts, Hannig is making a concerted effort to escape the time warp that has entrapped Disney's restaurants, steering toward market-inspired cuisine wherever possible. Hannig's initial, and most notable, makeovers—the **California Grill**, **Coral Reef**, **Chef Mickey's** and **'Ohana**—are winning raves from vacationers and locals alike. Watch for continued success now that **Spoodles** at the BoardWalk Resort has opened.

Still, there are an unfortunate number of middling or lesser restaurants operated by the Disney Company. For most people, it's one thing to lay out six or eight bucks at an amusement park for an average burger with fries and soft drink, but it's quite another to spend $30 or more for a bland Moroccan dinner at Epcot's **Restaurant Marrakesh** that proves only marginally better than

RESTAURANTS

the burger. Too many Orlando visitors forget one simple fact: you don't need a passport to leave Walt Disney World and eat at some of the numerous restaurants that offer better value for dollar. One general Fielding's rule of thumb: if the number of dollar signs we designate for a restaurant exceeds the number of stars, it's overpriced.

AUTHOR'S OBSERVATION

Somebody likes Mickey's cooking. The current annual shopping list for Walt Disney World's kitchens must generate 7 million hamburgers, 5 million hot dogs, 5 million pounds of french fries and 265,000 pounds of popcorn.

Our restaurant listings are broken down into four, primarily location-based groups:

The Disney Theme Park Restaurants

This list is composed of sit-down, waiter-served restaurants within Disney's three main parks. Other Disney theme park eating options are featured in "Walt Disney World Theme Parks."

Disney Resort Restaurants

Dining locations at the Disney-owned resorts, excluding the Swan and Dolphin hotels.

Lake Buena Vista, Pleasure Island and Crossroads Area

The restaurants located in the Swan and Dolphin, in the "Official Hotels of Walt Disney World," at the Disney Village Marketplace, and those situated just off World property in the Crossroads Mall area.

International Drive and Around Orlando

Restaurants situated along or near International Drive, north of Sea World, facilities located inside Universal Studios and nearby.

In every instance, restaurants were visited anonymously and all meals were paid for by Fielding's.

INSIDER'S TIP

Florida residents can join "Disney's Dining Experience," a program developed to entice locals into the Disney restaurants by offering a 20 percent discount off food and drink. The card covers all Disney Resort eateries and most of the theme park venues, and members also are invited to wine tastings, special demonstrations and celebrity chef dinners. Annual membership fee is $40 (and includes half-price admission to Pleasure Island). Call ☎ (407) 828-5792 for more information.

Disney's Food and Fun Plan

Continuing Disney's theme of all-inclusive vacations, the company has created a pair of dining and recreation programs that lock down Walt Disney

World meal and recreation prices to a daily rate of $58 for adults, or $21 for children ages 3 to 9, including tax and gratuity, not including alcoholic beverages.

Designed for guests of the Disney Resorts, the **Food 'n Fun Plan** includes two meals daily (your choice of breakfast, lunch or dinner) at selected Disney eateries, and unlimited use of selected Disney recreational facilities. The operative word here is selected. For instance, although a number of excellent dining facilities are included (such as Artist Point, Cape May Cafe, Bonfamille's and Boatwright's), high-end Disney establishments are excluded, including the California Grill, Narcoosee's, Coral Reef, Bistro de Paris and, of course, Victoria and Albert's. Character meals are in, the Polynesian Luau and Hoop Dee Doo Revue are out. Similarly, the recreational activities include sailboats and water sprites, horseback riding and tennis, but exclude water skiing, parasailing, golf, and golf or tennis lessons.

Disney's Dining Club is a similar package, but is extended to guests of the non-Disney Resorts that are part of Disney's Travel Company, including the Swan, the Dolphin, the "Official Hotels of Walt Disney World," and a few other central Florida hostelries. Priced identically to Food 'n Fun, the Dining Club offers the same meal plan, but limits recreation to the water activities found at Disney Village Marketplace only (it also provides free parking at the theme parks).

The packages don't make sense if they are used strictly for dining. Although it's possible to spend $30 to $40 (including tax and tip, excluding alcohol) for a huge dinner at some of these restaurants, it's difficult to spend $20 for breakfast or lunch at most of them in order to total $58. Instead, the value of these plans lies in the recreational corner, but only if you plan to utilize these features extensively. Therefore, the plans make sense only on days you're not touring the theme parks. Since the packages only have a two-day minimum, you should consider signing your crew up with these plans for the two or three days (in a row) that you plan to concentrate your activities within the resorts. Go over the list of dining locations covered by the plan, compare it with the prices and recommendations listed in Fielding's, and schedule your itinerary accordingly.

In addition to the two-night minimum, the Food 'n Fun Plan and Dining Club must be booked for every person in your party over the age of 2. Plan carefully before committing to these programs, either of which may be added to your vacation even after you've arrived in Orlando.

Disney Theme Park Restaurants

"The issue is, would our restaurants survive without the theme parks?"

—**Dieter Hannig, Vice President of Walt Disney World Food and Dining**

Sit-down dining at Disney's theme parks can be a frustrating experience. From noon until about 2 p.m., all of the best food options will be socked with guests, which means you must plan (and book) your meals in advance. Needless to say, coordinating your dining reservation with what slots are available, the lines for rides and an assortment of grumbling stomachs can be a pretty heady set of obstacles to harmonize. So much for spontaneity.

Nowhere is this problem better exemplified than at **The Magic Kingdom**, where the sheer quantity of guests seems to torpedo any chef with higher aspirations. If the options listed below don't seem adequate, you are left with three choices: go with the flow and opt for fast food (and potentially survive with your wallet intact), or bring your own food stocked from neighboring grocery stores (against the Disney rules, but the discrete are tolerated), or hop on the monorail to visit one of the resort restaurants outlined in the next section. The Grand Floridian has the best array, lead by the moderately expensive **Narcoosee's**; the **Grand Floridian Cafe** is reliable and possesses a moderately priced, something-to-please-everyone menu, and the resort's **Garden View Lounge** serves an elegant high tea daily from 3 p.m. to 6 p.m. (the Grand Tea, with trifle and champagne, is $18.50; seating on a first-come, first-served basis only). The **Whispering Canyon Cafe** at the Wilderness Lodge (accessed by pleasant boatride), provides a hearty, all-you-can-eat lunch, popular with families but rarely overflowing with guests, while the **Concourse Steakhouse** at the Contemporary Resort serves an adequate, if pricey steak for lunch.

Epcot and the **Disney-MGM Studios** offer a better selection of sit-down options within their gates, although planning ahead will yield the best results. Restaurants to book several days or weeks in advance include the **San Angel Inn**, **L'Originale Alfredo di Roma** and **Coral Reef** at Epcot, and the **Sci Fi Dine-In Theater** and the **50's Prime Time Cafe** at the Studios. If good food at a reasonable price is a priority, take the *FriendShip* to the Boardwalk Resort and enjoy the flavorful food offered at Spoodles.

In all instances, reservations are made through Disney's central dining reservation number: ☎ *(407) WDW-DINE*, which is staffed from 7 a.m. to 10 p.m. daily (until 8 p.m. on Saturday and Sunday). Because you will likely spend a few minutes waiting for an attendant, you're best off having a general dining itinerary and backup plan when you call; mornings are when the lines are least busy and evenings when they are most tied up. Dining reservations may be made up to 60 days in advance. Note that the Discover Card and Diners Club are not accepted at the Disney restaurants.

AUTHOR'S OBSERVATION

Because of the sheer quantity of guests fed by the Disney Company, rushed food is a common annoyance at most restaurants in the theme parks. If you want a casual meal, take your time going over the menu, alert your waiter that you want a leisurely meal, and then split your beverage and food orders into two or three separate requests. Of course, if you're on a tight schedule and want to get in and out quickly, your server will likely be happy to accommodate you.

Au Petit Cafe   **$$**   ★★★

Epcot (World Showcase).
French cuisine. Specialties: French onion soup, salads, sandwiches and light entrées.
Lunch: Noon–4 p.m., entrées $4–$16.
Dinner: 4–9 p.m., entrées $4–$16.
Of Epcot's three side-by-side French dining establishments (which seemingly share the same kitchen), Au Petit Cafe tackles the simplest menu, and by keeping its sights low, comes the closest to reproducing its chosen food theme—streetside Paris. The open-air dining area can be stifling in summer, and seatings are on a first-come, first-served basis, which means a line is ever-present, but otherwise this is one of Epcot's better values, particularly if you're open to a lighter meal. L'entrecote topped with bordelaise is quite filling and the salad nicoise is reliable. The chicken breast and vegetables in puff pastry is a satisfying entree; desserts are painfully hard to resist. Best asset, though, is the prime locale for people-watching. Features: outside dining, wine and beer only. Reservations not accepted. Credit cards: A, MC, V.

Biergarten   **$$**   ★★

Epcot (World Showcase).
German cuisine. Specialties: German sausages, kraut and salad, served buffet-style.
Lunch: Noon–3 p.m., entrées $10.
Dinner: 4–9 p.m., entrées $15.
A year-round commemoration of Octoberfest, Epcot's huge Biergarten feature a festive all-you-can-eat buffet and oompah music all in a village setting. The communal tables seat eight, and the food is uninspiring, if inoffensive—it's hard to muck up bratwurst and sauerkraut. Potato salad, lentil salad, spaetzle and baked chicken round out the limited selection. Dessert is not included in the price, but the apple strudel awash in vanilla sauce is tasty. Beck's beer (by the bottle or litre), a decent selection of H. Schmitt Sohne wines, as well as Underberg and other traditional

German liqueurs keep the spirits high, particularly when the polka dancing gets serious. Reservations recommended. Credit cards: A, MC, V.

Bistro de Paris $$$ ★★★★

Epcot (World Showcase).
French cuisine. Specialties: Rack of lamb, grilled beef tenderloin, seafood casserole.
Dinner: 6–9 p.m., entrées $21–$27.

Epcot's most intimate dining experience is staged by this bistro reached via a spiral staircase that winds to the quiet second floor of the French pavilion. Candles and soft chandelier lighting accent the plush surroundings, while elegant gold frames embellish artwork and mirrors. Appetizers include a duck foie gras salad spiked with artichoke hearts and a subtle escargot casserole. The short list of entrées is consistently good. Try the grilled tenderloin of beef topped with green peppercorn sauce, or the rack of lamb for two. The red snapper with potato scales and red wine lobster sauce on sautéed leeks is acclaimed by many. One of two restaurants overseen by the likes of three of France's best-known chefs (Paul Bocuse, Gaston Lenotre and Roger Verge). Reservations can be tight, as are the seating arrangements, but request a window seat overlooking the lagoon and keep your fingers crossed. Reservations recommended. Credit cards: A, MC, V.

Chefs de France $$$ ★★★

Epcot (World Showcase), Disney Theme.
French cuisine. Specialties: Sauteed tenderloin of beef, braised duck, broiled salmon.
Dinner: 5–9 p.m., entrées $16–$25.

French nouvelle cuisine is celebrated adequately at this, the largest of Epcot's three French establishments. Like the Bistro de Paris upstairs (which serves comparable food in a better environment), the menu is the creation of three top cuisiniers: Paul Bocuse, Gaston Lenotre and Roger Verge, who are theoretically responsible for overseeing the operation—some wonder how often they visit. The escargot in butter and garlic is a good starter (also available for the same price at Au Petit Cafe next door), while broiled salmon in sorrel cream sauce, and sautéed tenderloin of beef drizzled in raisins and brandy are solid choices. Desserts herald French classics, heavy on the ice cream dishes. Hurried, manic service is a recurring problem, and count on feeling cramped, otherwise this is a fair representation of French cuisine—though the affable staff and smokeless surroundings would never be stomached on the real Boulevard Saint Michel. Reservations recommended. Credit cards: A, MC, V.

Coral Reef Restaurant $$$ ★★★★

Epcot (Living Seas Pavilion).
Seafood cuisine. Specialties: Seafood Provencale, clambake, grilled tuna and salmon.
Lunch: 11 a.m.–2:45 p.m., entrées $15–$26.
Dinner: 4:30–9 p.m., entrées $17–$29.

With one of the most spectacular and unique settings anywhere, and food that almost lives up to it, Coral Reef is Epcot's seafood restaurant to end all. The multi-tiered dining area faces The Living Sea's 5.7-million gallon salt water aquarium, where eight-inch-thick acrylic provides a window into the 27-foot-deep undersea environment. The $6–$10 first course choices include cream of lobster soup, sautéed mussels in a spicy red sauce, and a dynamite shrimp cocktail served on watercress with a side of wasabi mustard sorbet. The entree selection is equally diverse, with kudos to the bright seafood Provencale and the clambake with chunks of alligator meat thrown in for a local taste treat. The food is generally excellent, but the prices may make you flinch. Although the aquarium setting is awesome (if a tad austere), Disney officials were considering a remodel for the restaurant that would further build on the undersea theme by constructing a faux coral reef around the dining room to blend in with the viewing windows. If Coral Reef is a dining experience you want to count on, reserve a table before you arrive in Orlando; the restaurant is often completely booked days in advance. Features: wine and beer only. Reservations recommended. Credit cards: A, MC, V.

50's Prime Time Cafe $$ ★ ★

Disney-MGM Studios (Lakeside Circle)
Specialties: Meatloaf, pot roast, broiled chicken, daily fish specials.
Lunch: 11 a.m.–3:30 p.m., entrées $10–$18.
Dinner: 4–9 p.m., entrées $13–$21.

Perhaps nowhere else in Walt Disney World does theme triumph over food with greater panache than at this Disney-MGM Studios tribute to the "Beaver" era (although the nearby Sci-Fi Dine-In is a close second in this thankless category). The hysterical environment is composed of a series of interconnecting rooms designed to look like June Cleaver's kitchen, complete with formica, garish wallpaper, tchotchke, and dozens of television sets where the black-and-white sitcoms never stop. The cast members waiting on tables are known as either Brother or Sis, and devote a lot of energy to playing out the retro concept, plus the meat-and-potatoes menu doesn't miss a beat (kids love its unstinting hollowness). The chicken pot pie tastes as good as frozen, but the burgers are a notch above the park's other fast-food versions and the peanut butter and jelly shake isn't half-bad. The "Magnificent Meatloaf" may be PTA-approved, but at $12.50 a plate, just how badly do you want to recall this nightmarish vision? The adjacent Tune In Lounge, a '50s-style wood-paneled den, is the comfy bar area—a good spot to sample the scene without committing to a meal. Typically, most or all of the dining slots are locked up for the day by the time the park opens its gates; if you want to count on it, book a table before you arrive in Orlando. And don't forget to wash your hands! Reservations recommended. Credit cards: A, MC, V.

Hollywood Brown Derby, The $$$ ★ ★ ★

Disney-MGM Studios.
American cuisine. Specialties: Cobb salad, garlic basil pasta, baked grouper, filets mignon, sandwiches (lunch).
Lunch: 11:30 a.m.–3:45 p.m., entrées $9–$16.
Dinner: 4–9 p.m., entrées $17–$24.

The best food at Disney-MGM Studios is served at this loving recreation of the famous Hollywood Brown Derby, right down to the trademark Cobb salad swamped with French dressing. The palm-lined walls are adorned by 1600 duplicates of the original restaurant's framed celebrity caricatures, and cast members playing Hollywood agents and "wannabes" flit from table to table. The menu doesn't reach for the stars, but the roast chicken, baked grouper over pasta and filet mignon are nicely prepared. A "Value Meal" selection is available from 4 to 5:30 p.m. daily, and includes a salad, entree and dessert for $15.75. One caveat: Disney's priority seating system is at its rockiest at this restaurant; on both occasions I dined here, my wait exceeded the reservation time by more than 20 minutes. Watch for a possible menu makeover that would embrace a lighter, California-inspired cuisine (without giving up the Cobb salad). Reservations recommended. Credit cards: A, MC, V.

King Stefan's Banquet Hall   **$$$**   ★

The Magic Kingdom (Fantasyland).
American cuisine. Specialties: Red meat, breast of chicken, seafood pasta.
Lunch: 11:30 a.m.–2:45 p.m., entrées $11–$17.
Dinner: 4 p.m.–park closing, entrées $21–$26.

The lure of dining at Cinderella's Castle is great, but you'll pay for the privilege in more ways than one. The decor in this medieval-themed restaurant is magisterial, but some visitors wonder why it was named after Sleeping Beauty's father. The food served here is among Walt Disney World's most uninspired and overpriced. The brief menu focuses on steaks, with a single chicken and fish entree; sandwiches are also offered at lunch ($11–$12). I suspect Disney executives can't agree on a permanent solution for this mess: despite miserable food, a limited number of seats, and an awkward entry area, the demand keeps the restaurant busy around the clock—the morning character breakfast here is possibly the hottest ticket Mickey flashes—so why mess with success? Still, keep your eye out for a makeover in 1997 that may find the establishment renamed Cinderella's and offering better food. If you want one of the room's eight prized window tables overlooking Fantasyland, request it at the time of your reservation, and again when you arrive at the podium. If meeting Cinderella is important, she periodically waltzes by the ground-floor entrance. No alcohol is served. Reservations recommended. Credit cards: A, MC, V.

L'Originale Alfredo di Roma Ristorante   **$$$**   ★ ★ ★

Epcot (World Showcase).
Italian cuisine. Specialties: Fettuccine Alfredo, pasta dishes, salmon, veal.
Lunch: Noon–4:15 p.m., entrées $8–$16.
Dinner: 4:15–9 p.m., entrées $10–$25.

Dependable pasta is served up at Epcot's plush Italian eatery, in a dining room lined with latticework and trompe l'oeil murals depicting the southern countryside. The original Alfredo (De Lelio) opened his famous Roman ristorante in 1914, and his descendants have conspired with Mickey to reproduce the attraction at Epcot. A responsibly high-fat Fettucine Alfredo (using loads of butter flown in from Italy) is the star attraction, but Bolognese, Pomodoro and Carbonara sauces are also offered, and use the same fresh fettucine. The lasagna with veal and cream sauce is excellent, and other meat entrées include chicken baked in focaccia, grilled veal chop in a Chianti and black truffle sauce, and a braised rack of lamb. In addition to a daily fish selection, there's a tasty grilled salmon with rattatouille. Strolling singers perform arias at dinner, and the atmosphere is genuinely festive. This is one of Epcot's more-popular dining experiences; book early to ensure a table. Reservations recommended. Credit cards: A, MC, V.

Liberty Tree Tavern   **$$**   ★★

The Magic Kingdom (Liberty Square).
American cuisine. Specialties: Grilled fish, traditional roast turkey dinner, pot roast, sea-
food pasta, sandwiches, salads.
Lunch: 11:30 a.m.–2:45 p.m., entrées $10–$15.

Have a hankering for a traditional Thanksgiving meal in the heat of summer? This
Liberty Square dining hall lays out a daily Pilgrim's Feast for lunch, with roast tur-
key, dressing, mashed potatoes and sautéed vegetables. Pot roast, a grilled fish of
the day, and a decent Cape Cod pasta topped with shrimp and vegetables, sand-
wiches and salads are also available. The darkish atmosphere is early American Colo-
nial, with themed rooms decorated by items linked to six of the era's major figures:
Paul Revere, Betsy Ross, Ben Franklin, John Paul Jones, George Washington and
Thomas Jefferson. The adequate food adds up to probably the best of The Magic
Kingdom's meager selection of sit-down restaurants. No alcohol; a character dinner
is served nightly. Reservations recommended. Credit cards: A, MC, V.

Mama Melrose's Ristorante Italiano   **$$$**   ★★

Disney-MGM Studios.
Italian cuisine. Specialties: Pizza, pasta, tenderloin of beef, chicken marsala, fresh fish.
Lunch: 11:30 a.m.–3:45 p.m., entrées $9–$16.
Dinner: 4 p.m.–park closing, entrées $12–$23.

With a New York-style facade and red-checkered tablecloths, Mama Melrose's is a
light-hearted and friendly spot for simple Italian food. Try the chicken marsala,
which comes with a side of pasta, or the grilled tenderloin of beef in a red wine,
tomato and garlic sauce. Thin crust pizzas are fine, and baked in a brick, hickory
wood-burning oven. Dissenters claim the prices are too steep for the play-it-safe
menu, but it's a sure bet for families, and the easiest of Disney-MGM Studios' four
sit-downs to obtain a last-minute table. A makeover is under discussion that may
reduce the menu's heavy cream and butter offerings, as well as an exterior face-lift
to incorporate awnings, French doors and outside chairs. Mama Melrose's is open
for dinner only when the park is scheduled to stay open until 8 p.m. or later. Reservations recommended. Credit cards: A, MC, V.

Nine Dragons   **$$$**   ★★

Epcot (World Showcase).
Chinese cuisine. Specialties: Kung Pao chicken, shrimp ambrosia, moo gu gai pan, sweet
and sour pork.
Lunch: Noon–4:30 p.m., entrées $9–$18.
Dinner: 4:45–9 p.m., entrées $11–$24.

A couple of decades ago, Nine Dragons might have been considered one of the bet-
ter Chinese restaurants on the East Coast. In the '90s, however, its food is over-
shadowed by any number of less-expensive Chinese dining rooms found elsewhere
in the region. In spite of the truly elegant, ornate backdrop of painted ceilings, black
lacquer chairs, delicate paper lanterns, rich reds and gleaming golds, the menu will
please only the most undemanding customers. The Cantonese-heavy selection is
not as extensive as that at most Chinese diners; surprisingly, only one stir-fried gar-
den vegetable plate is available. A few Szechuan dishes are offered, with the Kang
Bao chicken being a spicy standout. I suspect a big reason why the restaurant keeps

its tables turning is that, short of a burger at the American pavilion, this is as risky an international venture as some Epcot visitors are willing to try; as such, it does keep the kids happy, but don't expect anything you can't get at home for half the price. The lunch and dinner menu is identical, except for the prices; an early bird set-menu is available: $13.95, 4-6 p.m. Reservations recommended. Credit cards: A, MC, V.

Restaurant Akershus $$ ★★★
Epcot (World Showcase).
International cuisine. Specialties: Hot and cold buffet featuring salmon, meatballs, smoked pork, venison, Norwegian cheeses, salads.
Lunch: Noon–4 p.m., prix fixe $12.
Dinner: 4:15–9 p.m., prix fixe $18.
Although a tad overpriced for dinner, Restaurant Akershus is one of Epcot's best lunch deals, and an easy way to sample Norwegian cuisine that most Americans know little about. The diverse smorgasbord includes a lengthy cold section: gravlaks in mustard, smoked mackerel, a variety of salads and a tasty smoked salmon and scrambled eggs dish. Hot items include smoked pork, lamb and cabbage, venison strips in cream, and sweet mashed rutabagas; a variety of hearty breads. Ringnes beer, Norwegian liqueurs and heavy desserts top off the selection. A good bet when other restaurants are jammed. Credit cards: A, MC, V.

Restaurant Marrakesh $$ ★★
Epcot (World Showcase).
International cuisine. Specialties: Shish kebab, couscous, lamb, tangine of grouper or chicken.
Lunch: Noon–4 p.m., entrées $10–$13.
Dinner: 4:15–9 p.m., entrées $14–$20.
A number of Walt Disney World visitors enjoy Restaurant Marrakesh as an exotic culinary excursion—I, too, find the menu tantalizing, but the actual food strikes me as overpriced and disappointing, a poor facsimile when compared to the real thing. The couscous, a Moroccan staple topped with chicken, lamb or vegetables is safe, but the roasted lamb meshoui and the chicken brochette are neutered for the American palate. Where the restaurant scores is in its entertainment—belly dancers accompanied by a small live band—the lush decor is seductive as well. In all, not unpleasant, and ambitious, but not what it should be. Reservations recommended. Credit cards: A, MC, V.

Rose and Crown Pub and Dining $$$ ★★
Epcot (World Showcase).
English cuisine. Specialties: Fish and chips, beef with Yorkshire pudding, cottage pie, vegetable curry.
Lunch: Noon–3:15 p.m., entrées $10–$12.
Dinner: 4:30–9 p.m., entrées $13–$21.
British food usually suffers a bad rap, and although the Rose and Crown does nothing to improve the country's bruised culinary reputation, it does spin out the classics—fish and chips, prime rib and yorkshire pudding, steak and kidney pie—in faultless fashion. A few unexpected choices pop onto the menu: a decent vegetable curry is one, while the walnut breast of chicken in stilton cream is a rich order. Des-

serts are best—decadent sherry trifle and a tasty apple-blackberry crumble are trundled out for approval (they get mine). A smaller menu is available at the Rose and Crown's pub, where a cheese plate or Scotch egg can be pondered over a half-yard of ale. A traditional tea is also served at 4 p.m. daily for $9.95. Some tables provide good viewing spots for IllumiNations, but the competition for them can be fierce. Reservations recommended. Credit cards: A, MC, V.

San Angel Inn $$$ ★ ★ ★

Epcot (World Showcase).
Mexican cuisine. Specialties: Carne asada, fillet of red snapper, chicken mole, enchiladas, chiles rellenos.
Lunch: 11:30 a.m.–4 p.m., entrées $10–$16.
Dinner: 4:30–9 p.m., entrées $14–$23.

Epcot's most extravagant decor is reserved for Mexico's San Angel Inn, where guests dine in a nighttime cantina setting beneath an Aztec pyramid and smoldering volcano. The food doesn't live up to the room—it's expensive and mostly ordinary—but it manages to please most visitors. The menu offers chicken enchiladas, chile rellenos and tacos al carbon, with several grilled beef selections gently embellished by Mexican seasonings. Kudos for placing chicken mole (a muddy, love-it-or-hate-it sauce of ground chocolate and 20 spices) and a vibrant poached red snapper on the menu; they're among the most adventurous taste sensations laid out at Epcot by Disney chefs. The Dos Equis are a cold respite from pounding the World Showcase pavement, the prefab margaritas less so. A scaled-down (and less expensive) selection of Mexican favorites is available at the nearby Cantina de San Angel. The seductive ambiance keeps this restaurant very popular; reserve ahead of your Epcot visit if you want to be assured of a table. Reservations recommended. Credit cards: A, MC, V.

Sci-Fi Dine-In Theater $$ ★ ★

Disney-MGM Studios.
American cuisine. Specialties: Burgers and sandwiches (lunch), roast turkey, barbecued pork ribs, pasta with chicken, steak (dinner).
Lunch: 10:30 a.m.–3:45 p.m., entrées $9–$14.
Dinner: 4 p.m.–park closing, entrées $11–$23.

The Disney-MGM Studios' most popular meal ticket is this tribute to drive-in entertainment—a huge sound stage occupied by an ersatz drive-in movie theater and a bevy of '50s-style pastel-and-chrome convertibles that seat six diners apiece. The screen is brightened by a panoply of wacky newsreel footage and previews for grade-Z horror and sci-fi epics; kids are spellbound, but since virtually all seating arrangements face forward, all the oddly serene interaction is with the screen, rather than with other diners. The food is better than the greasy pizza slices usually served at drive-ins, but not much. The menu is burger- and sandwich-heavy at lunch; try "The Thing They Called Seafood" (scallops and shrimp in a creamy basil sauce over penne pasta) or "The Towering Terror" (barbecued pork ribs) for dinner. With hosts on roller skates and a star-filled night sky, it's an amusing scene. For a less-expensive deal, visit for a late afternoon milk-shake break rather than an actual meal. If you want to sit in a car, you need to make your request at the time of your reservation, and again when you show up. A number of non-car tables line the walls, but these are generally set aside for walk-up traffic. Note that odd-numbered parties will have one diner seated solo in the two-passenger rows. Book your reservation well in advance of your front gate arrival. Reservations recommended. Credit cards: A, MC, V.

Tempura Kiku $$$ ★★★

Epcot (World Showcase).
Japanese cuisine. Specialties: Chicken, shrimp and vegetable tempura, sushi.
Lunch: Noon–3:45 p.m., entrées $10–$12.
Dinner: 4:30–9 p.m., entrées $15–$23.
Vying with Bistro de Paris as Epcot's most intimate dining experience, this is a little-heralded, first-come, first-served, 26-seat dining area adjoining the Teppanyaki Dining Rooms in Japan's pavilion. Seating is counter-style at a square bar, where a coterie of cooks prepare the food as you watch. The appetizers include a short list of nicely prepared sushi and sashimi. The entrées are limited to tempura—chunks of chicken, shrimp and vegetables dipped in a light batter and quickly fried—and sumashi soup and steamed rice accompany your order. Tempura is not fancy or dynamic, but the Disney version is as good as it gets. However, this is one of several Epcot restaurants wherein not-inexpensive lunch prices are nearly doubled for dinner, and for a marginally larger plate of food. The Yakatori House, in a lovely garden setting just below Tempura Kiku, is a decent fast-food alternative for a scaled-down and less-expensive menu of tempura, curry and skewered meats. Reservations not accepted. Credit cards: DC, MC, V.

Teppanyaki Dining Room $$$ ★★★

Epcot (World Showcase).
Japanese cuisine. Specialties: Grilled steak, chicken, shrimp.
Lunch: Noon–3:45 p.m., entrées $10–$17.
Dinner: 4:30–9 p.m., entrées $15–$28.
The Americanized, Benihana-style version of Japan's steakhouses is reproduced at the Teppanyaki Dining Room, where communal, eight-person tables surround a gleaming teppan grill. Once your meal is ordered, your private chef comes to the table and begins his show—the food preparation includes sight gags and fancy knife-work, with the results being fairly ordinary grilled beef, seafood and poultry, with sides of fried vegetables and steamed rice. The dinner prices are steep, but if a knife-juggling, Benihana-style experience is what you had in mind, Teppanyaki is the place to go. A $15.50 early bird special is offered daily from 4:30 p.m. to 6 p.m. Reservations recommended. Credit cards: A, MC, V.

Tony's Town Square $$$ ★★

The Magic Kingdom (Main Street USA).
Italian cuisine. Specialties: Frittata, sandwiches and calzone (lunch), spaghetti with meatballs, seafood penne, turkey piccata (dinner).
Breakfast: 8:30 a.m.–10:45 a.m., entrées $4–$10.
Lunch: Noon–2:45 p.m., entrées $9–$16.
Dinner: 3:45 p.m.–park closing, entrées $17–$23.
Positioned right near the exit from The Magic Kingdom, Tony's Town Square takes its cue from Lady in the Tramp, duplicating the location of the canine couple's first date. The lunch menu features frittatas, salads and pasta, with a nice Mufalata and

other sandwiches. At dinner, the pricey entree list includes linguine sautéed with prosciutto, artichoke hearts, cream and cheese, chicken Florentine, as well as a steak and lobster combo and, of course, spaghetti and meatballs for any lovers who want to try the noodle-sharing-kiss perfected by Lady and the Tramp. The New York trattoria ambience is pleasant. No alcohol served. Reservations recommended. Credit cards: A, MC, V.

Disney Resort Restaurants

The resorts are where the Disney Company's dining overhaul has made its first impact. When Orlando residents who previously avoided Walt Disney World offerings began turning up at the **California Grill** in 1995, Disney could claim a certifiable win. The California Grill was an important benchmark for a number of reasons. This was where Disney began working with market-inspired cuisine—a menu that evolved weekly based on the fresh ingredients available at any given time. Further, though not inexpensive, the restaurant continues to be reasonably in step with how this kind of food might be priced in other parts of the country. The only bad news (for us) is that the restaurant has been discovered: it was chosen as the winner of *Orlando Magazine's* annual readers poll and reservations are now genuinely difficult to obtain on short notice.

Not to fear. Most of Disney's resorts now have at least one good restaurant available, and market-inspired cuisine is the new buzzword bounding onto the menus of a number of these locations. In all instances, reservations are a good idea (☎ *[407] WDW-DINE*), but are particularly recommended for several popular spots other than the California Grill: **Ariel's**, **Artist Point**, **Narcoosee's**, **Victoria & Albert's** and the **Yachtsman Steakhouse**.

A few 1996 changes are worth noting. **Crockett's Tavern**, the only sit-down spot at Fort Wilderness, was closed down during the summer, as was the much-maligned **Tangaroa Terrace** at the Polynesian; an announcement was pending as to what Disney would do with the sites. The Polynesian's **Coral Isle Cafe** was scheduled to reopen in late 1996 as **Kona's** with a coffee-roasting machine on the premises—sounds promising. Two new restaurants, **Spoodles** at the BoardWalk and **Seasons** at the Disney Institute are generating very favorable buzz. **Chef Mickey's**, previously situated at the Disney Village Marketplace, has been moved to the Contemporary Resort, where it has become home to a very popular pair of character meals (see "Character Dining" later in this chapter).

Ariel's $$$ ★★★★

Disney's Beach Club Resort.
Seafood cuisine. Specialties: Fresh menu daily features Maine lobster, shellfish, surf and turf.
Dinner: 6–10 p.m., entrées $18–$30.
Named after the perky star of *The Little Mermaid*, this colorfully decorated room edges the other Disney seafoodery (Epcot's Coral Reef) for the sheer quality and creativity of its preparations. The menu highlights both classic and local seafood preparations—the latter is cheekily referred to as "Floribbean." In addition to can't-miss daily specials, try the lush paella, or the pasta wrapped around lobster and shrimp and sautéed effortlessly in garlic, wine, lemon and butter. Two-pound Maine lobsters come steamed, or baked with crabmeat, and a mean porterhouse is available for landlubbers. Four tables are positioned next to a 2500-gallon aquarium writhing with neon-hued tropical reef fish; request this spot if you have children in your party—otherwise, this is an elegant restaurant more suited for adults. The ceiling is decorated with fish mobiles and suspended bubbles, while the walls display scenes from Ariel's movie. The wine list is excellent, and focuses on California selections—try a "wine flight," four samples for $8–$10. Without question, one of the three or four best Disney dining experiences, exemplified by the hefty repeat business from locals. Features: rated wine cellar. Reservations recommended. Credit cards: A, MC, V.

Artist Point $$$ ★★★★

Disney's Wilderness Lodge.
American cuisine. Specialties: Prime rib, venison, lamb, salmon, trout, wild game appetizers.
Dinner: 5:30–10 p.m., entrées $15–$26.
A restaurant that lives up to and beyond its elaborately themed resort home, Artist Point is one of Disney's more ambitious dining establishments, highlighting the field-and-stream vistas of the Pacific Northwest in a soaring dining room decorated with vast canvasses of Rocky Mountain scenery and cast-iron chandeliers. Enormous windows overlook the lodge's waterfall or out through slash pines onto Bay Lake—somehow managing to exude the rustic milieu of a backwoods park lodge without cartoony pretense (could it be how the windows tastefully imitate Frank Lloyd Wright's stained-glass pieces?). The menu changes seasonally, but regulars include a succulent, pan-seared rainbow trout with pancette and lentils, a venison chop embraced by rabbit sausage, and a fine, simple salad of field greens, Oregon pears, spiced walnuts and raspberries. Most items are cooked over the room's gently smol-

dering hardwood fire. The unique (for Florida) wine list embraces the hearty merlots and pinot noirs produced in Oregon and Washington by Willamette Valley, Columbia and Hogue Cellars; the adjoining Territory Lounge is one of Disney's best bars, and serves a not-half-bad microbrew. The dynamic food and atmosphere are not for all tastes, but heaven for those looking for something unique. A character meal is held here daily for breakfast. Features: rated wine cellar. Reservations recommended. Credit cards: A, MC, V.

Boatwright's Dining Hall $$ ★★★

Disney's Dixie Landings Resort.

Cajun cuisine. Specialties: Prime rib, roast pork loin, baby back ribs, barbecued chicken.

Breakfast: 7–11:30 a.m., entrées $5–$8.

Dinner: 5–10 p.m., entrées $10–$18.

Imaginatively themed to resemble a late-1800s, Louisiana shipbuilding shop, Boatwright's is one of Walt Disney World's best dining values, but is known primarily only to the guests overnighting at Dixie Landings. The pleasing decor includes a huge hull suspended from the ceiling and walls covered in antique tools, but what keeps the praise flowing is the rich menu that focuses on rural Southern ingredients. The meat-heavy selection includes roast loin of pork swathed in braised red onions and mustard, a grilled fillet of catfish, and several juicy cuts of beef. Dixie Beer welcomes true Southerners, while the thick, Blackened Voodoo Lager splendidly complements the barbecue dishes. Enjoy delectable bananas Foster for dessert, or come early for the vibrant Cajun breakfast. Reservations recommended. Credit cards: A, MC, V.

Bonfamille's Cafe $$ ★★★

Disney's Port Orleans Resort.

Specialties: Prime rib, barbecue ribs, salmon, chicken and Andouille sausage gumbo, jambalaya.

Breakfast: 7–11 a.m., entrées $5–$8.

Dinner: 5–10 p.m., entrées $10–$19.

The French Quarter mood is decidedly low-key, but otherwise Bonfamille's gingerly bearhugs Creole cooking, if not with absolute respect for the volume of spices traditionally spooned into a pot of jambalaya. Steaks and barbecued ribs top the entree list, but don't skip the appetizers, such as the rich crawfish pasta or spunky gumbo, any combination of which can make a worthwhile meal. The hearty breakfast selection includes a skillet filled with eggs and your choice of andouille sausage, crawfish or blackened chicken; or you can go for broke with the indulgent French toast—a baguette swamped by sweet custard and deep fried... argh! Disney officials are discussing a name change (to the Alligator Cannery?) and a rehab that would provide a cross between a Texas rib joint and a Bourbon Street seafood house; if so, one wonders if Michael Eisner has ever experienced firsthand Bourbon around midnight? Reservations recommended. Credit cards: A, MC, V.

INSIDER'S TIP

Best burger in central Florida? According to an Orlando Magazine survey of its readers, Jungle Jim's, located just outside Walt Disney World in the Crossroads Mall Shopping Center, tops the list, with hearty burgers assembled 63 different ways. One warped favorite is the Fertility Burger—"not endorsed by Planned Parenthood"—and heaped with cajun sauce, buffalo-wing sauce, sliced jalapenos, jack and cheddar cheese, sour cream and cream cheese. Wow!

California Grill $$$ ★★★★★

Disney's Contemporary Resort.
American cuisine. Specialties: California-style pizzas, grilled beef, chicken and fish, salads, sushi; market-inspired menu changes.
Dinner: 5:30–10 p.m., entrées $9–$27.

Disney's great success story of 1995 was the debut of this inspired dining room with a view, named one of America's top 10 new restaurants by Esquire magazine. Situated at the summit of the Contemporary Resort and overlooking The Magic Kingdom and Seven Seas Lagoon, the California Grill theme echoes Wolfgang Puck's eateries such as Spago's, that became all the rave in Los Angeles in the late '80s. Not only is Puck's modernist decor amusingly mimed, but the Grill's kitchen produces a more-than-adequate spin on California cuisine, with Asian and Mediterranean accents featured in many dishes. A first course might encompass a light rock-shrimp and lemongrass soup, or goat cheese ravioli with Shiitake mushrooms, basil and sun-dried tomatoes, or button clams steamed in lime and chili pepper (two diners could order four or five of these, all under $10 apiece, for a dazzling light meal). Main course selections include spicy braised lamb shank afloat in a tarn of Thai-style red curried lentils, or an elegant platter of sushi, or the Atlantic salmon baked in a black olive crust, or—my favorite—the grilled pork tenderloin with polenta and Crimini mushrooms smothered in Balsamic vinegar. The market-inspired menu changes weekly (fall brings a multi-colored plate of mouth-watering tomatoes). Although the restaurant is not inexpensive, if you're not famished, you can order a sparkling salad of field greens, a designer brick-oven baked pizza, and an excellent new-wave California wine all for under $25. The only drawback is the restaurant's popularity—it attracts a significant number of Orlandoans, who awarded it their top slot in a Spring 1996 *Orlando Magazine* readers' poll. This is one to book before your trip commences. Everyone wants a choice window seat for The Magic Kingdom fireworks, but savvy repeaters know a seat at the counter provides an opportunity to see the kitchen show in action, and to receive an occasional treat. The bar and lounge area stays open until midnight, serving a scaled-down menu of pizzas, burgers, salads and sushi. The wine list is top-notch at any hour, and the desserts are heavenly. Features: rated wine cellar, late dining. Reservations recommended. Credit cards: A, MC, V.

Cape May Cafe $$ ★★★

Disney's Beach Club Resort, Disney Resort.

American cuisine. Specialties: Clams, mussels, barbecue ribs, grilled chicken.
Dinner: 5:30–9:30 p.m., prix fixe $19.

Of the various Walt Disney World buffets, this clambake is one of the best. Disney follows the Yacht and Beach Club's eastern seaboard theme to its delightful pinnacle—the New England ambiance is complete with beach umbrellas and sandcastles, and the food's pretty dependable, too. Start with peel-and-eat shrimp or one of several thick chowders, then proceed to the steamed clams, mussels, baked fish, marinated grilled chicken, barbecued pork ribs, sausage and corn on the cob. Bookended by a salad bar and dessert table, for sheer variety, the buffet selection is impressive, the adult price is $18.95, juniors ages 7 to 11 are $9.50 and children ages 3 to 6 are $4.50. Steamed Maine lobster is available at an additional charge. A character breakfast is held here daily. Reservations recommended. Credit cards: A, MC, V.

Captain's Tavern $$ ★★

Disney's Caribbean Beach Resort.
American cuisine. Specialties: Braised lamb shank, rib-eye steak, grilled pork ribs, daily seafood catch.
Dinner: 5–10 p.m., entrées $12–$16.

In theory, the Captain's Tavern showcases Caribbean cuisine, but despite selections that promise Trinidad chicken and Aruba scallops, the actual region is woefully misrepresented at this uninspired diner overlooking the Caribbean Beach Resort's bustling food court. Best options are the braised St. Croix lamb shank and the grilled pork ribs, smoked and marinated in apricot and pepper. Meals are served on tin and wood platters to denote a pirate theme. Good as a fallback if you're staying at the Caribbean Beach, otherwise not worth the trip. Reservations recommended. Credit cards: A, MC, V.

Concourse Steakhouse $$$ ★★

Disney's Contemporary Resort.
American cuisine. Specialties: New York strip, T-bone, top sirloin and other steaks, breast of chicken, shrimp pasta, roasted salmon.
Breakfast: 7–11 a.m., entrées $6–$11.
Lunch: 11:45 a.m.–2:30 p.m., entrées $7–$19.
Dinner: 5:30–10 p.m., entrées $14–$22.

Uneventful steakhouse food tendered in a make-or-break location on the floor of the Contemporary Resort's atrium—kids and geeks (this one included) love it that the monorail sails overhead every few minutes; anyone looking for a more intimate dining experience will curse the rumbling trains and the high noise level from the nearby lobby. Otherwise, filet mignon, T-bone and prime rib are the passable lead items, each roasted over oak wood for a smoky flavor. A fresh seafood entree is offered daily, and Atlantic coast salmon is served over pasta. A Caesar salad is available as an entree or side portion. Breakfasts includes eggs, bacon and pancakes, with a "Nova" platter of salmon, red onions, capers, tomatoes and cream cheese for a toasted bagel. Reservations recommended. Credit cards: A, MC, V.

Flagler's $$$$ ★★★

Disney's Grand Floridian Resort.
Italian cuisine. Specialties: Pasta, grilled fish and lobster, veal scaloppine, beef tenderloin.
Dinner: 5:30–10 p.m., entrées $20–$45.

Named after Henry Flagler, the turn-of-the-century entrepreneur who built a railroad down Florida's east coast to develop Palm Beach and other resorts, this Grand Floridian diner is all pretense and show, with food that struggles to live up to highfalutin prices. The signature item among the short antipasti menu is the sautéed jumbo shrimp flamed in anisette, garlic, artichoke and cream. Pasta dishes are modeled after Old World classics—I liked the rich Penne Marco Polo, shrimp, artichoke hearts, mushrooms and broccoli folded into a Parmesan cream sauce. Veal scaloppine, chicken cacciatore, grilled swordfish served with portobello mushrooms, and a grilled beef tenderloin with green peppercorns are the main entrées, all of which are served with a dinner salad. The elegant setting sometimes includes singing waiters. In spite of (or because of?) the carping, Flagler's is tentatively scheduled for a makeover and name change that would incorporate a wine room and bar, an open kitchen and a bakery station. Reservations recommended. Credit cards: A, MC, V.

Grand Floridian Cafe $$ ★ ★ ★

Disney's Grand Floridian Resort.
American cuisine. Specialties: New York strip steak, filet mignon, seafood platter, blackened catfish, pasta.
Breakfast: 7–11:15 a.m., entrées $4–$14.
Lunch: 11:30 a.m.–5 p.m., entrées $8–$17.
Dinner: 5–11 p.m., entrées $8–$25.

One of the better Walt Disney World secrets is the Grand Floridian's sunny cafe, which offers a good selection of Florida-themed food and Florida-style ambience; it's also one of the only Disney eateries open past 10 p.m. The breakfast menu features a vast selection of egg dishes (I found the hash tasty, if salty); early risers on a tight schedule can usually get from the restaurant to The Magic Kingdom entrance in about 10 minutes. Lunch is better than any offered at The Magic Kingdom, and features entree salads, pastas, sandwiches and a can't-miss Floribbean burger topped with guacamole, bacon, jack cheese and jerk sauce. The dinner menu adds steaks, barbecued ribs and a nice blackened catfish. A easy way to sample the elegant Grand Floridian Resort on a modest budget. Features: late dining. Reservations recommended. Credit cards: A, MC, V.

INSIDER'S TIP

Invoking a Mary Poppins theme, the Grand Floridian Beach Resort serves tea in the Garden View Lounge against a backdrop of potted palms. The United Kingdom pavilion at Epcot also serves a proper British tea at 4 p.m. daily. Afternoon tea worthy of a stuffy Victorian novella can be obtained at the Peabody Orlando, in the atrium lobby that serves as the afternoon swimming locale for the five Peabody ducks.

Narcoossee's $$$$ ★ ★ ★ ★

Disney's Grand Floridian Beach Resort.
American cuisine. Specialties: Steaks and seafood.
Lunch: 11:30 a.m.–3 p.m., entrées $7–$20.
Dinner: 5–10 p.m., entrées $17–$35.

RESTAURANTS

This elegant, octagonal dining room is surrounded by a veranda and is perched idyl-lically along the shoreline facing The Magic Kingdom. While steak and seafood menus are a dime-a-dozen in Walt Disney World, this is where Mickey pulls out the stops. Appetizers include local favorites: hickory smoked baby back ribs, Key West conch fritters, and deep-fried gator tail nuggets. Although Narcoosee's is known for mouth-watering steaks, the thick pair of grilled lamb chops astride an eggplant crouton, the grouper swathed in mustard and rosemary hollandaise, and a swordfish steak marinated in hazelnut oil and garlic are all worthy contenders for your atten-tion. Though the pricey selection hardly breaks new ground, the grilling and prep-aration are given their full due—if that's what you're looking for, look no further. Though Narcoossee's is popular as is, Disney executives are discussing tinkering with the menu to incorporate a Pacific Rim seafood selection. Reservations recom-mended. Credit cards: A, MC, V.

'Ohana $$ ★ ★ ★

Disney's Polynesian Resort.
Polynesian cuisine. Specialties: Grilled beef, pork sausage, chicken, ribs and shrimp.
Dinner: 5–10 p.m., prix fixe $20.

Kids love this jovial all-you-can-eat spot that feature a Polynesian theme for its indoor luau-style feast. An 18-foot fire pit in the center of the room produces long skewers of sausage, grilled beef, chicken, turkey, ribs and, as a finishing touch, huge shrimp (save room); salads, stir-fried veggies, rice and noodles also are included. The bounty of food slides onto your table's lazy susan with alarming regularity—no one goes away hungry from here. Polynesian serenades, Hula Hoop contests and coconut races keep the pace rousing; make sure you're seated in the main dining room for maximum effect. Although not cheap, 'Ohana is an ideal splurge for fam-ilies. Adults are $19.75; juniors ages 12 to 16 are $13; children ages 3 to 11 are $8. A character breakfast is held here every morning. Reservations recommended. Credit cards: A, MC, V.

Olivia's Cafe $$ ★ ★ ★

Disney's Old Key West Resort.
American cuisine. Specialties: Seasonal fish specials, prime rib, chicken, meatloaf.
Breakfast: 7:30–11 a.m., entrées $6–$10.
Lunch: Noon–5 p.m., entrées $7–$10.
Dinner: 5–10 p.m., entrées $10–$19.

Visited almost exclusively by the families staying at the Disney time-share property, Key West-themed Olivia's is a pleasant respite from pace of theme park and resort dining; and its seasonal menu received an overhaul in late 1995 to good effect. Reg-ular items include angel hair pasta with vegetables, goat cheese and croutons, grilled pork chop with plum barbecue sauce and a side of andouille sausage, and Caesar sal-ads capped with chicken or shrimp. The juicy burgers are a modest $6.75 for lunch or dinner; in fact, most items are priced below other comparable Walt Disney World restaurants. Often overlooked and usually easy to get into, the restaurant offers character breakfast Sunday and Wednesday mornings. Reservations recommended. Credit cards: A, MC, V.

Seasons   **$$$**   ★ ★ ★

The Disney Institute.
Specialties: New Florida cuisine.
Breakfast: 7–11 a.m., entrées $5–$8.
Lunch: 11:30 a.m.–2:30 p.m., entrées $8–$13.
Dinner: 5:30–10 p.m., entrées $9–$15.

Originally conceived as an opportunity to explore a different cuisine nightly, Seasons soon evolved into a more traditional restaurant experience, exploring the best of Nuevo Florida. It delivers some of the best bang for your buck of the Disney resort eateries, with delicious "home grown" entrées like a pan-seared chicken breast in an avocado beurre blanc and topped by potato-tomato relish, a brisk Gulf Coast bouillabaisse served over Yukon gold potatoes, and a London broil marinated in St. Augustine peppers. The four individual dining rooms are airy, and themed to the four seasons, but otherwise the focus is what's on your plate. It's possible to walk to Seasons via a ten-minute path from the Village Marketplace. Reservations recommended. Credit cards: A, MC, V.

Spoodles   **$$**   ★ ★ ★ ★

Disney's Boardwalk Resort.
Mediterranean cuisine.
Breakfast: 7–11 a.m., entrées $5–$10.
Lunch: Noon–2 p.m., entrées $7–$13.
Dinner: 5–10 p.m., entrées $10–$22.

The latest inspiration bubbling forth from Disney's food department is the self-titled "cuisine of the sun"—flavors and styles associated with the Mediterranean, including coastal French, Spanish, Italian and Greek influences. The vegetarian-friendly menu features a selection of 13 tapas, smaller portions perfect for sampling—a couple could share a half-dozen choices, priced from $4 to 6, for a dynamic light meal. Spicy shrimp, portobello mushrooms in truffle oil and octopus are popular favorites. Sicilian pizzas toast in the oak-burning oven, and the entrées include rib eyes, lamb chops and braised veal chops, all cooked in spices imported from Provence, Morocco and Tunisia. The wine list showcases Mediterranean vintages, and the show kitchen sparkles. Mornings are saluted with cappuccinos, frittatas and breakfast pizzas. All signs point to Spoodles as yet another fresh impulse. Reservations recommended. Credit cards: A, MC, V.

<table>
<tr><td colspan="2" align="center">**DISNEY RESTAURANTS WITH
EXCELLENT WINE LISTS**</td></tr>
<tr><td>*Ariel's*</td><td>*Disney's Beach Club Resort*</td></tr>
<tr><td>*Artist's Point*</td><td>*Disney's Wilderness Lodge*</td></tr>
<tr><td>*California Grill*</td><td>*Disney's Contemporary Resort*</td></tr>
<tr><td>*Victoria and Albert's*</td><td>*Disney's Grand Floridian Beach Resort*</td></tr>
<tr><td>*Yachtsman Steakhouse*</td><td>*Disney's Yacht Club Resort*</td></tr>
</table>

RESTAURANTS

Victoria & Albert's   **$$$**   ★ ★ ★ ★ ★

Disney's Grand Floridian Beach Resort, ☎ *(407) 939-7707.*
Specialties: Daily chef specials include game, poultry, fish and beef.
Dinner: Two seatings nightly, prix fixe $80.

Though easily the most expensive restaurant in the Orlando area, Victoria &
Albert's rewards its guests with unparalleled service in an elegant formal dining
room tucked away in Disney's Grand Floridian. Scott Hunnel, the executive chef,
compiles a new gourmet menu nightly, personalized and sealed in gold wax, but
he'll work to accommodate your input if you call a few days prior to your seating.
You are waited on by "Victoria," a maid, and "Albert," a butler, who pamper you
relentlessly through seven courses of indulgent Continental cuisine served on Royal
Doulton china with Sambonet silver and Schott-Zweisel crystal, as a harpist plucks
gently in the background. A typical night begins with a choice of appetizers—cof-
fee-spiced bobwhite quail on angel hair pasta in a vanilla-scented cream, or perhaps
vermouth-poached scallops in a delicate rice-noodle basket. A lobster consommé
with chive crepes may follow, and the entree list might include a Dungeness crab
stuffed with shrimp on a ginger-cilantro beurre blanc, or a rack of lamb topped with
gourmandise cheese. A plate of royal stilton is accompanied by a burgundy poached
pear, and then dessert—a pumpkin rum souffle or bananas Foster? The Royal Wine
Pairing, featuring a selection designed to enhance each course, is available for $30
and well worth considering, though the restaurant's standard wine list is top-
drawer, with an array of fine aperitifs and cordials to finish your meal (a snifter of
Louis XIII cognac runs $100). The restaurant has two seatings nightly: one at 6
p.m., and a second at 9 p.m. (during July–August, there is usually just one seating
at 7 p.m.). Victoria & Albert's kitchen is open to guests most nights via the popular
chef's table; guests may interact with Hunnel and ask questions during the meal
preparation. The chef's table seats six, and is priced $100 per person (or $130 with
the Royal Wine Pairing). Victoria & Albert's is an expensive, one-of-a-kind experi-
ence—a place for a very special birthday or anniversary. Features: rated wine cellar.
Jacket requested. Reservations required. Credit cards: A, MC, V.

Whispering Canyon Cafe   **$$**   ★ ★ ★

Disney's Wilderness Lodge.
American cuisine. Specialties: Rotisserie chicken, pork spareribs, braised lamb shank, bar-
becue beef brisket and veal ribs.
Breakfast: 7:30–11 a.m., entrées $9.
Lunch: 11:30 a.m.–3 p.m., prix fixe $11.
Dinner: 5–10 p.m., prix fixe $17–$19.

This rustic, frontier-style room overlooks the majestic Wilderness Lodge lobby, providing a nightly all-you-can-eat stampede. Family dining is the specialty, with lazy
susans loaded with your choice of apple-rosemary rotisserie chicken, maple-garlic
pork spareribs, grilled sausage, braised lamb shank, and smoked barbecue beef brisket or veal ribs (pick any two). Side dishes include a green salad, steamed vegetables,
corn on the cob and herbed potatoes. Culinary arts may not be pushed forward
here, but the food is dependable, the service quite friendly, and the entire experience perfect for grub-starved families. The fixed-price dinner is $16.50 for adults

RESTAURANTS

(or $18.50 to sample all of the entrées) and $6.50 for children ages 3–11; a catch of the day is also available, and a stir-fry veggie skillet ($11.95) is offered for vegetarians. Reservations recommended. Credit cards: A, MC, V.

Yacht Club Galley $$ ★ ★ ★

Disney's Yacht Club Resort.
American cuisine. Specialties: Prime rib, pot roast, pastas (dinner); fish and chips, hot and cold sandwiches (lunch).
Lunch: 11:30 a.m.–3 p.m., entrées $8–$12.
Dinner: 5–10 p.m., entrées $9–$19.
The Yacht Club Galley successfully intermingles the Yacht and Beach Club's New England theme with dishes featuring both Cajun and south-of-the-border accents. Lunch choices encompass salads, hot and cold sandwiches, fish and chips and a pair of pasta dishes. At dinner, the seafood sampler includes shrimp, scallops and a crab cake, or you can try one of several beef dishes—T-bone, prime rib and pot roast are the chief preparations; a sprightly pasta primavera is also available. The environment is defined by brass, wood and nautical accouterments; one of the better resort diners. Reservations recommended. Credit cards: A, MC, V.

Yachtsman Steakhouse $$$ ★ ★ ★ ★

Disney's Yacht Club Resort.
American cuisine. Specialties: Filet mignon, prime rib, porterhouse and strip steaks, Chateaubriand, lamb chops.
Dinner: 5:30–10 p.m., entrées $17–$27.
The menu is simple and to the point: five different cuts of beef, hand-selected and impeccably prepared over hardwood fires. The 20-ounce porterhouse is a monster, and the bone-in Kansas City strip steak is not for the timid; lighter eaters will be happy with the filet mignon, available in a yachtsman or yachtress size—ugh. The slow-roasted prime rib is satisfying, while the chateaubriand for two is an elegant and romantic feast complemented with both a bearnaise and bordelaise sauce. The "smashed" potatoes (with cheese and garlic) are a signature item, but a tall order since the meat comes with a baked potato; other sides are similarly robust. If beef isn't your style, lamb chops, breast of chicken and a daily fish special are also available, but this is truly a carnivore's paradise. It all comes with a hefty price tag, but when Orlandoans want their steak prepared by Mickey, this is where they come, so reserve early. Good beer selection, too. Reservations recommended. Credit cards: A, MC, V.

Lake Buena Vista, Pleasure Island and Crossroads Area

This area covers three very different varieties of eating establishments. Since all serve the same basic clientele (mostly tourists, with a few locals thrown in for good measure), and since they are located in the same area near the eastern edge of Walt Disney World, these restaurants are best grouped together.

The restaurants offered by the "Official Hotels of Walt Disney World" are a far-ranging bunch: from the very classy, expensive **Arthur's 27** on top of the Buena Vista Palace, to the numerous and assorted cafes usually located in the basements of the hotels. Then there's the Disney Village Marketplace and Pleasure Island; this area is a vibrant and always-busy hub during the evening, and offers several theme-dining experiences, notably **Planet Hollywood** and the newly opened **Rainforest Cafe**. Just outside the entrance to Disney Village is Crossroads Mall, with everything from **Burger King** and other fast-food pit stops, to **Pebbles**, a terrific choice for reasonably priced upscale cuisine.

The area truly has something to fit every taste bud, and any budget.

AUTHOR'S OBSERVATION

Dinner shows are a popular Orlando phenomenon. The accent is on entertainment, not food, so we've listed them under "Dinner Theaters" in "Universal, Sea World and Other Attractions." Disney also offers two dinner shows: the long-running Hoop Dee Doo Revue and Polynesian Luau; both are covered in that same chapter.

INSIDER'S TIP

Although discounts for the Disney restaurants are rare, coupons for other dining locations are abundant. If you are eating at any non-Disney facility, leaf through the guides and coupon books that litter your hotel's foyer. Call the restaurant directly to ask what deals it offers; only a few don't provide some kind of incentive. Admittedly, not all the restaurants offering discounts provide a first-rate dining experience, but they will usually translate to a better deal than most of the Disney eateries.

Arthur's 27   **$$$$**   ★ ★ ★ ★ ★

1900 Buena Vista Drive, Lake Buena Vista, 32830, just off I-4 at Exit 27, ☎ *(407) 827-3450. Associated hotel: Buena Vista Palace.*
American cuisine.
Dinner: 6–10 p.m., entrées $24–$30.

Haute cuisine at the 27th-floor apex of the Buena Vista Palace. The panorama is unbeatable, the alcove-seating intimate, but the food (though top-dollar) follows in lock-step. Appetizers run the gamut from crabcakes topped by frizzled leeks and basil oil to a truffle ravioli filled with veal and wild mushrooms; these and other starters average $5–$12. The menu changes every month or two to reflect seasonal availabilities and chef K. David Clawson's whims, but three regular highlights include the blackened tuna loin with a mango scotch bonnet salsa, the herb mustard-encrusted rack of lamb, and the filet of beef tenderloin with grilled portobello, shallot jelly and salsify. A better deal are the three prix-fixe meals: four courses are $49, five $55, or the six-course version, $60; a low-fat/low-cholesterol spa cuisine menu is also available. Desserts include a magical lemon tart enclosed in shortbread, and a triple-threat chocolate combo of ice cream, cake and mousse. A strong wine list will satisfy true devotees. One of the best views in the area, but note that only a few tables face the Disney fireworks and these are hot commodities. One of the region's very best, and one that draws heavily from outside the park; reservations not required, but a good idea on weekends. Features: rated wine cellar. Jacket requested. Reservations recommended. Credit cards: A, DC, D, MC, V.

Fireworks Factory $$$ ★★★

1630 Buena Vista Drive (Pleasure Island), Lake Buena Vista, 32830, next to the Disney Village Marketplace, ☎ *(407) 934-8989.*
American cuisine. Specialties: Barbecued and smoked items, steaks, ribs and seafood.
Lunch: 11:30 a.m.–4 p.m., entrées $7–$14.
Dinner: 4 p.m.–2 a.m., entrées $14–$25.
A dynamite (pun intended) theme—a fireworks factory after a match was mislaid—is the scene of this noisy, 400-seat Pleasure Island barbecue joint. The decor has to be seen to be believed: blown-out red brick walls, crates of TNT, vintage fireworks signage and exposed red pipes. The cayenne-heavy menu includes a tasty rock shrimp quesadilla appetizer (roasted green chiles, pepperjack and cheddar cheese, topped with cilantro lime cream), a creamy smoked chicken fettucine, and popular applewood-smoked baby back ribs. Steaks, mesquite smoked chicken and grilled pork chops fill out the selection. Regular complaints focus on the wait (long) and service (treadmill), but this busy spot is otherwise popular for its reliably pungent food well into the wee hours. Part of the Levy Restaurant chain. Features: late dining. Reservations recommended. Credit cards: A, MC, V.

Fulton's Crab House $$$

1670 Buena Vista Drive (Pleasure Island), Lake Buena Vista, 32830, next to Disney Village Marketplace, ☎ *(407) 934-2628.*
Seafood cuisine. Specialties: Daily fish specials.
Lunch: 11:30 a.m.–4 p.m., entrées $9–$11.
Dinner: 5 p.m.–midnight, entrées $15–$35.
The elegant Empress Lilly, a turn-of-the-century riverboat replica, underwent a complete interior redesign in 1996 and its 485-seat restaurant is now operated by Levy Restaurants of Chicago. Fresh fish is flown in daily from Hawaii and elsewhere for the Fulton menu; selections might include Great Lakes walleye pike, Copper River king salmon, Alaskan soft prawns and, of course, crabs—soft shell, dungeness, and Florida stone crabs, with the Alaskan red king crab claws a menu highlight. A variety of sauces and cooking methods are available for these and other seafood items. A limited lunch menu is served in the lounge, though an expanded policy is being explored. A character breakfast is served daily. Given the location, appeal and success of both the Portobello Yacht Club and Fireworks Factory, Levy's other Disney operations, Fulton's should be a sure-fire hit. Features: late dining. Reservations recommended. Credit cards: A, MC, V.

Hemingways $$$ ★★★★

1 Grand Cypress Boulevard, Lake Buena Vista, 32836, just off State Route 535; from I-4 use Exit 27, ☎ *(407) 239-3854. Associated hotel: Hyatt Regency Grand Cypress.*

American cuisine. Specialties: Steaks, poultry and seafood with Key West accents.
Lunch: 11:30 a.m.–2:30 p.m., entrées $9–$17.
Dinner: 6–10:15 p.m., entrées $20–$28.

Named after Ernest Hemingways, this exotic Grand Cypress restaurant is perched atop rocks, away from the main resort structure, and ringed by waterfalls and lush greenery overlooking the grotto-lined pool. The dining rooms are topped by purring ceiling fans, and furnishings use wicker and floral patterns. Entree favorites include the ever-popular beer-battered coconut shrimp, Maryland-style crab cakes spiked with Cajun tartar sauce, and a robust paella overflowing with fruits of the sea. In keeping with the theme, a good rum selection is proffered, along with Papa Dobles, the drink Hemingway made famous at the Floridita in Havana. A splurge, but what a beautiful and relaxed setting in which to set your wallet free. Open for lunch Tue.–Sat. only. Reservations recommended. Credit cards: A, DC, D, MC, V.

Juan and Only's Bar and Jail   SS   ★★

1500 Epcot Resorts Boulevard, Lake Buena Vista, 32830, just off Buena Vista Drive, between Epcot and the Disney-MGM Studios, ☎ (407) 934-4889. Associated hotel: Walt Disney World Dolphin.
Mexican cuisine. Specialties: Fajitas, pork adobado, carne asada, margaritas.
Dinner: 6–11 p.m., entrées $13–$20.

A south-of-the-border restaurant with an excessive jail setting adorned by pinatas and Mexican hats, along with a cumbersome back story to explain Juan and Only's "history." The margaritas aren't bad, and the food is appropriately spicy, but it's also grease-laden and tired. The jail theme makes some visitors feel imprisoned by the unambitious menu. A few of the corner tables face the Disney-MGM Studios' fireworks show; the adjoining bar can be lively. Reservations recommended. Credit cards: DC, D, MC, V.

Jungle Jim's   S   ★★

12501 State Road 535, Lake Buena Vista, in Crossroads Mall, next to I-4 at Exit 27, ☎ (407) 827-1257.
American cuisine. Specialties: Burgers, grilled chicken sandwiches, exotic drinks.
Lunch: 11 a.m.–11 p.m., entrées $6–$16.
Dinner: 11 a.m.–11 p.m., entrées $6–$16.

Burgers, from conventional to outrageous, are the focus at Jungle Jim's. Try the Henhouse: a fried egg is mounted on a 1/3-pound hunk of ground beef, then smothered with sautéed mushrooms, cheddar cheese and bacon. The menu also features a selection of grilled chicken sandwiches (and sometimes equally wacky—the chicken, bacon, cheddar and peanut better version is reported to be tasty, though I wimped out). Huge salads and a few steak, seafood and pasta dishes round out the "official" dinner menu, but locals say, stick with the burgers and sandwiches. Warning: the frou-frou libation marketing is laid on thick—happy hour is 4–7 p.m.; the bar is open until 2 a.m. nightly with food service available after the tables shut down. Jungle Jim's also has locations at the Church Street Market, and at 8255 International Drive. Sit-down meal service is offered until midnight Fri. and Sat., until 1 a.m. Sun. Features: late dining. Reservations not accepted. Credit cards: A, DC, D, MC, V.

Outback Restaurant $$$ ★★★

1900 Buena Vista Drive, Lake Buena Vista, 32830, across the street from the Disney Village Marketplace, ☎ (407) 827-3430. Associated hotel: Buena Vista Palace.
Seafood cuisine. Specialties: Lobster, steak and seafood.
Dinner: 5:30–11 p.m., entrées $13–$33.

This Australian-themed steakhouse features Aboriginal designs, a multi-level waterfall and weathered woodwork for a rustic-chic atmosphere popular with conventioneers looking for a big-ticket splurge. Highlights include grilled steaks, pork chops, jumbo shrimp, a rack of lamb or roasted prime rib au jus; a 30-ounce Dundee cut of grilled prime rib can be shared for $29.95. Fried gator tail is available as an appetizer, served with spicy remoulade sauce, or the adventurous can try the kangaroo; a short list of pastas is tendered for saner appetites. The Maine lobster is priced a whopping $55 for a three-to-four pounder (yes, you can share it); or for $65 you can buy a five-to-six pound lobster and receive a permanent wall plaque in the restaurant, but only if you finish it solo. Not affiliated with the national chain of Outback Steakhouses. Reservations recommended. Credit cards: A, DC, D, MC, V.

Palio $$$ ★★★

1200 Epcot Resorts Boulevard, Lake Buena Vista, 32830, just off Buena Vista Drive, between Epcot and the Disney-MGM Studios, ☎ (407) 934-1610. Associated hotel: Walt Disney World Swan.
Italian cuisine. Specialties: Grilled items.
Dinner: 6–11 p.m., entrées $12–$33.

Upscale and colorfully draped in banners and flags, bustling Palio features a wood-fired brick oven to embrace the culinary length and breadth of Italy. The menu begins with an extensive selection of appetizers, including carpaccio with Parmesan cheese, sautéed calamari, and grilled portobello mushrooms; the antipasto trolley is a good value. The thin-crust pizzas are unspectacular, but offer the best chance for a moderately priced meal. Entrees include traditional favorites, and are generally quite good; try the veal scaloppine in marsala served with gnocchi, the osso buco in white wine and vegetables, or the red snapper sautéed with mushrooms, artichoke hearts, olives and roasted peppers. Diners are welcomed by a wonderful bowl of garlic breads and a glass of chianti—a nice touch, but the lengthy wine list offers better. In short, Palio aims high with simple food and is priced to match, delivering solid country trattoria cooking in a congenial resort setting. Reservations recommended. Credit cards: A, DC, D, MC, V.

Pebbles $$ ★★★

12551 State Route 535, Lake Buena Vista, 32819, in Crossroads Mall, next to I-4 at Exit 27, ☎ (407) 827-1111.
American cuisine. Specialties: Contemporary American, grilled meats, pastas, burgers and salads.
Lunch: 11 a.m.–11 p.m., entrées $6–$20.
Dinner: 11 a.m.–11 p.m., entrées $6–$20.

Immensely popular, Pebbles blends California cuisine with simple surroundings and no-nonsense service to deliver better value than virtually any eatery inside The Magic Kingdom across the street—nowhere else in the area does gourmet mingle so respectably with casual. The dozen or so pastas are uniformly strong; try the sea scallops over lemon pesto angel hair, or the wild mushroom penne topped by smoked duck. Among the entrées, the basil crusted lamb is so popular the kitchen boosted it last year from a half-rack to a full. Leave room for the signature gold-brick sundae—ice cream with a chocolate pecan shell, carmelized sugar and strawberries. No reservations, but parties of six or fewer can put their name on the priority seating list by calling just before they leave for dinner. Without a doubt, the favorite overall restaurant of Orlandoans; also locations in downtown Orlando, Winter Park and Longwood. Reservations not accepted. Credit cards: A, DC, D, MC, V.

Planet Hollywood   **$$**   ★ ★

1506 Buena Vista Drive (Pleasure Island), Lake Buena Vista, 32830, next to the Disney Village Marketplace, ☎ (407) 827-7827.
American cuisine. Specialties: Grilled meats, burgers, pizza, sandwiches and salads.
Lunch: 11 a.m.–1 a.m., entrées $8–$19.
Dinner: 11 a.m.–1 a.m., entrées $8–$19.

You're unlikely to dine with the stars, who show up only long enough to snap the requisite photos proving they were there. Even the famous co-owners—Bruce, Arnold, Demi and Sylvester—don't exactly keep tabs on the kitchen. But you're still in for a Hollywood-style treat at the Orlando branch of this renowned dining spot situated in a three-story globe next to Pleasure Island with a flying saucer colliding into the front door. Inside, brand-name movie memorabilia clutters the halls and walls and dangles from the domed ceiling. The interior is noisy and overflowing with bodies and video monitors endlessly unspool previews of upcoming films. Food quality, in relation to the prices, is not unreasonable, though it obviously plays second banana to the decor. The something-to-please-everyone menu includes burgers, fajitas, pizzas, pastas (the Thai shrimp linguini was fine), sandwiches and "grilled platters" for bigger appetites; salads are large, if pedestrian. The Cap'n Crunch-coated fried chicken has to be tasted to be believed. There is always a line, which can reach epic lengths in the evening and on weekends, so try late afternoon. The merchandise store will sell you just about anything with the restaurant's logo on it. Incidentally, Orlando is the home to Planet Hollywood's corporate offices. Features: late dining. Reservations not accepted. Credit cards: A, DC, D, MC, V.

Portobello Yacht Club   **$$$**   ★ ★ ★

1650 Buena Vista Drive (Pleasure Island), Lake Buena Vista, 32830, next to the Disney Village Marketplace, ☎ (407) 934-8888.
Italian cuisine. Specialties: Nouveau pizza, pasta, grilled meats.
Lunch: 11:30 a.m.–4 p.m., entrées $5–$10.
Dinner: 4 p.m.–midnight, entrées $13–$24.

Resoundingly popular with locals—always a good sign in a theme park—the Portobello Yacht Club has a homey, Key West nautical ambiance and a Northern Italian cooking-style and surprisingly, the setting works splendidly. The salad of roasted portobello mushrooms, field greens and shaved Parmesan is a great start, while the bruschetta with prosciutto, gorgonzola and cabernet onions is imaginative. The pizzas crusts are cracker-thin and crisp, which doesn't work for all tastes and, ranging $7–$9, they are more an appetizer concept than a meal. The pasta list is topped by a house specialty—spaghettini brimming with Alaskan crab, scallops, clams, shrimp and mussels in a sauce of tomatoes, garlic, olive oil, wine and herbs. Entrees include grilled steaks, chicken and daily seafood specials, as well as a succulent skewer of shrimp toppled onto a plate of pasta and vegetables in roasted garlic cream. Portobello is expensive, but the line of fans is ever-present. The current first-come, first-serve seating policy is under discussion. Operated by Chicago's Levy Brothers family. Features: late dining. Reservations not accepted. Credit cards: A, MC, V.

Rainforest Cafe $$

1800 East Buena Vista Drive; Disney Village Marketplace, Lake Buena Vista, 32830, Located next to Pleasure Island, ☎ *(407) 827-8500.*
American cuisine. Specialties: Pastas, salads, signature sandwiches and desserts.
Lunch: 10:30 a.m.–4 p.m., entrées $8–$18.
Dinner: 4–11 p.m., entrées $8–$18.

Part of a quickly expanding Minneapolis-based chain, the 620-seat Rainforest Cafe turns environmental awareness into "eatertainment" (their term, not mine). Housed under a 60-foot-high erupting volcano—most vivid at night—the jungle-themed environment inside features waterfalls, thunder, lightning and simulated rain showers. Interspersed throughout the 30,000-square-foot building are unconvincing animated mechanical props: a talking tree, a crocodile, mammoth butterflies and a group of apes that will keep kids enthralled. The food is similarly family-friendly, Rasta Pasta is bowties with grilled chicken and spinach in a garlic cream sauce; the Rumble in the Jungle pita pocket sandwich engulfs a Caesar salad tossed with turkey and cranberry relish; Jamaica Me Crazy is hefty, spiced pork chops with red beans and rice. Though the restaurant takes pride in using fresh or organic veggies and beef that is not produced on deforested land, the food is churned out of the kitchen much the same as in other mass-production eateries. The omnipotent sound effects—thunder, animal noises, rainfall and music—successfully stifle any hope of thoughtful conversation…which is fine for children, many of whom will think they've entered Tiki Room heaven. Otherwise, most adults will be content to sample the experience at the restaurant's Magic Mushroom Juice and Coffee Bar, where tropical libations are served under a vast mushroom cap to those who mount the humorous bar stools shaped like animal legs. Keep a little cash handy for the trip through the trademark retail area on the way out. Reservations not accepted. Credit cards: A, DC, D, MC, V.

Sum Chow's $$$$ ★★★★

1500 Epcot Resorts Boulevard, Lake Buena Vista, 32830, just off Buena Vista Drive, between Epcot and Disney-MGM Studios, ☎ *(407) 934-4000. Associated hotel: Walt Disney World Dolphin.*
Chinese cuisine. Specialties: Upscale Pacific Rim, seafood, chicken, pork.
Dinner: 6–10 p.m., entrées $25–$34.

An elegant, tastefully colorful Michael Graves-designed interior greets diners, embellished by Oriental screens, black lacquer tables and flower arrangements. A few say the way-'90s cuisine featured here has peaked, but most sing its praises, particularly the chef's table where diners are dazzled by Christopher Salansky's kitchen prowess. The rest of us can sit back and enjoy Poem of the Sea—tender chunks of Maine lobster in a herb garlic sauce over sweet peppers and black truffles—or the sesame-crusted, roasted spring lamb Canton. A 12-piece sushi sampler goes for $27. Sum Chow's is tucked away in the Dolphin basement and is often overlooked, partly because it closes for private functions at the drop of a hat, but well worth the investment for serious "foodies." Reservations recommended. Credit cards: A, DC, D, MC, V.

International Drive and Around Orlando

Sheer variety is the theme for the busy International Drive corridor. Several of the big hotels have some of Orlando's best: **Dux** at the Peabody Orlando and **Atlantis** at the Stouffer Renaissance both draw a sizable number of visitors from Orlando. Then there are the stand-alone facilities, most of which are heavy on the theme, such as the **Hard Rock Cafe**. But even along this thoroughfare you'll find somewhat more intimate locations, and a few special places where food and decor live up to and complement each other, including **Cafe Tu Tu Tango** and **Ming Court**. For a trip off the beaten path, head to the lovely, untouristed **Chatham's Place** or **Oak Ridge Cafe**.

Visitors staying along U.S. 192 will have a tougher time finding quality food. The delightful, perhaps under-appreciated **Basil's** along 192 went belly-up in 1996, but the nearby **Hooters** is thriving.

AUTHOR'S OBSERVATION

If food is an important part of your trip, or if you will be staying in the region over an extended period of time, obtain the Zagat Survey of central Florida/Gulf Coast restaurants. The book is edited by local foodies and uses consumer ratings (and their pithy comments) to review more than 300 area eateries in the Orlando area alone.

INSIDER'S TIP

*Looking for a late-night caffeine jolt? The coffee craze taking over most of America hasn't left Orlando behind. The local favorite is **Barnie's Coffee and Tea Co.**, with several locations around the city. **Yab Yum** and **Chapter's**, both downtown, are the place for young intellectuals and poets.*

Cafe Tu Tu Tango   **$$**   ★★★

8625 International Drive, Orlando, 32821, half-mile south of Sand Lake Boulevard,
☎ *(407) 248-2222.*
American cuisine. Specialties: Soups, frittatas, salads, thin-crust pizzas, kebabs.
Lunch: 11:30 a.m.–3 p.m., entrées $3–$8.
Dinner: 3–11 p.m., entrées $3–$8.
Orlando's freshest theme-dining concept is this tribute to starving artists located in the heart of International Drive. The building is slick on the outside, but offers a polished Bohemian artist's loft inside, where three painters work nightly (you can

talk to them and purchase their artwork). In addition, tarot card readers ply their trade, and belly dancers swivel hips. Further establishing its chic credentials, the menu features only tapas—appetizers designed to be shared and ordered in quantity. Highlights include Cajun chicken egg rolls, a Barcelona stir fry (shrimp, calamari, chicken, andouille sausage mushrooms and peppers), skewers of sautéed mushrooms, and a creamed spinach and wild mushroom pizza. Light eaters can have a varied meal on a budget, though the hungry can rack up a substantial bill with ease (and watch those sangrias!). The lunch menu adds sandwiches to the mix—try the "Tango" melt chili tuna or the Cuban mojo steak. While Cafe Tu Tu Range verges on pretension, it's all done in good humor and the food is frequently quite tasty. At an average price of $6 each, and about two or three tapas necessary for an average meal (plus soup and/or salad, expect to spend about $15 per person, not including drinks. Open until 1 a.m. Fri.–Sat. Reservations recommended. Credit cards: A, DC, D, MC, V.

Chatham's Place   **$$$**   ★ ★ ★ ★

7575 Dr. Phillips Boulevard, Suite 150 South, Orlando, 32819, just west of I-4 (Exit 29) near Universal Studios, ☎ (407) 345-2992.
American cuisine. Specialties: Rack of lamb, Florida black grouper.
Lunch: Noon–1:30 p.m., entrées $7–$13.
Dinner: 6–9 p.m., entrées $17–$27.
Lodged in a nondescript office complex just south of Universal, and with a simple interior decor, Chatham's Place doesn't strike one as a place for great food. But Orlando's "foodies" know this family-owned operation for its short, but sweet menu that tackles New American cuisine with subtlety and grace. The mouth-watering signature item and hands-down favorite is the sautéed Florida black grouper, topped with pecans and scallions. It deserves the praise, but the rack of lamb and baked jumbo shrimp are every bit as tantalizing. The desserts are dangerously good. Definitely worth looking up for a relaxed and informal meal. Lunch Mon.–Fri. only; open until 10 p.m. Fri.–Sat. Features: wine and beer only. Reservations recommended. Credit cards: A, DC, D, MC, V.

Dux   **$$$**   ★ ★ ★ ★ ★

9801 International Drive, International Drive, 32819, Exit 29 off I-4; just north of the Beeline, ☎ (407) 352-4000. Associated hotel: Peabody Orlando.
Specialties: Wild game and seafood.
Dinner: 6–10 p.m., entrées $23–$32. Closed: Sun.
The name refers to the one item that is never found on the menu of this formal, fine-dining establishment at the Peabody Orlando, home to the five famous Peabody ducks. The globally inspired food fuses French, Asian and Southwest elements for a dynamic (and seasonal) selection of epicurean delights. The appetizer that draws the most praise is the smoked lump crabcakes, while delightful entrées include the seared yellowfin tuna and roast prime rib of veal embellished with sage, lemon and black olives. The chandelier-lighted dining room is refined and formal, with textured walls, florid mirrors and duck-themed artwork leading down to candlelit tables. In addition to AAA Four Diamond and Mobil Four-Star designations, *Orlando Magazine* readers selected Dux as their favorite hotel restaurant of 1996.

Expensive, but an excellent choice for that special meal. Open until 11 p.m. Fri.–
Sat. Features: rated wine cellar. Jacket requested. Credit cards: A, DC, D, MC, V.

Hard Rock Cafe   **$$**   ★ ★

5800 Kirkman Road, Orlando, 32819, next to Universal Studios main entrance,
☎ *(407) 351-7625.*
American cuisine. Specialties: Burgers and barbecue.
Lunch: 11 a.m.–2 a.m., entrées $7–$20.
Dinner: 11 a.m.–2 a.m., entrées $7–$20.
From London to Tijuana, diners worldwide have learned to look to the Hard Rock
Cafe for food served in an ear-ringing atmosphere. Entrée salads, oversized sand-
wiches and burgers lead the menu choices, but fajitas, barbecued ribs and a strip
steak are also available. As for the busy and always-loud atmosphere, the collection
of guitars, jackets, gold records and other recording artifacts is worth a look-see for
music fans, but otherwise, if you have only one overdone theme dining experience
in you, Planet Hollywood provides the better slice of cultural, er... enrichment. On
the other hand, at Hard Rock, you might get to join in a bicep-flashing rendition of
"Y.M.C.A." Features: late dining. Reservations not accepted. Credit cards: A, MC, V.

Lombard's Landing   **$$**   ★ ★ ★

Universal Studios (near Earthquake), Orlando, 32819, in Universal Studios (theme park
admission required), ☎ *(407) 354-6400.*
Seafood cuisine. Specialties: Daily fish specials, sandwiches, pastas.
Lunch: 11 a.m.–park closing, entrées $9–$19.
Dinner: 11 a.m.–park closing, entrées $9–$19.
The best of several restaurants on the Universal property, Lombard's Landing is a
Fisherman's Wharf-themed fish-house overlooking the park's central lagoon. A sea-
worthy selection of daily fish specials can be prepared grilled, blackened or baked,
and the menu also features a nice collection of San Francisco-style starters such as
sautéed mussels, shrimp Louie, steamed littleneck clams and spring rolls. Steaks and
sandwiches are also offered, and several pasta dishes are memorable; I enjoyed the
cioppino, though the ravioli with pesto, sun-dried tomatoes and pine nuts was hard
to resist. Lombard's could use a better beer and wine selection to complement the
food, but otherwise it's an above-average theme park diner. Reservations recommended. Credit cards: D, MC, V.

Ming Court   **$$$**   ★ ★ ★

9188 International Drive, Orlando, 32819, three-quarters a mile south of Sand Lake
Boulevard, near Convention Center, ☎ *(407) 351-9988.*
Chinese cuisine. Specialties: Gourmet Chinese.
Lunch: 11 a.m.–2:30 p.m., entrées $5–$8.
Dinner: 4:30 p.m.–midnight, entrées $10–$25.
An undulating white wall wraps around the garden of this elegant gourmet Chinese
restaurant, which draws a mix of tourists, conventioneers and locals. The lengthy
dinner menu includes spicy kung pao chicken, grilled Szechwan-style filet mignon,
punchy mu shu pork, and fish plucked live from the kitchen's bubbling tanks; a dim
sum menu may also be requested. Or come for lunch, when the selection of beauti-
fully prepared dim sum appetizers are rolled out in carts and the pace is more
relaxed. At any hour, the Western-style dessert menu is luxuriant. Ming Court's

slap-dash evening service, particularly at these prices, is a drawback; otherwise, this is the place for a refined Chinese culinary experience. Features: late dining. Reservations recommended. Credit cards: A, DC, D, MC, V.

Numero Uno $$ ★★★
2499 South Orange Avenue, Orlando, 32806, one quarter mile south of Kaley Avenue (Exit 35 from I-4), ☎ *(407) 841-3840.*
Italian cuisine. Specialties: Paella, roasted meats.
Lunch: 11 a.m.–3 p.m., entrées $4–$6.
Dinner: 5–9:30 p.m., entrées $8–$20. Closed: Sun.
Although better Cuban food might be had closer to Miami, no-frills Numero Uno is perhaps Orlando's best spot for roast pork smothered in onions and garlic sauce. Steak, chicken and fish are also available, and all come with a salad and your choice of fried plantain or yucca. The house specialty, paella valenciana, is the traditional Spanish dish of seafood and chicken, oven-cooked in saffron rice ($35 for two); allow an hour and 15 minutes' preparation time. The decor and ambience is spare, but that keeps the prices down and the focus on the food, as it should be. Reservations are taken only for parties of five or more, or for parties planning to order the paella. Located just outside downtown. Lunch is Mon.–Fri. only; open for dinner until 10 p.m. on Fri. Features: wine and beer only. Reservations not accepted. Credit cards: A, D, MC, V.

Oak Ridge Cafe $ ★★★
2340 West Oak Ridge Road, 32809, from I-4, take John Young, three miles south to Oak Ridge, right on Texas to 3rd driveway, ☎ *(407) 240-2341.*
American cuisine.
Lunch: 11 a.m.–3 p.m., entrées $3–$6.
Dinner: 3–10 p.m., entrées $8–$11. Closed: Sun.

Possibly Orlando's best-kept secret, the Oak Ridge Cafe is where Victoria and Albert's chef goes to eat off-duty. Other equally-savvy Orlandoans come for the fried mushroom appetizer, a poached salmon beurre blanc, or the pork and shrimp pasta—all served at unbeatable prices by William Fulgoni, the creative chef/owner. This off-the-beaten track find, in a weathered strip mall setting, may be Orlando's tastiest bargain. Open until 11 p.m. Fri.–Sat. Reservations recommended. Credit cards: A, DC, D, MC, V.

Passage to India $$ ★★★
5532 International Drive, Orlando, 32819, one quarter mile north of Kirkman Road, ☎ *(407) 351-3456.*
Indian cuisine. Specialties: Curries, Tandoor specialties.
Lunch: 11:30 a.m.–3 p.m., entrées $7–$10.
Dinner: 3 p.m.–midnight, entrées $9–$20.
Few Orlando visitors think of Indian cuisine as part of their Disney vacation, but this low-key restaurant, located in a strip mall near the northern terminus of International Drive, is a strong contender for the region's best curried and tandoori oven dishes. Among my favorites: lamb or chicken vindaloo, cooked in a lovely Goan sauce with potatoes, and any of the roasted tandoori offerings. The clay tandoor ovens are used for meats marinated for a day or more in a yogurt-and-spice mixture to provide succulent results. The restaurant also features an extensive vegetarian

selection. The dinner menu is available throughout the day, the lunch combo specials, priced $6.95–$9.95, are a bargain. Two evening combos are available for $16.95–$19.95. Accented by brass, Indian rugs and beautifully carved wooden screens, this restaurant may not offer world travel on an Epcot scale, but Passage to India definitely qualifies as a worthy escape. Features: wine and beer only, late dining. Reservations recommended. Credit cards: A, DC, D, MC, V.

Rio Bravo Cantina   **$$**   ★★

2809 West Irlo Bronson Highway (U.S. 192), Kissimmee, 32741, four miles east of State Road 535, ☎ (407) 847-2244.
Mexican cuisine.
Dinner: 4–11 p.m., entrées $6–$13.

The atmosphere at this surprisingly decent Mexican chain eatery is festive—old neon signs, cactus and Cuban music—and the food delivers the goods more often than not. Fajitas are the focus (including a dynamic vegetarian version), but the sprightly honey-lime grilled chicken salad, the carne asada and the sangria all deserve mention. The usual suspects (burritos, enchiladas and tacos) are rounded up in various combinations, but it's safe to stray a bit from the tried-and-true. Live mariachi bands on Friday and Saturday evenings, and a Sunday brunch (*11 a.m.– 3 p.m.*); the bar stays open until midnight nightly with full menu service available. Features: Sunday brunch, late dining. Reservations not accepted. Credit cards: A, CB, DC, D, MC, V.

Character Dining

The sheer number of Disney animated characters milling about the parks and resorts makes it fairly improbable that you will have a Mickey-less vacation. Still, many of the character encounters guests experience are fleeting at best—the Mad Hatter glimpsed out of the corner of an eye, Roger Rabbit sighted through a clutch of moppets. The solution for those who want to make sure they come home with an autograph book loaded with ink? The increasingly popular Disney character-dining program.

The events, which started as character breakfasts a few years ago, have grown into a mini-industry within the Disney empire. As a rule, the food is unexceptional, but the ability to have Mickey Mouse stop at your table, mug for photos, and devote personalized attention to your children adds up to a very special event for most any pre-teen. You'll need to allow at least an hour for the meal—the characters (usually four to a meal at the Disney facilities, less at some of the others) will work around the entire room, but one table at a time.

One small warning, however. Very young children, such as those under 5 years of age, will sometimes recoil in horror at the sight of a seven-foot-tall, mute Pluto. The wail of tears and frustration I've observed on more than one occasion is unfortunate for parent and child alike. The best solution is to make sure Disney doesn't inadvertently slip your kid a hidden mickey—allow your child to observe these larger-than-life creatures from a distance first, providing them a chance to establish a comfort level. This process may take more than one encounter spread over more than one day. It also helps to advise your child that the masked characters do not speak, although Pocahontas, Cinderella, et al, will be happy to converse. Fortunately, the Disney villains are usually not seen at character meals.

Finally, due to the growing popularity of these events, the specific locations, characters and times are scheduled to change (as well as the prices, of course).

Disney Theme Park Character Dining

Each of the three main Disney parks offer daily character dining experiences. They are enormously popular, with the daily character breakfast held in **King Stefan's Banquet Hall** (on the parapet of Cinderella Castle) topping the list—seatings for this cherished event book up nearly two months in advance.

Theme park admission is not included in the price of a character meal at the parks. Therefore, if you are utilizing single-day park admissions or a Four Day Value Pass, you'll want to coordinate your character dining reservation with the actual date of your park touring. Obviously, if you are using a Park Hopper or Be Our Guest pass, you can dine at a theme park restaurant and then move onto another park, if you wish.

To book a table for all Disney theme park character meals, call ☎ *(407) WDW-DINE* as soon as your travel dates are set. Since you can make dining reservations up to 60 days in advance, you're best off calling on the day your preferred dining date is exactly two months away, particularly for the breakfast at King Stefan's Banquet Hall, where the tables are rarely booked less than seven weeks in advance and cancellations or no-shows are rare. If you arrive to the parks without a reservation, remaining tables can be booked via same-day priority seatings by contacting Guest Relations in person or by phone at the theme parks directly:

The Magic Kingdom: ☎ *(407) 824-4521*

Epcot: ☎ *(407) 560-6646*

Disney-MGM Studios: ☎ *(407) 560-4665*

King Stefan's Banquet Hall–The Magic Kingdom

Needless to say, the ability to eat inside Cinderella's house is the prime sales point, but the relatively small number of tables conspires to keep this ticket very hot. Mickey and Cinderella are the regulars, but Snow White, Alice of Wonderland and others also put in appearances. Breakfast only: 8:30–10 a.m. (opens at 7:30 a.m. on Surprise Mornings). If possible, select a dining slot as late in the morning as possible to allow for touring the Kingdom when it's least busy before sitting down for a meal. Adults: $14.95; children ages 3 to 11, $7.95.

Crystal Palace–The Magic Kingdom

The most recent theme park addition to the roster of character dining locations features Winnie the Pooh, Tigger and Eeyore, too. Breakfast with the characters is served from 8 a.m. to 10:45 a.m. (beginning at 7:30 a.m. on Surprise Mornings); adults, $12.95; children ages 3 to 11, $7.95. A character lunch is served from 11:30 a.m. to 3:15 p.m.; adults, $14.95; children $7.95. Finally, a character dinner is served from 4 p.m. to closing; adults, $19.50; children, $9.95. All meals are served buffet style.

Liberty Tree Tavern–The Magic Kingdom

Mickey and friends hang out at the character dinner served in Liberty Square's main eatery. Meal served family style. Daily, 4 p.m. to closing. Adults, $19.50; children ages 3 to 11, $9.95.

Garden Grill–Epcot

The Garden Grill has a unique setting, rotating above the boat ride through The Land Pavilion; table service. The cast of characters includes Mickey, Minnie, Chip and Dale. Breakfast is served from 8:30 to 11 a.m. (beginning at 7:30 a.m. on Surprise Mornings); adults, $14.95; children ages 3 to 11 $7.95. Lunch starts at 11:15 a.m., shifts to a dinner selection at 4 p.m. and the restaurant is open until 7:30 p.m.; either meal, adults, $16.95; children, $9.95.

Soundstage Restaurant–The Disney-MGM Studios

Since this restaurant is based at the Studio, it shouldn't be any surprise that the Soundstage hosts what may be the best-attended character meal: Aladdin, the Genie, Pocahontas, Captain John Smith, Meeko and Radcliff are among the usual attendees; Quasimodo (from Hunchback) started making appearances as this book went to press. Buffet breakfast served 8:30 to 10:30 a.m. (beginning at 7:30 a.m. on Surprise Mornings). Adults, $12.95; children ages 3 to 11, $7.95.

Disney Resort Character Dining

If you're unable to secure a reservation at one of the theme parks' character dining events, don't despair. The Disney Resorts now offer six locations for character meals, and tables for these meals are rarely booked up more than a few days in advance. An added benefit over theme park dining is that you won't be shaving valuable hours off your touring itinerary if you schedule a meal for a day when you're not visiting the parks. The general reservation number for all of these meals is ☎ (407) WDW-DINE and tables may be reserved up to 60 days in advance.

In addition to being less-heavily booked, meals at the resorts do not require theme park admission. Therefore, one can schedule a meal at one of these locations without burning up valuable theme park touring time. Ideally, schedule a character breakfast for the morning of your departure; the meal makes a terrific farewell for children.

If, after perusing this section, you're still striking out on your quest to find a table with the stars, additional dining locations are based at the non-Disney resorts (within Walt Disney World) in the next section.

Artist Point–Wilderness Lodge

The resort character meal is set in a superb environment, overlooking the forest at the edge of Bay Lake. Goofy, Pluto, Chip and Dale are the featured celebrities, with an all-you-can-eat breakfast served daily from 7:30 to 11:30 a.m. Adults, $13.50; children ages 3 to 11, $8.25.

Cape May Cafe–Beach Club Resort

The daily buffet breakfast here is hosted by Admiral Goofy and his crew (usually Chip and Dale and a surprise guest), daily from 7:30 to 11 a.m. Adults, $13.50; children ages 3 to 11, $8.50.

Chef Mickey's Restaurant–Contemporary Resort

This restaurant (recently moved from the Village Marketplace) delivers one of the best food experiences among the selection of character dining events. A 100-foot-long buffet table features carved items, chicken and fish and an extensive salad bar and dessert table is available. Chief stars include Mickey (of course), along with Minnie, Goofy, Chip and Dale. Breakfast daily, 7 to 11:30 a.m.; adults, $13.95; children ages 3 to 11, $7.95. Dinner daily, 5 to 9:30 p.m.; adults, $17.95; children $7.95.

Mickey's Tropical Luau–Polynesian Resort

This is the most lavish character meal—a show set at the same dinner theater location that serves up the Polynesian Revue, at the resort's Luau Cove. As with the Revue, which follows soon after the Luau, food quality is mediocre—you're definitely paying for the entertainment. The event begins nightly at 4:30 p.m. and is priced a stiff $30 for adults, and $14 for children ages 3 to 11.

'Ohana–Polynesian Resort

"Minnie's Menehune Breakfast," named after the shy, mythical creatures of the Hawaiian Islands, is hosted by Minnie and friends. Breakfast daily, 7:30 a.m. to 11 a.m. Adults, $13.50; children ages 3 to 11, $8.25.

1900 Park Fare–Grand Floridian Beach Resort

A lively and popular breakfast, starring Mary Poppins, Goofy, Pluto, Chip and Dale, served daily 7:30 to 11:30 a.m.; adults, $14.95; children ages 3 to 11, $9.95. 1900 Park Fare is also the location for a character dinner hosted by Mickey and Minnie, nightly between 5:30 and 9 p.m.; adults, $19.95; children, $9.95.

Olivia's Cafe–Old Key West Resort

Low-key, tasty breakfast featuring Winnie the Pooh and Tigger, on Sundays and Wednesdays only, 7:30 to 10:15 a.m. Adults, $11.95; children ages 3 to 11, $7.95.

Non-Disney Resort Character Dining

The Swan, Dolphin and Disney Village resorts have recently gotten in on the character action, and now feature meals starring the Disney characters. Additionally, Universal has instituted a character meal, albeit one that features *its* stars—the Flintstones, Woody Woodpecker, et al. As a rule, obtaining a table for any of these meals is much easier, and although reservations are suggested by calling the resort directly, they are rarely necessary. Note that most of these meals are *not* served daily.

Baskerville's–Best Western Grosvenor Resort

The least-expensive character dining experiences in the World. Buffet breakfast served Tuesdays, Thursdays and Saturdays featuring Pluto and Goofy, 8 to 10 a.m.; adults, $9.95, children three to 12, $5.95. Prime rib buffet dinner served Wednesdays with Chip and Dale in attendance, 7:30 to 9:30 p.m.; adults, $14.95; children ages 3 to 12, $9.95. Baskerville's also hosts a popular Saturday night Murder Watch Mystery Theater starring Sherlock Holmes — guests help solve a crime that unfolds over dinner. $30 for adults, or $35 including unlimited beer and wine; $14.95 for children age 12 and under (tax and gratuity included). Showtime: 5:45 p.m. Reservations: ☎ *(800) 624-4109 or (407) 828-4444.*

County Fair Restaurant–Hilton Lake Buena Vista

Sunday breakfast buffet with Minnie, Pluto and Goofy. 8:30 to 11 a.m. Adults, $13.50; children ages 4 to 11, $7.95. No reservations accepted; first-come first-served seating (8:30 to 9:00 is busiest). Information: ☎ *(407) 827-4000.*

Fulton's Crabhouse–Disney Village Marketplace

Breakfast is served daily, hosted by Captain Mickey and his crew: Minnie, Goofy, Chip and Dale. Two seatings, at 8 a.m. and 10 a.m. Adults, $12.95; children ages 3 to 12, $7.95. A good bet for a last-minute reservation. ☎ *(407) 934-2628.*

Garden Grove Cafe–Walt Disney World Swan Resort

À la carte breakfast, starring Goofy and Pluto, available Saturday from 8 to 11 a.m. An à la carte character dinner is served on Monday and Friday with Rafiki and Timon, and on Thursday nights with Winnie the Pooh and Tigger, served from 6 to 10 p.m. Reservations: ☎ *(407) 934-3000, ext. 1618.*

Harry's Safari Grill–Walt Disney World Dolphin Resort

Goofy, Pluto, Chip and Dale star at this colorful but pricey brunch, held Sundays only, 8:30 a.m. to noon. Adults, $15.50; children ages 3 to 12, $9.25. Reservations: ☎ *(407) 934-4858.*

Watercress Cafe–Buena Vista Palace Resort

Sunday buffet brunch from 7 to 10:30 a.m. with Minnie, Goofy and Pluto. Adults, $11.95; children 12 and under, $6.95. No reservations accepted; first-come, first-served seating. ☎ *(407) 827-2727.*

Universal Studios

An all-you-can-eat breakfast buffet with appearances by Fred Flintstone, Woody Woodpecker, Yogi Bear, George Jetson and other Hanna-Barbera characters. Served Tuesdays, Wednesdays and Thursdays from 8 to 9 a.m. only, in the International Food Bazaar next to Back to the Future. Reservations required 24 hours in advance: ☎ *(407) 354-6339.* Adults, $13.50; children ages 3 to nine, $8.75 (theme park admission also required).

OBSTACLES AND OPPORTUNITIES

Walt's Fairy Tale

"Walt Disney World has become a pilgrimage site partly because of the brilliance of its cross-referential marketing and partly because its utopian aspects appeal strongly to real peoples' real needs in late capitalist society. The (Walt Disney) Company—especially at its theme parks—produces, packages, and sells experiences and memories as commodities."

—**Stephen M. Fjellman,** *Vinyl Leaves*
Walt Disney World and America (1992, Westview Press).

As its massive advertising campaign will remind you time and again, Walt Disney World is a special place.

An elegant, turn-of-the-century train station is juxtaposed against a sleek monorail. Mickey, Donald and Pluto canvass the pavement of Fantasyland while, next door in Liberty Square, the Hall of Presidents brings to life onto a single stage every elected leader of our country. Situated on a velvety curl of sand on the Seven Seas Lagoon, the Polynesian Resort echoes a *National Geographic*-style memory of a destination most of us have only dreamed about. The other side of the same lake is rimmed by the opulent Grand Floridian Beach Resort, another vaguely recollected signpost, this time possibly from our grandparents' vacations to coastal Florida almost a century ago.

What is this dreamland—this resort built on the hinge linking fantasy and history, the real and the imagined?

Colorful birds add to the beauty of many of the city's theme parks.

Of course, much of what Walt Disney World is today grew out of Disneyland, in Anaheim, California. In his 1976 biography about Walt Disney, Bob Thomas wrote that the idea for Disneyland had its inception "on the Sunday mornings when (Disney) took Diane and Sharon to amusement parks after Sunday school. As his daughters went on the rides, Walt studied the boredom of other parents, and he noted the squalor of the parks—paint cracking on carousel horses, the grounds dirty and littered, the ride operators cheerless and unfriendly."

Annoyed by the raucous clientele, trash-strewn walkways and the smell of stale beer, Walt Disney began to envision a unique attraction for families. The idea began to take shape formally in a 1948 memo, wherein Walt called the proposed allurement Mickey Mouse Park. The thrust of this concept centered around the Main Village and the Western Village (eventually to become Main Street, USA and Frontierland). But the early ideas also incorporated a toy-repair shop, a candy factory, a working post office and, of course, a railroad circling the park. Later, a visit to Tivoli Gardens in Copenhagen—an amusement park that was immaculate, brightly colored and friendly—further stoked Walt's creative fires.

Walt's amusement park would be similarly clean and tidy, and it would offer trees and carefully manicured gardens—these by themselves would be a departure for an American amusement park. Rather than build carnival-type rides that spun in circles, Walt wanted adventures that followed a linear storyline, rides that took you someplace. He wanted a land inhabited by the characters from his films, not just Mickey and Donald, but Davy Crockett, and others. Above all, he wanted to evoke a happier era, one defined by the warm embrace of Main Street, USA.

In the early 1950s, these were revolutionary concepts, and Walt struggled with money men in order to raise the capital he needed. Eventually, with funding from the fledgling ABC television network, which initially held a 35 percent ownership of Disneyland, Walt's vision became a reality, and Disneyland opened its doors on July 13, 1955.

Walt had successfully created an environment carefully cut off from the real world. Beyond the main gate, guests were transported into a real-life fantasy. The freeways and traffic of Los Angeles literally disappeared, even though the ceaseless stream of cars was but a stone's throw from the edge of the park. When it came time to devise more thrilling adventures, they debuted in the shape of bobsleds racing down the slopes of the Matterhorn Peak (realized in 1/100 size), and later via a rocket ship adventure through Space Mountain. Neither ride was typical of the roller coasters offered at other amusement parks.

From afar, Disneyland soon began to represent *what* America was, and the park drew prestigious guests from around the world: former Presidents Truman and Eisenhower, the Kennedys, King Hussein of Jordan, India's Prime Minister Nehru, King Mohammed V of Morocco, and Vice President Nixon (a frequent guest). Of course, the requisite Hollywood celebrities all toured the park and showered it with acclaim that provided vast amounts of free publicity. The attraction became such a must-see that in 1960 when Nikita Khrushchev, the premier of Russia, visited the United States, a headline-sparking international "incident" occurred when he was told he could not visit Disneyland because of security precautions.

But if the United States was becoming defined by Disney, what was Disneyland? The pat corporate response would probably be something to the effect, "It's the happiest place on earth." And, indeed, guests seem to wander Disney's parks with a few millimeters of air separating the soles of their shoes from the pavement. One can visit the nation's real historical attractions—you can stand in Colonial Williamsburg or other locales that gave birth to the United States—but it's not the same as standing amid a crowd of people in Main Street or Frontierland. Mike Wallace wrote a 1985 piece for the *Radical History Review* titled "Mickey Mouse History: Portraying the Past at Disney World." In it, Wallace addressed Disney's ability (need?) to shape our collective stories into a history we can all live with, a "vacuum cleaned" chronicle of who we are as a nation and people. "Walt's approach to the past," wrote Wallace, "was thus not to reproduce it, but to improve it."

Some of this is a reflection of the idealism that arose during Walt Disney's formative years in the Midwest—simpler times to be sure—yet Walt's upbringing (as the son of a carpenter and farmer) was hardly easy. Much of his vision is undoubtedly a reflection of the social environment during which Disneyland was conceived and built, during the early 1950s, when the United States was trying to put memories of World War II to rest and the Cold War heightened a need for proverbial escape. It's worth noting that important highlights of recent U.S. history—the Vietnam War, the Watergate scandal, America's response to the Iraqi invasion of Kuwait—are barely glimpsed within Disney's borders; the company has not yet found a way to address (and sanitize) these events for its customers who, after all, are paying to be entertained.

But, if Disneyland had been a simple tweaking of our collective history, or just another amusement park, it would not have gone on to emerge as the international success it quickly became. The crowning genius was that Walt Disney knew how to breathe life into the stories and fantasies of our childhood—and not just the fairy tales that lulled us to sleep. After entering the front gates, one would proceed down Main Street toward the drawbridge of

Sleeping Beauty's Castle. Our dreams of fearlessly exploring deepest Africa were realized by turning left and entering Adventureland, home of the Jungle Cruise. A 10- or 12-year-old's most basic wish—a driver's license—could be momentarily appeased by turning right and entering Tomorrowland, where the Autopia puttered away.

Inside Disneyland, disparate pieces with shadowy links to reality—the Mark Twain Steamboat and the Pirates of the Caribbean, the Matterhorn Bobsleds and the Submarine Voyage—were joined together to produce a seamless whole. What Walt and his team of *imagineers* created was a unique convergence of history and fantasy, rewriting them both, almost as if creating a film story, and providing them a stage, until the merger allowed each to become the other. And in developing Walt Disney World, Walt used a much bigger canvas in order to tell his story.

Walt's creation is not special because Michael Eisner and his staff spend millions to tell us it is. Walt Disney World is a special place because there is nowhere else like it in the real world. It is an original.

We Are the World

Most first-time visitors seem a little vague as to exactly what Disney's World encompasses. Many assume Walt Disney World is The Magic Kingdom, or vice versa. However, the Kingdom actually occupies less than one half of one percent of the World's territory, and at any given time probably no more than a quarter of all guests are actually touring The Magic Kingdom. So, what else makes up Walt's unique World? Where do the theme parks end and the resorts begin? What requires a ticket and what is free?

First, Walt Disney World represents a 30,500-acre parcel of land, 47 square miles, all owned by the Disney Company. About half of it (mostly the southern portion) remains relatively untouched and is inaccessible to visitors. The northern edge of the World's territory was the area first developed, but resorts and theme parks have been built progressively farther south. The "town" of Lake Buena Vista, which exists primarily as a technicality and has virtually no permanent residents, occupies the eastern edge of the World, around and north of Disney Village, which is primarily a locale for hotels, shopping and restaurants; neither town exists beyond serving the needs of Disney's guests.

AUTHOR'S OBSERVATION

At the time Disney bought his Florida property, about three-quarters of the land was usually submerged or swampy during the rainy summer season. The system of lakes and waterways that now controls the park's former wetlands is ingenious, and extensive. A total of 55 miles of canals lace the property, and water flow and levels are monitored by satellites and electronic sensors. Bay Lake probably looks something like what Walt saw when he first toured the property, albeit with the addition of white sand beaches, a couple resorts and a campground. But in 1967, the area in front (south) of The Magic Kingdom's entrance-to-be was little more than a low-lying bog. To create the Seven Seas Lagoon, this 200-acre patch was dug to accommodate the present 10-foot-deep lake, and in the process, eight million cubic yards of earth were moved. Similarly, Epcot's World Showcase Lagoon was originally a collapse sinkhole that was dredged to create the current lake, except for a pair of "islands" that were actually extremely tangled heaps of roots that could not be easily removed.

Within Walt Disney World are three primary theme parks, each requiring a full day or more of touring: the 107-acre **Magic Kingdom**, the 154-acre **Disney-MGM Studios** and the 300-acre **Epcot**. In addition, two major water parks—**Blizzard Beach** and **Typhoon Lagoon**—and one smaller one, **River Country**, provide more diversion. Each of these requires several hours to tour. There is a miniature zoo, **Discovery Island**, situated in Bay Lake, and a nighttime entertainment complex, **Pleasure Island**, situated next to Disney Village. All of these represent gated, paid-admission activities.

Walt Disney World also provides a growing selection of more specialized diversions—miniature and full-size golf, shopping, restaurants and movie theaters. Although most of these are Disney-developed and owned, the company also used the Village area to augment its relationships with other providers. For instance, **Planet Hollywood** and **Rainforest Cafe** are lavish eateries built and operated by outsiders, as is the cinema, the **AMC Pleasure Island**. Most of the customers for these activities are World visitors from out-of-state, but the evolving mission at Disney Village Marketplace is obviously to attract locals by providing more traditional entertainment, including less-intensive offerings than are provided at the theme parks.

AUTHOR'S OBSERVATION

The industry trade publication Amusement Business *made the following Disney attendance estimates for the 1995 calendar year: The Magic Kingdom, 12.9 million admissions; Epcot, 10.7 million admissions; the Disney-MGM Studios, 9.5 million admissions. However, some industry analysts feel these numbers are very conservative estimates. Disney stopped releasing attendance figures publicly a while back due to the dramatic impact it had on company stock prices. However, the company reported that fiscal 1995 was a "record attendance" year for the Orlando parks, and initial figures show that 1996, buoyed by a cold, vacation-inspiring winter in the Northeast, was set to follow a similar trend.*

Anyone can utilize Walt Disney World's road system, most of which is open to the public 24 hours a day, although three huge parking areas, one located at the **Ticket and Transportation Center**, one at Epcot and one at the Disney-MGM Studios, each charge a $5 parking fee. If you are staying at a Disney Resort or at the Swan and Dolphin, the parking fee is waived. If you are staying at a non-Disney hotel and want to visit one of the resorts or restaurants north of the Ticket and Transportation Center main entrance, the control point on World Drive, you will not be charged for parking, but you must identify your destination. For more information on navigating via public or Walt Disney transport, or using your own set of wheels, see "Transportation" in "Planning Your Trip."

Of course, Walt Disney World features 15 impressive Disney-owned resorts, offering more than 16,000 rooms. These facilities are discussed in detail within the "Accommodations" chapter, and touring the marvelously themed hotel properties is an enjoyable (and free) activity in itself. In addition to the Disney-owned resorts, there are the "Official Hotels of Walt Disney World" surrounding Disney Village, plus the Westin- and Sheraton-managed Swan and Dolphin near Epcot.

The following section encompasses the daunting, nitty-gritty of preparing to visit the Disney theme parks. Keep in mind, there's a light at the end of the tunnel—the parks themselves.

If at any point during your Disney tour you experience obstacles that are unexpected, seem out-of-the-norm or feel downright unreasonable, the **Guest Relations** desk at each park is the answer. The problem-solving staff deals with everything from lost children to botched dining reservations with friendly solutions geared toward keeping guests happy. The cast members are also a terrific source of information for more specific questions not addressed within these pages. They are the parks' great unsung heroes.

OBSTACLES AND OPPORTUNITIES

Tickets

Purchasing your Disney admission tickets should be one of the simpler hurdles you will face. Unfortunately, it's not always so, and more frequently it resembles a tussle in the Briar Patch. Part of this has legitimately grown out of the multiplying quantity of activities Walt Disney World furnishes its guests. But the Disney Company doesn't make the options obvious, particularly for first-timers, and seems increasingly determined to lock guests into an all-inclusive package, whereby Orlando's other attractions are completely bypassed in favor of an exclusively Disney vacation. Some comfort may be taken in the fact that most of the multiday passes have no expiration date, thereby providing the possibility of getting your money's worth on a later sojourn, if not on this one.

AUTHOR'S OBSERVATION

On opening day in 1971, a seven-ride coupon book and admission to The Magic Kingdom was priced $4.75 for adults; an 11-ride booklet was $5.75.

Visiting Walt Disney World is not cheap. A family of two adults and two children can expect to spend an average of more than a hundred dollars a day on admission tickets alone. Although Disney makes a beguiling array of ticket packages available, don't be fooled: The prime directive here is to maneuver money out of your wallet and into the Mouse's. That said, you'll be better prepared if you arrive in Orlando with some basic touring decisions made ahead of time. As you read through the attractions chapters in this book, be realistic as to how much you think you can incorporate into your vacation. Refer to the chart "How the Big Attractions Compare" in the "Introduction and Overview" section for an idea of how much time to budget for each park. Keep in mind, when 12 to 14 hours is advised for a thorough immersion into The Magic Kingdom, trying to do it in 10 will mean cutting sights and attractions from your tour of the park. Be sure to allow time for eating, resting and travel between the parks. Don't forget, this is a vacation, not an incursion on foreign soil. Still, Disney tickets are land mines to be reckoned with.

INSIDER TIP

If you are a Florida resident, Disney provides a broad spectrum of annual ticket options just for you. The Annual Passport is sold at a slight discount to those who can prove in-state residency. Also available are Seasonal Passports (valid during nonpeak periods), Single Park Annual Passports (valid for a year at one of the three main parks), and an Annual Epcot Passport (valid after 4 p.m. only, at a further reduced rate). Lastly, Florida residents also receive a discount on single-day park admission tickets during nonpeak periods.

Let's start with the basics. Prices for one-day admission tickets including tax, at the time of publication, were as follows (children are defined as ages 3 to 9):

The Magic Kingdom *or* Epcot *or* Disney-MGM Studios:	**$40.81, adult;**	**$32.86, child**
Blizzard Beach *or* Typhoon Lagoon:	**$25.39, adult;**	**$19.03, child**
River Country:	**$15.64, adult;**	**$12.19, child**
Discovery Island:	**$11.61, adult;**	**$6.31, child**
River Country and Discovery Island combo:	**$20.09, adult;**	**$14.31, child**
Pleasure Island:	**$17.97, all ages**	

Obviously, if you're planning a one-day side trip through Walt Disney World, a single-day admission is just the ticket. The same (times two) probably applies if you are spending only two days at the Disney parks. However, if you anticipate spending *three* or more days touring the Disney parks, you'll want to consider the following, multiday options. As you read, notice that the per-day price of the various options increases based on the level of flexibility offered. And, as a reminder, as with all things Disney, you can count on not only the prices, but the actual pass structure, to change in due time.

1. Four-Day Value Pass

This is the basic, least-flexible and least-expensive multiday pass now offered by Disney. It provides one admission to each of the three main parks (The Magic Kingdom, Epcot and Disney-MGM Studios), and a fourth admission for a second day at one of these three parks. It does not allow for "park hopping" although, conceivably, you could use two of the admissions in one day to visit two parks (and thus making it a three-day pass). The admissions never expire, so if you are planning to spend just three days at the three main parks, this is still a good option because you'll have a remaining admission for a future visit. (For comparison, three single-day adult admissions tallies to $122.43.) Price: $136.74, adult; $109.18, children ages 3 to 9.

2. Four-Day Park Hopper Pass

Like the Value Pass, the Park Hopper never expires, but you are allowed to "hop" between the three main parks each day you use the pass. This increases your touring flexibility, and is still less expensive than single-day admissions. (For comparison, four single-day adult tickets would total $163.24.) Potentially, this means you can visit one park in the morning, another in the afternoon, and can tour the third in the evening, all in the same day, for just one admission. Again, the Four-Day Hopper may still be a good choice even if you are only spending three days at the Disney parks. Price: $152.64, adult; $121.90, children ages 3 to 9.

3. Five-Day World Hopper Pass

Now the decision gets trickier. Like the Four-Day Hopper, the Five-Day version allows you to bounce among the three main parks any five days you choose. But the Five-Day also includes unlimited admission to all three water parks, Discovery Island and Pleasure Island for seven *consecutive* days beginning the first time the passport is used. The five admissions to the three main parks are still valid indefinitely. The Five-Day World Hopper is priced slightly higher than five single-day tickets to the three main parks (five single day, adult admissions would be $204.05), but you also receive come-and-go privileges at the other parks. If you are staying at a Disney Resort for seven days or more, you'll probably get your money's worth with this pass. If you're scheduling a five- or six-day trip, you should get out a calculator after planning your theme park itinerary to decide whether this package works for you. If the Five-Day Hopper is only a few dollars more than purchasing tickets you might better utilize, the convenience of this package probably makes it worth the extra expense. Price: $207.76, adult; $166.42, children ages 3 to 9.

4. Be Our Guest Pass

The plot thickens. A recent addition to the family of Disney ticket options, this is an inclusive, length-of-stay pass for guests of Disney Resorts. Offering the same features of the Five-Day Hopper, this pass features unlimited admission to all the attractions (including the water parks and Pleasure Island) for exactly the length of your visit. For example, if you're staying at a Disney property for three nights, the Be Our Guest Pass would be in effect the morning of your arrival through the night of your check-out—four days in all. If you plan to limit your Orlando touring strictly to the Disney parks and are staying at a Disney Resort, this may be your best ticket option for a three- or four-day visit.

You should *not* buy this option, however, if you want to visit Universal, Sea World, or any other, non-Disney attractions. Because the pass must match the number of nights you are staying, the expiration date on the Be Our Guest Pass will be ticking closer every minute you're touring attractions outside Walt Disney World. Additionally, if you plan to stay within World boundaries for your entire trip, yet you are not planning a theme park-intensive vacation and want to have time to relax with a book or play a game of golf, you'll be squandering this pass when you are not using the parks. Also note that if you arrive in Walt Disney World the first day of your trip in the afternoon or evening and/or if you depart on your last day well before dusk, you are again shaving value off this option. While the five-day Be Our Guest Pass is slightly less expensive than the Five-Day Hopper, keep in mind that it is valid only during your stay and has no value following the night of your checkout. If you are staying five or six nights (six or seven days), the Five-Day Hopper will be less expensive and is probably a better option. The bottom line, in other words, is that you are paying a premium for this option because of its versatility *within* the World's borders. A two-day, one-night Be Our Guest Pass is priced $95.40, adult; $76.32, child. The per-day Be Our Guest price drops for each additional day you stay: a five-day, four-night pass is priced $204.58, adult; $164.30, children ages 3 to 9.

5. Annual Passport

This option works best under two circumstances: either you are planning an additional trip(s) to the area within 365 days of the date of issue, or you are scheduling a visit of more than a week and know in advance you'll want to spend several days in each of the three main parks. The standard annual pass is not valid beyond the three main parks, although it does allow for complimentary parking if you are not a Disney Resort guest. It is strictly nontransferable. Price: $250.16, adult; $217.30, children ages 3 to 9.

6. Premium Annual Passport

The *denouement.* As with the standard annual pass, the Premium version allows unlimited admission to the three main parks for 365 days, but also is valid at the water parks, Discovery Island and Pleasure Island. The price makes it prohibitive to all but the rich, or the most ardent devotees of Walt Disney World. Price: $348.74, adult; $306.34, children ages 3 to 9.

INSIDER TIP

Other than at AAA, Disney tickets are generally not discounted. If you are offered Disney tickets at a reduced price, take heed: they may be black-market passes (multiday passes are not transferable between parties, but some guests resell their unused admissions to scalpers). Two exceptions include tickets for the Disney-MGM Studios and Pleasure Island, which the Disney Company has begun selling at a discount off-property, presumably to stave off competition from Universal Studios and Church Street Station, where tickets are easily obtainable at lower-than-gate rates.

AUTHOR'S OBSERVATION

If you aren't exactly sure which of the various Disney passes you should purchase, err on the side of fewer days and less flexibility. If you realize after the start of your trip that you might be better served by another pass structure, Disney allows guests to upgrade (by paying the difference between the pass you have and the one you want), as long as you have at least one admission day remaining on your ticket. By contrast, Disney will not downgrade passes to a lower price ticket once they are purchased.

The early morning lines at the Disney ticket booths can be long; try to purchase your Disney admissions prior to arrival in Orlando (fortunately, photos are no longer used on passes). Some, but not all, branches of the American Automobile Association sell Disney tickets at a slight discount off the front gate price. AAA also sells discounted tickets for Universal, Sea World and a few other attractions. You can also obtain a small discount on Disney tickets if you are a Magic Kingdom Club member (see "Planning Your Trip"). Alternatively, theme park tickets are available at the Disney Store, found in malls across the country; one is conveniently located at the Orlando International Airport. Park tickets are available at the Disney Resorts, and at most other area hotels. At the theme parks and the Ticket and Transportation Center, major credit cards, traveler's checks, personal checks (with driver's license and credit card for identification) and Disney Resort identification cards are all accepted for purchasing admission tickets and passes. None of the admission media sold at Disneyland in California is valid at the Orlando parks, and vice versa.

Finally, you may also purchase your multiday passes by mail through *Walt Disney World, Box 10,030, Lake Buena Vista, Florida 32830-0030*, attention Ticket Mail Order. Send check or money order for the total amount, including $2 for shipping and handling of your order, and allow three to four weeks for delivery. Single day park admissions are not sold by mail.

INSIDER TIP

The always-courteous Walt Disney World phone information attendants have a wealth of information at their fingertips regarding the resorts, restaurants and, of course the Disney theme parks. However, don't expect them to fork over the know-how to secure the best deals. They are trained to process your call efficiently and close the sale if possible, without divulging truly worthwhile insider tips that might save you money or time. Your best bet is to save your dime for very specific questions, rather than using them as a general information source. Park information and brochures: ☎ (407) 824-4321. *Hotels and accommodations:* ☎ (407) WDI-SNEY. *Dining reservations:* ☎ (407) WDW-DINE.

OBSTACLES AND OPPORTUNITIES

AUTHOR'S OBSERVATION

Disney recently abandoned the policy of attaching photos to annual pass-ports in favor of a slightly Orwellian, high-tech system that went into effect spring of 1996. The new biometric readers measure the exact dimensions of a guest's first and second fingers the first time the pass is used; the pass is then encoded so that fingers of anyone presenting the pass for admission must exactly match the original guest's measurements. Disney plans to extend the system to encompass all multiday admission tickets. The company says it initiated the system to eliminate ticket theft, but the bigger reason is probably to control scalping of unused admissions. The pass is not punched or stamped, so only the original guest definitively knows the quantity of admissions left. Hence, if you return home with a single park admission remaining on your nontransferable Five-Day Hopper, your Aunt Tilly won't be able utilize the nonexpiring admission when she visits the World on her trip—only you will.

What Day to Visit

The biggest turnstile-spinner for The Magic Kingdom, Epcot and the Disney-MGM Studios within any given week is the **Surprise Morning** policy (see below). Regardless of whether you are staying at a Disney Resort or not, familiarize yourself with this early admission program and use it to steer away from the heftiest crowds at the three main parks.

During the summer, as a general rule, the Disney theme parks are at their busiest during the week. This is because the parks draw from a vast region of the country, and many summer visitors plan weeklong trips, but use Saturday and Sunday to travel to and from Orlando. Additionally, the main parks do not draw heavily from Orlando residents during the summer, who might otherwise impact weekend traffic.

However, from September through May, the equation changes. Central Florida residents tend to visit the Disney parks more during the less-crowded off-season, and primarily during the weekend. Therefore, from fall through spring, the day-by-day attendance tends to peak on weekends and dips slightly mid-week.

One important exception is the water parks. During the hot summer, Blizzard Beach, Typhoon Lagoon and even River Country draw a substantial number of locals who use their weekends off to visit the water environments. Therefore, Saturday and Sunday attendance from May to September tends to be equal to the mid-week periods. During winter months, the water parks are visited almost exclusively by out-of-towners and crowds are rarely a problem, but busiest on Tuesdays, Wednesdays and Thursdays.

Hours of Operation, Rope-Drop and Closed Attractions

If ever there were a formal misinformation policy in effect at Disney headquarters, this would probably be it. And I, as one of its victims, can assure you this is one of the more annoying ambushes that visitors must face.

One year, with a group of three in-laws in tow, I made plans for us to take in Disneyland together. My familiarity with Disney's parks, they reasoned, made me a suitable tour guide. I called three days prior to our planned visit to determine the exact opening time—9 a.m., I was told—and we planned our trip to arrive at the front gate at 8:30 a.m. I stressed to my cousins the importance of walking down Main Street just as the park first opened, getting into position for the "rope drop" in order to have a crack at several of the big rides before the lines became too long.

We drove into Disneyland's parking lot at 8:20 a.m., only to discover the gates to the park had opened an hour ahead of schedule. By the time we had parked the car, shuttled to the entrance, and purchased tickets, it was 8:45 a.m. when we finally sauntered onto Main Street. My family members weren't too upset, until they saw that the line for our first ride, Splash Mountain, already topped an hour-long wait. The day went downhill from there as the lines became progressively longer. Each time we arrived at a popular attraction and discovered the wait time, I received a (marginally) good-humored chastising about my "misunderstanding" with the Disney phone attendant. On the way out that night, I stopped by Guest Relations and was told that, yes, the scheduled opening time had been changed only the day before, due to a late-breaking forecast of higher-than-previously anticipated park attendance.

I learned my lesson and now bestow this gold-plated wisdom on you. "Rope drop" is that special moment when the park and its rides first open. It leads to a period—15 minutes on a busy day, up to an hour on a slow day—when there is little or no waiting for attractions. As the touring suggestions later in this chapter attest, the best time to be in the parks is when they open. Even if you are not a Space Mountain devotee, you'll be able to see and do more in that first hour than you will, per-hour, for the rest of the day. Don't miss it.

To ensure that you, unlike me, have the correct hours of operation, call ☎ *(407) 824-4321 the night before* you plan to visit each of the parks. As a not-worth-the-paper-it's-printed-on rule, the three main parks *usually* open at 9 a.m. *most* days when the Disney Company *anticipates* moderate or light touring. However, on days when the crowds flow thick and fast, particularly during the summer or around holiday periods, watch for openings at 8 a.m. or earlier.

The correct opening time matches when the rope actually drops, permitting guests on the attractions. At The Magic Kingdom, Main Street, USA usually opens a half-hour earlier. Rouse your spouse, friends or family at the wee hours of the morning, and be positioned inside the parks in time for the rope drop.

Finally, if you haven't previously discovered which park attractions are closed for their annual maintenance, the night before call ☎ *(407) 824-4321* to check. This will help you adapt our touring itineraries to your visit, and will help cushion the disappointment if a major attraction is down for rehab.

The Surprise Morning Policy

Prior to researching this book, I had never overnighted at a Disney Resort. In visiting both Disneyland and Walt Disney World, I slogged it out with everyone else, arriving at the parks at the "official" opening time, rushing to all the big rides I could conquer in the first hour the park was open, then cursing under my breath for the rest of the day as lines became progressively more untenable. Then I learned of the ultimate perk bestowed on Disney Resort guests: the Surprise Morning.

Surprise Mornings works like this: Every day of the week, 52 weeks a year, one of the three main Disney parks opens its gates 60 to 90 minutes prior to its scheduled opening time—but only for guests staying at a Disney Resort, or at the Swan and Dolphin hotels. The result? Waits of five minutes or less for popular rides such as Space Mountain and the Tower of Terror. Even Dumbo, that evil, child-magnet, becomes a walk-on attraction. Until the gates open for everyone else. Then, in a matter of minutes on most days, the parks become a packed wallow.

Needless to say, this perk alone—one money can't buy—is for many folks worth the price of admission to a Disney Resort. In the first 60 to 90 minutes before the park is open to the general public, you are virtually assured of spending more time on the actual rides than you will in the lines. Later in the afternoon, as waits for major attractions top an hour or more (on an average day), the reverse will be true. However, keep in mind that not everything in park is available for touring at the earlier hour. At The Magic Kingdom, Surprise Morning guests can roam through Main Street, USA, Tomorrowland and Fantasyland. This represents almost half the park's attractions, and is more than enough to keep one occupied until the gates open to the general public. The current schedule for Surprise Mornings, subject to the whims of a Hidden Mickey, are:

SUNDAY	**Disney-MGM Studios**
MONDAY	**The Magic Kingdom**
TUESDAY	**Epcot**

WEDNESDAY	Disney-MGM Studios
THURSDAY	The Magic Kingdom
FRIDAY	Epcot
SATURDAY	The Magic Kingdom

If you are *not* staying at a Disney Resort or the Swan/Dolphin, it's important to *avoid* the parks on the above days; the early entry policy is such a draw that the three parks log higher-than-usual attendance figures on days the policy is in effect. Therefore, Thursday is generally busier at The Magic Kingdom than Wednesday, and so on. In fact, some World-ly visitors take this one step further by using the Surprise Morning to visit a park early, but stay only until it opens to the general public; they then dash to one of the other parks for the balance of the day where crowds are usually thinner. Note that although the "Official Hotels" provide some Disney perks, they do *not* participate in the Surprise Morning program.

Phone ahead to verify the Surprise Morning schedule before locking down your plans. ☎ *(407) 824-4321.* For additional hints on beating the crowds, turn to "Touring Strategies" later in this chapter.

Suggested Theme Park Itineraries and Cost

The biggest unknown facing most first-time visitors is the amount of time to allot for a trip to Walt Disney World and how much it will all cost. Airfare (if you plan to fly), hotel and food will eat up the lion's share of your budget, and these costs are addressed in chapters two, three and four, respectively. But for reasons you can now understand, theme park tickets are a vast gray area to most folks, which is why many visitors end up spending more for admissions than they need to. The key is to plan your theme park itinerary before you purchase your tickets, preferably before you even begin your trip, and then calculate which Disney ticket option is most economical.

To assist you in planning your own custom trip, we have designed three sample Disney-intensive itineraries. One covers eight nights and includes one day to visit either Universal Studios or Sea World; the second is a relaxed six-night visit that allows time for the best of Walt Disney World at an unhurried pace; and the third is an action-packed, four-night visit. Each of these agendas works well for first-time visitors, though the eight-night visit obviously allows a chance to see virtually all of Walt Disney World's theme parks and a little beyond. If it's been a decade or more since your last visit (i.e., pre-Disney-MGM Studios), these three itineraries will also work well for you. In each instance, the suggested itineraries take advantage of Surprise Mornings, and the six- and four-night versions can easily be done without a rented car. All admission prices and packages *include* tax. They do *not* factor in additional discounts that can be obtained from AAA, the Magic Kingdom Club, etc.

An Eight-Night, Mostly Disney Orlando Itinerary

This itinerary is designed for the visitor who wants a complete tour of Walt Disney World and a small taste of what lies beyond World borders. It allows sufficient time for shopping and recreational activities such as golf, swimming or fishing; you might even have a few hours by the pool to finish that novel you carted along. You could easily incorporate activities outside the World, such as Church Street Station, a dinner theater or a boat trip through Winter Park, although each of these activities will add to the cost of your tickets outlined below. Also note that this agenda incorporates a second day at Epcot (see "The Two-Day Plan" in "Epcot"), and a few hours on a second day to return to The Magic Kingdom to revisit your favorite rides.

SATURDAY:	Arrive in the afternoon, spend the evening at Pleasure Island.
SUNDAY:	Spend the day and evening at the Disney-MGM Studios.
MONDAY:	Spend the morning at Blizzard Beach; your afternoon and evening are free.
TUESDAY:	Spend the day at Epcot; evening free.
WEDNESDAY:	Spend the day and evening at Universal Studios *or* Sea World.
THURSDAY:	Spend the morning at Typhoon Lagoon, the afternoon at Discovery Island; evening free.
FRIDAY:	Spend the day and evening at The Magic Kingdom.
SATURDAY:	Spend the morning at The Magic Kingdom, the afternoon and evening at Epcot.
SUNDAY:	Return home in the morning or afternoon.

The cost of your theme park tickets for this vacation will vary greatly depending on the type of ticket plan you use. For instance, you could purchase a **Premium Annual Passport**, which would be valid at all of the Disney parks for one year starting the first day of your trip. Including one admission to Universal Studios or Sea World*, the total cost would be $389.55 for each adult and $339.20 for each child, ages 3 to 9. This plan makes sense only if you know you'll be visiting Walt Disney World again within the year.

If you select Disney's all-inclusive **Be Our Guest** plan, and purchase admission to Universal or Sea World, this itinerary would be priced $338.67 per adult and $271.15 per child.

Purchasing **individual theme park tickets** (10 total) would cost $325.22 per adult, and $259.50 per child. Alternatively, you could shave $16.91 per adult and $11.03 per child off this option by substituting River Country for Typhoon Lagoon on Thursday (using a River Country/Discovery Island combo ticket).

Disney's **Four-Day Park Hopper**, plus individual tickets purchased for Blizzard Beach, Typhoon Lagoon, Discovery Island and Universal or Sea World, would be priced $273.81 per adults, and $217.10 per children. You could make the same water park substitution outlined above to save a little money.

Disney's **Five-Day World Hopper Pass**, plus admission to Universal or Sea World, would cost $248.57 per adult and $199.28 per child. You would have one (of your five) admission tickets to the three main Disney parks left at the conclusion of your trip; it never expires.

Obviously, with the theme park scenario outlined above, the Five-Day World Hopper would be the ideal package to purchase. It's not quite as flexible as the Be Our Guest plan, but it is still versatile enough to maximize your theme park touring.

*Adult admission to Sea World is priced about a dollar less than Universal Studios; a child admission is almost the same at both parks.

A Six-Night, Exclusively Disney Orlando Itinerary

This itinerary provides a somewhat tighter introduction to Walt Disney World, but still allows time for a fairly comprehensive experience at all the Disney theme parks. There is some free time for shopping and recreational activities, but not enough time for any major excursions outside the World. This itinerary can easily be accomplished without a rental car if you are staying at a Disney Resort. As with the previous itinerary, it allows a second day at both Epcot and The Magic Kingdom.

THURSDAY:	Arrive in the afternoon, spend the evening at Pleasure Island.
FRIDAY:	Spend the day at Epcot; your evening is free.
SATURDAY:	Spend the morning at Blizzard Beach or Typhoon Lagoon; afternoon and evening free.
SUNDAY:	Spend the day and evening at the Disney-MGM Studios.
MONDAY:	Spend the day and evening at The Magic Kingdom.
TUESDAY:	Spend the morning at The Magic Kingdom, the afternoon and evening at Epcot.
WEDNESDAY:	Spend the morning at Blizzard Beach or Typhoon Lagoon, return home in the afternoon.

Again, the price of your theme park admissions will vary greatly based on the admission package you select. In this scenario, if you purchase **individual theme park admissions** (eight total), the cost would be $272.80 for each adult, and $220.33 for each child, ages 3 to 9.

If you select Disney's all-inclusive **Be Our Guest** plan, this itinerary would be priced $255.46 per adult and $204.58 per child.

Purchasing a **Four-Day Park Hopper** ticket along with the individual water park and Pleasure Island admissions would total $221.39 per adult, and $177.93 per child.

A **Five-Day World Hopper**, which would cover all of the parks outlined in this itinerary, would be priced $207.76 per adult, and $166.42 per child. You would have one remaining admission to the three main parks at the end of your trip; it never expires.

A Four-Night, Exclusively Disney Orlando Itinerary

This plan is for those who want to conquer all three main parks in three intensive days, plus Pleasure Island and one of the water parks. Note that it doesn't include any free time for golf, dinner shows, shopping, swimming or other activities outside the theme parks. If you follow this itinerary, you won't spend much time in your hotel beyond the time you're asleep.

WEDNESDAY:	Arrive in the afternoon, spend the evening at Pleasure Island.
THURSDAY:	Spend the day and evening at the Disney-MGM Studios.
FRIDAY:	Spend the day and evening at Epcot.
SATURDAY:	Spend the day and evening at The Magic Kingdom.
SUNDAY:	Spend the morning at Blizzard Beach or Typhoon Lagoon, return home in the afternoon.

In this scenario, the **Five-Day World Hopper** would be a less-effective package; it would cost $207.76 for each adult and 166.42 for each child, ages 3 to 9. This would allow you all the flexibility of the Be Our Guest package, plus you would have two admissions to the three main parks left over; they never expire.

If you choose Disney's all-inclusive **Be Our Guest** plan, it would cost $204.58 per adult, and $164.30 per child.

You could buy a **Four-Day Value Pass** and individual admissions to the water park and Pleasure Island for $180.10 per adult and $146.18 per child. You would have one admission to the three main parks left over.

If you purchase **individual theme park tickets** (five total), it would be priced $165.79 per adult and $135.58 per child. The disadvantage of the least-expensive plan here is that if you decided to visit (or revisit) a Disney park not listed in the itinerary above, you would have to add that to your cost, whereas by using the Five-Day World Hopper or Be Our Guest plan, your ticket cost wouldn't change. You pay for the level of touring flexibility your ticket provides.

Obviously every person planning a Disney vacation will have a slightly different agenda, but use these touring models as a starting point to create your ideal Walt Disney World trip.

AUTHOR'S OBSERVATION

A $2500 admission ticket that was too good to be true? You betcha. In June 1996, as plans began to solidify for The Magic Kingdom's 25th anniversary, the Orlando Sentinel reported that Disney officials actively investigated the possibility of selling a "Mother of all Passes," a one-time-only offer of a 25-year, all-park passport for $2500, plus tax. The ticket would come with a limited edition watch and lithograph, a letter from Michael Eisner, and your name engraved in a brick near Cinderella Castle. The figure may sound outrageous, but you do the math—a premium annual adult passport purchased at today's prices for 25 years would cost $8225, plus tax. Unlimited admissions to Disney's Orlando parks (including those that have yet to be built) was apparently too valuable to price at just $100 a year.

Meeting the Characters

Over the past several years, Disney's ongoing market research has determined that Walt Disney World visitors place a high priority on meeting the company's animated mascots. The array of costumed "toons" is not limited to Mickey and Minnie; the VIP list also includes Goofy, Chip and Dale, Tigger and Pooh. The ever-burgeoning cast also features Alice of Wonderland, Baloo the Bear, Scrooge McDuck (Donald's Uncle) and a number of more obscure stars. True aficionados know that an autograph from Mickey Mouse is easy to obtain, but cornering Roger Rabbit takes a little more effort, and Donald Duck's scrawl warrants a combination of luck and an all-out search party. Though Dopey is a regular, if you can get a pen into the hands of all Seven Dwarfs, the gods are truly smiling on you.

Since the list of appearances changes daily based on season, anticipated park attendance, special events, the release of new animated Disney films, and factors that are beyond the scope of this book, your best bet for character interaction is to stop by **Guest Relations** on your way into a given park. They will tell you the necessary who/when/where in effect for that day. Another sure-fire option for character encounters of the third kind is the character meals held both in the parks and at several of the resorts (see: "Restaurants"). Beyond this, a few generalizations can be made:

The Magic Kingdom

Due to high demand and the expectations of guests, appearances at the Kingdom are shuffled more regularly than anywhere else, but usually a number will be positioned in Town Square each morning as you enter the park; look for Minnie next to SunTrust Bank. Cinderella regularly pops down to the lobby area of King Stefan's Banquet Hall. The revamped Mickey's Toontown Fair is designed to accommodate 1400 character greetings per hour, and offers a selection of the VIPs. Another new character area, Ariel's Grotto, was in development at press time, and scheduled to be built in the space between Dumbo and 20,0000 Leagues in Fantasyland.

Epcot

The characters are used to draw patrons (especially families) into the deepest reaches of Epcot, i.e., the far side of World Showcase Lagoon. The character department assigns the stars by theme, for instance Pinocchio (who is based on a German fairy tale) hangs out at Germany, Pocahontas at America, Jasmine (from *Aladdin*) at Morocco, Beauty and the Beast at the International Gateway (next to France), and Winnie the Pooh, Mary Poppins and Alice frequent the United Kingdom. Additionally, a few characters will usually show up at Innoventions during the evening hours.

Disney-MGM Studios

Mickey Mouse is stationed in front of the Beverly Sunset Theater, where a line is usually in place for autographs and photos. Mickey Avenue behind the Great Movie Ride is usually enlivened with a variety of roving stars, but at press time, the situation was in flux due to the pending move of the entrance to the Studio's Tram Tour to Mickey Avenue.

Dining

If you come to Walt Disney World expecting cuisine limited to typical amusement-park fare—hot dogs, hamburgers and the like—you're in for a pleasant surprise. Spurred on by the international scope of Epcot, Disney has endeavored to raise the dining standards at its theme parks, particularly at Epcot, to a relatively distinguished level. Unfortunately, if you come to the parks expecting a memorable food experience on par with big city dining, you're in for an pricey disappointment.

Cost, in fact, is the chief complaint of most guests who rely on Mickey's kitchen. It's not that the food is unexceptional (though it sometimes is), nor that it's always expensive but, instead, that too often you don't get what you pay for. A family of four can easily shell out upwards of $75 for lunch and more than $100 for dinner (including tax and tip) at one of Epcot's average-priced restaurants. The same quality of food, by contrast, can usually be had for as little as half the price just outside World boundaries.

A second common complaint is that dining at the theme parks requires fortitude. The first obstacle is simply obtaining a table: on an *average*-attendance day at Epcot, you can expect all lunch-time dining slots and most or all dinner seatings will be gone within an hour after the park has opened. The solution? Make your dining-reservations at Guest Relations immediately when you enter each park (see "Transportation, Arrival and Orientation"). Better yet, you may make theme park dining reservations up to 60 days in advance of your visit by phone. ☎ *(407) WDW-DINE*. In addition, you no longer need to be staying at a Disney Resort to take advantage of this option.

Then there's Disney's reservation system itself. When you confirm your reservation, you will be given a priority seating number and time. Unfortunately, that time won't always match the point you actually sit down, and undeserved waits of up to a half-hour past reservation time are not unheard of. The solution? After contending for years with no-shows and latecomers, Disney is working on making the system more efficient, and it promises relief is on the immediate horizon.

Still, on the good side, most of the Disney restaurants share a delightful common element: elaborate, themed decor. From Epcot's evocative **San Angel Inn**, set in a Mexican cantina against a backdrop of a smoldering volcano, to the **Sci-Fi Dine-In Theater**, where guests sit in surrogate 1950s-era convertibles positioned beneath a drive-in movie screen, the Disney dining experience always aspires to live up to the dazzling rides just next door. In my opinion, these settings sometimes justify the added expense and hassle.

The Disney theme park eateries are broken into two groups: sit-down dining options with waiter service (listed in the "Restaurants" chapter), and fast-food spots that are listed in the chapter with the various theme parks under "Eating." Note that only Disney's three main parks, and Pleasure Island, have sit-down facilities. The water parks and other attractions offer only fast-food items.

Pets

Animals (other than seeing-eye dogs) are not allowed into the theme parks or Disney Resorts and, for the record, it's against Florida law to leave a pet in a closed car. Therefore, bringing Fido with you on your Orlando vacation is an exercise your animal would rather not experience.

However, if you have decided to lug your pet along, there are four, 24-hour kennels located within Walt Disney World: at the Ticket and Transportation Center, at the entrances to Epcot and the Disney-MGM Studios, and at Fort Wilderness campground. Boarding fees are $6 per day, per pet, or $11 to overnight ($9 for Disney Resort guests). A few Fort Wilderness campsites are designated for pets; you may have your animal at one of these locations for an additional $3 per day, but you must request a pet site at the time of your reservation.

Guided Tours

The Disney Company has developed an interesting series of behind-the-scenes tours for each of its three main parks. While the guided tours are appealing for any guest, they're particularly valuable for repeat visitors who want to glimpse what goes on beyond the purview of most guests.

Except for the Backstage at The Land at Epcot, these tours need to be booked in advance. The Backstage Magic tour is popular enough to have its limited number of slots filled up to two months in advance. All tours require attendees to be age 16 or older, except for the Keys to the Kingdom tour, which allows kids 10 years of age and older to attend, and Backstage at The Land, which allows anyone age 3 and up. Also note that except for the Backstage Magic tour and the Dive Quest tour, your theme park admission is not included; you will need to purchase it on top of the price listed below (tax is included in all prices below). American Express cardholders receive a 20 percent discount on each of these tours. For additional information and reservations, call ☎ *(407) WDW-TOUR*.

Backstage Magic

The lollapalooza of the bunch, the seven-hour Backstage Magic tour provides history, trivia and insight into all three of the main parks, including a visit to the access tunnels and *utilidor* systems underneath The Magic Kingdom, as well as the computer controls for Body Wars at Epcot. Transportation between the three parks (via bus) is included, as is lunch. Mondays, Wednesdays and Fridays only; book at least two months in advance. Meets at 8:45 a.m. at Epcot. Cost: $160 per person.

Keys to the Kingdom

The tour offers a four-hour circuit of The Magic Kingdom along with a healthy dose of Walt's philosophies and design inspirations. The tour visits the underground tunnels, explains the unique vacuum system for trash collection and sorting, and goes behind the scenes of five rides for an in-depth look at how the attractions work. This tour overlaps somewhat with the Backstage Magic tour. Meets at 10:15 a.m. daily. Cost: $45 per person (theme park admission not included).

D.E.E.P. - Dolphin Encounter and Exploration Program

This tour offers opportunities for interaction and observation of the dolphins housed in Epcot's Living Seas tank. Guests spend three hours backstage as "guest researchers" for the marine biologists, and learn about the behavior and training of dolphins. This is not a swim-with-the-dolphins course, nor are visitors allowed to touch the animals. Meets Monday through Friday at 8:45 a.m. Cost: $45 per person (theme park admission not included).

Dive Quest

This 2.5-hour scuba program allows certified divers to plunge into the 24-foot-deep tank at Epcot's Living Seas pavilion. Guests spend 30 to 40 minutes in the tank, observing the roughly 65 species in captivity, waving at the nondiving guests on the other side of the glass (note, guests taking this course do not enter the tank through the vertical tube at Seabase Alpha). You must bring your diving certification card; meets daily at 4:30 and 5:30 p.m. Cost: $140 per person, including all equipment, plus a T-shirt, certificate and dive log-book stamp.

Gardens of the World

Three-hour tour of Epcot's World Showcase gardens with a Disney horticulturist who provides insight into the theming, practices and growing techniques used in Walt Disney World. Meets Tuesdays and Thursdays at 9:15 a.m. Cost: $25 per person (theme park admission not included).

Hidden Treasures

Another Epcot tour, Hidden Treasures offers two glimpses into the authenticity and attention to detail at World Showcase. The three-hour tour provides an overview of the design, architecture, culture and costuming at the various nations represented at Epcot. Meets Tuesdays and Saturdays at 9:15 a.m.; the Tuesday tour highlights the east side of World Showcase, Saturday takes on the west. Cost: $25 per person (theme park admission not included).

Backstage at The Land

A 45-minute walking tour through the greenhouses and laboratories of the Land pavilion. Highlights include fish farming, soil-free gardening and pest management for the 30 different crops grown at The Land. Held daily at one-hour intervals. No advance reservations accepted; you need to sign up inside the pavilion at the podium near the Green Thumb Emporium (slots fill up early in the morning). Cost: $6 for adults, $4 for children ages 3 to 9.

Inside Animation

An in-depth, 2.5-hour behind-the-scenes tour at the Disney-MGM Studios' animation department, with an opportunity for the guest to paint their own Mickey Mouse animation cel. Held Tuesdays and Thursdays at 9:15 a.m. Cost: $45 per person (theme park admission not included).

Kid's Programs

In the Disney Company's valiant attempt to continually diversify their product, Walt Disney World now offers special programs that take the kids off your hands for an extended period. Whether parents want a romantic night to themselves or a stressless shopping excursion, one of the following three programs may be ideal for both you and child alike. Any necessary theme park admission is included in the price of the course. Also see: "Families With Small Children" in "Planning Your Trip" for information on child-care services for children ages 4 to 12. All programs can be booked in advance by calling ☎ *(407) WDW-TOUR.*

Night Under the Sea

On Fridays, children ages 6 to 10 are invited to an overnight slumber party at Epcot's Living Seas pavilion. The event includes a visit to select Future World attractions, IllumiNations and a character breakfast in the morning at the Garden Grill Restaurant. The overnight experience starts at 7:30 p.m. on Friday; parents pick children up at 9:30 a.m. the following morning. Cost: $125 per child (includes breakfast and a Disney character sleeping bag).

Disney Day Camp

One morning (8:30 a.m. to noon) and one afternoon (1:30 to 5:30 p.m.) program is presented daily by the Disney University for children ages 7 to 9. The eight rotating field trips include "Face Magic" (makeup artistry and illusion), "Swamp Stomp" (a nature safari through a cypress swamp) and "Orient Express," a journey to Epcot's Japan and China pavilions for a look at the culture and life of the two Asian countries. All classes begin at North Studios at the Disney Institute. Cost: $49 per child for half-day session, or $79 for both the morning and afternoon class (including lunch).

Wonders

This program for kids ages 10 to 15 offered by the Disney University features four six-hour courses, including "Art Magic," which includes a behind-the-scenes tour of the Disney-MGM Studios' animation department and an opportunity to paint a Mickey Mouse cel; "Show Biz Magic," a backstage look at how the Disney stage shows are put on at all three parks; "Wildlife Adventure," a visit to Discovery Island for an in-depth look at the animals, and how Disney works with the ecosystem; "Passports," an adventurous mission to Epcot's World Showcase, where students collect clues about the different countries to solve a mystery. Each field trip meets at 9:30 a.m. at the Disney-MGM Studios on weekdays only. Cost: $79 per child (includes lunch).

A Special Event: The 25th Anniversary

As *Fielding's Walt Disney World and Orlando Area Theme Parks* went to press, a 15-month birthday bash to celebrate the 25th anniversary of Walt Disney World's October 1, 1971 opening was just revving up. Throughout 1997, crowds are expected to reach record levels as the Disney Company rolls out the red carpet for returning guests and welcomes new visitors—the theme being "Remember the Magic." In addition to dedicating several new attractions on October 1, 1996, including **Mickey's Toontown Fair** and the **Barnstormer**, the **BoardWalk Inn and Villas**, a revamped **World of Energy** at Epcot, and **World of Disney** (the world's largest Disney merchandise store) at the Village Marketplace, the company has several special attractions set for guests visiting during 1997.

The 25th Anniversary Welcome Center

Tucked into the same Main street building that formerly housed the Walt Disney Story, the new Welcome Center is a mixed bag, due to an errant 10-minute promotional film that hypes the Disney Institute, Disney Cruise Lines and Disney's Animal Kingdom. There are some interesting newspaper clipping and memorabilia from when the World originally opened on the way in to the theater, but most interesting for Disney-philes is the model of Animal Kingdom which lies at the theater's exit. My suggestion? If you're visiting The Magic Kingdom for the first time or if you're trying to do the whole park in a day, skip the exhibit and film. A rolled lithograph is handed out to visitors who fill out a survey that "registers" past and returning guests. The Welcome Center is located on the right, just as you enter Main Street (opposite City Hall).

Remember the Magic Parade

Beginning October 1, 1996 (and replacing Mickey Mania), the daily parade will receive a full makeover to become an "interactive spectacle" with giant floats inspired by *The Lion King*, *Cinderella*, *The Little Mermaid*, *Aladdin*, *Beauty and the Beast* and *Snow White*. 1400 past guests will be invited to take part in the parade each day.

Cinderella Castle Cake

With a touch of Christo, the Kingdom's landmark palace will be transformed into an oversized confection with 25 glowing candles, towering candy canes and red and pink "icing" to create the world's tallest birthday cake.

IllumiNations 25

An anniversary edition of the World's most popular nighttime event will be revamped to include musical themes from the Southern Hemisphere with a new-age lilt, and climax with a pyrotechnic show themed to "Circle of Life" and "The Lion King."

Our Favorite Hidden Mickey Locations

The domed planetarium ceiling of Epcot's Spaceship Earth contains a Mickey constellation.

The mural above Body Wars at Epcot contains the big cheese.

The mural facing Maelstrom's loading dock at Epcot contains a Viking wearing a Mickey Mouse cap.

The brick path leading to the Wedding Pavilion contains a stone Mickey.

In the African section of The Magic Kingdom's It's a Small World, look for mouse-ears in the purple-flowered vine.

Mickey can be found in the main balcony design used at the entrance to the Studios' Tower of Terror.

At the conclusion of Splash Mountain, look for Mickey in the pink clouds to the right of the steamboat.

Coping Strategies

With an average combined attendance of 100,000 guests daily at the three main parks, the crowds encountered at Walt Disney World can be truly monumental and overwhelming. How bad? Try one-to-two hour waits for the major attractions during peak season. Popular restaurants may be booked to capacity days, or even weeks prior to your arrival. Sobering traffic jams following the 9 p.m. performance of "IllumiNations" at Epcot. On the busiest days, the Disney Parks reach capacity and stop admitting guests. How does one cope?

Take it easy.

Appreciating Walt Disney World is all in the pacing. You can't do it all in one trip, but so many visitors become caught up in the notion that they must conquer the World in one visit. But the World is a very big place. Columbus couldn't do it all, and neither should you expect to.

Take time to smell the roses, or coffee, or whatever provides the stimulation you need to refresh your senses. And, in truth, the brilliant secret to Disney's creation is not in its size or scope, it's in the details. For instance, after the initial onslaught of starry-eyed arrivals at The Magic Kingdom has subsided (around noon), Main Street USA can finally be appreciated. Take a moment to glance up at the names adorning most of the second-story windows; most are those of individuals whose imprint on the Disney Company was usually buried within Walt's dominant shadow. One sign, for a shoemaker, says "no shoes too large to fit," perhaps this is a gentle nudge at Walt's legacy? Stop by the Penny Arcade, which supplements its stock of current video games with vintage lures, such as a Kiss-o-Meter and the Mute-o-Scope. Visit the 1870-era Harmony Barber Shop, a genuine, old-fashioned haircutting establishment, with a barbershop quartet, the Dapper Dans, providing music every hour. Most of these choice theme elements are missed by the stampede to see the Kingdom's "real" attractions.

Additionally, no touring plan can take into account the many variables that snag the best itinerary. Whether it's an unexpected parade blocking your route to the next must-see ride, or an opportune encounter with the Seven Dwarfs, maintaining a crack schedule is almost impossible. My advice? Like the old adage, when life gives you lemons... get out the sugar and ice! There's always a good time to be had someplace in the Disney parks. But if it's not happening where you are at a given moment, don't rush to the next action-packed ride for a quick fix. Instead, stop, gather your senses, and allow the experience to come to you. Leave room for spontaneity.

OBSTACLES AND OPPORTUNITIES

AUTHOR'S OBSERVATION

Aside from the specific days of the week recommended for park touring (see "Touring Itineraries"), save your visit to The Magic Kingdom for last, particularly if you have children in tow. Epcot has a decidedly educational bent, and represents a good, low-key start to your adventure. The pace picks up at the Disney-MGM Studios but, being somewhat smaller, it provides a slight break between the two big parks. Dessert is best savored last, and The Magic Kingdom is Disney's piece de resistance, a magical dollop of icing on Walt Disney World's rich feast.

In truth, as much as Fielding's and other guidebooks might suggest, there is no one perfect touring plan, only a plethora of suggestions that will help you pack the greatest quantity of rides into a single visit. But it's definitely worth developing a plan for your assault on each of the three main parks. As you read through the pages of *Fielding's Walt Disney World and Orlando*, you'll begin to develop your own list of "must sees." Take a moment to review the ingredients and instructions of the touring suggestions we provide, and then integrate your own priorities.

Lastly, here's a pleasant surprise. At the end of most major lines is a sign that estimates the probable wait time; on particularly busy days, these waits can mimic expeditions to the farthest reaches of the globe. But, Disney deliberately overestimates the probable wait times on their signs so as not to cause disappointment. If you arrive at Splash Mountain and the estimated wait time posted at the end of the line states 90 minutes, don't despair. You'll probably be settling into your log in about an hour, and when you disembark, you'll be refreshed and ready for new challenges.

Now, take a deep breath. We're going to Disney World!

THE MAGIC KINGDOM

The white heron can be seen around Orlando's many lakes.

Transportation, Arrival and Orientation

Unlike the other main theme parks, The Magic Kingdom does not have a parking lot at its front entrance. Therefore, if you are arriving by car, you will park at the **Ticket and Transportation Center** ($5 for non-Disney Resort guests), on the opposite side of the lake from the entrance. After parking—

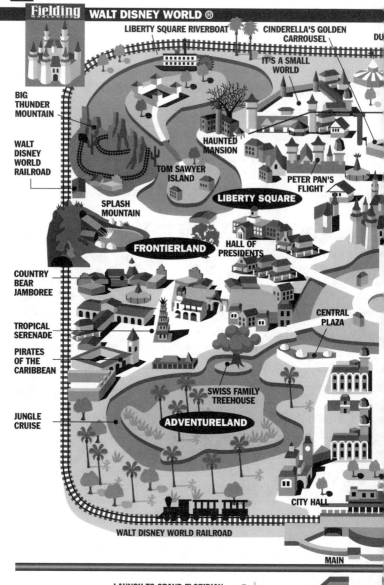

Fielding WORLDWIDE
WALT DISNEY WORLD ®

LIBERTY SQUARE RIVERBOAT

CINDERELLA'S GOLDEN CARROUSEL

DU

IT'S A SMALL WORLD

BIG THUNDER MOUNTAIN

WALT DISNEY WORLD RAILROAD

HAUNTED MANSION

TOM SAWYER ISLAND

PETER PAN'S FLIGHT

LIBERTY SQUARE

SPLASH MOUNTAIN

FRONTIERLAND

HALL OF PRESIDENTS

COUNTRY BEAR JAMBOREE

TROPICAL SERENADE

CENTRAL PLAZA

PIRATES OF THE CARIBBEAN

SWISS FAMILY TREEHOUSE

JUNGLE CRUISE

ADVENTURELAND

CITY HALL

WALT DISNEY WORLD RAILROAD

MAIN

LAUNCH TO GRAND FLORIDIAN AND POLYNESIAN RESORTS

SEVEN SEAS LAGOO

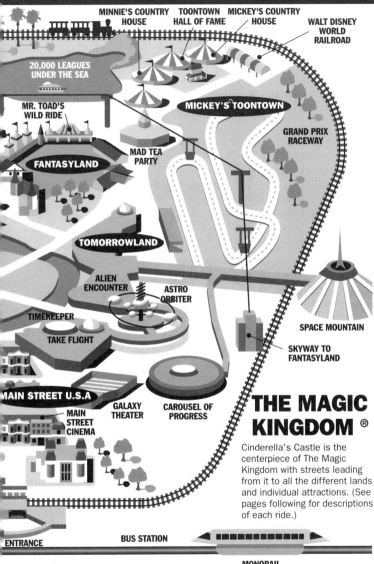

MINNIE'S COUNTRY
HOUSE

TOONTOWN
HALL OF FAME

MICKEY'S COUNTRY
HOUSE

WALT DISNEY
WORLD
RAILROAD

20,000 LEAGUES
UNDER THE SEA

MR. TOAD'S
WILD RIDE

MICKEY'S TOONTOWN

GRAND PRIX
RACEWAY

FANTASYLAND

MAD TEA
PARTY

TOMORROWLAND

ALIEN
ENCOUNTER

ASTRO
ORBITER

TIMEKEEPER

TAKE FLIGHT

SPACE MOUNTAIN

SKYWAY TO
FANTASYLAND

MAIN STREET U.S.A

MAIN
STREET
CINEMA

GALAXY
THEATER

CAROUSEL OF
PROGRESS

THE MAGIC
KINGDOM ®

Cinderella's Castle is the
centerpiece of The Magic
Kingdom with streets leading
from it to all the different lands
and individual attractions. (See
pages following for descriptions
of each ride.)

ENTRANCE

BUS STATION

MONORAIL

LAUNCH TO DISCOVERY
ISLAND & FORT
WILDERNESS

make sure to note the section you have landed in, the 12,256-space lot is alleged to be the second-largest in the world—you'll board one of the trams that ferry you to the hub of the Ticket and Transportation Center. You may purchase your park admissions here if you have not already done so, or you may hold on until arriving at the entrance to the Kingdom. Either way, if you are buying tickets, expect a wait.

From the Ticket and Transportation Center, you have two possible passages into The Magic Kingdom. One is the **Monorail**, which offers two routes around the lake to the park. One is a non-stop express, the other will make a stop at the Polynesian Beach and Grand Floridian Beach resorts. The non-stop is faster, of course, but the resort-bound monorail sometimes has a shorter wait and only takes about five minutes more to the Kingdom's main entrance. When operating at capacity (four trains each direction) the monorail can carry almost 12,000 people an hour. However, the shortest line is typically for the **ferry** leading straight across the Seven Seas Lagoon. These efficient behemoths haul 600 passengers at a time, and can cross the lake in a brisk five-and-a-half minutes, making four round-trips an hour during peak periods. They don't speed quite as fast as the monorail, but are frequently overlooked in the rush to get to the Kingdom.

INSIDER TIP

There's nothing quite like riding to The Magic Kingdom in the first-class section. The front cabin of the monorail is open to everyone, on a first-come, first-served basis. When your train comes into the station for boarding, ask one of the drivers if you may sit up front and you will be escorted to the captain if space is available. The front compartment comfortably seats six. Obviously, these prime seats are popular, but during the afternoon, and after the parks have finished clearing out guests for the day, the front cabin sometimes goes unoccupied.

If you're staying in a Disney Resort, the Disney Transportation System offers the fastest method to the Kingdom's entrance. The monorails, **buses** and boats all deposit their passengers directly at the main entrance, *not* at the Ticket and Transportation Center. Leave your car at your resort if you can. All non-Disney Resort buses, however, deposit passengers at the Ticket and Transportation Center.

The Magic Kingdom's layout is ingeniously simple: seven themed "lands" leading out from a central hub, very much like the spokes of a wagon wheel. The lands can also be thought of like the points of a compass: Main Street is south, Fantasyland is north, etc. The only entrance to the Kingdom is at the "bottom" of the wheel, through Main Street, USA, and a berm surrounds the entire park to shield us from the distractions of real life; our description of the lands begins with Main Street and circles the park in a clockwise fashion. The biggest attractions are positioned at the edges of the park, dispersing visitors into all corners of the property. However, the Kingdom's hub—Central Plaza in front of Cinderella Castle—is a major thoroughfare and can become jammed with pedestrians, particularly before and after parades, and as the park begins to shut down for the night.

AUTHOR'S OBSERVATION

In the planning stages for the design and layout of Disneyland, Walt employed the term "weenie" to describe how he would entice his crowds into all corners of the park (a frankfurter being what an animal trainer used to get a dog to perform tricks). Walt considered his most colorful attractions—the castle being perhaps the biggest and best example—a kind of oversize lollipop that would lure guests into the deepest reaches of his kingdom. "You've got to have a weenie at the end of every street," Walt would say. Can you spot some of the other "weenies" in the parks?

On entering the park through its main entrance, you'll be handed a guidebook and schedule of the day's entertainment offerings. Assuming you've arrived well before rope drop (see "Obstacles and Opportunities"), this is a good time to browse through the schedule. At the end of Main Street next to the Crystal Palace Restaurant is a **tip board** that provides updates about the wait times for various attractions. The estimates tend to be conservative, but are good for comparison purposes. Additional touring information is available at **Guest Relations** in **City Hall**, just to the left of the train station as you enter Main Street; this facility also handles lost and found, "lost parents," and can assist with reservations. An additional Guest Relations desk is located outside the park, to the right of the turnstiles as you enter. Two **guided tours** are available, Keys of the Kingdom and Backstage Magic; both need to be booked in advance of your arrival (see "Guided Tours" in "Obstacles and Opportunities").

Stroller and **wheelchair rental** is available just to the right of the main entrance, before you cross under the train station. A **diaper changing** and **nursing station** is located next to the Crystal Palace at the end of Main Street. **Lockers** are provided immediately under the Main Street train station. **Banking** needs can be handled to the left of the train station, at the SunTrust Bank next to City Hall (*open daily, 9 a.m. to 4 p.m.*); an **ATM** is located here, and also near the Space Mountain exit in Tomorrowland.

Ticket information is listed under "Tickets" in "Obstacles and Opportunities."

INSIDER TIP

There is a nursing and diaper changing facility in each of the three main Disney parks. Each make pleasant escapes for mothers, and they also sell a small selection of baby care items such as diapers, bottles and baby food. At The Magic Kingdom, the diaper changing facility is next to the Crystal Palace Restaurant on Main Street. At Epcot, the room is located at the Odyssey Center, the now-closed restaurant between the Mexico Pavilion and the World of Motion. At the Disney-MGM Studios, the facility can be found in the Guest Relations building next to the main entrance. Of course, there are also the unofficial nursing stations, the attractions that briefly afford mothers a certain level of privacy—at The Magic Kingdom, a prime spot is aboard the Haunted Mansion's "doom buggies," with the Tomorrowland Transit Authority and Skyway also providing decent respites from the crowds.

The Magic Kingdom Rope Drop and Surprise Morning Procedures

At The Magic Kingdom, several opening procedures are used to admit guests into the park. Typically, the "official" opening time is 9 a.m., or 8 a.m. on days when Disney expects high attendance. However, the main entrance is always open to the general public 30 minutes prior to that time, and Main Street will be open for touring during that time (the first Walt Disney World Railroad departure leaves the Main Street station at the official opening time).

On the days when the Surprise Morning policy is *not* in effect (at this writing, Sundays, Tuesdays, Wednesdays and Fridays), the rope will usually be in place around the perimeter of Central Plaza until the official opening time. If you want to be among the first on a particular ride, position yourself at the rope prior to the official opening time, facing the land you wish to visit first.

On Surprise Mornings (Mondays, Thursdays and Saturdays), when Disney Resort guests are admitted to the park early, the Kingdom typically opens 90 minutes prior to the "official" time. Confusingly, some brochures tell you the park will open 60 minutes early. Confirm the exact time the main entrance opens with your Disney Resort information staff. On these mornings, there is no real rope drop procedure, and Main Street, Fantasyland and Tomorrowland will be open for touring. Note that Space Mountain is not usually scheduled to begin operation until the official opening time, although it usually opens some time before that point.

On Surprise Mornings, the general public is still admitted to Main Street a half-hour ahead of the official opening time, but the rope extends across the end of the street, before you enter Central Plaza.

Always confirm the exact opening procedure with Disney Information. Call ☎ *(407) 824-4321* the night before your day at The Magic Kingdom. For more information on how the Surprise Morning program works, see "Obstacles and Opportunities."

INSIDER TIP

Dedicated thrill-seekers can usually visit all three of The Magic Kingdom's mountains–Space, Splash and Big Thunder–in about an hour, but only if you're in place for the rope drop. You must be able to keep up a brisk-paced clip; you'll walk from one side of the Kingdom to the other within this hour, a distance of about a half-mile. First, position yourself for the rope drop in Central Plaza; the entrance you want for Tomorrowland (there are several) is the main one, facing AstroOrbiter. As soon as the rope is dropped, head straight for Space Mountain, where you should be able to board with little or no wait. After riding Space Mountain, proceed back to Central Plaza and continue on through Adventureland to Big Thunder and Splash Mountains. On all but the Kingdom's most crowded days, you should be able to conquer all three mountains in about an hour (less on a slow day, slightly more on a busy day). On Surprise Mornings, this exercise will not work, regardless of whether you are a Disney Resort guest or not; lines will be firmly established within 10 to 20 minutes of the park's opening.

AUTHOR'S OBSERVATION

What's under The Magic Kingdom? Nine acres of offices and tunnels that connect the various lands out of the sight of guests. Although this area is sometimes referred to as a basement, the utilidors *(in DisneySpeak) were actually built at ground level due to the area's natural water table, with most of the Kingdom constructed above the corridors. The long hallways are filled with water lines, power cables, and huge pipes for the 60-mile-per-hour vacuum garbage collection system. Additionally, the underground passages are routinely used to provide access from "backstage" to the various lands, which helps ensure that Snow White doesn't commit a* faux pas *by walking through Tomorrowland to get to Fantasyland where she belongs.*

Main Street, USA

Entered via tunnels under the elevated, red brick Victorian Train Station, Main Street, USA is where your Magic Kingdom experience begins. Main Street is a disarming invitation into turn-of-the-century Americana, lovingly detailed in brick and gingerbread molding, kept sparkling clean (in a way the real Main Streets of this era never were). The passage is meant to evoke Anytown, but it probably bears more than a passing resemblance to one small town in particular: Marceline, Missouri, where Walt Disney spent four formative years of his life.

Town Square, filled with lawns, benches and a flagpole, is the plaza immediately beneath the railroad station. SunTrust Bank and City Hall (housing Guest Relations) are located west of Town Square on the left-hand side as you enter. The east side of the square features the Hospitality House, a building housing Disney memorabilia, including letters, sketches, rare photos and a few of the many Oscars won by Walt's films (next door, Disneyana Collectibles sells considerably less rare items). An immense Christmas tree is positioned at Town Square every December. At the opposite end of Main Street is Central Plaza and, of course, Cinderella Castle.

The buildings lining Main Street are real, and boast functioning office space for some of the Disney Company's many administrative employees. But a subtle trickery is at work here: a close look at the upper floors reveals the buildings aren't quite full-size. Walt had the facade of the second floor designed slightly smaller than the first, the third floor is slightly shorter than the height of the second. The effect—a technique known as foreshortening—adds to the mythical quality of Disney's brand of Americana. It may also reflect the larger-than-life stature Walt accorded his boyhood memories. In reality, the interiors of the buildings contain only one floor above the ground.

Main Street boasts the smallest quantity of rides of any of the Kingdom's major lands. As a result, many guests pass down the street in the morning and don't return until they are on their way out of the park. However, Main Street is also where parades conclude, briefly boosting afternoon attendance of this area, and in the half-hour before and after closing time, the street becomes clogged with foot traffic and shoppers.

Shopping is the prime activity here, and a bevy of purse-emptying opportunities awaits. Among the highlights is **Disneyana Collectibles**, which features both original animations cels and reproductions of classic Disney animation art; these items have skyrocketed in value over the past couple of decades. The Shadow Box displays a delicate, fading art: facial silhouettes cut from black paper, a portrait technique popular at the turn of the century. The **Harmony Barber Shop** is a functioning haircutting establishment in a vintage setting: $15 for a man's cut, $12 for a child, handled on a first-come, first-served basis. The shop also sells vintage shaving items. And, of course, the dazzling array presented at **Main Street Confectionery** attempts to satisfy the sweetest tooth—the specialty, fresh peanut brittle, is concocted daily. The biggest draw, however, is the **Emporium**, which stocks every imaginable T-shirt or stuffed character you could want. If you are looking for a generic Disney-character gift, the Emporium has the best selection. Keep in mind it is engulfed by shoppers at closing time.

INSIDER TIP

*One of the niftier perks Disney has recently added is **Package Pickup**. With this service, if you're staying at a Disney Resort, your shopping purchases can be delivered to your room free-of-charge by noon the following morning. This allows you to do your theme park touring without lugging cumbersome purchases around all day.*

If you want to spend time touring Main Street's shops, avoid the area before and after parades and during the park's closing hour. The least-congested shopping period is in the early morning when most visitors will be scooting past you to board rides while lines are still short, or in the early evening, well before foot-traffic out of the park become a stampede.

Walt Disney World Railroad

In real life, Walt Disney was an unabashed train aficionado. He built a miniature railroad in his back yard, and later designed a 1/8 scale model for the Disney Studio in Burbank, California. Were he alive today, this simple attraction and its counterpart at Disneyland would still be among Walt's favorites. The trains are driven by authentic, late 1920s-era steam engines built in the United States. The engines were in service as late as the 1960s hauling sugar cane in Mexico's Yucatan Peninsula before Disney scouts snared them for use at Walt Disney World in 1969.

The 1.5 mile track circles The Magic Kingdom, making two stops, one at Frontierland and another at Mickey's Toontown Fair. Unlike the route around Disneyland, the trip doesn't offer passage through the Grand Canyon and the Primeval World. As transportation between the lands, the railroad is rarely a shortcut, and should be thought of instead as a leisurely extension of Main Street, and an opportunity to "take a load off." *Length of ride:* 20 minutes. *Special note:* The Main Street Station is the least busy departure point for the train; many guests board the train in Frontierland and Mickey's Toontown Fair (back to Main Street) as their last attraction for the day. Strollers are not permitted on the railroad.

INSIDER TIP

In the early afternoon, the number of guests touring The Magic Kingdom hits its peak. You can best sidestep the crowds by devoting this time to the attractions with the shortest lines. In The Magic Kingdom, the usual list includes the Walt Disney World Railroad, the Main Street Cinema, Swiss Family Treehouse, Tropical Serenade, Tom Sawyer Island, the Hall of Presidents, Liberty Square Riverboat, It's a Small World, TakeFlight, Timekeeper, the Carousel of Progress and the Tomorrowland Transit Authority.

Main Street Cinema

The birth of Mickey Mouse—1928's *Steamboat Willy*—is on screen daily in this tiny cinema-in-the-round, where six screens exhibit some of the earliest Disney animated classics. *Length of show:* Stay as long as you like. *Special note:* There's no seating, but the cinema is air-conditioned, and surprisingly under-attended on hot summer afternoons.

Main Street Vehicles

A selection of turn-of-the-century transportation devices—jitneys, horseless carriages, horse-drawn trolleys, a double-decker omnibus and even a cherry-red fire engine—ply the route between Town Square and Central Plaza below Cinderella Castle, the hub of The Magic Kingdom. *Length of ride:* two to three minutes. *Special note:* Kids love 'em, but skip these less-than-rapid transit systems if a line has formed.

Adventureland

Beating drums, squawking parrots and the relentless putter of the Jungle Cruise boats provide the soundtrack, while thatched-roof shacks and luxuriant vines sweeping from the fronds of date palms create the ambience for Adventureland. Intriguingly situated between Main Street and Frontierland, The Magic Kingdom becomes its most international here, with territory where Indiana Jones and Tarzan might have once collided. The shops and rides have an African and South American atmosphere, with a little of the Caribbean, Middle and Far East thrown in for good measure. Draped by honeysuckle, hibiscus, palms, ferns and much more, exotic Adventureland tantalizes our senses with a lush, tropical ambience that is green and dark enough to seduce the most jaded traveler.

The **Adventureland Bazaar** is a conglomeration of a half-dozen shops that sell exotic wares of dubious value—shrunken heads, pith helmets and the like. Khaki clothing, Indonesian batiks, and ethnic jewelry help to round out the mix. Near the entrance to Pirates of the Caribbean is the **Caribbean Plaza**, another set of shops, this time focusing on pirate- and tropical-themed items.

Jungle Cruise

A giggly smash since it first opened, the Jungle Cruise was inspired by "The African Lion," one of Disney's True-Life nature documentaries shot in the 1950s. Today the cruise is a tongue-firmly-in-cheek ride through the wilds of Asia, Africa and the Amazon, narrated by skippers well-educated in cornball banter—including four different entertaining spiels. Some of the boat names are the Irrawaddy Irma, Orinoco Ida, Nile Nellie, Amazon Annie, etc. The animals—lions, hippos, crocodiles and bathing elephants—are intermittently believable, and the misty vegetation is dense, green and exotic, and most of it is real, making the Jungle Cruise a horticulturist's dream playground. But beware: the puns come fast and furious, and it's worth noting that the audio-animatronic humans seen on the Jungle Cruise are almost all people of color, fostering a pervasive "us and them" interpretation of Third-World countries. *Length of ride:* 10 minutes. *Special note:* Although disdained by some repeat visitors since the scripts never seem to change, the Jungle Cruise is a good bet for first-timers, and kids find it a hoot. Due to the laborious boarding process, however, lines move slowly and never let up. Ride the Jungle Cruise well before noon, or just before park closing.

Swiss Family Treehouse

Based on Disney's 1960 film adaptation of the Johann Wyss novel, this walk-through attraction surveys the Banyan treehouse built to house the shipwrecked Robinson family who became marooned in New Guinea. The nearly 100-foot-tall tree is not real—its trunk is constructed of painted concrete and the 300,000 leaves are made out of polyethylene—but real Spanish moss, running water, and antique props (sans audio-animatronic Robinsons) bring the environment to life. Length of tour: 8 to 10 minutes, depending on crowds. *Special note:* The Treehouse usually doesn't build a line outside its entrance, but when it does, the line tends to be short-lived. This is a good attraction to visit in conjunction with Tropical Serenade. If there's a wait of more than 10 minutes for the Tiki Birds, tour the Treehouse first.

Pirates of the Caribbean

An eerie set of catacombs and passages greet guests as they wait to board their time-traveling boats into the Spanish Main. From here, you are advised sonorously, "Dead men tell no tales," before plunging down a flume, through dark caves and into the middle of a cannonfire battle between a pirate ship and a stone fortress. The pirates win and plunder the port, which appears to be inhabited almost exclusively by women. The story is told using dozens of debauched audio-animatronic creations, some carefully detailed down to the hair on their legs.

Pirates of the Caribbean was the last ride to open at Disneyland with any significant input from Walt. Interestingly, he felt the concept of a pillaging by pirates was a little strong for the park, but he died a few months before the ride opened to immediate success in 1967. It remains an enduring classic, and a model use of Disney's storyboarding technique—that is, developing an attraction through a series of drawings, like a movie. Add in the richly detailed environment, costumes and special effects, and you have one of The Magic Kingdom's best, a one-of-a-kind original. *Length of ride:* nine minutes. *Special note:* Although the line for Pirates builds by late morning, the boats load quickly and keep the queue moving at a decent clip. If you miss the attraction in the morning, wait until the afternoon parade, which starts near the Pirates entrance, when the line is temporarily shorter.

Tropical Serenade

Previously known as the Enchanted Tiki Birds and set in a hexagonal, Polynesian hut, this attraction documents where audio-animatronics first took off. The show features a group of 225 singing, mechanical birds, flowers and tiki statues, led by a group of four, ethnically-stereotyped parrot-emcees adrift in a tropical environment. For many, however, this cankered Disney "classic" is strictly for the birds.

Things aren't helped much by the distraction of attendees who elect to walk out mid-show, previously unaware of what they were signing up for when they got in line. Young children enjoy the warbling birds, but for adults, the command "let's all sing like the birdies sing, tweet, tweet-tweet, tweet-tweet..." is grating. In short, this is one attraction that is long overdue for a serious overhaul. *Length of show:* 18 minutes (plus a pre-show). *Special note:* Except during the early afternoon on busy days, there is rarely a line longer than the number of seats available inside. Visit any time, and if the next show is more than 10 to 15 minutes away, visit the Swiss Family Robinson Treehouse first.

AUTHOR'S OBSERVATION

Audio animatronics was a word Disney coined to describe the animated, three-dimensional robots at the parks. The first, rudimentary appearance of the technique could be seen as far back as the Jungle Cruise, one of Disneyland's earliest adventures. Walt later had a wacky, unrealized concept for a Chinese restaurant that would be hosted by a Confucius-style mechanical man who would spout words of wisdom. But the first real leap into the computer-synchronized technique as it is known today came with Disneyland's 1963 opening of the Enchanted Tiki Room, which mated music, voices and sound effects to the movement of dozens of mechanical birds.

Frontierland

Seamlessly bordered by Adventureland and Liberty Square, the American frontier is displayed in its most optimistic guise in Frontierland, a sanguine monument to the pioneers who pushed the boundary of the country west to the Pacific Ocean. The land is actually an amalgamation of environments: the southwest around red-stone Big Thunder Mountain, the verdant midwest at the Rivers of America, and a fantasy landscape that supports Splash Mountain. Elements of the plains, Rockies and southwest are used to accent the architecture of Frontierland's exposed wood-and-stucco buildings.

Checkered shirts, leather vests and jeans are the typical costume for cast members who work this land. Hitching posts along wooden sidewalks provide a Gold Rush ambience. For a rugged backdrop, Disney's horticulturists have planted mesquite, century plants, saguaro cactus and pepper trees to lend a parched atmosphere. The Frontierland soundtrack is peppered by gunshots and the occasional whistle of the steamboat that docks in Liberty Square next door, and the scent wafting through the Trading Post area is that of leather and popcorn.

Frontierland is home to two of The Magic Kingdom's three mountains, Splash and Big Thunder, and the crowds for these two attractions solidify early and create a wall of bodies near their entrances by late morning. Frontierland is also where the afternoon parade begins, usually at 3 p.m., erupting from a cavity between Pirates of the Caribbean and Splash Mountain and then proceeding to Liberty Square, through Central Plaza and down Main Street. Hence, in the afternoon, Frontierland can be difficult to navigate.

Shopping in Frontierland is themed to western goods and apparel. The **Frontier Trading Post** stocks coonskin hats, Indian feather headdresses, peace pipes and turquoise jewelry. The stuffed characters from *Song of the South* are sold at the **Briar Patch**, situated near the Splash Mountain exit. Photos of your laughing/screaming log-crew are made available next door at **Splashdown Photo** as you exit the ride. The original "video" game, the **Frontierland Shootin' Arcade**, offers five shots for 25 cents and is a relatively elaborate shooting gallery—complete with sound effects, mist and a panorama set in a mid-19th-century ghost town—that teens particularly enjoy.

One of my favorite Magic Kingdom attractions, **Davy Crockett's Explorer Canoes**, has been shut down indefinitely. If it reopens in the near future, know that the canoes are one of the most pleasant experiences within the park: a ride not confined to a track, and gently propelled by your own muscle as you cruise around Tom Sawyer Island in the nine-foot-deep Rivers of America. If the canoes are operating during your visit, note that they are notoriously slow to load. The canoes, the Mike Fink Keelboats and the Liberty Square Riverboat each circles the same territory and features essentially the same sights; if you're trying to "do" the Kingdom in a day, select the one mode of transport that most appeals to you.

Big Thunder Mountain

The closest thing to a roller coaster in Walt Disney World, Big Thunder is a triumph of theme and thrills, a "runaway" train ride through an old west mining town gone amok (the Roadrunner would be right at home here, were it not for the wrong manufacturing label). The red rock "mountain" is made of steel and cement and towers to 197 feet in elevation—the highest point in The Magic Kingdom—and is covered with cactus and scrub. The Four Corners-style scenery is attractive, but you won't see much of it after you board the ride. The train drops into a mine shaft and pitch-black caves, then quickly ascends three different hills in its otherwise-downhill pursuit of kicks—the third climb occurs during an earthquake amid falling boulders and snickering bats. Although the train proceeds rapidly along its half-mile track— taking in a furious, 720-degree descending corkscrew at mid-point—most visitors are not taken aback by Big Thunder. The attraction is fairly tame for a roller coaster, placing an emphasis on the southwest theme and fun over intense thrills. A good viewing area is located just to the right of the entrance, near the attraction's exit. *Length of ride:* three minutes. *Special note:* Minimum height requirement, 40 inches. Big Thunder is one of the Kingdom's most popular attractions and the wait starts early and continues late. Make this your second or third attraction of the day, or wait to ride until just before park closing on a busy day. The ride also takes on a different ambience at night.

Country Bear Jamboree

With architecture set somewhere in the Rockies, but a cast from deepest Appalachia, the Country Bear Jamboree is a good-humored musical hoe-down featuring a cast of singing audio-animatronic animals. Banjos, fiddles, harmonicas and washboards are dragged out to accompany the motley crew of bluegrass and country performers, led by Henry, the group's suave, tall emcee. "Embarrassing" cornpone humor and wisecracks are muttered by the mounted buffalo, stag and moose on one wall (they're adorned with Christmas tree lights for the altered routine during December). The show is getting a bit rusty, but fortunately it isn't as long in the tooth as its avian counterpart, the Tropical Serenade around the corner, and pre-teens are tickled by the silly humor. *Length of show:* 16 minutes. *Special note:* the Jamboree maintains a devoted following and plays to packed houses from late-morning on. Try to time your arrival at the point guests are being admitted to the 480-seat theater. The pre-show area inside the entrance holds about 300 people—if that area is full, about 180 additional bodies outside will be admitted into the theater for the next performance. Also watch out for the flood of guests deposited on the area from the Hall of Presidents' exit, just across the way. Another good time to visit is just before or during the afternoon parade, which passes in front of the theater.

Diamond Horseshoe Saloon Revue

A western dance-hall saloon featuring a lively (and live) cast of cowboys, singers and comedians, Diamond Horseshoe provides a preview of the other western-themed Disney dining/theater extravaganza, the Hoop-Dee-Doo Revue (see: "Dinner Theaters" in "Universal, Sea World and Other Attractions"). Previously a sit-down attraction requiring advance reservations, Disney established a policy in 1995 that allows guests to come and go during the Diamond Horseshoe performance. The good news is that it's subsequently a lot easier to squeeze in if you don't mind standing—and you can stay for a few minutes or for the entire 30-minute show— but the spectacle has also been scaled back. The nearly continuous show times vary seasonally, but are scheduled a little tighter in the morning. Counter-service sandwiches, cookies and soft drinks are available.

Splash Mountain

Perhaps the best all-around attraction at The Magic Kingdom, Splash Mountain is the post-Disney ride that would most make Walt proud. When the *imagineers* set out to create a log flume—long a staple at many lesser parks—who could have expected they would triumph so spectacularly? Not content to simply haul guests up a hill for a single wet plummet back down, instead, Disney's log flume is set within the vivid Uncle Remus stories, basis for the 1946 plantation-set fantasy *Song of the South* starring Bobby Driscoll.

As we enter the ride, cackling Br'er Fox has enlisted ever-torpid Br'er Bear in an attempt to triumph over savvy and happy Br'er Rabbit. There's just one small deviation: here, the Briar Patch that serves as the story's pivotal destination now lies at the bottom of a 52-foot-high drop. Cresting this plunge, you'll swear you're going over a cliff—really a cleverly-disguised 45 degree slope. Inside Splash Mountain, the Uncle Remus story is played out by dozens of audio-animatronic creations to the tune of the film's classic music score, and one of the best surprises occurs in the tumble to the Laughing Place. *Length of ride:* 11 minutes. *Special note:* Minimum height requirement, 44 inches. Along with Space Mountain, this is the park's most popular ride and a long line forms 20 to 30 minutes after the park has opened. Make it your first or second attraction of the day; otherwise pray for a lull during afternoon parades or evening fireworks. For anyone nervous about heights or drops, the big plunge is scary for that one or two seconds at the top when you realize there's no turning back, and then it's all over—in a splash. After viewing hundreds of guests chuckling happily after the big drop, and never once observing someone who appeared permanently shaken, all I can say is work up the courage and ride Splash Mountain. There's a good chance you'll find it the highlight of your trip. And if you're worried about getting wet, note that few riders get soaked, but the brief spray is least toward the back of the eight-person log.

Tom Sawyer Island

Accessible only by motorized raft, the one-minute trip to Tom Sawyer Island is usually made by clever parents in search of a respite for their kids to burn off some sugar-fed energy. The "attractions" on the island include a barrel bridge, a fort filled with air guns and a pair of eerie caves—Injun Joe's and the Magnetic Mystery Mine. Both caves can be scary for small children, but don't miss the escape tunnel out of the fort. In short, kids under 14 or 15 love it, and emerge subdued. On less busy days, the island is a pleasant escape for all ages. Most of it is shaded, there are usually a few unoccupied benches, and Aunt Polly's Landing provides peanut butter sandwiches, fried chicken and other snacks for an excellent, uncrowded lunch stop. However, if the second, mainland raft-loading dock is in use, you are assured that the island is well-stocked with frenetic children. *Length of attraction:* Stay as long as you like, but allow at least 40 minutes for the round-trip raft ride and exploration time. *Special note:* Tom Sawyer Island is cleared and closed at dusk. Uptight parents beware—the most dangerous thing on the island for impressionable kids is the surfeit of Huck's signs using "misspelt werds, pour gramma and bakwerd letterz."

Walt Disney World Railroad

Smack dab between Splash and Big Thunder is the Frontierland station for the railroad circling the park. If you're exiting one of these rides and are headed directly for Mickey's Toontown Fair, the railroad will probably shave a couple minutes off your trip, otherwise, walking is faster to most other points within the park.

Liberty Square

The Liberty Tree, a 130-year-old transplanted live oak adorned with 13 lanterns that represent the original 13 colonies forms the centerpiece of Liberty Square, the patriotic and tranquil land adjoining Frontierland. The locale affectionately captures Colonial America with its cobblestone streets, brick and clapboard buildings topped by and flower boxes beneath shop windows, all celebrating the "Spirit of '76." The Fife and Drum Corps provides a musical backdrop throughout the day. Liberty Square boasts one of the park's most impressive achievements, the Hall of Presidents, as well as one of the park's most delightful attractions, the Haunted Mansion. But it is the Liberty Square Riverboat that serves as the dominant landmark.

Interesting shopping opportunities abound—the lace-curtained Olde World Antiques sells both made-to-order and brand-name perfumes, original decorative items and furnishings, as well as reproductions. **Yankee Trader** offers a diverse array of gourmet cooking items, including stoneware and country-themed dinnerware, a selection of jams and jellies, along with the requisite Disneyfied items, including that Mickey Mouse waffle iron you always wanted.

The Hall of Presidents

Housed in a replica of a Philadelphia meeting house, the distinguished voice of poet Maya Angelou graces this landmark attraction, revamped and updated in 1994. The program begins with a 70mm film illuminating the significance and history of the U.S. Constitution. Then a curtain rises for a "performance" by all 42 chief executives, from George Washington to Bill Clinton, each recreated via audio-animatronic robots. While the brief speeches are limited to Abraham Lincoln and Clinton, note that during these, the other presidents' eyes blink, their heads turn and nod, and a few whisper to each other—the detail is quite impressive. The 1994 overhaul for this production, coupled with the dignified narration by Angelou, makes for a moving and unique attraction. *Length of show:* 23 minutes. *Special note:* most kids under about 15 years of age would rather be plunging through Splash Mountain, but unless you're on a fast-paced tour, anyone old enough to recognize Lincoln will get something out of this special attraction. Lines sometimes appear long, but the theater accommodates more than 700 people each performance, a couple hundred more than can be held in the lobby area. Except on very busy afternoons, guests who arrive just a few minutes before show time won't be turned away.

The Haunted Mansion

Happily inhabited by 999 ghosts, ghouls and goblins—"But there's always room for one more... any volunteers?"—the Haunted Mansion is a grand collection of classic Disney special effects piled artfully on top of one another. The ride is housed in a re-created 18th-century Hudson River Valley chateau, complete with a graveyard full of tombstones engraved with silly puns. You are ushered into a portrait gallery, the doors close behind you, and the room stretches before your eyes, all narrated by a charmingly sarcastic "ghost host." Released from the extended room you continue to your "doom buggy," which spirits your through the rest of the house—past a ballroom with dancing ghosts, into an attic with a woman speaking from inside a crystal globe, and then out to the graveyard, where a vivid party rages under the light of the moon. The details are splendid—this is one ride where a repeat visit will conjure up loads of previously unseen sights—and the whole effect is one of mirth, making the attraction suitable for all ages. Watch out for the hitchhiking ghosts! *Length of ride:* 15 minutes, including pre-show and a brief walk-through section. *Special note:* Although lines move rapidly into the mansion, this ride is impacted by the nearby Hall of Presidents; if a performance by our elected leaders has just ejected several hundred people into the area, quite a few of them will descend on the Haunted Mansion—time your visit appropriately.

Liberty Square Riverboat

The gleaming, triple-decked *Richard F. Irvine* is a real, steam-driven paddle-wheel boat, albeit one tied to an underwater track that rings Tom Sawyer Island. There are a few effects in place on the back side of the island, a narrator and Dixieland music is played over the sound system, but the real reason for riding the leisurely Riverboat is the opportunity to relax away from the crowds on the concrete walkways. The dock is situated at Liberty Square, though this attraction is somewhat better linked to the Frontierland era and theme. *Length of ride:* 15 minutes. *Special note:* there's rarely a line longer than the capacity of the Riverboat, allowing guests to time their arrival for the point just as the craft is pulling up for loading.

Mike Fink Keelboats

Operated seasonally only, the *Bertha Mae* and the *Gullywhumper* sputter and wend their way around Tom Sawyer Island with a recorded spiel that attempts to lend a folksy air of backwoods authenticity. Passengers can sit on the enclosed main deck, or on the open top. *Length of ride:* 10 minutes. *Special note:* the line moves slowly for this attraction, peaking in the early afternoon; if you are a completist, hoping to conquer every ride in the park, hop aboard, otherwise, the Riverboat is a more appealing venture on the same Rivers of America.

Fantasyland

Graced by a magnificent dream castle and festooned with brightly colored ribbons, balloons and gold trim, Fantasyland is a favorite destination for many Magic Kingdom visitors. From Central Plaza, the 189-foot-high Cinderella Castle is the symbolic entrance—a timeless, romanticized vision of the medieval castles featured in countless fairy tales. Once we pass through the castle gates, Cinderella's Golden Carrousel beckons, its band organ hums classic Disney tunes along with a chorus of jubilant children. A village reminiscent of alpine Bavaria is draped around the Carrousel, and an easy-to-miss, but charming *Fountaine de Cendrillon* (Cinderella Fountain) can be spotted off to the left.

The two other primary entrances into Fantasyland yield a completely different impression. Entering through Liberty Square, the transition between lands—through a portico—is subtle rather than grand, and the continuity between architectural eras is sly and seductive. On the other hand, the wide passageway from Tomorrowland is impersonal and bland, and en route a loud soundtrack is provided by the puttering Raceway. There is also a pair of little-used routes into Fantasyland around the sides of the castle.

While many of Fantasyland's attractions are geared towards kids, a few are equally beloved by adults, particularly Peter Pan's Flight, which was also a personal favorite of Walt's. With its mixture of "dark house" rides, a merry-go-round and circling elephants and teacups, Fantasyland most mirrors a more typical amusement midway, albeit without the carnival barkers. Of course, everything is colored with the usual, glistening Disney touch.

Fantasyland has the greatest concentration of rides, and by lunchtime, it is packed. Most of the attractions have slow loading capabilities—this is one place where you are likely to see more people in line than strolling about. Three attractions, in particular, create problems: Dumbo, Peter Pan and 20,000 Leagues Under the Sea, all of which should be experienced early or late in the day. Because most visitors head first for the three big mountains, then converge on Fantasyland, the crowds here are thicker later in the morning, but do not let up until later in the afternoon, when tykes begin to burn out and wilted parents head for the hotel. Two touring options are recommended: families should see Fantasyland first thing in the morning, while older groups should wait until the afternoon attendance begins to ebb, usually after 4 or 5 p.m.

Shopping in Fantasyland strays well beyond the animated themes, notably at the **King's Gallery**, an expensive, but well-stocked collection of medieval and mythical items, including suits of armor and other "elegant" weaponry, oversized tapestries, clocks and hand-crafted jewelry. **Mickey's Christmas Carol** is a year-round Christmas accessory shop, heavily infiltrated by Disney characters, while **Tinker Bell's Treasures** sells stuffed animals and other toys, lavish dresses and a line of Madame Alexander dolls.

Ariel's Grotto is a new meet-and-greet area for the star of *The Little Mermaid*, located next to Dumbo (overlooking the 20,000 Leagues lagoon); try to visit first thing in the morning before the line builds (Ariel generally arrives at 10 a.m.).

AUTHOR'S OBSERVATION

Cinderella Castle is a focal point for The Magic Kingdom, but it also serves as a nerve center for the park. In addition to providing a major conduit down to the utilidors, a spiral stone staircase leads up to King Stefan's Banquet Hall, which serves meals overlooking the busy Carrousel area. Higher, the main spire contains a broadcast room, security rooms and television monitors, while an apartment—built for, but never used by the Disney family—sits idle. The castle itself is made of steel-reinforced fiberglass and paint.

Cinderella's Golden Carrousel

Although the Disney Company could have easily designed and built one from scratch, legend has it this glittering merry-go-round is a genuine, 1917 carousel built in Philadelphia, a tribute to the amusement-park craftsmen of a century ago. It was discovered by Disney scouts, refurbished, and scenes from the 1950 Disney *Cinderella* were painted for the 18-scene mural above the 90 galloping steeds. *Length of ride:* two minutes. *Special note:* Loading and unloading for this attraction takes longer than the ride itself; if you have children in tow and the carousel is a must, tackle it by mid-morning, or in the evening when it takes on an elegant aura.

Dumbo the Flying Elephant

Anchored by a baton-wielding Timothy Mouse, the agent who masterminds a circus career for the little elephant with big ears, Dumbo throws its weight around as the most popular Disney attraction for many small children. The ring of flying elephants circles 10 to 20 feet off the ground for a breathtakingly short trip, and holds little appeal for adults, other than providing the brief opportunity to observe pure, unmitigated joy in a 4- or 5-year-old's eyes. *Length of ride:* One-and-a-half minutes. *Special note:* The line for Dumbo may not appear long, but it is easily the slowest-moving in the park. Parents of small children should schedule this ride as the first of the day, or wait until evening when the toddler factor dwindles.

It's a Small World

A Disney "classic," It's a Small World was created for the 1964-1965 World's Fair and represents a children's version of themes the Disney Company gives a slightly more sophisticated (and commercialized) spin to in Epcot's World Showcase. A boat ride through an enormous, brightly lit warehouse, It's a Small World seeks to encapsulate the cultures of as many nations as possible. Curiously, Antarctica is represented, but the nations of Eastern Europe are overlooked. The homogenized, audio-animatronic dolls pay tribute to the concept of global harmony, each doll singing the same song. For a few minutes, the world's ills are invisible. This ride holds great appeal for children, but many adults ride it once, and are never able to banish the cloying song from their brain. *Length of ride:* 11 minutes. *Special note:* It's a Small World boasts a devoted following, but processes the lines quickly; the longest waits come mid-day. If you are attempting to conquer Fantasyland in a single gulp, make It's a Small World your last ride during a morning tour, or your first ride during an afternoon visit.

Legend of the Lion King

In 1994, the Disney Company took the unusual step of creating an attraction based around a movie still enjoying its commercial theatrical release. This allowed the company to promote the film's pending video release, its stuffed-toy characters and character-designed clothing. Now, with *Toy Story* and *Hunchback of Notre Dame* attractions firmly in place at the Disney-MGM Studios, the company seems intent on using this cross-marketing tool for much of its family product. The Legend of the Lion King is situated between Peter Pan's Flight, Cinderella's Castle and Snow White's Adventures, which may be a sly way of cementing the film as another Disney classic. (Who me, a cynic?) Legend of the Lion King is a "live" show, using a mixture of hand puppets, film footage and special effects to re-tell the story of Simba. Because of their familiarity with the film, children are big fans of this attraction; adults not in the company of pre-teens will probably want to place this lower on the priority list, possibly for second-day touring. For what it's worth, I rank the similar attraction at the Disney-MGM Studios, Voyage of the Little Mermaid, as slightly better, and easier to fit into a busy schedule. *Length of attraction:* 26 minutes with the pre-show. *Special note:* The theater accommodates 480 guests. On a slow day you may be able to arrive shortly before the scheduled performance time and secure a seat. Otherwise plan on a 30-to-45-minute wait, with early and midafternoon producing the biggest line.

Mad Tea Party

A favorite spot for people-watching, the Mad Tea Party draws a diverse group of guests who circle around on a giant, revolving table in garish teacups, all inspired by the animated film, *Alice in Wonderland.* A huge favorite with teenagers, the Mad Tea Party also encourages more rider participation than other Disney attractions. The faster you turn the wheel in the center of your teacup, the faster you spin — nausea is not unknown. Teenagers (including this one once) love to see just how fast they can twirl, much to the consternation of any hapless adult trapped in the whirling cup with them. You are forewarned. Otherwise, the attraction is perfectly pleasant, but not unlike the action found on a number of carnival rides. Don't miss the drunken doormouse who pops out of a central teapot. *Length of ride:* One-and-a-half minutes. *Special note:* Though not one of Fantasyland's most visited attractions, lines move slowly; ride by mid-morning or wait until late afternoon.

Mr. Toad's Wild Ride

One of Disney's two "dark house" attractions, Mr. Toad's Wild Ride is popular with kids, less so with adults. Based on the witty 1949 Disney film *The Adventures of Ichabod and Mr. Toad*, which was loosely based on Kenneth Grahame's book *The Wind in the Willows*, the ride is inspired by Mr. Toad's obsession with motorcars, and the wild late-night ride he experiences in a jalopy that turns out to have been stolen by wily weasels. Guests are passengers in his car, which goes, literally, to hell and back. The wildest element is neon and black lights, not the physical motion. *Length of ride:* Two-and-a-half minutes. *Special note:* Although he does have his devotees, Mr. Toad is not one of Fantasyland's most popular attractions. Lines move at a moderate clip, but are biggest mid-day.

Peter Pan's Flight

The one "must-see" attraction in Fantasyland. Children of all ages flock to this delightful, if brief interpretation of the 1953 Disney animated film. Guests board a pirate ship that follows Peter Pan into the air and sails away—over London on a moonlit night, off to Neverland, and into battle with Captain Hook. Peter Pan's Flight gives the "dark house" type ride a fresh new spin by allowing visitors to look down on the action—the ships are suspended from the track above—a technique adopted by Universal's E.T. Adventure to more elaborate effect. *Length of ride:* Three minutes. *Special note:* Peter Pan's Flight is the all-around most popular ride in Fantasyland and the line does not move quickly. Visit first thing in the morning, or wait until families have sufficiently cleared out of Fantasyland at the end of the afternoon

Skyway to Tomorrowland

Complementing the Swiss and alpine decor of Fantasyland, the modern Skyway was actually designed and built in Switzerland. A quick look to the right as you depart the station reveals that half of Fantasyland and Liberty Square are mostly composed of one big building. Since walking to the Tomorrowland station (near Space Mountain) is faster, the best reason for boarding is for the view, or for a private moment. *Length of ride:* Five minutes, one way. *Special note:* This is one of the slower-moving lines the park, although the Fantasyland station tends to be a little less busy than the Tomorrowland side. Strollers not permitted.

Snow White's Adventures

The folks at Disney seem at a loss as to what to do with this attraction. Little ones have always been unnerved by this recreation of the 1937 Disney animated classic, so in the 1980s, *imagineers* retooled it, and retitled it Snow White's Scary Adventures. Then, undoubtedly prompted by hostile customer feedback, the attraction was revamped again in 1995, to soften the terror factor for children. This "dark house" ride weaves through the haunted forest in a mine car, but the witch still makes more appearances than Snow White. The simple effects are enough to rattle the psyches of many 4- and 5-year-olds, so try to take them on Peter Pan and Mr. Toad first, to get them used to the darkened setting. *Length of ride:* Three minutes. *Special note:* Although not as popular as Peter Pan's Flight, Snow White still draws a good-sized crowd and does not process the line quickly. Ride by mid-morning, or wait until late afternoon when families begin to clear out.

20,000 Leagues Under the Sea

Based on the Jules Verne novel and a highly-entertaining 1954 Disney film, this elaborate submarine-themed attraction was scheduled for a long-promised upgrade in 1996 for as-yet-to-be-determined results. Previously, a couple of good effects, such as the one of "descending" into the depths, were offset by the vast quantity of cheesy ones—inflated plastic fish ascending from strings, an overly mechanical (and thoroughly unmenacing) giant squid and other deep-sea icons. Where the submarines disappear under a waterfall, a series of more intricate effects are produced, leading up to a volcanic eruption—the visuals are duplicated on each side of the 38-passenger subs. How many of these effects will remain after the renovation is not known, but an improved fantasy submarine ride at least holds promise. Pre-teens find this attraction engrossing and you should make room in your schedule to incorporate the ride if they want to experience it. *Length of ride:* Nine minutes. *Special note:* Second only to Dumbo in causing bottlenecks, the queue for 20K (as it is affectionately referred to by employees) becomes clogged with visitors soon after park opening and never lets up. You have to really want to see this attraction to make the usually immense line worthwhile on a busy day. Try to visit during the first hour the park is open, or wait until just before closing.

Mickey's Toontown Fair

What started as Mickey's Birthdayland (to celebrate the 60th anniversary of Mickey's first screen appearance in 1928), and evolved into Mickey's Starland, has finally become a full-fledged "land" in its own right. It is one of the most significant additions for the 25th Anniversary celebration underway at Walt Disney World.

The overhaul was instigated by Disney research, which showed that the key experience many World visitors count on is meeting the characters. Although three-acre Mickey's Starland was the one, dependable location for character interaction within the World, the demand was intense and generated long lines around the clock. Adding to the situation is that the tent-like structures built for Mickey's Birthdayland were designed to be temporary and always looked a bit like an afterthought.

With the addition of a delightful kiddie roller coaster, the new Mickey's Toontown Fair is a terrific improvement. The tent structures are still there, but they have been pushed into the background by a more interesting foreground. Mickey's country house received a face-lift, with a "remodeling-in-progress" kitchen, a sports-fanatic gameroom, and silhouette evidence that Pluto has chased a cat through the screen door of Mickey's cluttered bedroom. Minnie now receives equal billing through the construction of her own bungalow and flower garden, complete with a Martha Stewart-style work room and craft nook, and a milkmaid kitchen; the artsy-craftsy living room is filled with interactive gags and country music. A new play area, **Toon Park**, is filled with animal sculptures, and an interactive, leaping-water fountain, **Donald's Boat**, is perfect children's entertainment for hot days.

The key attraction, however, is the characters, and nine or more are usually on hand for greetings. The catch is that rather than strolling the streets, all the characters reside in the two tents behind Mickey and Minnie's houses, with lines to meet the group of your choice. Mickey Mouse is found in the **Judges Tent**, which is now set up to handle 1400 one-on-one encounters per hour in an air-conditioned area (which makes one wonder: just how *does* Mickey greet all those kids?). The line to meet Mickey moves relatively quickly, but can approach an hour on busy days (peak toon-greeting period is late morning to late-afternoon).

The **Hall of Fame** next door has three different staging areas, each containing four animated stars and room for a few dozen guests: one line leads to the Heroes (Pluto, Goofy, Minnie and, usually, Donald, all attired in farm fair duds), one to the Princesses (a rotating selection, including Snow White, Cinderella, Belle, Jasmine, Sleeping Beauty and sometimes Alice or Wendy), and one to the Villains (also a rotating crew, including Jafar, Prince John,

Sheriff of Nottingham, Cruela de Vil, Maleficent, B'rer Fox and Ratcliff). In order to see all three groups, you must wait in line for each, but be aware that the Princesses sometimes call it a day around 5 p.m. Since the lines here can top an hour on busy days, if seeing the characters is important, stop be first thing in the morning, or wait until evening, when younger visitors start leaving the park. The good news is that once you wait in line, you are guaranteed to have a few moments with the four characters for photos and autographs.

The Barnstormer

A delightful, pint-sized roller coaster, the Barnstormer is a gleeful spin through Goofy's Wiseacres Farm, complete with a gaggle of wide-eyed chickens that cluck in horror when the coaster crashes through the farmhouse. *Length of ride:* less than a minute. *Special note:* Although it's fun for all ages, the Barnstormer seats only 16 and the line crawls along slowly. If your children are too short for Big Thunder, you'll want to make the Barnstormer a priority, but try to visit in the first hour the park is open, or in the evening as children begin to clear out of Mickey's Toontown.

Walt Disney World Railroad

From the newly painted Mickey's Toontown Fair station, the WDW Railroad is the fastest route out of the park, particularly if the Main Street parade is about to begin.

Tomorrowland

Tomorrowland was intended by Walt as a serious complement to Main Street and Frontierland. Instead, the concrete 'burb was dated almost as soon as it was built, and it had the feel of "yesterday's view of tomorrow," in the words of author Stephen M. Fjellman. Unlike the other lands, Tomorrowland lacked both intimacy and immediacy, imagining a humorless *Jetsons* future already poorly anticipated by second-rate science fiction films of the 1960s. It was time for a new Disney vision, and in 1995 the company's *imagineers* delivered in spades. The shimmering makeover of Tomorrowland is an unqualified success.

Veering substantially away from the "city of the future" style of the old land, and toward a tongue-in-cheek future-past—that of Jules Verne and Buck Rogers—Tomorrowland now mixes a sexy camp aesthetic with a nostalgic tribute to science fiction visions created in the 1920s. Disney publicity perfectly characterizes this creation as "the future that never was," laid out in a dreamy collage of sleek lines and soaring obelisks, with Mars-like rock crags jutting against metallic buildings. The aural texture of Tomorrowland has also been refined: the inspired instrumental soundtrack wafting though the neighborhood is composed of Vangelis, Andreas Vollenweider and the "space-age bachelor pad" music of Esquivel.

With the openings of the ExtraTERRORestrial Alien Encounter and Time-keeper, Tomorrowland now justifies the mass of bodies that invade its promenade from the first minutes the park is open. Space Mountain continues to be the main draw, but many guests are spending more time in the revamped Tomorrowland, complicating touring plans for those trying to tackle it all in a day. In general, attendance peaks in Tomorrowland earlier than in Frontierland and Fantasyland, making mid-to-late afternoon visits ideal, but Space Mountain is busy from the git-go. Interestingly, although three Tomorrowland attractions (Space Mountain, ExtraTERRORestrial and Astro-Orbiter) generate long lines, most of the others either accommodate a high volume of traffic or have low demand, making them ideal for early afternoon touring, when most of the park's arteries are clogged.

Beyond T-shirts and trinkets, Tomorrowland offers little in the way of shopping. **Merchant of Venus** has futuristic toys and games, and souvenirs themed to ExtraTERRORestrial. **Star Traders** features character merchandise, clothing and sun-care products.

AstroOrbiter

Like Dumbo, the AstroOrbiter (previously known as StarJets) is an airy, "spinning in circles" attraction similar to more-traditional midway rides, only this one is gussied up with a hub of whirling planets and its flight path soars considerably higher than most rides of this nature. The view is good and the jets are fun, but the ride is over before you know it. *Length of ride:* One-and-a-half minutes. *Special note:* Lines don't always appear long, but they move very slowly. If you want to ride the AstroOrbiter, do it early in the morning, or just before closing, and by all means don't hop in line after the nearby Timekeeper has just deposited 650 bodies onto the avenue.

Take Flight

A light (very light) take on the history and romance of aviation, Take Flight glides past dioramas of early flight daredevils, onto a make-believe trip around the world, and then into the world of speed, featuring 70mm footage shot on planes and computer-generated graphics appropriated from the movie *Tron*. This ride began as an airline-sponsored tribute to flight (Delta abandoned the attraction in early 1996), but is one section of Tomorrowland that didn't benefit from the recent rehab—now the ride feels dated and stodgy. *Length of ride:* Five minutes. *Special note:* Take Flight rarely has a long line and is an easy attraction to slide in between the big rides, or while waiting for Timekeeper. Ride it anytime.

ExtraTERRORestrial Alien Encounter

Easily the most controversial attraction the Disney Company has assembled in years, ExtraTERRORestrial bears the unique distinction of having been shut down for a creative overhaul by Michael Eisner after it was first completed in 1995 because the Disney CEO thought it wasn't scary enough. A few thousand traumatized moppets and more than a few pissed-off parents later, it's safe to say the theater-oriented attraction adequately "toughens up" The Magic Kingdom and steels the company against the faint criticism it wasn't adult enough when compared to Universal. Which isn't to say *this* adult is a big fan of the sensory assault on display here.

Guests are ushered into a demonstration room at the Tomorrowland Interplanetary Convention Center, where audiences are prepared to experience an exhibition by X-S Tech, a corporation based on a distant planet which promises to do everything "with excess." An evil-looking robot, S.I.R., beams a cute and fuzzy alien "volunteer" from one glass cylinder to another, with increasingly disturbing results, then you are taken into the 132-seat theater for the real demonstration. Here, a restraining device is lowered onto your shoulders, pinning you in your seat. The plan is to beam an X-S representative, Chairman Clench, into the glass cylinder in the center of the 360-degree theater, but of course, something goes very wrong; the lights go out and guests are treated to a display of visual, aural and tactile special effects.

Loud and graphic, ExtraTERRORestrial is more unpleasant than scary, and the attraction posts significantly lower repeat customers than the park's other big rides. In fact, this attraction is not scary at all the second time around, although it is equally loud and annoying. *Length of attraction:* 19 minutes, including pre-show. *Special note:* There's a good reason 17 signs are posted at or near the entrance warning parents about the intensity of the alien encounter. Although many kids survive the demonstration unscathed, a quick look at the tear-streaked 7- to 8-year-old faces exiting most performances tells a different story. Also, the 48-inch height requirement is not strictly enforced by ride attendants. If you have a child under 10 years of age, send another adult in as a guinea pig. In addition, many guests make ExtraTERRORestrial their second attraction of the day, right after Space Mountain, and by mid-morning, queues are well-established. However, by early afternoon, lines begin to recede. Our recommendation: see ExtraTERRORestrial first thing in the morning, or wait until late afternoon. Also, be aware of the crowds that flood out of nearby Timekeeper every 20 minutes, many of whom beam directly over to the line for ExtraTERRORestrial.

Grand Prix Raceway

Many adults scratch their heads over the continuing appeal of this ride, but as anyone under the age of 14 or 15 knows, the ability to take the wheel of a car—even a miniature one—is quite empowering. The cars run on a track, limiting their steering capabilities, and the roadspeed tops out at about seven miles per hour. The engine noise is not quite deafening, but quite pervasive. If you have a driver's license, this attraction is imminently skippable. Children must be 52 inches tall to ride alone; otherwise they can drive with an adult as a passenger. *Length of ride:* The cars circle the 2/5-mile loop in three to four minutes. *Special note:* Few park attractions have as little appeal to grown-ups as this one, however, adults do get roped in by the 52-inch height requirement. Let your child do the driving, sit back and enjoy his or her delight. Lines build before noon and move slowly, but taper off late afternoon.

AUTHOR'S OBSERVATION

What Disney ride has produced the largest number of personal injury law-suits? The delightfully sordid 1994 tell-all, Mouse Tails: A Behind-the-Scenes Look at Disneyland, by David Koenig, is the ultimate insider's guide to The Magic Kingdom's West-Coast counterpart. Its pages detail the location and layout of Club 33 (the park's members-only bar and restaurant), whispers notorious scandals perpetrated by Disney employees (including at least one Peeping Tom), and even includes a chapter titled "Fatal Attractions," about the deaths—accidental and otherwise—that have occurred in the park. While we can't testify to the book's cover-to-cover veracity, it does make for an entertaining read. Oh, and based on California court records, Disneyland's Autopia (which is identical to The Magic Kingdom's Grand Prix Raceway) was responsible for 67 personal injury lawsuits from 1954 through 1992. The Mouse Tales list ranked the Matterhorn Bobsleds second and the Haunted Mansion third.

Skyway to Fantasyland

The colorful Skyway buckets highlight some of the best views of The Magic Kingdom, and make a nifty 90-degree turn at their mid-point. When they were built 25 years ago, this was the first such dogleg in use on this type of transport. The skyway lands in Fantasyland next to It's a Small World. *Length of ride:* Five minutes, one-way. *Special note:* Even without a line at the Skyway, walking is a faster way to reach Fantasyland. The line crawls along slowly—allow about 15 minutes from the bottom of the steps. Strollers are not permitted, and neither are round-trips.

Space Mountain

Promising a "trip out of this world," Space Mountain was a dazzling success when it opened in 1975, with astronauts Scott Carpenter, Gordon Cooper and Jim Irwin making the first lift-off. Since then the ride has thrilled and delighted millions of visitors. The mountain is a metal, Mount Fuji-like apparition, with a tangle of two nearly identical roller-coaster tracks that snake through its hollow super-structure. Riders are loaded into six-passenger jets, which climb a long hill to the star-filled ceiling of the darkened interior. Watch for the giant chocolate chip cookie amid the space debris. From here it's all downhill, with the rockets reaching speeds of 28 miles per hour (it feels faster) as they whip turbulently through the darkness.

For those nervous about tackling Space Mountain, you can obtain a glimpse of the inside of the attraction via the Tomorrowland Transit Authority, although the disembodied whoops and shrieks may further turn you off. The best bet is to work up to it via Big Thunder; if you are comfortable on this ride, Space Mountain is somewhat more tumultuous. Also note that the front-seat position in the jets is physically a little rougher, and psychologically more daunting—your request to sit in back will always be accommodated.

Length of ride: Two-and-a-half minutes. *Special note:* Children under 7 must be accompanied by an adult, and all guests must be 44 inches to ride. For couples tow-ing children under the minimum height requirement, see the switch-off section under "Families With Small Children," in "Planning Your Trip." With the possible exception of that Zip-a-Dee-Doo-Dah ride, Space Mountain is the attraction that draws the most repeat business in the park, and therefore, a few logistical strategies are in order. Within 15 minutes after the park has opened to the general public, a line will be solidly established. The queue builds through the morning, then ebbs and expands throughout the afternoon. During the last few hours the park is open, the line grows longer again, since many visitors opt to make Space Mountain their last ride of the day. If the attraction is high on your list, make it your first of the morning, preferably in the first few minutes the park is open, or else in the late afternoon when parades can lessen the wait. Ideally, be positioned for the rope drop at Central Plaza several minutes before the park officially opens, then sprint for the mountain. For those who wish to ride in the last hour the park is open, it's worth noting a little deception the greeting attendants perform nightly: much of the line for Space Mountain is held outside the main building as the park prepares to shut down, thus creating the appearance of a line longer than it really is. By doing this, attendants can cease operation of the ride soon after scheduled closing time; however, if you are in line at closing, you will be permitted to ride. Finally, "Surprise Morning" visitors are often surprised that Space Mountain is not technically among the attractions opened early for Disney Resort guests. Actually, the ride usually opens at some point during the early admission period, before the general public is admitted. Keep checking back between rides and you'll probably have the opportunity for a few ascents of the mountain before lines become long.

Timekeeper

Imported from Disneyland Paris, Timekeeper is a delightful addition to the new Tomorrowland. Using the park's CircleVision 360 theater, the film follows the exploits of a flying, time-traveling droid, 9-Eye, who transmits her drop-in observations of a medieval Scottish battlefield, a young Mozart playing a concert, da Vinci working with a model, and eventually hooks up with H.G. Wells and Jules Verne at the 1900 Paris Exposition for a trip into the future. The visuals are great, but what really makes the attraction work is the "live" presence of Timekeeper himself, a humanoid, wisecracking audio-animatronic scientist with a voice supplied by Robin Williams. Positioned at the front of the theater, the scientist lends a buoyant immediacy to the presentation the film might otherwise lack. *Length of attraction:* 16 minutes. *Special note:* Timekeeper is developing a big following, but lines for the attraction are usually accommodated whole by the 650-person theater-in-the-round. On all but the busiest afternoons, it's possible to get into the next performance (spaced at 20-minute intervals) without delay.

Tomorrowland Transit Authority

A pleasant tour of Tomorrowland is provided by these spiffed-up people-movers. The system purports to require no moving parts, uses very little energy to operate, and emits no pollution. *Length of ride:* 10 minutes. *Special note:* The Tomorrowland Transit Authority rarely has a line, providing a good opportunity to cool your jets in the hot afternoon. If you are headed for Timekeeper, but just missed the start of a performance, this attraction is a nice place to hang around until the next show.

Walt Disney's Carousel of Progress

Long one of Disney's most commercial conceits (and that's saying a lot), the Carousel of Progress debuted at the 1964–1965 World's Fair and features an ingenious design. A single, progressive storyline is told on four different sets, each representing a different era, that occupy the stationary hub of a merry-go-round. The audience, broken into separate theaters, circle around the stages to experience the full play. A single theme song bridges the shift from one set-piece to the next, all focusing on a mythical American family from the turn of the century to the present day. The nostalgic show is Disney and General Electric's take on progress — that is, a celebration of electricity and all it serves, including toasters, refrigerators, and televisions. With each new invention, the family on display is further "freed" from the burdens of life. Which means, by the end of the performance, the family can spend more time playing video games, thereby using more electricity. The Carousel of Progress is a fascinating glimpse into the marketing logic behind corporate sponsorship of Disney attractions: General Electric, Exxon, AT&T and other giant corporations (and entire countries, at Epcot) are allowed to weave their interpretation of how the world is a better place for their presence. *Length of attraction:* 18 minutes. *Special note:* Rarely a line, the Carousel is ideal for afternoon touring.

Eating

Eating is more a function than a celebration at The Magic Kingdom. Of the three main parks, sit-down dining options at the Kingdom are the most limited and, in terms of food quality, the least appealing. The sit-down eateries, the **Liberty Tree Tavern**, **Tony's Town Square** and **King Stefan's Banquet Hall** are described in detail under "Restaurants." Information on the popular **character meals** is also provided in "Restaurants." If you're planning to utilize one of these restaurants once you're in the park, go directly to the location you wish to eat at and make a reservation, or call ☎ *(407) WDW-DINE* prior to your arrival. Note that alcohol is not served anywhere within the park.

If you have your heart set on a sit-down meal during your day at The Magic Kingdom, my recommendation is to incorporate a midday meal into an afternoon break from theme-park touring. Restaurants located outside the park are less busy, more varied and considerably better in quality. Among the easiest lunch possibilities are the **Grand Floridian Cafe** and **Narcoossee's** at the Grand Floridian Beach Resort, the **Concourse Steakhouse** at the Contemporary and the **Whispering Canyon Cafe** at the Wilderness Lodge. Check the "Restaurants" chapter for other options within easy reach of the Disney Transportation System.

INSIDER TIP

At the risk of instigating an irate phone call from Michael Eisner, those on a budget can bring their own food into the Disney parks, providing one is discreet. The company's official policy is that outside food and drink is not allowed past the front gate of the three main parks, but attendants don't check bags. As long as you're not hauling an oversized Pepsi cooler, you'll be able to join the millions of other guests who have saved more than a few bucks by packing their own meal. Remember, alcohol is not sold anywhere within The Magic Kingdom's boundaries. On the other hand, outside food (other than glass containers and alcohol) is allowed into the water parks and onto Discovery Island.

However, if you want to see all of the park in one long day, I suggest you stay the more-typical amusement-park course by subsisting on fast food. Unfortunately, a number of guests feel that the quality of Disney's food is inferior to McDonald's. Additionally, even the "fast" food options can require an unreasonable chunk of time. From about 11:30 a.m. until around 2:30 p.m., food counters are jammed even on the least-busiest days. Still, my hat goes off to the enormous crew who have the unenviable task of feeding tens of thousands of people daily. That the park has begun to incorporate more health-conscious items such as salads and sandwiches into its menus is an improvement. A breakdown of some of the better eateries in the park includes:

Main Street, USA

The **Main Street Bake Shop** is an excellent early morning pit stop for those milling about waiting for the rope drop; it provides coffee, pastries, cookies and cinnamon rolls baked on the premises. **The Plaza Restaurant** serves cold sandwiches, and a good selection of burgers; its proximity to the **Plaza Ice Cream Parlor** guarantees a variety of milk shakes, immense sundaes and other ice cream desserts, including nonfat ice cream. **Casey's Corner** is themed to baseball, providing jumbo hot dogs, french fries and other fast food. A simple buffet is proffered at the **Crystal Palace**, but the facility is now consigned to the character dining program for all three meals (see "Character Meals" in "Restaurants").

Adventureland

The Mexican food served at **El Pirate y el Perico** is quite subpar—greasy and bland, while the **Egg Roll Wagon** is marginally better; fresh spears of pineapple are a better bet at **Aloha Isle**.

Frontierland

Aunt Polly's Landing is accessible only to those who raft over to Tom Sawyer's Island. This keeps the crowd down, but also limits the menu to peanut butter and jelly sandwiches, ham and cheese, fried chicken served cold, soft drinks and simple desserts; still, it offers a pleasant respite with a nice view of the river. The **Pecos Bill Cafe** is a popular for do-it-yourself burgers, barbecue-chicken sandwiches and salads, but keep an eye on the mounted animals on the wall.

Liberty Square

The **Columbia Harbour House** serves cold sandwiches and fried fish and chicken dishes, but is best for clam chowder. **Sleepy Hollow**, a snack stand located next to Olde World Antiques, is a good bet for anyone searching for a healthier snack. Tasty vegetarian chili is offered and whole wheat pita and potato bread wrap the preprepared sandwiches.

Fantasyland

The very busy **Pinocchio Village House** features a vegetarian pasta salad, a selection of burgers, and cold smoked-turkey sub sandwiches; decor centers on a collection of antique cuckoo clocks. **Lumiere's Kitchen** is the kiddie choice, offering chicken fillet, ham and muenster, and grilled cheese sandwiches and chicken nuggets.

Tomorrowland

Cosmic Ray's provides three menus with a huge seating area; one menu focuses on rotisserie chicken, another sticks to burgers, including turkey-burgers, while a third sells soups, sandwiches and tossed-to-order chicken and Caesar salads. The **Plaza Pavilion** is linked to the Plaza in Main Street, but offers a different menu, including Italian deli subs, pizza by the slice and fried chicken strips.

INSIDER TIP

When my niece and nephew joined me for theme-park research, their mother sent them to me with fanny packs filled with snacks. It wasn't until midway through our first day of touring—as I witnessed other parents becoming slaves to the Disney food-cart empire—that I saw the beauty of her plan. The kids had a say on what snacks they carted in their packs (a mix of both junk and more-healthful food), and control over when it was eaten. All I needed to spring for between meals was drinks.

The Magic Kingdom Touring Itineraries

Myth: At their best, Disney's theme parks are whimsical creations that invite us to wander aimlessly, bouncing from ride to ride for a day of fantasy and fun. Reality: Without a plan—be it mine, yours or Daisy Duck's—you will waste valuable hours as you become ensnared in crowds and sucked into endless lines. No single touring plan works perfectly for everyone, but we've broken down our touring suggestions for The Magic Kingdom into three groups, each with a goal of seeing most of the park in the course of one very long day. All three plans work best under the following circumstances:

a. You have purchased your tickets before you arrive at the Ticket and Transportation Center or The Magic Kingdom (see "Tickets," in "Obstacles and Opportunities").

b. You are positioned at the main entrance to the Kingdom—*not* the Ticket and Transportation Center—at least 30 to 45 minutes prior to the official opening time. Call ☎ *(407) 824-4321* the day before your visit to verify the opening time.

c. All members of your party are willing to follow the same touring itinerary. Members of your party can, of course, bow out of individual attractions they have no desire to ride.

d. If you are *not* a guest of a Disney Resort, that you tour The Magic Kingdom only on days when the Surprise Morning policy is not in effect: currently, Sundays, Tuesdays, Wednesdays and Fridays. Note that Sundays and Fridays are the least-busy days during the summer season. If you visit the park on a Surprise Morning (currently Mondays, Thursdays and Saturdays), you will find lines in place at all major attractions within minutes after the general public is admitted to the park.

In the preceding section, The Magic Kingdom's "lands" were discussed following a logical touring order: a clockwise pattern as one would encounter them on a map. This format is also used for the descriptions of Epcot and the Disney-MGM Studios that follow. Real life, however, is not so orderly, and neither are our touring suggestions. At several points, these itineraries will ask you to backtrack across the park, or to pass up attractions en route to others. This is not by accident. Crowds at the Kingdom ebb and flow throughout the average day, based on many underlying factors not readily apparent to first-timers. The Fielding's touring itineraries are designed to guide you to where the multitudes aren't, ideally at every given point of the day.

Among the more obvious causes for logjams and long lines are parades, shows and fireworks. By staying aware of these events, *especially* if you don't personally want to partake in them, you will have a leg up on the competition. Yet other, more subtle gremlins are at work here, too. One example is the attractions that accommodate a large number of people, and are situated next to a slow-loading ride. For instance, the auditorium containing **Timekeeper** holds 650 people for each 20-minute show cycle; the **AstroOrbiter** immediately facing Timekeeper's exit accommodates only 24 people every four minutes. Through the course of a busy day, one can observe the line for AstroOrbiter grow and shrink, again and again, with the length peaking every 20 minutes when — you guessed it — Timekeeper exits and a flood of guests surges toward the ride. Fielding's suggestion? After Timekeeper, you'll head to an attraction less likely to be bottlenecked at that particular moment. Other major attractions that dispense large numbers of people at once include the **Country Bear Jamboree**, the **Hall of Presidents** and **Legend of the Lion King**. In each case, the exits for these attractions affect the lines for rides in the immediate vicinity. Tips such as these are designed to help you get the most bang for your buck and maximize your limited touring time.

If you are staying at a Disney Resort and are able to take advantage of the Surprise Morning policy, by all means, do so. Logically, head for **Space Mountain** and **ExtraTERRORestrial** first—note that Space Mountain sometimes doesn't open immediately on Surprise Mornings. Then tour the **Fantasyland** attractions of your choice until the park opens to the general public. At that point, head straight for **Splash** and **Big Thunder** mountains which are not open during the Surprise Morning period, then follow the general plan itinerary outlined below, omitting the attractions you have already visited.

Although breaks are not incorporated into the touring suggestions that follow, they can be incorporated easily any time after noon, as the park reaches capacity. You can best visualize park attendance in the form of a bell curve, the peak period occupying a three- or four-hour window beginning about 11:30 a.m. At about 3 p.m. you will find the lines beginning to recede. This theory applies to Epcot and the Disney-MGM Studios, as well. Simply resume your touring itinerary where you left off.

The Ideal Plan

This itinerary is geared for those who want to try to see all of The Magic Kingdom in a single day, and are tall enough (at least 44 inches) to ride—or are not adverse to—the action-packed attractions. Because attendance (as little as 10,000 guests or as many as 90,000) and the number of hours the park remains open (until 6 p.m. on a slow day, or as late as 2 a.m. on a busy one) will affect how this plan operates, the number of attractions each reader actually experiences will vary. It is possible to see virtually the entire park in one long day, but this requires stamina, as well as the conviction to stick to the itinerary. A better plan is to see as much as you can in one, moderately paced day, incorporating an afternoon break, then return to the park another day for a few hours one morning or evening to take in rides you have missed or want to revisit.

1. Enter the Magic Kingdom and walk down Main Street, USA to **Central Plaza** for the rope drop. Ignore the sign that states that the (WDW) Railroad offers the fastest passage to Mickey's Toontown Fair and Frontierland.

2. When the rope drops, proceed quickly through Tomorrowland to **Space Mountain**.

3. After riding Space Mountain, swiftly *retrace* your steps back to Central Plaza, pass through Adventureland to **Big Thunder Mountain**. You can ride the WDW Railroad to Big Thunder from Mickey's Toontown Fair station to Frontierland instead of walking, but this will devour several invaluable minutes from your schedule.

4. Following Big Thunder, ride **Splash Mountain**, next door. At this point, you will have experienced the three rides that later in the day will involve the longest waits. On a moderately busy morning, these three rides will take about an hour if begun immediately when the park opens—or about three-to-four hours if attempted later in the afternoon.

5. Ride the **Jungle Cruise**, followed by **Pirates of the Caribbean**, then proceed to the **Haunted Mansion** in Frontierland. Keep an eye out en route to the Haunted Mansion to make sure that the Hall of Presidents hasn't just loosed an army of people from its exit; if it has, visit the Haunted Mansion after step 6.

6. See the **Country Bear Jamboree**. At this point, sometime shortly before lunch, the park will have reached its peak attendance for the day. Our itinerary continues, but switches gears to focus on the attractions boasting the shortest lines. Integrate your lunch stop where convenient.

7. Visit the **Hall of Presidents** and ride the **Liberty Square Riverboat**. Both of these 20- to 25-minute attractions, situated almost next to each other, have set starting/departure times; begin with the one that offers the shortest wait, then proceed to the other.

8. Go to Adventureland and visit the **Swiss Family Treehouse** and **Tropical Serenade** (aka the Enchanted Tiki Birds). As with the previous attractions, the Tiki Bird show is timed to pre-set intervals, 20 minutes apart. If the wait is less than 10 to 15 minutes for the next show, see the Tiki Birds first; otherwise, visit the Treehouse first (about 10 minutes to tour if there's no line), then visit the Tiki Birds.

9. Head for Tomorrowland and either ride the **Transit Authority** or see **Timekeeper**. Again, Timekeeper is set at 20-minute intervals; if the wait is more than 15 minutes, ride the Transit Authority first. Visit the **Carousel of Progress** and **Take Flight**. By this time, afternoon attendance should have peaked and lines will begin to shorten.

10. See the **ExtraTERRORestrial Alien Encounter**.

11. Take the **Skyway** to Fantasyland, or walk if the line extends to the bottom of the stairs, which equals about a 15-minute wait. Ride **It's a Small World**.

12. Ride **Mr. Toad's Wild Ride** and **Snow White's Adventures**, starting with the one offering the shortest wait since the attractions are next to each other.

13. At this point, most of the attractions you have left to see are in Fantasyland and Tomorrowland. If there are several, post-dusk hours remaining before closing time, you'll manage to visit most of the attractions without too many problems. If you have only an hour or so before the park closes, rank your desire to see **Legend of the Lion King** (allow at least a half-hour, *not* including the line), **Peter Pan's Flight**, **20,000 Leagues Under the Sea** and **AstroOrbiter**, as well as any rides you wish to revisit.

14. At the appointed closing time, ride attendants will not allow anyone to enter any existing lines. Proceed to **Main Street, USA**, where you may shop amid the throng. Take your time, the transportation system outside the park will be jammed.

What Did We Miss?

Following this tour by the number will omit **Tom Sawyer Island** (open only until dusk), **Mike Fink Keelboats** (open seasonally during daylight hours), **Mad Tea Party**, **Dumbo the Flying Elephant**, **Cinderella's Golden Carrousel**, **Mickey's Toontown Fair**, and the **Grand Prix Raceway**. While each of these rides has its fans, they should be included on your tour only if you have kids who are particularly interested in them. Tom Sawyer Island and the Raceway are very popular among 8- to 12-year-olds. The above itinerary does not incorporate breaks for parades or fireworks, which vary seasonally; integrate them at your own discretion, although if you do, you may need to eliminate most of the attractions listed beyond step 12.

For Seniors, and Anyone who Desires a Less Hectic Tour

The Ideal Plan above is not popular with some guests because the park's major thrill rides—The Three Mountains—are front-loaded into the itinerary. The quest to conquer the entire park in a single day also involves a great deal of walking. The touring plan below is a more leisurely introduction to the park. The tour cannot cover all the sights, but it does incorporate the major ones, and allows you to "work up to" the more thrilling adventures. This itinerary works well for people who want to spread their Magic Kingdom visit over two days—use this plan the first day, then follow the Ideal Plan the second day, omitting the attractions you have already visited unless you wish to ride them again. Also consult the "Rattle Ratings" in "Planning Your Trip," to help you decide which attractions might be more than you want to take in.

1. Enter the Magic Kingdom and proceed down Main Street to **Central Plaza** for the rope drop. Alternatively, you may wait for the **Walt Disney**

World Railroad's first train, which departs at the scheduled opening time and ride it to the Frontierland station for step 2.

2. When the rope drops, proceed quickly through Adventureland and board **Splash Mountain**.

3. After Splash Mountain, visit **Pirates of the Caribbean**, then **Jungle Cruise**.

4. Proceed through Frontierland to the **Haunted Mansion**.

5. Walk to Fantasyland and ride **Peter Pan's Flight**, then **It's a Small World**. Take the Skyway to Tomorrowland. By this point, the park will be approaching its peak attendance for the day; the itinerary switches gears to focus on attractions with the shortest wait.

6. Ride**Take Flight**, the **Carousel of Progress** and the **Tomorrowland Transit Authority**.

7. See **Timekeeper**. Integrate a lunch stop between the Tomorrowland rides, or during your walk over to Adventureland for step 8, where you will pass several restaurants and snack bars on the way.

8. In Adventureland, visit the **Swiss Family Treehouse** and **Tropical Serenade** (aka The Enchanted Tiki Birds). The tiki bird show is timed to pre-set intervals, 20 minutes apart. If the wait is less than 10 to 15 minutes for the next show, see the tiki birds first; otherwise, visit the treehouse first, about 10 minutes to tour if there's no line, then the tiki birds.

9. See the **Country Bear Jamboree**.

10. Experience the **Hall of Presidents** and **Liberty Square Riverboat**. Both of these 20- to 25-minute attractions, situated almost next to each other, have set starting/departure times; begin with the one offering the shortest wait, then proceed to the other.

11. The peak attendance period should be waning now. Although the line will probably still be lengthy, ride **Big Thunder Mountain** if you feel up to it. Take the **WDW Railroad** from the Frontierland station to Mickey's Toontown Fair.

12. Ride **Snow White's Adventure** and **Mr. Toad's Wild Ride**, starting with the one offering the shortest wait, since the attractions are next to each other.

13. At this point, most of the rides you have left to see are in Tomorrowland and Fantasyland. If there are several, post-dusk hours remaining before closing time, you will be able to see the rest of the major attractions without too much problem. If you have only an hour or so before the park closes, you will need to prioritize among **ExtraTERRORestrial**, **Space Mountain**, **AstroOrbiter**, **Legend of the Lion King** and **20,000 Leagues Under the Sea**, as well as any rides you wish to revisit.

14. At the appointed closing time, ride attendants will not allow guests to enter any existing lines. Proceed to Main Street, USA where you may shop amid the throng. Take your time, as the transportation system outside the park will be jammed.

What Did We Miss?

Following this tour by the number will leave out **Tom Sawyer's Island** (open only until dusk), **Mike Fink Keelboats** (open seasonally during daylight hours), **Cinderella's Golden Carrousel**, **Dumbo the Flying Elephant**, the **Grand Prix Raceway** and **Mickey's Toontown Fair**. While each of these rides has its fans, they should be included on your tour only if you have kids who are particularly interested in them. Tom Sawyer's Island and the Raceway are very popular among 8- to 12-year-olds. Note that this itinerary does not include breaks for parades or special shows. Additionally, if you maintain a casual pace throughout the day, you will be hard-pressed to visit most of the attractions listed beyond step 12.

For Families with Small Children

The key touring suggestion for smaller children is Fantasyland first, the place that is packed with the attractions that 3- to 8-year-olds most crave. Geographical and crowd flow logistics are at work here, too. In the first hour that The Magic Kingdom is open, there is a rush both east and west from Central Plaza to the three mountains; most of the park's guests then spread out from these points. Because Fantasyland's attractions to the North aren't perceived by adults in charge to be major rides with long lines, this area of the park doesn't become heavily trammeled until sometime before noon. However, several of Fantasyland's rides—particularly **20,000 Leagues Under the Sea**, **Dumbo the Flying Elephant**, **The Mad Tea Party** and **Cinderella's Golden Carrousel**—are slow-loading attractions, and once this area becomes inundated with guests around lunchtime, it becomes a vast mire of anxious toddlers. This itinerary bypasses both Space and Splash mountains, which require children to be at least 44 inches tall. Also note the "Terror Factor" chart in "Planning Your Trip," which will help you ferret out rides youngsters may welcome with open arms, but experience through a glaze of tears.

1. Enter The Magic Kingdom and procure a stroller just inside the entrance to the right of the train station, if necessary. Walk down Main Street to **Central Plaza** for the rope drop. Alternatively, sans stroller, you can take the **Walt Disney World Railroad's** first train, which departs at the scheduled opening time, and ride it to Mickey's Starland station for step 2, however this takes more time than the moderately-paced walk from Central Plaza and will cost you time you might use for another ride later.

2. At the rope drop, proceed quickly through Cinderella Castle to **Dumbo the Flying Elephant**.

3. After riding Dumbo, go straight to **Cinderella's Golden Carrousel**, then **Peter Pan's Flight**.

4. Ride **20,000 Leagues Under the Sea**. These first four attractions can be accomplished in about 70 to 80 minutes at the start of the day; later in the afternoon, they will easily soak up three hours or more. At this point, you will need to pry your youngsters away from Fantasyland. Let them know you will return later in the day.

5. Proceed to Adventureland and ride the **Jungle Cruise**, followed by **Pirates of the Caribbean**.

6. Head for Frontierland and the **Haunted Mansion**. Keep an eye out en route to make sure that the Hall of Presidents hasn't just released a crowd into the area; if so, visit the Haunted Mansion after step 7.

7. Ride *either* the **Liberty Square Riverboat** or the **Mike Fink Keelboats**, they both travel the same route, though the Keelboats are operated during peak season only. By now, the park will have reached its peak attendance for the day. You'll need to incorporate a lunch stop, or take your afternoon break soon. For the rest of the afternoon, this itinerary concentrates on the attractions with the shortest lines.

8. See the **Country Bear Jamboree** and the **Tropical Serenade** (aka the Enchanted Tiki Birds). These shows are timed to pre-set, 20-minute intervals; visit the one with the shortest wait to showtime first.

9. Take the raft to **Tom Sawyer Island**. Lunch at **Aunt Polly's**, on the island, is quieter and less-expensive than virtually anywhere else in the park.

10. At this point, it will be near the start of the **afternoon parade**, usually scheduled for 3 p.m. Stake out a position to enjoy the parade, preferably in the area near Tom Sawyer's dock.

11. After the parade, head straight for the Frontierland Station and take the **Walt Disney World Railroad** to Mickey's Toontown Fair station and meet the **characters**. Ride the **Barnstormer**. If your child is in a stroller you'll need to walk instead of taking the train, but in this case, visit Mickey's Toontown Fair following step 12.

12. Go to Tomorrowland and ride the **Transit Authority**, **Take Flight** and see **Timekeeper**. Ride the **Grand Prix Raceway**. If your children are less than 52 inches tall, you will need to ride the Grand Prix with them. At this point, the lines at major attractions will start to shrink.

13. Take the **Skyway** back to Fantasyland; if you have a stroller, walk instead. Ride **It's a Small World**.

14. Ride **Mr. Toad's Wild Ride** and **Snow White's Adventures**, starting with the one offering the shortest wait, since the attractions are next to each other.

15. Ride the **Mad Tea Party**. Follow this with the **Legend of the Lion King**.

16. If your child is tall enough (40 inches), proceed to Frontierland and ride **Big Thunder Mountain**.

What Did We Miss?

This tour successfully covers moppet territory, but it omits several attractions adults enjoy, including **Splash Mountain**, **Space Mountain**, **ExtraTERRORestrial Alien Encounter** and the **Hall of Presidents**. It also bypasses lesser attractions such as **AstroOrbiter**, **Swiss Family Treehouse** and the **Carousel of Progress**. Be aware that, if you maintain a casual pace, or incorporate the afternoon parade into your plans, you'll find it difficult to visit all of the rides listed beyond step 13.

EPCOT

Hot air balloon riders get a spectacular view of Orlando.

"Epcot is not at all empty of ideas. It has a coherent guiding philosophy, a central idea, straight from Walt: an unbounded belief in progress, powered by technology. Such a philosophy neatly fits the commercial needs of American corporations marketing their technology—a fact that certainly helped build Epcot. Epcot's image of the future is unfailingly sweet, a dictatorship of the nice, with no sense of the chaos, waste and confusion that make up the real world. It is a technologically inspired utopia of order and harmony. Epcot (like Disney World as a whole) has no answer for social problems—it just outlaws them, banishing them to the world outside. As a result, whether its designers intended it to or not, Epcot teaches specific social messages."

—Joe Flower, Prince of the Magic Kingdom.

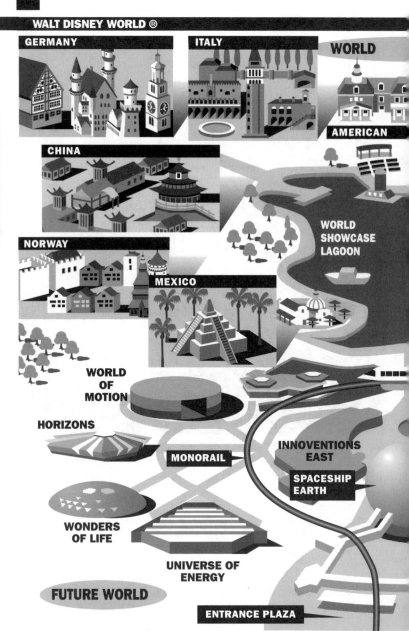

WALT DISNEY WORLD ®

EPCOT

GERMANY

ITALY

WORLD

AMERICAN

CHINA

WORLD
SHOWCASE
LAGOON

NORWAY

MEXICO

WORLD
OF
MOTION

HORIZONS

INNOVENTIONS
EAST

MONORAIL

SPACESHIP
EARTH

WONDERS
OF LIFE

UNIVERSE OF
ENERGY

FUTURE WORLD

ENTRANCE PLAZA

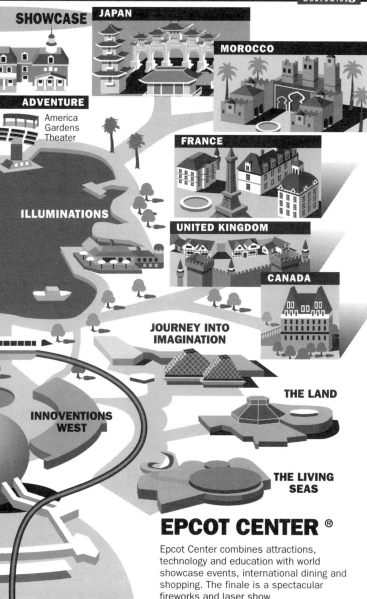

SHOWCASE

JAPAN

MOROCCO

ADVENTURE

America
Gardens
Theater

FRANCE

ILLUMINATIONS

UNITED KINGDOM

CANADA

JOURNEY INTO
IMAGINATION

THE LAND

INNOVENTIONS
WEST

THE LIVING
SEAS

EPCOT

EPCOT CENTER ®

Epcot Center combines attractions,
technology and education with world
showcase events, international dining and
shopping. The finale is a spectacular
fireworks and laser show.

Walt Disney's original concept for Epcot—the Experimental Prototype Community Of Tomorrow—was vastly different from what the Disney Company succeeded in producing after his death. Instead of a glass-domed, living technological utopia, Disney's upper-echelon envisioned a sort of two-pronged, permanent world's fair: one section, Future World, a tribute to technology and innovation, the other, World Showcase, devoted to an icon-based international community.

Most visitors gravitate to one half or the other in their touring. Dynamic Future World has more in the way of attractions, including some rides that aspire to educate as well as entertain. Positioned around a lake, World Showcase is more relaxed, with some attractions geared toward sit-down events in theaters; the focus is on international dining and shopping. A fireworks-laser-and-recorded-music-spectacular, IllumiNations, closes the park each night.

In retrospect, the park is an amazing conceit. Epcot was designed to operate as both a huge shopping mall as well as an opportunity for major corporations and countries to spin "their side" of the story. Behind the official portrayal of education and entertainment, the bottom line at Epcot is... the bottom line. The cash register begins ringing at the ticket office, where today's adult admission had climbed to more than $40.

AUTHOR'S OBSERVATION

How serious does the Disney Company take the corporate trade-off at Epcot? The company's stance is best exemplified by the Future World attraction, Horizons, which has spent much of the last few years in mothballs because no corporation has been willing to pony up the dough to make its operation cost-effective for Disney. In other words, your admission fee alone doesn't make it worthwhile for the company to keep the attraction open. The Disney image is sometimes hard to define, but Epcot is easy: counting seven corporate-sponsored Future World pavilions and 11 World Showcase participants, Epcot stands for Eighteen Perfect Commercials Of Today.

Nonetheless, Disney sells a unique product at Epcot. If you take the educational component with a grain of salt, and keep the corporate arm-twisting at arm's length, Epcot is a pleasant environment for a day or two of touring. Epcot boasts some genuinely good international restaurants, as well as excellent, seemingly spontaneous live entertainment, and a diverse array of shopping opportunities. Besides, where else can the phrase "meet me in Morocco for lunch" ring so delightfully?

The optimistic Disney concept of a miniaturized and harmonious world community is played out in an upbeat, unpatronizing fashion. Similarly, the idea that innovation can be celebrated spatially is a fascinating, singular achievement that the company continually refines and updates.

Transportation, Arrival and Orientation

Occupying a 300-acre swath of territory, centrally located Epcot is the all-around easiest Disney park to reach. If you're driving, the 12,155-space parking lot situated at the entrance is amply large; the parking toll is $5, or free to Disney Resort guests. The driving time from the Epcot Resorts—the Swan, Dolphin, BoardWalk, Yacht and Beach Club—and the nearby Caribbean Beach, Port Orleans and Dixie Landings is less than 10 minutes; allow 15 to 20 minutes from all other Disney hotels.

If you are using Walt Disney World transportation, the Resort **Monorail** ringing the Seven Seas Lagoon (with stops at the Contemporary, Polynesian and Grand Floridian Beach resorts) connects to the Epcot monorail at the Ticket and Transportation Center. Allow about 20 minutes from these hotels to Epcot's entrance (at peak periods, the Epcot monorail line ferries about 3000 passengers per hour, each direction). The All-Stars, Port Orleans, Dixie Landings, Caribbean Beach, Wilderness Lodge and campsites are all connected to Epcot's main entrance by bus; allow 15 to 20 minutes by bus.

An unofficial "secret" is that, unlike all of Disney's other parks, Epcot has a small rear entrance, the **International Gateway**, that connects the park by boat and footpath with the Epcot Resorts. This entrance lies between the French and British pavilions within the World Showcase portion of the park. If you are staying at one of the Epcot Resorts, it is a 10- to 15-minute walk (the boat ride is nominally faster) to this entrance, which also has a regular ticket facility. If you're combining a visit to the Disney-MGM Studios with Epcot on the same day, you can take the Epcot Resort launches from one park to the other. On Surprise Mornings, this rear entrance is open, but you will be directed straight to the Future World portion of Epcot until World Showcase opens later. There is no parking lot for this entrance, other than those provided for the Epcot Resorts.

Epcot's geographical layout differs from The Magic Kingdom's. **Spaceship Earth**, a 180-foot-high silver sphere, marks the park's northern main entrance. The park is composed of two "lands," **Future World** and **World Showcase**, each occupying one circle in a giant figure-eight formation. The two "lands" are dramatically different in concept, atmosphere and layout, and each individual loop is nearly the size of the Kingdom. Future World is devoted to technology, placing an emphasis on historical perspective, while World Showcase has a world's fair flavor, providing 11 pavilions, each sponsored by and themed to a different country. Future World's hub is the central fountain located between the two Innoventions buildings, while World Showcase rings a huge lake, and therefore has no central focal point.

As a rule, World Showcase does not open for touring until two hours after the park opens; similarly, most of Future World usually closes two hours prior to the rest of Epcot. Each evening, around World Showcase Lagoon, a fireworks, laser and music show, **IllumiNations**, marks the end of the Epcot day, usually at 9 p.m. Touring suggestions are listed below, under "Epcot Touring Itineraries." Plan on one-and-a-half to two days for a thorough exploration of the park.

You may purchase your admission tickets at the main entrance, but plan on a wait during the first hours the park is open. On admittance, you will be provided a guidebook and a schedule of the day's entertainment. Since most of the entertainment offerings are based in World Showcase (which opens later in the morning), you can hold off on reading through this until later. Just past Spaceship Earth is a tip board that provides updates about the wait times for various attractions. The time estimates tend to be conservative, but they're good for comparison purposes. Additional touring information is available at the **Guest Relations** office on the left, just past Spaceship Earth. Another Guest Relations office is located outside the park, on the right side of the main entrance, but this one draws crowds early in the morning). Five different, reservations-only guided tours provide additional insight into Epcot's operation, particularly the Living Seas pavilion (see "Guided Tours" in "Obstacles and Opportunities" for more information).

Stroller and **wheelchair rental** is available outside the park, west of the main entrance, or just inside Epcot, to the left of and before you reach Spaceship Earth. A **diaper changing** and **nursing station** is located at the Odyssey Center, on the border of Future World and the World Showcase between the World of Motion and Mexico pavilions. **Lockers** are based in the building immediately to the right of Spaceship Earth, or at the International Gateway entrance in the rear of the park. Two **ATMs** are found at Epcot: one is just outside the main entrance, in the building on the east side of the turnstiles, another is situated near the bridge between Future World and World Showcase.

Dining is a big part of the Epcot experience, but it requires advance planning. See "Eating" later in this section for more information. Epcot ticket information is listed under "Tickets" in "Obstacles and Opportunities."

Our Favorite Acronyms for Epcot

Every Person Comes Out Tired

Eisner's Paycheck Comes On Time

Every Plastic Costume Of Tomorrow

Our Favorite Acronyms for Epcot

Excruciating Polyester Costumes Of Torture

Every Pocketbook Comes Out Trashed

Every Parent Carries Out Toddler

Rope Drop and Surprise Morning Procedures

Two basic opening procedures are used to admit guests to Epcot. Typically, the "official" opening time is 9 a.m., or 8 a.m. on days when Disney expects high attendance. However, the main entrance is always open to the general public 30 minutes prior to this time, with Spaceship Earth and Innoventions available for early touring. On days when the Surprise Morning policy is *not* in effect (at this writing, Sundays, Mondays, Wednesdays, Thursdays and Saturdays), the rest of Future World opens at 9 a.m. World Showcase opens at 11 a.m., or 10 a.m. on days when Disney expects high attendance.

On Surprise Mornings (Tuesdays and Fridays), when Disney Resort guests are admitted early to the park, Epcot typically opens 90 minutes prior to the "official" time. Some brochures tell you that the park will open 60 minutes early; confirm the exact time the main entrance opens with your Disney Resort information staff. On these mornings, the following attractions will be open for early touring: Spaceship Earth, Living Seas, The Land and Journey Into Imagination (the International Gateway entrance is open on Surprise Mornings, but you will be ushered to the Future World section of the park until 11 a.m.).

Always confirm the exact opening procedure with Disney Information ☎ *(407) 824-4321* the night before your day at Epcot. For more information on how the Surprise Morning program works, see "Obstacles and Opportunities."

Future World

> *"With apologies to Marshall Macluhan, the medium is not the message. The message is far more important, and has a life of its own. The stone tablets that Moses carried down the mountain are lost in the dust of the Sinai. The message written on them survives thousands of years later."*

—Michael Eisner, CEO of the Walt Disney Company

With an aim to celebrate man's achievements in science, technology and creativity, Future World is anchored by a magnificent, 180-foot-high silver

geosphere, encircled by the monorail. This oversized golfball also marks the main entrance to Epcot, and it contains one of the park's best rides, **Spaceship Earth**. The multifaceted *geosphere* (a Disney-coined word) is breathtaking at night when it is bathed in purple and orange light.

Like Tomorrowland in The Magic Kingdom, without constant attention, the attractions in Future World are predestined to continually date and age right before the eyes of visitors. Two pavilions were added after Epcot's original opening: the Living Seas in 1986, and the $90 million Wonders of Life (featuring Body Wars, the park's first thrill ride) in 1989. In 1994, the Disney Company began a much-needed overhaul of Future World. The initial focus was on Spaceship Earth and CommuniCore (renamed Innoventions). Since then, Universe of Energy and World of Motion have been shuttered for improvements. There is rumor of a new space-themed pavilion to replace Horizons, but no concrete plans have been announced.

Each of the various pavilions has a slightly different operation. Both Horizons and Universe of Energy feature a single attraction, while the others have one or more ride-type enticements, as well as an exhibit area. While the exhibits are interesting to varying degrees, if you are trying to see all of Epcot in a day, you will not have time to linger long. The best exhibit area overall is **Innoventions**, a continually evolving, hands-on display focusing on the technological frontier.

Because it opens ahead of World Showcase, Epcot attendance tends to peak earlier in Future World. Viewing it as a bell curve, the most-crowded period of the day at Future World starts about 10:30 a.m. and continues until about 1 p.m. Most of the attractions in Future World close ahead of those in World Showcase (usually at 7 p.m.), although Spaceship Earth typically stays open until the start of IllumiNations.

Spaceship Earth

With the collaboration of Sci-Fi author Ray Bradbury, Disney *imagineers* created this ambitious, special-effects-laden overview of human progress and communications, narrated by actor Jeremy Irons. The track of continuously moving vehicles winds gradually higher inside the *geosphere*, passing audio-animatronic scenes of our first attempts at communication (cave painting, hieroglyphics, etc.) through the development of commerce and trade, and eventually into the future of human interaction. With a smart renovation completed in 1994, the edifying Spaceship Earth is one of the few Disney attractions that successfully melds education and entertainment into a single, memorable package. On the way out, you'll pass through Global Village, an exhibit of new communication technology.

Length of ride: 15 minutes. *Special note:* Spaceship Earth is the favorite Epcot ride of many adults, and most kids enjoy it pretty well, too. Fortunately, the loading procedure is relatively fast and, like Main Street in The Magic Kingdom, this attraction is usually open 30 minutes ahead of the rest of Epcot. Still, because of its position at the front of the park, many visitors opt to make this their first ride of the day and a line forms early in the morning. Later in the afternoon, there are periods when there is little or no line in place. If you have arrived late enough that the wait for Spaceship Earth tops 10 minutes or more, bypass the attraction and return after noon.

AUTHOR'S OBSERVATION

The 16-million-pound geosphere containing the Spaceship Earth ride is so-named because the big ball is not perfectly round, measuring 180 feet in height and 164 feet in diameter, and therefore it is not a sphere; nor is it one of Buckminster Fuller's geodesic domes, which is only half a sphere. The geosphere is positioned on six pylons sunk 100 feet into the ground, and the anodized aluminum exterior is created from 954 triangular panels of differing size and shape.

Universe of Energy

Previously a lumbering dirge about fossil fuel production sponsored by Exxon, the Universe of Energy was revamped for a major, and desperately needed overhaul in 1996. The main ride components—a combination of film and Audio-Animatronic dinosaurs, linked by unique moving theaters—are still there, but the update adds humor and Hollywood star power to help us feel more comfortable consuming Exxon's wares. The film section stars Ellen DeGeneres as herself, who dreams she's landed a role as a contestant on "Jeopardy" but all the categories concern energy, a subject she knows virtually nothing about. Bill Nye (the Science Guy) steps in to help by taking Ellen back to the Big Bang and the origins of fossil fuel, where an Audio-Animatronic Ellen does battle with a sea serpent with one-liners. The prehistoric setting has been spiffed up nicely and DeGeneres is now part of that unique Disney pantheon of Audio-Animatronic presidents, historic figures and toons. Though the attraction is still too long and the information delivered here won't be new to anyone with a sixth-grade education, Ellen delivers a nice dose of levity to the Future World arena. *Length of ride:* 39 minutes, including the eight-minute pre-show. *Special note:* Ellen's popularity will undoubtedly secure a new following for this ride and the peak attendance will probably start mid-morning and continue until late afternoon. However, this is one of Disney's higher capacity attractions; the theaters hold almost 600 guests for each performance, and a new theater is ready for boarding every 15 minutes (you will rarely have to wait more than 15 minutes).

The following three attractions are all situated in the **Wonders of Life** pavilion. The DNA towering at the entrance to the pavilion is 5.5 billion times actual size — just the right size for a human 6 million miles tall.

Body Wars

A mad dash through the human body, Body Wars takes off from the 1966 *Fantastic Voyage* storyline, that of scientists being miniaturized and injected into the bloodstream of a patient. In the fast-paced story, you have been sent into the body to retrieve a scientist, but things go awry, and white blood cells begin to attack. The turbulent ride is created by a 48-passenger motion simulator, identical to the one in use for Star Tours at the Disney-MGM Studios, and the vessel whooshes through the veins, heart and brain before being extracted from the body. The special effects in the film are quite realistic, and the experience is brief, but intense; seatbelts are required. Most visitors find Body Wars among the highlights of their Epcot touring, but the attraction has its detractors. Although the type of up-and-down motions is essentially the same as on Star Tours, owing to its more visceral visuals, Body Wars inspires motion sickness in some guests, most of whom, curiously, have no problem with Star Tours. Avoid Body Wars on a full stomach, and if you feel queasy midway through the experience, close your eyes and ride it out—i.e., it's the visual in combination with the movement that creates a problem. *Length of ride:* Four minutes. *Special note:* Until the Test Track opens in 1997, Body Wars is essentially the only thrill attraction at Epcot, and lines start early and run late. Try to ride it in the first 15 minutes the park is open, or wait until late afternoon. On busy days, be alert to the World of Energy next door, which finishes every 15 minutes, releasing up to 600 people into the immediate area.

AUTHOR'S OBSERVATION

The flight simulator technology in use for Star Tours and Body Wars was developed by a British company to train jet pilots. The sealed capsule simulates acceleration by reclining backward, deceleration is mimed by leaning forward, while tilts to one side or the other produce the sensation of turns. Combined with sound effects and dynamic film footage projected onto the front "window" of the capsule, the 40-person craft simulates pre-programmed motion in a breathtaking and believable fashion, though the capsule never leaves its stationary position. The same technology is in use at Sea World for Wild Arctic. Universal's Back to the Future attraction utilizes a different design: 12 of the eight-passenger DeLorians are situated in a giant theater setting with a single, stationary screen and sound system for the effects.

The Making of Me

Disney's sensitive sex-education course is a charming film starring Martin Short, presented at an intimate, 80-person theater inside the Wonders of Life pavilion. Alleged to be a pet project of Disney CEO Michael Eisner, the film is a reflection on the start of life, with Short's parents meeting and falling in love, and then the development and birth of baby Martin. Most open-minded parents are comfortable with the Disney version of events, although kids around age 8 to 12 usually writhe nervously during the very brief section alluding to intercourse (which is not really seen or discussed); the material goes over the heads of most younger children. Disney posts lots of warning signs to scare off the prudes, but many folks leave the theater wondering what all the fuss is about. *Length of show:* 14 minutes. *Special note:* The theater is very small and a line sometimes builds around midday.

Cranium Command

A whiz-bang combination of live-action, animated film footage, audio-animatronics and special effects, Cranium Command is a delightful theater attraction that many Wonders of Life visitors miss on their way to and from Body Wars. The humorous story concerns a young pilot, a Cranium Commando named Buzzy, "operating" an adolescent boy's brain through the course of a typical day. In the process, he must coordinate the efforts of the major organs (heart, stomach, etc.) in order to cope with everything that happens to the boy, including a chase, an encounter with a pretty girl, and a visit with the principal. The major organs are operated by a host of guest stars—Jon Lovitz, Charles Grodin, Dana Carvey and others—but the real star is Buzzy, an endearing audio-animatronic character audiences fall in love with. *Length of show:* 18 minutes, plus the five-minute pre-show that is integral to understanding the plot. *Special note:* The Cranium Command theater holds about 200 people. Although the attraction still lacks a large following, a line usually builds by late morning.

Horizons

Indirectly addressing the conundrum faced by imagineers building a time-locked Tomorrowland or Future World today, the implacably optimistic Horizons begins with a look at the hereafter as predicted by Jules Verne and other visionaries. Your suspended, four-passenger vehicle then visits a hemispheric 80-foot screen that presents dramatic film footage that simulates the sensation of flight. The ride then enters the future, with a glimpse of next-millennium transportation, food production and communities of tomorrow, including one on water and another in space. *Length of ride:* 15 minutes. *Special note:* Orphaned by its original sponsor in 1994, Horizons has spent most of the past couple of years shut down while Disney tries to find another financial partner for the day-to-day operation of this attraction. At press time, Disney's plan was to keep it open through the spring of 1997 during the World of Motion renovation, but don't be surprised if the attraction is temporarily shuttered during off-season periods. On busy days, be alert to the nearby World of Energy, which finishes every 15 minutes and releases up to 600 people into the immediate area. Otherwise, the continuously loading Horizons is one of Future World's less-busy attractions, a good bet almost any time.

Test Track

The most ambitious attraction set to debut at Walt Disney World in 1997 is the speed ride simulating the rigorous test process new vehicles undergo before being brought to market. The queuing area snakes through a series of 23 exhibits and videos that explain the why and how of vehicle performance tests implemented at General Motors, the attraction's sponsor. Guests then board the six-passenger, open-air cars which race up a hill to the upper level of the round building. Here the cars undergo a road surface test, a brake test around orange traffic cones, travel through hot and cold environmental chambers, demonstrate ride and handling on curves through a forest and then tackle a high-velocity barrier test before crashing out of the building into the employee parking lot. In this final stretch, the cars reach speeds expected to top 65 miles-per-hour on a steeply banked curve. *Length of ride:*

5 minutes, plus pre-show. *Special note:* Test Track will be one hot ticket from the day it opens, anticipated to be May 1997. Current estimates are that the ride will accommodate 1800 guests per hour—less than some other big attractions, so lines will probably reach epic proportions within an hour or so of the park's opening daily. If you are visiting Epcot after Test Track has opened, you'll want to make it your first attraction of the day. At press time, Disney had not determined minimum height requirements anticipated or whether Test Track will be part of the Surprise Morning program.

The following two attractions are based at the **Journey Into Imagination** pavilion.

Honey, I Shrunk the Audience

Spun off from the 1989 hit movie starring Rick Moranis, this 3-D film located in the Journey Into Imagination pavilion has quickly become the all-around most popular attraction at Epcot since its 1994 opening. Moranis recreates his role as Professor Szalinski who, in a visual slight-of-hand, is visiting Epcot's "Imagination Institute" with his family to receive an award as "Inventor of the Year." Absent-minded mishaps lead to the audience and theater being miniaturized for an astounding series of visual and tactile special effects. A hilarious thrill for all but the most impressionable. Parents should know that little ones can be moderately rattled by the sophisticated effects, which are more intense than the ones in the Muppet 3-D film at the Disney-MGM Studios; the high sound volume is also a put-off to some visitors. *Length of attraction:* 18 minutes, plus pre-show. *Special note:* Honey, I Shrunk the Audience has eclipsed Body Wars as the line to beat for early morning visitors. Although the theater accommodates almost 600, the show's popularity creates a thick bottleneck early in the day. Make the show your first attraction of the morning, or if you can't get into one of the first two or three performances, come back late in the afternoon when most guests have moved on to World Showcase.

Journey Into Imagination

The original focal point of the Imagination pavilion, this fanciful attraction is hosted by Dreamfinder, a red-bearded, artist-type who invites us to summon our creative powers for an expedition with his dragon-like creature Figment through the world of imagination. A colorful hit for some, an annoying miss for others, the pleasant Journey Into Imagination has its charms, but is beginning to feel a little tired. *Length of ride:* 13 minutes. *Special note:* This is a continuously loading attraction, and the line moves relatively quickly, but be alert to the exit of Honey, I Shrunk the Audience, which releases almost 600 guests into the area every 20 minutes. The ride exits near the entrance to Image Works, a colorful, interactive activity area; kids particularly enjoy spending time here.

The following three attractions are part of the six-acre **Land** pavilion.

Living with the Land

This two-part canopied boat ride is the centerpiece of The Land pavilion. The first portion of the tour is through a series of realistic dioramas addressing humankind's relationship with the land and how we have tried to mold the land to fit our needs.

The second part tours Epcot's greenhouse laboratory wherein biotechnology, hydroponics, aquaculture and other high-tech growing methods are used to control food production; many of the crops you see wind up on Epcot dining tables. This portion of the tour is narrated by a live "skipper" and the workers you pass are not audio animatrons, but real farmers working in a strangely unreal environment. One caveat: the boat passes quickly through the greenhouse and the script does not allow room for questions. If you are interested in the use of futuristic growing techniques, sign up for the informative walking tour (see "Guided Tours" in "Obstacles and Opportunities"). *Length of ride:* 13 minutes. *Special note:* Updated in 1994 and now one of Future World's more popular attractions, Living With the Land is located next to a huge food pavilion that is filled with diners at lunch. Many visitors board this ride just before or after their mid-day meal, creating substantial lines; try to visit by mid-morning, or wait until later in the afternoon.

Food Rocks

A fast-paced, educational parody performed by singing, audio-animatronic fruits and vegetables, Food Rocks is a lighthearted look at nutrition, aimed squarely at pre-teens of the MTV age. One highlight is the tune "Every bite you take" sung by the Refrigerator Police, with lyrics that include "...every cake you bake, every milk you shake, every egg you break, will be part of you." The original performers of the songs rerecorded the new lyrics to their hits, including Neil Moussaka ("Don't Take my Squash Away from Me"), and the Peach Boys ("Good Nutrition"). *Length of show:* 13 minutes. *Special note:* Although kids enjoy it, Food Rocks has yet to establish much of a following. You will almost always be seated for the next show, although on very busy days, the lunch crowd at the Sunshine Season Food Fair can stimulate some demand.

Circle of Life

A pro-environment view of the Earth from the pro-development Disney Company, Circle of Life is a live-action, 70mm film presentation book-ended by an appearance by the ever-popular Simba, from The Lion King. At the opening, Simba encounters Timon and Pumbaa, the film's lovable meerkat and warthog, who are clearing the forest for a Hakuna Matata Lakeside Village development. Simba shares with them an environmental message about the interdependent nature of life on earth against the backdrop of a live-action sequence. It's an important message, but never have developers received such favorable treatment as they do here in the charming guise of Timon and Pumbaa. *Length of show:* 15 minutes. Note: though aimed squarely at kids, most adults enjoy this optimistic fable. The 420-seat Harvest Theater rarely fills, although on very busy days it will operate at capacity during the lunch hour.

The Living Seas

Disney generally does an admirable job of taking established concepts, giving them a fresh creative overhaul, and blowing away the competition. The Living Seas is one of the few instances where the company lags behind—in this case, the pavilion is inferior to the admirable, marine-themed product provided at Sea World. Guests see a brief film presentation about humankind's interaction with the sea, and then enter a "hydrolator," a mock-elevator that descends into the depths. When you exit, you board a sea cab that crawls through an acrylic window-lined tube in Epcot's 5.7 million gallon saltwater environment. Roughly 65 species of marine life live in a huge tank that simulates the Caribbean Sea. After disembarking the very short ride through the tank, you may tour the two-story Sea Base Alpha, which features interesting exhibits covering diving technology, submersible vehicles, and more. If you are interested in exploring this pavilion further, two tours provide a backstage glimpse into The Living Seas (see "Guided Tours" in "Obstacles and Opportunities"). *Length of attraction:* Pre-show, 10 minutes. The ride in the sea cab lasts about three minutes. Allow 30 to 60 minutes to tour the exhibits. *Special note:* Guests encounter more hype than payoff here, but the best portion of Living Seas is the exhibit area—an area many guests bypass for other attractions. A line builds by late morning on busy days, but usually moves quickly, otherwise, tour the pavilion any time.

AUTHOR'S OBSERVATION

There are an estimated 175 costumes for Mickey Mouse, most of which are used for special occasions or photo shoots only. Among the favorites: a suit used for underwater appearances at Epcot's Living Seas pavilion (complete with scuba rigging), a formal tux with tails, an NFL series covering the major leagues, a running suit, and a outfit using African kente cloth.

Innoventions

For many visitors, particularly teens, the new Innoventions is the best part of Epcot. Featuring dozens of hands-on exhibits, Innoventions showcases a variety of products, most of which have yet to be commercially released. The manufacturers represented here are a diverse lot and much of the technology on display is virtual-reality-based. Among the most recent additions to Innoventions: Time Warner's interactive network service featuring movies-on-demand, home shopping and news exchange; a redesigned Apple Computer exhibit; a virtual-reality tour of St. Peter's Basilica in Italy; a Silicon Graphics station showcasing visual computing and modeling; a fusion lightbulb running on sulfur, and microwaves with a 10,000-hour lifespan; as well as computer software that allows blind users to hear what others see on screen.

Innoventions requires at least two hours to tour in its entirety, and is not designed for quick walk-throughs, a fact that escapes many guests bent on cramming it in as yet another attraction on a busy, single-day schedule. Additionally, although younger guests have latched onto Innoventions, the Disney company has found that many Epcot customers are "techno-phobes" who are intimidated by the sophisticated technology on display here. In 1996, Disney began to grapple with this dilemma by repositioning the huge exhibit as an evolving display that will show "how technology will change your life in the near future."

World Showcase

> *"Epcot is quite simply the world perfected. Each of your basic, more attractive nations, like France or Italy, has its own area, with a few landmarks reduced in size and cleaned up, so there's a few-stories-high Eiffel Tower and a nice little Doge's Palace, all without any rust or smells or decay. The countries with yucky political problems, like South Africa or Bosnia, just aren't included, which keeps things cheerful and teaches those countries a valuable lesson: If they want us to buy their souvenirs and sample their native cuisine, if they want a gift kiosk at Epcot, they're just going to have to behave. Just about anybody can get into the United Nations, but you need some nice porcelain wooden shoes or some delicious toffee if you ever hope to make it in Orlando."*

—**Libby Gelman-Waxner,** *Premiere Magazine*

Tastefully sown landscapes, global iconography, lavish promotional films, and international shopping and dining are among the highlights of Epcot's sprawling World Showcase arena. With one tame exception, there are no thrill rides here; the "land" is firmly devoted to the relaxed pleasure of travel and culture — something like a passport-less, round-the-world tour aboard an invisible cruise ship. Plus, the food is safe, the water good, and the bathrooms are clean. World Showcase successfully converts entire nations into miniature theme parks.

The whole effect is fascinating. Where else can one gaze at replicas of France's Eiffel Tower, a Moroccan *medina*, Japan's Haryuji Temple, Venice's Piazza San Marco and a German *Biergarten* in a single, sweeping glance? A stirring domestic attraction, the **American Adventure**, situated in a colonial-style edifice, forms the undeniable centerpiece of this view. Ostensibly, at Epcot, Disney seeks to define international harmony—with the United States positioned at the head of the table. And yet, the 11 nations that ring the 40-acre World Showcase Lagoon (linked by a 1.3-mile promenade) represent an Eurocentric, top-heavy view of the global community; the southern hemisphere (as well as the Third-World) don't make much of an appearance. Although there is always talk of another country being added to World Showcase to help round out the mix, the Disney Company hasn't yet found a nation that is a complement to the current selection—one that is willing to foot the bill, and that doesn't have awkward or potential political issues to reckon with. It is, admittedly, a delicate quandary.

One of the more delightful, less-heralded aspects of World Showcase is that the various pavilions are hosted by native representatives who work in Walt Disney World as part of a job-exchange program. Seemingly chosen for their sunny disposition, good looks and English fluency, these guest-employees have a unique role within the Disney caste system: they not only represent the company, but the home nation that sent them here.

The lovingly manicured grounds in World Showcase are a major focal point, with gardens designed to reflect the native flora of the various host countries. For a six-week period starting in mid-April, the popular **International Flower and Garden Festival** blossoms, and yields more than 3 million blooms, with floral displays, topiary exhibits and more. Green thumbs can obtain a closer look at the horticultural theming on the three-hour **Gardens of the World** tour held Tuesdays and Thursdays (see "Guided Tours" in "Obstacles and Opportunities").

There are two forms of transportation in the World Showcase portion of Epcot. Neither will speed you to another part of the park any more quickly than walking, but they can be helpful breaks during long days of touring. One is the **double-decker bus** system that rolls slowly around the lake along the World Showcase Promenade. There are four bus-stops: one in front of Norway, one at Italy, one at Morocco and the fourth near Canada, close to the main entrance to World Showcase. Otherwise you can board one of the 65-foot **FriendShips**, water taxis that ply the World Showcase Lagoon. The two boat routes both originate at the entrance to World Showcase; one travels to a dock near Morocco, the other to a dock at Germany.

World Showcase does not open until 11 a.m. (or 10 a.m. on days when Disney expects high park attendance). Because it opens later and many guests are preoccupied with their Future World touring, World Showcase doesn't become crowded until some time after noon. Viewed as a bell curve, the peak attendance for World Showcase starts around 12:30 p.m. and continues until about 4 p.m. when families begin to clear out of the park. The "land" receives an additional swarm of guests around 7 p.m., when Future World closes for the day and many visitors are on their way to restaurants. More specifically, the Mexico and Canada pavilions (being closest to the

World Showcase entrance) are busiest early in the day, before crowds have a chance to dissipate into the other countries around the lake; similarly, late afternoon and early evening seem to concentrate foot-traffic around France and Great Britain. The one attraction that generates any substantial line in World Showcase is the delightful **Maelstrom** in Norway; try to ride it before noon, or wait until just before IllumiNations. Most of the rest of the World Showcase attractions are positioned in theater settings with ample seating or standing capacity on all but the busiest days.

INSIDER TIP

*Many kids become antsy during any comprehensive tour of World Showcase. A solution? Purchase the **Passport Kit** at either Gateway Gifts or the Camera Center in Future World (beneath Spaceship Earth). The packet comes with a blank World Showcase passport and stickers that your children can insert into the booklet as they circle the lake, providing a simple, but engrossing activity. Although rather pricey, the $9 packet also contains some information about the culture and history of the 11 represented countries, and a Mickey Mouse button to boot.*

EPCOT

Mexico

Evocative inside and out, the Mexican pavilion is fringed by palm trees, and dominated by a six-story Mayan pyramid, with depictions of the Aztec serpent-head god, Quetzalcoatl, extending out from the walls of the stairway into the building. Inside, a small foyer contains an exhibit of pre-Columbian cultural items, **Reign of Glory**, though many visitors bypass this interesting display on their way inside. The romantic, indoor **Plaza de Los Amigos** is a seductive scene, designed and lit to provide a twilight ambience. Its *Mercado* (market) sells sombreros, serapes, woven baskets, pottery and carvings; a mariachi band performs hourly in the plaza. A lagoon-side outdoor eatery, **La Cantina de San Angel**, faces the pyramid and serves beer and adequate Mexican fast food.

El Rio del Tiempo (the River of Time) is one of two World Showcase rides. You'll board a boat (similar to those used in It's a Small World) that cruises past San Angel Inn diners, and beneath a softly rumbling volcano. The craft then glides through an assortment of Mexican scenes, thematically linked by dance, portrayed by audio-animatronic dolls and via rear-screen projection (and most of the film was scratched and filthy during my visits). At mid-point, the film footage shifts abruptly from native Mexican cultural scenes to vacation activities. While the attraction is colorful, the country deserves more dynamic representation than this boat ride presents. *Length of ride:* Five minutes. *Special note:* Roughly half of World Showcase's visitors encounter the Mexico pavilion before any other, making this country heavily toured around noon. Despite its rather simple nature, El Rio del Tiempo can develop a hefty line early on busy days. See it before noon or wait until evening on a big-attendance day; otherwise, skip it.

Norway

The most recent addition to World Showcase, the Norway pavilion combines structures with steep-pitched roofs and cobblestone streets, along with forest and sea, history and culture into a condensed replica of the Scandinavian country. Located in a detailed reproduction of a medieval church, the **Stave Church Gallery** celebrates Norway's culture and history; note the carved dragon heads adorning the eaves of the structure. The **Puffin's Roost** features a wonderful spread of crafts—heavy sweaters, pewter candlesticks, leather goods, a variety of trolls and, of course, Lego blocks. A recreation of 14th-century Akershus Castle contains the restaurant of the same name.

The ride next door, **Maelstrom**, is one of Epcot's highlights, a tantalizing blend of history, folklore and contemporary commerce, all themed to the sea. Guests board a 16-passenger Viking-style longboat that quickly ascends a hill and enters Norway's mythical world of trolls and forest goblins. A three-headed apparition sends you plummeting backwards through fjord country before your vessel plunges into a raging North Sea storm. It's delightful, but short. You exit the craft in a quaint fishing village which leads to a small theater playing a 70mm promotional film about Norway and its relationship with the sea. Many guests bypass the film, but it's only five minutes long, and provides a nifty introduction to the country's scenic grandeur, culture and trade. *Length of ride:* Five minutes, plus the film, which begins every seven or eight minutes. *Special note:* Because Maelstrom is the only real ride in World Showcase, a long line forms soon after 11 a.m. when it opens. Ride before noon, or wait until just before IllumiNations. Also note that busy afternoon performances of the nearby Wonders of China can release several hundred people into the area, further clogging the Maelstrom line.

China

Rosebushes and native trees accent the lovely China pavilion, where a ceremonial gate greets visitors to a half-size replica of the 15th-century, red-and-gold Temple of Heaven. The serene gardens and lotus ponds of the courtyard are beautiful, with the sound of a lute whispering gently in the background—an excellent place to enjoy red-bean ice cream, or a Tsing Tao beer. The **House of the Whispering Willows** showcases art and artifacts, on loan from the People's Republic of China. **Yong Feng Shangdian** is an immense shopping area that sells a huge selection of silk, jade, paper umbrellas and fans, wind chimes, porcelain, carved chests, lacquer furnishings and other imports.

Wonders of China is a CircleVision 360 film that tours some of the many scenic and cultural highlights of China. An actor/narrator plays Li Bai, a Chinese poet, who guides us through Shanghai, Suzhou, Beijing, the Forbidden City, the Great Wall, the Yangtze River and the Shilin Stone Forest. The 1981 production ignores both recent and politically sensitive issues (the Tibet situation, Tiananmen Square and the Yangtze River Dam all go unmentioned), but, Wonders of China is a fast-paced introduction to a vast country, and one of the highlights of World Showcase. *Length of show:* 18 minutes. *Special note:* The theater accommodates more than

500 standing guests so you will be admitted to the next performance on all but the busiest days.

AUTHOR'S OBSERVATION

CircleVision 360 is the Disney-developed cinema-in-the-round concept introduced at Disneyland in 1955, a response to the three-camera Cinerama system. The cinematography is accomplished using a 60-pound nine-camera mount, which is then shown using nine projectors in a cylindrical building. The effect can be breathtaking. In all three Walt Disney World CircleVision theaters—in the China and Canada pavilions at Epcot, and for Timekeeper at The Magic Kingdom—the best place to stand is not in the center, but near the "back" of the theater to the left as you enter. This allows one to see most of the screens at once.

Germany

One of Epcot's five, "attraction-less" pavilions, Germany exudes the boisterous charm of a year-round Octoberfest. The architecture is a pleasing compilation spanning several eras and regions: a facade drawn from Eltz Castle on the Mosel, a merchant's hall from southern Germany, a Bavarian-style beer hall. The central fountain in the *platz* celebrates St. George's slaying of the dragon, and every hour on the hour, a glockenspiel in the prominent village clock tower chimes merrily. Shopping opportunities in the German pavilion are spread over eight specialty shops, among them: **Weinkeller**, selling about 250 varieties of wines bottled by H. Schmitt Sohne, along with glassware and German cheeses; **Die Weihnachts Ecke** offers traditional Christmas ornaments and gifts, including nutcrackers; and **Der Teddybar**, a toy store featuring wooden playthings and building blocks, miniature trains, dolls and teddy bears. A unique selection is on display at **Volkskunst**, a small store devoted to timekeeping, including an array of cuckoo clocks, but also featuring ceramics, beer steins, Tyrolean scarves and wood carvings from Oberammergau.

Italy

More than any other country in World Showcase, the Italian pavilion is devoted to recreating a single locale, in this case, Venice, an obvious choice, since the city is probably what Americans most conjure when they think of Italy. The real Venice is also the most intimate of destinations, so Epcot has recreated its most public place: the Piazza San Marco. Miniatures of the pink and white Doge's Palace, the Campanile and the gold-leafed statues of San Marco are fronted by gondolas, tethered to striped poles in the lagoon. An Italian quartet sings hourly in the piazza, providing street entertainment. The stately back wall of the piazza is adorned with Mediterranean coastal vegetation—kumquat, olive and cypress are among the trees imported to enhance the setting. **La Cucina Italiana** sells wine, dried pastas and sauce, gourmet items, and a variety of cooking utensils. **Il Bel Cristallo** offers fine glassware, including famed Murano and Venetian glass, Capodimonte florals and figurines, and inlaid wooden musical boxes.

America

A single colonial structure in the Georgian style represents the United States for Epcot. Although the building is intricately detailed, there's little of interest beyond a formal rose garden around the exterior of the pavilion. **Heritage Manor Gifts** sells reproductions of turn-of-the-century Americana, while the open-air **American Gardens Theater** hosts sporadic concerts and special tapings of television events.

But inside the building sits what is probably the most compelling World Showcase attraction for Americans, **The American Adventure**, a dynamic multimedia presentation. The show encapsulates U.S. history, beginning with the Mayflower, and is told by audio-animatronic narrators, Ben Franklin and Mark Twain. A total of 25 lifelike characters including George Washington, John Muir, Susan B. Anthony and others, make up the cast of this story. The ambitious presentation gamely tackles a few of the difficult passages in America's history (not something that happens in the attractions at other World Showcase pavilions) although Disney ideology ensures an optimistic referendum on two-plus centuries of U.S. patriotism. The screen rising above and behind the characters uses film footage to provide a sort of time line and link for the disparate sequences. The American Adventure received a $2.5 million overhaul in 1992 that breathed new life and events into the mosaic of the country's history. The inclusive presentation finds room for Rosie the Riveter, abolitionist Frederick Douglass, and Nez Perce Indian Chief Joseph.

Equally fascinating is the unique technology used to create the computer-controlled attraction. The 72-foot-wide screen is the largest ever utilized for a rear-screen projection system. Underneath it, however, is not a stage, but a pit with a huge, 175-ton Lazy-Susan-type platform on which each of the 10 audio-animatronic sets are stationed. Each set rises and lowers for its sequence, then the platform turns quietly (out of sight) for the next set-piece. Seats toward the front of the theater provide the best view. *Length of show:* 29 minutes; show times (every 35 minutes) are posted out front. *Special note:* The 1000-seat American Adventure theater is large enough to accommodate demand for the attraction on all but the busiest days. However, during high season, afternoon performances can fill up as much as 30 minutes prior to the scheduled show time. During peak touring times, visit the American Adventure before 1 p.m. or wait until evening. An a cappella singing group, the Voices of Liberty, performs folk classics in the rotunda prior to most daytime performances.

Japan

Epcot's most tranquil pavilion is graced by a bright red, barnacle-encrusted *torii* ceremonial gate that rises out of the water on the pebble-and-stone-scattered shore of the World Showcase lagoon. Across the promenade, the pavilion's compact layout is accented by a five-story, blue-roofed pagoda—each level represents the traditional components of Buddhism: earth, water, fire, wind and sky. Facing the pagoda is a peaceful garden where water ripples through a bonsai, rock and grass environment; most of the other plants here are not indigenous to Japan. The Florida environment is too hostile for these cold-weather dwellers. Behind the garden is an elegant tea house, modeled after the 16th-century Katsura Imperial Summer Palace in Kyoto, which is occupied by **Yakitori House**—fast-food Japanese style. Next door is the White Egret Castle, replicating one part of Kyoto's Gosho Imperial Palace. Inside on the ground floor is the **Mitsukoshi Department Store**, which sells elaborate dolls, screens, kimonos, china, bonsai trees, wind chimes and much more. On the second floor are Japan's two sit-down restaurants, and a lounge (the Matsu No Ma) that overlooks the World Showcase lagoon. The second-floor deck provides an excellent, sometimes overlooked, vantage point for IllumiNations. The Bijutsu-Kan Gallery offers a revolving art show of both contemporary and traditional pieces.

Morocco

A replica of the Koutoubia Minaret of Marrakesh, a 12th-century prayer tower, forms the visual icon for the exotic Kingdom of Morocco. The Najjarine Fountain leads through the Bab Baoujouloud Gate of Fez to the *medina* (old city), which is composed of a *souk* (market) and a traditional Moroccan home. The ornate details in the mosaics of this pavilion can be spotted around every corner. Nineteen craftsmen were brought from Morocco to work with the nine tons of handmade tile imported to Orlando. Don't miss the waterwheel across the promenade that pours a stream through elevated gardens filled with olive trees, date palms and banana plants. In an innovative touch, stores in the Morocco pavilion barter with guests for a sale, so haggle for the best deal. **Casablanca Carpets** and the **Brass Bazaar** offer rugs and brass items. Leather goods and clothing, woven baskets and that fez you always wanted are available at **Tangier Traders**. A **Gallery of Arts and History** is located just outside the gate, while the Moorish Cafe offers Moroccan mint tea.

France

Le Belle Époque, "the beautiful era" of the late 19th century, when French architecture and art hit its stride, is swooningly revisited in the French Pavilion. A 1/10-scale Eiffel Tower soars above the three-story Gallic buildings, each fronted with stone and topped with copper or slate mansard roofs. In a delightful touch of French Impressionism, a quiet park styled after the Bois de Boulogne depicts the setting for Georges Serat's "Sunday Afternoon on the Island of La Grande Jatte"; flowering crape myrtles and pleached sycamores provide the backdrop. In the heart of this Paris, no fewer than three restaurants including a sidewalk cafe and a *boulangerie* offer *gastronomique* delights at all price points. The art nouveau **Plume et Palette** presents a selection of original art, tapestries and crystal pieces. **La Maison du Vin** is one of several World Showcase wine shops, with a reasonable charge for wine tastings where you keep the glass, while **La Signature** sells perfumes, bath products and apparel. The **Galerie des Halles** features an iron-and-glass, barrel-roofed ceiling that is a tribute to the now-gone *Les Halles*, and markets cookies, chocolates and inexpensive souvenirs.

Impressions de France is unquestionably the best of the four main film presentations at World Showcase. Featuring a glorious music soundtrack by Saint-Saens, Debussy and Satie, the film sweeps gracefully through the French countryside, the Alps, castles and Paris to a soaring climax as the camera climbs the Eiffel Tower against the strains of Saint-Saens' *Organ Symphony*. The eye-filling images, a tourist bureau's dream, encompass five, wrap-around screens in the sit-down **Palais du**

Cinema. The staff of **Galerie des Halles** on the way out is routinely bombarded for requests for videotapes of the film and soundtrack, and it's difficult to imagine viewers leaving the theater without booking a trip to France on the spot. *Length of show:* 18 minutes. *Special note:* Impressions de France is shown in a 350-seat theater that plays to capacity audiences on moderately busy afternoons. However, you generally will be seated for the next performance. During peak touring periods see the film before 1 p.m. or during the evening.

United Kingdom

A diverse selection of eight architectural styles covering four centuries are at work in this pavilion, a delight for fans of the Merchant-Ivory films and Anglophiles in general. The town square leads to a formal English garden, surrounded by a recreation of Shakespeare's Anne Hathaway thatch-roof cottage (note the perennial and herb garden) and buildings constructed in classic Tudor, Victorian and Georgian styles. The classic cherry-red phone booths along the promenade cheerfully complete the tourist clichè, and accept your calling card, as well. Without a central attraction, shopping is the main focus of activity here. The R. Twinings and Company is represented at The **Tea Caddy**, which also features biscuits, hard candy and a regal selection of teapots. Pringle of Scotland sells an array of imported wool and cashmere sweaters, along with scarves, kilts and other dress items. British games and playthings are sold at **The Toy Soldier**, along with wooden boats and a line of collector's dolls. **Lords and Ladies** provides an eclectic array of dart boards, fragrances, tobacco, pottery, limited-edition chess sets and much more. The emporium also creates detailed genealogy charts. Bass Export, Guinness and Harp are among the selections at the atmospheric **Rose and Crown Pub** across the promenade.

Canada

A curious amalgam of icons and themes, the Canadian pavilion's best asset—an inviting rock gorge with a thundering waterfall—has the least to do with the nation's culture or people. But it is a memorable and realistic recreation of Canada's natural environment, as is the manicured garden next door a lush take on Vancouver Island's Butchart Gardens—see if you can spot the three fake conifers among the deodar cedars, Fraser firs, willow, birch and red maple trees that form a park-like setting. The mansard-roofed *Hotel du Canada*, styled after Ottawa's Chateau Laurier, towers (courtesy of forced perspective) over the rocky landscape, while Eskimo culture is represented by totem poles that surround the courtyard. A log cabin contains **Northwest Mercantile**, which sells Indian and Eskimo crafts and clothing, maple syrup, fur vests and sheepskins; **La Boutique des Provinces** represents French Canada with jewelry, fashions and figurines.

O Canada! is the featured attraction, a rousing CircleVision 360 film that plays in a theater entered via a mine shaft lined with flickering lanterns. The film pays tribute to the country's coast-to-coast natural wonders, as well as its attractive cities. A highlight is the takeoff of thousands of Canada snow geese which seems to surround the audience, as does a herd of reindeer that stampedes on all nine screens. *Length of show:* 18 minutes. *Special note:* Because of its position close to the World Showcase entrance, Canada tends to become crowded earlier than most other pavilions.

Try to see it before noon, or wait until late afternoon. The theater accommodates more than 600 people, and you will usually be admitted to the next performance on all but the busiest afternoons.

IlluminNations

Epcot's most popular daily event is **IllumiNations**, a culminating show of fireworks, laser and music held at the park's official closing time each night, usually 9 p.m., but the schedule varies somewhat during holiday periods. The 15-minute performance occurs in and above the World Showcase Lagoon and can be seen, to varying degrees, from any point around the lake. During busy seasons, guests begin claiming the best viewpoints 30 to 60 minutes before the performance.

Because most evening visitors stay for IllumiNations and a mad dash for the exits occurs at the conclusion of the performance, plan your viewing location with regard to your exit. If you're staying at one of the Epcot Resorts, you'll want to be near the International Gateway between France and Great Britain. Otherwise, you'll be exiting through the main gates, and want to position yourself close to Innoventions between Mexico and Canada. Not coincidentally, in both cases, these are the most popular viewing areas. Several small islands in the southern portion of the lake block some of the show from view, particularly from points near the promenade in front of China, Morocco and France.

Two ideal, but very popular, locations for viewing IllumiNations are from the Cantina de San Angel in front of Mexico and the outdoor pub of the Rose and Crown in front of Great Britain. Both spots offer table service, among the earliest to be locked down. Two choice parks lie immediately south of Great Britain: one is an island linked by two bridges near the International Gateway, the other is a small terrace a few feet from the Rose and Crown that is sometimes roped off, but still accessible. Neither of these spots, however, is clandestine and will be solidly occupied well before the performance.

INSIDER TIP

Honeymooners and boat enthusiasts alike may want to consider springing for viewing IllumiNations from aboard Breathless, *a vintage, 1934 Chris Craft speedboat based at the Yacht and Beach Club Resort dock. The romantic, one-hour cruise over to Epcot's World Showcase Lagoon runs $110 for up to seven passengers, and can be arranged for by calling* ☎ (407) 934-6112.

If getting away quickly is less important than a good view claimed closer to show time, the best general area is in front of either the German or Italian pavilions. In both cases, these are the farthest you can be from the main exit, but tend to offer good spots just before show time, and fairly close to the action.

IllumiNations received a makeover for Walt Disney World's 25th Anniversary. The basic content of lights, lasers and fireworks is mostly the same (there's a fresh new soundtrack), but one significant change is that some of the fireworks are now launched from the area behind the Italian, American and Japanese pavilions. If you are situated along the walkway in front of these pavilions, you are engulfed by the spectacle. On the other hand, if you are inside the lounge of the Japanese pavilion (previously a good viewing location), you will miss part of the action.

INSIDER TIP

If you missed IllumiNations during your Epcot tour but don't want to use a theme park admission to see it, here's a free tip. Unofficially, the International Gateway entrance opens to the public at the moment IllumiNations begins. Although it is difficult to obtain a good viewing location as the show is starting, you can see most of the sizzle as it unfolds above the water, free of charge.

Eating

Dining at Epcot is a major part of the "international" experience, à la Disney. During your visit, try to plan on one sit-down meal, preferably an early afternoon lunch. Though prices can be somewhat steep, fortunately, dining attire can be termed theme park informal at all Epcot restaurants. You may make restaurant reservations up to 60 days in advance by calling ☎ *(407) WDW-DINE.* If you have not made a reservation prior to arriving at Epcot, proceed directly to the reservations desk at Guest Relations, immediately to the left of Spaceship Earth just inside the front entrance. They will suggest that you use the WorldKey terminals next door, but dealing directly with a live body in front of you is easier.

Because of the quantity of dining options available, be sure to read through the "Restaurants" chapter in advance to make sure your desires are served. Disney cast members will not usually offer recommendations among the different eateries. The most popular Epcot restaurants include the Coral Reef, San Angel Inn, L'Originale Alfredo di Roma and Chefs de France. If reservations are solidly booked at all locations—not at all uncommon—one of the better options is France's **Au Petit Cafe**, which offers waiter service, but first-come, first-serve seating only (see "Restaurants"). If you don't wish to splurge on a sit-down meal, fast food and cafeteria-style dining is listed below.

Most of the full-service restaurants have reasonably priced **children's menus**. However, as I learned with my young niece and nephew who assisted me during the research for this book, most pre-teens are unconcerned with elegant settings or unusual food they might not see at home. I didn't realize it at the time, but when we dropped more than $50 on an underwhelming dinner at the Nine Dragons restaurant, the experience was no more exciting for them than the $17 lunch earlier in the day at Sunshine Season Food Fair. If you're on a budget, and want to splurge on one meal kids will enjoy, do it on your visit the Disney-MGM Studios, where the '50s Prime Time Cafe and Sci-Fi Dine-In Theater deliver the best package of dining-as-theme-park experience. Information on Epcot's **character meals**, provided at the Garden Grill Restaurant, is covered in the "Restaurants" chapter.

Only a few eating options of any kind exist in the Future World half of Epcot. The best location is the **Sunshine Season Food Fare**, a series of fast-food counters on the lower level of The Land pavilion. The combined offering is diverse and features the added benefit of being relatively wholesome and reasonably-priced. Choices include barbecue chicken and ribs, pastas, sandwiches, soups, salads, stuffed baked potatoes and a bakery (open early for bagels and cinnamon rolls). Overall, this is a good choice for families with differing taste buds to satisfy. One caveat, this food mall is quite busy from about noon until 2 p.m.

Innoventions features the large **Electric Umbrella**, which provides hamburgers, hot dogs, chicken sandwiches and salads; outdoor seating is sometimes available. Nearby, **Pasta Piazza Ristorante** offers pizza, pasta and antipasto salads in a bright, neon setting. Lighter fare is served at **Pure and Simple** in the Wonders of Life pavilion, including fruit-topped waffles, muffins, juices, sandwiches and frozen yogurt, while desserts, coffee, cappuccino, pastries and gourmet items are available at **Fountain View Espresso and Bakery** in Innoventions.

In World Showcase, the Mexico pavilion features the **Cantina de San Angel**, which offers tacos al carbon, chicken tacos, salads, Dos Equis beer and margaritas—in a setting perfectly situated alongside the lagoon. In Norway, the **Kringla Bakeri og Kafe** provides open-face sandwiches, delicious Norwegian pastries and Ringnes Beer. China's **Lotus Blossom Cafe** serves simple lunch and dinner items such as eggrolls, stir fry, sweet and sour pork, soup, and tasty red-bean ice cream as well as Tsing Tao beer. Snack-oriented **Sommerfest** in Germany sells pretzels, Bratwurst sandwiches, apple strudel, Black Forest cake, beer and wine. In America, the **Liberty Inn** offers burgers, hot dogs, rotisserie chicken and grilled chicken sandwiches.

Japan provides two good options. The **Yakitori House** features soup, teriyaki and yakitori in a lovely setting while the **Matsu No Ma Lounge** serves sushi and appetizers along with specialty drinks and Kirin beer, all in a location that provides an excellent viewing area for IllumiNations. Morocco's **Moorish Cafe** sells sweet Moroccan mint tea, coffee and pastries. An excellent (though pricey) spot for a late morning or evening snack, the busy **Boulangerie Patisserie** in France is the place for a dazzling array of croissants, brioches, fruit tarts, chocolate eclairs, quiche and espresso. The **Rose and Crown Pub** of the United Kingdom offers a selection of beers on tap, as well as cheese plates, Scotch eggs, steak-and-kidney pie, and chicken-and-leek quiche. Canada's **Le Cellier** is a cafeteria-style dining room, featuring prime rib, poached salmon, pork-and-potato pie, cheddar cheese soup, maple syrup pie and more. Le Cellier is a popular selection for those who did not secure a reservation at a waiter-service restaurant, but still want an upscale meal.

Epcot Touring Itineraries

Developing an all-purpose touring itinerary for Epcot presents unique challenges. The entire park really requires the better part of two days to see, but most visitors want to experience it in one day. Unfortunately, this is easier said than done. No two visitors are alike in their priorities and interests, and because Epcot offers such a broad range of attractions and exhibits, it seems impossible to suggest the perfect touring equation. Add in the sheer size of the park and you have a tour guide's nightmare.

A few generalizations can be made. Children gravitate to Epcot's limited number of rides, most of which are in Future World. Shoppers and culture-buffs will enjoy World Showcase touring more than others. Beyond these generalities, however, guest preferences vary. Epcot boasts one distinct touring advantage over most other "amusement" parks: much of both Future World and World Showcase is composed of walk-through or hands-on exhibits that you can either partake of or easily bypass. Both of our suggested itineraries focus on attractions; you may insert all the additional exhibit touring you wish.

As with The Magic Kingdom itineraries, these plans work best under the following circumstances:

a. You have purchased your tickets before you arrive at the park (see: "Tickets" in "Obstacles and Opportunities").

b. You are positioned at the Main Entrance to Epcot at least 30 to 45 minutes prior to the official opening time. Call ☎ *(407) 824-4321* the day before you visit to verify the opening time.

c. All members of your party are willing to follow the same touring itinerary; they can, of course, bow out of individual attractions they have no desire to ride.

d. If you are not a guest of a Disney Resort, that you tour Epcot only on the five days when the Surprise Morning policy is not in effect: Sundays, Mondays, Wednesdays, Thursdays and Saturdays (Saturdays and Sundays being the least busy days for touring). If you visit Epcot on a Surprise Morning (currently Tuesdays and Fridays), you will find lines already in place at several major attractions by the time the general public is admitted.

A Special Note

In the spring of 1997, Disney will debut one of its most ambitious attractions ever at Epcot: the **Test Track** at the old World of Motion pavilion. Sure to be a huge draw from the first day of operation, the ride will change traffic patterns in the park, making some elements of our touring itineraries obsolete. If you are visiting Epcot after the attraction has opened, we recommended that you ride the Test Track first thing in the morning. At publication time, it wasn't established whether the ride would be part of the Surprise Morning program. At the point the Test Track opens, Horizons is scheduled to be mothballed indefinitely.

The One-Day Plan

This itinerary is geared for those who want to devote no more than one long day (at least 12 hours) to Epcot. While it takes in almost all of the major attractions, it allows very little time for shopping, meals and live entertainment, and provides time for only a cursory glance at the numerous exhibit areas.

If you are a Disney Resort guest and are able to visit Epcot on a **Surprise Morning** (see "Obstacles and Opportunities") by all means, do so. However, because Body Wars does not open early on Surprise Mornings, you'll need to delay step 2 until 9 a.m. (following steps 3 and 4). Additionally, it will be advantageous to tour the rest of the Wonders of Life pavilion (Cranium Command and the Making of Me) at that point, before returning to the itinerary steps below.

1. Enter Epcot at the moment the gates open to the general public; on non-Surprise Mornings, this will usually be 8:30 a.m. (even when advertised as 9 a.m.). Proceed straight to **Spaceship Earth** and ride. After Spaceship Earth, spend a few minutes touring the **Global Neighborhood** exhibit and exit the building. If you have not made **lunch reservations**, go to the Guest Relations office to do so, preferably for some time between 12:30 and 1 p.m. By following this itinerary, you will be in World Showcase, in the vicinity of China, at that time; the best sit-down choice would be the **San Angel Inn** in nearby Mexico. (Nine Dragons, Bedridden and L'Originale Alfredo di Roma are also nearby.)

2. Enter Innoventions East and go through the building to the exit facing the **Wonders of Life** pavilion. When the rest of Future World opens at 9 a.m., go straight to Wonders of Life and ride **Body Wars**.

3. Following Body Wars, bypass the rest of the Wonders of Life pavilion for now and go directly to the **Journey Into Imagination** pavilion and see **Honey, I Shrunk The Audience**. You should arrive in time to see the second performance of the day. At this point, you will have experienced the three attractions that later will require the longest waits; on a moderately busy day, these first three steps will take about 80 minutes first thing in the morning while later on, they will require two to three hours.

4. Proceed quickly out of the theater and ride **Journey Into Imagination**; walk through the Imagination pavilion.

5. Ride **Living With the Land**.

6. Visit **The Living Seas** pavilion. Depending on how long you spend visiting the Imagination, Land and Seas pavilions, the World Showcase portion of the park should be open by this time. Aim to enter **World Showcase** right as the rope drops usually at 11:00 a.m.

7. Go to **Mexico** and ride **El Rio del Tiempo**.

8. Go to **Norway** and ride **Maelstrom**. You will have time to stay for the brief film after the ride.

9. Go to **China** and see **Wonders of China**. At this point, you will be approaching your lunch reservation. Proceed to your restaurant.

10. After lunch, return to Future World and go to the **Universe of Energy**. If the wait for the next performance exceeds 10 minutes, go to step 11, and return to Universe of Energy after the Wonders of Life pavilion.

11. Revisit the **Wonders of Life** pavilion to see **The Making of Me** and **Cranium Command**; start with the attraction that has the shortest wait.

12. Ride **Horizons**.

13. At this time, you'll have toured most of Future World, with the exception of **Innoventions**. Visit the two sides at your leisure, then finish your tour of the World Showcase.

14. Go to **Canada**; see **O Canada**! Visit the **United Kingdom** pavilion.

15. Go to **France**; see **Impressions de France**.

16. You now have five countries to visit during your remaining time in Epcot: **Morocco**, **Japan**, **America**, **Italy** and **Germany**. Although each has its appeal, the **American Adventure** is the don't-miss attraction of the five; tour the other four in the time remaining before IllumiNations. This will also be the period you'll be contemplating dinner. (Sommerfest in Germany or Yakitori House in Japan are your best choices in this area for a quick meal.

17. Stake out a viewing location for **IllumiNations** (usually at 9 p.m.) 20 to 30 minutes prior to showtime (see: "IllumiNations" earlier in this chapter for ideal viewing positions).

What Did We Miss?

Following this itinerary step by step will eliminate **The Circle of Life** and **Food Rocks**. While it visits all of the exhibit areas within Future World, this itinerary allows little time to explore hands-on and walk-through demonstrations. It also provides only a brief period to visit Morocco, Japan, Italy and Germany before IllumiNations.

The Two-Day Plan

This plan entails less backtracking than the one-day itinerary, and splits Epcot into two logical servings, each consuming a more leisurely eight to 10 hours. The itinerary focuses Future World touring into the morning and afternoon of the first day, and World Showcase in the afternoon and evening of the second day. You will have ample time to tour the exhibits and view entertainment throughout both days. It provides for one sit-down meal in the park each day, although it's possible to incorporate more (or less) if you wish. If you are a Disney Resort guest and are able to visit on a Surprise Morning, you can still use the following plan for day one, and you will be finished with your first day of touring about mid-afternoon. The Surprise Morning policy does not affect the operational hours of World Showcase.

Few pre-teens and some young adults will have the patience for two full days of touring at Epcot. If you have children in tow but want to make sure you cover all of Epcot, make a slight adjustment to the following plan. Follow the day one itinerary, but tackle the American Adventure at the end of your first day at Epcot. Then on your second day at Epcot, begin your touring around 2 p.m. (rather than 10:30 a.m.) and follow the day two itinerary (omitting step 15). This will allow time to visit a water park or another half-day activity in the morning of your second day, and still see all of Epcot.

If agriculture and whole foods are of interest to you, go to The Land between steps 2 and 3 and make a late-morning or early afternoon reservation for the Backstage at the Land tour (see: "Guided Tours" in "Obstacles and Opportunities" for more information).

Day One

1. If you have not already done so, when the gates open go to Guest Relations and make **lunch reservations**, preferably for some time between noon and 1 p.m., ideally at the Coral Reef Restaurant, the only full-service restaurant in **Future World**.

2. Proceed directly to **Spaceship Earth** and ride. Visit the **Global Neighborhood** on your way out.

3. Go to the **Journey Into Imagination** pavilion and see **Honey, I Shrunk the Audience**. Ride **Journey Into Imagination** and tour the **Image Works** exhibits.

4. Ride **Living With the Land**. See **The Circle of Life** and **Food Rocks**.

5. Tour **The Living Seas** pavilion until your **lunch** reservation. Proceed to your restaurant.

6. Visit **Innoventions** East and West.

7. Ride **Horizons**.

8. See the **Universe of Energy**.

9. Go to the **Wonders of Life** pavilion. See **Cranium Command**, the **Anacomical Players** and **The Making of Me**, tour the exhibits.

10. Ride **Body Wars**. Go to **Guest Relations** and confirm what time World Showcase will open on your second day in Epcot; make a dinner reservation for the second day for some time between 6 and 7 p.m. at one of the restaurants in World Showcase.

Day Two

1. Arrive at Epcot around 10:30 a.m. and be at the **World Showcase** entrance by the time it is scheduled to open, usually 11 a.m. Browse through the day's entertainment schedule and coordinate live entertainment into your touring plans.

2. Ride **El Rio del Tiempo** and tour the **Mexico** pavilion

3. Ride **Maelstrom** and tour the **Norway** pavilion.

4. See **Wonders of China** and tour the **China** pavilion. By now, you'll be thinking about lunch. Choose one of the World Showcase eateries that does not require a reservation.

5. Proceed to the **America** pavilion and see the **American Adventure**.

6. Over the course of the afternoon, visit the rest of the countries: **Germany**, **Italy**, **Japan**, **Morocco**, **France**, the **United Kingdom** and **Canada**. You may also have time to visit any Future World rides you missed or want to try again before your **dinner** reservation.

7. Following dinner, find a spot to enjoy **IllumiNations**.

THE DISNEY-MGM STUDIOS

Fireworks are the grand finale for many festive events in Orlando.

Promising a "Hollywood that never was and always will be," the Disney-MGM Studios have been a successful addition to the Walt Disney World family of parks. Much more light-hearted in tone than Epcot, the Disney-MGM Studios are designed to compete head-on with Universal's nearby attraction—although the two are very different in style and approach. A visit to both studios on one trip is a rewarding study in contrasts, with little overlap. What the two parks share is a cheeky, flip tone that guests enjoy—even Michael Eisner is not beyond gentle ribbing at the Disney park, and a video monitor in the waiting area for one attraction features David Letterman who

WALT DISNEY WORLD ®

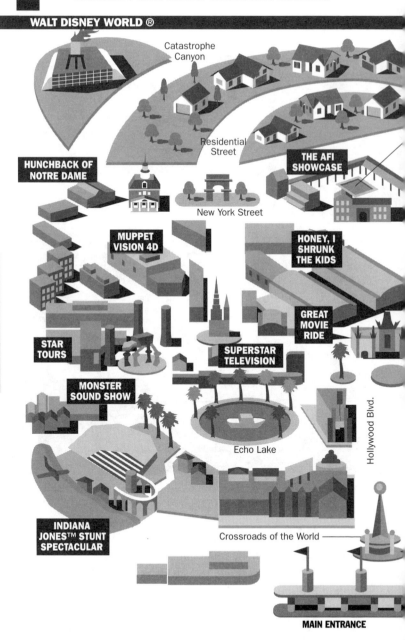

Catastrophe
Canyon

Residential
Street

**HUNCHBACK OF
NOTRE DAME**

**THE AFI
SHOWCASE**

New York Street

**MUPPET
VISION 4D**

**HONEY, I
SHRUNK
THE KIDS**

**GREAT
MOVIE
RIDE**

**STAR
TOURS**

**SUPERSTAR
TELEVISION**

**MONSTER
SOUND SHOW**

THE DISNEY-MGM
STUDIOS

Hollywood Blvd.

Echo Lake

**INDIANA
JONES™ STUNT
SPECTACULAR**

Crossroads of the World —

MAIN ENTRANCE

DISNEY-MGM STUDIOS ®

Disney-MGM Studios re-creates Hollywood's golden era and takes guests on behind the scenes tours of the world of animation, television and movies. Shops, restaurants and architecture are Tinseltown-inspired.

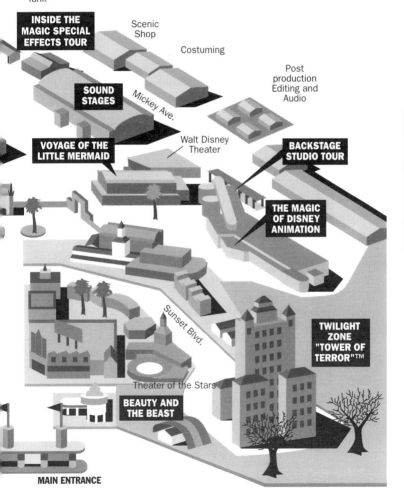

Water effects Tank

INSIDE THE MAGIC SPECIAL EFFECTS TOUR

Scenic Shop

Costuming

Post production Editing and Audio

SOUND STAGES

Mickey Ave.

VOYAGE OF THE LITTLE MERMAID

Walt Disney Theater

BACKSTAGE STUDIO TOUR

THE MAGIC OF DISNEY ANIMATION

Sunset Blvd.

TWILIGHT ZONE "TOWER OF TERROR"™

Theater of the Stars

BEAUTY AND THE BEAST

MAIN ENTRANCE

advises guests "if you break anything, security guards in mouse suits will beat you senseless."

As a former Los Angeles resident, I find the effect of Disney's vision of Hollywood enchanting—the re-creation presented here is loving and detailed. Cast members pose as Clark Gable or Carol Lombard for passing guests—they'll vamp for pictures and sign autographs—as well as movie directors and over-the-top gossip columnists. A number of buildings are Tinseltown archetypes that recall a golden era, but others are deliberate replicas of specific landmarks from the '30s, '40s and '50s (and a few are actually savvy, renamed knock-offs). The sleek curves of the Pan Pacific Theater have become the main entrance to the Studios, with the Crossroads of the World monument adorned here by a waving Mickey. Farmer's Market (of Fairfax Avenue fame) is replicated here as the Sunset Ranch Market, while a gleaming 1947 Buick sits parked in front of Oscar's Super Service, a vintage gas station providing fill-ups for 34 cents a gallon.

Although much of the movie information disseminated at the Studios is general in nature with a high priority placed on entertainment, the observant guest can pick up a wealth of knowledge about how films are created. For instance, the technique of "forced perspective" is showcased on New York Street where, at one end of the block, a group of skyscraper facades a few feet apart creates a multi-mile illusion of depth. One of the park's best features is a three-minute short starring Bette Midler as a music teacher who wins the lottery, loses her ticket, and the wild chase that follows; the entire film—including subway train and station—was produced on the Orlando back lot and sound stages. Visitors can walk through the collection of props and tricks that were compiled to tell the madcap story.

AUTHOR'S OBSERVATION

The Disney-MGM Studios' production facility has been the location for such films as Oscar, Ernest Saves Christmas and Passenger 57 (using the studio's full-size mock-up of a 747), while some of the television productions shot here include selected episodes of "Star Search," "Wheel of Fortune" and "Siskel & Ebert."

The Disney-MGM Studios were originally conceived as a pavilion within Epcot. But as Universal's plans for an Orlando studio tour attraction rolled forward, Disney stayed competitive by expanding the concept to encompass a new theme park "gate" for Walt Disney World. At its 1989 opening, many observers were struck by the fact that the Disney-MGM Studios admission price was (and continues to be) equal to that of The Magic Kingdom and Epcot—both were bigger parks that provided substantially more touring opportunities. However, the Disney Company has spent much of the '90s adding to its newest park, with major rides such as **Twilight Zone Tower of Terror** and **Star Tours** debuting to popular acclaim. The Studio now adds up to a full day of entertainment and light-hearted education around the theme of movie-making, creating one of Disney's (and Orlando's) best attractions.

The studio tour is segmented into three distinct attractions, each taking place in a different portion of the park: the **Backstage Studio Tour**, a tram ride through the back lot; **Inside the Magic**, which tours the soundstage area and highlights special effects; and the **Magic of Disney Animation**, which visits a portion of the studio's growing (and functioning) animation department. Two sit-down attractions highlight filmmaking: the **Indiana Jones Stunt Spectacular** and the **Monster Sound Show**. **SuperStar Television** apes the hustle bustle of a live television show for a sit-down audience, while a restaurant, the **'50s Prime Time Cafe**, recreates the Ozzie and Harriet kitchen-that-never-was, complete with black-and-white sitcom reruns and acres of Formica table tops, where diners scarf down meatloaf and mashed potatoes.

Transportation, Arrival and Orientation

Although visitors to the Disney-MGM Studios were hampered by an inadequately sized parking lot at the park's 1989 opening, an expansion has doubled the number of parking spaces. There are two entrances for this lot, one opposite the Swan and BoardWalk hotels on Buena Vista Drive, and a southern entrance from World Drive near Maingate and U.S. 192. The lot is less than 10 minutes by car from the All-Stars, Caribbean Beach or Epcot Resorts; allow 15 to 20 minutes from the other Disney properties.

All of the Disney properties except the Epcot Resorts offer a bus route to the Studios; transit times are comparable to the driving times listed above. The Epcot Resorts access the park by boat; allow 10 to 15 minutes from the Swan, Dolphin and BoardWalk, a little longer from the Yacht and Beach Club (a footpath linking the Studios with the nearby BoardWalk is also under discussion).

The layout of the park appears, at first glance, to be a little more haphazard than other Disney operations. In reality, Disney's creative team obviously has learned from the crowd-flow problems at Epcot, and the Studios bear some resemblance to the hub-and-spoke structure of The Magic Kingdom. Guests enter the park via Hollywood Boulevard, and the Great Movie Ride, located inside a replica of Grauman's Chinese Theater, is the hub at the end of this main street. Several vaguely defined "lands" lead away from this central hub: Echo Lake and New York Street are to the east (left); Sunset Boulevard and the Animation Courtyard are to the west; Mickey Avenue and the Sound Stages are south, just beyond the Chinese Theater.

When you enter the park, you'll be handed a guidebook and schedule of the day's entertainment offerings. Unlike at Epcot and the Kingdom, "rope drop" here is simply when the turnstiles start spinning, at which point the entire park is open for business. On Surprise Mornings, four attractions will be open for touring: The Great Movie Ride, The Tower of Terror, Star Tours and MuppetVision 4-D. Usually musical entertainment provides a diversion at the park entrance prior to the actual gate-opening. At the end of Hollywood Boulevard, on the right, is a **tip board** that provides estimates as to how long the waits are for various attractions. The time estimates tend to be conservative, but they're good for comparison purposes. Additional touring information is provided at **Guest Relations**, just to the left of the main entrance gates. A behind-the-scenes glimpse into the inner-workings of the animation department (beyond what is provided to the general public) is available; this reservations-only Inside Animation tour is described more fully under "Guided Tours" in "Obstacles and Opportunities."

A **diaper changing** and **nursing station** is provided next to Guest Relations. **Stroller** and **wheelchair rental** is located at Oscar's Super Service, just inside the main entrance; **lockers** are made available next door to this location. An **ATM** is situated outside the park to the right of the main entrance as you enter.

Ticket information is listed under "Tickets" in "Obstacles and Opportunities."

Hollywood Boulevard, Sunset Boulevard, Shopping and Characters

Disney has endeavored to break up the park's layout with "lands" similar to The Magic Kingdom, but the "lands" are ill-defined and of marginal use. Guests enter the via **Hollywood Boulevard**, and continue down the street to the **Chinese Theater**, where **Sunset Boulevard** extends off to the right, and **Echo Lake** to the left. However, beyond that point, the themed areas become more vague.

As might be expected, shopping within the Disney-MGM Studios sticks to movie themes and items that embrace the '30s and '40s. Most of the Studios' shops are concentrated along Hollywood and Sunset, the best of which is probably **Sid Cahuenga's One-of-a-Kind Shop**, located just to the left of the main entrance. In addition to props and the personal items of stars, Sid Cahuenga's is the only location in the World that sells photos of Walt Disney (on occasion, the store even proffers an authentic Walt signature for collectors). The requisite Disney T-shirts and character merchandise is laid out at

Mickey's of Hollywood across the street, while just down Hollywood Boulevard, **Celebrity 5 & 10** sells more general movie-themed items.

Around the corner on Sunset, look to **Legends of Hollywood** for movie-oriented books, and Disney's animated and other classic films on video, as well as reproductions of popular one sheets and black-and-white stills. The selection of Disneyana proffered further along Sunset at **Mouse About Town** and **Sunset Club Coutures** is unique in Walt Disney World; among the wares are limited edition and one-of-a-kind watches, and stylish Disney apparel. **Once Upon a Time** next door is brimming with more vintage Disney memorabilia, including snow globes, ceramics and delightful marionettes, all festooned with famous characters from Disney's classics.

Highlights throughout the rest of the park include the **Animation Gallery** next to the entrance for the Magic of Disney Animation; most of the pieces for sale are reproductions of classic Disney scenes, but an occasional original sneaks onto the walls. The **Costume Shop**, next to the Sci-Fi Dine-In Theater, produces an array of T-shirts, masks and hats for year-round Halloween needs. The exit for Star Tours passes through **Endor Vendors**, a current selection of the best Star Wars toys and accessories.

Disney character autograph sessions are more-or-less continuous in front of the **Beverly Sunset Theater**—Mickey Mouse is usually present—while other characters are known to loiter on Mickey Avenue, behind the Chinese Theater. For other character information, consult with the Guest Relations desk on your way in. The afternoon **Toy Story Parade** emanates from near Star Tours, proceeds past Echo Lake to the Chinese Theater and ends at the entrance to the park. An evening fireworks show, **Sorcery in the Sky**, is performed at 9 p.m. on selected nights.

The following section addresses the park's attractions in a clockwise pattern, beginning with **The Great Movie Ride**, which is close to the center of the park.

Rides, Attractions and Tours

The Great Movie Ride

The original showpiece attraction, the Great Movie Ride is housed in a gigantic soundstage with a facade based on Grauman's Chinese Theater of Hollywood. Chinoiserie reigns supreme inside, where a long indoor queuing area winds past a lobby display of famous movie props including Sam's piano from *Casablanca* and a pair of ruby slippers from *The Wizard of Oz*, and then through a theater with a movie screen that plays previews from Hollywood's golden age. Guests board 70-passenger mechanized trams with live guides to tour the rest of the soundstage, which is broken into sets representing scenes from classic movies. The elaborate production involves 50 audio-animatronic creations that perform as you roll by, and the films covered include Busby Berkeley's *Footlight Parade, Singin' in the Rain, Public Enemy, Raiders of the Lost Ark, Mary Poppins* and others. One highlight is when the tram enters the narrow confines of the *Nostromo* set, where Ripley keeps *Alien* at bay—a sequence that can unnerve small children. In another scene, your tram operator becomes engulfed by the action. After touring the sets, the tram enters a theater featuring a fast-paced, three-minute clips assemblage by Oscar-winner Chuck Braverman.

In spite of a couple of flat sections—the short *Tarzan* sequence is particularly plastic—the Great Movie Ride is an impressive Disney creation, with several sequences remarkable in their detail; the finale in Oz is a dazzler. *Length of attraction:* 20 minutes. *Special note:* Although crowds have thinned following the addition of other park attractions, the Great Movie Ride is still a major draw. Because of its front-and-center position at the end of Hollywood Boulevard, the ride is the first attraction in view for guests and lines establish early in the day. Our suggestion? Wait until the end of your touring day, when guests are beginning to leave; frequently the line is much shorter during the last few hours the park is open.

SuperStar Television

Offering the flip side of the Great Movie Ride, SuperStar Television invites a few guests to have the opportunity to act in contemporary and classic TV scenes, in front of a live audience. In the pre-show waiting area, about 28 visitors are chosen (usually from the front of the lobby) to act out the set pieces. Those chosen to participate will be acting "opposite" Lucille Ball ("I Love Lucy"), Tim Allen ("Home Improvement") and others, all courtesy of blue-screen technology and creative editing in the television facility's booth. The fast-paced, make-believe television show that follows is produced and aired live for the 1000-person audience inside the theater. One of the most entertaining attractions at the park, popular with all ages (the horse head prop used for the "Bonanza" segment is the same as the one used in *The Godfather*). *Length of show:* 25 minutes. *Special note:* Because SuperStar is held in a large venue, you will almost always be accommodated for the next show, allowing you to fit it into your schedule at any time. Be aware, however, that the nearby Indiana Jones Stunt Spectacular releases up to 2000 guests into the Echo Lake area when it exits. If you want to be chosen for the performance, arrive at least 20 minutes before show time and make yourself obvious to the casting directors near the front of the waiting area.

INSIDER TIP

Although no regular television shows are in production at this writing, a few specials and one-time events will use the Disney-MGM Studio's soundstage and production facilities. Tickets are usually available for these tapings on a first-come first-serve basis, on the morning of the taping. Call ☎ (407) 824-4321 the night before your visit to see what may be scheduled. Or, check the tip board at the junction of Hollywood and Sunset Boulevards when you first arrive at the park.

The Monster Sound Show

A humorous exercise in how sound effects are produced. Here, volunteers are asked to assist in creating the effects for a comic, two-minute haunted-house clip starring Chevy Chase and Martin Short. The guest Foley artists—named after Jack Foley, an early Hollywood sound effects technician)—along with the 270-person audience, first view the short as originally intended. Then the audience and volunteers receive a brief lesson on how to create the approximately 100 sound effects—wind, thunder, footsteps, etc.—that went into the original soundtrack. The student Foley artists then perform the effects when the clip is replayed; the entertainment value is usually provided by the gloriously out-of-synch sound effects produced by the guests. If the visiting Foley artists are actually talented, much of the humor is lost. On the way out, the SoundWorks exhibit is a post-show demonstration area that allows the rest of audience to get in on the action. *Length of show:* 12 minutes. *Special note:* though the theater is relatively small, the show turns over quickly so waits are rarely longer than 15 to 20 minutes. However, if a performance of the Indiana Jones Stunt Spectacular has just concluded, the waiting area will be filled beyond the theater's capacity; come back later.

Indiana Jones Epic Stunt Spectacular

Disney pulls out all the stops for this wildly popular show, held in an enormous 2000-seat theater, the biggest in Walt Disney World. The show begins with six audience members who are selected (enthusiasm counts) by an oh-so-perky host to be a part of the live demonstration of stunt techniques. The backdrop is straight out of the Indiana Jones films: a Cairo street market, a desert landscape, and 1940s-era cars and a tank. Stunts performed in the films (and a few new tricks) are displayed at a rapid clip. *Length of show:* 30 minutes. *Special note:* Although the theater seating is huge, only the first and possibly second show of the morning play to less-than-capacity audiences. Obtaining a seat for afternoon shows requires you to enter the theater 20 to 30 minutes before show time on a moderately busy day. Try to fit in the Stunt Spectacular before noon, or wait until the last performance of the day. Also, if you aren't among the first guests out of the theater, head for a different part of the park to avoid the crowds.

THE DISNEY-MGM STUDIOS

INSIDER TIP

A number of the attractions at the Disney-MGM Studios are outdoor shows that can be uncomfortably hot during mid-day summer performances. If you are touring Disney during warm-weather months, try to see these shows before noon or closer to dusk when the temperature begins to cool down. The outdoor attractions include Indiana Jones Stunt Spectacular, Hunchback of Notre Dame, Honey I Shrunk the Kids Movie Set, Backstage Studio Tour, and Beauty and the Beast.

Star Tours

Universal may have Steven Spielberg, but one of Disney's creative partners is George Lucas, who lends his Star Wars characters and special effects to this dynamic

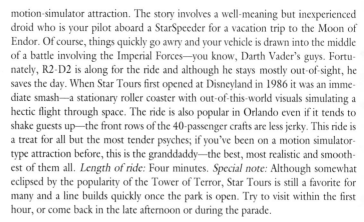

motion-simulator attraction. The story involves a well-meaning but inexperienced droid who is your pilot aboard a StarSpeeder for a vacation trip to the Moon of Endor. Of course, things quickly go awry and your vehicle is drawn into the middle of a battle involving the Imperial Forces—you know, Darth Vader's guys. Fortunately, R2-D2 is along for the ride and although he stays mostly out-of-sight, he saves the day. When Star Tours first opened at Disneyland in 1986 it was an immediate smash—a stationary roller coaster with out-of-this-world visuals simulating a hectic flight through space. The ride is also popular in Orlando even if it tends to shake guests up—the front rows of the 40-passenger crafts are less jerky. This ride is a treat for all but the most tender psyches; if you've been on a motion simulator-type attraction before, this is the granddaddy—the best, most realistic and smoothest of them all. *Length of ride:* Four minutes. *Special note:* Although somewhat eclipsed by the popularity of the Tower of Terror, Star Tours is still a favorite for many and a line builds quickly once the park is open. Try to visit within the first hour, or come back in the late afternoon or during the parade.

MuppetVision 4-D

Like Epcot's Honey, I Shrunk the Audience, this is a 3-D film presentation, but some creature has mischievously changed the title to reflect the extra-sensory activities taking place off the screen. The story (and it's dubious, at best) begins in the laboratory of Dr. Bunson Honeydew, who has created a sprite—"the spirit of 3-D"—to somehow assist in our enjoyment of a typically delirious Muppefied musical show. The huge on-screen cast is augmented by the perpetually grousing balcony critics, Waldorf and Stadler, and the Swedish Chef, who mans both the projection booth and a loaded cannon behind the audience. Early on, Kermit assures us that they will "not resort to any cheap 3-D tricks," but never has the well-meaning frog been so terribly wrong—watch out for Fozzie Bear's corsage. I confess, I am a card-carrying member of the Muppets' fan club, but who isn't? Kermit, Miss Piggy and the rest of the cast entertain kids, but somehow never shortchange the adults who've come along for the ride. This attraction is enthusiastically recommended for all, regardless of the age of your traveling companions. Don't miss the movie posters in the waiting area, among them *Closet Encounters of the Worst Kind* starring Miss Piggy—"in space, no one can find their shoes." *Length of show:* 17 minutes, plus delightful pre-show. *Special note:* MuppetVision 4-D vies with the Tower of Terror as the most popular attraction at the park. Although it plays in a 582-seat theater, try to see it in the first hour after the park opens, or else during the hours before closing; the afternoon parade can sometimes reduce the length of the line, while the exit of the nearby Hunchback stage show can extend it.

Hunchback of Notre Dame—A Musical Adventure

Disney-MGM Studios' newest live attraction, the Hunchback of Notre Dame opened summer 1996 to coincide with the theatrical release of Disney's animated movie of the same name, replacing the Spirit of Pocahontas show briefly performed on this stage. As in the movie, Victor Hugo's one-eyed, misshapen monster emerges in the Disney version as "a gee-whiz cuddly creature with the innocence of E.T. and the loyalty of Lassie" (in the words of *Variety's* Jeremy Gerard). The play-within-a-play structure finds gypsies, lead by Clopin, retelling the medieval story of bellringer Quasimodo and beautiful Esmerelda, set against a vibrant backdrop of the catacombs of 15th-century Paris. The fast-paced show uses a 21-member cast, impressive Broadway-style lighting design, three-foot-tall puppets that transform into humans, and diverse special effects to recreate scenes featuring falling snow and molten lead. The expanded, 1500-seat Backlot Theater has been covered and a 40-foot runway now extends from the stage into the seating area. *Length of show:* 32 minutes. *Special note:* Currently set for five performances daily, afternoon productions will usually fill well before show time; try to fit the first or last Hunchback performance of the day into your schedule.

Honey, I Shrunk the Kids Movie Set

Inspired by the movie of the same name, this imaginative, 11,000-square-foot play area allows children a fantasy adventure as if they had been miniaturized to a few inches high, and dropped into their backyard. Blades of grass tower 30 feet into the sky, a roll of film can be climbed through to a slide made of "film," an immense hose leaks water onto initially unsuspecting passersby. From a distance, adults will enjoy the whimsy, otherwise this playground is strictly for kids. *Length of attraction:* Stay as long as you like, but most children will want at least 20 minutes to explore. *Special note:* Always busy, the shrunken movie set has a maximum moppet capacity of about 250, which is usually reached by late morning and can continue into the mid or late afternoon. Disney controls attendance by creating a line when the playground gets crowded. If you have children under 12 or 13 years of age, this will be a highlight of their day; try to visit in the first hour or two the park is open, or wait until dusk. Also beware of when the nearby Hunchback stage show exits, releasing 1500 people into the surrounding area.

Inside the Magic: Special Effects and Production Tour

An interesting walking tour through the Disney-MGM Studios' sound-stage area. The first stop is an outdoor water tank where a naval battle is re-enacted with the assistance of a pair of volunteers who get drenched in the process; the pyrotechnics display is videotaped and played back. The tour continues into the long series of sound stages, where the bumblebee ride from *Honey, I Shrunk the Kids* is recreated utilizing a matte-shot and two children from the audience—complete with critical appraisal from "Siskel and Ebert" (the duo are a Disney commodity). The tour continues through the working sound stages where a soundproofed passageway allows visitors to observe any actual productions at work. The concluding section uses a madcap three-minute short, "The Lottery" starring Bette Midler, to show how props, sets, camerawork and special effects are combined in the Orlando studio to create an action-filled New York scene. Among the other props on display are a 1/24 model of the *USS Alabama* from *Crimson Tide*, matte paintings from *Dick Tracy* and more. *Length of attraction:* 40 minutes. *Special note:* Make a bathroom stop before entering the queue for this tour. The line moves relatively quickly for this attraction, so it can be toured almost anytime; since most of it is conducted indoors, try it in the early afternoon when rides are mobbed and lines hot.

Making of Toy Story

Added immediately after *Toy Story* landed on movie screens to overwhelming success, this exhibit supplements the animation tour by focusing on the computer technology used in the creation of the movie. Unfortunately, the attraction does little to explain the daunting complexities of computer animation, and instead serves as a bloated, hastily-assembled promo for the film. *Length of attraction:* 25 minutes, with guests admitted to the tour every 15 minutes. *Special note:* if you've seen the actual film *Toy Story*, you've seen half of this clip-heavy attraction. A low touring priority for all but die-hard animation buffs; visit anytime.

Voyage of the Little Mermaid

Like Legend of the Lion King at The Magic Kingdom, Voyage of the Little Mermaid is a multimedia remake of the popular 1989 animated film. Stationed in a 400 person theater, hand puppets, full-size costumes, black lights, lasers and film are combined to create a stage setting from "under the sea." Tactile special effects like wind, rain and bubbles add to the sensory experience; one highlight is the 12-foot-high Ursula slithering around the stage to perform "Poor Unfortunate Soul." *Length of show:* 18 minutes, plus pre-show. *Special note:* Although the show is a bit of a *Cliff Notes* interpretation, the charming Voyage of the Little Mermaid continues to be the must-see attraction for many pre-teen visitors and a line forms astonishingly quickly after the park opens. If you have young ones with you, try to get into the first or second performance of the morning, otherwise wait until the afternoon parade starts, or later when families begin to clear out of the park. Keep in mind that doors to the theater close several minutes prior to the time posted out front.

Backstage Studio Tour

This attraction surveys the Disney-MGM Studios back lot, which is otherwise inaccessible to guests, and travels through Catastrophe Canyon. Visitors board 200-passenger trams in the waiting area, and travel past the wardrobe department—the world's largest, we are informed—a prop construction and crafts warehouse, and along a residential street facade. Among the rusting artifacts on the way: the helicopter from *Blue Thunder*, a trolley car from *Who Framed Roger Rabbit?* and other items. Then the tram continues to Catastrophe Canyon—in theory, a "live" set built to look like the red rock southwest. We're told the filmmakers are on a break, but a sudden rain storm leads to a flash flood, then an earthquake that rocks the tram, followed by an oil-tanker explosion hot enough and close enough to rattle the most composed customers. While visitors reposition hairdos and regain equanimity, the tram proceeds calmly out of the structure to see the mechanics of how the two-minute show is produced including the hydraulics, gas for the explosions, and air cannons for the water. *Length of attraction:* 15 minutes. *Special note:* Ironically, this tour is one of the less-educational offerings at the Studios unless you consider the nitty-gritty of water cannon operation fascinating, but it is entertaining and the only opportunity to see the Disney-MGM Studios backlot area. A line usually forms by late morning, but it moves relatively quickly. The trams are spaced about five minutes apart on a busy day. If the midday wait tops 20 or 30 minutes, come back in the late afternoon when the line will have receded. Also note that the unloading area for the trams is several hundred yards from the entrance; following the tram ride, it's possible to continue your studio tour with Inside the Magic, next door to the tram exit.

Magic of Disney Animation

The most genuinely informative of the three studio tours, and the one that brings you closest to an actual, working production facility, the animation tour is an excellent walk-through exhibit that sheds light on the many nuances that make the difference between good animation and classics such as *Beauty and the Beast*. Since the park opened, this facility has grown to produce a sizable chunk of Disney's animated output, and during 1996–1997 will be responsible for most of the work going into *The Legend of Mulan*. The tour begins with a hilarious nine-minute video featuring Robin Williams and Walter Cronkite—one of them wants to be reincarnated as Peter Pan—that provides an introduction into the process. You then proceed into the glass-walled animation studio, where a non-audio-animatronic staff works in front of your eyes. Keep in mind few animators are at work on weekends, but otherwise you'll be in the midst of a functioning production facility. The Williams and Cronkite show (an unlikely pairing that truly works) continues on overhead monitors to explain the various stages of production, but you don't have to rush through this area; linger as long as you want and join the next walk-through tour when it enters the facility 10 minutes later. The glassed-in area exits into a 140-seat theater where a reel of classic Disney animation from the beginning up through *Aladdin* is played. *Length of attraction:* Allow at least 30 minutes. *Special note:* For visitors interested in how films are really made, this tour is the best offering at the Disney-MGM Studios. On busy days, a line builds by late-morning, and continues into late afternoon; try to visit the animation tour in the first two hours the park is open.

AUTHOR'S OBSERVATION

The music for Disney's animated classics is almost as famous as the pictures themselves. My favorite is a compendium titled "Stay Awake," an ambitious project headed by producer Hal Wilner. There are pleasing interpretations you might expect, such as Bonnie Raitt singing "Baby Mine" from Dumbo, Harry Nilsson skipping through "Zip-a-Dee-Doo-Dah" from Song of the South, and "I Wan'na Be Like You" from Jungle Book strummed joyously by Los Lobos. And then there are the covers straight out of left field: "Someday My Prince Will Come," from Snow White and the Seven Dwarfs sung by Sinead O'Connor, and "I Wonder" from Sleeping Beauty, rendered by Yma Sumac are two potent examples. But the wildest of the lot is the warped reading Tom Waits provides to "Heigh Ho," from Snow White, creating a boozy, clattering jangle of sinister dreams.

The Twilight Zone Tower of Terror

The delightfully crumbling Hollywood Tower Hotel looms 13 stories above Sunset Boulevard, and houses one of Disney's best rides. Patterned after the "free-fall"

attractions in place at other amusement parks, the Tower of Terror is much more than a single, weightless plunge; Disney imagineers add a storyline, a ghoulish "Twilight Zone"-themed atmosphere, snazzy visual effects and a few other surprises to create an excellent adventure. As at the Haunted Mansion, visitors are ushered into a room—in this case, a cramped library—where a bolt of lightning strikes and the lights go out. A lone black-and-white television set plays the "Twilight Zone" theme and a Rod Serling look-alike introduces the plot of tonight's episode. Two minutes later, when the television segment is over, another door opens and you wander into the basement of the hotel, where boilers rumble and moan, and where one of four elevators waits for you to personally live out the rest of the episode.

A triumph of style over substance, the brilliance of Tower of Terror is in the details. Note the lightning-scarred front of the decrepit hotel, where neon lettering flickers; at night this is an eerie apparition. In the exterior courtyard, a lumbering ballroom jazz score sets the sleazy mood, while the hotel lobby rots with dust and decay. All of it combines to mold a humorously unsettling ambience for your spine-tingling exploration of the hotel's upper floors. *Length of ride:* 11 minutes, including the pre-show in the library. *Special note:* Of all the rides, this is the don't-miss attraction. The 13-story drop is sudden, but over in a flash, and gently cushioned at its conclusion; the special effects in the tower are truly splendid—amusing and creepy, rather than scary. The Tower of Terror is also the Studio's most popular attraction, and a line forms within 15 minutes after the park opens to the general public. Make it your first attraction of the day, or wait until the last hour the park is open. Also, beware of the nearby Theater of the Stars; when Beauty and the Beast exits, up to 1500 people flow into the area immediately next door to the Tower.

AUTHOR'S OBSERVATION

What's the highest point within Walt Disney World? The apex of the 27-story Dolphin Hotel reaches 250 feet in the air, a "mountain" visible from any elevated point within the World. The Tower of Terror climbs to 199 feet in height, Big Thunder Mountain is 197 feet and Cinderella Castle reaches 189 feet. Spaceship Earth and Space Mountain both top 180 feet, while the Earffel Tower (the water tower at the Disney-MGM Studios) is 130 feet high, and Summit Plummet at Blizzard Beach soars to 120 feet.

Beauty and the Beast

Disney's Broadway musical got its start here at the 1500-seat Theater of the Stars. The story tells of beautiful Belle, who is imprisoned by the Beast, but eventually falls in love with him, transforming him into a prince; of the several musical numbers, "Be Our Guest" is the show-stopper. Though the Broadway version is told on a bigger (and full-length) scale, this is a sufficient "greatest hits" interpretation of the animated film that became an instant classic. *Length of show:* 25 minutes. *Special note:* This long-running show continues to be one of the park's more popular attractions. Despite the theater's size, you'll want to plan on arriving 10 to 20 minutes prior to show time for afternoon performances. Optimally, try to see the first performance of the day. If you've seen the Broadway show, this attraction may be skipped.

Eating

Several entertaining dining options exist within the Disney-MGM Studios. The **Hollywood Brown Derby** serves good food in a glamorous, old-Hollywood setting, while kids adore the wacky themed eateries such as the '50s **Prime Time Cafe** and **Sci-Fi Dine-In Theater**. These three sit-down facilities (plus **Mama Melrose's Ristorante Italiano**) are listed in the "Restaurants" chapter. Due to their popularity, you'll need to make dining reservations by phone ☎ *(407) WDW-DINE,* up to 60 days in advance. Otherwise, when you arrive at the park, proceed directly to the Dining Reservation Booth, on the right side of Hollywood Boulevard, at the junction with Sunset Boulevard. Be aware that within an hour after the park has opened, most lunchtime reservation slots will be gone. Information on the **character breakfast** served at Soundstage Restaurant is also listed in the "Restaurants" chapter.

Among counter-service options, the enormous **Soundstage Restaurant** is a good choice for a fast lunch or dinner. This elaborately decorated facility themed to both *Pocahontas* and *Aladdin* has three counters that sell deep-dish pizza, pasta, meatball subs, tortellini soup, salads, turkey and other sandwiches. Upstairs from the Soundstage Restaurant, the **Catwalk Bar** offers drinks and appetizers. Art deco and murals set the mood at **Hollywood and Vine**, which serves meals all day, cafeteria-style; breakfast is scrambled eggs, pancakes and french toast, while roast chicken and baby back ribs are the lunch and dinner specialties. The **Commissary** is a recent lunch-and-dinner addition, providing burgers, chicken and tortillas, chili and salads. The *S.S. Down the Hatch* contains **Min and Bill's Dockside Diner**, a delightful eatery offering turkey sandwiches, shrimp and vegetable cocktails, seafood and pasta salads, fruit and yogurt. The 600-seat **Backlot Express** is the park's largest dining facility, with a paint-splattered back-lot ambience—burgers, chicken sandwiches, salads, and chili are the main provisions for lunch and dinner. A quick breakfast can be procured at **Starring Rolls Bakery**, which sells muffins, croissants, pastries and cookies to accompany hot coffee or tea.

Touring Itinerary

Unlike The Magic Kingdom and Epcot, the Disney-MGM Studios can be conquered in a single day. Still, you can spend a sizable chunk of time waiting in lines if you approach the park with a *laissez-faire* attitude. With few exceptions, the Studio's attractions have broad-based appeal for all ages; hour-long waits at rides are not uncommon during the middle of the day on moderately busy afternoons. We believe that our touring itinerary serves almost everyone's needs. The itinerary works best under the following circumstances:

a. You have purchased your tickets before you arrive in the park (see: "Tickets," in "Obstacles and Opportunities").

b. You are positioned at the main entrance to the Studios 30 to 45 minutes prior to the official opening time. Call ☎ *(407) 824-4321* the night before to verify the opening time.

c. All members of your party are willing to follow the touring plan; they can, of course, bow out of individual attractions they have no desire to ride.

d. If you are *not* a guest of a Disney Resort, that you tour the park only on days when the Surprise Morning policy is not in effect: Mondays, Tuesdays, Thursdays, Fridays and Saturdays (Fridays and Saturdays are the least busy days, particularly during the summer). If you visit on a Surprise Morning (currently Sundays and Wednesdays), you will find lines already in place at all major attractions from the moment the general public is admitted.

e. You have made dining reservations *the day before* you tour the studios by calling ☎ *(407) WDW-DINE.* The in-park dining reservation booth is small and the number of tables available at Studio restaurants is woefully inadequate for the demand.

If you are traveling with any children under 40 inches in height, they will not be able to ride the Tower of Terror. Instead, begin your itinerary with the following adjustment: make the Voyage of the Little Mermaid and Star Tours your first and second attractions of the day. The first Little Mermaid performance is sometimes not until 45 minutes after the park has opened; in this case, ride Star Tours first, then see the Little Mermaid. After these two attractions, follow the itinerary from step 3.

Similarly, if you are wary of unsettling rides, work up to both the Tower of Terror and Star Tours, rather than front-loading them into the beginning of the day as outlined below. If so, make the Great Movie Ride and Little Mermaid your first two attractions, then follow the itinerary from step 3 and incorporate the Tower of Terror and Star Tours toward the end of the day when crowds begin to thin. Be assured that while both rides are thrilling, neither is as rough as Space Mountain.

Another hint: because most park attractions are scheduled stage performances that play to large numbers of people, stay one step ahead of the crowd by anticipating where bottlenecks might occur. The Indiana Jones Stunt show is the biggest draw, seating 2000 people for each show. When the stunt show is over, these people exit and many head directly for the nearest attractions. If you're sitting next to an exit and are among the very first to leave the stunt show theater, choosing your next attraction won't be a problem. If you're buried amid the throng, your best option is to head for an attraction on the opposite side of the park, such as Inside the Magic or the Backstage Studio Tour. Similarly, when you want to see the Monster Sound Show and SuperStar Television (the attractions closest to the stunt show), the shortest lines will usually be found while the stunt show is in progress.

The All-Purpose Plan

1. Enter the park and take a right down Sunset Boulevard and head straight for the **Tower of Terror**.

2. After riding the Tower of Terror, head back down Sunset Boulevard, cross the park to ride **Star Tours**.

3. From Star Tours, take a left into New York Street and see **Muppet Vision 4D**. These first three attractions, the most popular in the park, will require about 80 to 90 minutes on an average-attendance day; later on, they will swallow up three hours or more.

4. At this point, you'll want to browse through the entertainment schedule to plot your next moves leading up to lunch. Unless there's a long wait until the next show, try seeing the **Indiana Jones Epic Stunt Spectacular** now.

5. Incorporate the following attractions into the period before and after lunch: **The Monster Sound Show**, **Superstar Television**, **Hunchback of Notre Dame**, **Inside the Magic** and **The Making of Toy Story**.

6. If children are a part of your trip, let them burn off some energy at the **Honey, I Shrunk the Kids Movie Set**. Additionally, they'll want to see the afternoon **Toy Story Parade** (check your entertainment schedule for time).

7. Take the **Backstage Studio Tour**.

8. Visit the **Magic of Disney Animation**.

9. Experience **The Great Movie Ride**.

10. See **Beauty and the Beast** and **Voyage of the Little Mermaid**.

11. Have dinner and revisit any attractions you want to see again until the evening **Sorcery in the Sky** show.

THE DISNEY-MGM STUDIOS

THE DISNEY-MGM STUDIOS

DISNEY'S OTHER PARKS

Florida's east coast beaches are an hour from Orlando.

Typhoon Lagoon

> *A furious storm once roared 'cross the sea*
> *Catching ships in its path, helpless to flee*
> *Instead of a certain and watery doom*
> *The winds swept them here to Typhoon Lagoon!*

As Disney's manufactured legends go, this waterpark's origins constitute one of the more fanciful stories—a jungle oasis littered with maritime flotsam and jetsam carried inland by a fierce typhoon. After a volcanic eruption and earthquake, the enterprising "locals" turned their mangled landscape into a tourist attraction in the form of a huge water park. A shrimp boat from Safen Sound Florida, the *Miss Tilly*, sits perched atop 95-foot Mount Mayday, the crag that juts above the lagoon. The boat erupts in a soaring geyser of water every 30 minutes.

Opened in 1989 with a breathtaking price tag of $92 million, Walt himself would be proud of the fictional residents of Typhoon Lagoon—or more to the point, the crew of imagineers whose creative impulses were allowed to run wild in creating this unique water theme park. The illogical landscape includes bat caves, dinosaur bone remains, rusty anchors, an upside-down ship and other exotica, resulting in a bizarre tropical ambience something like "Gilligan's Island" on hallucinogens.

The popularity of Typhoon Lagoon hasn't waned following the opening of the larger, more thrill-oriented Blizzard Beach in 1995. The park can still reach capacity by within an hour after opening, particularly during the summer months when both locals and visitors are looking to escape the intense Florida heat and humidity. Although the park usually reopens to let in additional guests later in the afternoon (and is open into the evening during the summer and other busy periods), it's best to arrive a few minutes prior to the official opening time to ensure some time before the lines for slides become longer than the slides themselves.

The centerpiece of the park is the 2.5-acre, blue **Typhoon Lagoon** itself, a 2.75-million gallon swimming pool with a serious wave machine. For 40-minute periods, small oscillating waves roll through the lagoon. But these are calm reprieves between the 80-minute periods when five-foot waves big enough to body surf wash across the lagoon every 90 seconds. A pair of adjoining tidal pools are the alternative for those who simply wish to bob in the water.

Three-foot-deep **Castaway Creek** is a 2100-foot, slow-current waterway that winds through the park and into the **Forgotten Grotto**, a misty jungle environment (allow about 25 minutes to float the entire circuit of the river). Encircling a *Poseidon*-like capsized tanker, **Shark Reef** is a swim-through aquarium featuring, yes, small sharks, rays and tropical fish—snorkeling equipment and lessons are provided for the swim into this saltwater environment. An underwater viewing area for non-swimmers is cleverly disguised in the portholes of the overturned boat. This attraction is quite popular and, unfortunately, by late morning, humans seem to outnumber the fish. Try to visit Shark Reef during the first hour the park is open. **Ketchakiddie Creek** provides slides, waterfalls and a grotto for children under 48 inches (children must be accompanied by an adult).

A certain highlight for most guests is the imposing, 30-mile-per-hour **Humunga Kowabunga**, a pair of identical 214-foot-long slides that drop precipitously down the slope of Mount Mayday. Sitting down at the brink of these plunges requires an act of courage, but the decent is easy—and over in seconds. Somewhat more tame and scenic is the trio of 300-foot-long storm slides: the **Jib Jammer**, **Rudder Buster** and **Stern Burner**. The slides snake through rock caves, waterfalls and past palm trees, and guests land gently in a bubbling pool at the bottom of the slope. Two inner-tube rides—**Keelhaul Falls** and **Mayday Falls**—are designed for single riders, while **Gangplank Falls** is designed for groups of up to four. These whitewater troughs wind at a moderate clip through the lush scenery. At 460 feet, the Mayday inner-tube ride is the longest and most popular. A newer attraction, **Bay Slide** is designed for children under 48 inches. Red nautical pennants differentiate the thrill factor for the various rides, and the four-pennant Humunga Kowabunga is a doozie.

Two food counters, **Leaning Palms** and **Typhoon Tilly's Galley and Grog**, provide a simple menu of burgers, sandwiches, hot dogs and salads. Beer, wine coolers, frozen yogurt and ice cream are also available. **Singapore Sal's** sells theme merchandise, along with bathing suits, towels, water cameras, suntan lotion and sandals.

DISNEY'S OTHER PARKS

INSIDER TIP

Coolers are allowed into Disney's water parks, but no glass bottles are allowed. Alcohol may not be brought in, but beer and wine is for sale inside the park. Rafts, tubes and mats are provided for the various slides. Personal swimming accouterments such as fins or mats are not permitted.

Typhoon Lagoon ticket information is provided under "Tickets" in "Obstacles and Opportunities." Children under the age of 10 must be accompanied by an adult to visit Typhoon Lagoon; Humunga Kowabunga has a 48-inch height requirement.

INSIDER TIP

Lockers are available at all of the water parks, but can be completely gone by mid morning. Try to limit what you bring along to essential items. Avoid wearing jewelry—a surprising amount goes down the drain at the parks. Robbery is uncommon, so bring only the cash you expect to need for food and drinks, a change of clothes, suntan lotion and a towel, and you can get by without a locker. Light footwear is helpful for tender soles, but not absolutely necessary; "flip flops" are ideal. Lockers at the water parks are priced an exorbitant $3 per day, plus $2 deposit. Towels may be rented, and life jackets are provided free of charge with a deposit.

Blizzard Beach

When Blizzard Beach opened in 1995, Disney *imagineers* could be certified as positively warped or brilliant, depending on your point of view. I happily opt for the latter opinion. Sticking with Disney's proven design policy of establishing a back story for their conceptual themes, the loopy Blizzard Beach idea goes something like this: a freak snowstorm hits central Florida and transforms a rock crag into an unlikely ski resort—until the sun comes out and turns the slopes into a slick collection of water slides.

Nowhere else does Disney pull off the merger of theme and content as delightfully as at this 66-acre water park—for the moment, the world's largest. Although some of the slides plunging down the slopes of Mount Gushmore are quite daunting, there's enough to see and do here that all but the few guests who don't want to get their feet wet will be satisfied. Chief among the pleasures is enjoying the details, including the ski lift that climbs to the top of Gushmore, the icicles that drip off the "warming" huts, the ski poles left behind on a particularly steep slope.

The immediate success of this water park is such that during the summer months, the facility quickly reaches maximum capacity and it is not unusual for the front gates to close within an hour after opening. Fortunately, the turnstiles usually reopen by mid-afternoon. Disney is trying to deal with capacity and crowding issues by adding more slides, but for the foreseeable future it's safe to say you should be at the park entrance before the scheduled opening time (other than during the dead of Florida's winter).

INSIDER TIP

Summer thunderstorms in central Florida are not at all uncommon in the early afternoon, and all three water parks close temporarily during inclement weather. Except under unusual circumstances, admission is nonrefundable, but you will be readmitted later in the day if the park reopens. The hours following a rainstorm can be pleasantly uncrowded.

In addition to the ski lift, three sets of stairs permit you to climb to the top of the mountain where the best slides originate. The two big rides at Blizzard Beach are most impressive—you are advised to work up to them. **Summit Plummet** towers horrifyingly *above* Mount Gushmore; it starts on a ski jump platform 120 feet up (making it the world's highest water slide) and heads straight down into the mountain and out at its base. If the ride seems like it's over in a flash, it's because riders attain speeds of up to 60 miles-per-hour on the briefly free-falling 300-foot chute, making Summit Plummet also the world's fastest water slide. Next door, the **Slush Gusher** doesn't appear quite as intimidating. The actual descent is even scarier than Summit Plummet—momentary weightlessness occurs after cresting the third plunge—it may leave you breathless for a few short seconds.

AUTHOR'S OBSERVATION

The speeds attained on some of the more spectacular water slides invite bathing suits to do their own thing. Women are advised to tackle the faster rides in a one-piece, or be quick-witted at the bottom for some expeditious rearranging. Swim attire with rivets or buckles are not permitted on the slides.

To term the other slides more moderate would be damning them with faint praise. Each slide is marked by ski trail-type signs that announce the not-always-apparent "difficulty" (i.e., Summit Plummet and Slush Gusher are "Black Diamond" runs). **Runoff Rapids** is a trio of water troughs for inner tubes that winds down the back side of Mount Gushmore; the enclosed trough is best, but usually has the longest line. **Snow Stormers** provides a fast, slalom-style descent aboard mats, while **Teamboat Springs** is an enjoyable family-style raft ride down a quarter-mile chute. **Cool Runners** is a new addition—a pair of slides through a mogul area. Late 1996 should see the opening of the **Double Dipper** fast-paced tube ride off the summit, modeled after the Slush Gusher.

The meandering **Cross Country Creek** is a 3000-foot slow-moving stream that encircles the mountain. Midway along the 30-to-40-minute ride you'll cut under an ice cave that drips with chilled water; there are several designated areas to enter the creek. A huge pool, **Melt-Away Bay**, is equipped with a wave machine that's not as aggressive as the one at Typhoon Lagoon. One side of the pool is fronted by rock cliffs and dripping snow, while the other leads to a white sand beach. The **Ski Patrol Training Camp** offers smaller thrills for pre-teens, and younger children are catered to at **Tike's Peak**, another carefully monitored play area.

Fast food is served near the park entrance at the **Lottawatta Lodge**, which offers burgers, chicken, pizza, pasta, salads, beer and wine coolers. Two smaller stands, **Avalunch** and the **Warming Hut**, provide foot-long hot dogs, Italian sausage, ice cream and snow cones. Themed merchandise featuring the park's logo—an alligator on skis with legs akimbo—is available at the **Beach Haus**, also near the main entrance. The shop also sells bathing suits, sunglasses, suntan lotion, water cameras and sandals. **Lost and Found** and a **Guest Relations** desk is provided next to the ticket office.

Blizzard Beach ticket information is provided under "Tickets" in "Tickets" in "Obstacles and Opportunities." Children under the age of 10 must be accompanied by an adult to visit Blizzard Beach; several of the slides have a 48-inch height requirement.

River Country

The first water park that Disney built, River Country has the ambience of an old-fashioned swimming hole—a trip to a bygone era when an automobile tire swinging from a tree branch was a 12-year-old's afternoon entertainment. The artificial rock landscaping is somewhat reminiscent of the American Southwest, as well as Big Thunder Mountain, with cypress and slash pines completing the environment. Quite attractive and pleasant—an escape from hectic theme park touring—River Country is ideal for a late-afternoon visit following a morning sojourn at The Magic Kingdom.

The central feature of River Country is **Bay Cove**, a cordoned-off section of Bay Lake. The cove has rope swings, suspended car tires, and a ship's boom to drop swimmers into the water. Two white sand beaches wrap around Bay Cove; one is designed as a children's play area with a wading pool. A vivid blue 330,000-gallon swimming pool offers cool refreshment. The big attractions are the two slides: **White Water Rapids**, a tube ride down a gently turbulent steam, and the faster **Whoop-'n-Holler Hollow**, a pair of adjacent corkscrew slides (one is 100 feet longer than the other) that zip riders quickly into Bay Cove. A 1/5-mile nature trail winds through the lake's cypress swamp.

In recent years, River Country has been eclipsed by the size and number of slides at Typhoon Lagoon and Blizzard Beach, parks that offer an undeniably bigger experience. But River Country is more integrated into its natural surroundings, and most pre-teens will have every bit as much fun with the

Tom Sawyer-esque environment. Those who want their water parks festooned with a variety of fast slides will want to steer toward Disney's other two parks first; on the other hand River Country can be less crowded and is priced below Typhoon Lagoon and Blizzard Beach. Like the two bigger parks, between Easter and September, River Country can reach its maximum capacity by late morning, but around 2 or 3 p.m. the park starts to clear out. When the two bigger parks fill early in the morning, guests head straight for River Country, causing it to close soon after. River Country is closed Mondays and Tuesdays during most non-summer months.

River Country ticket information is provided under "Tickets," earlier in this chapter. Children under 10 years of age must be accompanied by an adult.

Discovery Island

Disney's first foray into creating a real (not audio-animatronic) zoo is an 11-acre park in the middle of Bay Lake. The island features more than 100 species of animals and a lush array of tropical foliage, and the facility has been officially designated as a zoological park by the American Association of Zoological Parks and Aquariums. As such, Discovery Island may be a sneak preview of the company's grand scheme to create **Disney's Animal Kingdom** (set to open in 1998). Before the park was created, the entire island was leveled, and a boardwalk and paved walkway was added for touring. Boulders, trees and bamboo were brought in, the topography was sculpted to allow for waterfalls and streams.

When you arrive at Discovery Island's dock and ticket booth, pick up a map and check the day's schedule of Animal Encounter shows. Two intimate seating areas near the boat dock provide venues for the three 15-minute shows: **Feathered Friends** (parrots and birds of prey), **Native Neighbors** (Florida wildlife) and **Reptile Relations** (alligators and snakes). Coordinate performance times with the 45-minute walking tour of the enclosures. The birds and animals on display include the southern bald eagle, great blue heron, ring-tail lemur, muntjac deer, Patagonian cavy, Galapagos tortoise and American alligator. A walk-through aviary, nearly one acre in size, features the United States' largest breeding colony of scarlet ibis. There is also a glass-enclosed nursery complex and animal hospital where babies are raised.

For what's on display, Discovery Island is a pricey excursion. The enclosures can be toured in under an hour, while all three animal shows can be experienced in another hour. For this roughly two-hour experience, the adult admission price is $11.61 (children ages 3 to 9 are $6.31). If you have a established zoo to visit at home, Discovery Island is not a bargain. However, if you are so deprived, and are truly devoted to visiting animal enclosures, and have a surfeit of time in Orlando available, go ahead and spring for the trip. Discovery Island's best attribute is that most Walt Disney World visitors skip the attraction, even though they may have free admission to see it (Discovery Island admission is part of the Five-Day World Hopper or Be Our Guest pass structure). If you're looking for a pleasant and leisurely escape from the crowds, this might be the ticket.

Access to Discovery Island is provided by watercrafts that depart from the docks at the Wilderness Lodge and Contemporary Resort, as well as from The Magic Kingdom, every 15 minutes or so. The park is only open during daylight hours, so check with your resort's guest services desk or call ☎ *(407) 824-4321* for exact hours. You can picnic on the island's small beach; a snack bar, the **Thirsty Perch**, is available for sandwiches, hot dogs, ice cream, soft drinks and beer. **Explorer's Outpost** sells T-shirts and a small selection of gift items.

Pleasure Island

Trumpeted by the same marquee as the destination where lost boys were turned into braying donkeys in the film *Pinocchio*, Pleasure Island was a major part of Disney's 1989 expansion activities. But other than its name, the six-acre island has nothing to do with the famous wooden puppet. Instead, Pleasure Island is an adult- and music-oriented amusement park—its "lands" are nightclubs, one themed to country music, another to jazz, and so on. There is probably something to please everyone on at least one of these eight stages, and the entertainment isn't limited strictly to music.

Disney didn't come up with the nightclub-as-theme park notion (that honor lies with Orlando's Church Street Station; see "Universal, Sea World and Other Attractions"), but the company accomplished one of its typically inspired overhauls of an existing concept to come up with a veritable original. The guests on most evenings are about 85 percent out-of-towners, although on Thursday nights, Disney cast members are admitted free. Friday is the island's busiest night.

Pleasure Island's clubs include the **Comedy Warehouse**, which features improv humor based on audience suggestions and delivered by a cast of five comedians and a musician; out of respect for the few families visiting early in the evening, the first two shows skew the humor at a "PG" level, while later performances may be more risqué. Glistening bell-bottom pants define the cast-member outfits at the three-level **8 Trax**, which celebrates '70s and '80s rock and dance hits, including a "YMCA" line dance nightly. Boasting a sophisticated sound-and-light system, **Mannequins Dance Palace** is a '90s disco, with a rotating dance floor and stage performances featuring the island's dance company; on Thursday nights, Mannequins is filled to the gills with

Disney employees. The **Jazz Club** features live jazz, bluegrass and occasional jam sessions; a dessert and appetizer-style menu supplements the cocktail bar. The **Neon Armadillo Music Saloon** is the island's country-and-western dance bar, with live music performed nightly amid the cactus-and-neon decor. The largest venue on the island is the **Rock & Roll Beach Club**, where live bands play a wide range of pop music; a local group, Panama, has proven immensely popular since it debuted in spring 1995, and now plays five nights a week to a packed house. The **West End Stage** is a large outdoor platform at the "top" of the island, with performances throughout the evening, culminating in the nightly 11:45 p.m. New Year's Eve show filled with confetti, laser and fireworks.

The most delightful offering at Pleasure Island is a one-of-a-kind club that a surprising number of visitors skip because its entertainment virtues aren't readily apparent to those making a quick pass through. **The Adventurers Club** is a night-long, mostly-scripted performance by eight talented actors who interact with each other, and with guests, in a 1930s British setting meant to evoke a private social club for world explorers. The decor is astounding: the walls are covered with spears, shrunken heads, mounted animal heads, statues, trophies, books and letters, and loads of photos that provide background on the eccentric cast of characters. Among the club members present are Inga, the Swedish maid; Fletcher Hodges, the club's curator; Hathaway Brown, the chairperson and world-renowned ichthyologist; and Camilia Perkins, the flustered club president. A series of six individual performances by the cast is held in the library (no two shows are alike), and there's also the Mask Room, which provides a glimpse into what today's *imagineers* might do if they were to overhaul those damned Tiki Birds at The Magic Kingdom (yes, audio-animatronics are at play here). Twice nightly, new members are inducted into the club, which has a theme song and secret hand signal. One could legitimately spend the entire night in the Adventurers Club for a unique and entertaining evening — I suspect some guests do. The best of the jolly bartenders, by the way, is Nash. *Kungaloosh!*

It's possible to sample all of Pleasure Island in a single night, but it pays to start early. The island usually opens at 7 p.m., although other than the Rock & Roll Beach Club, Adventurers Club and Comedy Warehouse, the venues don't get rolling until about 8 p.m. Whenever you arrive, head down to the Comedy Warehouse first and get in line for the next show. The performances are scheduled about every 70 minutes, with the first one around 7:15 p.m. Since the seating capacity inside is quite limited, most Pleasure Island visitors are not able to see the comedy show during their evening; the line becomes progressively longer during the course of the night. After Comedy Warehouse, proceed through the seven other clubs, with a goal to be at or near the West End Stage for the 11:45 p.m. New Year's Eve Show.

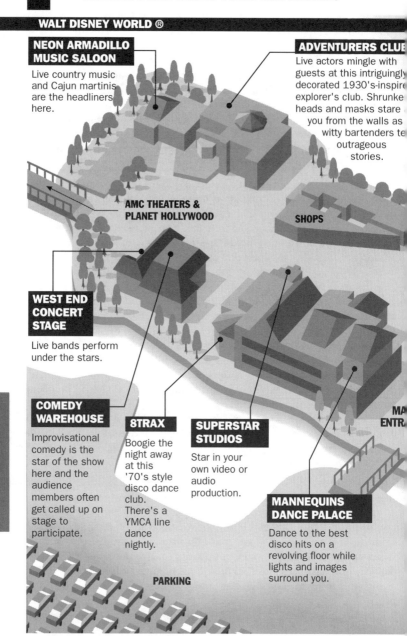

NEON ARMADILLO MUSIC SALOON

Live country music and Cajun martinis are the headliners here.

ADVENTURERS CLUB

Live actors mingle with guests at this intriguingly decorated 1930's-inspire explorer's club. Shrunke heads and masks stare you from the walls as witty bartenders te outrageous stories.

AMC THEATERS & PLANET HOLLYWOOD

SHOPS

WEST END CONCERT STAGE

Live bands perform under the stars.

COMEDY WAREHOUSE

Improvisational comedy is the star of the show here and the audience members often get called up on stage to participate.

8TRAX

Boogie the night away at this '70's style disco dance club. There's a YMCA line dance nightly.

SUPERSTAR STUDIOS

Star in your own video or audio production.

MA ENTR

MANNEQUINS DANCE PALACE

Dance to the best disco hits on a revolving floor while lights and images surround you.

PARKING

PLEASURE ISLAND ®

Pleasure Island is an adult and music-oriented amusement park featuring nightclubs of different themes. There's something for everyone from country music to rock, disco, comedy and jazz. Dancing in the street is almost a nightly happening here.

THE ROCK 'N ROLL BEACH CLUB

Live bands play classic rock from the 50's to the 90's at this fun club.

FIREWORKS FACTORY

Chow down on barbecue specialties and explosive drinks.

LAKE BUENA VISTA

FULTON'S CRAB HOUSE

Fresh fish and crabs from Hawai and Alaska are specialties.

PLEASURE ISLAND JAZZ COMPANY

Live jazz is featured in this contemporary jazz club.

PORTOBELLO YACHT CLUB

Savor delicious Northern Italian specialties.

VALET PARKING

DISNEY VILLAGE MARKET PLACE

CE

DISNEY'S OTHER PARKS

Pleasure Island isn't for all tastes; Disney has made a concerted effort to seduce a younger audience it may have feared was slipping off Walt Disney World's property to visit Church Street Station or other local nightclubs. The music at Pleasure Island is geared toward a contemporary sound, even at the jazz club; if loud, pop music grates on your ears, you probably won't enjoy a majority of what is offered here. However, if you have purchased a multiday pass wherein Pleasure Island admission is included, try to carve out at least a couple of hours to tour the island early some evening. Alternately, it's possible to walk through the island during the day without purchasing a ticket; the paid-admission period doesn't start up until 7 p.m.

Excluding the island's **Fireworks Factory**, **Portobello Yacht Club**, **Fulton's Crabhouse** and the sit-down eateries located around Disney Village Marketplace (all discussed in the "Restaurants" chapter), you'll find a few snack stands selling pizzas, sausages, frozen yogurt, cappuccino and other treats. Visit the shops for interesting souvenirs—the shops are open during the day, without requiring a ticket. **Avigator's Supply** sells Adventurers Club-themed clothing, including T-shirts and tote bags, and other aviation themed gifts; **Suspended Animation** proffers Disney's cartoon art, primarily reproductions, but sometimes original cels as well.

The ticket to Pleasure Island is priced at $17.97, but unlimited admission is included with the purchase of a Five-Day World Hopper or Be Our Guest pass (see: "Tickets " in "Obstacles and Opportunities"). Also note that Disney frequently features discount coupons for Pleasure Island in local publications—a play aimed at staying competitive with Church Street Station. These deals are generally targeted to visitors *not* staying at the Disney Resorts, so keep your eyes peeled in the entertainment guides that clutter the hallways of the non-Disney hotels. American Automobile Association members can purchase discounted admission at the AAA office in Orlando at *4300 East Colonial Drive.*

Children under 18 are admitted to Pleasure Island, but must be accompanied by an adult (there is no child admission price). In order to drink alcohol on the premises, one needs to show identification upon entering, at which time guests will be given a wrist band (drink prices average $4 to $5, but check into the drink of the day). Otherwise, only one club, Mannequins, requires all visitors to be 21 years of age to enter. Smoking is allowed throughout the island except inside the Adventurers Club and the Comedy Warehouse.

UNIVERSAL STUDIOS, SEA WORLD AND OTHER ATTRACTIONS

Aerial view of Universal Studios, which covers 400 acres.

Coupons and Discount Offers

There is a reason why locals refer to Orlando as the "coupon capital of the world." Unlike their mouse-eared competition, Universal Studios, Sea World and virtually every other central Florida theme park provide a variety of admission discounts. These are easy enough to locate so that, as a general rule, if you paid full price for your admission, you overpaid. In fact, the only problem seems to be making sure that you obtained the absolute lowest price for your tickets.

In addition to the coupon-laced fliers found in wall rack displays located at every non-Disney Orlando lodging facility, several publications are designed with visitors in mind and contain dozens of discount offers. *See Orlando* is probably the best known and features a wealth of coupons providing one to six dollars off admission at most area attractions, and a number of restaurant deals as well. A recent issue had a coupon for Capone's Dinner and Show that provided a healthy $11.65 off each adult admission. Your American Automobile Association membership card can help you get good discounts, although some attractions require you to purchase tickets at an AAA office in advance.

An important and groundbreaking Orlando alliance was announced in March 1996. The five-day **Vacation Value Pass**, a discount package starring three International Drive theme parks—**Universal Studios**, **Sea World** and **Wet 'n Wild**—each of which had tired of vying for the tourist scraps discarded by the big Mouse machine. Since none of these parks competes directly with another, the "united we stand" alliance makes perfect sense and creates a true Orlando alternative to the Disney vacation. The five-day Vacation Value Pass is priced (tax included) $95.35 for adults and $77.33 for children ages 3 to 9, and must be used over five consecutive days. Also available is a four-park, seven-day version that adds Tampa's **Busch Gardens** into the mix, and is priced $127.15 for adults, and $102.77 for children. However, both passes deserve closer analysis before you pony up the dough.

If you are comparing the five-day I-Drive package with Disney's Five-Day World Hopper, it looks like a terrific deal; the Vacation Value Pass is less than half the cost of the World Hopper. But, one must compare apples to apples. The Disney pass not only provides five days' admission to its three main parks (theme parks that require about four days to properly tour), it also allows an additional seven consecutive days unlimited admission to the three Disney water parks, Pleasure Island and Discovery Island. It's not a stretch to expect six or seven days nonstop entertainment value out of the Five-Day World Hopper with little "down" time. By contrast, the three I-Drive parks can realistically be tackled in about three unhurried days (or two long days on a rushed schedule). Beyond Universal, Sea World and Wet 'n Wild (and Busch Gardens), there are no ancillary parks involved in the five-day arrangement.

Therefore, since five days are more than one really needs in the three I-Drive parks, a more valuable comparison is with the single-day admission price for the parks, which totals to $106.16 for adults, and $85.75 for children ages 3 to 9. To go one step further, by utilizing some of the many discount coupons littering the I-Drive hotels, you can shave another $5 to 10 off your combined one-day park admissions. In sum, if you are definitely planning to see all three parks and can cover them in a single day each, the five-day Vacation Value Pass is a wash compared with single-park admissions. But if you plan to return a second day to any of these facilities, the come-and-go privileges of the Vacation Value Pass provides an added level of touring flexibility and save you money as well. The same logic applies to the seven-day Vacation Value Pass.

The Vacation Value passes do make sense for Orlando's repeat guests who have experienced most or all of Walt Disney World on a previous trip, and want to see the city's other attractions with the Disney parks taking a back seat. And, in the near future, as Universal's **E-Zone** and **Islands of Adventure** come on line (see "TomorrOrlando" in "Introduction and Overview"), the merit of a Disney alternative will begin to have more concrete value. The I-Drive corridor will begin to delineate its own image to outsiders as a separate Orlando experience from the one concocted by Walt.

Beyond the Vacation Value Pass, ticket prices are discussed under the individual attractions. Unless otherwise noted, Visa, MasterCard and American Express are accepted for all attractions.

The **Orlando Convention and Visitor's Bureau** is open from 8 a.m. to 8 p.m. daily (except Christmas Day) and can assist with any number of questions; the bureau also sells discounted attraction tickets and maintains a hotel availability list updated daily. It is located at *8723 International Drive, at the corner of International Drive and Australian Court.* ☎ *(407) 363-5872.*

Universal Studios

Universal Studios' $650 million Florida production facility is, like the Disney-MGM Studios, more theme park than actual movie studio, but it's a pretty spiffy theme park nonetheless.

Most visitors hardly seem to mind that there's little actual moviemaking taking place here—they're here to "ride the movies" as the park's billboards say. With an inventory of hit films like *E.T.*, *Back to the Future* and *Jaws* (all directed or produced by Steven Spielberg, a consultant for the park since it first opened), Universal has a potent roster of source material to inspire its rides. Like Disney, Universal increasingly supplements its inventory of productions with franchises owned by other studios, inspiring attractions linked to *Beetlejuice*, *Ghostbusters* and *Terminator*, among others. *SeaQuest* filmed here during its network run, and the movie *Parenthood* was also shot at Universal's Orlando facilities. **Nickelodeon** produces 90 percent of its on-air material here and **America's Health Network** opened offices here in 1996. By 1998, **E! Entertainment** is slated to produce some of its on-air material here.

UNIVERSAL STUDIOS FLORIDA ®

More theme park than movie studio, Universal Studios takes visitors behind the scenes of their favorite movies and TV shows. Where else can you experience an earthquake, King Kong and Jaws all on the same day?

SCREEN TEST VIDEO ADVENTURE

KONGFRONTATION

GHOSTBUSTERS SPOOKTACULAR

SOUND STAGES

"MURDER, SHE WROTE" MYSTERY THEATER

NEW YORK

PRODUCTION CENTRAL

MCA RECORDING STUDIOS

THE BLUES BROTHERS

THE BONEYARD

FUNTASTIC WORLD OF HANNA-BARBERA

NICKELODEON STUDIOS

ADVENTURES OF ROCKY & BULLWINKLE

HOLLYWOOD

HITCHCOCK'S 3-D THEATER

PRODUCTION STUDIO TRAM TOUR

THE FRONT LOT

TERMINATOR 2 3-D

LUCY, A TRIBUTE

Exit to Turkey Lake Rd.

MAIN ENTRANCE

PARKING

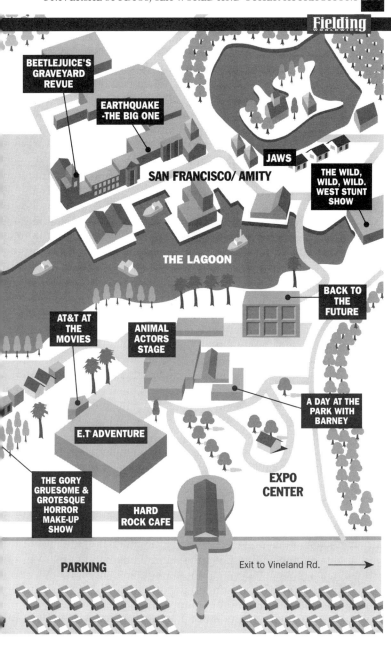

Fielding

BEETLEJUICE'S GRAVEYARD REVUE

EARTHQUAKE -THE BIG ONE

JAWS

SAN FRANCISCO/ AMITY

THE WILD, WILD, WILD. WEST STUNT SHOW

THE LAGOON

BACK TO THE FUTURE

AT&T AT THE MOVIES

ANIMAL ACTORS STAGE

A DAY AT THE PARK WITH BARNEY

E.T ADVENTURE

THE GORY GRUESOME & GROTESQUE HORROR MAKE-UP SHOW

HARD ROCK CAFE

EXPO CENTER

PARKING

Exit to Vineland Rd. ⟶

In recent years, however, most actual production has been limited to television specials and commercial work.

"Jaws," Universal Studios, recreates the scariest scenes from the movie.

The entertainment focus at Universal Studios is different enough from the Disney-MGM version that the two parks exist comfortably only a few miles from each other with little overlap. Many visitors spend a day at each studio during a single Orlando trip. Few can avoid comparing the two parks. At its 1990 opening, pundits noted that Universal played at a higher pitch and its rides would be enjoyed most by teens and young adults, while the Disney-MGM focus was on shows that would appeal to a general family audience.

In subsequent years, both parks have added attractions to diversify their appeal but, not surprisingly, they still maintain their own unique identities. In seemingly every area where the parks could inadvertently (or purposefully) duplicate one another, they have each attempted to go their own way. The motion simulator rides at Walt Disney World (**Star Tours** and **Body Wars**) have a completely different design from the two at Universal (**Back to the Future** and the **Funtastic World of Hanna-Barbera**); the stunt shows at the parks are told on a vastly different scale; and from a bonafide educational standpoint, Universal excels at explaining special effects, while Disney triumphs in the animation department.

Before the end of the century, following the opening of **E-Zone** in 1998 and **Islands of Adventure** in 1999, and two hotels with a combined construction cost topping $750 million, Universal will start to have a resort that may genuinely compete with Disney's empire well beyond the head-to-head battle now taking place only at the studio-themed attractions. Perhaps no personalities better symbolize the competition-to-come than Mickey Mouse on one side and the Terminator on the other.

Tickets, Hours of Operation, and When to Visit

Universal's ticket prices are kept identical to Disney's one-day prices for their three main parks; when Disney announces a rate increase, Universal immediately matches the new price. At the time of publication, the rates for Universal (tax included) were $40.81 for adults, and $32.86 for children ages 3 to 9. A two-day pass is $58.30 and $46.64, respectively; the admissions have no expiration date. During low season, typically, mid-September through mid-December and January through mid-February, the park provides incentives for a return visit the following day; the dates and specifics of these offers change regularly but can sometimes result in a second day at the park for free. An annual pass is available for $73.14, children $62.54.

Unlike Disney, Universal has a more aggressive discounting policy. Coupons are found in some of the visitor publications, and reduced-price admissions are available throughout the area's ticket counters and hotel desks. Show your AAA membership card at the main gate and receive $3 off each admission, although purchasing Universal tickets at a AAA office will usually net a bigger discount. The AAA card also earns members a 10% discount at park gift shops and restaurants. Universal is also part of the five- and seven-day Vacation Value Pass program (see "Coupons and Discount Offers," above).

Universal typically opens at 9 a.m. daily; during peak periods, the park may open its gates earlier. Closing hours vary seasonally, but the park is generally open until 6 or 7 p.m. in the winter months, and as late as 10 p.m. during the summer; call ☎ *(407) 363-8000* the day before you plan to visit to determine exact hours of operation. During less-busy periods, some of Universal's secondary attractions do not begin operating until an hour or more after the park's gates have opened. This won't detract from your tour since the big lures (Terminator 2 3-D and Back to the Future, among others) usually open when the front gates do. Consult your entertainment schedule when you enter the park to verify what is open when and adapt your itinerary accordingly.

INSIDER TIP

In an effort to keep pace with Disney Resort guest privileges, Universal has instituted a new early admission policy similar to Disney's Surprise Morning program. By staying in one of the Universal Travel Company-affiliated hotels (currently numbering more than a dozen), you are provided admission one hour ahead of the official gate opening at Universal, when E.T., Back to the Future and Terminator 2 3-D are open early (on Thursdays and Sundays). For additional information on this program, call the Universal City Travel Company, ☎ (800) 224-3838.

Because the park requires at least one long day to experience, we recommend arriving 20 to 30 minutes prior to the gate opening to park your car, purchase tickets and look over the day's entertainment schedule (also see the "Universal Studios Touring Itinerary" below). You can purchase your admission tickets prior to the day you visit, either at the gate or at one of the numerous brokers positioned in hotels and other locations along the I-Drive and U.S. 192 corridors. During peak season (summer, Christmas, Easter), advance purchasing will save waiting in line 20 minutes or more the morning you arrive.

Unlike Walt Disney World, Universal continues to draw a large portion of its visitors from the neighboring area and, accordingly, tends to be somewhat busier on weekends, making weekdays ideal for touring.

Universal's general information number is ☎ *(407) 363-8000*.

Transportation, Arrival and Orientation

Universal Studios is located near the intersection of I-4 and the Florida Turnpike, about seven miles southwest of downtown Orlando and eight miles northeast of the Disney Village area. From Walt Disney World or Kissimmee, take I-4 eastbound to exit 29 or 30B and follow the signs to Universal—from the Disney Village/Crossroads area, the drive takes 20 to 25 minutes, a little longer from the Disney-owned resorts or Kissimmee. From the International Drive area, proceed north on International and left on Kirkman to the main entrance; allow 15 to 20 minutes from an I-Drive hotel to the Universal parking lot.

Parking in Universal's 7000-car lot is $5 per vehicle. In preparation for the opening of E-Zone, a 9000-car, multi-level structure is scheduled for completion by fall 1996. Universal is well-connected via public transportation to hotels and other attractions along the I-Drive corridor. However, there is no courtesy bus system linking the Walt Disney World resorts with Universal Studios.

An **ATM** is located outside the main entrance, to the right of the **Guest Services** window; more extensive **banking** services are provided by the First Union National Bank located just inside the main entrance—the bank can handle currency exchange, cash advances and traveler's check cashing, even on Sundays. The **Studio Kennel** is adjacent to the main entrance and provides pet accommodations for $5 per day (not including food). **Lockers** are available outside the group entrance and inside the main entrance. **Stroller** and **wheelchair rental** is provided for $6 per day, just inside the main entrance.

With somewhat more success than the Disney-MGM Studios, Universal has attempted to split its park into various "lands," including the Front Lot, Production Central, Hollywood, New York, Expo Center and the curiously bicoastal San Francisco/Amity. Again, however, these definitions are of minimal use in navigating the park, so rides and shows are described in a clockwise order, as one would encounter them on a map. Families with small children will find the most attractions geared toward younger audiences focused in Expo Center near the Hard Rock Cafe entrance, where Barney, Fievel and E.T. reside.

Information on the park's **character breakfast**, which provides early admittance to E.T. Adventure, is provided under "Restaurants."

VIP Tours

Universal has two types of guided tours available—one is expensive, the other is exclusive and more expensive still.

The standard **VIP Tour** is $95.40 per person (tax and park admission included) and is a four-hour walking tour of Universal that includes priority seating/admittance for *up to* seven attractions. Unlike Disney's Backstage Magic or other World tours, this is not a behind-the-scenes circuit, but instead, an opportunity to see more of Universal for four hours by jumping ahead of the lines. Group size varies, but can total up to 15 persons.

The **Exclusive VIP Tour** is a *private* eight-hour tour for a group of up to 15 persons. Again, the main perk here is an opportunity to jump ahead of the lines, but no other guests will be mixed in with your group and you can customize the list of attractions on your itinerary to some degree. Regardless of the size of your party, the flat fee for the exclusive tour is $954, including tax and park admission.

In both cases, you're paying a premium to minimize your waits in line. If money is no object, the standard tour is probably worth it, particularly during peak season when the park's lines can top an hour or more for each major attraction. However, priced more than twice the cost of the usual (undiscounted) adult admission, the VIP Tour makes for an expensive outing. As for the exclusive tour, this option is strictly for the well-heeled, although compared with adult gate admission of $40.81, the per-person price of $63.60 for a *full* group of 15 is a good deal for the advantage of skipping lines on one of the park's busier days.

The VIP Tour office is open from 9 a.m. to 6 p.m., Monday through Friday. Most tours leave around 10 a.m. and noon. Reservations are required, preferably with 72 hours' notice, but Universal will try to accommodate you on a standard tour on a space-available basis without reservations. Additional information and reservations, ☎ *(407) 363-8295.*

Rides, Attractions and Shows

Kongfrontation, Universal Studios, gives visitors a closeup look at King Kong.

Universal is laid out in a series of themed areas vaguely resembling the lots of a real studio. You'll see a New York street scene, a Hollywood area and a lagoon that doubles as the San Francisco wharf on one side and the New England home of Jaws on the other. The detailing is absolutely on-par with the creativity at work at the Disney-MGM Studios.

There's little guarantee that a film or television show will actually be in production while you are visiting, but it doesn't hurt to call ☎ *(407) 363-8000* for current production information. When you arrive at the studios, check the production board at the main entrance for a list of that day's shooting schedule.

The Boneyard has a few rusting props from films, but also includes a fun recreation of the T-Rex from *Jurassic Park* and a Jeep for a paid-fee photo op.

Rides and shows are listed in a clockwise fashion, starting with the attraction closest to the main entrance.

Lucy: A Tribute

A well-executed walk-through museum housing memorabilia from Lucille Ball and the "I Love Lucy" television series, including letters, costumes, scripts and television monitors featuring classic clips and home movies. A computer-generated Lucy trivia game provides a challenge for die-hard buffs. *Length of tour:* Allow 15 to 20 minutes. *Special note:* Rarely crowded, the Lucy museum is a good place to ditch the afternoon heat.

Alfred Hitchcock: The Art of Making Movies

This walking tour uses the films of Alfred Hitchcock as a vehicle to explain commonly-utilized trick camera effects, particularly rear- or blue-screen projection. The tour begins in a theater, where 3-D effects from Hitchcock's films are shown, including *The Birds* and *Dial M for Murder*. From the theater, the tour proceeds to a soundstage designed to recreate other famous moments, including the shower scene from *Psycho*, the merry-go-round sequence from *Strangers on a Train*, and the climactic fall from the Statue of Liberty in *Saboteur*, each using volunteers from the audience as stand-ins for the real actors. You have to pay close attention to the guide's spiel to fully appreciate the techniques showcased, but the tour is a decent introduction to the tricks of the trade. Upstairs, the illusions continue with mock-ups from *Rear Window* and *Vertigo*. *Length of tour:* About 40 minutes. *Special note:* Its position near the park entrance makes this particular attraction somewhat more crowded during morning hours. Try to visit in the afternoon when other attractions are operating at full capacity. Some young children may be frightened by the mayhem on display.

Production Studio Tram Tour

Universal's Orlando tram tour is neither comparable to either the one featured at its Hollywood studios, nor to the Backstage Studio Tour that Disney has installed at its Florida facility. The ride is simply a brief narrated tour of the same area you walk through on your way to the attractions; if the tram visited more real sets and shooting locations, it would be somewhat more interesting. *Length of ride:* About 20 minutes. *Special note:* First thing in the morning, the tram tour is a nice introduction to the park; *however*, this is a poor use of the prized hour or two before major attractions become inundated with crowds (furthermore, mornings are also just about the only time there's a line for this attraction). Take the tram in the middle of the day, and only if you are looking for a break from walking and don't mind a re-tread of areas you have already visited.

Nickelodeon Studios

One of Universal's smarter concepts is the tie-in with the Nickelodeon channel, but the attraction it inspired—a walk-through tour for the younger set—is lengthy and not as engrossing as one might hope. The impressive 90,000-square-foot studio features two soundstages with seating for 250, where roughly 90 percent of Nickelodeon's programming is filmed, although most is not taped before a live audience. The Game Lab is an interactive area for kids, but be forewarned that one young visitor will be "slimed." The *Gak* and *Goo* (cooked on the premises) continues to flow outside Nick's studios, where the green slime geyser erupts every 10 minutes. *Length of tour:* About 45 minutes. *Special note:* The studios are typically in production during the week and seats for shows, when available, are handed out on the day of taping; check with the Guest Relations desk. Otherwise this attraction is minor; if you're visiting without pre-teens, skip it, particularly since the information delivered overlaps to some extent with the superior Hitchcock exhibit. Nickelodeon tours usually don't start until 10 a.m. Recorded production information, ☎ *(407) 363-8586.*

Funtastic World of Hanna-Barbera

The gentlest of Orlando's motion simulator rides, this one is a fast-paced trip through the animation of Hanna-Barbera studios. A five-minute pre-show introduces Bill Hanna and Joe Barbera, who provide a stilted overview as to how their animation is produced. You are then ushered into a 96-seat theater with 24 individual simulator vehicles for an animated chase sequence starring the Flintstones, Jetsons, Yogi Bear and other cartoon characters. The ride exits into an interactive play-area themed to the Hanna-Barbera characters. *Length of ride:* Five minutes, plus the pre-show. *Special note:* Although aimed squarely at pre-teens, the riders must meet a 40-inch minimum height requirement for the motion-simulator vehicles; children under 40 inches tall are allowed to watch the movie from a stationary vehicle at the front of the theater. If you are unsure about whether you want to tackle Back to the Future, Hanna Barbera is a mild introduction to the type of action found on the bigger attraction. However, the ride may be a letdown following a visit to the considerably more intense Back to the Future. This is one of the slower-loading rides at Universal; if lines appear long, come back later in the day.

Murder She Wrote Mystery Theater

Fans of Jessica Fletcher rejoice—at Universal, the now-canceled television hit (at 12 seasons, the longest-running detective series in history) lives on. The attraction goes into the mechanics of the post-production process—where all of the elements (film, dialogue, effects and music) come together in the editing room. Audience recruits are asked to assist in the compilation of a climactic "Murder She Wrote" whodunit, with often-hilarious results. *Length of attraction:* 35 minutes. *Special note:*

Although not a must-see attraction, this is one of Universal's better "how-to-make-a-movie" presentations. A long line is unusual, except on very busy afternoons; in any case the attraction makes for an ideal visit during the middle of the day. Note that the first show sometimes doesn't start until noon.

Ghostbusters Spooktacular

The popular 1984 movie is the inspiration for this fast-paced and funny look at special effects. The gimmick is a pitch from a salesman for a Ghostbusters franchise, with a live demonstration of the ectoplasmic containment center at the Temple of Gozer from the film. A New York city official comes on to the scene, ready to expose the salesman as a fraud, and disconnects the containment unit to prove it. Needless to say, things go quickly awry and the movie's cast of characters materializes for a series of eye-popping effects involving explosions, lasers and 11 tons of liquid nitrogen. *Length of show:* 15 minutes, plus pre-show. *Special note:* Ghostbusters is one of the park's more popular attractions and a line is not unusual. Try to visit before noon, or wait until late afternoon.

Kongfrontation

An immense soundstage with a New York facade houses this impressive, larger-than-life attraction featuring one of Hollywood's biggest stars. The waiting area tours a graffiti-laced subway station, where we are informed of King Kong's ongoing Manhattan rampage and are told to evacuate to Roosevelt Island. You'll board a 45-person aerial tram that makes a notably circuitous trip to tour a series of burned-out buildings, broken water mains, before running into interference by the agitated, love-struck ape. He howls and screams, fondles an oil tanker, shakes your tram and, worst of all, his breath smells of bananas. Not terribly frightening except to impressionable children, the technology used to create this huge attraction is more interesting than the ride itself. The technology may also be the cause of the infamous breakdowns that seem to occur here more than at any other Universal attraction. *Length of ride:* Five minutes. *Special note:* Kongfrontation is worth seeing, but the ride logs fewer repeat visitors than other park attractions, and therefore lines are usually in place only during the late morning and early afternoon. If you don't see it before noon, wait until mid-afternoon when lines have noticeably diminished. If the line extends out the front doors of the building, it's long.

AUTHOR'S OBSERVATION

The computer-animated King Kong figure used in Kongfrontation is the largest audio-animatronic-type creature ever built: He is four stories tall, weighs six tons and has an arm span of 54 feet. The big ape is made of steel, plastic, fabric and 7000 pounds of fur, and he can perform 46 motions.

Beetlejuice's Graveyard Revue

This loud, brassy show stars some of Universal's '30s-era creeps—Dracula, Werewolf, Phantom of the Opera, Frankenstein and his Bride—who are joined by host Beetlejuice, the "ghoul of cool," for a series of musical numbers and small-scale pyrotechnics. Cornball and camp reign supreme amid the one-minute renditions of standards such as "Great Balls of Fire" and "When a Man Loves a Woman," and kids love its relentless, cartoon-style energy. If not offended by a mini-skirted Bride of Frankenstein or an earring-studded Dracula, some adults love it too. *Length of show:* 20 minutes. *Special note:* Performed in an open-air (but covered) 1250-seat amphitheater, the Revue is performed up to eight times on busy days, but rarely reaches capacity long before show time. This is a good choice for early or mid-afternoon.

Earthquake: The Big One

Based on the sudsy 1974 disaster epic, this ride is one of the park's signature attractions—a spectacular, simulated 8.3-magnitude earthquake that occurs while aboard an underground subway. Universal adds an educational element to the mayhem by having host Charlton Heston explain the use of blue screens, matte paintings and miniatures in "Earthquake's" Oscar-winning effects; three separate pre-shows are featured, including a final segment that uses audience volunteers. Then guests board a 220-passenger BART train for the climax of the show: pulling into a San Francisco underground station just in time for a gut-wrenching temblor that produces explosions, a 65,000-gallon flood, and the sudden onslaught by another subway train on the opposite track. *Length of attraction:* 20 minutes, including pre-shows. *Special note:* The effects are real enough to produce anxiety among guests who are previously inclined to dislike disaster scenarios; young children might be alarmed. Accommodating more than 2000 guests hourly, Earthquake doesn't reach maximum capacity except midday on very busy afternoons. On these occasions, visit the attraction before noon, or wait until late afternoon.

Jaws

What a hoot! Universal's Jaws attraction has a decidedly checkered past. The shark appearance on the Universal Tram Tour in Hollywood is a thrill-less sideshow, and when the Jaws ride originally opened here in Florida, it was beset by mechanical problems and breakdowns. In 1993, however, the Orlando attraction was completely overhauled. Now it is one of the most entertaining rides in the region, aided by over-the-top boat skippers who gleefully out-perform their tongue-in-cheek counterparts at Disney's Jungle Cruise.

Guests board a 46-passenger boat for a pleasant tour of Amity Bay, but quickly come across a sinking boat that has been savaged by a shark. The tell-tale John Williams score trumpets in the background and a great white fin slices through the water toward you, rocking the boat as it passes underneath. A dark seaside warehouse marks the next close encounter, which leads to an explosive finale, straight from the conclusion of *Jaws 2* (fortunately, he doesn't eat a helicopter this time). You will probably get splashed, particularly if you are sitting on the left side of the boat (facing forward). *Length of ride:* Five minutes. *Special note:* Jaws is one of Universal's more popular attractions, but can process upwards of 2000 people per hour when all six boats are plying the lagoon. Try to visit before noon, or wait until late afternoon; beware of the exiting crowd from the nearby Stunt Show. The triumphant adventure is all in jest and most guests depart cheering and laughing, but pre-teens can be alarmed by the nonstop menace on display here.

> ### AUTHOR'S OBSERVATION
> *The 32-foot, three-ton sharks used for Jaws are made of steel and fiberglass and are wrapped in a latex skin; the teeth are made of urethane. Universal claims these sharks move through the water at 20 feet per second, and thrust with power equal to a 727 jet engine.*

The Wild Wild West Stunt Show

A collection of stunts is put forth as hillbillies invade a western set for this thigh-slapper. The five actors go through their "greatest oater hits" routine with split-second timing to make for a moderately amusing performance—fistfights, bullwhips, shoot-outs, pratfalls, acrobatics and horse stunts are featured. *Length of show:* About 18 minutes. *Special note:* The Stunt Show is told on a smaller scale than either the Indiana Jones version at Disney-MGM or the Stuntacular at Universal, but the intimacy (the theater seats 1200) makes it just as enjoyable. See it anytime, preferably during the early afternoon when other attractions are overflowing.

Back to the Future

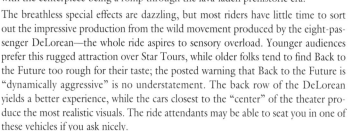

The showpiece attraction of Universal Studios is this motion-simulator ride based on the hit 1985 movie and its sequels. Two characters are carried over from the movies: the mad scientist Doc Brown (Christopher Lloyd) and Biff Tannen (Tom Wilson), the bad-boy villain. The frenetic backstory (explained on television screens as you wait to board) amounts to little, but it helps to know that the reason you are chasing Biff through time is that by rear-ending his DeLorean you'll return to the present. Or something like that. Along the way, you zoom through space and time, with the centerpiece being a romp through the lava-laden prehistoric era.

The breathless special effects are dazzling, but most riders have little time to sort out the impressive production from the wild movement produced by the eight-passenger DeLorean—the whole ride aspires to sensory overload. Younger audiences prefer this rugged attraction over Star Tours, while older folks tend to find Back to the Future too rough for their taste; the posted warning that Back to the Future is "dynamically aggressive" is no understatement. The back row of the DeLorean yields a better experience, while the cars closest to the "center" of the theater produce the most realistic visuals. The ride attendants may be able to seat you in one of these vehicles if you ask nicely.

Length of ride: Five minutes, plus pre-show. *Special note:* Back to the Future has a 40-inch minimum height requirement, and some children who clear that mark may still find the experience daunting. Prior to the debut of the Terminator attraction, this was Universal's most popular ride. Despite turning more than 2000 guests per hour, waits exceeding 60 minutes are not uncommon even on moderately busy days. Although Terminator 2 3-D will siphon some of the early morning demand from this ride, Back to the Future should still be tackled in the first half-hour that the park is open, or else wait until the park's closing hour when crowds start to thin. Also be on the lookout for the exit of both the Wild West Stunt Show and the Animal Actors Stage, each of which can release over a thousand guests into the area.

AUTHOR'S OBSERVATION

The crisp and realistic projected image for Back to the Future is the combined result of several processes never before utilized together. The image was shot on 70mm film using the Omnimax process, the largest film frame ever created, allowing for minute detail. It was transferred onto laserdisc so that the projected image would not degenerate in time with scratches or film breaks. The image is projected onto an 80-foot diameter hemispherical screen; the DeLoreans' guests ride in are so close to the curved screen that passengers who look straight ahead during the ride will not see the edges of the image—experiencing a completely engulfing visual.

Barney Show at Universal Studios delights the toddler set.

A Day in the Park with Barney

To the delight of preschoolers, the purple dinosaur has invaded Universal. The pre-show area includes a hands-on interactive playground in a park-like setting, which leads to a magical waterfall and the 400-seat Barney Theater. The theater-in-the-round showcases Barney and his most popular songs, augmented by a wealth of special effects simulating the four seasons, clouds and stars. After the show, children are invited into Barney's back yard, which features "cause-and-effect" activities designed to stimulate creative thinking. The centerpiece of the play area is Barney's Treehouse, with slides and tunnels for exploration. *Length of attraction:* Allow 25 minutes for the show, plus additional time for the play area. *Special note:* Barney's fans tend to put the dinosaur at the top of their agenda for the day, so lines peak by mid-morning. Try to visit in the first hour the park is open, or wait until after lunch, when demand begins to fall off.

Animal Actors Stage

Universal's most unpredictable attraction is this pleasant series of performing animals, including descendants or relatives of Babe (the pig), Benji, Lassie and Beethoven among the huge cast. While most of the tricks are fairly pedestrian, kids love the show and humor is frequently supplied by the animals' unplanned antics. The show is performed in a 1200-seat theater. *Length of show:* 20 to 30 minutes. *Special note:* With fewer performances than the other two major shows, this show can be a hot ticket, particularly on busy days. If you have children in tow, try to see the first or second performance of the day, and arrive 10 to 20 minutes before show time.

Fievel's Playland

Named after Orlando's *other* resident animated rodent (Fievel Mousekewitz of *An American Tale*), this 18,000-square-foot play area is a hit with pre-teens, who enjoy its collection of oversized props, including a 200-foot water slide experienced on a sardine-can raft that runs through a maze of sewer pipes. Similar to Disney's *Honey I Shrunk the Kids* attraction, Fievel's has the advantage of being an open play area and therefore doesn't have a line to enter (although the wet slide on a raft can develop a long wait). *Length of tour:* Allow 20 to 30 minutes for children to explore the area. *Special note:* On hot or busy days, the 15-second raft-ride develops a major line; the slide is fun, but not large enough to endure a long wait.

E.T. Adventure, Universal Studios, features the beloved bicycle scene.

E.T. Adventure

Steven Spielberg helped create this ride, a lavish continuation of the storyline from the immensely popular 1982 film. Guests board "bicycles"—suspended gondolas that, like Disney's Peter Pan ride, fly over and through a series of detailed sets—and E.T. rides along in the basket up front. After escaping police officers, the bicycles sail into space, eventually landing on E.T.'s home, the Green Planet, where a series of goofy-looking Day-Glo aliens thank you for saving their planet (although exactly how you did it is never explained). With names such as Gurgles, Squirtals and Churtles for E.T.'s relatives, this attraction pushes the "cute" button, but is elaborate enough to keep most visitors sufficiently entertained. Parents should note that some very young children can be a little fearful of the imagined peril experienced on this ride. *Length of ride:* Five minutes, plus pre-show. *Special note:* E.T. remains one of Universal's most popular attractions and lines build by mid-morning and don't let up until mid afternoon. Try to ride in the first hour or two the park is open, or else wait until pre-teens start to clear out of the park in the late afternoon. Also, be aware that the line for E.T. is a little deceiving; after the two-minute pre-show, you enter another waiting area in an air-conditioned forest. If this path is full for its entire length, prepare for a 30-minute wait prior to boarding the actual ride. Watch out for the exit of the nearby Animal Actors Stage, which can release up to 1200 guests into the area.

AT&T at the Movies

A museum of interactive-computer exhibits involving the use of sound and featuring a host of clips from Universal-owned franchises. *Length of tour:* 10 to 20 minutes. *Special note:* Rarely busy, so visit during the apex of the afternoon when lines for the big attractions have become unreasonably long.

The Gory Gruesome and Grotesque Horror Makeup Show

An amusing exploration into the art of make-up for horror films is staged with a ghastly series of delightfully oozing effects. Gaping wounds, severed limbs and transformation scenes from "An American Werewolf in London" and "The Fly" are featured, along with Linda Blair's rotating head from "The Exorcist." All is presented in good... er, taste. *Length of show:* 20 minutes. *Special note:* Although warnings are posted regarding the "intense nature" of this attraction for younger audiences, most kids weaned on television find this exhibit a hoot. On less-busy days, the first performance may not be scheduled until noon, otherwise, visit any time.

Terminator 2 3-D—Battle Across Time

When it came time for Universal to produce a spectacular 3-D film attraction, the company (knowing Disney set the standard with Honey I Shrunk the Audience) pulled out all the stops. The $60 million attraction opened in April 1996 and quickly became the park's must-see event. Not unlike Disney's 3-D productions, T2 3-D features tactile effects that build on the illusion. Where this attraction comes out ahead is by adding yet another layer of depth—real-life actors plunge out of the screen, including a Schwarzenegger lookalike on a motorcycle, and when the theater "descends" into Cyberdyne Systems, additional screens increase the scope and depth of the presentation. The overall effect of the complex production has allowed Universal to raise industry standards a notch higher.

Length of attraction: 20 minutes, including pre-show. *Special note:* Although the bloodshed is toned down, T2 3-D is a sequel (of sorts) to violent, R-rated theatrical releases; the attraction is intense and not suitable for many pre-teens. How long are the lines? The good news is that a whopping 2400 guests per hour can be accommodated in this theater. But, as the new kid on the Universal block, lines build early and stay long throughout busy days. Try to see T2 3-D in the first half-hour the park is open, or wait until late afternoon when attendance starts to wane.

Dynamite Nights Stuntacular, Universal Studios, features a changing roster of stuntpeople demonstrating daring feats.

Dynamite Nights' Stuntacular

The day at Universal usually closes with this loud stunt show performed on the park's eight-acre lagoon. The script endeavors to detail the pursuit of drug smugglers on the water by water-ski and motorboat-equipped police; it ends in a 60-foot stunt boat jump through a wall of fire, explosions and fireworks. Although the stunts and effects on display here are fairly prodigious, the storyline is weak, made all the more difficult by the fact that the lagoon area is big, making it hard for you to see all of the smoke-engulfed action from virtually any point along its perimeter. *Length of show:* 15 minutes. *Special note:* The actual show time varies seasonally, and a second performance is added on busy days before dusk. The best spots to situate your party are close to the "center" of the lagoon near Lombard's Landing, or near the Animal Actor's Stage on the opposite side of the lagoon. Keep an eye out for the "splash zones"—places where water may land on viewers. As with Epcot's IllumiNations, the conclusion of the Stuntacular is marked by a mad dash for the parking lot—a time-consuming process on busy nights.

Eating

Universal has a surprisingly decent assortment of eateries. The two sit-down options, **Lombard's Landing** (easily one of the best restaurants in any area theme park) and the **Hard Rock Cafe**, are detailed in the "Restaurants" chapter. Both are ideal for an evening dinner, but note they receive an influx of diners when the Stuntacular concludes, and at the Hard Rock Cafe it can be just plain hard to obtain a table on most nights.

Near the main entrance, the **Beverly Hills Boulangerie** is a good place to start the day; the shop offers fresh-baked pastries, muffins, croissants, sandwiches and coffee. Proceeding counter-clockwise around the park, the **Studio Stars Restaurant**, across from the Bone Yard, provides an all-you-can-eat buffet featuring salads, burgers, sandwiches, seafood and a number of Italian dishes, as well as sit-down service. Opposite Kongfrontation, **Finnegan's Bar and Grill** serves shepherd's pie, bangers and coddles, corned beef and cabbage, and features a nice array of beers on tap or by the bottle—this pub is one of the more-used filming locations within Universal. Italian fast-food is offered at **Louie's,** and **Richter's Burger Company** across from Earthquake, of course, sells hamburgers and chicken sandwiches, and offers a well-stocked fixin's bar.

The **International Food Bazaar** next to Back to the Future is the spot for gyros, sweet and sour chicken, bratwurst and pizza. Tex-Mex food and margaritas set the tone at **Cafe La Bamba**. For an afternoon ice cream soda or malt, stop by **Schwab's Pharmacy**, a '40s-era Hollywood drug-store and soda shop, or visit **Mel's Drive-In**, modeled after the *American Graffiti* diner, for burgers, fries and shakes.

Universal Studios Touring Itinerary

Seeing all of Universal in one day requires determination and a nimble itinerary. On the positive side, there are enough "big" rides to spread out the demand for fast-paced thrills. On the other hand, because the park caters to a narrower demographic than Disney, most visitors have the same basic agenda. For parents traveling with small children, you'll want to make some minor adjustments to the initial portion of this itinerary, noted at the end of this section.

At 444 acres, including parking and production areas that are off-limits to guests Universal is a big facility—larger than the Disney-MGM Studios—so this itinerary focuses on the attractions and leaves minimal time for the secondary exhibit areas such as Lucy and AT&T at the Movies. As at the Disney-MGM Studios, be alert to the show times for the park's three large-scale shows (**Beetlejuice's Graveyard Revue**, the **Wild West Stunt Show** and the **Animal Actors Stage**). Since some of Universal's best rides are located near the exits for these shows, their lines can become quickly inundated (another reason for keeping your schedule flexible).

This plan works best under the following conditions:

a. You have purchased your tickets before you arrive at the front gate (see: "Tickets, Hours of Operation and When to Visit" above).

b. You are positioned at the main entrance 20 to 30 minutes prior to the scheduled opening time; call ☎ *(407) 363-8000* to verify the opening time.

c. All members of your party are willing to follow the same touring itinerary. They can, of course, bow out of any attractions they have no desire to ride.

When you enter the park, look at the brochure containing the day's entertainment schedule; of Universal's three large-scale shows, you'll want to plan to attend one that starts between 11 and 11:30 a.m. for step 5.

1. When the park gates open, proceed quickly down Hollywood Boulevard (the first right after you enter) to **Terminator 2 3-D**.

2. After experiencing the Terminator, continue down Hollywood Boulevard to see **Back to the Future**.

3. Ride **E.T. Adventure**. At this point, about an hour-and-a-half after the park has opened, you will have experienced three rides which, later in the afternoon, will require two-to-three hours to see.

4. After E.T., head around the lagoon to the right and ride **Jaws**, then **Earthquake**.

5. At this point, check your entertainment schedule and head for one of the park's three large-scale shows: **Beetlejuice's Graveyard Revue**, the **Wild**

West Stunt Show or the **Animal Actors Stage**, all of which are within a five-minute walk from Earthquake.

6.   After seeing one or two of the shows, ride **Kongfrontation**.

7.   You will be nearing lunchtime at this point. The park's best sit-down eatery, **Lombard's Landing**, is nearby, as are several counter-style spots.

8.   During the next few hours, during the heat of the day, you'll want to tackle the following indoor attractions, most of which will have little or no wait: **Ghostbusters**, the **Murder She Wrote Mystery Theater**, **Alfred Hitchcock: the Art of Making Movies** and the **Gory Gruesome and Grotesque Makeup Show**. Keep an eye on your watch for the next step.

9.   Coordinate the remaining one or two of the three large-scale shows you have not seen into your late afternoon schedule: **Beetlejuice's Graveyard Revue**, the **Wild West Stunt Show** and the **Animal Actors Stage**.

10. Ride the **Funtastic World of Hanna-Barbera** and revisit any attractions you wish to see again before the start of the **Dynamite Nights Stuntacular**.

What Did We Miss?

Following this itinerary by the letter will omit the following attractions: **Lucy: A Tribute** (easy to visit on your way out of the park), the **Production Studio Tram Tour**, **Nickelodeon Studios**, the **Day in the Park With Barney** show, **Fievel's Playground** and **AT&T at the Movies**. You may also find a limited amount of time to complete steps 9 and 10 prior to the start of the Dynamite Nights Stuntacular show.

If you are visiting Universal with small children under 8 or 9 years of age, you'll want to make some adjustments to the schedule. At the beginning of the day, make **E.T. Adventure** your first attraction, followed by **A Day in the Park with Barney**. Then follow the itinerary from step 4, omitting attractions that might be too intense. Tackle **Back to the Future** and **Terminator 2 3-D** at the end of the day, employing the switch-off technique if your child is not up for them (see: "Families with Small Children" in "Planning Your Trip").

Sea World

Marine life and the environment is celebrated at Sea World, symbolized by the Shamu family of balletic killer whales. No ordinary aquarium, in addition to housing sharks, dolphins, sea turtles, manatees and other denizens of the deep, Orlando's Sea World is also home to polar bears, penguins and a large collection of tropical birds. The animal antics are scripted, but not performed by audio-animatrons, and an environmentally correct theme is woven into most of the park's shows and attractions. In fact, Sea World has a comprehensive animal-rescue and marine research program that extends to its sister parks in Cleveland, San Antonio and the original park in San Diego. Sea World also hosts an educational program for Orlando schoolchildren.

Sea World's Killer Whale Show is still its most popular.

The attraction, the world's largest marine life park, encompasses 135 acres, making it slightly larger than The Magic Kingdom. But similarities between the two parks end there. In addition to embracing an educational component, low-key Sea World has few lines and rarely feels crowded, despite an annual attendance that exceeds 4 million. Indeed, when you find yourself waiting for an attraction, it will probably be in a shaded seating area, not in an endlessly switchbacking queue.

The park has not grown without a few bumps along the road to success. Sea World was constructed at a cost of $150 million, and opened right on the heals of The Magic Kingdom. Only two years younger than the Disney operation, Sea World endured the late '80s under the looming threat of bankruptcy by its then-owner Harcourt Brace Jovanovich. The park was purchased by the Anheuser-Busch company (the nation's number two theme park operator), in 1989. Anheuser-Busch spent the early part of the '90s adding impressive new exhibits, including the world's largest **manatee** enclosure and **Wild Arctic**, a motion-simulator helicopter ride that deposits guests into an impressive arctic-themed environment. In 1996, Sea World added **Key West**, a "land" themed around Bahamian architecture with animal habitats devoted to dolphins, stingrays and sea-turtle encounters. Although it still has occasional conflicts in its mission (the "Baywatch" franchise is the cheesiest example) on the whole, Sea World's aggressive and well-executed

SEA WORLD ®

Sea World is the world's largest marine life park, encompassing 135 acres. No ordinary aquarium, it also features sharks, killer whales and polar bears.

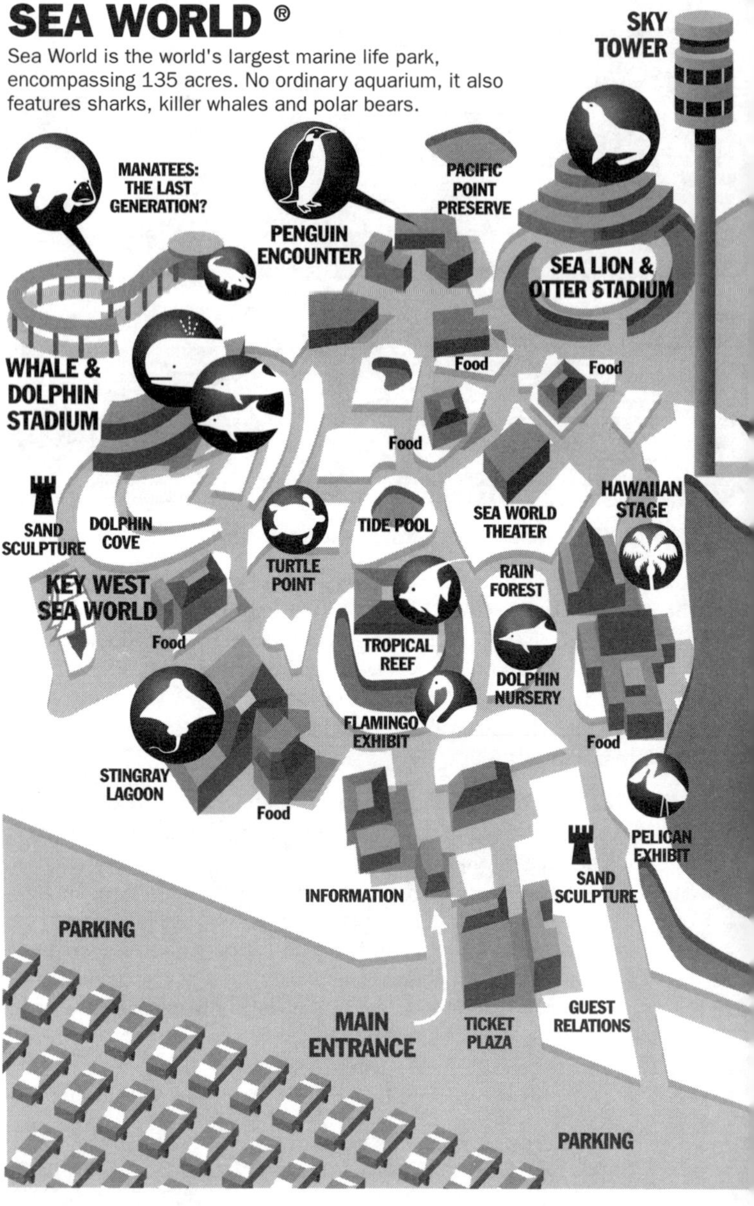

SKY TOWER

MANATEES: THE LAST GENERATION?

PENGUIN ENCOUNTER

PACIFIC POINT PRESERVE

SEA LION & OTTER STADIUM

WHALE & DOLPHIN STADIUM

Food

Food

Food

SAND SCULPTURE

DOLPHIN COVE

TURTLE POINT

TIDE POOL

SEA WORLD THEATER

HAWAIIAN STAGE

KEY WEST SEA WORLD

Food

RAIN FOREST

TROPICAL REEF

DOLPHIN NURSERY

STINGRAY LAGOON

FLAMINGO EXHIBIT

Food

Food

PELICAN EXHIBIT

INFORMATION

SAND SCULPTURE

PARKING

MAIN ENTRANCE

TICKET PLAZA

GUEST RELATIONS

PARKING

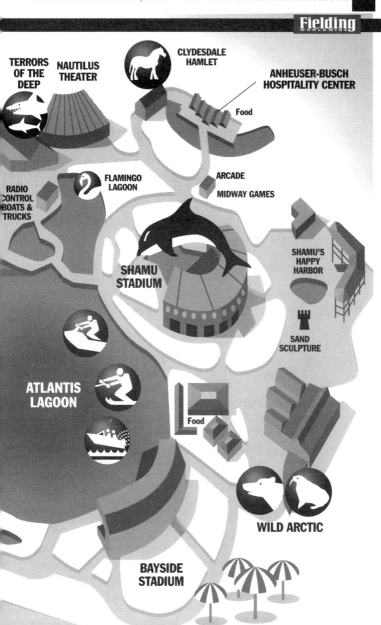

TERRORS OF THE DEEP

NAUTILUS THEATER

CLYDESDALE HAMLET

ANHEUSER-BUSCH HOSPITALITY CENTER

Food

RADIO CONTROL BOATS & TRUCKS

FLAMINGO LAGOON

ARCADE

MIDWAY GAMES

SHAMU'S HAPPY HARBOR

SHAMU STADIUM

SAND SCULPTURE

ATLANTIS LAGOON

Food

WILD ARCTIC

BAYSIDE STADIUM

expansion during the '90s has made the marine park one of the country's premier zoological attractions.

In short, the success and operation of Sea World provides Disney an excellent role model as it prepares its wild animal park for public consumption.

Tickets, Hours of Operation and When to Visit

Although the one-day ticket is priced slightly below the three main Disney parks and Universal, Sea World is still a fairly expensive excursion for families. Check for discount coupons prior to purchasing your tickets. Adult admission (tax included) is $39.95, children ages 3 to 9 are $32.80 each, and seniors 55 and up are $35.95. Budget a few extra bucks for animal food, which is sold at the enclosures for dolphins, sea lions and elsewhere.

A two-day ticket is also available for an additional $5. Annual passes are priced at $74.15, or $63.55 for children. Flash your AAA membership card and save an additional 10 percent off each ticket. Sea World is part of the five- and seven-day Vacation Value Pass policy (see "Coupons and Discount Offers" at the beginning of this chapter). Or, if you plan to tour both Sea World and Busch Gardens in Tampa during your vacation, the two parks (which are both owned by Anheuser-Busch) have a package for visiting both facilities on separate days within a week: $70.10 per adult, $56.55 per child.

Sea World usually opens at 9 a.m. daily. Closing hours vary seasonally, but the park generally stays open until 7 p.m. during winter months, and as late as 10 p.m. during the summer. Sea World can easily be seen in a single day, and during the summer when the park is open well into the night, it is ideal for afternoon/evening visits. Because most of its attractions are in a theater setting and shade is plentiful, strolling through Sea World is less intense than some of the other theme parks. For those on a tight schedule, it can be preceded by a morning visit to a water park.

Sea World's general information number is ☎ *(407) 351-3600*, or *(800) 327-2424.*

Transportation, Arrival and Orientation

Sea World is located at 7007 Sea World Drive, just off International Drive, near the junction of I-4 and the Beeline, about four miles northeast of Disney Village and five miles south of Universal Studios. From Walt Disney World, take I-4 east to exit 27A and follow the signs to Sea World; allow 10 to 15 minutes from Disney Village to Sea World's entrance. Parking is $5 per vehicle.

An **ATM** is located near the main entrance ticket window; foreign currency exchange is handled at the Guest Relations window nearby. Self-service **pet kennels** are located just outside the main entrance and are priced at $4 for the day (an attendant is on duty during park hours). **Lockers** are available adjacent to Shamu Emporium, just to the right as you enter the park. **Stroller** and **wheelchair rental** can be found at the Information Center on the left, just after you enter the main gate.

Sea World is predominantly made up of two types of attractions: walk-through exhibits and scheduled, stadium shows. Because of this, there are few long lines, a refreshing change of pace from the Disney and Universal operations. Several of the shows are well-worth seeing, so it's important to pick up a show schedule when you enter the park (see the Sea World "Touring Itinerary" below). Unlike the Disney and Universal section, all Sea World shows and attractions are described below alphabetically, rather than in a geographical order as one would encounter them on a map.

Sea World's layout has grown to wrap all the way around a 17-acre lagoon. The 400-foot **Sky Tower** is built in the lagoon's center and, for $3 per person to ride up to the top, provides a revolving, 360-degree panorama of the area. Information about the park's **Aloha Polynesian Luau** is provided under "Dinner Theaters" later in this chapter.

Scheduled Shows

Baywatch at Sea World

In 1995, Sea World replaced the Atlantis Ski Show at the 5000-seat Bayside Stadium with this show inspired by television's "Baywatch" to similarly mindless results. The jiggles take a back seat to the Cypress Gardens-style water ski and aerial stunts, complete with police boats, sirens, explosions and musical numbers, all narrated by star David Hasselhoff, who gets to perform one of his own musical numbers. The show keeps kids enthralled, otherwise this is one of the park's less, er... educational moments. *Length of show:* 30 minutes.

Big Splash Bash

A Broadway-style special effects and song-and-dance extravaganza, Big Splash Bash pays homage to water in an air-conditioned, 2400-seat indoor theater. The lost city of Atlantis and the mysteries of the Bermuda Triangle provide a backdrop for the production, with ultraviolet lasers, pyrotechnics, puppets, the park's trademark "dancing waters" and a cast of 14 (human) dancers delivering the action. *Length of show:* 25 minutes.

Hawaiian Rhythms

Calling all grass skirt and lei fans. The lead-in to the nightly Aloha Polynesian Luau, Hawaiian Rhythms is a pleasant, if insubstantial, revue of south seas dancing and music. If you're planning to attend the nightly dinner theater show, you can skip this since there's a fair amount of overlap. *Length of show:* 25 minutes.

Hotel Clyde and Seamore

Easily one of Sea World's most popular attractions, this sea lion, walrus and otter show is played for laughs amid a rollicking message of environmental awareness. Two animal trainers play the littering humans, Harry and Foible, who display less brain power than their animal counterparts. The stadium seats 4000 guests, but can fill to capacity in advance of the show on busy days. *Length of show:* 25 minutes, but arrive a few minutes early to take in the pre-show antics.

Mermaids, Myths and Monsters

Sea World's counterpart to Disney's IllumiNations is this nighttime show with music, lasers and fireworks that utilizes a 60-foot "screen" of water to project images of mermaids, sea serpents and King Neptune himself. A pleasant way to welcome the night, or to conclude your day of touring. Performed at the Atlantis Water Ski Stadium. *Length of show:* 20 minutes.

Shamu World Focus

A 1.7 million-gallon tank is the backdrop for this impressive display of the intelligence of killer whales (aka orcas), that includes at least two younger stars born at the park since 1993. The 16-by-20-foot "ShamuVision" video monitors fed with shots from four live cameras magnify some of the high-octane action in the huge 5600-seat arena, and also allows actress Jane Seymour to provide insight into the natural habitat of these creatures. While the stunts are grand just based on the size of the whales alone, few things are as spectacular as watching Shamu nose the trainers straight up into the air. A few lucky guests are chosen to be a part of the performance—you'll long to be a kid again for the opportunity. A killer whale research and breeding habitat backstage, **Shamu: Close Up**, provides additional insight into the training procedures and the park's successful breeding program. Sea World press refers to this as the largest and most sophisticated marine research facility in the world. This exhibit is best visited *during* the Shamu show when it's less likely to be mobbed. *Length of show:* 25 minutes. *Special note:* Easily the park's most popular attraction, the huge stadium can fill up well before show time, so arrive early to secure the seat you want. But beware—Shamu is trained to splash as far into the arena as possible, usually reaching the promenade level, 14 rows back. Routinely, the announcer advises the crowd of this fact, but a mass exodus for higher ground occurs immediately following the first big splash. An evening version of this show, Shamu Night Magic, is performed most evenings and features a somewhat flashier plot set against a rock music soundtrack.

AUTHOR'S OBSERVATION

If you are carrying a still or video camera, you are well advised to steer clear of the designated "splash zones," particularly at Shamu Stadium. Saltwater is the fastest way to deteriorate the mechanism of a camera, and Shamu happily sloshes the audience as many as 14 rows back.

Whale and Dolphin Discovery

The third of Sea World's three big animal shows, this one features six performing dolphins and two false killer whales (they're all black and sleeker than regular orcas). The show includes flips, high jumps and trainers water-skiing on the dolphins against a calypso-themed set named Discovery Cove, and surrounded by a 3500-

seat stadium. A child is picked out of the audience to participate in the dolphin interaction. *Length of show:* 25 minutes.

AUTHOR'S OBSERVATION

Averaging eight to 10 feet long, and weighing 300 to 650 pounds, bottlenose dolphins live in pods or herds of up to 15 animals in temperate or tropical waters throughout the world. Dolphins rank themselves and establish dominance by smacking their tails against the water, butting heads, snapping their jaws, and by demonstrating threatening postures and gestures. The dolphin life span is estimated at up to 20 years.

Window to the Sea

The Sea World Theater is the venue used for this self-promoting collection of video clips about the park's ecological focus and how it rescues hundred of beached marine animals annually (many of which soon make it into the Sea World animal collection). Sea World's mission is fine, but this image-buffing presentation is strictly a secondary attraction compared with the parks' other shows. Equally secondary is the **Water Fantasy**—fribbling computer-synchronized music, water and lights—that plays in this same theater, usually in the afternoon. Length of both shows: 20 minutes.

AUTHOR'S OBSERVATIONS

Sea turtles, one of the few saltwater-adapted reptiles, are found in warm and temperate seas throughout the world and can live 80 years or more. Of the eight species of sea turtle, one (the loggerhead) is threatened, while the other seven species are endangered. The Kemp's ridley is probably the most endangered sea turtle, with only 300 to 350 females nesting each year. Sea turtle hunting was a major industry in Key West until the '70s, when federal legislation was enacted to protect the animals. Poachers stealing eggs (which are laid on beaches) are thought to be the key to declining populations today.

Walk-through Attractions

Key West

Sea World's newest addition is a five-acre, Bahamian-themed attraction fringed by stands of palm trees, hibiscus and bougainvillea, and a replication of Key West's Duval Street. The compound actually encloses three separate animal habitats. The 600,000-gallon **Dolphin Cove** is home to two dozen Atlantic bottlenose dolphins and features coral formations that create swim-through tunnels seen from an underwater viewing area. A wave machine adds an additional element of realism, producing rolling breakers that crash onto a sandy beach. Park specialists hope that the enormous pool will encourage dolphin courtship and mating, and the long swimming patterns necessary for nursing young. **Sea Turtle Point** features endangered and threatened green, loggerhead and hawksbill turtles against a backdrop of a sand dune. **Stingray Lagoon** (which existed prior to the Key West addition) has been doubled in size and features a variety of docile rays—almost 200 *batoids*—that can be touched and fed; a new nursery cove exhibits newborns.

Manatees: The Last Generation

The gentle and endangered manatee is displayed in this unique 300,000-gallon lagoon—perhaps the world's best window into the lifestyles of these creatures, thought to number only 2400 in the wild today. Here, a 126-foot-long underwater viewing area allows visitors to observe manatees lolling about in a 3.5-acre tank. Surrounded by limestone, this artificial lagoon mimics the crystal-clear waters only a few miles from Orlando—the lagoons where manatees naturally thrive. While it's still a mystery as to how they were once mistaken for mermaids, the term "sea cow" begins to make more sense when you watch these slow and cumbersome mammals in their environment. Allow 20 to 30 minutes to tour the entire enclosure, which includes a brief theater presentation, and the **Alligator Habitat**, a marsh displaying trolling shore birds, turtles and American alligators. *Special note:* The manatees continue to be one of Sea World's premiere attractions, and one of the few to develop lines at midday. Avoid visiting the exhibit immediately following the exit of the nearby Whale and Dolphin Discovery, which can release up to 3500 guests into the area.

AUTHOR'S OBSERVATION

In 1995, a female manatee was struck by a power boat, an all-too-common occurrence in Florida's waterways. X-rays showed the animal had sustained cracked ribs that punctured and collapsed a lung, creating buoyancy problems that made eating difficult. Sea World worked with a local wetsuit manufacturer to create a manatee flotation device—a wetsuit with flotation inserts. The manatee, nicknamed "Fathom" (for the company that produced the wetsuit) now wears a bright neoprene wrap, and floats and eats with ease at Sea World's manatee habitat.

Pacific Point Preserve

A delightful and scenic Pacific coastal environment for pinnipeds—California sea lions, and harbor and fur seals—complete with crashing waves, rock outcrops and a beach. An underwater viewing area lets you observe the subaqueous shenanigans. You can feed the animals—fish are $1 for a small tray, and last about 15 seconds in the hands of a child. After purchasing fish, step around to left of enclosure where children can drop fish into the mouths of the seals. This is always a noisy and lively area. *Special note:* Watch for the exit of the nearby Hotel Clyde and Seamore Show.

Penguin Encounter

Ever see a bird fly—underwater? The majestic, orange-streaked king, the delightful chinstrap, and other penguins are among the 200 brightly marked inhabitants of this popular indoor exhibit. The Encounter features an extensive underwater viewing area for observation of the birds' submarine antics. A moving walkway provides the first pass, but a stationary viewing area allows a longer take. If it seems chilly, it is—the air temperature behind the glass is kept at 34° while the water is a brisk 45°, all cool enough to keep the snow (produced on the premises) chunky. The glacial habitat features puffins and murres next door, other Arctic avians that aren't certified for takeoff. *Special note:* Penguin Encounter can become inundated with visitors following the exit of either the nearby Whale and Dolphin Show or Hotel Clyde and Seamore.

Terrors of the Deep

Everything you always wanted to know about the mean and nasties of the deep is on display here in a quartet of darkly lit tanks enclosing 917,000 gallons of water, set against a soundtrack of foreboding sounds. The exhibit contains barracudas, green moray eels, massive groupers, poisonous pufferfish and scorpionfish and, of course, an assortment of fierce-looking sharks—nurse, yellow, bull and brown. The experience of following a moving walkway through a clear acrylic-lined tunnel engulfed by 450 tons of water makes you feel as though you are truly underwater with the sharks. You may want to allow time for a second pass. This excellent attraction is superior to the similar (though larger) Living Seas exhibit at Epcot. *Special note:* Beware the exit of the nearby Shamu or Hotel Clyde and Seamore Shows.

Sea World offers a closeup view of dolphins.

Tropical Reef

This indoor, 160,000-gallon, man-made coral reef structure features more than 1000 colorful tropical fish, including vivid yellow sergeant majors, blue surgeons, graceful French angels, butterfly fish and even infant sharks. Supplementing the huge main tank are 17 mini-aquariums that contain king crabs, conch, moray eels, lobsters and other individual species. Outside is the **Caribbean Tide Pool**, a collection of sea urchins, sea cucumbers, starfish, crabs and anemones, while around the corner is the **Dolphin Community Pool**, which underwent a 1996 makeover (following the opening of the larger Key West exhibit) to become a sick-bay and nursing station for mothers. *Special note:* Many guests make this group of tanks their first stop on the way in; try visiting in the afternoon.

Wild Arctic

A big hit since it opened in 1995, this smartly conceived trip to the frozen reaches begins with a motion-simulator ride aboard a helicopter. The 60-seat chopper flies out of a hanger and into the vast Arctic landscape, offering glimpses of narwhals, walruses and other marine life en route. The craft briefly sets down on the edge of a glacier, until a rumbling starts and propels the helicopter over the calving precipice. All is not lost, and you soon disembark at the exhibit area, Base Station Wild Arctic—a spectacular indoor environment simulating the Arctic milieu from inside the skeletal remains of an ice-encrusted, creaking sailing ship. Wrapped in rock outcrops and ice floes, three separate pools (900,000 gallons of 50-degree seawater in all) contain polar bears, white beluga whales and walruses, all of which can be viewed from both above and below the surging water level. This is a splendid and unique signature attraction for Sea World, as well as a cool respite from summer heat.

Length of ride: Four minutes, plus walk-through exhibit (allow 30 minutes). *Special note:* A line for the motion simulator ride forms immediately following the conclusion of each Shamu performance when more than 5000 visitors can flood out of the stadium; conversely, during Shamu World Focus the lines are shortest for Wild Arctic. Also watch for the exit of the nearby Ski Stadium shows. The ride portion of this attraction has a 42-inch minimum height requirement; if you don't want to partake in the helicopter trip to the Arctic (roughly comparable to Star Tours in its impact), you can bypass the simulators and proceed directly to the exhibit area. A nifty bonus for *imagineer* wannabees is that near the exit to the attraction on the right, before the gift shop, is a "flight observation deck" where you can see the ride in action—from its exterior.

AUTHOR'S OBSERVATION

Once called sea canaries, beluga whales are actually born gray, attaining their white coloration as they age—a camouflage from predators amid the ice floes of the frozen Arctic. Belugas can weigh from 1500 to 3300 pounds, and measure 10 to 15 feet in length; they feed on squid, octopus, shrimp and bottom-dwelling fish.

Also at Sea World

Pre-teens find the three-acre **Shamu's Happy Harbor** play area a delight, regardless of the size of crowds. Best time to visit is in the morning, before the first Shamu performance exits. **Clydesdale Hamlet** is a frequently overlooked corral of magnificent Clydesdale horses; if you're wondering why there are horses at Sea World, remember who owns the park. Which leads us to the **Anheuser-Busch Hospitality Center**, which offers free beer samples daily starting at 11 a.m.

Eating

Full-service dining is featured at **Bimini Bay Cafe**, which offers light, tropic-infused seafood and traditional cuisine. This pleasant, usually uncrowded setting overlooking the main lagoon offers conch chowder, fried gator nuggets, and crab quiche. A children's menu is also available.

The fast-food sold at Sea World is as good as or better than what is served at most other area theme parks. Best bet is **Mango Joe's Cafe**, located between Shamu and Wild Arctic, which features fajitas, salads, sandwiches and key lime pie. Near the sky tower is the **Waterfront Sandwich Grill** and **Smokehouse Chicken and Ribs**, offering barbecue and turkey sandwiches, burgers and brisket dinners. Information about the **Aloha Polynesian Luau** is provided under "Dinner Theaters" later in this chapter.

Sea World Touring Itinerary

Polar Bears at Sea World live in a re-created polar environment.

Because so much of the Sea World agenda focuses on scheduled performances in large arenas, it is difficult to outline an hour-by-hour itinerary. Too much depends on when and how many performances each show is scheduled for on a given day. Additionally, because Sea World doesn't require a dawn-to-dusk commitment like some of the other area attractions, many visitors choose to enter the park at noon or later, which means they encounter entirely different traffic patterns from the guests who arrive first thing in the morning. A few basic touring suggestions can help you best enjoy the park.

Sea World offers an ingenious courtesy at the Information Desk near the park entrance—a computer-generated itinerary based on when you enter the park. The agenda plots a path for you to see every scheduled show in the hours remaining until the park closes that particular day; then you work in exhibits in the time between shows. However, the recommended show schedule is not necessarily the most expedient. Because the park maximizes its profits from dining and shopping by keeping you on the premises longer, the suggested agenda Sea World provides for its guests spreads out the touring schedule to encompass an entire day. Nor does the schedule account for personal tastes. I suggest you skip the park's recommended itinerary and craft your own.

Although it's possible to tour the park in a clockwise (or counter-clockwise) fashion, at some point you'll probably find yourself backtracking or skipping a show to maintain forward momentum. The park's scheduled performance highlights in order of priority are: **Shamu**, **Hotel Clyde and Seamore** and the **Whale & Dolphin Discovery**. When you arrive, plot a schedule that will seat you at these three shows during the first two or three hours you are in the park. Remember, these shows may be performed as few as three times on a slow day. Allow at least 10 to 15 minutes to exit each show and walk to the next, which may be on the other side of the park. Kids also enjoy **Baywatch** and **Mermaids, Myths and Monsters**; incorporate these and the other remaining shows based on how long you want to stay in the park.

Don't forget to allow time to view exhibits. Although virtually all of the park's marine enclosures are worth touring, don't miss **Manatees: The Last Generation**, **Penguin Encounter**, **Terrors of the Deep** and **Wild Arctic**. Avoid Wild Arctic following the exit of Shamu. If you have kids along, you'll want to allow some play time for **Shamu's Happy Harbor**. Again, visit the remaining exhibits based on how long you want to stay in the park.

Guided Tours

At present, two guided tours are offered at Sea World, but more are reportedly in the works. The **Bird's Eye View Tour** is provided once daily at 12:30 p.m.; participants journey to up to 15 different park locations to feed the exotic collection of winged residents, some of which are endangered species. The **Polar Expedition Tour** is a "pole-to-pole" trip behind the scenes of two of the park's best exhibits: the polar bears of Wild Arctic, and the aviary of Penguin Encounter. The Polar tour is usually provided several times daily but the schedule changes frequently.

Reservations are not accepted for the guided tours and spaces are filled on a first-come, first-served basis. Each tour lasts one hour and is priced $5 per adult, $4 per child ages 3 to 9 (park admission not included). Call the tour

office the day before your Sea World visit to obtain exact times and itineraries, ☎ *(407) 363-2398.*

Orlando's Other Theme Parks

Wet 'n Wild

*The Surge, a five passenger tube ride through 600 ft. of exciting, banked curves
is Wet 'N' Wild's newest attraction.*

Staking a claim as both the world's first as well as the nation's best-attend-
ed water park, Wet 'n Wild continues to be the throbbing epicenter of teen
Orlando—a dubious honor for parents caught in the crossfire, but a notable
draw for young adults. Kids love this park and, during summer months, a
third or more of its visitors are locals. Of the region's water parks, the 25-
acre Wet 'n Wild also wins the award for the greatest quantity and variety of
slides in one location. Although compact, this park has many individual attractions and it has never reached its maximum capacity. When the Disney
parks fill up, Wet 'n Wild is almost sure to still have its ticket booth open.

INSIDER TIP

*If thrilling slides are what you are looking for, Orlando's four major water
parks are priced within a few dollars of each other, but offer a varying quantity of slide-type attractions. Not counting children's play areas, wave pools
or river floats, Wet 'n Wild has the largest number of rides with 10, while
Blizzard Beach and Water Mania both feature seven, and Typhoon Lagoon
has five. River Country, which is priced about $10 below the undiscounted
adult price of the other parks, has four rides.*

The only thing missing at Wet 'n Wild is a theme. Just as The Magic Kingdom is more than your typical amusement park back home, Disney's three water parks offer a lavish unifying concept that allows each to become more than the sum of its parts. At Wet 'n Wild, the park's personality is determined primarily by its rides (exciting), and customers (predominantly teenagers). But make no mistake, the park has a lot to offer and it stays busy in all but the coldest winter months.

Wet 'n Wild's noteworthy attractions include the thrilling **Black Hole**, a completely enclosed, pitch-black slide for two-person tubes that descend from the imposing flying saucer-like tower toward the rear of the park. The **Bubba Tub** is a popular family tube slide that becomes momentarily airborne as it flies over its two humps. The new **Fuji Flyer** is an exciting toboggan-style plunge down 450 feet of banked curves and speed-enhancing straightaways. The unique **Knee Ski** (the only ride of its type in the country) is a cable-towed kneeboard ride around the park's adjacent lake; watching riders in protective gear wipe out on the water is an entertainment in itself. The ultimate thrill is the harrowing **Bomb Bay**, where guests are dropped out of a capsule straight down onto a near-vertical slide. Also offered are the **Surf Lagoon**, which surges with four-foot waves, and the short **Lazy River** float, which loops through one end of the park. Your Wet 'n Wild ticket includes free admission to the **Congo River Miniature Golf** course next door.

Wet 'n Wild is the only one of Orlando's water parks that does not close during the winter months for annual maintenance. The park shuts down during inclement weather, which is not uncommon during summer months. Hours vary seasonally, but the park opens between 9 and 10 a.m. daily, and closes at 5 p.m. from November through March, and stays open later (as late as 11 p.m.) during the balance of the year. Call to determine the exact hours on the day you want to visit.

Adult admission (including tax) is $25.39; children ages 3 to 9 are $20.09; seniors 55 and over are $12.70. One noteworthy Wet 'n Wild feature is that admission is half-price during the last few hours the park is open (after 5 p.m. during summer months, otherwise after 3 p.m.). Wet 'n Wild is also part of the five- and seven-day Vacation Value Pass alliance (see "Coupons and Discount Offers" at the beginning of this chapter for details). Parking is $4; lockers are $4, plus a $3 deposit. An ATM is located next to the gift shop near the entrance. Picnic lunches may be brought in, but alcohol and glass containers may not. Beer and wine are sold at the park's fast-food stands. Wet 'n Wild is located at 6200 International Drive, two miles south of Universal Studios, two miles north of Sea World. Information, ☎ *(407) 351-9453 or (800) 992-9453.*

AUTHOR'S OBSERVATION

Wet 'n Wild's creator, George Millay, was one of the founders of Sea World in San Diego in the early '60s. He left the Sea World organization in the mid-1970s to build his concept of a participatory water theme park. Orlando's Wet 'n Wild was the world's first water park, and opened its doors in 1977 to overnight success.

Water Mania

WaterMania features 36 acres of waterslides, wave pools, thrill slides, kiddie pools, bumper boats, volleyball courts and picnic areas.

Another one of Orlando's five water parks, Water Mania lies just a stone's throw from the Disney property on U.S. 192. Promising "more splash for less cash" and a nifty simulated surfing experience, the park is actually priced almost identically to Wet 'n Wild, but Water Mania circulates discount coupons taking up to $4 off the gate admission (River Country, though smaller and less ride-oriented, is still cheaper). Like Wet 'n Wild, there is no connecting theme between the numerous attractions and, compared with the Disney operations, Water Mania subsequently delivers a similarly sterile water park experience.

Still, during the summer, this 36-acre facility provides the one thing locals and visitors desire: an escape from the heat—the park is visited by up to 4000 people a day during the summer months. The atmosphere is noticeably more family-oriented than at Wet 'n Wild; no alcohol is sold or allowed on the premises, and the heavily utilized three-acre picnic area in back features volleyball and basketball courts. Water Mania also boasts that it never reaches capacity, so when the Disney facilities have filled, you can still make your way to this park and be assured of getting in.

The unique highlight of the park is **Wipe Out**, the only surfing simulator in the Southeastern United States. One at a time, guests ride on a boogie board to surf the continuous wave formation. Surfing familiarity is not required to ride, but it helps; inexperienced riders get spit out of the wave after 30 seconds or so, wiping out into a lagoon. The park's other unusual ride is **The Banana Peel**, a two-passenger tube that plunges to the base of a 176-foot slide.

Water Mania's other attractions are variations of rides available at the other parks: **The Screamer** offers a seven-story free-fall drop, while the **Double Bozerker** next door is a twin-humped speed slide. Several family-style rides are featured, including **Cruisin' Creek**, an 850-foot-long river winding through the park, and a 720,000-gallon **wave pool** (bigger than Wet 'n Wild's). The children's play area is popular, as well as the basin containing **Barnacle Bob's Bumper Boats**. A miniature golf course next door, **The Big Chipper**, is $1 with Water Mania admission.

Water Mania's operational schedule varies seasonally, but the park typically opens at 9:30 or 10 a.m. and closes around dusk; the park is usually down for maintenance in December and January. Like the other water parks, Water Mania shuts down during inclement weather. Adult admission (including tax) is $25.63, children ages 3 to 12 are $19.21. Parking is $3; lockers are $4.28, plus $2 deposit. Picnic lunches may be brought in, but alcohol and glass containers are prohibited. The park is located at 6073 U.S. 192, a half-mile east of I-4, outside Kissimmee. Information, ☎ *(407) 396-2626 or (800) 527-3092.*

Splendid China

 Splendid China is a curiosity of the first order—a theme park based on miniaturized replicas of China's cultural and architectural highlights. The facility had its genesis in a similar park built in Shenzen, China (near Hong Kong) in 1989. There, Chinese and other citizens strolled respectfully amid a lavish (if sanitized) re-creation of their country's history. The park's creators (which are pointedly, and repeatedly, said to *not* be the Chinese government) decided to share their great concept on the other side of the world, and promote Chinese tourism to boot. Where better to mount this production than the theme-park capital of the world?

Not surprisingly, the Orlando park, said to have cost $100 million to build, has suffered a different fate since its 1993 opening; some visitors have walked away with "souvenirs" from the models, the grass is frequently mottled, and a few of the miniature Chinese citizens depicted have been decapitated or knocked over. Some of the ambient music is less than authentic—low-grade synthesizer music that cheapens the setting. Further, attentive visitors will note that China's less-pristine recent historical footnotes are frequently downplayed in favor of the country's architectural highlights. Buddhists and human-rights activists, in particular, have repeatedly protested the park, which includes a replica of Tibet's Potola Palace.

Splendid China in Kissimmee features 60 Chinese landmarks replicated in detail. China's best entertainers perform acrobatics and dances.

Nonetheless, though it may be the black sheep of capitalist Orlando, 76-acre Splendid China presents a unique image of a land of astonishing diversity and scope. The detailed craftsmanship that went into creating the park is impressive: approximately 120 artisans spent over two years building the miniaturized country. Live entertainment from China, featuring dancers and acrobats in authentic costumes, help round out the mix.

Perhaps Splendid China's greatest strength (and most unenviable marketing obstacle) lies in the fact that it isn't what visitors to Orlando expect. The park doesn't boast any rides or fast-paced entertainments; it's subdued even when compared with its likeliest competition—Epcot's World Showcase. But for many, particularly seniors, Splendid China is a breath of fresh air amid the usual clutter of bigger, faster, wilder attractions.

In summer, 1996, the admission gate to Splendid China was relocated to help boost the lagging sales at the park's atmospheric shopping area. **Chinatown** (formerly named Suzhou Gardens), is now open to the general public and can be visited without purchasing an admission. Originally a full-size replica of a 13th-century commercial district, the new Chinatown is meant to embrace a microcosm of urban Chinatowns all over the United States.

The village is lovingly detailed and contains a number of shops and restaurants. Cloisonnè jewelry, silk clothing, porcelain, jade, herbs, bonsai and wind chimes are among the imported offerings for sale. A 12-minute video presentation, "This is Splendid China," shown in the makeshift **Harmony Hall Theater**, is a good introduction to the actual sights of China.

The second touring area, the paid-admission **Exhibit Park**, contains the miniatures and, like the country itself, is intimidating in its size. To visit all 57 exhibits, allow at least two hours; more if you stop for any of the several shows offered along the route. The guidemap provided at the front entrance numbers all of the exhibits in a logical walking tour and notes those of special interest if you only want to see the highlights.

Perhaps the most impressive recreation is also the biggest: **The Great Wall**, created using some 6 million, tiny, hand-laid bricks and stretching more than a half-mile along one side of the park's perimeter. Other sights include the 15th-century, 9999-room **Imperial Palace** and **Forbidden City**; the underground cave housing the magnificent **Terra Cotta Warriors** of Xi'an; the 35-foot **Leshan Grand Buddha Statue** modeled after the 24-story sculpture carved into a mountain; and the pink and white **Potola Palace**, Tibet's capital and the center of one of China's contemporary diplomatic tussles.

Although each of the exhibits posts a one-paragraph explanation of what one is viewing, two options are available for guided tours. You may take a two-hour guided walking tour of the park for $5 per person, or up to five persons can take a two-hour, golf-cart tour of Splendid China for $48.15 (tax included). A color souvenir book provides additional background and is available at Chinatown's gift shops. Sporadically scheduled but free tram service provides relief for tired soles (and a much-abbreviated tour of the park).

A 900-seat outdoor, covered amphitheater, the **Temple of Light Theater**, is located toward the rear of the park, and is the setting for some of the entertainment offerings provided throughout the day. Other performances are scheduled in other venues located within the park. The schedule changes daily (in part based on the visa requirements of the Chinese-native performers), but typically includes a costume show, music, dance and ballet, acrobats, martial arts and magic shows; an entertainment guide is provided at the park entrance.

Splendid China has several eating facilities, but not all are operated daily. **Suzhou Pearl** is the park's most authentic restaurant, with a relatively expensive menu featuring gourmet Chinese selections. The **Seven Flavors** in Chinatown and **Wind and Rain Court** next to the Temple of Light Theater both offer cafeteria-style dining with Chinese dishes and a smattering of western selections. There are food carts with snacks and drinks scattered throughout the Exhibit Park area.

Since virtually all of Splendid China's exhibits are outside in a minimally shaded environment, visitors should wear cool clothing and sun hats, drink plenty of water. In fact, touring the park in the late afternoon and early evening is an excellent plan. During busy season, Splendid China is sometimes open after dark when the lighted miniatures become a fairyland.

Hours: Varies seasonally, but open daily. Adult admission (tax included) is $23.55; children ages 5 to 12, $13.90; seniors 55 and older, $21.20; children 4 and under are free. Parking is free. Wheelchairs and baby strollers may be rented at the main entrance for $5. There is an ATM machine located at Guest Services, near the main entrance. Splendid China is located at 3000 Splendid China Boulevard, two miles west of Disney's "Maingate" on U.S. 192, and three miles west of I-4 via exit 25B. Information, ☎ *(407) 397-8800* or *(800) 244-6226.*

Gatorland

You gotta love Gatorland. Equal parts hokey and educational, shameless and interesting, the family-owned attraction harkens back to another era of Florida tourism, when billboards announced roadside tourist traps with gleeful hype. In the '90s, Gatorland, like most of the area's secondary attractions, has been forced to evolve in order to avoid being trampled by Mickey. Today, Gatorland has subsequently engineered one of the region's more successful makeovers. Wisely, instead of re-inventing its attractions with high-tech thrill rides, the Godwin family has polished its wares, added an educational angle, and built a nifty boardwalk into the real swamp behind the facility. The result is a small but entertaining theme park requiring only a couple of hours to tour.

Gatorland opened in 1949 as an alligator farm, and harvesting the meat and skin is still done on the premises today; the farm also produces the only artificially inseminated alligator hatchlings. The entrance to the attraction—through the enormous jaws of a fiberglass gator—is a classic, and leads right into the ticket booth (and a gift shop, of course). Beyond the entrance lie the enormous ponds that house the bulk of the 50-plus-acre park's approximately 4000 American alligators. A series of cages contains monkeys, crocodiles, a black bear and Florida white-tail deer. Three 15-minute shows are scheduled throughout the day; in order of increasing absurdity, they are the **Snakes of Florida** show, the **Gator Wrestling** show and the **Gator Jumparoo**. In the latter performance, chicken carcasses are strung out over the main pond where languid alligators eventually lunge pathetically for the meat (the best show is usually the first of the morning when gators are hungriest).

wild-
life

Gatorland in nearby Kissimmee has more than 5000 alligators and crocodiles.

The highlight of the park is a 10-acre alligator breeding marsh behind the main facility. In 1991, a 2000-foot elevated boardwalk was extended through this area for guests. Since then, an increasing number of birds, drawn by the nesting gators, have been using the marsh; a three-story observation tower provides additional views. March through August finds hundreds of wading birds building nests and rearing their young, including snowy and cattle egrets, green and little blue herons, anhingas and others. Late August and early September is gator hatching period.

INSIDER TIP

A noteworthy period to tour Gatorland is mornings in May, when the gators bellow their loud mating call. This low, guttural sound is also produced when the Space Shuttle breaks the sound barrier on an approach to a Florida landing. During summer months, the gators are known to hover at the bottom of the ponds as a way of escaping the region's intense heat.

A narrow gauge railroad circles most of Gatorland and provides a little history; the free train ride takes about 10 minutes. The park has a snack bar inside an old-fashioned Florida "cracker" house, **Pearl's Smokehouse**, featuring deep-fried gator nuggets and smoked gator ribs, chicken sandwiches and soft drinks. The recently refurbished, swamp-themed gift shop at the entrance features alligator leather items and other Florida souvenirs.

Gatorland is open daily from 8 a.m. to dusk, rain or shine. Admission (tax included) is $12.67 for adults, and $9.49 for children ages 3 to 9; seniors over 55 are $10.13. Parking is free. Wheelchair and stroller rental is $3.50. The park is located at 14501 South Orange Blossom Trail (U.S. 441), four miles north of U.S. 192 and Kissimmee. Information, ☎ *(407) 855-5496* or *(800) 393-5297.*

Church Street Station

Church Street Station is a block long entertainment/restaurant complex in the heart of downtown Orlando.

One of the more ingenious original concepts to spring up in Orlando was Church Street Station, a nightclub and amusement park rolled into one, block-long entertainment complex that recycled a series of quaint late-19th-century buildings.

The Church Street facility developed by entrepreneur Bob Snow opened in 1974 as Rosie O'Grady's, in a run-down section of downtown Orlando next to the train tracks. Against all odds, the lively bar was a fast success and business boomed. Snow bought adjoining dilapidated buildings to add to his creation, which reached its apex with the 1982 completion of the ornate Cheyenne Saloon. Long on turn-of-the-century ambiance, the operation today is made up of a series of interconnecting saloons and dance halls. So successful was Snow's endeavor that it fueled both the revitalization of downtown Orlando and, of course, inspired a Disney copycat—Pleasure Island.

A major difference with the Disney venture is that Church Street Station is built within and around a restored area of downtown Orlando—the architecture is authentic, late-1800s Victorian, with real antiques and embellishments. But beyond architectural considerations, both complexes have their own distinct personalities, defined largely by their guests: Church Street draws a hefty number of locals, creating a genuine street-party atmosphere, particularly on Friday and Saturday nights, while Pleasure Island is frequented mostly by out-of-towners.

AUTHOR'S OBSERVATION

Some of the antiques on hand at Church Street Station are quite impressive. Inside the Cheyenne Saloon is a collection of ornate antique guns, one set once owned by Jesse James, while the solid rosewood pool tables upstairs are 1885 Brunswick authentics. The front bar at Apple Annie's Courtyard is reconstructed from an 18th-century French communion rail, and some of the booths were once church pews. But some of the choicest "props" are the steel-backed, green velvet chairs once used by Al Capone and situated at one table of Lili Marlene's Aviator's Pub and Restaurant—the steel reinforcement helped guard against an unexpected shot in the back.

Another important distinction is that much of Church Street can be visited without purchasing admission, which means that you can stop by early one evening and test the waters before buying a ticket. Free of admission charges, you can stroll through **Commander Ragtime's** video and midway games area, and into the vast **Exchange Shopping Emporium** (open until 11 p.m.), as well as **Apple Annie's Courtyard**, an airy, wrought iron-wrapped indoor Victorian garden serving fruit and ice cream drinks. Several restaurants are available, including the plush but pricey **Lili Marlene's**, and the area immediately surrounding the Church Street Station complex features a number of other clubs and bars. A romantic horse-drawn carriage circuits nearby Lake Eola Park.

What your Church Street ticket buys you is admission to the four clubs, the most famous of which is **Rosie O'Grady's Good Time Emporium**, an ornate, turn-of-the-century saloon featuring banjos, Dixieland Jazz, can-can girls, Charleston dancers and singing waiters. The festive room is decorated with antique brass chandeliers, etched mirrors and leaded glass. Opened in 1982, the **Cheyenne Saloon and Opera House** is a three-level tribute to the Old West, with a nightly Grand Old Opry-style country jamboree keeping the large dance floor bustling—the six chandeliers overhead are from the Philadelphia Mint (circa 1895), and adorned with the imprint of coins minted during the era. Rock music from the '50s through the '90s is performed live in the **Orchid Garden Ballroom**, which features an elevated dance floor surrounded by wrought-iron balconies and balustrades, brick floor, and stained and beveled glass. **Phineas Phogg's Dance Club** is a high-energy disco set amid ballooning memorabilia of the past and present; this club doesn't start jumping until around midnight, and guests must be 21 or older. Phogg's version of happy hour on Wednesdays, Nickel Beer Night, is very popular with locals.

The live shows at Rosie O'Grady's, the Orchid Garden and the Cheyenne Saloon last 45 to 60 minutes each and are staggered throughout the evening, but it can be a little difficult (due to overlapping performances) to map out an efficient schedule. If you want to sample each of the three, obtain the showtime schedule at the ticket booth and ask one of the employees to provide some input. Allow about four hours—more if you plan to include a sit-down meal. Keep in mind the restaurants do not take reservations.

Church Street Station opens daily at 11 a.m. with paid-admission activities beginning about 7 p.m.; the joint shuts down at 1 a.m. Sundays through Thursdays, and is open until 2 a.m. Fridays and Saturdays. Admission (tax included) is $17.97 per adult, children ages 4 through 12 are $11.61; discount coupons are widely available, as is an annual pass. Church Street Station is located in downtown Orlando, at the intersection of Garland Avenue and Church Street two blocks east of I-4 (use Exit 38 from I-4 and follow the signs). There are several parking garages in the immediate vicinity; most charge a flat $5 during the evening. Many of the non-Disney area hotels provide transportation to and from Church Street, a worthy inquiry if you're planning on drinking along with the crowd. Additional information, ☎ *(407) 422-2434.*

Medieval Times' dinner and tournament takes participants back to the days of knights in armor, chivalry and regal feasts.

Dinner Theaters

"Orlando may have lost an orchestra due to lack of interest, the bal-
let may be running into bad times, but like Vegas did with casinos, the
tourist ghetto has sprouted a mutated strain of dinner theater as a
bigger, better, louder Dinner Show Experience. Are there lessons here?
Maybe the ballet wouldn't be in trouble if only they would sling hash
during 'Swan Lake.' Maybe the symphony would still be around if only
they offered free beer. If there's one thing high culture can learn from
the packed houses of dinner theater, it's promise them anything, but
give them ribs."

—Liz Langley, Orlando Weekly

Once known as the last bastion of almost-retired soap stars, the Orlando
dinner-theater scene has evolved into something more than uninspired reviv-
als of *Camelot* performed for a sea of blue hair. Instead, for sheer, grandiose
diversion, the food-and-entertainment spectacle executed nightly in Orlando has almost no equal. At least 12 semi-permanent productions are in place,
and visitors flock to them in droves, lured by the promise of both all-you-
can-eat grub and flashy entertainment. In the past year alone, two more
mammoth food halls have opened—**American Gladiators** and **Pirates Dinner
Adventure**—each seemingly equating bigger with better.

The food is not what draws people to Orlando's dinner theaters—the cuisine is basic but generally served in great quantities. Most of the theaters
offer vegetarian meals, but you'll need to make the request at the time of
your reservation. Unlimited beer and wine is included, including the special
alcoholic beverages noted below (the wine can be deadly); most outfits provide a cash bar for stronger enticements.

Selecting one venue to recommend above the fray isn't easy. A lot depends
on your personal taste (do you prefer your gladiators in gleaming chainmail
or Day-Glo Spandex?). Whether you have kids along is another factor, as
well as your tolerance for being roped into performing alongside the paid
cast. But I'll pass along three observations: **Arabian Nights** has been selected
by the *Orlando Sentinel's* Osceola edition readers as the best dinner show in
town three years in a row, while the dinner theater locals choose to take their
out-of-town guests to is **Sleuth's**, according to *Orlando Magazine.* But,
when Prince William and Prince Harry of Great Britain visited Orlando a
couple years ago with their mother Diana, their single favorite experience of
the whole trip was Disney's long-running **Hoop Dee Doo Revue**.

Discount coupons abound for all of these shows except the two Disney
productions (the Polynesian Luau and the Hoop Dee Doo Revue). During
spring 1996, tickets for **King Henry's Feast** were discounted by as much as

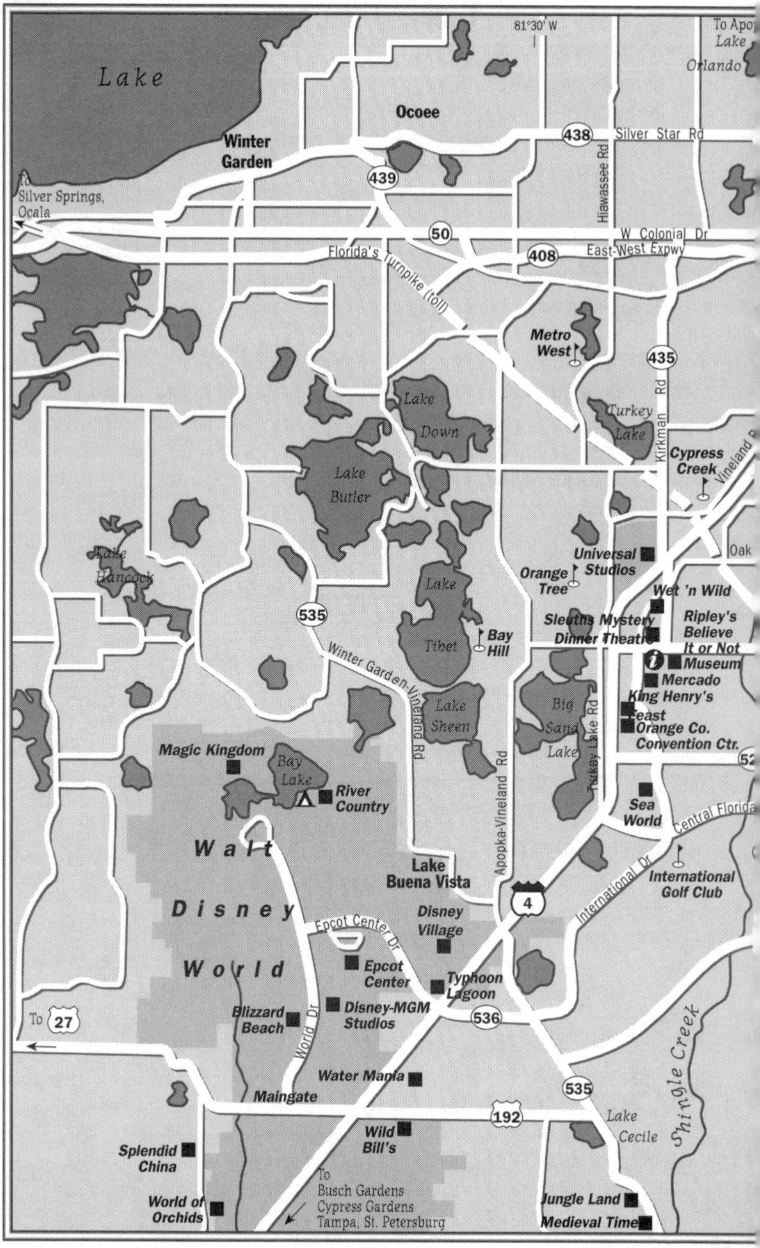

UNIVERSAL STUDIOS, SEA WORLD AND OTHER ATTRACTIONS

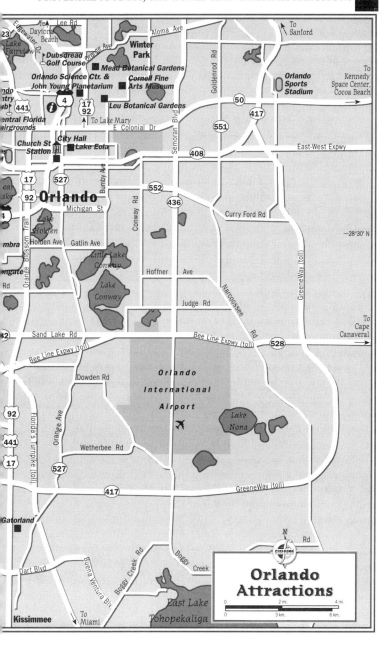

Orlando Attractions

$8.40 off the gate admission price. Not to be undersold, **Capone's** dropped its price from $35.99 to $24.34 for coupon-holders. Leaf through the local visitor publications for coupons before buying your tickets, or purchase admission at your hotel or at one of the "discount dealers" that line the U.S. 192 and I-Drive corridors, including the **Orlando Convention and Visitor's Bureau** office at 8723 International Drive. Prices listed below include tax, but not gratuity; nor do they include the cost of the requisite photos taken of guests that are offered for sale (or blackmail) at the end of the evening. Reservations are "required" for all dinner theaters, but this is primarily to gauge food preparations; if you arrive at show time and seats are still available, you will not be turned away.

Except as noted, the theaters offer nightly performances (times vary seasonally), and some schedule up to three shows on evenings when demand is high. All admission/dinner prices include tax.

Aloha Polynesian Luau

Adults are $31.75; juniors ages 8 to 12, $21.15; children ages 3 to 7, $10.55. Sea World park admission is not required.
Reservations, ☎ (407) 351-3600.
Sea World's two-hour indoor luau show features music by the Hawaiian Rhythms, a Samoan fire-knife dance, and hula demonstrations. Roast pork loin, mahi mahi, sweet-and-sour chicken, and one complementary mai tai are the featured food and drink items; the meal is served family-style at tables seating eight or 12 in a dining area that holds 276. A shell lei is provided on arrival.

American Gladiators - Orlando Live

Adults, $34.95; children ages 3 to 12, $21.50, including gratuity. It's also possible to attend the show without purchasing dinner: adults $27.95; children ages 3 to 12, $15.95.
Reservations, ☎ (407) 390-0000 or (800) 228-8534.
A 90-minute recreation of the television show that opened for Christmas 1995, American Gladiators is played out in a 1600-seat arena bedecked in red, white and blue, and features such events as Powerball, Jousting, the Wall and Whiplash (nothing like a little choreographed physical aggression to round out a family vacation, eh?). The muscle-and-Spandex performers—Hawk, Turbo, Siren, Jazz and others—mingle with the audience between exertions. The high-testosterone show also includes dance numbers, explosions and other special effects; the food is "healthier," and features a chicken entree.

Arabian Nights

Adults, $39.54; children ages 3 to 11, $25.63.
Reservations, ☎ (407) 239-9223 or (800) 553-6116.
More than 50 horses are the focus of this popular two-hour show, including Lippizans, Andalusians, Quarter Horses and Arabians. The show has a storyline (something about a genie, a gossamered princess, and a knight in shining armor), but the real attraction is the horses; their riders recreate the chariot race from "Ben Hur," perform Wild West stunts, and close with a musical tribute to the U.S.A. A tiered, 1200-person seating area surrounds the 56,000-square-foot arena, the world's larg-

est indoor equestrian facility. Prime rib or vegetable lasagna are the main meal offerings; beer and wine are served and a cash bar is available for other drinks.

Capone's Dinner Show

Adults, $35.99; children ages 3 to 12, $18 (including mandatory gratuity).
Reservations, ☎ *(407) 397-2378 or (800) 220-8428.*
The focus here is on gangsters and gams, circa 1931 Chicago. Admittance to Capone's 350-seat speakeasy and cabaret is via a secret password and leads to a small-scale musical featuring singing and dancing, and a bit of action. Lasagna, stuffed shells, Italian sausage, baked chicken and ham are served buffet-style; beer, sangria and rum runners are available. *Length of show:* one hour and 45 minutes; heavily reliant on audience participation.

Hoop Dee Doo Revue

Adults, $38.16; children ages 3 to 11, $19.08.
Reservations, ☎ *(407) 939-3463.*
Enormously popular for many years, the Hoop Dee Doo is performed in Pioneer Hall, a barn-like structure within Disney's Wilderness Campground facility. The 90-minute "Hee Haw"-style storyline is better developed than some, and concerns a roving troupe of eight performers on a circuit of the Old West. There's a wholesome romance and plenty of slapstick humor making the sum effect *almost* charming. The food includes fried chicken, barbecued ribs, corn, baked beans, wine and beer. Tables for this show are booked weeks in advance during the summer and other busy periods; if you want to see Hoop Dee Doo, call Disney's reservation office as soon as your travel plans have firmed and lock down a slot. Pioneer Hall has no parking facilities, so guests must take a bus from the parking lot in front of the Wilderness Campground entrance to the Hoop Dee Doo (a situation that is currently under discussion within the Disney organization); allow at least 20 minutes from the campground parking lot to the Hall.

King Henry's Feast

Adults, $37.05; children ages 3 to 11, $23.27.
Reservations, ☎ *(407) 351-5151 or (800) 883-8181.*
It's King Henry VIII's birthday, and you're invited! The celebration features 16th-century-style delights such as sword-swallowing, jesters, juggling, battling knights and a trapeze artist. The two-hour show is performed in a 650-seat castle/theater with guests seated at long, wooden tables where they are served baked chicken, sliced pork, and a potato leek soup; beer and wine are served along with soft drinks.

Mark Two Dinner Theater

Evening prices, $32.50 to $40, depending on table location; matinees, $27.50 to $35.00 (including tax); children ages 12 and under, $5 off.
Reservations, ☎ *(407) 843-6275 or (800) 726-6275.*
The single traditional dinner show experience in town, the 324-seat Mark Two is the only equity theater company in Orlando, and has produced more than 100 musicals since its 1986 opening. Each show runs six to seven weeks and is performed evenings Wednesday through Sunday, with matinees Wednesday, Thursday and Saturday. The meal is served before the curtain goes up, with dessert at intermission; featured menu items are prime rib, chicken, fish and pasta. Upcoming pro-

ductions scheduled include "I Do I Do," "Zorba," "Crazy for You," and "Gypsy." Tables seat two or four apiece.

Medieval Times Dinner and Tournament

Adults, $37.40; children ages 3 to 12, $24.56.
Reservations, ☎ (407) 239-0214 or (800) 229-8300.

A 90-minute show involving hand-to-hand combat, precision equestrian drills and jousting by handsome, color-coded knights. As for food, the feast is provided without silverware so that you can enjoy the authentic pleasure of ripping apart a whole roasted chicken with your bare hands. Beer, a "fruity wine cocktail" and soft drinks are provided, along with a cash bar. For an extra buck, you get to tour the ever-so-appetizing torture chamber. Also note: you are required to wear a paper crown, its color signifying which of six knights you are expected to cheer. This is part of the chain of similarly named attractions in Dallas, Los Angeles, Chicago and New Jersey.

Polynesian Luau

Adults, $36.04; children ages 3 to 11, $19.08. A late afternoon show, Mickey's Tropical Luau, is geared for kids with somewhat reduced prices: adults, $31.80; children ages 3 to 11, $14.84.
Reservations, ☎ (407) WDW-DINE.

A 90-minute South Seas music and dance revue a' la Mickey—and probably the most castmember skin you'll see exposed within Walt Disney World territory—is performed nightly at this outdoor theater next to Disney's Polynesian Resort. Colorful costumes, fire eating, ceremonial drums, ukulele music and hula dancing are the focus of the performance, held at a cove on the shore of the Seven Seas Lagoon. The food includes roast pork, chicken cooked in coconut milk, and marinated salmon sushi, easily among the more adventurous dinner theater menus.

Sleuths Mystery Dinner Show

Adults, $35.99; children ages 3 to 11, $24.33.
Reservations, ☎ (407) 363-1985 or (800) 393-1895.

This show features a 2.5-hour comedy-mystery. The cast (in character) greets you as an invited guest to an English drawing room complete with gargoyles and secret panels. Between dinner courses that offer Cornish game hen, a murder takes place and you are invited to help solve the whodunit. Red herrings litter the scene, and guests are allowed to ponder the mystery between acts (the solutions are harder than one might think), then interrogate the crew before casting their vote. Two smallish theaters (one seats 100, the other 170) make the experience much more intimate than the other dinner spectacles, and reservations are wise. Eight scripts are played in rotation, and repeat guests can call to find out which story is scheduled. The chemistry of the audience can make or break this show.

Wild Bill's Wild West Dinner Extravaganza

Adults, $36.33; children ages 3 to 11, $21.35.
Reservations, ☎ (407) 351-5151 or (800) 883-8181.

Wild Bill and Miss Kitty host this two-hour western-themed spectacle which is flashier although less intimate than Disney's Hoop Dee Doo. Set in an 1870s-style, 650-seat cavalry mess hall, Wild Bill's traveling show features can can dancers, as well as

Native American dancers, rodeo tricks and sing-alongs. Audience participation is mandatory and includes a bleating and mooing contest; you'll wear a cardboard cowboy hat. Fried chicken and barbecue ribs are the featured entree.

Around Orlando

Groups such as the Southern Ballet perform often in Orlando.

"This is a city well aware that, for many foreign visitors, Orlando represents the face of America, and it wants to make a good impression. The streets are clean, the fountains bubble, vibrant landscaping is lovingly maintained, and the band shell in downtown's picture-perfect Lake Eola Park is almost always in use. Orlando and Walt Disney World grew up together, and the city has tried to duplicate the theme parks to create one seamless experience."

—Jeff Truesdell, Editor, *Orlando Weekly*

Contrary to popular rumor, entertainment in Orlando is not limited to the region's theme parks—though with the 1994 crash of the city's symphony due to lack of funding, it's probably wise not to set one's sights too high. For current entertainment information, pick up a copy of the free *Orlando Weekly* (available on Thursdays), or the Friday edition of the *Orlando Sentinel*, where a "Calendar" section provides extended entertainment listings.

Lake Eola Park is the city's pride and joy. A 1995 *Orlando Magazine* reader's poll covering the "Best of Orlando" found Lake Eola tops in almost every category asking readers to name a place. Readers voted Lake Eola Park the best place to pop the question, best place to hear live music, best place to unwind, best place to take out-of-towners, best place for people-watching, and the best place for in-line skating (even though it's not officially allowed). Originally dedicated in 1892, the inner-city park fell on hard times during the 1970s. Through the determination of frustrated residents, its rebirth has been a victory that has helped spur the revitalization of downtown Orlando. The trademark jello-mold style fountain is restored, a playground has been built, and the park is once again safe for families. A half-mile brick walkway circles the lake, or you may rent a two-person, swan-shaped pedal boat—either route is rewarding. The lakeside Disney Amphitheater is home to Orlando's annual spring **Shakespeare Festival** as well as host to regular music events.

International Drive is Orlando's tourist hub, and it throbs with activity from early morning until late at night. Many smaller attractions are located along this corridor, with Sea World and Universal Studios anchoring either end, about four miles apart. If you're up for accommodations with a taste of Orlando as it once might have been, try overnighting at the **Courtyard at Lake Lucerne**, three residences near downtown that have been lovingly restored to their Victorian and art deco eras (see "Other Possibilities" in "Hotels and Accommodations").

Finally, it's a pleasure to note that a genuine nature preserve lies in the forests smack dab between Walt Disney World and Orlando. The **Tibet-Butler Reserve**, located along the Winter Garden Vineland Road (State Route 535) offers trails, interpretive programs and the chance to see alligators and bald eagles in their natural habitat.

For additional information, call the Orlando/Orange County Convention and Visitors Bureau ☎ *(407) 363-5872.*

Museums and Exhibits

Orange County Historical Museum ★★

812 East Rollins Street, Orlando, 32803, from I-4, take Exit 43; go east on Princeton a half-mile to Loch Haven Park, ☎ *(407) 897-6350.*
Hours: 9 a.m.–5 p.m.
Special hours: Sunday: noon–5 p.m.

An interesting trip into central Florida's past. Highlights include Fire Station No. 3, a brick structure built in 1926 and now Orlando's oldest standing fire station, complete with a ladder truck and horse-powered steamer; a turn-of-the-century newspaper pressroom; and an exhibit that captures the enormous changes in central Florida created by the all-important citrus industry. Admission: $2 adults; $1.50 seniors; $1 children.

Orlando Museum of Art ★★★★

2416 North Mills Avenue, Orlando, 32803, I-4 to Exit 43 East; follow Princeton to Loch Haven Park, ☎ *(407) 896-4231.*
Hours: 10 a.m.–5 p.m.
Special hours: The museum will be closed January-April 1997. Closed: Mon.

In 1996-1997, the Orlando Museum of Art underwent a major expansion, in large part to accommodate the Imperial Tombs of China exhibition. The last stop on a five-city U.S. tour, this collection of antiquities, jewels and priceless relics is considered by Chinese officials to be the most important exhibition to leave Chinese soil, and displays some of the glittering artifacts meant to accompany the emperors and their courts into the next world. Spanning 2500 years and nine dynasties, highlights include the entire throne room from the Qing Dynasty's (A.D. 1644 to A.D. 1911) Shenyang Palace, containing a six-foot-high, gold-lacquered throne. Also on exhibit are four life-size terra-cotta warriors and a chariot horse found guarding the tomb of Qin Shi-huang-di (259 B.C. to 210 B.C.), the first emperor of China, as well as a magnificent jade burial suit assembled for Lui Sui, Prince of Liang, from 2007 pieces of gleaming jade stitched together with more than two pounds of gold thread (and estimated to have taken 10 years to construct). More than 200 other rare objects such as bronze and silver vessels, cloisonnè, precious jewels will be part of the show. The Chinese exhibition will be on display from May 2, 1997, through Sept. 15, 1997. The regular collection which will be on display through Dec. 31, 1996, and then goes back on display after Imperial Tombs closes, includes 19th- and 20th-century American art. The holdings include Floridians John Singer Sargent, George Innes and Milton Avery, and a worthy trove of pre-Columbian and African artifacts. The Orlando Museum of Art was founded in 1924 and was cited by *Newsweek* as one of the best museums in the south. There is also a Disney-sponsored, hands-on "Art Encounter" that helps children appreciate the museum's collection. Admission for Imperial Tombs of China: $12 adults; $10 seniors and students; $6 children ages 4 to 16. Imperial Tombs of China hours: Sun.–Thurs., 9 a.m. to 10 p.m.; Fri.–Sat., 9 a.m.–11 p.m. Regular hours and general admission vary, call the number listed above to confirm. Admission: $4 adults; $2 children age 4–11.

Orlando Science Center ★★★

810 East Rollins Street, Orlando, 32803, quarter-mile east of I-4 at Exit 43, in Loch Haven Park, ☎ *(407) 896-7151.*
Hours: 9 a.m.–5 p.m.
Special hours: Friday: 9 a.m.–9 p.m.; Sunday: noon–5 p.m.

A kid-friendly excursion into the world of science, this interactive museum invites youngsters to feel their way through an assortment of simple experiments that help to demystify tornados, wetlands and other natural phenomena. The museum also hosts visiting shows—a dinosaur exhibit, featuring a 22-foot-high Tyrannosaurus Rex, will be in place through December 1996—and a major expansion will be complete by February 1997. Admission includes a ticket to the museum's planetarium show. Admission: $6.50 adults, $5.50 children age 3–11.

Trainland ★★

8255 International Drive, Orlando, 32819, quarter-mile south of Sand Lake Road, behind Ripley's Believe It or Not, ☎ *(407) 363-9002.*
Hours: 10 a.m.–10 p.m.
Special hours: Sunday: 10 a.m. to 6 p.m.

Here's a concept the mouse hasn't appropriated... yet. Containing one of the largest G-gauge model train layouts and a Rocky Mountain theme, Trainland features a 14-foot-long wooden trestle, a Santa's Village, a replica of Pike's Peak and other requisite miniatures in a train-lover's ideal fantasy layout, covering 5000 square feet in all. A scavenger hunt for details keeps older kids enthralled, and a steam locomotive for real-life passengers is in the works. Admission: $6.36 adult; $5.30 senior; $4.24 child age 4–12.

Parks and Gardens

Harry P. Leu Gardens

1920 North Forest Avenue, Orlando, 32803, Use Exit 43 from I-4 to Princeton East; go right on Mills, left on Virginia, left on Forest to Leu Gardens, ☎ (407) 246-2620. Hours: 9 a.m.–5 p.m.

An off-the-beaten track Orlando treasure, Leu Gardens is a 50-acre botanical paradise on the edge of Lake Rowena. The garden is known for its camellias—the largest documented collection in the East, with more than 200 varieties that bloom from October to March. Hibiscus, ginger, azaelias and orchids are also lovingly cultivated, guaranteeing that something in flower year-round. A 50-foot floral clock imported from Scotland overlooks the largest formal rose garden south of Atlanta, and a network of paths circuit the gardens. Tours of the Leu House, a restored, late-19th-century farmhouse, are provided every 30 minutes. Admission: $3 adults; $1 children age 6–16.

Theaters

Civic Theatre of Central Florida, The

1001 East Princeton Street, Orlando, 32803, East Princeton at North Mills Avenue, ☎ (407) 896-7365.

A complex of three theaters seating from 140 to 400, the Civic Theatre of Central Florida is a year-round production facility for an impressive variety of plays and musicals. Among the highlights are a free Monday Night Playreading Series; a Radical Classics Series featuring the work of Joe Orton, George Bernard Shaw and others; a Family Classics series performed on weekends fall through spring, and a Summer Musical series. Call for additional information about performances. Admission: Prices vary.

Theme/Amusement Parks

Mystery Fun House

5767 Major Boulevard, Orlando, 32819, use Exit 30B from I-4; north on Kirkman half-mile, right on Major, ☎ (407) 351-3355.
Hours: 10 a.m.–11 p.m.

An old-fashioned carnival fun house is the main feature of this antiquated entertainment complex across the street from Universal Studios and next to the Radisson Twin Towers hotel complex. Inside the fun house is a maze of dark corridors and chambers that tour a hall of mirrors; a spinning, walk-thorugh drum; an Egyptian pyramid tomb with disorienting, tilted floors; and other thrills. Your enjoyment of the fun house is roughly proportionate to the pleasure you take in having things jump out at you in the dark; those who enjoy vibrating floors, air guns and pitch-black hallways will be in hog heaven. Also on the property is a laser tag game called "Starbase Omega" (allow 30 minutes), and a sub-par, dinosaur-themed miniature golf course called "Jurassic Putt"—one of Orlando's more shopworn attractions. Admission to the Fun House is $8.43; laser tag and mini golf are additional (each of the three attractions can be purchased via a discounted combo ticket), or you can hang out in the extensive video arcade. Admission: $8.43 all ages (Fun House only).

Ripley's Believe It or Not ★★

8201 International Drive, Orlando, 32819, quarter-mile south of Sand Lake Road,
☎ *(407) 363-4418.*
Hours: 10 a.m.–11 p.m.

A time-honored gallery of the odd and the obscure, Ripley's is a museum for both trivia freaks and for those impressed by the absurd lengths people will go to be noticed. Some visitors find the exhibit hoakey, but most are entertained by the assemblage of cultural perversities and minutia. Be warned that many kids used to the fast pace of other theme parks won't have the patience for an in-depth tour. The rotating exhibits may include a three-legged ukelele player, a full-size car made from more than 1 million matchsticks, a Mona Lisa made from croutons, and a Lincoln portrait fashioned from human hair, plus the usual assortment of shrunken heads and curious animal remains. But the the most spectacular sight is the most permanent one: a corner of the museum's tilted exterior facade appears to be sinking dramatically into a Florida sinkhole! Admission: $10.55 adults; $7.37 children age 4–12.

Terror on Church Street takes visitors on a frightening adventure to witness the most horrifying scenes of all time.

Terror on Church Street ★★

135 South Orange Avenue, Orlando, 32801, corner of Church Street and Orange Avenue, in downtown Orlando, ☎ *(407) 649-3327.*

Hours: 7 p.m.–midnight

Special hours: Friday and Saturday, open until 1 a.m.

An elaborate horror show that originated on a Buenos Aires stage in 1987 and later set up permanent camps in Madrid, Rome and Mexico City, Terror on Church Street is the Orlando franchise, situated next to the Church Street Station complex in the "dead center" of downtown Orlando. The multimedia, participatory fright-show incorporates live actors, elaborate sets and special lighting and aural effects to create a chilling atmosphere punctuated by several genuine scares. Guests explore the labyrinth of 23 individual sets in groups of eight; a full tour requires about 20 minutes, although a "chicken-out" exit midway means that all members of your group may not make it to the end together. This underdog Orlando attraction opened in 1991 and has gradually built a solid reputation by delivering the creeps with a good dose of humor; it now entertains a quarter-million thrill-seekers annually. Although teens love it, children under 10 must be accompanied by parent. Admission: $12.72 adult; $10.60 age 17 and under.

Around Winter Park

Winter Park's main thoroughfare, Park Avenue, is lined with specialty shops.

Incorporated in 1886, and predestined from the start by its location and by land speculators to become an affluent haven for winter dodgers from the northeast, Winter Park is a posh day trip away from the jangle of activities in Walt Disney World.

The most scenic attraction in town is the sparkling string of lakes connected by slender canals that dot the residential district, creating the exclusive aura for which the community is most known. Deep, narrow housing lots allowed for maximum lake frontage along these jewels, and public access to long stretches of the shoreline is frequently blocked by the homes. The roads that circuit these neighborhoods are lined with enormous oaks draped with Spanish moss. Get a peek at the town's wealthiest denizens via the **Scenic Boat Tour**, voted by *Orlando Magazine* readers as the "best-kept secret" among things to do.

For a glimpse of Winter Park's history, visit the well-preserved 1882 railroad depot, the town's first building, and the store at the corner of Park and Welbourne, which housed the community's first mercantile establishment and post office. **Rollins College** was founded in 1885 and was the first institution of higher learning in the state, drawing lectures, recitals and exhibitions by famed artists and others from the northeast—Mister Rogers of public TV fame is one of its alumni. The **Charles Hosmer Morse Museum** houses a collection of rare Tiffany glass—"the most comprehensive and most interesting Tiffany collection anywhere," according to the curator of the Met's American Decorative Arts. The **Albin Polasek Galleries** houses a collection of the late Czechoslovakian artist's religious paintings and sculptures in his home.

As befits Beverly Hills or any other exclusive burb, the ultimate draw here is shopping and browsing. Over the past decade, **Park Avenue** has become central Florida's most upscale shopping area—a tony hub for the Gap and Laura Ashley, and everything in between. While some of this has been at the expense of locally owned independent shops, you'll have a far more pleasant window-shopping experience here than at your average mall back home. Keep in mind, though, that some smaller stores are closed Sundays, while the museums are shuttered Mondays. On Saturday mornings, the **Winter Park Farmer's Market** just off Park Avenue has been a quaint tradition since 1979, soliciting locals who sell fruit and vegetables, herbs, flowers, houseplants and butterfly cocoons at the corner of New York and Lyman Avenues. Afterward, stop by the delectable Petit Four, the town's preeminent bakery, where the almond croissant is a particular delight.

Three miles west of Winter Park is another special enclave—**Eatonville**, the first municipality in the United States incorporated by African Americans, and hometown of author Zora Neale Hurston, who celebrated her central Florida upbringing in her 1942 autobiography, *Dust Tracks on a Road*. The community was incorporated in 1887, and soon after the front page of the *Eatonville Speaker* proclaimed: "Lots to actual settlers (colored): 44 x 100, can be bought for thirty-five dollars cash; and fifty on time... all the necessary adjuncts of a full-fledged city, all colored, and not a white family in the whole city!" The town, enormously proud of its heritage, commemorates its famous writer, community and culture with the **Zora Neale Hurston Festival** at the end of January each year. A small art museum, also named in her honor, is located at 227 East Kennedy Boulevard, which lies between Exits 46 and 47 on I-4. Information, ☎ *(407) 647-3307.*

Winter Park is located five miles north of downtown Orlando, two miles east of I-4. From the Walt Disney World area, take I-4 east to Fairbanks Avenue (Exit 45) and head right to Park Avenue; free parking is found on Morse Boulevard. The city features more than 20 restaurants, including the charming sidewalk cafe **Brandywine's**, or the open-air patio, **The Briarpatch**. More upscale meals are offered by the acclaimed **Maison and Jardin** in nearby Altamonte Springs. Several lodging options are available, the most captivating being the **Park Plaza Hotel**, a New Orleans-style inn embellished in wrought-iron balconies (see "Other Possibilities" in "Hotels and Accommodations").

For additional information, stop by the **Winter Park Chamber of Commerce**, located on New York Street next to Central Park, or call, ☎ *(407) 644-8281.*

Museums and Exhibits

Charles Hosmer Morse Museum of Art, The   ★★★★

445 Park Avenue North, Winter Park, 32789, use Exit 45 from I-4; east on Fairbanks to Park Avenue; go left six blocks, ☎ *(407) 645-5311.*

Hours: 9:30 a.m.–4 p.m.

Special hours: Sunday: 1–4 p.m.; closed holidays. Closed: Mon.

One of central Florida's most important museums, the Morse collection embraces American decorative arts of the late-19th and early 20th centuries. The recently expanded museum's shining focus is its collection of Tiffany glass pieces, including a number of one-of-a-kind works crafted by the artist himself. Stained-glass windows, a unique "Electrolier" (an electrified chandolier), a column of glass daffodils, and a wealth of jewelry are among the highlights. The rest of the museum is occupied by some of the rotating collection of American Art Pottery (including Rookwood), sculpture, furniture (Stickley and others) and paintings. Docents available for tours. Admission: $3 for adults; $1 for students; children under 12 free.

Cornell Fine Arts Museum   ★★★

1000 Holt Avenue, Winter Park, 32789, from I-4, use the Fairbanks Avenue east exit; go right on Park, left on Holt, ☎ *(407) 646-2526.*

Hours: 10 a.m.–5 p.m.

Special hours: Saturday and Sunday: 1-5 p.m. Closed: Mon.

Housing a surprisingly diverse collection of artwork spanning from the Italian Renaissance to American contemporaries, the Cornell is located on the grounds of Rollins College, on the shores of Lake Virginia. Among the notables: a set of tapestries by Alexander Calder, "Europa Crowned by Genius" by Pietro Liberi, "Madonna and Child Enthroned" by Cosimo Rosselli, as well as works by Herman Herzog, Red Grooms, Jonas Lie, Thomas Sully and many others. Traveling shows regularly supplement the permanent collection. Admission: free.

Tours

Winter Park Scenic Boat Tour ★ ★ ★

*312 Morse Boulevard, Winter Park, 32789, from I-4, take Fairbanks Exit east to Park; go
left, then right on Morse, ☎ (407) 644-4056.*
Hours: 10 a.m.–4 p.m.

One of central Florida's oldest attractions, this pleasant pontoon boat tour visits the
backyards of Winter Park's rich and sometimes famous residents who live on the
town's 17 interconnecting lakes. The one-hour tour begins from Lake Osceola,
named after the local Indian chief, and the elegant lakeside mansions (which usually
can't be seen from the road) are quickly established as the major focus. Philip
Crosby, Margaret Mitchell, Hugh McKean, Horace Grant and the Kraft family are
among the current or former wealthy denizens, and boats pass close to the sublime
Isle of Scicily, which is about as prime as real estate comes in central Florida. Wildlife, including cormorants, osprey and the occasional owl, can be spotted, and the
boats also travel down several of the narrow and evocative canals lined with moss-
draped cypress trees, ferns and bamboo. The raft of stale jokes told by the fleet's
skippers are part of the fun. Boats leave every hour on the hour; canoe and rowboat
rentals are also available at the boat dock. Admission: $6 adults; $3 children age 2–
11.

Scenic boat tour in Winter Park cruises through a chain of lakes.

Around Kissimmee

Once a cow town, now a theme park gateway *and* cow town, Kissimmee
has a split personality that almost defies description. The community is one
of the region's major beef and dairy producers, and cattle auctions and rode-

os are still an institution even if they are invisible to most outsiders. On Kissimmee's outskirts, Mormons operate a cattle ranch 10 times larger than Walt Disney World. But while cattle used to be the major trade, today the big business is in hotels and motels, with nearly 30,000 rooms. A sizable number of chain eateries throw open their troughs. Agriculture, engineering and plastics (Tupperware is based here — but sorry, no factory tours) are also part of the economy.

World of Orchids is the first permanent indoor display simulating the tropics. It boasts thousands of flowering orchids and gardens.

The actual downtown lies just south of U.S. 192 at Main, and contains Kissimmee's faintest glimmer of personality, but few visitors ever see it. Instead, most stick to 192 (aka, the Irlo Bronson Memorial Highway, or Vine Street), which is lined by the hotels and motels. Kissimmee is frequently linked with neighboring St. Cloud; the two towns have a combined population of about 42,000, but the region triples in size when peak-season visitors are taken into account. Disney's new **Celebration** community is springing up on the outskirts of Kissimmee, on 192, although the development lies within the Walt Disney World borders.

Beyond the scope of this book are the many minor attractions—paintball, bungee jumping, go carts and more—along the 192 alley. One drive down the glittering, neon-entwined highway, and all of Kissimmee's temptations will become obvious. Two big area events include the **Silver Spurs Rodeo** held in February and July, and the **Kissimmee Bluegrass Festival** held in March. The **Houston Astros** warm up for the season at Kissimmee's Osceola County Stadium in March (see "Spring Training" in "After the Theme Parks"). For additional information on these or other special events, call the **Kissimmee Tourist Information Center**, ☎ *(800) 327-9159.*

Details about the assortment of dinner theaters constructed in and near Kissimmee are outlined under "Dinner Theaters" earlier in this chapter.

Children's Activities

Green Meadows Farm ★★

1368 South Poinciana Boulevard, Kissimmee, 34746, from I-4, take Exit 25A and head east on U.S. 192 three miles; right on Poinciana, go five miles south, ☎ *(407) 846-0770. Hours: 9:30 a.m.–5:30 p.m.*

A charming country attraction geared to educating pre-teens and their parents about farm animals, Green Meadows is a grassy, 40-acre farm shaded by Spanish moss-draped oaks. The two-hour guided tours are segregated by age to allow the experience to be tailored for various levels; all visitors get a chance to pet, hug, pick up or feed the animals—and everyone grabs an udder for a first-hand opportunity to milk cows. The tractor-drawn hayrides are a big hit. An excellent stop for 3 to 5-year-olds, most of whom have difficulty keeping up with the pace and scope of the Disney attractions, but are overjoyed with the authentic experience delivered here. Last full tour begins before 4 p.m. daily; small gift shop and snack bar on the premises. Admission: $13 age 3 through adult; $9 for seniors.

Parks and Gardens

Cypress Island ★★★

1541 Scotty's Road, Kissimmee, 34741, from the Turnpike, take Exit #244 to Shady Lane; follow the signs to the dock, ☎ *(407) 933-2704. Hours: 9 a.m.–dusk*

A 200-acre island in the missle of Kissimmee's Lake Tohopekaliga ("Toho" for short), Cypress Island provided sanctuary to the Seminole Indians, central Florida's original settlers. The island is now a privately owned, landscaped park, with 200-

year-old oaks and cypress dripping with Spanish moss. A number of transplanted animals—llamas, rheas, emus, Sicilian donkeys, Barbados mountain sheep and others—roam part of the island freely, while another area shelters Florida bobcats and other cats. While on Cypress Island, guests can walk a two-mile nature trail around the island's perimeter, visit a petting zoo, and picnic; other options (not included in the general admission price) include SwampBuggy rides, a nighttime airboat gator photo safari and horseback riding. Call for reservations. Admission: $24 adults; $17 children 3–12.

World of Orchids, A ★ ★

2501 Old Lake Wilson Road (State Route 545), Kissimmee, 34747, from I-4, take Exit 25 (U.S. 192) west two miles to Route 545; turn right and proceed one mile south, ☎ *(407) 396-1887.*

Hours: 9:30 a.m.–5:30 p.m.

Special hours: Closed major holidays.

A unique tribute to the hardy but ugly plant with the luxuriant flowers, World of Orchids is the first observatory specifically designed to display orchids; it's also a year-round, commercial growing facility housing up to 20,000 plants. The main touring area is a 3/4-acre indoor greenhouse, landscaped with paths, streams and a waterfall and made more tropical by the sight of colorful parrots. While many of the lush plants are permanently positioned, the staff rotates the orchids cultivated in an adjacent greenhouse and other flowering plants into this facility as they bloom, ensuring guests will always encounter hundreds of flowers, some of them quite rare. Several 45-minute tours are provided daily. A short nature walk navigates a portion of the 10-acre property outside, which overlooks the western border of Walt Disney World. The gift shop (no admission required) sells orchid plants both retail and wholesale, as well as orchid-related artwork, books and gardening supplies. While the admission price is exhorbitant, orchid-lovers will find this attraction an out-of-the-way delight. Annual Orchid Fairs conducted mid March and late June. Admission: $9.58 adults; under 16 free.

Theme/Amusement Parks

JungleLand ★

4580 West Irlo Bronson Highway (U.S. 192), Kissimmee, 34746, two miles east of State Route 535, ☎ *(407) 396-1012.*

Hours: 9 a.m.–5 p.m.

Special hours: Extended hours in spring and summer.

This old-fashioned attraction has a small collection of wildlife, including several cats (lynx, serval, bobcat), rheas, emus, lemurs, orangutans and, of course, alligators; all of the animals are sadly kept in unattractive cages. A gator wrestling and reptile show is performed several times daily in a small arena. The former owners were ordered to shut down in 1994 after their animal licenses were revoked for not properly caring for the animals. This is one attraction unlikely to survive for long in the shadow of the mouse once Disney's animal theme park opens. Admission: $10.65 adult; $7.44 children age 3–11.

UNIVERSAL STUDIOS, SEA WORLD AND OTHER ATTRACTIONS

Points West

The Wilderness River Cruise at Weeki Wachee Spring is a 30 minute tour past otters, raccoons, blue herons and endangered wood storks.

The low-lying hills west of Orlando create one of central Florida's least populated stretches—miles of desolate scrub and swampland lead away from the Disney property, graced by the occasional citrus grove. A small stand of grapes surrounds the pleasant **Lakeside Winery**, and the **Florida Citrus Tower** nearby provides excellent views from its 226-foot summit; otherwise, you'll probably avoid this territory.

Farther west, however, is an oasis—the Gulf of Mexico and its gentle beaches. The twin-city **Tampa Bay** area includes Tampa and St. Petersburg, a bustling combination that has produced one of the nation's fastest-growing economies. Cigar production was a major industry around the turn-of-the-century, and leaving behind a large Cuban community that still resides in Ybor City, on the fringe of downtown Tampa, while tourism spurred by the beaches was another source of income during the '40s and '50s. In recent years, tourism has staged a revival, and the recent resurgence of cigar smoking may further prompt once-lagging (and now mechanized) cigar production.

Tampa Bay hosts the region's best collection of art museums, including the **Museum of Fine Arts** and the **Salvador Dali Museum** in St. Petersburg, and the **Tampa Museum of Art** and a **Museum of African-American Art**. The Tampa Bay Hotel (now the University of Tampa) is a spectacular palace built in 1891 and is topped by 13 minarets that dominate the downtown silhouette. But the real draw to Tampa Bay for Orlando visitors beyond **Busch Gardens** is the wealth of sublime beaches. **Caladesi Island State Park** is a protected barrier reef island with three miles of undisturbed sand; you'll need a boat to visit Caladesi—call Clearwater Ferry Service, ☎ *(813) 442-7433*. Nearby, **Honeymoon Island State Park** is almost as nice, and connected via the Dunedin Causeway to the town of Clearwater. **Indian Rocks Beach**, **Madeira Beach** and **St. Pete Beach** are resort communities on other, road-connected barrier islands west of St. Petersburg, each boasting comely strips of sand; additional information available by calling the Gulf Beaches Chamber of Commerce, ☎ *(813) 595-4575*.

Farther south lies **Anna Maria Key** and **Longboat Key** off the coast from Sarasota. These offer lovely beaches but, positioned over 140 miles from Orlando, are probably farther than a Disney day-tripper will want to travel for surf and sand.

Lakeland, along the I-4 en route to Tampa, claims the largest construction designed by **Frank Lloyd Wright**, a series of austere structures on the Florida College Campus (at Ingraham and McDonald), and completed in 1946. Chosen as one of the nation's 10 most livable cities by *Money* in 1996, Lakeland is also the spring home of the **Detroit Tigers**, who play at the Jokey Marchant Stadium every March. Other teams training in this area include the **Philadelphia Phillies** (Clearwater), the **Pittsburgh Pirates** (Bradenton), the **Cincinnati Reds** (Plant City), the **Chicago White Sox** (Sarasota) and the **New York Yankees** (Tampa); see "Spring Training" in "After the Theme Parks" for additional details.

For additional Tampa Bay information, call the Tampa/Hillsborough Convention and Visitors Association, ☎ *(813) 223-1111* or *(800) 448-2672*, or the St. Petersburg Chamber of Commerce, ☎ *(813) 821-4069*.

Busch Gardens

Half zoo, half thrill-ride emporium, if ever a theme park could be accused of schizophrenia, Busch Gardens might be the one. If the 335-acre Anheuser-Busch facility never quite completely melds its two identities, it still delivers a potent day's worth of entertainment in Tampa, about 68 miles west of Disney Village. Roller-coaster fanatics, in particular, will have a field day at the park, which contains the best collection of gravity-defying, steel-tracked doozies in the Southeast. The zoo is the nation's fourth-largest, with more than 2800 animals representing 320 species in an array of naturalistic habitats; the bird collection, in particular, is impressive.

The current facility grew out of a brewery, where the Anheuser-Busch company began offering tastings and tours in 1959. Over time, the Busch family's burgeoning exotic animal collection was moved to the site and, by the 1970s, the zoo had eclipsed the brewery in terms of public interest.

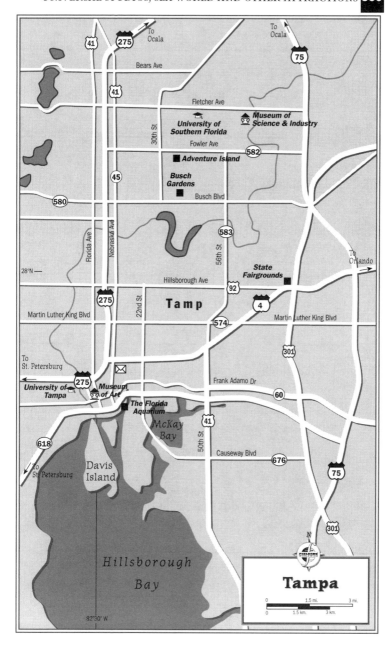

Busch Gardens altered again in 1976 with the introduction of Python, the park's first roller-coaster attraction. Today, Busch is the biggest tourist attraction on Florida's west coast, drawing 3.5 million visitors annually.

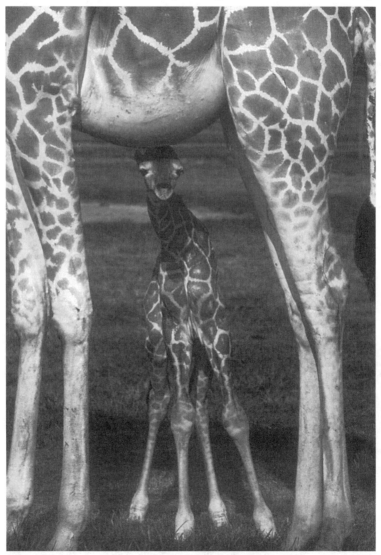

Busch Gardens is a 300-acre African-themed park in nearby Tampa. Free-roaming exotic animals are part of the seven different experiences.

Busch Gardens is segmented into different "lands" based on nine geographical regions of turn-of-the-century Africa; the rides are interspersed throughout most of these areas, as are the animal exhibits. Among the park's themed lands are **Morocco** (which recreates a *medina*), **Nairobi**, **Timbuktu**, **Congo** and **Stanleyville**. The most recent is addition Egypt, a seven-acre themed area that features a lavish, special effects-enhanced walk-through tour of **Tut's Tomb** as it might have been encountered in the 1920s, a **Sand Dig** area for youngsters to unearth buried antiquities, and **Montu**, perhaps the region's most harrowing thrill ride.

Busch's layout, in a continuous circle, defies efficient touring—you must either tackle rides and exhibits in the order you encounter them, or backtrack repeatedly. The scheduled shows also complicate matters. Fortunately, the park is rarely crowded and, outside summer, guests will confront relatively few lines at all when visiting during the week.

In order of increasing thrill, the roller coasters include the yellow-and-avocado **Python**, which features a double spiral corkscrew, and the **Scorpion**, named after its coiling conclusion—a 360-degree wrap that comes to a screeching, dizzying halt. Both of these rides are fun, but last under 90 seconds apiece. Winding elegantly through the rear of the park, the salmon-and-teal **Kumba**, opened in 1993 to great success as the largest and fastest roller coaster in the Southeast. The coaster produces a lion-like roar as it streaks down the tracks along countless loops and spirals, at least once providing momentary weightlessness on its furious, three-minute dash.

Named after the hawk-headed, human-bodied Egyptian warrior god, **Montu** differs from the other Busch coasters in that it's the world's tallest and longest *inverted* roller coaster—that is, the cars hang underneath the track and your legs dangle off the edge of your seat. The "flying" sensation delivered in the first row is particularly breathtaking. There are several first-ever elements, including the largest vertical loop on an inverted coaster (104 feet), and an "Immelman," the world's first inverse diving loop. Montu reels along its twirling, 4000-foot track at speeds topping 60 miles-per-hour. The ride opened in 1996 to immediate popularity and long lines are not uncommon on weekends or during the summer (make it your first or last attraction of the day); Montu can accommodate 1700 guests hourly when all three trains are in operation. All four of the Busch roller coasters have minimum height requirements of between 42 and 52 inches.

Somewhat tamer thrills are offered by the three giddy water rides, which are listed here in increasing level of wetness. **Stanley Falls** is a pleasant log-flume ride that culminates in a 40-foot drop. The **Tanganyika Tidal Wave** is a 20-passenger boat ride through a tranquil, orchid-laced jungle, which leads to an absurd plunge over a 55-foot brink creating a wall of water that engulfs an observation bridge—all to the tune of the "1812 Overture." White-water thrills are provided by the **Congo River Rapids**, where 12-passenger rafts drift along a swift river current through an obstacle course of geysers, waterfalls, and dripping caves. Watch out for the gang of bystanders who can plop a quarter into water guns to further assault river runners. At all three water attractions, riders are assured of getting wet—you may emerge soaked... but that's the point.

Land of the Dragons is a children's area, with rides geared toward kids under 7 or 8 years of age. A few more rides—typical of a carnival midway—are found in Timbuktu, while **Questor** is a five-minute motion-simulator ride that takes visitors in search of a mythical crystal. There is also the **Trans-Veldt Railway**, a train that makes a pair of loops through the park and stops at three stations en route. A 1.1-mile **Skyride** carries passengers from the Crown Colony area to Congo on the other side of the park.

The train and skyride provide views of the 60-acre **Serengeti Plain** animal enclosure, which features hippos, lions, rhinos, impalas, gazelles, baboons, zebras—nearly 500 African animals in all. Unfortunately, much of this area can be seen only via the clunky, suspended **Monorail**, a 10-minute tour accompanied by rote, "live" narration. The monorail speeds by the animals as if the objective was to get you back to the boarding station as quickly as possible. Additionally, the spacious "veldt" is divided by concrete walls and fences, hardly creating the naturalistic environment the park strives for elsewhere.

Myombe Reserve: the Great Ape Domain is featured at Busch Gardens.

Far better is the **Myombe Reserve**, a lush habitat for six western lowland go-rillas and seven chimpanzees. The state-of-the-art primate enclosure features waterfalls and bamboo, and large viewing windows that bring viewers close to the animals. **Claw Island** is also a nicely detailed habitat for Bengal tigers including the extremely rare white tigers. A **Living Dragons** enclosure is home to Asian water monitors, crocodile monitors, rhinoceros iguanas and green iguanas. The **Aldabra Tortoise Habitat** is a recent addition and features six is-land tortoises, while the popular walk-through **Koala Habitat** provides close encounters with the cuddly looking Australian bears. A variety of **Safari Classes** for all ages are offered by the park's conservation and education de-partment; call ☎ *(813) 987-5555* for more information.

Hollywood Live on Ice is Busch Garden's live entertainment show.

The entertainment schedule is presented to guests on arrival and includes individual "Animal Enrichment" presentations that focus on elephants, ti-gers, orangutans, warthogs and others. The two big animal shows are the **World of Birds** (see it when you pick up your free beer at the Hospitality House next door), and **Dolphins of the Deep**, which is similar to the dolphin show at Sea World. The park's other big show is the flashy, 35-minute ex-travaganza, **Hollywood Live on Ice**, silver-screen-themed ice capades played out at the 1200-seat Moroccan Palace Theater. The self-guided **Brewery Tour** is overlooked by many guests, but is a good place to ditch the crowds and/or heat in the middle of the day.

AUTHOR'S OBSERVATION

In terms of identity, Busch Gardens may soon be forced to make an all or nothing commitment to its zoological facilities, currently ranked as the fourth-largest in the United States. Disney's Wild Animal Kingdom will be certifiable competition for all regional animal parks, and a clear mission focus will be essential for the Tampa theme park as it enters the 21st century. With the debut of bigger and better coasters at Busch, the animals seem to be emerging as an afterthought—a sideshow attraction.

INSIDER TIP

An efficient touring itinerary for Busch Gardens is most easily summed up: coasters first. The biggest line is for Montu, followed by Kumba, so make these your first stops of the morning. Because the coasters are located at opposite ends of the park, take the Skyride to Kumba after Montu. If it's a hot day, cool off with one of the water rides, then, when lines become untenable at the north end of the park, work your way back through to the east side of the park, through Timbuktu and Nairobi, visiting Myombe Reserve and the Brewery in the heat of the afternoon. Then head back through Stanleyville to revisit the water rides and coasters you didn't catch in the early morning. Finish off your day with Questor, the spirited motion-simulator ride near the park entrance.

Tanganyika Tidal Wave, Busch Gardens

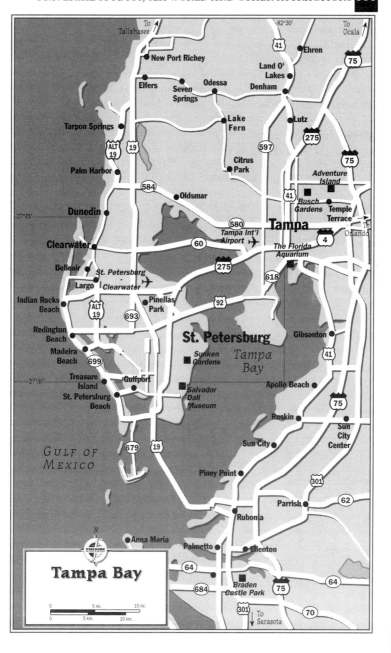

Tampa Bay

Busch Gardens is open daily from 9:30 a.m. to 6 p.m., except during the summer and select holiday periods when hours are extended. Adult admission (tax included) is $36.15; children ages 3 to 9 are $29.75; seniors 50 and over are $32.55 (admission includes all rides, shows and attractions); a combo ticket for Busch Gardens and Sea World is also available, and Busch is a part of the seven-day Vacation Value Pass program (see "Coupons and Discount Offers" earlier in this chapter). A Surf 'n Safari ticket which includes same-day admission to the Adventure Island water park next door is $45.60 for adults, $38.94 for children. Members of AAA receive a 10 percent discount. Parking in the 3400-space lot is $4. Wheelchairs and baby strollers may be rented at the main entrance for $4 per vehicle. Busch Gardens is located at the corner of Busch Boulevard and 40th Street, eight miles northeast of downtown Tampa. From Orlando, follow I-4 west to I-75 north, using Exit 54 an follow the signs (allow about 75 minutes from Orlando). Additional information, ☎ *(813) 987-5000.*

Other Attractions West of Orlando

Theme/Amusement Parks

Adventure Island   ★★

10001 McKinley Drive, Tampa, 33674, located at the corner of 46th Street and Bougainvillea Avenue, next to Busch Gardens, ☎ *(813) 987-5600.*
Hours: 10 a.m.–5 p.m.
Special hours: Extended hours during summer; operated seasonally.
The major water theme park on Florida's "left coast," Adventure Island is a 36-acre play area for all ages, conveniently located adjacent to Busch Gardens. The park features nine water slides, including the 700-foot Key West Rapids, a 1995 addition to the park that drops down six stories of water-driven twists and turns, as well as the formidable Tampa Typhoon, a 76-foot, near-weightless drop. The park also features Rambling Bayou for a leisurely tube float, a surf lagoon with five-foot waves, and a children's play area, Fabian's Funport; an 11-court sand volleyball area is also available. Open mid-March through October, with extended hours during peak season; a combo ticket with Busch Gardens can be purchased. Parking $2. Admission: $22.21 adults; $20.09 children age 3–9.

Weeki Wachee Spring   ★★

6131 Commercial Way, Spring Hill, 34606, from I-75, take Exit 61; head west 20 miles on State Route 50, follow the signs, ☎ *(800) 678-9335.*
Hours: 9:30 a.m.–5:30 p.m.
Special hours: Extended hours in summer.
This 200-acre sister park to Silver Springs in Ocala is subtitled the "City of Mermaids," based on its long-standing tradition of live underwater performances featuring a cast of fish-tailed maidens. The underwater theater is located at the site of a natural artesian spring that pumps 170 million gallons of fresh water to the surface every 24 hours—creating perfect underwater viewing conditions. In 1947, Newton Perry, an ex-Navy frogman, built the first underwater theater, which was 15 feet underwater. The attraction celebrates its 50th anniversary in 1997, and the current

production, "Pocahontas Meets the Little Mermaid," combines Greek mythology with American folklore and uses "high-tech" neon costuming and "space age" bathing caps for the mermaids. A 15-foot-long seaweed moster also makes an appearance. The theme park also hosts two 20-minute avian shows: one focuses on birds of prey, the other on macaws and cockatoos. As at Silver Springs, Weeki Wachee features a 30-minute Wilderness River Cruise aboard quiet, electric-powered boats, passing North American river otters, raccoons, great blue herons and, sometimes, endangered wood storks. A petting zoo is also available. A water theme park, Buccaneer Bay, is located next door to Weeki Wachee (separate admission required; operated March through Labor Day only). Admission: $17.97 adults; $13.73 children age 3–10.

Weeki Wachee Spring, the 200-acre sister park to Silver Spring, is subtitled "City of Mermaids," for its tradition of live underwater performances.

Winery

Lakeridge Winery and Vineyards ★★

19239 U.S. 27 North, Clermont, 34711, ☎ *(352) 394-8627.*

Hours: 10 a.m.–5 p.m.

Special hours: Sunday: noon-5 p.m.

The Clermont area was the center of Floridian viticulture efforts at the turn of the century, expanding to more than 5000 cultivated acres during the 1920s, but Pierce's Disease killed off most of the vineyards during the 1930s. Today, with the advent of new, disease-resistant varieties, winemaker Jeanne Burgess makes bracing, fruity wines from the grapes grown in the sandy, clay-based soils of central Florida. Currently 34 of the winery's 127 acres have been planted with Stover, Suwannee, Blanc Du Bois and Muscadine varieties, yielding much of the all-Florida grapes for the winery's reds, whites and champagnes. Tours and wine tastings are available daily, and a gift shop and picnic area are also on site. Admission: free.

Points East

Florida's shimmering east coast, lined by a long series of breathtaking barrier islands, is capped by one truly unique tourist attraction: **Kennedy Space Center**—the only departure gate in the United States for manned space flights.

It's a little-acknowledged piece of history, but Orlando was already growing in the late '50s and early '60s before Walt Disney came on the scene (who chose Orlando for his theme park in 1965 in large part due to the region's existing expansion). The pre-Disney growth was fueled largely by NASA's commitment to the space race and, later, to land on the moon. To this day, many Kennedy Space Center employees are Orlando residents who make the trek along the Beeline Expressway to work each day. The highway courses straight and unswerving through a mostly undeveloped territory of inhospitable swamp and brush, though one small community a few miles to the north, **Christmas**, maintains a Yuletide industry of posting Christmas Cards; just south of town is a remote 28,000-acre wilderness area, the **Tosohatchee State Preserve**.

The major communities on either side of Kennedy Space Center (Daytona Beach, 50 miles to the north, and Melbourne, 25 miles to the south) are beyond the reach of this book. But delightful **Cocoa Beach** is the place young Floridians holiday, an always percolating, slightly funky hangout lying on a wash of loamy sand. The 800-foot **Cocoa Beach Pier** is the town's centerpiece, and ideal tanning territory sprawls north and south from here. Surfing conditions are among the best in Florida, and inspire a neon-trimmed, 24-hour retail oasis, **Ron Jon Surf Shop**. The Cocoa Beach Chamber of Commerce produces a nicely detailed map (complete with hurricane evacuation routes!) of the area south of Kennedy Space Center. For this and other information, ☎ *(407) 459-2200*.

In sum, an eastbound sojourn from Orlando—to Kennedy Space Center in the morning, to the beaches or the wildlife refuge in the afternoon, and for shopping and dining at the Cocoa Beach Pier in the evening—is an excellent deviation from an otherwise-theme-park-full vacation.

Kennedy Space Center and Cape Canaveral

Short of seeing an actual liftoff, few sights can match the thrill of standing below NASA's **Space Shuttle**. For any Florida visitor wanting a glimpse of *the* real thing—something genuinely authentic, that hasn't been manufactured

Kennedy Center

| 0 | 5 mi. | 10 mi. |
| 0 | 5 km. | 10 km. |

To Daytona Beach

95 1

Eldora

Turtle Mound

Canaveral

ATLANTIC

Oak Hill

OCEAN

Scottsmoor

National

Lake Harney

Seashore

Mims

Merritt Island Nat'l Wildlife Refuge

Space Shuttle Launch Pads

46

Vehicle Assembly Building

Titusville

St. John's Nat'l Wildlife Refuge

John F Kennedy Space Center

50

405

Visitors Center

Christmas

407

528

Banana River

520

Beeline Expressway

Courtenay

1 3

To Orlando

Beeline Expwy

Cape Canaveral

524 Cocoa

Merritt Island 520

Lake Poinsett

Rockledge

Cocoa Beach

Georgiana A1A

Lake Winder

95 Lotus

Satellite Beach

Tropic

441

Indian Harbour Beach

Lake Washington

518

Melbourne

Indialantic

N

192

West Melbourne

Brevard Zoological Park

1

Sawgrass Lake

To Fort Pierce

solely for the purpose of generating tourism revenue—nothing tops the Space Shuttle. A visit to see Kennedy Space Center is Orlando's best day trip.

Kennedy Space Center's Rocket Garden is a favorite with visitors.

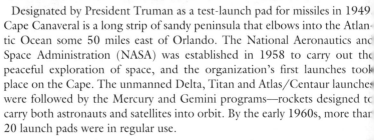

Designated by President Truman as a test-launch pad for missiles in 1949, Cape Canaveral is a long strip of sandy peninsula that elbows into the Atlantic Ocean some 50 miles east of Orlando. The National Aeronautics and Space Administration (NASA) was established in 1958 to carry out the peaceful exploration of space, and the organization's first launches took place on the Cape. The unmanned Delta, Titan and Atlas/Centaur launches were followed by the Mercury and Gemini programs—rockets designed to carry both astronauts and satellites into orbit. By the early 1960s, more than 20 launch pads were in regular use.

In 1962, the north end of Merritt Island just inland from Cape Canaveral was developed for liftoffs, and on Dec. 21, 1968, Apollo 8 was launched from this new base, which was eventually named Kennedy Space Center. After a brief lull at the conclusion of the Apollo era, the reusable Space Shuttle made its debut, and its maiden flight took place in 1981. All subsequent launches have taken off from Kennedy at either Pad A or B, after being assembled for flight in the massive Vehicle Assembly Building, visible for miles around.

Kennedy Space Center and Cape Canaveral is the only place in the Western Hemisphere from where humans have been flung into space, and NASA has been providing public tours of the site since 1963. The initial tours were rudimentary—a self-guiding booklet handed to passing Sunday motorists—but by 1964, 400,000 visitors a year were exploring the area. As NASA segued from the Mercury and Gemini launches to the Apollo moon exploration program, the agency recognized the need for a permanent visitor's center and a 70-acre site was selected on Merritt Island. A bus tour was developed to take guests to the major points of interest, and on Aug. 1, 1967, a 20,000-square-foot visitor center was opened for business. The success and popularity of the facility is such that more than 2 million visitors a year now tour the site, making it one of the most popular tourist attractions in the state. Best of all, the space complex is one of the region's least-expensive attractions.

AUTHOR'S OBSERVATION

*To move the fully assembled Shuttle to the launch pad, Kennedy Space Center uses **Crawler Transporters**, the largest tractors on earth–designed to carry 14.5 million pounds on their platform, and powered by powerful diesel electric generators. A hydraulic system can raise either end of the platform by up to six feet, allowing the Shuttle to remain upright as the Transporter rolls up to the launch pad. Using a crew of 26, the Transporter moves the Shuttle at a top speed of one mile per hour, a seven-hour process to transfer the Shuttle the three miles from the Vehicle Assembly Building to the launch pads.*

Compared to the competition in Orlando, as a tourist attraction, Kennedy Space Center Visitor Center has felt stodgy and unpolished, awash in unrealized potential. The entire facility was in need of an overhaul to update the presentations and bring it in line with the slick attractions the region has become known for. So in 1996, following several years of declining attendance, the Center's private operator under NASA, Delaware North Parks, began a two-year, $70 million expansion, the centerpiece of which will be a building (opening December 1996) to house a newly refurbished, 363-foot-tall Saturn V moon rocket. Other exhibits will open throughout 1997, but the star of the show, will likely remain the Space Shuttle, and it's a sight to behold.

At present, a pair of two-hour bus tours are provided and are the central focus of any visit. Keep in mind that the tours vary daily based on the activity at the Center on the date you visit. You could encounter Shuttle-less launch pads, or you could luck out by visiting on a day when a vehicle is being hauled to the pads via the gargantuan "Crawler Transporter." The **Red Tour** stops at a bluff one mile from the Shuttle launch pads, as well as well as at the new Apollo/Saturn V Center. The Red Tour is the more popular circuit and departs every 15 minutes. The **Blue Tour** visits Cape Canaveral Air Force Station, the location of the space program during the '50s and '60s. Enthusiasts will want to take in both tours, which start at 9:30 a.m. and continue departing throughout the day until two hours before dusk. For each tour, tickets are $7 (tax included), children ages 3 to 11 are $4. Buy tickets as soon as you arrive to ensure that you get the time slot you want.

In 1985, a pair of **IMAX theaters** opened next to the Visitor Center and feature a revolving slate of older IMAX films shown on massive theater screens. Unfortunately, during my visit, the image projected for *The Dream is Alive* was scratched and dirty—hardly the presentation warranted by these excellent films that explore the environment and NASA's mission. For each film, tickets are $4, children ages 3 to 11 are $2.

The free **Visitor Center** contains a number of interesting exhibits including a full-size, walk-through replica of the **Space Shuttle**, an **Astronauts Memorial**, and a **Rocket Garden** of eight authentic rockets from the past. Two food counters are available for breakfast or lunch, and a souvenir store stocks space-related gifts and accessories.

Kennedy Space Center is open daily from 9 a.m. to dusk *except* on the day of a launch, in which case the facility re-opens approximately two hours after liftoff. Free wheelchairs are provided, and all exhibits and tours are handicapped-accessible. Parking is free. From Orlando, take the Beeline east (State Route 528) and follow the signs after Titusville. Additional information, ☎ *(407) 452-2121*. Launch information within Florida only, ☎ *(800) 572-4636*.

Kennedy Space Center educates visitors on the space program.

Space Shuttle Launch Viewing

Viewing a Space Shuttle launch is both easier and more difficult than one might expect. Easier, because the taxpayer-funded NASA uses the spectacular Shuttle liftoffs as a public relations tool—by making the events accessible to those who are footing the bill. But with launches routinely scrubbed at the last minute and advance reservations necessary for the best viewing areas, it's not uncommon to expend a fair amount of time, and still return home without anything to show for the effort.

AUTHOR'S OBSERVATION

During the mid-1990s, NASA has been exploring the possibility of privatizing the Space Shuttle operation, making the agency a paying customer for the services of a privately operated fleet of Shuttles. The goal would be to make the Shuttle's operation more cost-efficient—savings of $700 million out of the current $3.2 billion annual budget are projected—but critics claim the savings may come at the expense of safety oversight. In 1995, a study commissioned by NASA concluded that the odds of a Shuttle launch catastrophe had improved from 1 in 73 prior to the Challenger disaster to 1 in 219 today.

Two pads (A and B) are used for all Shuttle launches at Kennedy Space Center; both are about 13 miles east of Titusville. A "launch window"—the time-frame within which the liftoff can commence—is announced several months prior to each scheduled launch; the window can last anywhere from a few minutes to several hours. To obtain a front-row seat, you'll want to secure a launch-viewing pass, which are available two ways.

NASA allows a limited number of cars onto its property to view the launch from a distance of about four miles on the Causeway over the Banana River—a spectacular, unobstructed viewing area. To obtain a free car pass, write to NASA Public Affairs, P.A. Pass, Kennedy Space Center, Florida, 32899. NASA begins issuing the car passes about one month prior to the launch on a first-come, first-served basis. If the launch is scrubbed, the car pass is valid for the reschedule date.

A a bus is available from the Visitor Center to the same location. These launch viewing tickets may be reserved by phone up to seven days in advance, but must be picked up and paid for in person *two days prior* to the launch. There is no mail order service and tickets that are not picked up go on sale to the general public the day before the launch. Tickets are priced $7 for adults and $4 for children ages 3 to 11. If the liftoff is scrubbed after you board the bus, the ticket cannot be re-used. Launch viewing reservations, ☎ *(407) 449-4400.*

If you have not obtained a viewing pass, there are two prime areas for watching the liftoff. For mid-to-late morning, afternoon or nighttime launches, the best location is the shoreline along the **Indian River**, just outside **Titusville**. This spot doesn't work well for early morning launches because you'll be looking straight into the sun. From this area, the Vehicle Assembly Building and both launch pads are clearly visible. From Orlando, take Route 528 (the Beeline) east to Route 407, and then proceed North on U.S. 1, choosing a spot along the shore before Titusville. The intersection of U.S. 1 and State Route 50 is where the locals congregate.

For early morning viewings when the sun is low on the horizon, the best spot is **Jetty Park**, a county facility located at the beach near the Air Force base entrance and about 13 miles south of the Kennedy launch pads. You won't be able to see the ignition blast, but you will have a view of the shuttle moments after liftoff. This location also works for unmanned launches that take off from Cape Canaveral, only a few miles from Jetty Park. From Orlando, take State Route 528 (the Beeline) east toward Cocoa Beach, taking a left on King Boulevard after crossing Merritt Island. The park is about 2.5 miles north of the Cocoa Beach Pier.

The easiest way to see the Shuttle liftoff is to overnight in the area—there are 8300 motel and hotel rooms between Titusville and Palm Bay, 40 miles south of the launching area—but this can be a crapshoot, since launches are sometimes delayed for days on end. Local accommodation information can be obtained by calling the Titusville Chamber of Commerce, ☎ *(407) 267-3036;* or the Cocoa Beach Chamber of Commerce, ☎ *(407) 459-2200.*

The (normally) one-hour trip on the Beeline from Orlando to the coast becomes clogged with cars in the hours prior to a Shuttle liftoff; allow *at least* two hours to make the 50-mile trip from Orlando to the viewing areas. Most local radio stations broadcast launch information and some go live for the final countdown. Keep in mind that high humidity levels or clouds will decrease the viewing opportunities. Crisp winter mornings are usually best, and the shuttle can even be seen from the Orlando area if conditions warrant. Nighttime launches are always spectacular.

The return home of the Space Shuttle, when it's scheduled to take place at the Kennedy landing strip, is easy to watch. The parking lot at the Visitor Center is open to the public for landings and the Shuttle streaks close to the site on its final approach. The liftoff of the unmanned Titan rocket from Cape Canaveral can usually be viewed from this parking lot during business hours.

AUTHOR'S OBSERVATION

The glistening white cloud that emerges from the base of the Shuttle at liftoff is not smoke or exhaust, but steam—the byproduct of water released from spouts located above the flame trench at the base of the Shuttle. During a 20-second period following ignition, more than 300,000 gallons of water are dumped onto the pad area beneath the Shuttle, providing both sound suppression and cooling.

For 24-hour recorded launch information contact ☎ *(800) KSC-INFO* (accessible from within Florida only). From outside the state, launch and ticket information, ☎ *(407) 452-2121.*

Other Attractions East of Orlando

Kennedy Space Center is NASA's site for shuttle and other launches. The space museum offers visitors a look at space technology.

Museums and Exhibits

U.S. Astronaut Hall of Fame ★★

6225 Vectorspace Boulevard, Titusville, 32780, just off State Route 405, en route to Kennedy Space Center, ☎ *(407) 269-6100.*

Hours: 9 a.m.–5 p.m.

Special hours: Extended hours during summer.

An interesting adjunct to Kennedy Space Center, which lies a few miles east, this family friendly museum is dedicated primarily to the stories of the nation's astronauts, but offers interactive exhibits to keep children transfixed. The 15-minute video highlights the manned spaceflight program, and the "Shuttle to Tomorrow" provides a 20-minute presentation aboard a full-scale space shuttle replica. The museum also contains a pair of motion simulator rides: 3D-360, a mock jet that soars, banks and rolls, and the G Force Trainer, an intense, stomach-unsettling ride that spins fiercely to simulate up to 4-G's. The Hall of Fame is also the home of U.S. Space Camp, a nonprofit educational facility designed to promote space science education; 4th- to 7th-grade children are trained like real astronauts in Space Camp's five-day, hands-on programs. Admission: $10.55 adults; $6.31 children age 4–12.

Parks and Gardens

Merritt Island National Wildlife Refuge   ★★★

P.O. Box 6504, Titusville, 32782, visitor center located four miles east of Titusville on State Route 402, *(407) 861-0667.*
Hours: 8 a.m.–4:30 p.m.
Special hours: Closed Sunday May through October.

Sharing a common boundary with NASA's Kennedy Space Center, Merritt Island is home to several of the nation's rarest and most endangered species of wildlife. The West Indian (or Florida) manatee, southern bald eagle, Florida scrub jay and loggerhead turtle are among the regulars who use the 25-mile-long barrier island as a refuge, though many other species can be spotted by the patient observer. The open water area provides winter breeding ground for 23 species of migratory waterfowl, while the marsh areas attract snails, crabs, clams, fish, shore birds, raptors and alligators. A six-mile driving tour, the Black Point Wildlife Drive, is a one-way car loop that is best taken in the early morning or late afternoon when wildlife is most active. Three walking trails are also maintained: The longest, the five-mile Cruickshank Trail, circuits a shallow water marsh facing the Indian River. Begin your visit by stopping at the Visitor Center to orient yourself and to pick up brochures and trail guides. The best viewing season is October through March, when the greatest concentration of wildlife is on hand. The waterfowl count is highest in January; warm days in February bring out the alligators; the manatee population peaks in April; and sea turtles nest May through July.

Shopping

Cocoa Beach Pier   ★★★

401 Meade Avenue, Cocoa Beach, a half-mile north of State Route 520, just off North Atlantic Boulevard, *(407) 783-7549.*
Hours: 6 a.m.–1 a.m.

A historic Florida landmark extending 800 feet over the Atlantic Ocean, Cocoa Beach Pier has been successfully positioned as a dining and shopping destination. Drawing a wide cross-section of locals and visitors, the pier is perfect for people-watching or fishing (no license required; rental equipment available).

Ron Jon Surf Shop   ★★

4151 North Atlantic Avenue, Cocoa Beach, 32931, in the heart of Cocoa Beach, at the intersection of State Route 520, ☎ *(407) 799-8888.*
Special hours: Open 24 hours, 365 days a year.

The self-proclaimed "largest attraction" in the area, this 52,000-square-foot, art deco retail institution is for surfers, "wannabees" and hangers-on (i.e., the rest of us.) Stocking a veritable smorgasbord of paraphernalia linked to either the sun or water, Ron Jon's selection goes far beyond surfboards and flip flops and includes scuba equipment, running shoes, rollerblades and bicycles. Even trendier pursuits, such as boomerangs, are featured. There are, of course, racks and racks of sunny clothing, and the Ron Jon logo screams from a bazillion different T-shirts, mugs and visors. The store also rents in-line skates, beach bikes, surfboads by the hour, day or week. The helpful dudes and dude-ettes that toil 24 hours a day to serve the shop's 1.3 million annual visitors are seemingly kept awake by the store's surfeit of neon-bright colors—the staff makes Ron Jon the most professional surfing retail outfit around.

Points North

One of the most attractive portions of Florida is the pine-and-lake-dotted region that stretches north of Orlando, culminating in the 383,000-acre **Ocala National Forest**. The area is awash in curious trivia: it's the home to one of the nation's oldest spiritualist communities, and the lakeside town of Clermont purports to hold more triathlons than any other community in the world as well as housing a miniature of the White House at its wax museum.

INSIDER TIP

The Yalaha Country Bakery is a delightful place to begin a driving tour of the small towns north of Orlando. Situated on County Road 48, along the shores of Lake Harris, the bakery is fronted by a mural of intertwining fruits and flowers, and the smell of fresh bread wafting through the thick air. The shop is headed by master baker and pastry chef Max Klopfer, from Bavaria, who uses traditional baking methods and German ovens to create 15 varieties of bread, plus an assortment of pretzels, tortes and other tasty goods. The tiny hamlet of Yalaha is three miles east of State Route 27.

Referring to anything as lakeside, actually, is almost a misnomer since most everything is on or near a body of water. **Lake County** boasts more than 200 square miles of its 1200-square-mile territory is under water—well over a thousand individual tarns, bayous and ponds. There are quirky towns such as Altoona and Howey-in-the-Hills that haven't noticed (or don't care about) the invasion of theme parks a few miles to the south, but several other communities are worth a day trip from Orlando.

A chief lure is Starbucks-less **Mt. Dora** (also see "Bicycling" in "After the Theme Parks"), where the '90s have brought a bevy of independent java joints to mingle with the antique shops, bookstores and graceful, turn-of-the-century homes. Gourmet coffee beans are even sold at the Mt. Dora flea market, out on U.S. 441. The 8000-person community is situated among rolling hills on the shores of Lake Dora, which is connected to Lake Eustis by a cypress-lined canal that 1930s sportswriter Grantland Rice once termed "the most beautiful half-mile of water in the world." Otters, bobcats and snowy white egrets are among the canal's more unusual wildlife, and lovely trails are found at Palm Island Park.

But the key activity in Mt. Dora is "antiqueing," which climaxes dizzyingly at **Renninger's Antique Center**, a series of about 150 independently operated booths connected under one roof, and termed the largest antique selection in the state. A tour of this flea market is supplemented by stores selling local crafts, as well as boutiques and art galleries. Don't miss the **Lakeside Inn**, an 1883 hotel that was a favorite retreat of President and Mrs. Coolidge. Stop by the **Mt. Dora Chamber of Commerce** at *341 Alexander Street*, for additional information and a map of the historic sights; ☎ *(352) 383-2165*.

Positioned on the fringe of Lake Monroe, Sanford represents the upriver terminus of the navigable St. John's River, and the southern terminus of Amtrak's Auto Train (see "Getting There" in "Planning Your Trip"). The turn-of-the-century downtown was recently restored and offers antique and crafts stores; the big news is a 1.5 million-square-foot regional mall, **Seminole Towne Square**, that opened in 1995. Just west of Sanford is the 109-acre **Central Florida Zoological Park**, while nearby **Katie's Wekiva River Landing** serves as a put-in point for canoes to explore the St. John's.

For all of central Florida's well-entrenched religious organizations, few communities come as a greater surprise than **Cassadaga**, a 300-strong spiritualist headquarters listed on the National Historic Register. The camp was founded in 1875 by George Colby, who was looking for a winter home for his followers, and settled on this tract of land, which he had envisioned in a dream. Today, about half of the hamlet is made up of practicing healers and mediums who work out of their homes, and they welcome outsiders to stroll through the peaceful, five-block-square community—it's probably the second-largest spiritualist camp in the country, following Colby's original home in Lillydale, New York.

You can stock up on Edgar Cayce books, or locate a medium by stopping at the **Cassadaga Camp Bookstore and Information Center**, where a bulletin board posts the names of residents who are available for readings or spiritual consultations. This unofficial town hub also provides flyers for workshops and special events. The Colby Memorial Temple holds services Sundays at 10:30 a.m. and Wednesdays at 7:30 p.m. The gatherings are unconventional services designed to solicit messages from beyond. Cassadaga is one mile east of I-4 at Exit 54, about 30 miles northeast of downtown Orlando. The bookstore is open daily and located at *1112 Stevens Street*, on the right as you enter town; ☎ *(904) 228-2880*.

For overnighting, try the **Higgans House** in Sanford, which offers bed-and-breakfast style rooms in a quaint, Victorian-era setting (see "Other Possibilities" in "Hotels and Accommodations").

Silver Springs

Silver Springs is perhaps the one theme park that can most accurately claim to be Florida's oldest tourist attraction. And, for once, the hyperbole doesn't oversell the destination.

Florida's oldest attraction, Silver Springs, is famous for its glass-bottom boat rides and jungle cruise.

The 350-acre riparian park wraps around the headwaters of the crystal clear **Silver River**, a series of seven artesian spring formations—the largest in the world—that pour forth some combined 880 million gallons of 99.8 percent pure, fresh water per day. In the early 1500s, Timucuan Indians lived on the land, and Spaniard Hernando de Sota perused the territory in 1539, looking to exploit its resources. In the 1860s, conventional steamboats brought tourists upriver to visit the scenic headwaters, but in 1878, Hullam Jones created the glass-bottom boat here by installing a glass viewing box on the flat bottom of a dugout canoe. Jones' invention provided a unique window to the moonlike underwater environment, which revealed fish, turtles, crustaceans and fossils more than 10,000 years old. In 1925, the Department of the Interior declared Silver Springs a Registered National Landmark.

Besides its role as a flowering tourist attraction, Silver Springs served another master in the 20th century—Hollywood. Since the 1930s, a number of directors have used the crystalline waters as a "back lot" for films requiring underwater scenes, including six of the Johnny Weissmuller *Tarzan* movies, *The Yearling* and, perhaps most famously, much of the archetypal 3-D monster film, *Creature From the Black Lagoon* (Ricou Browning, who played the creature, reportedly still lives within a mile of the springs today). More than 100 episodes of "Sea Hunt" starring Lloyd Bridges were shot here during its television run from 1958 to 1961.

Today, low-key Silver Springs is popular among seniors, many of whom bring their pre-teen relatives to tour the beautifully landscaped grounds. Unlike Cypress Gardens, Silver Springs doesn't feel hopelessly locked in a time warp and, coupled with a drive through nearby Ocala National Forest, makes for a relaxing Orlando day trip.

UNIVERSAL STUDIOS, SEA WORLD
AND OTHER ATTRACTIONS

The 20-minute **Glass-Bottom Boat** tour remains an institution at Silver Springs—a friendly glide in electric-powered crafts over the gaping caverns that imperceptibly produce the immense flow of water into the river. This is a good place to begin your visit as it provides an overview of the park's history and layout, but if a line has formed, come back later in the day. Just to the left of the glass-bottom boats is a platform overlooking the largest of the sources, **Mammoth Springs**, which produces the bulk—550 million gallons per day—of the Silver River.

Continuing to the left is a series of landscaped gardens and lawns, which lead to the **Lost River Voyage**, a 25-minute boat ride that cruises farther down the cypress tree-lined river, passing raccoons, rhesus monkeys and, if you're lucky, alligators, which have been known to munch on the raccoons in front of gasping guests—the boat visits an "outpost" where a rehabilitation and breeding program for animals and birds of prey is under way. Near this boat dock is the **Jeep Safari**, a less-enthralling ride through a 35-acre block of enclosures for deer, Brazilian tapirs, and African waterbuck; the 15-minute excursion climaxes with a ride through a pit of alligators.

INSIDER TIP

"To gauge the length of an alligator that is mostly underwater, measure the distance from the tip of his nose to his eyes," says pontoon-boat Captain Charlie Patrick, and multiply the inches times 12. If the distance is six inches, the alligator is about six feet long.

The other wing of the park, to the right of the glass-bottom boats, is called Cypress Island. The 20-minute **Jungle Cruise**, leaves from a dock here, and takes guests in a boat past a series of large enclosures along the banks of the Fort King Waterway. Giraffes, zebras, aoudads and white-handed gibbons are on display. There are three animal shows on the island: **Reptiles of the World** (snakes and lizards), **Amazing Pets** (cats and dogs) and **Creature Feature** (bats, scorpions, a five-pound marine toad and giant Madagascar hissing cockroaches). Also found here is the 16-foot crocodile, **Sobek**, believed to be the largest American crocodile in captivity, and **Archbishop Hanna**, one of 17 enamel-white American alligators.

AUTHOR'S OBSERVATION

White alligators are so rare that there aren't even legends about them in the southern U.S. The porcelain white gator at Silver Springs is seven feet long and has soft blue eyes—which indicate pigment, making it a leucistic animal, rather than a true albino. The alligator is one of 17 discovered in a Louisiana marsh in 1987.

Silver Springs is open daily from 9 a.m. to 5:30 p.m.; hours are extended during the summer and over holiday weekends. Adult admission (tax included) is $29.63; children ages 3 to 10 are $20.09 (including tax). AAA members receive a discount, and a combo ticket with Wild Waters, a seasonal water-theme park next door, is also available. Parking is free. From Orlando, take the Florida Turnpike north to I-75; at Ocala, use Exit 69, and follow State Route 40 for 10 miles—Silver Springs is on the right. Additional information: ☎ *(904) 236-2121* or *(800) 234-7458.*

Other Attractions North of Orlando

Central Florida Zoological Park   ★★

3755 North U.S. 17/92, Lake Monroe, 32747, use Exit 52 from I-4; the zoo is a quarter-mile southeast on Lake Monroe, ☎ (407) 323-4450.
Hours: 9 a.m.–5 p.m.
A low-key, 29-acre facility two miles west of Sanford, the Central Florida Zoo features a couple of hundred animals, many common to the area, as well as elephants, hippos and bald eagles. The zoo boasts a large herpetarium (reptiles and amphibians), and has an extensive collection of smaller, endangered cats, including caracals, servals, cheetahs and jaguarundis. Elephant demonstrations are held at 11 a.m. and 2 p.m. daily; alligator snapping turtles are displayed at 11:15 a.m. and 2:15 p.m.; feedings around 3 p.m. A pleasant picnic area is located outside the zoo entrance. Admission: $7 adults; $4 seniors; $3 children age 3–12.

Ocala National Forest   ★★★★

45621 State Highway 19, Altoona, 32702, 45 miles northwest of Orlando, ☎ (904) 669-7495.
Hours: 9 a.m.–5 p.m.
Just an hour northeast of Orlando is the 383,000-acre Ocala National Forest. Sparsely developed and home to a series of freshwater springs, Ocala is a natural paradise, and the region is an easy day or overnight trip from Orlando for hiking, canoeing, fishing, birdwatching and more. Sand, slash and longleaf pines cover much of the gently rolling hills—the highest point is about 125 feet above sea level. Common wildlife includes reclusive black bears, alligators, eagles and osprey. Ocala's major hike is the Florida National Scenic Trail, a multiweek, still-under-construction odyssey that cuts through the National Forest on its way to Lake Okeechobee to the south, and Tallahassee to the northwest; the portion through Ocala is complete, and popular. Less-awesome pursuits on foot are also available: The Salt Springs Trail is a two-mile round-trip through cypress and pine forests to the Salt Springs Run, a freshwater river flowing at a rate of 52 million gallons per day; the St. Francis Trail begins at the River Forest Group Camp and offers two hikes—a 2.8-mile excursion to a natural spring, and a seven-mile trek through diverse terrain and six different ecosystems to the site of St. Francis, a once-booming pioneer town near the forest's southeast corner; and a pair of trails that lead to Lake Eaton and a nearby collapse sinkhole. Watersports and rentals are primarily based at the Salt Springs Marina, along State Route 19. Mid-November through mid-January is hunting season (by permit) throughout the forest; hikers and anyone

venturing off the main roads during this period should wear or carry articles of fluorescent orange color. For information, write, call or stop by the Visitor Center at the southern entrance (address above), or at the center along Route 40, near the town of Ocala.

AUTHOR'S OBSERVATION

Spanish Moss is neither moss, nor Spanish. The plant, which drapes gracefully from the boughs of oaks and other local trees, is actually a member of the pineapple family. Though many visitors want to take the moss home for decorating, it's infested with mites.

Sports/Recreation

Katie's Wekiva River Landing

190 Katie's Cove, Sanford, 32771, from I-4, take Exit 51, follow State Road 46 west for 5 miles; right on Wekiva Park Drive one mile, ☎ *(407) 628-1482.*

Hours: 7:45 a.m.–5:30 p.m.

Special hours: Extended hours during summer.

One of central Florida's most genuine escapes is provided by Katie Moncrief, who offers both guided and solo excursions along the scenic Wekiva River and its tributaries, much of which has been designated a Florida State Canoe Trail (also see "Why Orlando?" in "Introduction and Overview"). Though only a half-hour north of Orlando, you'll see plenty of birds and turtles, occasionally an alligator and, if you're really lucky, some of the manatees who "winter" in the St. John's River. Trips range from two hours to all-day and overnight adventures; all levels of ability can be accommodated. Rates, including canoe rental, life preservers and transportation to put-in point, with a minimum of four guests, start at $16.05 (including tax) for adults, with children ages 3 to 12 half-price. During warm weather, carry bug repellent and plenty of fluids; wear your bathing suit under shorts and bring a towel (a plastic bag is wise for keys, wallet and camera). Log cabins and campsites also available.

AUTHOR'S OBSERVATION

The oldest and largest cypress tree in the world resides in Big Tree Park just outside Sanford. Named "The Senator," the bald cypress is estimated to be 3500 years old.

Points South

The backbone of hills south of Orlando give weight to the southernmost reach of the Bible Belt, a region of vast citrus groves and steaming factories that reek of processed oranges. The numerous lakes make **water-skiing** the unofficial sport, celebrated proudly by **Cypress Gardens**. And peninsular Flor ida reaches its highest point here, at **Iron Mountain** which, at 298 feet, is the highest rise for hundreds of miles.

Bok Tower Gardens is a natural historic landmark located on Iron Mountain, the Florida peninsula's highest point.

Lake Wales has a curious claim to fame: on North Wales Drive (at North Avenue), cars roll "uphill" from the bottom of **Spook Hill**, an optical illusion that makes kids giggle, and adults reach for the parking brake (the phenomenon is said to be rooted in a Seminole Indian legend). Less curious is the ringing in your ears—the glorious carillon at **Bok Tower Gardens** that chimes every half-hour, beckoning visitors to the peaceful gardens unfettered by garish entertainments. One of Lake Wales' quirkiest establishments is **Chalet Suzanne**, a soup production plant and country inn with impossibly unique guest rooms—and an acclaimed restaurant with sky high prices (see "Other Possibilities" in "Hotels and Accommodations").

Two baseball teams use this region for Spring Training: the **Cleveland Indians**, who play at Winter Haven's Chain O' Lakes Stadium, and the **Kansas City Royals**, who play in Davenport's Baseball City Stadium. See "Spring Training" in "After the Theme Parks" for more information.

Miami is about 236 miles south of Orlando, a four-hour drive down the Florida turnpike. But that's another book.

Cypress Gardens

Conjure the picture of a water-borne chorus line of curvaceous women in one-piece bathing suits and where are you?

For many Americans, this trademark Cypress Gardens image of babes on water skis defined Florida from the 1940s on. When the visual was revived in 1982 by the rock group the Go Go's, who pasted their five heads onto the bodies of the water skiers to promote their album *Vacation*, another generation was presented with this tantalizing, loopy and once-risqué vision.

Credit owner Dick Pope with engraving this image into our brains—he was a master at public relations and once proclaimed himself the "Man Who Invented Florida." But credit Pope's wife Julie with the original concept of charging admission to their lakeside garden attraction to watch pretty girls on water skis. After several soldiers saw a promotional photo of water-skiers and had come to see the show, she rounded up her children and friends to produce one on the fly—and the following weekend, legend has it, 800 soldiers showed up for more. The park's tradition of parasol-clad southern belles posing on rambling lawns had an equally accidental beginning, when a major freeze in 1940 had damaged much of the gardens and the enterprising Pope dressed her employees in the extravagant hoopskirts to hide dead foliage.

Dick was the tireless entrepreneur, and he initiated their move to the town of Winter Haven—which sits along a chain of 14 interconnecting lakes. The park got its start when Pope read a *Good Housekeeping* article about a man who opened his house to the paying public. He imagined a Florida botanical wonderland and spent the early '30s with his wife building the property, opening on Jan. 2, 1936. He photographed the park and his posing beauties relentlessly, aiming a "ceaseless barrage" of the images to newspapers and magazines nationwide. In the early '60s, the *Saturday Evening Post* gushed that one of his cheesecake shots alone made 3760 papers. Absurd staged events—to announce the queen of citrus, or of good posture—were almost daily occurrences. And Pope's unflinching promotion of his beloved gardens wasn't limited to photos; an early billboard proclaimed simply, "If it isn't Florida's most unusual beauty spot, your admission gladly refunded."

AUTHOR'S OBSERVATION

Dick Pope referred to his favorite form of marketing as the "OPM system"– other people's money. The formula entailed tie-ins with other businesses; for instance, currently the Ames company sells "The Official Lawn and Garden Tool of Cypress Gardens." A little free exposure would also be provided by offering the gardens as a stage for a morning television show. The coup de grace would be an endless volley of publicity stunts to generate text and photo fodder for the many publications looking for filler. The sum of these parts was an unequaled, inexpensive publicity and promotion machine.

Today, the 200-acre Cypress Gardens is still pretty unusual, all right. The park quietly celebrated its 60th anniversary in 1996—though it doesn't look a day over 50. And, as long as we're tallying the numbers, the day I visited the gardens, I was the only person touring the attraction who appeared to be under 50 years of age.

How many visitors the park receives is a subject of local debate. Cypress Gardens benefited from the initial rush of tourists that swamped the region following the opening of The Magic Kingdom, but by the 1980s, with Dick Pope's health failing, the family sold Cypress Gardens to Harcourt Brace Jovanovich, which in turn sold it (and Sea World) in 1989 to Anheuser-Busch. Insiders point to a decade of declining attendance that lead to Anheuser-Busch selling the operation in 1995 to a management group. The attraction appeals to many area seniors, the nostalgic and the green-thumbs, and draws a number of European visitors in the summer who appreciate the tastefully landscaped grounds.

The main draw, of course, is the original **16-acre garden**, which contains 8000 varieties of plants and flowers culled from 90 countries. On your way into the park, pick up an entertainment schedule and map. The original gardens are located to the right of the entrance, which is also where you can begin a 15-minute tour of the shoreline canals via 18-passenger electric boats that wind through the cypress trees. At the rear of this section is the infamous **Florida-shaped pool**, constructed by Pope for the 1953 Busby Berkeley movie, *Easy to Love*, starring Esther Williams. Note the prominent gazebo, which is made of a leftover WWII satellite dish mounted on pillars from a cigar factory; the southern belles are usually positioned here. The **Pontoon Lake Cruise** (admission, $3.45), provides a 30-minute excursion around Lake Eloise and through nearby Lake Summit.

A pair of large, lakeside bleachers near the park entrance mark the location of the water ski extravaganza, **Totally Mardi Gras**. Julie Pope's first water ski show was performed in 1942 and in the ensuing decades, Cypress Gardens has attracted and developed talented athletes. The 30-minute show currently embraces a Mardi Gras theme, which primarily seems an excuse to justify the colorful costumes. Featuring "aqua maids" and "gauchos" the show incorporates water ski and boat stunts, and climaxes with the world's only five-tier human pyramid.

Cypress Gardens in Winter Haven features many unique shows and exhibits.

To the left of the main entrance are a series of shows and exhibits. The best include the butterfly exhibit, **Wings of Wonder**, which showcases about 1000 specimens in a glassed conservatory. **Moscow on Ice Live** is a spunky 30-minute ice show performed by a troupe of professional skaters from Russia. The **Reptile Discovery Program** is an educational show featuring lizards, alligators and a 14-foot albino python. The **Island in the Sky** is a unique, 153-foot-high platform that rises from the ground and revolves around a Styrofoam volcano and yields excellent views. But my favorite is the **Cypress Roots Museum**, which is loaded with memorabilia dating back to the park's opening, including historical photos, newspaper clippings, original costumes and more.

Among the park's yearly festivals are the **Spring Flower Festival** with 19 larger-than-life topiaries and 30,000 floral bed annuals, and animated light-pieces and fireworks at night; the summer-long **Victorian Garden Party**, which displays 80 life-size ivy and fig-vine topiary figures; the **Mum Festival** in November, which is composed of 2.5 million blooms representing 20 cascading and garden varieties of mums; and the **Poinsettia Festival and Garden of Lights**, which runs from Thanksgiving through the first week of January.

Cypress Gardens features both sit-down and cafeteria style dining options, and a mini-mall at the entrance that sells park souvenirs and gardening paraphernalia.

Cypress Gardens is open daily from 9:30 a.m. to 5:30 p.m. Admission (tax included) is $29.63 for adults, seniors 55 and up are $24.33. During 1996, to celebrate the 60th anniversary, up to two children per paying adult ages 6 to 12 are admitted free; each additional child is $19.02 (children 5 and under are always free); a children's admission policy for 1997 had not been determined at press time. An annual pass is available. Virtually all of the park is wheelchair-accessible; strollers and wheelchairs are rented for $5. Parking is free. Cypress Gardens is located near Winter Haven on the shores of Lake Eloise, about 35 miles south of Lake Buena Vista. From Orlando take I-4 west to U.S. 27 south, and State Route 540 west; Cypress Gardens is on the left. Additional information, ☎ *(800) 282-2123* or *(941) 324-2111.*

Other Attractions South of Orlando

Museums and Exhibits

Fantasy of Flight ★★

> *1400 Broadway Boulevard, Southeast, Polk City, 33868, use Exit 21 off I-4; go north on State Route 559 to Polk City, follow the signs,* ☎ *(941) 984-3500.*
> *Hours: 9 a.m.–5 p.m.*
> *Special hours: Extended hours during summer and peak season.*
> A museum dedicated to aviation history, Fantasy of Flight houses the world's largest private collection of vintage aircraft, the horde of aviation enthusiast Kermit Weeks, who began accumulating the planes in the late 1970s. Among the 30-plus planes on display are the *Curtiss Jenny* and other World War I aircraft, a Lockheed *Vega, Boe-*

ing 100, a replica of the *Spirit of St. Louis*, a British *Spitfire* and other World War
II survivors, a *MIG-15*, and the last four-engine airworthy *Short Sunderland Flying
Boat*, the centerpiece of the collection. Four separate "immersion experiences"
reprise man's first flights including a World War II B-17 bombing mission and aerial
battle over the Pacific. A ride on the Fightertown Flight Simulator is $6.31 (tax
included). The art deco buildings contain a diner, and the gift shop features one-of-
a-kind vintage aviation antiquities and other souvenirs. General admission: $12.
Admission: $9.49 adults; $8.43 seniors; $7.37 children age 5–10.

Parks and Gardens

Bok Tower Gardens   ★ ★ ★

*1151 Tower Boulevard, Lake Wales, 33853, three miles noth of Lake Wales, off County
Road 17A, near Cypress Gardens,* ☎ *(941) 676-1408.*
Hours: 8 a.m.–6 p.m.

Publisher and author Edward Bok built this 157-acre paradise in the rolling hills 55
miles south of Orlando, and dedicated it to the American people in 1929, when
Mickey Mouse was making his celluloid debut. The serene gardens envelope peninsular Florida's highest point, Iron Mountain (298 feet above sea level), and are
capped by a singing bell tower made of pink and gray Georgia marble and Florida
coquina stone. Designated as a National Historic Landmark the tower houses a carillon that includes 57 bronze bells weighing from 17 pounds to almost 12 tons. The
carillon is one of the world's best, and a 45-minute recital is performed daily at 3
p.m. by resident carillonneur Milford Myhre. Guided walking tours are available
daily at noon and 2 p.m. mid-January through mid-April (Sundays at 2 p.m. only).
Though the tower is not open for touring, the verdant grounds are beautifully
maintained, offering a peaceful respite for relaxation, meditation. reading, birdwatching and picnicing. Admission: $4 adults; $1 children age 5–12.

AFTER THE THEME PARKS

Activities In and Around the World

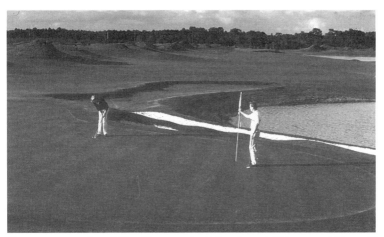

There are more than 100 golf courses in Orlando and 100 more within a 45 minute drive.

Golf

"Sure, the first vision the name Orlando conjures is of a giant, smiling rodent with oversize ears, floppy shoes and a falsetto voice. He towers over this central Florida burg, which really is like Las Vegas—minus the card, roulette and craps tables. But look past the tinsel and you can find a golfing oasis."

—**Larry Dorman**, *The New York Times*

Florida has more than 1000 golf courses—more than any other state—and they run the gamut from public courses primed for beginners to the Grand Cypress' triumphant homage to the classic Old Course of St. Andrews in Scotland, where the game was first played. The flat Florida landscape means that the best courses are usually constructed with a fleet of earth-movers. And the pursuit of new and exciting golf experiences has pushed course development farther into the once-virgin woods, but the result has been the emergence of courses such as Disney's isolated **Osprey Ridge**, where the leveled forests yield idyllic communions with the designer links.

Walt Disney World features the best spread of greens: five 18-hole, 72-par courses, and one nine-hole walking course—99 holes in all—each of which is open to nonguests, although visitors overnighting at a Disney Resort receive preferential tee times and lower greens fees. The Championship greens are meticulously maintained, particularly in the days leading up to the Oldsmobile Golf Classic, a PGA Tour stop every October.

INSIDER TIP

You, too, can play in a PGA tournament. For those willing to cough up $5000–the minimum one-year membership fee–you can buy a place alongside the pros in the Walt Disney World Oldsmobile Golf Classic. For additional information, call ☎ (407) 824-2250.

The two original courses—both designed by Joe Lee and dating to The Magic Kingdom's 1971 opening—are the **Palm** and the **Magnolia**, located around Shades of Green Resort, just opposite the Polynesian Resort, with the hum of the monorail nearby. Each has the look and feel of a more-traditional Florida course, and one features an infamous, not-so-hidden Mickey (aka, the Mousetrap). The Palm is a challenging classic amid a surfeit of water hazards; the 18th hole is rated the fourth-hardest on the PGA Tour, and holes six and 10 are also among the toughest in Walt Disney World. Generally regarded as one of the country's top 100 designs, the Palm has a Slope Rating topping out at 133, with a layout playing at 6957/6461/6029/5311 yards.

The lengthy Magnolia next door features one bunker after another—the fourth hole alone has 11 lining the fairway. But the biggest challenge comes on the 17th, a 400-yard par four that is practically engulfed by water over its entire length. The greens are ringed by magnolia trees throughout, and the course features a Slope Rating of 133 with a layout extending 7190/6642/6091/5232 yards.

AUTHOR'S OBSERVATION

Jack Nicklaus won the first Walt Disney World open in 1971, shooting 15-under 273 over four rounds at the Magnolia course and prompting Disney to modify the two-month-old course by moving back the tees on four holes. The following year, Nicklaus came back, shot 21 under par and captured the second tournament, winning by an astounding nine shots. In 1973, Nicklaus won his third Disney tournament, the only golfer to do so.

The **Lake Buena Vista** course sprawls over a large belt that is bordered by the Key West Vacation Club, the Port Orleans Resort and the Disney Institute, yet is more modest in yardage. Also designed by Joe Lee, the links are tightly constructed within the trees, and flow with the landscape, creating Disney's most beginner-friendly course, and also serves as home base for the Institute's golf program. The Slope Rating is 128, and the layout measures 6819/6268/5919/5194 yards.

The newcomers are the spectacular greens created in 1992 that stretch well into the woods beyond Fort Wilderness; both feature acclaimed architecture. Pete Dye's **Eagle Pines** course is famous for allowing water into play on all but two of the holes, though it features a lower profile and is accessible to beginner-intermediates. The fairways trail off gracefully to scrub areas dusted with pine needles, providing a serene natural ambiance. The Slope Rating is 131 with a layout playing 6772/6309/5520/4838 yards — Disney's shortest course.

Osprey Ridge is a long course with several remote holes that produce an even more placid, naturalistic environment. Tom Fazio's dramatic contouring produces tees up to 25 feet above the basic grade, which (coupled with the large greens) make club selection an essential component. With a Slope Rating of 135, and a course measuring 7101/6680/6103/5402 yards, this is probably the most prodigious (and currently the most popular) of Disney's five golf courses.

Rates for the Palm, Magnolia and Lake Buena Vista courses are $90.10 (including tax) year-round for Disney Resort guests and Magic Kingdom Club members, or $100.70 for visitors staying off-property. Greens fees are higher January through April at the popular Osprey Ridge and Eagle Pines courses: $111.30 for Disney Resort guests, $127.20 for those staying off-property (all rates include cart rental). Afternoon "twilight" slots are less expensive: $42.40–53.00 after 3 p.m. (after 2 p.m. November through February). Rental clubs start at $22, and lessons are priced $50 per half-hour session, or $150 for a playing session. Juniors are half-price.

The Disney courses are very popular and tee times should be booked as soon as your travel dates have firmed to obtain the best slots. The month of

January, in particular, and during the Oldsmobile Classic in October, can be very difficult periods to secure a reservation. If you're staying *off* the Disney property, your options will be further limited: during the January-April peak season, you may lock down reservations only four days in advance. One piece of tee-procuring advice, Mondays and Tuesdays tend to be the least-busy days. ☎ *(407) 824-2270;* this number also handles lessons.

A round at the nine-hole, par-36 **Oak Trail** is $25.44 (tax included), or $33.92 for two rounds. Prices do not include cart rental; the course is designed for walking. Children are half-price. Rental clubs for Oak Trail are priced a modest $5.

AUTHOR'S OBSERVATION

Central Florida is known as the "Lightning Capital of the World," with a series of thunderstorms rolling almost daily through the area during summer months. Though the usual advice—stay off the golf course—applies as always, everyone should avoid pools and lakes, lone trees in open areas, elevated zones, and wire fences or other metallic objects that draw lightning.

Outside Mickey's domain, there are more than a hundred courses within a 45-minute drive of downtown Orlando. At some resorts, you have to stay to play, but sometimes a humble letter of introduction from a golf pro back home will procure a tee time. In addition, the many public courses should keep all but the pickiest fanatic happy. Among the region's best golf facilities are:

Bay Hill Club and Lodge

☎ *(800) 523-5999 or (407) 876-2429.*

Arnold Palmer's winter home (he plays and eats lunch here almost every day) and home to the Bay Hill Invitational in March—not coincidentally, possibly the finest course in the area. 27 challenging holes await players, all providing a 72 par game; the three nine-hole layouts (Challenger, Champion and Charger) range from 5065 to 7114 yards. Some find the rustic, 58-room lodge (which you need to overnight in to play here) a tad frumpy, and locked in the early 1960s; jackets are required during the evening. Nonetheless, a 1996 *Conde Nast Traveler* readers' poll selected Bay Hill's staff as the single best in North America—a spiffy pro shop, too. Bay Hill is located three miles west of Universal Studios on Lake Tibet Butler (just off the Apopka-Vineland Road). Greens fees are included in the overnight rates.

Black Bear Golf Club

☎ *(800) 423-2718 or (352) 357-4732.*

This central Florida newcomer designed by Pete Dye opened in November 1995. Black Bear is a fun, 18-hole course offering six sets of tees measuring from 5080 to 7002 yards. The par-72 layout features 175 acres of gently rolling greens and striking elevation changes—the sparse land is mowed to fairway height, lacks roughs and, outside the lake-engulfed 10th, features little water (its best asset: no forced carries). The recessed, inverted greens inspire solitude, and cart paths are at a minimum, encouraging a casual, walking game. A 19th "bye" hole is available as a shoot-out for friendly tie-breakers. Located in Eustis, near Mt. Dora, 40 minutes north of Orlando. Greens fees: $40 Monday through Thursday, $45 Friday through Sunday.

Falcon's Fire

☎ *(407) 397-2777.*

A friendly, Rees Jones-signature course located in Kissimmee, Falcon's Fire is an 18-hole, 72 par offering a landscape of gently rolling greens, large lakes and fairways bordered by oversize mounds. The eighth hole is a delight, or a terror, depending on your ability to sail a tee shot over a body of water to the green, where seven bunkers guard front and back—"Falcon's Pride" is one of the most difficult par threes in the area. The course plays 5417/6080/6473/6901 yards. Located two miles east of I-4 off U.S. 192. Greens fees: $52–$78, discounts for twilight play.

Hyatt Regency Grand Cypress

☎ *(800) 790-7377 or (407) 239-1975.*

Universally regarded as one of the best golf resorts in the country, though the 45 Jack Nicklaus-designed holes are limited to guests only. The resort offers three excellent nine-hole layouts—the North, South and East Nines—which can be played in various pleasing 72 par combinations, ranging from 5821 to 6993 yards. The clincher is the New Course, a stateside tribute to St. Andrews' Old Course, right down to an 18th-hole copy of the Valley of Sin amid heather-lined fairways. There's little water coming into play, but the almost-treeless site is studded by 145 bunkers, double greens and stone walls. This time-consuming round requires creativity and intuition to play. The course layout is 5314/6181/6773 yards. The resort also features a nine-hole pitch-and-putt green, and a high-tech, biomechanic school: the Grand Cypress Academy of Golf (private lessons are available for non-guests). Located immediately north of the Disney Village area, just off Walt Disney World property. Greens fees and cart: $125 for guests, or $150 if you can swing it as a nonguest.

Marriott's Orlando World Center

☎ *(407) 238-8660.*

Water, water everywhere. Wrapping around the towering 27-story hotel, this par-71 is designed by Joe Lee, architect of three Disney courses, and adds plenty of trees and approximately 80 bunkers to the ever-present water hazards to keep this short course interesting. The course layout measures 4988/5956/6307 yards. The John Jacobs Practical Golf School is available on the premises for lessons. Located just off State Route 536 (Epcot Center Drive), two miles south of Lake Buena Vista. Greens fees and cart, $60–100; twilight and nine-hole rates, $40–65.

Orange Lake Country Club

☎ *(800) 877-6522 or (407) 239-0000.*

This 27-hole championship course is spread over 357 acres—all three layouts par at 72. In any union, the game isn't long, and abundant water and slender, short fairways add to the challenge. The three layouts can be combined for courses from

5322 to 6667 yards. A good budget choice; greens fees and cart, $30–$60; twilight rates, $17–$26. Located on U.S. 192, four miles west of Disney's Maingate entrance.

For die-hards willing to venture further for their fairway satiation, two other courses come highly recommended, but are both a 90-minute drive west from Orlando. The **Innisbrook Hilton Resort** in Tarpon Springs features the famous Copperhead Course and two other excellent layouts; you need to stay at the resort to play: ☎ *(800) 221-2424* or *(813) 942-2000*. Just north of Tampa, in Brookville, 60-foot elevation changes mark **Pine Barrons at World Woods**, a scrappy, isolated paean to Pine Valley in the middle of nowhere— "might be the finest public course in this or any other state," wrote *The New York Times* ☎ *(904) 796-5500*.

Golfpac will book the land portion of golf packages throughout the state, securing preferential tee times at most of the area resorts. Free 72-page brochure. ☎ *(800) 327-0878* or *(407) 260-2288*.

INSIDER TIP

Some Orlandoans rank **Lake Nona**, *located within spitting distance of the Orlando International Airport, as the best central Florida golf course. With a dazzling Tom Fazio design, and celebrities such as Michael Jordan, Sylvester Stallone and George Bush popping by for a round, this course is also one of the most exclusive. Currently, nonmembers must enroll in the $1500-a-day David Leadbetter Golf Academy to get a crack at these links.*

Course	Type	Yds	Par	Phone
Brevard County				
Baytree National Golf Links **National Drive, Melbourne 32940** *1/2 mile east of I-95 on Wickham Road Exit 73*	Public	7063-6469	72	*(407) 259-9060*
The Savannahs at Sykes Creek **3915 Savannahs Trail, Merritt Island 32953** *3 miles north of Bee Line on Route 3 to Hail Road*	Municipal	6700-5600	72	*(407) 455-1375*
Spessard Holland Golf Club **2374 Oak Street, Melbourne Beach 32951** *3 miles south of 192 on A1A*	Public	5211	67	*(407) 952-4529*
Turtle Creek Golf Club **1278 Admiralty Boulevard, Rockledge 32955** *I-95 at Exit 74 (Fiske Boulevard)*	Semi-Private	6686-6177	72	*(407) 632-2520*
Volusia County				
Golf Club at Cypress Head **6231 Whispering Lake, Port Orange 32129** *I-95 to Exit 85, west to Airport Road, south 2.4 miles*	Public	6814-4971	72	*(904) 756-5449*

Course	Type	Yds	Par	Phone
DeBary Golf & Country Club *300 Plantation Club Drive, P.O. Box 975, DeBary 32713* *Off Highway 17-92, 1 mile north of downtown DeBary*	Semi-Private	6776-5060	72	*(407) 668-2061*
Halifax Plantation *4000 Old Dixie Highway, Ormond Beach 32174* *I-95, exit 90 East, south 1.5 mi. on Old Dixie Highway*	Semi-Private	7128-4971	72	*(904) 676-9600*
Indigo Lakes Golf Club *301 Indigo Drive, Daytona Beach 32114* *1/4 mile east of 95 on Rou; 92*	Resort	7168-6176	72	*(904) 254-3607*
LPGA International *300 Champions Drive, Daytona Beach 32124* *I-95 to 92 West, north on LPGA Boulevard (11 Street) 5 miles to Champion Drive*	Municipal	7008-5131	72	*(904) 274-3880*
Marion County				
Golden Ocala Golf & Country Club *7800 U.S. Highway N.W., Ocala 32675* *On Highway 27, 3-1/2 miles west of I-75 (exit 70)*	Public	6735-6197	72	*(904) 629-6229*
Orange County				
Dubsdread Golf Club *549 West Par Avenue, Orlando 32804* *1 mile west of I-4 on Par Avenue*	Municipal	6055-5575	71	*(407) 246-3636*
Eastwood Golf Club *13950 Golf Way Boulevard, Orlando 32828* *2 miles south of E-W Expressway on Alafaya*	Semi-Private	7176-5393	72	*(407) 281-4653*
Forest Lake Golf Club of Ocoee *10521 Clarcona/Ocoee Road, Ocoee 34761* *Highway 50 west to Hiwassee, north to Clarcona/Ocoee Road*	Public	7003-5024	72	*(407) 654-4653*
International Golf Club *6351 International Drive, Orlando 32821* *1.5 miles south to Sea World*	Resort	6496-5077	72	*(407) 239-6909*
Marriott's Orlando WC˙ *World Center Drive, Orlando 32821* *I-4 to Exit 26A, 536 east 1 mile*	Resort	6307-5048	71	*(407) 238-8660*
Orange Lake Country Club˙ *8505 Irlo Bronson Parkway, Kissimmee 32741* *I-4 to Exit 192-W, 5 miles*	Semi-Private	6700-6400	70	*(407) 239-1050*
Zellwood Station Country Club *Highway 441 North, Zellwood 32798* *5 miles north of Apopka on 441*	Semi-Private	6400-5377	72	*(407) 886-3303*

Course	Type	Yds	Par	Phone
Osceola County				
Falcon's Fire Golf Club` 3200 Seralago Boulevard, Kissimmee 34746 2 miles east of I-4, on north side of Highway 192	Resort	6901- 5417	72	(407) 239-5445
Kissimmee Bay Country Club 2801 Kissimmee Bay Boulevard, Kissimmee 34744 Highway 192 east to Boggy Creek Road, east on Fortune	Semi-Private	6846- 5171	71	(407) 348-4653
Kissimmee Golf Club 3103 Florida Coach Drive, Kissimmee 34741 Route 192 to Hoagland Boulevard, south 2.5 miles	Semi-Private	6653- 5120	72	(407) 847-2816
The Oaks 3232 S. Bermuda Avenue, Kissimmee 34741 Route South Kissimmee on South Bermuda Avenue	Semi-Private	6942- 5021	72	(407) 933-4055
Poinciana Golf & Racquet Club 500 E. Cypress Parkway, Kissimmee 34759 Highway 192 to Poinciana Boulevard, 13 miles south	Resort	6700- 6014	72	(407) 933-5300
Remington Golf Club 2995 Remington Boulevard, Kissimmee 34744 Highway 192 east to Partin-Settlement Road, left on E. Lake Shore Drive, 2 miles	Public	7044- 4980	72	(407) 872-7919
Polk County				
Diamondback Golf Club 6501 SR 544 East, Haines City 33844 I-4 to US 27 south to 544, 6 miles	Semi-Private	6805- 6359	72	(941) 421-0437
Sandpiper Golf Club 6001 Sandpipers Drive, Lakeland 33809 I-4 to exit #19 - North, 1.5 miles on right	Semi-Private	6442- 5024	70	(941) 859-5461
The Ridge at Ridgewood Lakes 200 PGA Drive, Davenport 33837 I-4 to Exit 23, south 2.5 miles on east side	Public	7016- 5217	72	(941) 424-8688
Seminole County				
Ekana Golf Club 2199 Ekana Drive, Oviedo 32765 2.5 miles east on 419, Route on Lockwood Road	Semi-Private	6853- 5516	72	(407) 366-1211
Sabal Point Country Club 2662 Sabal Club Way, Longwood 32779 I-4 to 434 West to Wekiva Springs Road, 1/2 mile North	Semi-Private	6603- 5278	72	(407) 869-4622
Timacuan Golf & Country Club 550 Timacuan Boulevard, Lake Mary 3274. I-4 Exit 50, Lake Mary Boulevard to Rine	Semi-Private	7023- 5401	72	(407) 321-0010

Course	Type	Yds	Par	Phone
Lake County				
Black Bear Country Club* 24505 Calusa Boulevard, Eustis 32736 I-4 to 46 West 13 miles, north on 437	Semi-Private	7004- 5103	72	*(904) 357-4732*
Clerbrook Resort Golf Club 20005 U.S. Highway 27, Clermont 34711 On U.S. 27, 1 mile south of Florida Turnpike	Semi-Private	5154- 4805	67	*(904) 394-6165*
Country Club of Mount Dora 1900 Country Club Boulevard, Mount Dora 32757 1 mile north of Highway 46 on 4411	Semi-Private	6612- 5709	72	*(904) 735-2263*
Deer Island Golfer's Club 17450 Deer Island Road, Tavares 32778 441 North through Zellwood, west on Sadler (448), follow signs	Semi-Private	6676- 5298	72	*(904) 343-6741*
Mission Inn Golf & Tennis Resort *10400 C.R. 48, Howey-In-The-Hills 34737* *Florida Turnpike Exits (northbound) #285, (south-* *bound) #289, to SR 19N*	Resort	6879- 6852	72	*(904) 324-3885*

* Discussed in text

Miniature Golf

In 1996, Disney delivered its delightful version of miniature golf, **Fantasia Gardens Miniature Golf**, the world's largest miniature golf facility. High on interactive whimsy, the 18-hole "adventure" course is themed to the 1941 film classic, "Fantasia," and features ornate topiaries embodying the film's animated characters, along with dancing fountains and vivid flower beds. The third hole is a frolic, with your ball bouncing down chimes, while tricky hole 10 is the crux, with Bacchus egging on golfers up a steep ramp. Next door, an 18-hole "challenge" course, **Fantasia Fairways**, emphasizes skill over chance, offering exaggerated contours, water hazards and sand bunkers over a series of par-three and par-four holes shaped in dogleg bends. The Fairways course is like a miniature version of a real golf course with flags, and children under 10 can be a little frustrated with the level of challenge.

Located opposite the Walt Disney World Swan, Fantasia Gardens and Fantasia Fairways opened to immediate success—so much so that Disney quickly hiked the prices to keep the demand at bay (more courses are reportedly in the works). The courses are open daily from 10 a.m. to midnight, but are busiest in the evening, particularly as the parks begin to shut down. Allow 45 to 60 minutes to play the Gardens course, and 75 to 90 minutes for the Fairways. A round at either of the courses including club rental is $9.54 for adults, $8.48 for children age 3 to 9 (including tax). There is no direct transportation to Fantasia Gardens. The easiest way to reach the courses is to take

Disney bus or boat transportation to the Swan; Fantasia Gardens is a five-minute walk from there (there is no path from the nearby Disney-MGM Studios parking area). The BoardWalk, Dolphin, Yacht and Beach Club are a 10-to-15 minute walk. ☎ *(407) 560-8760.*

Duffers are tickled by **Pirate's Cove Adventure Golf**, a tropically embroidered landscape of caves, palms and toilet-bowl-cleaner-blue waterfalls and ponds. Pirate's Cove offers two locations to putt away: immediately next to I-4 in Lake Buena Vista (at Exit 27), and at 8501 International Drive, just south of Wet 'n Wild, both are open 9 a.m. to 11:30 p.m. daily. Both locations feature two 18-hole courses (one geared for younger golfers). One round for adults, $7.42; children ages 4 to 12, $6.36; discounts for two rounds or more. ☎ *(407) 827-1242,* or the I-Drive location, ☎ *(407) 352-7378.*

Fishing

The waters of Walt Disney World were stocked with 70,000 largemouth bass prior to the opening of The Magic Kingdom, and the creatures have multiplied in quantity and expanded in size during the ensuing quarter-century. Several options for recreational fishing are available, and they don't require a license within World boundaries.

Enthusiastically embracing the low-tech, Tom-and-Huck era of backwoods fishing excursions, the **Ol' Man Island Fishin' Hole** at Dixie Landings is a rustic testimony to Walt's beloved boyhood memories. The pond is stocked with blue gill, largemouth bass and catfish up to 15 pounds, and all fish are released back to the water. Old-fashioned cane poles and bait, plus use of the dock are $3.50 per hour, or $12.50 per hour for a family of up to six. You may bring your own pole and bait, but the hourly rate still applies. Hours: 9 a.m. to 3 p.m. ☎ *(407) 934-5409.*

Dixie Landings' two-hour fishing trips down the adjacent **Sassagoula River** were discontinued indefinitely in May 1996 due to a Reedy Creek environmental research project; they may have been re-established by the time you read this: ☎ *(407) 934-5409.*

Two-hour guided fishing trips on **Bay Lake** and the **Seven Seas Lagoon** are available with pickups from the marinas at any of the four resorts and the campground lining the two lakes. The price for the trip is $137 for up to five guests, including equipment, bait and refreshments (shiners are extra). The two-hour trips leave at 8 a.m., 11:30 a.m. and 3 p.m. daily. Reservations (up to two weeks in advance) necessary: ☎ *(407) 824-2621*.

Captain Jack's Guided Bass Tours provides two-hour, catch-and-release fishing excursions from the Disney Village Marketplace marina. The guided tours stick to the small lake facing the Marketplace and Pleasure Island, rather than heading up the canals, and bass up to 14 pounds have been caught, though two to five pounds is the rule. The trip is priced $137 for a group of up to five anglers, and includes all equipment; there are usually two trips daily, one at 6:30 a.m. and another at 9 a.m. Reservations necessary: ☎ *(407) 828-2461*.

To fish *outside* Walt Disney World, you'll need to procure a fishing license, unless you're under 16 years of age—which runs $16.50 for seven days, or $31.50 for a full year (fresh water and salt water fishing require separate licenses). Fishing licenses are available at any WalMart, Kmart and most area sporting-goods and bait-and-tackle stores.

AUTHOR'S OBSERVATION

Orlando is richly endowed with freshwater lakes, many of them sinkholes in the unreliable limestone soil. The city boasts 77 lakes and 56 miles of shoreline in all.

Watersports

Many of the Disney Resorts have a selection of watersport activities available, but the lakeside resorts—the **Wilderness Lodge**, **Polynesian**, **Contemporary** and **Grand Floridian Beach**—have the largest selection. These include a variety of motorized and sail boats such as Aqua Fins, Aqua Cats, Water Sprites, Canopy and Pontoon Boats, Sea Rayders and Hobie Cats, but each resort has its own unique selection. For instance, canoes and water-skiing is found at the Wilderness Lodge, while the largest Hobie Cats (16 feet) are based at the Polynesian. Rentals are by the half or full hour, and motorized prices top out at $30 per 30 minutes for the three-person Sea Rayders, which can crank out 25 to 30 miles-per-hour from their 90 horsepower engines— the fastest rental boats on the property. For more information, call your Disney Resort and ask for the watersports desk.

Florida's many lakes provide great opportunities for water skiing.

Swimming is available at all of the Disney Resorts, with the extensive Yacht and Beach Club facilities, named **Stormalong Bay**, topping the list. In addition to a nifty water slide through the fallen mast of a shipwreck, the three-acre pool features a sandbar and interconnecting lagoons spiced by gentle whirlpools and waterfalls. The **Wilderness Lodge** also boasts an excellent pool, set against the woods and overlooking Bay Lake, while the planned make-over of the **Polynesian** facilities in late 1996 will probably build splendidly on the tropical theme. Note that at all Disney Resorts, use of the pool facilities is reserved for the guests of that resort (see "12 Best Hotel Swimming Facilities" in "Hotels and Accommodations"). Outside the pools, guests staying at the resorts lining **Bay Lake** (the Contemporary, Wilderness Lodge and Fort Wilderness) and the **Seven Seas Lagoon** (the Polynesian and Grand Floridian Beach) may use the freshwater lakes for swimming. However, the Seven Seas Lagoon is occasionally closed to bathers when the lake's bacteria count becomes problematic. One of the best spots for lap swimming is the sprawling pool at the **Peabody Orlando**.

Parasailing is offered at the Contemporary Resort marina. The four- to six-minute flight over Bay Lake or the Seven Seas Lagoon is $60. Reservations should be made several days in advance; call the Contemporary's water sports desk: ☎ *(407) 824-1000, extension 3586.*

So you can practice your audition for Cypress Gardens, **water-skiing** is available on the Seven Seas Lagoon or Bay Lake. One-hour trips with an instructor on board depart daily from the four resorts and the campground lining the lakes, and accommodate all levels of ability. The boat rental and instructor is $86.92 and the crafts hold up to five skiers; trips depart beginning at 8:45 a.m. Reservations (up to two weeks in advance) necessary: ☎ *(407) 824-2621.*

AUTHOR'S OBSERVATION

Disney stunned many in the travel industry with its 1994 announcement that it would abandon the Big Red Boat and build two new mega-cruise ships as part of the Disney Cruise Lines portion of the company. The two ships— 85,000 tons each and with berths for 2400 passengers—will be larger than any other cruise liner in operation and are being built by the Fincantieri shipyard in Trieste, Italy. In addition to reflecting various, tried-and-true Disney motifs aboard, a prime stop will include a stop at a Disney-owned, themed island off the coast of Florida, allowing the company to own all of the destination's concessions, as well as control the flow of ganja. The ships will sail from a home dock of Port Canaveral, 50 miles east of Walt Disney World, with the first vessel scheduled to begin operation in January 1998.

Bicycling

Bicycles are available from many resorts as an alternate means of transportation but don't count on cycling Disney's main roads.

Walt Disney World should contain ideal cycling territory, but surprisingly few bike paths are available and, despite hosting an underattended Tampa-to-Mickey century in 1994, the Disney Company expressly forbids cyclists on the main roads or even in the parking lots. The best area for bicycling is around **Fort Wilderness**, where nine miles of campground roads may be toured, as well as a 3/4-mile path that connects the **Wilderness Lodge** with the campground. There's also a dirt path along the lake. At either location, Huffy three-speeds and beach cruisers make up the selection. Rental prices are $3.50 per hour, with day rates $10 at the campground (return by 4 p.m.), or $8 at the Lodge (return by 6 p.m.). **Fort Wilderness Bike Barn**: ☎ *(407) 824-2742*. The Lodge's **Teton Boat and Bike Rental** shop: ☎ *(407) 824-1256*.

Bike rentals are available at two other Walt Disney World locations: the **Caribbean Beach Resort** and **Port Orleans Resort**—in both instances you're limited to riding around on the hotel property. Equipment and prices are comparable to the aforementioned.

Outside Walt Disney World, the biking situation is moderately better, and the mouse isn't perpetually looking over your shoulder. Unfortunately, due to insurance and liability problems, most local bicycling stores won't rent bikes. However, there are two small operations near the start of a pair of lovely bike trails.

Bruce Chamberlain's **West Orange Trail Bikes and Blades** rents Raleigh mountain bikes and hybrids in the converted train station at the head of the **West Orange Trail**, on State Route 50, just east of the Turnpike overpass: ☎ *(407) 877-0600*. Rates are $5 for the first hour, $4 for the second, and $3 for each additional hour; prices include helmet and water bottle. The West Orange Trail initially was a five-mile route near the south shore of Lake Apopka that continued to Winter Garden, but an extension was under construction in late 1996 to lengthen the route as far as the town of Apopka, an additional 10 miles away.

Just east of downtown Orlando, at 5307 East Colonial Drive (aka State Road 50, a half-mile west of State Road 436), is **Cycle Path**: ☎ *(407) 282-5344*. Cycle Path rents Gary Fisher Tassajaras for $12 per day, or $20 for a 24-hour period; helmet, lock and water bottle are included. The rental shop is a quarter-mile from the start of the **Cady Way Trail**. This 3.5-mile path is a local favorite, and begins behind the Fashion Square Mall and winds up in Winter Park. Cady Way draws an average of more than 6000 cyclists, skaters and joggers weekly. Both of these two bike rental outfits also carry inline skates for rental.

There are also a few less-trafficked roads for bicycling. **State Route 545**, which runs north and south between U.S. 192 and the Turnpike, just west of Walt Disney World, is a pleasant 17-mile passage through marsh and rolling cattle country (and less busy than the nearby State Route 535). The **Apopka-Vineland Road** that begins in Lake Buena Vista is another excellent north-south route; nearby **Windermere** offers lovely countryside and lakes for further exploration.

Farther afield, **Lake County**, northwest of Orlando, is developing into Florida's biking mecca, with Mt. Dora its unofficial capital. The town hosts the state's largest cycling event every October—the **Mt. Dora Bike Fest**—and the three-day event draws nearly 2000 riders. Outside town, the lake-dotted country features gently rolling hills through orange groves and along cypress-lined shores, with a minimum of vehicular traffic to contend with; however, neither of the two local bike-repair shops rent bikes.

An enticing development in Lake County are the **rail trails**—abandoned railway corridors that are being converted into recreational trails. The planned **South Lake Scenic Trail** began construction in summer 1996 and eventually will be a 20-mile route that will connect the Van Fleet State Trail in Sumter County to the West Orange Trail, near Orlando. Mountain biking is problematic for most of the year unless you have a high tolerance for mud baths. Off-roading is best in the winter, when rainstorms are infrequent.

The friendly **Florida Freewheelers Club**, since 1973 the state's largest biking organization, hosts about 25 rides each month, primarily in Lake County, and invites visitors to participate in their excursions. Club cyclists meet every Saturday and Sunday at various starting points near Orlando, with road rides ranging from 25 to 60 miles. It also produces two notable annual events: the 17-year-old **Horrible Hundred** in November, a fully supported, hill-choked century—"the hardest in the state" as per a spokesperson; and the **Florida Safari**, a three- or six-day, fully supported tour held in April. For additional information, particularly regarding last-minute scheduling of ATB rides, or to request a copy of their bimonthly newsletter: ☎ *(407) 788-3446.*

If you bring your own bike into town and find yourself in need of service or supplies, **Bikeworks** has four area locations and their staff will also assist with route recommendations. The location closest to Walt Disney World is at *12473 South Orange Blossom Trail:* ☎ *(407) 438-8484.*

Tennis

Five Disney resorts provide tennis courts. Officially, they're designated for Disney resort guests only, but if a court is open, you probably won't be turned away. The facilities are lead by the **Contemporary**, which features six green-clay Har-Tru courts, at $12.72 per hour. Rackets are available for $4 per day. A tennis pro is on-site daily (hours vary); lessons are $40 per hour, or $35 per hour for a playing partner. Court reservations and additional information: ☎ *(407) 824-3578.*

The **Grand Floridian** has two Har-Tru courts, and similar services, but rackets are priced $5 per hour. A tennis pro is on-site from 8 a.m. to 4 p.m. daily. Ball machine $10 per half-hour. Reservations for the Grand Floridian's courts are recommended (up to 2 weeks in advance); ☎ *(407) 824-3000, extension 2134.*

The **Disney Institute** has a more intensive program where a tennis clinic is available, which also features the Har-Tru courts. Tennis instruction is by Peter Burwash International (see: "The Disney Institute" under "Accommodations").

There are more than 800 tennis courts in and around Orlando.

Two lighted, hard-surface courts are available at the **Yacht and Beach Club**, and are free, officially, to guests staying at that property. The courts are unattended and available on a first-come, first-serve basis only; racket and ball rental is available at the resort's Ship Shape Health Club. **Fort Wilderness Campground** also has a pair of low-tech courts; these are open to the public on a first-come, first-served basis, and are also unattended, which leads to a lot of kids skirmishing throughout the area.

Finally, the Contemporary Resort provides **Disney's Racquet Club**, which underwent a full makeover in 1994-1995. The high-tech courts are made of hydrogrid clay that are kept moist by a subterranean irrigation system. Court rentals are $12.72 per hour, and racquets can be rented for $4; private instruction is available at $20 per half-hour. Courts may be reserved 24 hours in advance: ☎ *(407) 824-3578.*

Health Clubs

Within Walt Disney World, easily the best facility and equipment resides at the Disney Institute's state-of-the-art **Sports and Fitness Center**, which features a full range of Cybex weight and strength-training apparatus, including the prototype Human Performance Center, an advanced computer fitness test that measures balance, agility, etc. (the Institute is a test center for Cybex' latest inventions). The facility also features an indoor exercise pool, an NBA indoor gym designed by Bill Walton, and a full-service spa with hydrotherapy, aromatherapy and massage. Free-weights, bikes, treadmills, rowing machines, and interactive stairmasters help round out the mix. The center is free to guests of the Institute; otherwise the cost is $15 per day, or $35 for your length of stay for guests of the Disney Resorts. Open 7 a.m. to 8 p.m. daily. ☎ *(407) 827-4455.*

The Yacht and Beach Club's **Ship Shape Health Club** is open to Disney Resort guests only, with lower rates afforded to Yacht and Beach Club residents. The facility features Next Generation Nautilus and Hammer Strength equipment, along with an entire room of cardio-vascular machines. There is a co-ed steam room, sauna and Jacuzzi, and a massage can be procured for $40 per half hour, or $60 for a full hour. Yacht and Beach Club guests pay $7 per day or $12 for a length of stay pass to use the facility; guests staying at other Disney Resorts pay $10 per day, or $20 for the length of stay. Family memberships (age 13 and up) are also available. Open daily 6 a.m. to 9 p.m. ☎ *(407) 934-3256.*

The Contemporary Resort houses the **Olympiad Health Club**, which offers Nautilus and Life Circuit machines, treadmills, bikes, rowers, stairmasters, and hand weights. A tanning bed and dry sauna is also available. Massage is $40 for a half-hour, or $60 for a full. The Olympiad is open to all Disney Resort guests, and is priced $8.50 per day, or $16 for your length of stay; a family length of stay pass (ages 13 and up) is $20. Open 6:30 a.m. to 8 p.m. daily. ☎ *(407) 824-3410.*

INSIDER TIP

Although a Walt Disney World Marathon is now conducted every January (see "Special Events" in "Planning Your Trip"), Disney does a mediocre job acknowledging the needs of joggers on its property and discourages anyone from jogging on the roads at any hour. The oldest trail is still the best: a 1.5-mile path through the woods surrounding **Fort Wilderness Campground***; part paved, part gravel, the jogging course starts across from the petting farm, and features a series of fitness stations en route. The* **Dixie Landings/ Port Orleans** *pathways are another decent spot, but your options are still limited. Or try the local's choice,* **Lake Eola Park***, which provides a pleasant setting on the edge of downtown Orlando. The busy 3.5-mile* **Cady Way Trail** *is a lovely path from Orlando to Winter Park; it starts behind the Fashion Square Mall. A local jogger's store, the* **Track Shack** *maintains a recorded hotline listing local runs (primarily 5K events):* ☎ *(407) 896-5473.*

Also within the World's borders is **Body by Jake** at the Dolphin (and shared by the Swan), which features Polaris Ultra and Sprint Weight System equipment, along with stairmasters, lifecycles and treadmills. Personal trainers and massage are also available, for $45 for a half-hour, or $65 for a full hour. The facility is available for a daily rate of $10 per guest, or guests may pre-buy unlimited visits to Body by Jake for $5 per day per room for the length of a Swan/Dolphin stay (not including massage and personal training).

Lake Eola's fountain is a prominent downtown Orlando landmark.

Horseback Riding

Walt Disney World offers 45-minute guided tours through the woods behind the **Fort Wilderness Campground**. Trips are conducted at a walking pace, and riders must be at least 9 years of age, with a maximum weight of 250 pounds. If you're not staying at the campground, be sure to allow plenty of commuting time to get to the stables, which are located next to the parking lot. The 45-minute tours are priced $17 per rider. Reservations are necessary and can be made up to two weeks in advance: ☎ *(407) 824-2832.*

More-serious riders will want to head off Walt Disney World property to the **Grand Cypress Equestrian Center** at the Hyatt Regency Grand Cypress.

The center, which in 1994 became the first U.S. training facility recognized by the British Horse Society, offers novice to advanced trail rides ($30–$90) and private lessons covering hunter, jumper, dressage, equitation and western styles as costs of $45 for a half-hour, $75 for a full. Many other courses are available. ☎ *(800) 835-7377* or *(407) 239-1938.*

The **Poinciana Riding Stables** has 750 acres of wooded property along sandy trails. The facility offers beginner's rides, as well as lessons and 90-minute trail rides (by reservation) for more experienced riders. Hayrides and pony rides are also available. The Poinciana Riding Stables are open daily from 9 a.m. and located at 3705 South Poinciana Boulevard, 12 miles south of U.S. 192 outside Kissimmee. ☎ *(407) 847-4343.*

Balloon Rides

What better way to experience The Magic Kingdom than from the still morning air—a thousand feet up? Doug Cleghorn is the "Balloonmeister" at **Orange Blossom Balloons**, which provides one-hour dawn flights over Walt Disney World and the surrounding area, depending on which way the wind blows. Guests participate in the inflation and launch process and celebrate their flight afterwards with a champagne toast and breakfast buffet at the Disney Village Travelodge Hotel, which also serves as the 6 a.m. pickup point. Allow three to four hours for the entire event. Adults, $159; children ages 5 to 12, $116 (including tax). Information and reservations: ☎ *(407) 239-7677.*

Spring Training

The **Grapefruit League**—the annual migration of most of the nation's Major League Baseball teams to Florida—takes place each March, and several of the sites for Spring Training are within easy reach of the Orlando area.

The simplest team to see has traditionally been the **Houston Astros**, which plays in the Osceola County Stadium in Kissimmee. The general admission $6.50 tickets for the 5180-seat stadium are not hard to come by, but it doesn't hurt to call ahead to make reservations. The team arrives in February and plays through the end of March, but exact dates for 1997 had not been set at press time. You can call the stadium directly for game information:

☎ *(407) 933-5500.* Osceola County Stadium is located just off U.S. 192, behind the Silver Spurs Rodeo facility.

The **Atlanta Braves** are tentatively scheduled to move into the new Disney sports complex for 1997, but this was not confirmed at press time; call ☎ *(407) 824-4321* for an update. The **Kansas City Royals** play in Haines City at Baseball City Stadium, about 20 miles southwest of Lake Buena Vista. Ticket information: ☎ *(813) 424-7211.*

Additional information on other teams can be obtained by calling the **Sports Hall of Fame** in Lake City: ☎ *(904) 758-1310.*

Shopping

Walt Disney World's best shopping area is the **Disney Village Marketplace**, a bustling open-air mall with a surfeit of Disney character exotica spread between about 15 stores. Beyond the usual T-shirts and assorted Mickey Mouse geegaws, The City sells Mossimo and No Fear clothing; Discover offers a selection of nature-themed items to wear, read or play with; the Christmas Chalet is a year-round holiday store with American and European handcrafted tree-trimming ornaments; and 2R's Reading and Writing retails best selling novels, music, videos, cards and gifts. One of my favorite stores is the Gourmet Pantry, which sells wine and beer, gourmet cooking supplies (including mouse-shaped pasta), deli items, and has a toothsome bakery selection accompanied by an espresso machine. It's a quiet place for a newspaper, coffee and bagel in the morning if you're staying at one of the nearby Disney Village hotels. The Disney Village Marketplace and adjacent Pleasure Island (which also has a few shops) feature a number of restaurants, and the lakeside complex is connected by bus to most Disney Resorts, or via boat to the Port Orleans and Dixie Landings Resorts. Shopping inside the theme parks is addressed in the respective chapters.

Outside Walt Disney World, one billboard you'll see repeatedly during your stay advertises the **Belz Factory Outlet World**, the nation's largest "non-anchored" factory outlet center, positioned near the northern end of International Drive (Exit 30 off I-4) at 5401 Oakridge Avenue. Among the featured shops are Calvin Klein, Guess, Anne Klein, OshKosh, Harve Bernard, Bass Shoe, Levis and Fieldcrest Cannon. Belz is open daily from 10 a.m. to 9 p.m., Sundays until 6 p.m. ☎ *(407) 352-9600.*

The Florida Mall, located at the intersection of Sand Lake Road and Orange Blossom Trail, currently houses Belk Lindsey, Dillard's, JCPenney, Gayfers and Sears as its anchor stores, with a Saks Fifth Avenue scheduled to open in late 1996. Among the 200 other stores are The Gap, Limited, Victoria's Secret, Warner Brothers Studio Store and Godiva Chocolatier. The Florida Mall is open daily from 10 a.m. to 9:30 p.m.; Sundays from 11 a.m. to 6 p.m. ☎ *(407) 851-6255.*

The region's best antique shopping is found in the **Orlando Antique District** (aka Antique Row) on North Orange Avenue, between Virginia and Princeton. About 40 shops are located in a three block strip just north of downtown Orlando, including: **Annie's Antiques**, an antique mall with a variety of glassware and fine furniture ☎ *(407) 896-3344;* **Flo's Attic**, which deals strictly in turn of the century Duncan Phyfe and Chippendale mahogany furnishings ☎ *(407) 895-1800;* and **A and T Antiques**, which features pine and primitive oak furniture ☎ *(407) 896-9831.* Most of the shops are open 9 a.m. to 5 p.m., Mondays through Saturdays, and most dealers will package and ship purchases.

Flea World—no it's not a Disney insect attraction—bills itself as America's largest flea market, with more than 1700 dealer booths under one roof. A kiddie amusement park, Fun World, is adjacent. Flea World is located in Sanford, near Exit 49 off I-4, and is open Friday, Saturday and Sunday, 8 a.m. to 5 p.m. ☎ *(407) 330-1792.*

Perhaps the single most pleasant shopping district, however, is **Park Avenue**, in Winter Park, a thoroughfare that boasts more than 100 clothiers, bookstores, art and antique galleries and jewelers (use Exit 45 off I-4). Among the name brands lining the street are Williams-Sonoma, Banana Republic, Foot Locker, Laura Ashley and others, but the specialty shops, lead by the Center Street Gallery offer the best surprises. Most shops are open Monday through Saturday, 10 a.m. to 5:30 p.m., with a number of the bigger stores open on Sunday afternoons, as well. ☎ *(407) 644-8281.*

Shopping for Disney Animation Art

The summit of Disney collectibles is the hand-painted cels that make a fleeting appearance in the company's animated classics. The last of Disney's hand-drawn feature films was *The Little Mermaid* in 1989. Films from 1991's *Beauty on the Beast* forward were drawn on computer screens, then transferred directly to film (skipping the cel process), now making the cels truly an unpracticed artform, at least with regard to the Disney Company. The value of original cels began to skyrocket during the 1970s, and it's now quite difficult to obtain anything from the 1940s or earlier. To further expand the wealth of financial potential for this market, in the 1980s, Disney began supplementing its original animation art with limited reproductions. These have also steadily climbed in value, but leave a number of would-be collectors a little vague as to what they are buying.

Original Production Cels are the real thing, a one-of-a-kind painting of a character(s) on acetate that appeared against a separate background in an animated film for a fraction of a second. Most of the cels produced prior to 1940's *Pinocchio* were created using flammable cellulose nitrate and were either destroyed, wiped clean and reused or, more commonly, disintegrated in time. The cels that survived from *Snow White and the Seven Dwarfs* and the shorts of the 1930s are few and far between. One that traded hands recently, a scene from *Orphan's Benefit*, a 1934 Donald Duck short, sold for a record $286,000. After 1940, the company used a more durable cellulose acetate, although the millions of original cels produced in the ensuing several decades are quite rare.

Disney Art Editions was established in 1973 to control the company's inventory of remaining original cels and to maximize the return by letting the last of the stock dribble out slowly. It sets the prices of any piece it releases into the market—therefore, one scene from a film might have a dozen or more similar images, but each will be priced the same whether sold in a Walt Disney World location, a Disney Store around the country, or an authorized Disney animation art dealer. After the image is sold onto the open market, it's value is dictated by demand. The oldest cels commonly found in Disney's animation galleries today are typically from *The Jungle Book*, the last animated film personally supervised by Walt. These, and images from *Who Framed Roger Rabbit* and *The Little Mermaid*, sell for $2500 and up—for the moment. If an original production cel is what you want, but the prices for those used in feature films is out of your league, consider a cel from Disney's recent television work. These cels (for "Winnie the Pooh" and other shows) are still painted by hand, though they are somewhat lower quality and value.

The company has subsequently introduced **Hand-Inked-Line Limited-Edition Cels**, which are acetate cel reproductions made in the same fashion as the originals—by hand. These are produced in editions of about 350 each and are priced in the $1500 to $3000 range. One step closer to the original film is the **Xerographic-Line Limited-Edition Cels**, which are similar in appearance and value, but instead the character outline is not hand-inked, but photographically copied onto the acetate from the original pre-production sketch, then painted with the colors used in the finished film. These are produced in limited editions of about 500, and priced between $1600 and $3200. Lower down the pricing ladder are **Serigraph Cels**, which are cel reproductions printed using a silk-screen process in un-numbered, limited editions of 5000; these price from $275 to $650.

Five stores within Walt Disney World sell original animation artwork, with possibly the largest collection contained at the **Art of Disney** in the Disney Village Marketplace. Another **Art of Disney** store is located on the second floor of the Centorium at Epcot, and the **Animation Gallery** at the Disney-MGM Studios also features a good selection. A smattering of collectibles is found at **Suspended Animation** at Pleasure Island. A fifth store, **Disneyana** at the Magic Kingdom, was scheduled to be replaced by the 25th Anniversary exhibit in October 1996; a new location for Disneyana had not been determined at press time. Several other stores sell original posters from Disney films. These are limited in number, and the early titles like *Snow White* and *Bambi* fetch prices into the thousands of dollars, but Disney does not have control over the release of these items to the general public for sale.

If there is a specific image or character you are trying to procure, any of these five stores will happily call the others to see if they can locate what you are looking for. An excellent resource of information about the production of Disney's animated classics is *Of Mice and Men*, by Leonard Maltin (1987, NAL Dutton).

The Art of Disney in the Disney Village Marketplace holds an annual one-day **Cel Event** in early June to clear out many of the odds and ends—a number of good values can be had. The exact date for the 1997 event had not been set at press time. For additional information, call the Art of Disney ☎ *(407) 828-3929*.

A Disney Wedding

With fairy-tale endings a prerequisite for virtually all of the animated fantasies that pour forth from the Disney Studio, the 1994 construction of a Disney **Wedding Pavilion** was bound to happen sooner or later. If you've always wanted Goofy as your ring bearer, now you can have him.

The 250-seat, nondenominational facility—a glass-enclosed, Victorian-style summer house—sits on a tiny island along the shores of the Seven Seas Lagoon, between the Grand Floridian Beach and Polynesian Resorts. The coup de grace is that Cinderella Castle sparkles in the distance behind the wedding alter, and the monorail buzzes over the parking lot.

Actually, Disney's wedding planners can assist with creative nuptial gatherings that go well beyond the scope of the new wedding pavilion. In addition o utilizing the facilities at the various resorts, weddings can been conducted in the theme parks after closing (how about taking the plunge at midnight aboard the Tower of Terror?), and a 60-foot Cinderella Castle replica and glass coach with horses can be procured for the reception. **Franck's**—a recreation of the dizzy wedding coordinator's studio from Disney's *Father of the Bride*—is the salon built to assist in the planning and execution of the ceremony, be it a Las Vegas-style quickie or a custom-designed show rivaling a Broadway production.

The price of a Disney wedding starts at $2300 for a bare-bones ceremony, and quickly spirals heavenward from there. Disney's wedding planners: ☎ *(407) 828-3400.*

AUTHOR'S OBSERVATION

Although Disney's Wedding Pavilion opened in July 1995, Disney has been organizing weddings on the property since 1991, with 3500 ceremonies conducted to date. Since the opening of the pavilion, more than 1200 weddings are now performed annually.

INDEX

Fielding's Walt Disney World and Orlando

Reader Survey

We want to make sure future editions of *Fielding's Walt Disney World and Orlando* are a valuable resource for our readers. Please assist us by providing feedback about your particular experience. When completed, mail to Fielding Worldwide, Attn: Walt Disney World and Orlando, 308 South Catalina, Redondo Beach, CA 90277.

Name (optional):

Street Address (optional):

City/State/Zip:

Number of adults traveling in your party: Age range:

Number of children: Age range:

Was this your first visit to Walt Disney World:

If not, in what year was your last visit:

Primary method of transportation to Orlando:

Did you rent a car in Orlando:

Did you book a package vacation:

If so, with whom:

Name of hotel you stayed in:

Number of nights you stayed:

The primary consideration in choosing this hotel was:

On a scale of five (five being best), please rate your hotel accommodations by:

    Quality of room furnishings and amenities
    (good bedding? voice mail?):

    Level of maintenance
    (ripped carpet? problems responded to quickly?):

    Strength of hotel staff (courteous? resourceful?):

    Pool area and recreational facilities
    (relaxing? a diverse selection?):

    Location (convenient to activities? congested?):

    Decor and overall appeal (dated? fresh?):

Did you feel your accommodations were overpriced, underpriced, or right on:

Your favorite restaurant visited on this trip (and why):

Your least favorite restaurant (and why):

After you arrived in Orlando, approximately what percentage of your waking hours were spent *within* Walt Disney World:

Which Disney admission ticket package did you purchase for the majority of your group:

Approximately how many hours did you spend (not including breaks) inside the following parks:

    The Magic Kingdom:

    Epcot:

    The Disney-MGM Studios:

    Typhoon Lagoon:

    Blizzard Beach:

    River Country:

    Discovery Island:

    Pleasure Island:

    Universal Studios:

    Sea World:

    Other:

    Other:

    Other:

Did you use any of the touring itineraries contained in this guide:

If so, what was your general experience using the itineraries (indicate which plans you used):

What was your favorite activity, *outside of theme parks*, within Walt Disney World:

What was your favorite activity, *outside of theme parks*, outside Walt Disney World:

How soon do you plan to revisit Walt Disney World and/or Orlando:

What one thing would you do differently if you were doing this trip again:

Suggestions for how we can make next year's guide more valuable to readers:

Order Your Guide to Travel and Adventure

Title	Price	Title	Price
Fielding's Alaska Cruises and the Inside Passage	$18.95	Fielding's London Agenda	$14.95
Fielding's The Amazon	$16.95	Fielding's Los Angeles	$16.95
Fielding's Asia's Top Dive Sites	$19.95	Fielding's Malaysia & Singapore	$16.95
Fielding's Australia	$16.95	Fielding's Mexico	$18.95
Fielding's Bahamas	$16.95	Fielding's New Orleans Agenda	$16.95
Fielding's Baja	$18.95	Fielding's New York Agenda	$16.95
Fielding's Bermuda	$16.95	Fielding's New Zealand	$16.95
Fielding's Borneo	$18.95	Fielding's Paris Agenda	$14.95
Fielding's Budget Europe	$17.95	Fielding's Portugal	$16.95
Fielding's Caribbean	$18.95	Fielding's Paradors, Pousadas and Charming Villages	$18.95
Fielding's Caribbean Cruises	$18.95	Fielding's Rome Agenda	$14.95
Fielding's Disney World and Orlando	$18.95	Fielding's San Diego Agenda	$14.95
Fielding's Diving Indonesia	$19.95	Fielding's Southeast Asia	$18.95
Fielding's Eastern Caribbean	$17.95	Fielding's Southern Vietnam on 2 Wheels	$15.95
Fielding's England	$17.95	Fielding's Spain	$18.95
Fielding's Europe	$18.95	Fielding's Surfing Indonesia	$19.95
Fielding's European Cruises	$18.95	Fielding's Sydney Agenda	$16.95
Fielding's Far East	$18.95	Fielding's Thailand, Cambodia, Laos and Myanmar	$18.95
Fielding's France	$18.95	Fielding's Vacation Places Rated	$19.95
Fielding's Freewheelin' USA	$18.95	Fielding's Vietnam	$17.95
Fielding's Hawaii	$18.95	Fielding's Western Caribbean	$18.95
Fielding's Italy	$18.95	Fielding's The World's Most Dangerous Places	$19.95
Fielding's Kenya	$16.95	Fielding's Worldwide Cruises '97	$19.95
Fielding's Las Vegas Agenda	$14.95		

To place an order: call toll-free 1-800-FW-2-GUIDE
(VISA, MasterCard and American Express accepted)
or send your check or money order to:
Fielding Worldwide, Inc., 308 S. Catalina Avenue, Redondo Beach, CA 90277
http://www.fieldingtravel.com
Add $2.00 per book for shipping & handling (sorry, no COD's), allow 2–6 weeks for delivery

FIELDING'S
WORLDWIDE CRUISES '97

"Recommended without reservation."

—*Philadelphia Inquirer*

This totally new, encyclopedic volume is the definitive guide for choosing the perfect cruise. It's really two books in one, with ratings of 178 ships and profiles of 58 cruise lines, as well as the lowdown on the 220 most visited ports around the world. Written by Shirley Slater and Harry Basch, a husband-and-wife travel-writing team whose work has been published internationally, the text is both urbane and engaging and packed with valuable insider information.

Reviews of 178 ships, and 220 ports of call, with 200 b/w photos and 23 helpful maps.

- **Essential data:** All the facts the reader needs to choose the right ship and the right destination; supplemented with maps, charts and tables.
- **Important info to know beforehand:** What to wear, how to select a cabin, how to book a table, how to avoid seasickness, and more.
- **Special-interest choices:** The best cruises for families, singles, fitness fans and couch potatoes; plus descriptions of elegant sailing vessels, paddle-wheel steamers and riverboats.

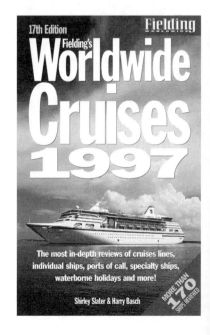

17th Edition

Fielding
WORLDWIDE

Fielding's

Worldwide Cruises 1997

The most in-depth reviews of cruises lines, individual ships, ports of call, specialty ships, waterborne holidays and more!

MORE THAN 170 SHIPS REVIEWED

Shirley Slater & Harry Basch

1024 pages, 5-3/8" x 8-3/8", 312 b/w photos, 23 maps
August 1996

$19.95

UK £10.95 CAN $23.95 AUS $24.95
ISBN 1-56952-115-8
Replaces ISBN#1-56952-073-9

Fielding
WORLDWIDE

NEW FIELDINGWEAR!

Now that you own a Fielding travel guide, you have graduated from being a tourist to full-fledged traveler! Celebrate your elevated position by proudly wearing one of these heavy-duty, all-cotton shirts, selected by our authors for their comfort and durability (and their ability to hide dirt). Choose from three styles—radical "World Tour," politically correct "Do the World Right," and elegant "All-Access."

Important Note: Fielding authors have field-tested these shirts and have found that they can be swapped for much more than their purchase price in free drinks at some of the world's hottest clubs and in-spots. They also make great gifts.

WORLD TOUR

Hit the hard road with a travel fashion statement for out times. Visit all 35 of Mr. D.P.'s favorite nasty spots (listed on the back), or just look like you're going to. This is the real McCoy, worn by mujahadeen, mercenaries, UN peacekeepers and the authors of Fielding's The World's Most Dangerous Places. Black, XL, heavy-duty 100% cotton. Made in the USA. $18.00.

DO THE WORLD RIGHT

Start your next adventure wearing Fielding's polically correct "Do the World Right" shirt, complete with freaked-out red globe and blasting white type. A shirt that tells the world that within that high-mileage, overly educated body beats the heart of a true party animal. Only for adrenline junkies, hard-core travelers and seekers of knowledge. Black, XL, heavy-duty 100% cotton. Made in the USA. $18.00.

ALL ACCESS

Strike terror into the snootiest maitre'd, make concierges cringe, or just use this elegant shirt as the ultimate party invitation. The combination of the understated red Fielding logo embroidered on a jet-black golf shirt will get you into the snobiest embassy party or jumping night spot. An elegant casual shirt for those who travel in style and comfort. Black, XL or L, 100% pre-shrunk cotton, embroidered Fielding Travel Guide logo on front. Made in the U.S.A. $29.00.

Name:

Address:

City:

State: Zip:

Telephone:
Shirt Name:
Quantity:

For each shirt add $4 shipping and handling. California residents add $1.50 sales tax.
Allow 2 to 4 weeks for delivery.
Send check or money order with your order form to:

Fielding Worldwide, Inc.
308 South Catalina Ave.
Redondo Beach, CA 90277

                    or
order your shirts by phone,:
1-800-FW-2-GUIDE
Visa, MC, AMex accepted

International Conversions

TEMPERATURE

To convert °F to °C, subtract 32 and divide by 1.8. To convert °C to °F, multiply by 1.8 and add 32.

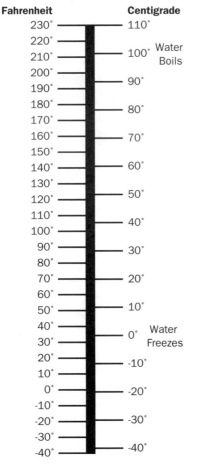

Fahrenheit — **Centigrade** scale

230° — 110°
220° —
210° — 100° Water Boils
200° —
190° — 90°
180° — 80°
170° —
160° — 70°
150° —
140° — 60°
130° —
120° — 50°
110° —
100° — 40°
90° — 30°
80° —
70° — 20°
60° —
50° — 10°
40° — 0° Water Freezes
30° —
20° — -10°
10° —
0° — -20°
-10° —
-20° — -30°
-30° —
-40° — -40°

WEIGHTS & MEASURES

LENGTH

1 km	=	0.62 miles
1 mile	=	1.609 km
1 meter	=	1.2936 yards
1 meter	=	3.28 feet
1 yard	=	0.9144 meters
1 yard	=	3 feet
1 foot	=	30.48 centimeters
1 centimeter	=	0.39 inch
1 inch	=	2.54 centimeters

AREA

1 square km	=	0.3861 square miles
1 square mile	=	2.590 square km
1 hectare	=	2.47 acres
1 acre	=	0.405 hectare

VOLUME

1 cubic meter	=	1.307 cubic yards
1 cubic yard	=	0.765 cubic meter
1 cubic yard	=	27 cubic feet
1 cubic foot	=	0.028 cubic meter
1 cubic centimeter	=	0.061 cubic inch
1 cubic inch	=	16.387 cubic centimeters

CAPACITY

1 gallon	=	3.785 liters
1 quart	=	0.94635 liters
1 liter	=	1.057 quarts
1 pint	=	473 milliliters
1 fluid ounce	=	29.573 milliliters

MASS and WEIGHT

1 metric ton	=	1.102 short tons
1 metric ton	=	1000 kilograms
1 short ton	=	.90718 metric ton
1 long ton	=	1.016 metric tons
1 long ton	=	2240 pounds
1 pound	=	0.4536 kilograms
1 kilogram	=	2.2046 pounds
1 ounce	=	28.35 grams
1 gram	=	0.035 ounce
1 milligram	=	0.015 grain

cm 0 1 2 3 4 5 6 7 8 9 10

Inch 0 1 2 3 4